ESSAYS IN ACCOUNTING THEORY

Volume I

AMERICAN ACCOUNTING ASSOCIATION

The By-Laws of the American Accounting Association state that the first purpose of the Association shall be "to initiate, encourage, and sponsor research in accounting and to publish or aid in the publication of the results of research." In harmony with this objective, the publication of the Studies in Accounting Research is aimed at encouraging and publishing research. This series is an outgrowth of the research program initiated by the Association in 1965. Under this program research projects and authors are selected by the Director of Research, who is assisted by a Research Advisory Committee.

This project was based on the author's lifework over nearly a half century, in which accounting issues are analyzed from an interdisciplinary perspective, in particular from the standpoint of such basic disciplines as scientific methodology, philosophy, ethics, logic, mathematics, economics, and behavioral science. In preparing the materials for this publication, the author was assisted by a Project Advisory Committee consisting of Yuji Ijiri (Carnegie-Mellon University, chairperson), Edward V. McIntyre (Florida State University), and Stephen A. Zeff (Rice University), as well as by AAA Publications Director, Janet G. Nuñez.

This publication was approved by Theodore J. Mock (University of Southern California), 1982-84 Director of Research. The Research Advisory Committee (1982-83) at the time of publication approval was composed of Joel S. Demski (Stanford University), Daniel L. Jensen (Ohio State University), James C. McKeown (University of Illinois), James A. Ohlson (University of California, Berkeley), Lawrence Revsine (Northwestern University), and William F. Wright (University of Minnesota), in addition to the Director of Research.

ESSAYS IN ACCOUNTING THEORY

Volume I

by
Carl Thomas Devine

AMERICAN ACCOUNTING ASSOCIATION
1985

TABLE OF CONTENTS

TABLE OF CONTENTS

Foreword

These essays may or may not belong to what is generally considered to be the field of accounting, but they are related to what accountants do, and, if the definition is not too rigid, they form a book. Many of the essays are repetitious and, in spite of the complicated jargon of modern scientific method, the message is comparatively simple. Accountants are concerned with individuals striving for objectives. Accountants attempt to furnish an information-control system that helps these individuals attain their goals. In the process accountants identify events that promise to be pertinent to future decisions and actions; they select aspects of these events that promise to be useful, and they construct conventions for measuring and reporting relevant aspects of the selected events. In short, accounting is a part of behavioral science.

The reader is warned of numerous footnotes and long quotations that add up to a form of intellectual name-dropping. In part, these notes are a stubborn reaction to the general callousness of many current writers, who all too often quote a late, easily-reached article or, worse, do not quote at all. The reader should be warned also of the vocabulary that is currently popular in business and behavioral science. This vocabulary, when combined with technical accounting terms and the writer's weakness for complicated grammatical forms, may result in slow and difficult reading. However, intellectual workers in related fields often express their research output with this vocabulary, so a little additional effort in this direction may prove to be beneficial.

There is a monumental debt to a host of bright and interested students who responded to being treated as rational beings. A debt of equal magnitude is due my colleagues and former colleagues who, between weary classroom sessions, have spent innumerable smoke-filled hours arguing and wrangling an endless succession of problems. The list is a long one. Laura MacAdams, Al Tener, Sue Heines, Everette Hong, Jeremiah Lockwood, Oscar Nelson, Fred Woodbridge, Edwin Lamb, Robert Dinman, Malcolm Pye, James Lanham, Lawrence Benninger, Richard Mattessich, Billy Goetz, David Green, Jr., Charles Horngren, George Sorter, Sidney Davidson, Hadibroto, Tan Hian Kie, Rogo, Rosalinda Atienza, and members of the Ivory-Tower Committee: Maurice Moonitz, Myron Gordon, Carl Nelson, Paul Kircher and Charles Bastable. The following teachers deserve special notice: Benton Talbot, who insisted that being a bookworm is a respectable activity for a mature human being; William A. Paton, whose no-nonsense approach to intellectual activity was a pleasant awakening; A.P. Ushenko, who encouraged minds to be a little erratic and to develop mutations in the form of useful insights. For Drue and Steve, who somehow refrained from mutiny.

1

Essay One

Accounting —
Toward a Suitable Philosophy

". . . the problem of the philosopher is not about the world but about experience." [1]

It seems appropriate to begin a series of essays devoted to accounting theory with the most general discussion. Such a beginning permits the reader to appraise the writer's system of values and to make allowances for peculiar attitudes and bias. Such a discussion may help to unify the accepted beliefs of a profession. Practically all thoughts worth having and beliefs worth holding are based on a series of preconceptions which are remnants of several philosophical systems. Thus, a thoughtful review of various competing philosophical systems may help to organize and clarify the attitudes of many professional, practice-oriented accountants. At the very least such a discussion should help the reader escape the rigid boundaries and constraints of an occupational area. At the more practical level, some competing information systems have well-developed structures that deserve to be treated as philosophies. In fact, management science and its related branches such as operations research attempt to differentiate their product by the unity of method by which all problems are approached. Meanwhile, it is probably safe to say that the philosophical probing carried on by most accountants is far too well characterized by the shallow and pompous tirades frequently published on accounting as an art *versus* accounting as a science.

The purpose of this essay is to set forth at least one acceptable approach for those who practice an information-control system such as accounting. In the course of this task a number of competing views are examined. To introduce such a vast and poorly-organized territory, we shall begin at a fairly low level of abstraction by observing what those interested in the field of management science appear to hold. As it turns out, the philosophical background for an effective management science program is almost directly applicable to the field of accounting. This overall view is outlined briefly and is followed by an overview of some of the broader implications. Further coverage of scientific method and the organic conception of organizations may be found in subsequent essays. For those readers with little interest in the philosophical aspects of accounting this overview may be adequate for an understanding of the more traditional essays that follow.

As a preliminary step, it should be repeated that management scientists are committed to a thorough-going scientific approach and to the thesis that the unity of scientific method is unquestionably applicable to all their problems. Kits of mathematical and ob-

---

[1] Hector Hawton, *Philosophy for Pleasure* (New York: Fawcett Publications, Inc., 1956), p. 178. Thurstone states: "A scientific law is not to be thought of as having an independent existence which some scientist is fortunate to stumble upon. A scientific law is not a part of nature. It is only a way of comprehending nature." Louis Leon Thurstone, *Multiple-Factor Analysis: A Development and Expansion of the Vectors of Mind* (Chicago: University of Chicago Press, 1974), reprinted in *Readings in Philosophy of Science*, ed. Philip P. Wiener (New York: Charles Scribner's Sons, 1953), p. 193.

servational instruments are available, but they are applied *after* the problem has been subjected to scientific analysis and the pertinent relationships placed in a framework (model) that can be solved in either analytic or approximate fashion. Undoubtedly some practitioners are overly quick to reach into the medicine cabinet before adequate diagnosis, and obviously the scientific appraisal is sometimes twisted to help fit the specific types of models which the researcher prefers or manipulates with confidence. These cases should not obscure the accepted ideal of the unity of method that underlies all problems regardless of the specific procedures employed.

The so-called scientific approach is appropriate for accounting and operations research, in particular, and for business research in general. Uniformities in experiences (the sensible data) are observed, inferred, defined, classified and related to other simple observations of the same general kind. These simple interpretations (facts) are then combined and arranged to form higher-level and more complicated constructs, which are related to one another by constitutive definitions made up of intervening variables and relationships expressed as equations or as less definite explications of various kinds. In order to avoid constructs that tend to orbit in metaphysical space it seems desirable to require that all constructs be related in such a way that they may be 'reduced' to the relatively simple data of the sensible world. Thus many constructs may be defined only in terms of others, e.g., net worth, but we require that such constructs be tied to the world of sensible data directly by rules of correspondence (operational definitions) or, by constitutive definition and intervening variables, to other constructs that may in turn be so reduced. A good definition then is one that interacts with other definitions and directly or indirectly has sharp, well-defined rules of correspondence (instructions) for connecting it to the sensible data.

The research specialist, or indeed anyone who thinks seriously, will sometimes be able to travel on constitutive definitions and relations in the abstract theoretical space for long stretches without returning to the mundane field of observational data. New relationships may be assumed or deduced, and new definitions may be formed from other abstract definitions. Hypotheses are said to be "operationally meaningful" in the sense that they may be tested for relative truth or falsity by experiment or direct observation of the data. Hypotheses may relate to nonempirical constructs, but unless they can be reduced to empirical data they are often characterized as pseudo-propositions or nonsense statements. 'Meaning' is therefore defined in terms of possibilities for (or sometimes methods of) verification or by 'habits to respond' and 'nonsense' statements are not necessarily 'nonsense' in the usual sense but are incapable of reduction to data of the sensible world. They are without sense content, i.e., they have no effective rules of correspondence tying them directly or indirectly to observational data.

The above description is essentially that of scientific method. Such a method consists of the repeated *interaction* of hypotheses and deductions from the abstract area with observations and inferences from the sensible data.[2] We shall return to a more detailed dis-

---

[2] Physics has a highly developed theoretical area in which long and complicated journeys may be taken without visiting constructs that are directly tied to observables by operational rules. A usable approach to the meaning of theory can be constructed from this interaction of abstraction and observation. "Laws describe regularities and are employed in order to explain and predict particular occurrences and phenomena. But often we wish an explanation of the regularity itself. One way of achieving this in science is to *deduce* the law which describes this regularity from some other law of a higher degree of generality . . . typically, a whole family of laws . . . may be deduced from a very few laws of high generality. When this is achieved, these highly general laws will be a *theory* for the family of laws which are deducible from them . . . ." *Philosophy of Science,* eds. Arthur Danto and Sidney Morgenbesser (New York: Meridian Books, Inc. 1960), p. 178. Unfortunately, rules for determining degrees of generality are not too well developed. Moreover, facts themselves are interpretations, so that the operationally meaningful approach is not as clear-cut as it seems.

cussion later in connection with operationism, logical empiricism, and pragmatism as schools of thought.

Thus the task facing accountants and similar systems specialists includes observing the environment, searching the environment for behavior patterns, and (usually) imputing objectives and goals to those who establish the patterns. In the typical case accountants have adopted a kind of teleological approach which observes actions, infers ends, accepts the prevailing social valuation of the worthiness of such ends, and recognizes acceptable patterns that tend to accomplish desirable goals. Accountants then accept as their proper domain the gathering and reporting of information that will facilitate movement toward such goals and retard actions that will lead to unacceptable objectives.

A teleological approach is always subject to certain dangers. Behavior patterns may be searched for uniformities in orthodox scientific ways. These uniformities may indeed suggest goal-searching activities and permit highly confirmable inferences as to the goals themselves. Once we infer the objectives we feed the inferences (inferred goals) back into our system as 'causes' of the behavioral actions. This approach is not objectionable in itself, but, as is pointed out later, it may lead to a 'volitional' philosophy in which all causes are related to personalities. Thus we may have gods pushing the sun across the sky and regulating all sorts of other things. The danger is due to a tendency toward anthropomorphism in which one imputes personal volition to the behavior of the physical world or, worse, imputes supposed divine-like behavior to human beings. The objection to anthropomorphism is not that it is demonstrably false (It may be true!), but that in the past it has not furthered fruitful investigation and does not seem very likely to do so.

Practitioners of operations research have sometimes been accused of constructing simplified models and placing them between the individual and some sort of assumed 'real' world.[3] Such models are simplified so that the limited powers of the human mind can grasp the relationships. They are then solved and presented with the hope that the solutions will have some carry-over application to the 'real' situation. This criticism has also been leveled at accountants. Accountants have a long-established tradition for abstracting entities, tracing only limited aspects of business decisions, and recording only a few of the many events that enter into the biography of an organization. They have therefore been accused of dealing with "shadows," "adumbrations," and, at a practical level, "ghosts of long-departed assets."

The accounting structure is certainly a highly abstract model of the relations, properties, and events of an organization. (The concept of asset, for example, abstracts from almost all aspects of a string of events except probable service potential of a limited sort.) The point that critics overlook is that knowledge of the 'outside' world and one's view of life itself is a model composed of the interactions of memory and sense organs. In effect the 'world' is a model constructed from the reports of sense perceptors. Such a model may be highly simplified so that we can solve it or at least cope with it. Or the solipsist may be correct: the individual's model may indeed be the entire world. Luckily, as an accountant one can afford the luxury of the skeptic and withhold judgment. To impute an external world with things-in-themselves is gratuitous, but at times it may prove to be useful and reassuring to do so. Let us now turn to more traditional philosophical questions.

---

[3] Kenneth Boulding has recently taken an untenable position in this regard. His outraged concern over the present lack of respect for nonquantitative methods has influenced him to take an extreme anti-model-making view. See "Evidences for an Administrative Science," *Administrative Science Quarterly*, June 1958.

Metaphysics and Solipsism

The fashion for many centuries was to erect from a few assumptions a metaphysical structure that would explain everything that might come before the human mind. The effect was to speculate about the universe behind the physical universe: to fill in by speculation the gaps in knowledge that were not filled by scientific inquiry. These philosophical systems were discussed and one by one became less popular, not because they were proved to be false but because other philosphers did not agree with the initial assumptions or non-philosophers became bored with discussing them and turned to other speculative systems. Metaphysics has indeed suffered a decline in this century in spite of a seemingly legitimate function of trying to provide a framework independent of the experience it hopes to interpret — a sort of model for the empirical world.

It is probably true that only in rare cases in the fields of esthetics, ethics and morals have broad metaphysical systems been effective in any way. According to Carnap: "Metaphysicians cannot avoid making their propositions nonverifiable, because if they made them verifiable, the decision about the truth or falsehood of their doctrines would depend upon experience and therefore belong to the region of empirical science."[4] Metaphysicians have often asserted that they have a new kind of knowledge that is somehow more fundamental than and superior to knowledge derived from experience. Such an attitude seems out of place in a pragmatic service field such as accounting. This point normally would not deserve mention, yet to many accountants there is something hypnotic about debit and credit that sometimes leads to mystical attitudes and expressions. For example, some accountants have spoken of attached and embodied costs, have preserved equity among periods and units of production, have insisted on measuring *true* income or finding *true* cost, have argued that revenue is composed in part of costs, and have held appropriate rites over expired costs.

Opposed in some respects to these grandiose metaphysical systems is the doctrine of solipsism, which is treated with intellectual respect by most philosophers but which has little or no effect on what men think or how they proceed with the business of living. This simple doctrine obviously cannot be refuted, and in the words of Hawton, "It is not merely logically irrefutable; it is obviously true. What you and I would regard as 'Professor Dingle' is not given to us in experience . . . which we call seeing him, hearing him."[5] The point to be emphasized is that the solipsistic approach makes no representations about external objects and beings, and the importance of it in modern philosophy is that it

---

[4] Reported by Hector Hawton, *op. cit.*, p. 165. Russell has pointed out that there is no reason to believe that everything is related to everything else, and Hawton emphasizes that to a grandiose metaphysician the success of science which had, at best, a dinky philosophical structure, was startling. "It became apparent that the experimentalists were working on profitable lines, but why they should obtain such good results was something of a puzzle. It was extremely difficult to find a theoretical justification for the procedure they followed so successfully." *Ibid.*, p. 131. White emphasizes the 20th-century reaction against the "absolute" and metaphysics generally. Hegelian metaphysics with its "world spirit" (absolute idea) with goals and a soul of its own, was probably the apex of metaphysical thought. White also discusses the factors that probably led to the growth of such ideas. Accountants are more committed to Russell's view that events can be partially controlled than to the Hegelian view of inexorable historical process. See Morton White, *The Age of Analysis* (New York: The New American Library, 1955), Chapter I.

[5] *Ibid.*, p. 170. See Herbert Dingle, *Through Science to Philosophy*, 1936 Lowell Institute Lectures (Oxford: The Clarendon Press, 1937). In the same tradition as Johnson's pedi-answer to Berkeley is Morris Cohen's " . . . my safety and my continued sanity depend upon recognizing that the automobile and its driver are realities having a history and purpose independent of my own." *Reason and Nature* (Glencoe: The Free Press, Publishers, 1953), p. 63. A more pedestrian operational view is expressed by Thurstone. "While the ideal constructs of science do not imply physical reality, they do not deny the possibility of some degree of correspondence with physical reality." *Op. cit.*, p. 193.

shows that such assumptions are unnecessary for rational activity. Such things as matter, space, events and Dingle himself, are mental constructs made up of experiences, and there is no necessity for assigning 'existence' or 'objectivity' or 'reality' or any other high-sounding word to them. Solipsism is not likely to be a useful theory for auditors who are committed to 'verifiable objective' evidence. While it may be that a Crusoe could be a scientist and test his own hypotheses by observation and replication, the basis of auditing is the use of independent ability and the expression of independent opinion. Thus we shall accept without proof the assumption of interpersonal existence and the collateral assumption that objectivity may be defined operationally as the agreement of trained observers.

Operationism

This writer's own subjective approach to philosophy and his framework for investigating and correlating information is essentially that of operationism. It is believed that goal-oriented operationism is an effective set of assumptions and judgments for investigating the essentials of accounting theory. This method of viewing and organizing experience is closely related to the doctrines of empiricism, behaviorism, pragmatism, and instrumentalism.[6] Operationism makes use of logic and mathematics but realizes that these branches are tautological and can yield information about the world only by making implications more readily discernible, by showing consistency, and by helping to avoid contradiction. Operationism is empirical in that it accepts experiences, looks for uniformities and tries to find relations among them. Even the question as to whether the knowledge is real or a mirage is not important to operationism; reality is a matter of classification and definition.

> Raw experience is "the given" . . . . We cannot classify and arrange until we have invented some scheme of classification. To do this we must invent abstract terms (concepts), and, because we must possess them before we can apply them, they are *a priori* . . . . Is it real or a mirage? That is simply a question of classification. We invent the term "reality" and define it in such a way that what does not fit is "mirage." . . . What is orderly we call "real," . . . . The category "unreal" is a temporary pigeon-hole for otherwise unclassified experiences.[7]

---

[6] An interesting classification was made by William James. "Empiricism, Skepticism, Naturalism, Positivism, and Pragmatism are typical thought movements of the worldly, tough-minded variety. Respect for the facts of experience, open-mindedness, an experimental trial-and-error attitude . . . distinguish them from the more impatient, imaginative . . . thinkers in the tender-minded camp. Among the latter are speculative metaphysicians, institutionists, rationalists, and absolute idealists." Herbert Feigl, "Logical Empiricism," *Readings in Philosophical Analysis*, eds. Herbert Feigl and Wilfrid Sellars (New York: Appleton-Century-Crofts, Inc., 1949), pp. 3-4. See also Morton White, *The Age of Analysis, op. cit.*, p. 136.

[7] Hawton, *op.cit.*, pp. 173-174. Hawton is describing Lewis's position. See also Clarence Irving Lewis, *Mind and the World Order* (New York: Dover Publications, Inc., 1956), Chapter I. Scientists must make assumptions which are not completely supported by observation. " . . . 'it is a metaphysical presupposition of science that the world is predictable' . . . ." Arthur Pap, "Does Science Have Metaphysical Presuppositions?" *Readings in Philosophy of Science, op. cit.*, p. 484. Bertrand Russell concludes that: "We must . . . accept analogy — in the sense in which it goes beyond experience — as an independent premise of scientific knowledge." *Human Knowledge, Its Scope and Limits* (New York: Simon & Schuster, 1948), p. 193. In fact many philosophers have discussed the *metaphysics of science*.

Most of these so-called 'metaphysical' presuppositions are currently useful *assumptions* that help scientific prediction and are not considered to be immutable truths. The relations of logic may be called 'metaphysical' or they may be considered to be coventions based on convincing experience that they work. Sidney Hook published *The Metaphysics of Pragmatism* (Chicago: The Open Court Publishing Co.) in 1927, and Nicholas Dopuch has expanded the title to "Metaphysics of Pragmatism and Accountancy," in *The Accounting Review*, April 1962. Unfortunately Dopuch betrays a penchant for the older semi-Hegelian metaphysics with such statements as "natural process," "The world has ends within its own process," "The world does not guarantee progress," etc. Such statements are flagrant examples of reification and their usefulness is doubtful.

Perhaps the outstanding difference between operationism and the various early forms
of positivism is that the former does not weaken its own case by trying to explain everything empirically. Stevens states the case.

> The blemish on positivism was that in its reaction against rational metaphysics it pretended to
> base *everything* in science on experience. Operationism, however, acknowledges the role of
> the rational methods of mathematics and logic — formal disciplines which do not appeal to
> experience for verification, but only to conventions. Science uses these formal systems as
> models for representing its data . . . . When it is a matter of the significance of *empirical*
> rather than of *formal* propositions, needless to say operationism adopts an uncompromising
> positivistic attitude.[8]

Thus one who holds to the operational approach may have strong personal opinions
about poetry, art, religion, ethics and the like, but he realizes that these opinions depend
on value judgments, and are not subject to the *usual* tests of truth or falsity and therefore
to the rules of logical inference. The early operational approach set forth by Bridgman
was more rigid in this respect and insisted that concepts which did not give a series of instructions for identifying and characterizing them were nonsense statements.[9] If it is not
possible to find operations to yield an answer to a question it is, by definition, meaningless and without sense content. For those accustomed to thinking in abstract terms it is extremely difficult to adjust to a strictly operational approach, but the adjustment is not
quite so severe when one realizes that there are *mental* operations. "In general, we mean
by any concept nothing more than a set of operations; *the concept is synonymous with the
corresponding set of operations* . . . if the concept is mental, as of mathematical continuity, the operations are mental operations . . ."[10]

A little reflection will show that some fantastically stupid questions with no possibility
of operational validity are not nonsense or meaningless in the broad, everyday sense.
Their psychological effects may be tremendous. Demagogues make wide use of such statements, and inevitably most religious statements are nonoperational. Ayers, a staunch logical positivist, takes an operationist viewpoint and offers the following comment on preference statements (value judgments).

> . . . it does not follow . . . that two persons cannot significantly disagree about a question of
> value . . . . there can be disagreement without formal contradiction . . . . since the expres-

---

[8] S. S. Stevens, "Psychology and the Science of Science," *Psychological Bulletin*, 36, pp. 221-263. Quoted
from the reprint in *Readings in Philosophy of Science*, ed. Philip P. Wiener (New York: Charles Scribner's
Sons, 1953), p. 166. An example of the early positivist view: " . . . science claims for its heritage the whole domain to which the word knowledge can be legitimately applied . . . ." Karl Pearson, *The Grammar of Science*, p.
312. Morris Cohen expresses the more mellow view of a typical operationist: "The dogma that all reality is sensory or can be apprehended through sense organs alone is as gratuitous as the assumption that all reality is
audible, or that all reality is odorous." *Op. cit.*, p. 197. To an extreme empiricist such as Mill and his disciples,
Pearson, Bridgman, etc., the *a priori* aspects of logic and mathematics are also the result of experience. Those
conventions that survive meet the needs of those who interpret experience and are themselves the result of induction. P. W. Bridgman states: "Mathematics thus appears to be ultimately just as truly an empirical science as
physics or chemistry . . . ." *The Nature of Physical Theory* (New York: Dover Publications, 1936), p. 52.
[9] P. W. Bridgman, *The Logic of Modern Physics* (New York: The Macmillan Company, 1928, 1960). Feigl
feels that the foundations of operationism precede Bridgman by a half century: He cites C. S. Peirce, "How to
Make Our Ideas Clear," *Popular Science Monthly*, January 1878. See Herbert Feigl, *op. cit.*, p. 508.
[10] *Ibid.*, p. 5. Notice also: "To adopt the operational point of view . . . means a far-reaching change in all
our habits of thought . . . . In some respects thinking becomes simpler, because certain old generalizations and
idealizations become incapable of use; for instance, many of the speculations of the early natural philosophers
become simply unreadable." (p. 31.) As an exercise accountants may wish to examine operationally the doctrine
that all costs are recovered *pro rata* when revenues are insufficient to cover all costs.

sion of a value judgment is not a proposition, the question of falsehood does not here arise . . . . if a man said that thrift was a virtue, and another replied that it was a vice, they would not on this theory be disputing with one another. One would be saying that he approved of thrift, and the other that *he* didn't; and there is no reason why both these statements should not be true.[11]

Operationism is closely related to the behaviorist movement in psychology, but again it does not deny the possible existence and importance of such things as emotions, self, etc. Stevens states: "Like positivism, behaviorism erred in denying too much. Operationism does not deny images, for example, but asks: What is the operational definition of the term 'image'?"[12] Accountants have, in fact, a long behaviorist tradition for observing business and economic behavior and trying to furnish information that encourages certain forms of behavior. At the present time accounting seems to be moving in the direction of more observations of this type, and fortunately decisions as to the reality of self, ego, etc., are seldom required.

Clearly operationism is not a form of monism, for until the fundamental irreducible substance is capable of being tested empirically, the individual must make his own speculations. What about dualism? Until things-in-themselves and other such monstrosities can be put to test and subjected to meaningful empirical tests they remain in the field of speculation. What about universals? The individual is at liberty to believe in them or not. For most purposes the following statement fits. "For an empiricist, universals are symbolical devices for grouping particulars. The sparrow can be analysed into sense-data; bundles of sense-data can be regrouped and handed over to various departments for study . . . ."[13]

Operationism has been criticized because it is essentially reductive in outlook. That is, it assumes that meaningful sentences can be reduced to atomic units, or to the physical language, or to statements that result in propositions that can be operationally tested for truth or falsity, e.g., propositions in the usual logical sense. How then can one ever generalize with such a philosophy? How can induction be applied? How do scientists generalize? Stevens has treated this problem.

The process of generalization proceeds on the basis of the notion of classes . . . no empirical proposition is ever without some element of generality. Classification can proceed only when we have criteria defining the conditions for class-inclusion, and these criteria are essentially operational tests . . . Here we resort to that fundamental operation we have already called discrimination. If we can discriminate crucial differences between Dobbin and other animals

---

[11] Alfred Jules Ayer, *Language, Truth and Logic* (New York: Dover Publications, Inc., 1946), pp. 21-22, 110. Notice the following expression of value judgments with respect to science. " . . . what higher and more spiritual goals could any man have than those involved in and implied by the whole enterprise of pure science — cooperation, understanding, respect, truth, and a life guided by reason? Such a goal as eternal bliss in some heavenly hereafter is almost crudely hedonistic in comparison." "Science and Its Critics," Harold E. McCarthy, *The Humanist XII*, Vol. 2, 1952. Reprinted in *Readings in Philosophy of Science, op. cit.*, p. 437. Many nonscientists with a humanist orientation will no doubt have different preference statements.

[12] S. S. Stevens, *op. cit.*, p. 166. The early stages of behaviorism were in fact so dogmatic in their refusal to admit nonobservables that C. D. Broad is reported to have classed behaviorism among "theories so silly that only very learned men would have thought of them." Quoted from Hector Hawton, *op. cit.*, p. 167.

[13] Hector Hawton, *op. cit.*, p. 178. " . . . life *has* been lived without absolute certainties. It may be true that some people are unhappy without the illusion of certainty, but it is also true that no human being can live rationally until he has freed himself from illusion." Harold E. McCarthy, *op. cit.*, p. 437. For teaching purposes and for memory work it is sometimes useful to abstract from certain influences and treat the remainder as dogma. It is probably safe to say that this device has an extremely limited range of usefulness before it begins to do more harm than good by inhibiting an inquiring mind. Consider, for example, the convention of debit and credit, which is usually presented to elementary students as an absolute dogma.

we have named horses . . . . On the basis of elementary discriminations, then, we make out first rudimentary classes and in doing so we have made the first step toward generalization. From there we advance to form classes of classes and to discover the relations between classes — always, at the empirical level, in keeping with operational criteria.[14]

Operationism is related to a number of other philosophical movements, but it is practically identical with pragmatism and is closely related to logical empiricism (scientific empiricism). Logical empiricism is a more moderate version of what was known as logical positivism and was developed primarily by the members of the Vienna Circle.[15] Two kinds of statements are recognized: those that are empirical in content and can be verified as to truth or falsity, and those that are formal sentences of syntax and are true by convention (stipulation). That is to say, formal sentences have no empirical content and are subject to the rules for manipulating sentences to get new sentences, i.e., the rules of logic and inference. Stevens traces the foundations of the system to Wittgenstein, who "made clear the *formal* nature of logic and showed that the rules and proofs of syntax should have no reference to the meaning (empirical designation) of symbols; and . . . showed that the sentences of metaphysics are pseudo propositions."[16]

This philosophy is a generalization of the axiomatic approach to mathematics, statistics, mechanics, and biology. Certainly much of the model-making that has overwhelmed the social sciences is related to constructing and interpreting abstract systems. The widely-used technique is to construct an abstract set of symbols and specify the rules of transformation that will be permitted for manipulating these symbols. Theorems are proved, and a whole superstructure that bears no necessary relationship to anything empirical is developed.[17] Some controversy exists over whether the rules adopted for manipulating symbols (logical rules) are completely arbitrary. Positivists usually take the position that the selection is *conventional* but is not a matter of indifference. Certain rules of inference and transformation yield a more useful — rich — framework for making interpretations and are therefore pragmatically more desirable than others. An instrumentalist or empiricist, such as Mill, may argue that the conventions that have been adopted for logic, and have survived, are those that led to useful interpretations. Thus the rules of logic are related to the needs of goal-seeking individuals and are the result of experience. They may have been developed through idle curiosity, but their survival depends on the richness of the interpretations that can be applied to them and to their general usefulness.[18]

The second step conceptually, if not historically, is concerned with finding interpretations of the symbols in terms of properties and relationships that can be sensed or can be reduced to other data that can be sensed.[19] Advocates of logical empiricism tend to call interpretation or the assignment of empirical meaning to symbols 'semantics,' and they have tried to develop a rigorous approach to this area. Mathematics consists only of symbols and rules for manipulating the symbols, and accordingly has no relation to the world of experience. Geometry, for example, is completely abstract until interpretations of some kind are made to relate it to what we think of as triangles, circles and other products of our senses.

The first reactions of such practical people as accountants are likely to range from disinterest to mild resentment, but as Wilder points out:

It reduces mathematics to a strictly "formal" process, with no direct reference to any "real" interpretation of the symbols involved. It has the advantages that accrue from avoiding er-

---

Footnotes on following page

rors due to varied interpretations of terms or unsuitable connotations, such as are frequently made in the use of ordinary language . . . .[20]

It should be clear that theorems proved in the more general calculus may be carried over and applied validly in all proper interpretations. An economy of effort may result, and the

---

[14] S. S. Stevens, *op. cit.*, p. 168. Moritz Schlick speaks of "certain primitive acts of recognition . . . so that each component can be identified as belonging to a definite class and assigned to a corresponding symbol." "Description and Explanation," *Readings in Philosophy of Science, op. cit.*, p. 470. Originally published in *Philosophy of Nature,* trans. Amethe von Zeppelin (New York: Philosophical Library, 1949).

[15] This group of intellectuals (Schlick, Neurath, Carnap, Frank, Brunswik, and others) began their discussions in the mid-'20s and set forth the outlines for logical positivism, which among other things attempts to eliminate metaphysics (in general, nonoperational statements) and replace it with a study of the language and methodology of science. The works of Carnap and Brunswik are cited frequently in subsequent essays.

[16] S. S. Stevens, *op. cit.*, pp. 169-170.

[17] "A Mathematical System is any set of strings of recognizable marks in which some of the strings are taken initially and the remainder derived from these by operations performed according to rules which are independent of the meanings assigned to the marks." C. I. Lewis, *Survey of Symbolic Logic* (Berkeley: University of California Press, 1918), p. 355. Or the voice of A. P. Ushenko, crying in the wilderness: " . . . the whole field of logic and mathematics consists of tautologies derived from other tautologies by means of tautologies." *The Theory of Logic* (New York: Harper & Brothers Publishers, 1936), p. 131.

[18] This insistence on a sharp distinction between syntax — the rules and the symbols — and the meaning of the symbols has been emphasized by logical empiricists, but this so-called axiomatic treatment of any subject has many advocates in other fields. Hilbert in mathematics along with Peano, Whitehead and Russell are representative. Kolmogorov and Savage in statistics, Hempel and Margenau in physics, Papandreou and Arrow in economics, Hull and Guilford in psychology, Lazarsfeld and Lerner in sociology make use of similar methods. Mattessich and Chambers have been trying to bring the approach to the field of accounting. See R. J. Chambers, "Blueprint for a Theory of Accounting," *Accounting Research*, January, 1955, and "Detail for a Blueprint," *The Accounting Review*, April, 1957. For Mattessich, see: "Towards a General and Axiomatic Foundation of Accountancy — With an Introduction to the Matrix Formulation of Accounting Systems," *The Accounting Review*, October, 1956; and in the same journal, "Mathematical Models in Business Accounting," July, 1958. and in the same journal, "Mathematical Models in Business Accounting," July, 1958.

[19] "If Σ is an axiom system, then an *interpretation* of Σ is the assignment of meanings to the undefined technical terms of Σ in such a way that the axioms become true statements for all values of the variables . . . . As a rule, we shall use the word 'model' to denote the *result* of the assignment of meanings to the undefined terms." Raymond L. Wilder, *Introduction to the Foundations of Mathematics* (New York: John Wiley & Sons, Inc., 1952), pp. 24-25. The separation of the calculus from the interpretation is emphasized by Andreas G. Papandreou: " . . . one could start with a calculus (any calculus) and attempt to give it an interpretation (i.e., assign meaning to the symbols) which would turn it into a deductive system." *Economics as a Science* (Chicago: J. B. Lippincott Company, 1958), p. 14. This remark by Alfred Tarski should keep us from overemphasizing the separation: "In contemporary methodology we investigate deductive theories as wholes as well as the sentences which constitute them; we consider the symbols and expressions of which these sentences are composed, properties and set of expressions and sentences . . . and even relations between expressions and the things which the expressions 'talk about' . . . " *Introduction to Logic* (New York: Oxford University Press, 1946), pp. 138-139. Each of these references is a very good source of information for those wishing an introduction to axiomatic method and symbolic systems. Another general discussion may be found in Patrick Suppes, *Introduction to Logic* (Princeton: D. Van Nostrand Company, Inc., 1957), especially Chapter 12. For a more sophisticated approach with discussions of meta-languages, see Rudolf Carnap, *Introduction to Symbolic Logic and Its Applications* (New York: Dover Publications, Inc., 1958). Most nonspecialists, such as accountants, will profit greatly from Charles W. Morris, "Foundations of the Theory of Signs," *International Encyclopedia of Unified Science* (Chicago: University of Chicago Press, 1955).

[20] Raymond Wilder, *op. cit.*, p. 200. Richard Mattessich gives more detail. "It introduces great generality, which produces highly economical working . . . in the setting up of accounting models . . . . It liberates the structure from the facade . . . . It opens new perspectives . . . . Features which have been hidden behind the technical language . . . are revealed by the much more general and fundamental language of mathematics. It brings a more rigorous order into what some call 'the art of ordering' . . . . It may facilitate the translation of concepts of one branch of accountancy into the concepts of another branch . . . . " "Towards a General and Axiomatic Foundation of Accountancy," *op. cit.*, pp. 329-330. It forces most psychological vagaries into the area of interpretation (semantics) and thereby banishes most psychological ambiguities from logic, i.e., the syntactical area.

help of specialists in proving such theorems may be used by those who are in the applied fields and are less adept at abstract proofs. Such a division clearly helps the cause of specialization yet in a paradoxical manner yields more generality. The fundamental calculus permits use of developments in other fields and, in fact, makes it easier for those in related fields to understand the specialized jargon of another. Thus a mathematician may understand more quickly and perhaps be able to make substantive contributions to accounting if the latter is approached as an interpretation of a set of abstract axioms.

Recently there has been a movement — led by some remaining members of the Vienna Circle — toward the unity of all sciences, and the results so far have been two volumes of the *International Encyclopedia of Unified Science*. The idea of the unity of science seems to be akin to such adventures as the search for the fundamental substance of matter, life or thought. The unifying structure is, of course, language under the title of Semiotic and slightly broadened from the narrow concept of language. The partitioning of any science or investigation into the formal (calculus) portion and the interpretation forms a starting point. The concept of language is expanded and classified so that the formal part is syntax (logic), the relation of the signs to experiential objects is 'semantics,' and the behavioral influence is 'pragmatics.' The language of science then becomes a generalized theory of signs including their designata and their relations to the folks who use them.[21]

We will not be concerned more with this subject at this point. An essay on the elementary aspects of semantics is included in this group, and two essays on logic and scientific method are included. While no essay on pragmatics is available, the relationship of this area to behavioral psychology and therefore to the essay on some behavioral aspects of accounting should be clear. It is hoped that these essays will indicate the extent to which scientific method is employed by accountants.

Holistic and Atomistic Views

A well-known controversy arises about an acceptable organizing principle for investigation in accounting. The reduction principle is usually associated with the view that a field or subject can be completely explained without remainder by explaining its constitutive parts. The opposing view assumes that the organism has properties not assignable to its parts and is known as the organic or holistic approach. Moreover, it is argued that peculiar properties are conferred on the parts by their relationship to one another and to the whole as a functioning organism.[22] The reductive approach was apparently aimed at freeing investigation from animistic remnants that hampered physicists for centuries, but when human beings are involved we are faced with adaptive behavior in the form of purpose. An instrumentalist approach that tries to describe and evaluate each part with reference to its contribution to the objectives of the entire organism is certainly inescapable. The organic (holistic) scientist studies the parts but insists that the whole is not entirely explained by this limited study, and, as Schwab emphasizes, the properties of the parts are

[21] The most comprehensive, easily digested treatment is by Charles W. Morris. "Foundations of the Theory of Signs," in the *International Encyclopedia of Unified Science, op. cit.*, pp. 77-137.

[22] A number of economists adopt opposing views on this matter. "As Koopmans points out, a full characterization of each individual's behavior logically implies a knowledge of *group behavior*; there is nothing left out. The rejection of the organism approach to social problems has been a fairly complete, and to my mind, salutary rejection of mysticism." Kenneth Arrow, "Mathematical Models in the Social Sciences," *The Policy Sciences* (Palo Alto: Stanford University Press, 1951), p. 133. But see Rutledge Vining: ". . . in a positive sense the aggregate has an existence over and above . . . individual units and behavior characteristics that may not be deducible from the behavior of these component parts." "Koopmans on the Choice of Variables to be Studied and of Methods of Measurement," *The Review of Economics and Statistics*, January, 1949, pp. 77-86.

treated as if they were conferred by their place in the organization. He adds: " . . . biologists and psychologists adherent to . . . anti-principles have an extremely hard time being faithful. The word and the notion of function creep in time and again; so does 'teleology' in the guise of 'drive,' 'anticipation,' 'adaptive value,' 'operant behavior'."[23] It is also interesting to note that the growth of cybernetics with emphasis on objectives and feedback has given impetus to the holistic-teleologic movement.

For one who uses a causal approach to science these ends or goals function as causes in the thinking process. Braithwaite, for example, points out their similarity to Aristotle's final causes functioning as immediate causes, and suggests that those who use the holistic approach postulate the goal-striving property in the organism.[24] The use of "to postulate" in this connection may be misleading and perhaps unfair to one committed to operationism. If the fruits of observation and theory formation indicate that the behavior of the parts can be predicted with the required degree of certainty by reference to such theoretical constructs as goal striving, operant behavior or other forms of organic behavior, we may use the construct in our investigations and explanations on a tentative basis until subsequent evidence makes its usefulness doubtful. The term 'postulate' may give the impression that such constructs and constitutive relations are made up at will and are therefore arbitrary.

With the use of goal-striving, objectives, ends, drives, etc., as theoretical constructs, operationists are not concerned with the old debate as to whether future explanations must be entirely in physico-chemical terms. All they need to assert is that there are uniformities in the observed system and that the particular theoretical construct helps predict the future state of the system.

To some extent the holistic-atomistic controversy arises from poor definitions and bad verbalization. The difference tends to disappear as the parts are more carefully described and defined. A broad view describes the individual notes and related symbols in a musical composition, for example, by a number of properties and relationships. Among these defining properties is the possible position of the part with respect to other parts and its relationship to them. To explicate a part without considering how it functions in its environment — relates to all sorts of other parts — is to over-apply the rules of abstraction and shear off properties and relations that may be important. Now it is clear that a complete description of the environment — all possible properties and relations — would be a description of the totality of our experiences and more! This problem also arises in connection with causation. If the view is broad enough, everything may be the cause of everything else. Thus we must construct a gap between the system and its environment and limit the forces that we let impinge on it. Usually we limit the bounds of the organism and its objectives, and then abstract from those properties and relationships that are not immediately related to the desired context.

This controversy over the holistic and atomistic approaches has implications for the accounting profession. The entity-organization problem may be viewed as an area of interest, but within such an area there are usually many sub-groups whose interests may be related but may also be in sharp conflict. We must remember that the entire concept of organizational objectives is highly abstract and is, in fact, a type of reification. However behavior attributed to organizations does exhibit certain patterns, and these patterns may be

[23] Joseph J. Schwab, "What do Scientists Do?" *Behavioral Science*, January, 1960, p. 10.
[24] " . . . writers . . . agree in postulating something in the organism which is present whenever goal-directed behavior is taking place and which is to explain it in the ordinary causal way . . . ." R. B. Braithwaite, *Scientific Explanation* (New York: Harper & Brothers, 1960), p. 326.

studied and predicted. We are certainly able to study patterns for individuals within the organization and to appraise the resultant influence of each.

It appears that accountants are forced to use methods of observation and measurement that are both aggregative and distributive. At times they may wish to estimate future income for the organization as a whole. More often they try to relate expected revenues and expenses to parts of the firm and to aggregate the individual streams. The rate of future expenditures, for example, can often be estimated best by referring to specific asset replacements necessary to preserve the revenue stream. Accountants operate in both directions, and one of the most difficult tasks is to find a basis for distributing a stream of favorable circumstances to individual assets. They do impute contributions on a more or less incremental basis to decisions, but, as is emphasized later, they then tend to impute excess contributions over cost of implementation to the general organizational environment. The usual procedure therefore uses an incremental approach that imputes all the increase to the specific event or decision and none to the remainder of the organization. After a decision has been made, however, the accounting procedure assigns benefit equal only to implementation costs to the specific assets or decisions and assigns the excess (if any) to the organization. This strange set of rules is responsible for considerable misunderstanding among both accountants and nonaccountants.

Criteria for Rule Selection

Philosophical and theoretical inquiry usually attempts to find general relationships, definitions and sentences. This statement needs special emphasis in the accounting field and in any similar field that grows up piecemeal and in answer to all sorts of demands for specialized information. The result in current professional jargon is a profession of numerous partially integrated rules that have been adopted to meet all kinds of 'brush fires,' i.e., specific points pressing for immediate answers. Accountants sometimes argue such theoretical points as direct costing versus full costing, or current costing versus replacement depreciation, without establishing any general criteria for assessing superiority or any standards for judgment. The arguments are often far too long, too loud, and too indecisive. Surely, there is enough in common in the problems of an information service such as accounting to permit generalizations and establish standards to which individual techniques and procedures should conform.

An adequate theorist from a field with any philosophical maturity should be able to give guidance and suggest answers to questions such as the following. What should be our criteria for preferring rule collection A over rule collection B? How are such criteria of superiority derived and judged? The standards for judging the adequacy, consistency and adaptability of rules and collections of rules are considered to be more general than the individual rules themselves. The search for generality is a major part of philosophical and scientific inquiry, and a science is considered to be well developed if its individual problems and situations can be 'explained by' (shown to be consistent with) relatively general propositions.

We assume a preference for rules that have clear-cut operational instructions for applying them to the sensible world. Preference is also presumed for rich interpretations with 'rules of correspondence' that are easy to follow and apply. Second, we feel that superior rules should lead to results that encourage progress in goal-seeking activities toward worthy objectives.

Criteria for superiority are standards of worthiness and are therefore value judgments. These assessments of worth are not controlled directly by logic and cannot be entirely settled by appeal to some sort of logical or scientific court. Logic and scientific method help us observe relevant data and search the resulting experiences for uniformities, objectives, etc., with a clearer insight. But what is accepted as desirable behavior for members of a profession — or indeed by a member of any society — is the result of subjective evaluation by individuals and especially by leaders of the relevant group. In later essays it is argued that standards for such evaluations are conditioned by the ideology in which they operate. While ethical and esthetical values may be *studied* by logical and scientific methods, they themselves are not logical propositions and are not scientifically determined.[25]

In the following essay we will discuss some of the criteria for an effective information-control system. Society has granted members of the accounting profession the responsibility for furnishing useful and dependable reports covering important segments of human activity. How do we sense (read) the extent of society's commission and how do we go about discharging our commission? Shall we let governmental agencies determine the ethical framework and operate our profession under the price system? Do members of the profession have special obligations for integrity and truthfulness and for helping maintain equity among contending groups in society? These are questions that should concern the accounting theorist as well as the social philosopher.

---

[25] This view is counter to that held by some positivists. " . . . the final ends of all personal conduct are provided by man's inherited desires or drives (his instincts), and therefore all problems of conduct are scientific problems . . . . The problem of what end is ethical is meaningless since no method of verifying any solution of it is conceivable." Burnham Putnam Beckwith, *Marginal-Cost Price-Output Control* (New York: Columbia University Press, 1955), pp. 11-12. However, our view is not necessarily opposed to the view held by those with "outer direction." Outer direction may or may not be influential in shaping the ideology, e.g., the standards and mores of the social group.

Essay Two

Comments on Accounting
and Its Environment

The thesis expressed in this essay is that the foundations upon which specific doctrines of accounting rest are inferences and assumptions related to the needs of goal-striving individuals. Thus it is argued that any theory of accounting depends for its validity on propositions in the broad area of human needs and human behavior and that any statement of accounting theory must be derivable from this more general set of relationships and propositions. Theory is often considered to be the entire complex of logical rules, primitive terms, semantic rules of correspondence, interpretations, definitions, theorems, etc., necessary to explain (Put the inquiring mind to rest.) behavioral or physical observations. In this spirit, the position expressed here is that the definitional boundaries of the profession are relatively unimportant except for establishing lines of professional jurisdiction. The important boundary, from the point of view of methodology, seems to be between the symbolic apparatus and the statements that tie this apparatus to the data of the empirical world. It is argued, therefore, that the important and critical boundary tends to separate the psychological features of human beings striving for their goals and attempting to satisfy their needs from the more conventional apparatus of logic and mathematics. According to this view, the generalizations of accounting must be subjected to the discipline of logic and scientific method, but in addition they must be deducible from more inclusive generalizations from the fields of individual and group behavior.

If accounting principles are rules derived from behavioral and social generalizations, then their usefulness and their consistency must be appraised in the broader context of goal-striving activities and worthy social ends. Their derivability is thus the result of applying acceptable logical and empirical procedures to broad social objectives in order to establish desirable rules for the more limited activities of gathering, classifying and reporting certain kinds of data. The machinery for investigating and appraising accounting principles, then, is related to finding whether the accounting rules are consistent with (harmonize with) those broader principles. This use of 'consistent with' is related to the use of the term in logic but is applied here primarily to determine whether certain accounting rules tend to accomplish acceptable goals — facilitate action toward desirable ends. The methodology of accounting therefore includes procedures and devices for appraising and evaluating worthy ends, for isolating and encouraging acceptable means of accomplishing such ends, and for establishing the routines necessary to adjust the two and permit enough flexibility to meet changing technologies and shifting social objectives.[1]

---

[1] Thus the following statement by J. F. Blair in his excellent article, "In Quest of an Audit Principle," seems to be overly restrictive. "It is uniformity of purpose we are seeking, not uniformity of practice — that is uniformity of ends, not of means." *The Journal of Accountancy*, February, 1947, p. 118. A. C. Littleton quotes this statement with approval and makes perhaps his own greatest contribution by discussing the adaptation of feasible means to accomplish desirable ends. See *Structure of Accounting Theory* (American Accounting Association, 1953), pp. 176 ff.

It is usually a thankless task to prepare a series of statements that are considered to be basic in any sense for a profession or branch of learning. Such lists are at best pretentious and are subject to criticism at practically every stage. The following list is accompanied by the feeling that the individual statements are far too loose and unsophisticated. Nevertheless, it is presented to emphasize some presuppositions that require attention before we are able to discuss the more familiar topics such as debit and credit. It should be observed that these statements are 'interpretations' and are at the semantic level in the sense that they refer to the relationship of the observer to the empirical world. Many readers may wish to prepare their own lists and may wish to begin with statements about acceptable forms of logic and acceptable rules of transformation and inference. For the benefit of the "meta-physicians of pragmatism" it should be emphasized that the following statements *presume* a succession of experiences, the ability of the observer to correlate these experiences, to arrange them in some sort of order, and to develop uniformities among them. Thus the unstated primordial methaphysical ooze assumes an entity with the ability to have experiences and to discriminate and classify them. For ordinary purposes we make the usual assumptions of science, including the assumption of observers and external data, but these assumptions are not necessary.

The following list attempts to avoid substantive material and to concentrate on some useful assumptions for establishing a methodology for accounting.

Some Observations and Generalizations:

1. We are able to organize our experiences so that we can discriminate entities and separate them from other entities and from their environment.
2. We can observe the experiences assigned to these entities — their behavior.
3. We observe uniformities (patterns) in behavior, *and* we propose an explanation, i.e., we infer goal-seeking activities, purposive and adaptive behavior.
4. We can infer from common behavior that some goals are considered to be more desirable than others, and we are able to weigh this evidence and to rank the relative strength of these goals.
5. We can infer from action of the entities the kind of information reports that stimulate them toward objectives and those that deter them.
6. We can observe the adaptability of these entities and infer that it is possible to 'educate' them to use different kinds of information.
7. We can devise procedures and schemes to help them accomplish desirable objectives.
8. Information is not always costless in terms of other objectives that must be sacrificed in order to procure it.
9. Interpersonal comparisons can be made.

Event-Recognition Rules and Entity Selection

It should be emphasized that the above statements are extremely general and may be applied to disciplines other than accounting. It is the intention now to review a number of tentative statements that might serve as a framework for accounting as it is usually conceived and defined.

We could begin such a series of statements by assuming some sort of fundamental *flow* or some kind of fundamental *rights* and attempt to build the accounting structure on this foundation.[2] The difficulty with such a beginning is that it gives no guides for determining which events should be recorded and which events should be neglected.

Our first problem seems to be to select from the more general social disciplines an area of interest and need — an entity. The selection of an entity is one of the more primitive accounting notions that involves: (a) recognition that certain individuals have worthy objectives; (b) that their progress toward these socially desirable ends requires adaptive behavior with some choice as to both means and ends; (c) that these choices may be improved by certain information. The objectives may be diverse. Simple scorekeeping may suffice if the objective is to determine the winner of a contest. If it is desirable to predict future winners and to improve performance, we may wish historical records of individual accomplishment in batting, pitching, fielding, throwing, etc. In such cases, as in most others, a number of entities — areas of interest — are interwoven. Records of achievement to be compared with objectives may be accumulated (accounted for) by individual players under varying conditions, individual groups of players, e.g., pitchers or left-hand batters, and for the entire team or for the entire league. The reader may or may not wish to exclude such information services from his definition of accounting, but many problems are common to both. Objectives are specified. Activities required to accomplish these objectives are identified. Convenient measures of performance of these activities are assigned. These measures are applied to those who are responsible for the activities and have some degree of control over them. The information is then gathered, summarized, and reported so that it should help attain objectives more effectively.

Clearly specifying and ranking objectives may be a major problem in some types of accounting. In some cases the task may seem relatively easy, and a few reports may suffice. In most cases, we may need a large number of progress reports that range from salesmen's records, product-sales records, production records, to efficiency and cost reports and liquidity statements. The objectives in some of these instances may be so complex and interrelated that the establishment of numerous intermediate and sub-objectives in the forms of standards, quotas and potentials may be desirable. Progress toward these targets may then be accounted for and reported. In the meantime the profession must be concerned with harmony of the sub-objectives among themselves and with more general goals.

In the operations of even a simple organization there are many events that do not seem to be relevant to immediate objectives. Cost considerations mean that we cannot record every event that impinges on the organization, and we must accordingly make a selection. This selection of events to be recorded is a matter of assigning subjective utilities and estimating probabilities. The fact that a ball player frequents bars at all hours of the night is a material piece of information that should call for measuring and reporting unless we may assume that the effects are reflected in some other measure of his accomplishment and capability. In a similar manner the senility of a corporate president would seem to be an event (or series of events) of importance to at least some other members of the organization. Perhaps the effects of this turn of events will show up elsewhere in the reports with

---

[2] I am unable to build a satisfactory structure on such primitive terms. Richard Mattessich has made an important contribution by considering a series of events to be a "flow" and with the help of some axioms, definitions and requirements, built an axiomatic structure for accounting. From our viewpoint he might well have begun with objectives, and proceeded to needs, and then to events. See Richard Mattessich, "Towards a General and Axiomatic Foundation of Accountancy — With an Introduction to the Matrix Formulation of Accounting Systems," *Accounting Research*, October, 1957, pp. 328-355. Consider the following statement from Alfred North Whitehead: "They are *our* axioms . . . not *the* axioms . . .," *A Philosopher Looks at Science* (New York: Philosophical Library, Inc., 1965), p. 38.

less direct reference. If so, our problem becomes that of choosing which means of disclosure yields the largest probable advantage.

The problem of finding rules for determining which events require recognition (and when) is a major problem of accounting. What we obviously try to do is to recognize those events relevant to objectives. In some cases we fall short of the mark when we apply definite rules of procedure. That is to say, our selection of operational rules is sometimes faulty even if we are lucky or astute enough to identify and appraise objectives and probable behavioral reactions correctly.

The selection of rules for determining which events will be relevant to objectives and to future decisions is a difficult task, but it is precisely at this level that real progress may be made by those interested in improving the practical operation of accounting. We are faced with evaluating the probable effects of such events as wars, revolutions, price-level changes, new products, technological advances, changes in ability of competing firms, conflict of interest among our own managers, changes in the general liquidity of the economy, and new tax policies, along with other internal events such as increasing conservatism of our management, inability of salesmen to adjust to changing times, inflexibility of our engineers, etc.

There is a cost (sacrifice) attached to extending our recognition rules to more and more events. The evaluation problem becomes more difficult, and the probability estimates become more diverse. The accountants' competence becomes more limited. The point to be emphasized is that critical examination and appraisal of the event-admission rules is a proper subject for investigation by accounting theorists. We may wish to argue such accounting problems as the price-level problem, but we should fit the arguments into the broader background by specifying exactly which objectives are involved, and exactly what decisions will be influenced, and identify precisely the individuals who make the decisions and hope to attain the objectives. Only then can we explore possible influences of available alternatives and experiment with competing recognition and reporting rules. Clearly (as Professor Sorter points out), there is something wrong with an information-control system that insists on recognizing the exchange of a dime for a glue pot and is silent about unfilled orders, expansion plans and the state of the industry.

Our task is not complete, by any means, when we adopt acceptable event-admission rules that give consideration to objectives, alternative information schemes, and cost. But at least we have completed a number of steps and have a basis for continuing. Our next step is concerned with determining which aspects of the events will be measured and reported. What dimensions shall we recognize? And how many? In accumulating pitching records we may wish to recognize wildness, ability to work long stretches (complete games), ability to work long and often (innings pitched), deceptiveness (strikeouts), ability to win (won-and-lost records), and remaining years of effectiveness (age and trend of performance). Many may wonder if accountants do as well.

To the extent that the enterprise objective is that of a bailor, we may devise a set of rules that admits events which are concerned with accepting responsibility for objects and with release from such responsibility. The objectives are clear; the event-admission rules are clear; and the dimensions are clear. But suppose we wish to recognize some damage that may occur. Clearly an expansion of the instructions is necessary to locate responsibility and to measure the deterioration.

Consider now the steward who is given a collection of properties along with a charge which includes in its provision: (a) increase the fund by operations if possible; (b) keep track of the claimants to the fund and their rights; (c) exercise freedom in the composition of the items of the fund but preserve enough liquidity so that control is not lost; (d) be kind to workers and pay them at least the current wage rate; (e) make products that are reliable and yield customer satisfaction; (f) keep the properties in such good physical shape that they will add to the beauty and dignity of the community; (g) keep the organization operating, and (h) support good works generally, take part in civil affairs, and operate in harmony with accepted social standards.

A little reflection on typical managerial responsibilities indicates that we accountants have taken an extremely limited attitude regarding our task of furnishing useful, dependable information. In fact we have permitted large parts of our domain to go by default to others. What reports do we render of good works? Participation in civil affairs? Wage obligations? Customer satisfaction? Obviously there is more to accountability than finding acceptable rules for measuring the amount of profit earned, and there are more objectives than profit maximization and survival.[3]

It is interesting to note that such information is given more or less outside the narrow double-entry system by judicious classification and arrangement. Some index of customer satisfaction is given by the amount of returns and allowances and in fact by the volume of sales itself. The degree of liquidity is indicated in a crude way by classification (grouping) and by presentation in statements. The condition of the properties may sometimes be inferred from the volume of maintenance expenditures, capital expenditures and book value related to original cost. So far we have done a poor job of reporting esthetic values.

The charge to do good works, be socially and morally worthy, and be public-spirited citizens has not been carefully measured and reported by accountants. Some indication of the contributions to worthy causes may be found in appropriate accounts, and the contributions to taxing agents are sometimes set forth. The contribution of the firm by allowing executives time off for public affairs is ordinarily not isolated. The contributions of employees on their own time are usually chronicled in such auxiliary reporting devices as presidents' reports, house organs, etc. Our conclusion should be obvious: Accountants must develop selection rules for the objectives themselves as well as for individual events. In practice, accountants often select objectives indirectly by selecting first a reference group, e.g., businessmen, and then adopting the values of this group.

Events and Values

The discussion in the preceding section emphasizes that accountants must be selective in determining which events are to be measured and recorded. The criteria for recognition are related to objectives. Objectives may be diverse and some events may affect more than one objective. It is the contention of this section that the concept of value (with some modification) is a sort of common denominator applicable to many diverse objectives and that the value construct (in some form or other) is an essential part of accounting.

In establishing an order among various constructs we maintain that objectives come first and are the guiding beacons for event admission and measurement. The concept of value is related to expected *favorable* prospects and is, of course, highly subjective. Value therefore is related to objectives, for favorable prospects are not definable except in terms of 'matters of concern,' and 'worth' is definable only in ability to further objectives. Valuation then turns out to offer a framework for assigning subjective utilities to different conditions, i.e., to sources of objective-fulfilling potential. This relationship is empha-

---

[3] Those who follow Luther and accept the Protestant ethic will no doubt feel that the presence of profits and increasing wealth reflect the reward of God for generally doing good works. Whether our current measures of income and wealth are acceptable measures of Christian behavior is debatable. Certainly the conclusion that large accounting profits inevitably imply commendable social and moral behavior is not entirely warranted.

sized because some accountants have apparently felt that value determination in some way is an ultimate of accounting. If valuation and accounting for values are designed to serve as a medium for reducing objective-potential to a common denominator, it seems that such values must be internal in the sense of being subjective assessments. We ask then: What do market values, costs, etc., have to do with our problem? To toss off glib references to profit maximization as the single objective of a composite organization may lead to a dismal measuring service. We need to do some thinking about weighing and harmonizing the goals of different individuals acting alone, in groups and sub-groups. Still it is possible that the economist's crude concept of external market value and the accountant's equally crude measurement rules together will provide an acceptable approximation for defining and weighing objectives.

The problem of subjective values is itself difficult enough, and it is complicated further by the necessity for weighing interpersonal considerations arising from the interaction of different individuals and groups within the entity. Our method of procedure here is similar to that employed by measuring specialists everywhere: we simplify the problem by searching for related constructs until finally we can substitute one with approximately the same meaning that can be identified, classified and measured. A considerable part of accounting and economic controversy is concerned with whether their simplified models are close enough to be useful in reaching decisions. This activity is legitimate theory in the sense that it is concerned with whether the rules of correspondence do or do not define the mental constructs that we wish to measure and relate to our objectives. 'Market value' may not be quite the phenomenon we wish to use, but perhaps it can be substituted for a more complex structure. The rules for measuring market value may be relatively simple, and the substitution may be acceptable. In a similar fashion *cost* to an entity is sometimes more easily handled than subjective value to the entity, and is therefore substituted. A legitimate theoretical activity is concerned with whether 'cost' as identified and measured by rules adopted by the accountant can be substituted with profit for the kind of value constructs that are appropriate for making decisions and meeting objectives. The historical − aboriginal − replacement − alternative − current − purchasing power discussion of cost should be judged against this broader framework. Notice that agreement is not a necessary condition for theory. Equally honest individuals may appraise needs and means in different ways and assign different weights.

Let us return to the problem of deciding which events are to be admitted and which omitted by constructing a crude analogy. The status of an entity in relation to the objectives of its members at any point of time may be represented by a panorama of hills and mountains of favorable prospects (goal-satisfying potential) along with depressions for unfavorable prospects. Some of these favorable hills arising above the wasteland we agree to recognize, measure (evaluate) and report as assets. Other favorable circumstances (e.g., morale) may indeed rise as high as some of the mountains, but accountants have agreed, for some obscure set of reasons, not to treat them as assets. We need to examine these rules for determining which service potentials should be recognized and which omitted. We also need to scrutinize the additional rules for reducing these mounds of favorable prospects (and sloughs) to common denominators and for measuring their elevations and depressions.

We could examine whether a report that nets the prospects (gives the algebraic total) would be adequate, but the usefulness of classification for suggesting additional dimensions is apparent. Accountants usually assume that indicating the type (source) of service potential, e.g., shelter, is useful. Some degree of liquidity is usually necessary for attaining objectives, and the accountant's procedures in this area need review. Our accepted methods disclose liquidity features by classification or by refusing to recognize an increase in favorable prospects unless it is accompanied by additional liquidity — realization. Perhaps we should try to scale liquidity directly into our value system instead of building it on a go/no-go basis into our definition of realized income.

Let us now turn to an examination of some rules for value recognition that are currently in use and comment briefly on measurement devices and assumptions. These instructions are not always clear-cut, and they are sometimes difficult to apply. Favorable situations that are common to all firms, such as good mountain air or stable governments, are usually considered to be a general rise in the plateau not subject to measurement and treatment as assets. In other cases, such as a donated factory, the donation may appear to be a mound worth capitalizing, but the attendant low lands of unfavorable wage efficiency, high transportation costs, etc., may mean that the gift has no substantial overall potential. In some cases the expected favorable circumstances must be differential in the sense that they are peculiar to the specific organization. Yet this test is not often applied, and we find buildings being treated as assets even though all competitors also have shelter. In these cases, we usually explain the position by pointing out that past effort in order to build may somehow be relevant to the future and be traced as the sacrifice in attaining desirable points of vantage.[4]

Measurement rules and models are discussed in later essays. At this point we emphasize that 'assets' are defined by accountants to include differential advantages that are related to potential to attain objectives. Thus the asset value to the members of an entity (e.g., recluses) may be different from the market value determined by marginal buyers and sellers in an external market. A very real difficulty that will concern us later is the process of finding an acceptable common denominator for all kinds of different potentials for satisfying all sorts of objectives. In some cases large sales may be a higher ranked objective than large profits, and monumental and impressive factory buildings may be more important than either. Power to dominate the industry or community is often a major goal. The extra cost of monumental buildings may be measured without difficulty, but clearly our measure of benefit in terms of product sales leaves much to be desired. Indeed, some objectives may be satiated quickly so that most of the benefits are received in a relatively short period. Thus we need to consider stability of goals for members of the entity and for society.

At last we may take a quick look at the bookkeeping phenomenon of double entry. Double-entry results from measuring two aspects of assets and adopting conventions and measurement rules that assure the equality of the numbers assigned to each aspect. We could just as well assign numbers to three qualities (properties) of events and have triple-entry or n qualities and have n-tuple entry. Or we could devise related pairs and have

---

[4] C. West Churchman has concerned himself with assets and has tended to relate them to power. "The concept [power] can be defined several ways within the means-end scheme . . . we may say that the power of an individual X is simply the measure of his ability to attain any one of a set of his desired goals . . . . This definition of power implies that the power of an individual depends on the choices he can make, on his state of knowledge, and on the goal he wants. Hence, one man may be more powerful than another because he wants less . . . . Our interest here, however, is in a concept of power that is independent of the individual's specific goals . . . . Although it may be possible to measure power in terms of potentiality of choice, we often find ourselves concentrating more on an individual's resources than on the actual choices themselves. This suggests a third definition of power. We shall call the resources assets, and define an asset as any aspect of an individual's environment that produces a potentiality of choice for a set of actions." *Prediction and Optimal Decision* (Englewood Cliffs: Prentice-Hall, Inc., 1961), pp. 323-324. The potentiality for choice instead of potentiality for satisfaction seems to be an unnecessary restriction and implicitly equates choices to objectives.

double-entry doubled. One pair might be our usual assets and source of assets while another might be a liquidity measure matched with a responsibility for liquidity, and still another a measure of esthetic values with equal credits to specific sources of such values.

These illustrations seem to be a little far-fetched, but it should be observed that accountants are far from agreed on the meaning of the credit dimension. On the other hand, they may be too well agreed and too insistent on the necessity for equality of assets and whatever other dimension is selected.

Some accountants hold to assets and sources of assets as *the* two dimensions worth recording; others use assets and claims, or equities; some seem to prefer assets and responsibilities for administering the assets; one at least appears to follow assets with restrictions on managerial freedom in manipulating the assets as the second dimension. Chambers has abandoned asset values as the primary dimension. He has suggested inputs equal outputs plus residues.[5]

It is not intended to discuss the relative merits of each such formulation. Later discussions will argue that single-entry or even no-entry accounting may be adequate for certain information gathering and reporting. Nevertheless, a digression on some aspects of double-entry as a method follows as an informal appendix.

---

[5] It is probably true that entity or fund theorists on the one hand may be distinguished from proprietary theorists on the other by their preferred fundamental equation. It seems that the form of the equation is not a fundamental mark of difference, i.e., there should be more important consequences of adopting these views. The degree of restriction in most cases is approximated by ordinal measurement, i.e., ranked classes without equal differences in restrictions. The approach of R. J. Chambers has interesting possibilities. "In the simplest case of a continuing entity inputs equal outputs plus residues . . . . The equality may be called the basic identity or axiom of accounting. If it is granted that the relationship between inputs and outputs and the size of residues are matters of importance, double-entry follows. If some aspects of these matters are practically less important single-entry accounting may suffice. For the purpose of recording inputs and outputs a convention is adopted. Inputs will be shown as credits; outputs and residues as debits." "Blueprint for a Theory of Accounting," *Accounting Research*, January 1955, pp. 22-23.

Appendix A to Accounting
and Its Environment

Exercise in Formulating Fundamental
Accounting Equation

In uninterpreted symbolic form we may express what is generally known as the fundamental accounting equation as:

$$(Z) \dashv x \dashv y[(N)xO(M)y]$$

In the usual jargon of logic this general equation may be read: for every Z there exists an x and there exists a y such that the property N assigned to x is always the relation O with the property M assigned to y. In order to develop this general statement for use in accounting, we must interpret the symbols and make the operators more definite.

To begin the interpretation of this general statement, we shall define z as any modification (event or transaction) that is worthy of recording. We have pointed out elsewhere that the establishment of a set of rules for determining which events in the empirical world are worthy of attention is a complicated matter that depends on objectives. The N and M may be interpreted as cardinal numbers assigned by measurement rules to x and to y, and the 'O' relation may be interpreted as the specific relation 'equal to.' Thus the later part of the expression asserts that the number assigned to x must be equal to the number assigned to y. When combined with (z), we assert the equality of x and y for every modification (event or transaction). The entity construct is an extension of the expression, 'for every z,' for the admission of any particular z into the collection requires the existence of class discrimination rules that together determine the boundaries of the entity. The formulation of such rules is not done automatically by some legerdemain of logic. These formulations are constructed with full attention to objectives and human needs.

The interpretation of x and y also relates directly to rules of correspondence that tie the symbolic letters to accounting concepts. These rules are not whimsical; they must be related to concepts and made operational. Thus, constructs may be related to other constructs containing intervening variables. We may interpret x to mean preferred states and interpret y to mean individuals who are able to enjoy these preferred states. Certainly the common interpretation assigns 'favorable prospects' to x and 'source of prospects' or 'right to enjoy prospects' or perhaps 'responsibility for administering prospects' to y.

It turns out that the concept of 'preferred states' is highly abstract and requires simplifying rules of measurement. The first level of simplification is to replace the diverse 'preferred states' with 'value,' a common denominator. By specifying only certain kinds of value, and calling the collection of specified values, 'assets,' we may interpret x as assets and y as source or responsibility for assets.

So far we have made no interpretation in terms of debits and credits. By specifying a suitable set of rules of correspondence between assets (and sources) on the one hand with debit and credit on the other, we can interpret the expression $(z) \dashv x \dashv y[(N) \, x \, O \, (M) \, y]$ to mean that for every recordable transaction (z) there exist at least one debit and at least one credit and the numbers assigned to debits must equal the numbers assigned to credits. The serious student should understand that it is possible to construct rules (conventions for assigning numbers) in which debits need not equal credits. For example, we might define debits as increases in either assets or sources of assets and credits as being decreases in either. The equality between assets and sources of assets could still hold, but the equality between debits and credits would not follow. Debit and credit are not identical to increase and decrease.

The interpretation in terms of debits and credits requires definitions of the verbal expressions 'debit' and 'credit'. These definitions may be constitutive definitions in the sense that they are defined in terms of other constructs such as assets, expenses, etc., or the definitions may be operational in the sense of giving instructions for identifying and using debits and credits, or they may be combinations of both. The latter case is clearly applicable. In the early stages of professional development, definitions were developed for 'account' and for 'balance,' and, with the ordinary usage of left and right, rules were developed such that debits are equal to credits. Thus, if an instance arises in practice in which the equality is not preserved, the lack of equality is attributed to the failure to follow the specified rules. When these rules are constructed to preserve equality of debits and credits, it is necessary to specify that assets and responsibility for assets have opposite balances. Which side is to represent which aspect is clearly conventional.

A further interpretation is required if we wish to subdivide the assets and their sources. First, rules must be given for making such classifications and deciding whether a particular instance is or is not a member of each specified class. These rules and their formation are exercises in practical pragmatics and must consider the reactions of humans and machines to data and their ability to discriminate and classify data. The rules of deductive logic may be applied to extend the rules to classes and aggregates.

Observe that in making the interpretation of (N) x O (M) y it was specified that the numbers to be assigned must be equal. This is not quite the same as specifying that only increases and decreases should be recorded. The case of increase and decrease of the same class on the same transaction z is usually trivial, and may be allowed to remain or may be ruled out by a more limited interpretation of z, a transaction or recordable modification.

Notice that a good part of accounting theory, as commonly understood, turns on the interpretation of recognizable transaction z, for z might be given such interpretations as changes in the degree of blueness, or degree of hardness, or degree of favoritism toward church activities instead of the usual subjective concept of favorable expectations. It should be clear that many difficult problems that face accountants and constitute accounting theory are related to: (a) specifying the rules for recognizing recordable events (This covers such practical activities as determining the entity and deciding which events are important.); (b) specifying what dimensions (aspects) of the events should be recorded; (c) adapting measurement rules for each dimension; and (d) giving instructions for collecting, classifying and reporting these measurements. The usual bookkeeping rules for debit and credit are a relatively minor part of (d).

Appendix B to Accounting
and Its Environment

Defense for Historical
Aspects of Accounting

Accountants have often been accused of looking at the past instead of into the future, and perhaps as a result, they have de-emphasized their close kinship to historians. Accounting information, it is argued, is always used for decisions that are made in the future about actions that will take place in the future. Unfortunately, those who have been most critical have given no instructions and no procedures for observing the future — the criticism has not been made operational.

An explanation (justification) of the accountant's position may begin with the statement that not even the most accomplished clairvoyants have ever learned anything from observing the future or by taking their clues for present action from the future. Extreme advocates of determinism and predestination seldom go so far as to argue that sources of present information are placed in one's future experiences in advance and are available to the mind before they take place. Some critics may insist that accountants should try to improve their approach by observing the 'present' and using its events for guidance, for, it has been argued, only the present has 'meaning.' Any useful definition of the present gets involved with mathematical limits and intervals far too short for meaningful psychological spans of recognition. If the present is defined as a period long enough for cognition, enough past must be included to allow coordination with existing experience. An instruction "to scan the present" is not very helpful.

Accountants observe the past and record some of its events simply because the past is the only segment available for observation. An accountant is therefore a special kind of historian; he selects events from the history of an entity by applying selection rules; he then applies measurement conventions and traces the effects of these events in terms of areas of interest — accounts. The legitimate criticism is not that accountants are historians. The legitimate objection is that the accountant's history is not relevant to the needs of those who must have information.

Isolated facts are of little interest to scientists, historians or other inquiring minds. The search is for uniformities in behavior and for possible patterns in such behavior. This extremely close relationship between science and history was emphasized by Karl Pearson, who long ago pointed out that science consisted of descriptions of the past plus *faith* that the descriptions will prove valid in the future. The faith that such relationships will recur corresponds to what philosophers know as induction — hypotheses about behavior in the future.

It is possible to observe relationships among events in the past without relating them *explicitly* to the future. Thus a static model may be set up from observed relationships and beliefs about such relationships, and changes can be inserted into the structural equations and parameters without explicit reference to time. Indirectly, these models are related to the future, for the reason for their formation is to find what would happen to the system if changes were introduced. Economists recently have concerned themselves with dynamics. This emphasis deserves mention inasmuch as the position taken here is that all information is about the past and that all useful information must be relevant to the future. To the human mind all events and activities seem to take place in a medium of time, so that the mere passage of time is sometimes advanced as an 'explanation' of all things that change. Clearly, to use time (or even history) as the sole independent variable carries aggregation to a fantastic limit and may take on anthropomorphic overtones. This is not to deny that many important investigations are concerned with the speed with which certain reactions occur and with ordering them as a prelude to assigning primitive causation. The entire purpose of examining the past for uniformities and relationships is to help with predictions about *events* in the future, and it goes without saying that precedence and persistence of relationships are of paramount importance. (Normally we predict probable events in the future and accept rather than predict that the 'future' will appear. In fact, a concept of future devoid of events may be an impossible concept.)

How then are accountants, or anyone else, able *to look* into the future? Clearly, no one looks into the future in any literal sense. What then are the specific instructions? One looks at uniformities in the past and assigns probability distributions to their expected persistence. One may enlarge his relevant past experience by analogy — a process that is also based on experience. Certainly there is no handy searchlight to be focused on the future. It is as if one 'looks' into the future by using mirrors pointed to the past. At best, inductions (hypotheses about the events of the future) are based on faith in the continuity of past relationships. Fortunately for mankind, many of these observed relationships have proved to be remarkably stable.

Consider once more the place of the recordkeeping function in modern social life. The function of keeping historical records — records can only be of the past — is to provide guides for future conduct. This is the function of history and of accounting, and it is the framework in which accounting and all other information services must operate. Once this purpose is understood, a framework can be constructed for developing an integrated accounting theory that includes a methodology for determining whether accounting hypotheses are consistent and which procedures are consistent with overall objectives. It turns out that the pertinent objection to accountants as historians is that they have sometimes concentrated on the wrong events — written bad history — by keeping records of events that are not helpful for making decisions and do not further accomplishment of desirable goals.

Accountants have, in fact, been slow to recognize their kinship with historians and have sometimes denied the historical function of their work. Some kind of record of accomplishment related to planned objectives would seem to be an essential ingredient of any control system. How far into the past the accountant must look for relevant clues and how he must weigh the clues are vital questions. In some instances a series of samples at 15-minute intervals in combination with the usual Shewhart and related quality-control apparatus may be sufficient. The accounting profession must do more, however. It should specify how it establishes its tolerances, and how many previous results need to be preserved and appraised to indicate trends, seasonals and other relevant influences with sufficient accuracy.

In fact, we may argue that the planning function is meaningless and futile without an appraisal of past behavior and projection of some of the patterns into the future. There is unfortunately a current tendency to call estimates based on past accounting information in the narrowest sense 'accounting estimates,' and to term estimates based less directly on the accounts 'engineering estimates' or 'managerial estimates.' Whence come the data and skills for making such nonaccounting estimates? The answer, in the absence of miraculous disclosure — an unsatisfactory basis for most business judgments — is of course that they use history that is not recorded directly in accounting records. They may be eclectic and select from a number of historians, including accountants, but select they do and the selections are from the past! Hypotheses may be set up and tested, but how does one suspect the relevance of the hypothesis to the problem at hand? Certainly, as soon as the hypothesis is confirmed or rejected it too becomes a part of the heritage from the past.

This somewhat extended discussion is given to emphasize that information about the historical past is imperative for control *and is also imperative for planning*. The separation of planning and control by some accountants is certainly over-drawn, for planning, by any definition, implies *concern* with the future course of events. In addition it implies that some aspects of the future are susceptible to influence and control or that reaction to them will offer opportunity for judgment and decision. In a similar manner it is future events, or reaction to assumed events, that are the objects of control. While it is impossible to learn from the future, it is equally impossible to control the past. (Unfortunately, some accountants and historians have been able to distort it!)

It has been said that every generation rewrites history to conform with its own needs. History then is rewritten as needs change, i.e., available records are resifted, reweighed and reinterpreted. The history that remains offers expected relevance to future conduct.[6]

---

[6] Those interested in the problems and philosophy of history will find *The Philosophy of History in Our Time* an exciting and useful book. (Hans Meyerhoff edited the anthology, published by Doubleday & Company, Inc., 1959.) Accounting history is written in a functional framework that constrains the writer no less than the Judeo-Christian religious framework, or than the rational structure of Hegel influenced historians to interpret events as clues to God's will or the rational spirit. Accountants, unlike institutional economists, would probably not identify their efforts with historicism: "The subject mater of history is human life in its totality and multiplicity . . ." (p. 10). Instead, accountants are probably nearer to Benedetto Croce: ". . . the past is dead except insofar as it is 'unified with an interest of the present life' " (p. 44). Most accountants would also agree with Meyerhoff's description of John Dewey's attitude: ". . . historical statements are like statements in any other discourse that claim to be true . . . and, despite their reference to the past, they are subject to the same kind of 'logic' which we use in ordinary language or in science." *Ibid.,* p. 162. The 'sociology of knowledge' aspects of history are discussed in Essay 6. Meyerhoff (p. 57) summarizes this view with this brief quotation from Jose Ortega y Gasset: "Man, in a word, has no nature; what he has . . . is history."

Essay Three

Accounting Profession — Simulation and Description

An attempt is made in this essay to point out the critical decision points in the accounting profession and to set up a descriptive model of how ideas may be introduced into the structure, how they become a part of the theoretical machinery and how they may be discarded. Similar discussions could consider the inflow and outflow of manpower, the expansion of services, or the monetary receipts. These flows are to some extent interdependent, but in this study no attempt is made to quantify the structural equations or to do more than guess at the form of related parameters. Such work would normally be undertaken by the equivalent in our profession of econometricians and probably would follow the general approach employed in industrial dynamics by Jay Forrester and others.[1]

Recently there has been some discussion of an accounting court and the desirability of having definite semi-judicial machinery for resolving conflict, admitting new ideas to respectability, and rejecting obsolete notions.[2] Before we accept a structure that cannot avoid the introduction of rigidity into the system, it may be useful to survey the accounting profession as it exists and to point out how the job of idea introduction is now being done.

The problem is complicated by the lack of sharp definitions for fundamental concepts such as idea and profession. For current purposes 'idea' is used as a title to indicate suggestions for additions, emendations, cancellations of procedures, objectives, methods, or other similar components of the profession. Thus, the concept of the all-inclusive earnings report may be treated as an idea although its emergence is related to many others, and the concept itself is a complex bundle of more elementary ones. The construct of the profession is also not a simple one. A number of variables operating on the concept are only partially determined or not determined at all by other variables within the system — they are more or less exogenous. Others are endogenous in the sense that they appear to be (with the present state of knowledge) completely determined by forces considered to be within the system. This difference depends on where the definitional boundaries of the system are drawn, but such a distinction between endogenous and exogenous means that the

---

[1] See, for example, Jay Forrester, "Industrial Dynamics, A Major Breakthrough for Decision Makers," *Harvard Business Review*, July - August, 1958, pp. 37-66. See also: *Industrial Dynamics* (New York: McGraw-Hill Book Company, Inc., 1961).

[2] Leonard Spacek, "The Need for an Accounting Court," *The Accounting Review*, July, 1958. The opposing view is presented here by DR Scott, who remains the most underrated philosopher of accounting. "The failure of accounts to adapt themselves to the changing needs of management was not due to a reactionary attitude on the part of accountants. Fundamentally, it was due to the fact that accountants have grown into the institutional framework of society. Over the centuries, business practice and the law have grown around the double-entry record. The social role played by accounting was such that it was freely available for the degree of experimentation which inevitably accompanied so radical an adjustment. A new technique [statistics] which had not yet become institutionalized lent itself readily to the process of experimentation." DR Scott, "The Influence of Statistics upon Accounting Technique and Theory," *The Accounting Review*, January, 1949, p. 83.

number of unknowns usually exceeds the number of equations so that the system is under-determined.[3]

We shall begin by assuming that the profession is in existence at the time of the investigation, so that one of the first steps is to determine the initial conditions and establish the relevant decision points so that prediction may be improved. It may be possible to establish the relationships in quantitative terms that will permit manipulation of the model to determine its reaction to controlled changes in variables and parameters. While the results are valid only for the model under consideration, a carefully constructed framework permits inference by analogy to the system itself so that new insights may be gained. Such an approach may suggest research to be undertaken in the actual system, or, if not, it may lead to useful results by allowing changes in the model that could not be introduced into the system except at high cost or by disrupting the system itself. In a profession, for example, it may be impossible to study the effects of certain changes without wholesale personnel changes — a procedure that is hardly feasible.

Setting forth initial conditions requires further attention, but at this point it is sufficient to accept the initial conditions as the state of the profession resulting from a process of historical selectivity. A brief discussion of Darwinian social selectivity is given elsewhere, and it is sufficient here to point out that the existence of a procedure is itself evidence that it met social needs more or less satisfactorily at some time. Certainly there are many institutions and ideas in existence that are unfortunate by all modern standards and in terms of alternatives that are now available. Such institutions and ideologies can be prolonged by men whose own interests instead of the interests of general society are furthered. In these cases our rejection processes are inadequate. Nevertheless, the residue that makes up the initial state of a system is the result of all sorts of past influences, and there is at least some presumption that it is serving social needs.

Certainly there is a presumption that what is done and how it is done have merit and relevance to needs that have arisen. Carried to an extreme, this attitude can become a universal 'answer' to all problems, for it tends to settle them in terms of the *status quo*. When such procedures clearly do not meet current needs, it is usually assumed that the needs of the times are changing faster than the profession is able to adjust to the changes. Inasmuch as stability itself is of utmost importance to those who must predict (All of us!), it is highly probable that any system will remain behind some current needs. That is to say, stability itself has important value, and certain changes that would normally make modifications in the system desirable are sometimes disregarded or are not considered until later in order to preserve an acceptable rate of change and cushion us from drastic discontinuities in our exploratory and predictive processes. Such decisions as to the rate of change are essentially incremental in nature and involve matching the sacrifice in maintaining order and stability with the sacrifice of having outdated procedures.[4] Clearly, any system must have perceptors that anticipate and appraise the two; sometimes, as in times of revolution, the perceptors and reactors are not acute enough to balance the sacrifices, so that more current methods become so valuable that the old predictive institutions are rapidly and unceremoniously discarded. As will be pointed out later, the passing of new legislation against the desires of the leaders of the accounting profession may be interpreted as such a revolution.

This kind of study is begun by assuming a level of wisdom, knowledge, information and technical procedures in the storage bins as a kind of intellectual heritage. We then try

Footnotes on following page

to locate and specify sources of storage capacity and valves for admitting new information and rejecting old. These levels may be compared with electric potentials in that they tend to resist new ideas at each source or gateway. In a similar manner an idea, once it has been admitted to the system, may become habitual and develop inertia-like tendencies to resist expulsion from the system.

The repositories of knowledge and also the admittance points for new ideas are summarized below. Some are passive repositories instead of active agents for introduction and expulsion, and in this characteristic they resemble problems of warehousing with the passive function of dead storage and active operations for admitting and shipping goods. The degree of each in a particular area may change from time to time, but it is probable that some areas remain primarily storage and others primarily active agents. This overview is concerned largely with the admittance and rejection, but some attention to the storage points is necessary for a discussion of tenacity in holding to the old and readiness to accept the new. Each point is composed of people and inanimate objects (books, etc.) whose importance is derived from their ability to influence people.

One of the first, and in this country relatively important, centers for idea processing is university and college departments of accounting instruction. These departments are the repository of much of the accumulated traditional knowledge and are, of course, active in injecting both new and old material into the system. The associations, through their leadership consensus, publications, research departments, and liaison groups, are especially important in integrating new problems with the old and devising new or modifying old conventions to cover new situations. The leaders of the large public firms perform similar functions. The controller's department of large firms is an important repository and injection point. While businessmen, credit men, investors, and others may be considered as exogenous to the system, it is also possible to consider them and their behavioral reactions as a part of an expanded system.

A number of related professions and professional groups work directly with accountants and with the output of the accounting system, and, while they are exogenous, their influence should be recognized and allowed for in structuring a profession. In this class are lawyers with their need to gather facts and opinions, and legislators with their need for certain kinds of regulation and control based on accounting output. Engineering groups and economists often develop independent theories that require new information and new

---

³ This discussion is not intended to set forth a blueprint for a mathematical description. Such a form may take the traditional form used by econometricians. The additional unknowns represent exogenous variables that take the form of parameters to be assigned value in the particular model. The system also contains a host of structural parameters which are in the nature of undetermined constants. An alternate approach used by Forrester makes use of difference equations and tends to give approximate answers instead of analytic solutions. Intervals are short enough so that interdependence among variables during a particular interval may be neglected. The resulting equations require solution in an ordered cycle and are set up to show storage levels, rates of change in levels and some hybrid auxiliary equations which function as rate equations. The initial conditions and equations are fed into a computer and new levels are computed at the end of the short interval. The results become the initial conditions for the succeeding period. Supplementary models can be developed and integrated for personnel, funds, training lags, facilities, etc.

⁴ The balancing of stability and adaptability is a fascinating study. DR Scott, who probably would have rated adaptability above temporal consistency, states: "Consistency and adaptation are both necessary in accounting in spite of the fact that they tend to contradict each other. If we accord them the rank of principles, they clearly are principles of a less general order than are justice, fairness and truth." "The Basis for Accounting Principles," *The Accounting Review*, December, 1941, p. 344. The use of "contradict" indicates that Scott employed a two-valued orientation and overlooked the broader functional range of the variables. The generality of the order apparently resolves conflicting principles.

reporting patterns. Taxing authorities and members of regulatory commissions bring problems to the profession for consultation and help in finding solutions.

While we are enumerating some influences on the profession, it seems desirable to add a note on the vehicles by which ideas and information are stored in the system and the vehicles by which new ideas are transmitted, promulgated and sold to members and users. Clearly, storage is carried on through books, publications of research groups, articles, monographs, releases, decisions, rulings, statutes, regulations and other devices of this sort. In addition, in spite of our seeming sophistication, many important items from the heritage of the past are carried in the minds of human carriers. Much of the feel for auditing and the adequacy of tests, for example, has been carried by individuals and imparted by individuals, with only minor help from the usual published vehicles. This set of devices consists of speeches that are not published, instruction made on the spot to junior employees, class instruction at colleges and in business or professional organizations, and the usual conferences, committee meetings and other small-group meetings that are so often used to convince and persuade others.

These vehicles should not be dismissed readily. Some kinds are extremely effective for transmitting to those with inferior knowledge. Others are in the nature of refreshers. Still others are developed to convince others of approximately the same background and are primarily argumentative in nature.

The problem is complicated further by hierarchies within each of the identified decision centers. In the university instruction centers, for example, the ranks of professors and instructors mean that there are status barriers to new ideas, and prestige is often associated with the elderly members of the firm who are often the least receptive to new ideas and the most reluctant to give up the old ways. A similar situation — with perhaps a great deal more authoritarianism — is found in the organizations of controllers and public accountants. Here the caution of the pocketbook and the status of position often stifle the younger men, who are fed into the organizations by universities and other institutions that attempt to encourage new thoughts and to adopt broader horizons of usefulness and responsibility. In the short struggle that ensues immediately after entering the profession it is little wonder that the desire for a living, for promotion, and for the favor of the reigning hierarchy tends to win out over the adventurous ideas of a rare but deserving instructor. In this connection the immediate problems of getting ahead in our success-oriented society may demand a function to express the receding importance of ideas from past training and the growing importance of ideas of present and immediate concern. Thus it appears that any mathematical formulation of these relations must use a discount factor of some kind either to discount the impact of past ideas or to expand the importance of present ones. Ideas from the new environment take on added importance, for their acceptance is related directly to the future success of the new member. At higher authoritative levels, current status has been reached by using existing ideas so that their importance tends to be magnified. The obvious result is that the rejection of outmoded ideas becomes more difficult. To the extent that new ideas are replacements, their admission must overcome the inertia of the tradition that the tried and true will continue to lead to success. The more mature members who have achieved their status by existing rules are those who have authority to reject or accept the new. The dice are loaded!

It seems desirable, therefore, to make a distinction between new ideas that do not displace ideas already integrated into the system and new ideas that are in addition to old, established lines of thought. Extensions of the latter type should tend to encounter less resistance for admission. While this factor may be considered separately, in many cases consideration is probably given automatically by adding the resistance to adopting the new to the resistance of abandoning the old. It is also possible that the two types of resistance are not additive. In any event, cases that call for partial abandonment or modification seem to merit special consideration.

The influence of authoritarianism on the speed of introduction and rejection of ideas calls for independent study. There is no question about the existence of a high degree of authoritarianism in business organizations, accounting offices, and regretfully, in university organizations. In most cases the presence of this factor is probably a strong deterrent to the introduction of new ideas and the rejection of old. This deterrent arises from the supposition that those in authority have succeeded with old techniques, and in the attempt to preserve their power they will not encourage wide discussion of alternative methods.[5] Certainly they are likely to be older; however, it has not been firmly established that age inevitably leads to greater reluctance to change. A more democratic process in almost all cases gives those younger and closer to the educational process more authority and thus may tend to yield a more flexible system.

It seems desirable to inquire about the origin of ideas and to speculate about their sources and about the conditions that encourage their birth. It is highly probable that many ideas in the field of accounting arise in response to problems found directly in practical work. Suppose, to illustrate, that a problem arises in the field of governmental control and requires information usually not furnished by the accounting system. The problem and the need for extension of procedures and attitudes are usually discussed first at the top or near the top of the management line. Such discussion may involve governmental regulators, accountants and perhaps highly-placed persons in the firm's public-accounting consultant. The development of new means to deal with the problems — the new idea — may be slow or fast depending on the ability of the personnel to absorb and discard. In some cases public accountants may not be consulted at all unless the controller's office needs help, while in other cases, the governmental agency may first ask for advice from leaders in both public and private accounting practice.

It is probable that members near the top of public accounting houses have the best chance to meet new problems and to develop new theory and techniques to meet the problems. The opportunities are there and the level of ability is relatively high. On the opposite side, it is well known that such leaders are extremely busy both intellectually and socially and are sometimes overly concerned with arriving at a compromise solution that is generally acceptable and with getting on with the job. Moreover, it is possible that a firm that specializes in accounting work may wish to amortize its investment in special knowledge and to enhance its reputation by keeping the information to itself as long as it can do so gracefully. It should be clear that general information cannot be concealed for long, and it is not meant to imply that such concealment is a general policy. Release of information about "how our firm did it" itself carries general prestige, helps enhance the reputation of the firm, and thus may be profitable in monetary units. To find time-lag factors in cases of this sort it is necessary to consider the vehicles such as speeches, discussions, articles,

---

[5] An opposing view deserves mention. It may be argued that those in power have tremendous ego needs and must introduce even flamboyant changes to maintain their status. In these cases junior members may develop a technique that permits those in authority to take credit for the new idea. Those who research this area must be on guard to isolate those who introduce the new ideas from those who have authority over their rejection or survival. One may speculate also about the higher status conferred by our society on those who exercise judgment on ideas as opposed to those who develop new concepts. Apparently the power to accept or reject is admired more than the extremely rare ability to generate. It seems incredible that ideas which do not lead to power have so little status in most cultures.

client's leakage and other forms of getting the problem and its tentative solution before a more general public.

It is interesting to return a moment to the professor's position in this general process. First, it should be pointed out that professors, like any other group of human beings, are not a homogenous group. Some have good problem perceptors and sharp abilities to extend the rules and conventions to meet new problems. Others are concerned more with methods of disseminating the accepted information quickly and efficiently. Both types are clearly helpful in speeding up the injection and rejection of ideas from the system. Some professors, unfortunately, fail to have either quality, view their function as training office clerks, and perceive the profession as it was a half-century ago. Clearly, any sophisticated simulation of a profession must study these distributions and fit some sort of distribution pattern to the variations.

Professors, at least in the more affluent schools, normally have more time to consider problems, to study corresponding difficulties in other areas, and to point out what extensions can be made without conflicting with existing theories. But how are professors stimulated and how does information come to them? First, they normally have more time for reading and integrating than high-level public or private accountants, so that written vehicles such as articles, releases, statutes, etc., are of particular importance. The professor learns what new problems are arising and how the profession is moving to meet them by talking with his colleagues, by belonging to and attending professional meetings, by joint meetings with public accountants and businessmen and others at the practical level. Professors should be closer to economists, statisticians, mathematicians, engineers and others than the practical man of accounting affairs, and these related fields should do much to keep him informed of new intellectual developments. To many overworked teachers these relationships are their chief reason for staying with the profession, but in far too many cases accounting teachers are either too narrow in their orientation or have not had sufficient professional experience to profit from their opportunities. One characteristic of a scholar is that he reads and digests new material with the hope of fitting it into a broader pattern of knowledge. The professional man may digest new material more efficiently, but he often uses it to meet an immediate problem.

We are then faced with the possibility that teachers of accounting should also be practicing accountants. If ideas come forth in response to problems, and problems are encountered primarily at the practical level, it seems to follow that a speed-up of new ideas would result from the development of the combination professor-practitioner. It seems clear that part-time practice at the proper level of difficulty should be helpful, but it is just as clear that such practice may infringe on the available time for mulling over theoretical problems and requirements. Thus the professor-practitioner may have less time for thinking and developing his ideas. There is a further danger that he will forfeit his position of trying to fit changes and new ideas into the *general* intellectual framework and accept the more pressing view-of-the-moment approach. The results may be a series of skirmishes with brush fires rather than the integrated and consistent system of principles and conventions that he should be trying to develop. Thus the simulationist — and the profession itself — is faced with the necessity to combine all sorts of practical techniques, specified objectives, and general theories.

Delays in the System

It is necessary as a preliminary step to identify the centers for admission, rejection and storage of ideas and to diagram their relationships. The problem of delays in the system is so important and they occur at so many points in the system that they deserve a separate discussion. Delays probably occur at all interchange points between individuals in the system, and, due to differences in perception time among individuals, any simulation should provide suitable distribution functions.

Schools have a particularly important part in delays. Suppose to begin that a given professor in a large staff somehow comes across an idea of merit. Assume also that he has completed the preliminary stage of convincing himself and working out details so that he will not appear ridiculous when he starts his active advocacy. This stage itself involves some delay, and even previous to this stage, there is usually delay in learning of the problem and arriving at the conclusion that the problem can be worked on with some chance of success. This professor will then bring the idea to his colleagues in an effort to get them to understand it and perhaps join him in advocating it. Normally he will bring it to his classes and observe student reaction.

When the idea is new, there may be a tendency for it to appear to be more difficult than some of the older, more familiar ideas. Thus the new extension tends to be introduced first at the more advanced levels and then to work its way down to the more elementary courses. The result tends to be a sort of last-in, first-out procedure in that the more advanced students finish sooner and therefore take the new ideas into practice more quickly. In this way the ideas are introduced outside more quickly, but the first students to leave have less time to assimilate them and to integrate them with the existing stockpile. While it is probably true that students will take up new ideas with more speed than professors, it is also probably true that unless fellow professors are convinced of the importance of a new idea, they will emphasize traditional ideas, and the student may remain unconvinced and therefore be lukewarm in his acceptance and advocacy.

Even if the student leaving the university has been fully convinced of the superiority of the new extension, his influence in the accounting profession for several years is likely to be very small. If most meritorious ideas came from the university professors, this delay would be serious indeed. The student graduate usually takes his place near the bottom of the accounting hierarchy in either public or private accounting. Of course, he has opportunities to discuss and advocate his ideas with men at slightly higher levels, but in the typical authoritarian structure his influence is often slow in developing.

There are internal delays of this sort at each level of leadership in universities, accounting offices, and among users of accounting products. Empirical studies should indicate that knowledge and ideas sift down from the top of the hierarchy with considerably more speed than they are likely to rise or to move crosswise. The delays in perceiving needs and delays in moving to find what solutions are effective may also be classified as internal delays, but they differ in that they are not delays brought about by the necessity to persuade. For research purposes it seems desirable to separate persuasion delays from those necessary to appraise the desirability of the extension.

A more direct route for the dissemination of new methods and ideas with considerably less delays may be found in the so-called executive training courses and seminars that are now so popular. These courses tend to give the professor access to managers and practitioners who are able to make immediate use of ideas. Moreover, members of the group have opportunities to try out the new information and to appraise the ideas of others in different contexts. While members of such sessions are often on the lookout for help with their immediate problems and therefore tend to slight the broader aspects, they still are subjected to new insights that can revolutionize their attitudes. There can be no question of the dissemination speed-up when such training is compared with the usual student route, and one should not become prejudiced by occasional blatant overselling of such courses on the wrong grounds.

Perhaps the fastest route for the introduction of new ideas by members of the professorial clan is by way of top-level consulting. Not only does the professor get material for new ideas from the problem environment, but he has an opportunity to get his own developed ideas into policy with less delay. Businessmen usually hire consultants with the hope of getting new ideas to which the firm has not previously had access. They are therefore in a mood to listen and, when convinced, in a position to act. Whereas the necessary time for dissemination through regular student channels might be in the order of ten years, it is conceivable that a few months would suffice if the ideas could be projected at higher levels. It is also probable that the financial position of the firm and the security of its officers may be relevant variables that influence the speed with which new ideas are received and accepted.

Constant urging from the dean's office for professorial lectures and speeches to groups that seem to offer little challenge is often irksome to the productive scholar. Yet it should be clear that this device is one of the best available to speed up the dissemination of new ideas from the professorial chair. It is important that professors use such opportunities effectively, with carefully prepared material tailored to fit the mood and ability of the audience. The prevailing mood has far too often blinded the speaker to his opportunities and has led to handing out the most banal pap with inspirational oratory and in a carnival spirit. These listeners often make up the kind of audience that the professor should be seeking. They are competent men at manipulating others and have demonstrated their competence in this direction. Often they are in need of new and fresh ideas in order to impress their superiors and to win promotion and prestige within their organizations. These folks may *need* new ideas to get ahead, and often they have not reached the stage where 'sound' judgment is identified with preservation of the *status quo*. An added advantage of such programs is that they tend to aggregate and snowball in the sense that they often help promote the ideas of struggling young men whose ideas are being put aside or diluted by their immediate superiors. This dilution and pushing aside by immediate superiors can be extremely important, for these superiors are essentially sifters who let pass upward what they think will benefit the firm or perhaps themselves. If they feel that their superiors are receptive they often will permit new ideas from fresh graduates to go up the line with more speed and without so much concern for their job security. Such sessions with middle and upper management may therefore prepare the way and increase the rate of progress.

Schools themselves differ tremendously in general quality and also in the perception of their responsibilities. The weaker schools require so much teaching and low-level practice from their members that the problem of idea development is often not treated as a matter of concern. It may be feasible to encourage the faculties of such institutions to keep abreast of new ideas, adopt modern materials and take part in new theory formation, but mediocrity in such schools is too often self-perpetuating. Bright, well-trained young men from the *avant-garde* institutions are extremely reluctant to go to academic graveyards, and the result is that these schools tend to hire products of similar institutions and to perpetuate views that are already antiquated. Threats to the job security of the older members through the introduction of new ideas are often not tolerated. The point to be emphasized here is that these institutions are a retarding (delaying) factor in idea dissemination, so we need some sort of scale to measure the variation and importance of such educational institutions. Corresponding scales must be developed for the wide variation in public accounting firms, with provision for discontinuity between national and some local firms, and among controllers' offices. It is probably fair to state that the difference in quality of internal accounting staffs is at least as great as it is in universities. It is not always true that the larger firms have the better staffs, for entire industries have a tradition for unimaginative accounting work. Blame in the case of railroad accounting is usually placed on regulatory systems that follow the 1907 and 1914 methods. Before turning to the area of government it should be emphasized that the faculties of important institutions have tremendous opportunities. They are in a position to perceive and estimate information needs for all kinds of future contingencies. Without the pressures of the profit motive and the need for immediate brush-fire relief, they can short-circuit the longer historical process without sacrificing their short-term personal income and without a personal stake in preserving the *status quo* or advocating specific changes.

The role of associations of public accountants, cost accountants, teachers of accounting, etc., and their organizational structures should be given some attention. As a rule, an association has influence far beyond the number of its members, and some sort of measure should be used to modify those areas of a profession that are subject to strong associations. Associations often are formed and operated by the most influential men in the profession. It does not follow that the leaders of a profession with demonstrated ability to influence people are also leaders in the development of new theory. In some instances the most reactionary members have captured professional associations and have set up what is in effect a self-perpetuating managerial elite. Such men are important for the propagation of ideas for they have both the organization for propagation and the demonstrated ability to convince their colleagues. Thus, it is indispensable for the discoverer of new theory to attempt to convince this group. In most cases the leadership of these organizations has been on the side of stability, but the pressures of those who use the output mean that they cannot be completely oblivious to new ideas and to professional change.

In the typical association the work is carried on by committees made up of appointees who are familiar with the problem areas and have some ability to develop new ideas. It is at this level that an intellectual has the best chance to operate and to have his ideas adopted. However, adoption by a committee is no guarantee of adoption by the association, because general veto power is usually kept by the leadership of the association.

Many organizations apparently have failed to realize the impact of the releases that are sent out with their approval, yet the rigidity of such releases may be comparable with the rigidity introduced by a court structure. These releases need careful examination, for their function is essentially one of stability and the development of conformity. Uninspired schools of business often look to the Association of Business Schools for detailed guidance, and correspondingly one finds many accounting offices and firms that follow institute releases with no serious attempt to criticize or modify them. Weak courses in accounting theory too often follow the releases in an uncritical manner. A hidden strength of such releases is due to the fact that those who do not wish to develop ideas, or are unable to do so, can use such guides as cookbooks to accomplish useful work. There is an added incentive to use authoritative pronouncements in that the personal onus of rejecting a client's plea can be shifted to the organization by citing an appropriate release. Thus the releases and other pronouncements of respected associations tend to become important carriers of ideas in a profession, and the problem of introducing new ideas becomes an important task for top-level committee personnel, who may be far removed from ordinary practitioners. Moreover, the introduction of changes may become difficult due to a fear that shifting positions will destroy the authoritative feeling for the pronouncement and for the organization. On the other hand, an advantage for introducing ideas arises from the definite and well-marked path that must be followed in order to get new ideas introduced. A knowledge of where to go for a hearing and who must be convinced may actually help the introduction of new theory. The procedure may be superior to formal judicial processes, for a court often requires an existing wrong of some kind before it will hear the case.

However the power of "insiders" to veto or expedite new ideas without wide publicity is probably greater in nonjudicial procedures.

So far we have not considered the influence of schools and public accountants directly on users of accounting output. Users of information introduce delays in the system by their failure to feel the need for new or better information. In some cases they do not know what new knowledge and techniques are in fact available or how the profession may be able to help them. Inasmuch as they are motivated by self-interest, it may be assumed that consumers of accounting will be interested in new developments. Moreover, it is in the self-interest of public accounting houses to call certain kinds of new information to the attention of their clients. (In some cases, unfortunately, there may be self-interest working to conceal bill-reducing improvements.) In spite of these obvious operations of the self-interest principle, clients often need education in the sense of explaining the latest techniques available to satisfy their needs. In some cases the client's own lawyers or engineers may recognize client needs and initiate the search for new theories and ideas.

What can be said about governmental agencies and their record for perceiving social needs for information? These agencies are themselves users of accounting output, and in addition they function as spokesmen for users that would otherwise be unorganized. The latter function is a primary objective of the Securities and Exchange Commission. This commission was set up originally because of the failure of the accounting profession to sense the needs and requirements of an industrial society and the lack of power to insist that its accounting standards be followed. This failure may have been due in part to the profession's identifying too closely with leaders of business who themselves had an interest in information different from that desired by the ordinary investor. There were many dissident voices in the accounting profession who lamented the inability to force conformance with acceptable standards, but the wisdom displayed by the leaders of the accounting profession at that time must be judged weak by almost any standards. Moreover, this lack of wisdom persisted, and the failure of professional leaders to see the seriousness of operating a professional service with *ad hoc* principles persisted until approximately World War II. Some argued that there were no accounting principles or, worse, that the principles were so obvious that there was no need to discuss them or make them available to the general public.[6]

The function of the Securities and Exchange Commission is most clearly seen as a perceiver of user needs and the enforcer of minimum acceptable disclosures to the unorganized investor group. In the former capacity it operates to discover problems and helps the profession initiate new and acceptable theory to meet the problems; and in the second capacity it acts to enforce minimum standards for the profession. That such a commission exists is, itself, evidence of the weakness of the public accounting profession. Yet its presence adds immeasurably to the effectiveness of the profession by adding sanction and authority to what professional leaders would like to do, and by helping police less responsible members of the profession. The limitations and dangers of such commissions and agencies are well known and will not be belabored here.

Many other agencies of regulation are concerned with accounting in connection with regulations that require accounting information. Such agencies are likely to sense needs for a somewhat limited purpose (seldom as broad as the interests of all investors), and as a

[6] Even after one allows for bias and bitterness, the statements of Howard C. Greer may prove to be shocking to younger generations of accountants. "Benchmarks and Beacons," *The Accounting Review*, January, 1956, pp. 3-14.

result they have sometimes hindered the progress of the profession perhaps as much as they have helped it. The income taxing process, for example, has dimensions — such as subsidies, penalties and the necessity for reducing the nuisance cost of collection — that do not appear in other parts of accounting. Thus some of the niceties of income measurement and matching expired cost with benefit may be casualties of desires to accomplish limited social goals and to keep amended returns at an acceptable level.

For some reason or other our experience with the regulatory agencies and their administration in the United States has not disclosed keen perception of needs and subsequent development of new and appropriate theory. Many insist that such an attitude is inevitable. Others hold that personnel has been generally incompetent or that delegated responsibilities have been so narrow that administrators lose interest in the broader aspects of social goals and professional responsibility.

Professional Service and the Price System

Some accountants have felt that a free price system will provide an automatic weighting of the relative importance of the groups contending for information. This group feels that the courts and the legislative process should set the ethical tone for any profession. Thus it is argued that members of a profession can follow their self-interest so long as they operate within the permissive legal boundaries. This approach removes the ethical flavor from a profession except in the rudimentary sense of legality, and tends to fit it into an enterprise system that attempts to harness the self-interest of individuals to do the world's work. As we shall point out below, such an approach is consistent with the informed electorate doctrine, the advocacy principle in law and the informed, economic-man approach to the marketplace. It must be admitted that a profession without guidance except from the money value of its products to individual users hardly qualifies as a profession, yet this pragmatic attitude is used with tremendous success in many areas of social endeavor.

The production and distribution of economic goods, as suggested before, is carried on largely through the mechanism of markets in which consumers are substantially in charge of the direction of production. If one supports the free-price system, one is committed to the belief that consumers are rational enough to sort out the exaggerated claims of producers and make decisions that will be generally satisfactory. When it is not feasible to determine quality by inspection, the government has stepped in, e.g., pure food laws, but a denial that the consumer is rational enough to use his purchasing power satisfactorily usually requires an agency or a board — an elite group — to decide what goods are to be produced and in what quantities. Self-interest is directed toward efficient activity, and informed buyers are supposed to weed out the rascals before serious harm is done.

The judiciary system is also based directly on the advocacy principle. It is assumed, with some support, that if each contending party is permitted to present his case in the best possible manner without concerning himself with abstract justice or ethics, the judge will be presented with the pertinent facts and issues. Further, it is presumed that judges are intelligent enough to separate the wheat from the chaff, and, with relevant facts and cases presented as the result of self-interest on the part of the contestants, they will reach acceptable decisions.

The present political system in America is based on a variation of the advocacy system. The selfish nature of human beings is assumed, and the problem is to direct it to acceptable social ends. Candidates with all kinds of axes to grind can be expected to present their claims in a forcible manner either within the party structure or against opposing parties. The resulting campaign verbiage seems fantastic to politicians from other countries. Our whole system assumes that the voter is astute enough to separate the ballyhoo from rational claims and to act accordingly. Notice that the satisfactory working of the system does not require that every member of the electorate be rational enough to make such decisions. There must, however, be enough folks so that each contending party is forced to show some signs of compromise and perhaps ameliorate some extreme claims in order to appeal to that group. Observe that if one denies that the voters as a group have the ability to select satisfactory programs, he is forced into defending decision making by elite groups, and a rough measure of his democratic spirit may be in terms of the size of the group that he feels should make such decisions.

The fact that every profession puts forth some sort of code of ethics indicates that most professional people do *not* hold an unrestrained price-system approach. One explanation for this modification of the price system is that the legal machinery is general and that the ethical code fills in the "specifics." Some may feel that such codes anticipate legal changes, smooth the effects of such changes when they do appear, and serve as models of what needs to be done at the legislative level. At an extreme position are those who feel that the primary function of a profession is to keep the price system from working in the area.[7]

Both views encounter difficulties. Most advocates of unmodified price allocation do not believe that a vital information service should be guided entirely by the squeak of the money wheel. In this case, what should be our professional policy if one solvent segment wants inventories carried at zero, and another equally eager and solvent portion of the market wishes stocks handled for costing purposes on the last-in, first-out basis? Those who favor the "market product" approach to the profession would probably feel that giving statements prepared with both assumptions is the proper attitude, at least until one group has established economic superiority. Are we then to prepare as many statements with as many conflicting assumptions as someone is willing to pay for or coerce someone else to pay for? Shall each different statement be labeled and identified with the purpose for which it is prepared? Is there any reason why a client (customer) cannot have a statement prepared to his specifications and present it to another interested party who would, if he knew matters, insist on different specifications? Should the accounting profession ignore such matters and adopt a *caveat emptor* attitude? Are we to disregard the fact that certain groups may be well organized and present their desires forcefully and with adequate buying power while groups that are more important in total strength are scattered and their cases are not forcibly presented? Should we modify when clients cannot appraise the values as we modify food and drug laws? Do managerial accountants have responsibilities to others? Is the motto "service, not profit" equivalent to the socialist's "production for use, not profit?"

The problems are not confined entirely to those who want to use the price system. One important problem that confronts the ethical school is: How does one assess client worthiness and need? Who makes these decisions for the profession? What are the criteria for decision? These topics are discussed briefly in the essay devoted to ethics and normative considerations and are only mentioned here. The remainder of the present discussion is devoted to speculation about the development of a profession and its boundary problems.

---

[7] The position of DR Scott and other Veblen disciples is that the price system is breaking down and must be replaced with 'professional' attitudes. The following statement sets forth the position and anticipates the recent flood of intrafirm-transfer-pricing articles by a few decades. "In a competitive system, the market adjusts the conflicting economic interests of all those who are competitors in the market. But when the typical unit of competitive enterpise became a complex group of varied interests, the market could not provide effective adjustments between them . . . the dependence upon accounts is much more direct and complete." "Accounting Principles and Cost Accounting," *The Journal of Accountancy*, February, 1939, p. 74. See also his "The Basis for Accounting Principles," *The Accounting Review*, December, 1941, pp. 341-349.

Some degree of integrity and competence is necessary to support the term 'professional,' and it is necessary to have standards. These norms (standards) help attain predictable results regardless of the particular individual who happens to do the work. It seems desirable, therefore, that the rules of the game should be consistent — at least not contradictory. It is often embarrassing to find that competent, ethical members of a profession may derive from identical data widely different answers to identical questions. Uniformity and consistency are therefore desirable, and the entire apparatus of accounting must be subjected to the rules of logic designed to expose certain kinds of contradictions. Yet there is a cost for uniformity and the problem becomes an incremental one.

It may be of interest to digress a moment and speculate about possible lines of development of accounting rules and doctrines. The following hypothesis does not pretend to meet all demands of objective history. Suppose that certain practices developed in response to needs and demands for accountability and reporting. Some degree of uniformity in behavior has developed and resulted in the presentation of systematic lists of existing procedures. These lists of uniform rules and procedures undoubtedly acted as guides for training new personnel and grew in stature until they reached the status of authoritative pronouncements. Individuals who mastered these authoritative rules found that they had something in common, organized and developed sanctions for enforcing the rules.

Up to this point the rules probably developed by observing uniformities in practice; but practice changes. Those rules that appeared time after time in succeeding lists were probably dignified by the term principles. If a rule no longer fitted the needs of those who employed accountants it was dropped from later lists. Thus a rule that survived and was included in later expressions of measurement folklore became permanent enough to be called a principle, given ancestral status, and accorded respect.

Moreover, a group of quasi-priests developed. These insiders made up the professional core of the art. Among other things, it was their duty to arbitrate the diverse demands of those who use professional products and to decide when a rule should be dropped, added, or modified. Thus it appeared as if this group were *creating* new principles. In one sense new principles were being created, but it should be clear that the group was (and is) extremely limited in its freedom to add, remove, and modify rules. The modifications must be in harmony with the social needs and desires unless the profession wishes to die quietly. It is possible to surround activities with ritual and mysticism and thereby perpetuate obsolete practices for long periods, but it seems reasonable to conclude that sooner or later other social groups look through the professional veil and stop their support for such practices. At any stage of development all professions undoubtedly have a number of outworn principles that have survived Darwinian selection, but these exceptions are probably relatively unimportant.

It should be clear that the actual things done by members of a profession crowd the boundaries of other professions. Project analyses and feasibility studies may be made by accountants, managers, engineers, and anyone else who has the time and feels competent to undertake the work. Determining the relevancy of specific costs to alternate decisions may be attempted by several groups. Actual professional boundaries are shifting and creeping to adapt to new conditions and to take advantage of weaknesses in neighboring fields. (Professional predators are not uncommon!) In addition to this dog-eat-dog elbowing at the margin, operations within the settled part of the profession are shifting to meet new conditions. Thus definitions need to be related to their environment, and temporal subscripts may be essential for understanding them. (Apparently some current school administrators still cling to a definition of accounting that should be correlated with the subscript '1900'.)

There is little doubt that accounting has been aggressive in adding to its empire. Perhaps an aggressive attitude is a universal attribute of new institutions and new fields of inquiry. Certainly sociology and political science have not been backward about extending their empires, and not so long ago economics (political economy) was a serious containment problem for historians and philosophers. Even within the field of accounting there have been upstarts who tended to upset the traditional divisions of the market. Almost before the financial accountants realized what was happening, aggressive managerial accountants have all but appropriated the budgeting and control (controllership) aspects of the field. Concurrently, the area of accounting had overflowed into the lucrative tax field, and within the field of accounting, tax accountants have placed their stamp on large parts of what had been general financial accounting. Lately we have seen the rise of internal auditing, which, according to its more enthusiastic supporters, includes everything of importance in accounting except the recording function. Moreover, internal auditors have not been entirely satisfied with appropriating business from within the profession; they have moved in on engineers, production men, treasurers, and research specialists.

Controllers during the Depression and immediately prior to World War II were in an extremely powerful position. They had the budgeting area pretty much to themselves, for market research was often immature and finance officers (including professors of finance) had not discovered capital budgeting. Moreover, controllers usually controlled the tax department (in spite of some protest from lawyers) at a time when taxes were becoming a major item in business operation. In some cases they sought the coordinating function usually reserved for managers at the very top. Since the war the controller has encountered some challenges. Lawyers used the "unauthorized practice of law" approach to limit the accountants' expansion in the fields of taxes, estates and trusts. Business schools added courses in business economics; industrial engineers modernized their weapons and supplied analytical material for the moribund production courses. Statistics provided new and exciting methods that extended probability theory to subjective values and decisions. But the greatest challenge undoubtedly came from those in computer technology and operations research. These developments are discussed elsewhere and are mentioned here only to support the contention that professional boundaries are fluid and sensitive.[8]

While boundaries may be sensitive and alive, academic discussion of scope and method tend to be sterile and dull. Except for those interested in the jurisdictional aspects of professional activity, boundary problems tend to be important primarily in determining the decisions that are under the control of the leaders of the profession (endogenous) and those that are made by outside decision makers (exogenous). Inside a profession the old-fashioned and elementary distinction between ends and means has enough usefulness to merit careful discussion. Some thought about the purposes of accounting — the ends — is usually rewarding and stimulates thinking about the decisions that have to be made, the personalities that may make these decisions, and the relevant factors for decision making. Attention to the vehicles — means — of accomplishing accounting purposes often gives a framework for discussion and permits specific practices to be placed in the broader mold formed by the objectives, so that they may be accepted or rejected on

---

[8] "It would be detrimental to those [areas of service] served as well as a brake on further development [of the profession], if each area of specialization were to be sharply limited by those trained and competent to operate in it. This would leave the twilight zones in between to be filled by less competent advisors . . . ." Donald P. Perry, *Public Accounting Practice and Accounting Education* (Boston: Harvard University, 1955), p. 25. Unfortunately, the more competent intellectuals do not always win!

the basis of conformance or nonconformance to these ends. Thus conventions and rules may be classed as means and placed against the general backdrop of objectives and evaluated accordingly. However, except for possible degrees of flexibility, careful distinction hardly seems necessary to support Gilman's sharp distinctions among rules, conventions, standards, and principles.[9]

---

[9] Stephen Gilman, *Accounting Concepts of Profit* (New York: The Ronald Press Company, 1939), especially Chapter 13. Cohen states: "The relation of means and ends coincides with that of cause and effect of the extent that both means and causes are antecedents which precede ends and effects as temporal consequences . . . . In the relation of purpose the value of the antecedent is subordinated to that of the consequent, while in the causal relation the antecedent is viewed as determining the nature of the consequence." Morris R. Cohen, *Reason and Nature* (Glencoe: The Free Press, 1953), p. 263.

Essay Four

Auditing — An Appraisal
and Some Recommendations

A large and important part of the accounting field is composed of procedures and attitudes known as auditing. This area appears to be deceptively simple because its procedures are so closely related to the evidentiary aspects of opinion formation and to accuracy in reporting. Auditing as an activity is carried on in order to get people to do certain things and to refrain from doing other things. The problems therefore are relatively easy to classify. First, objectives must be identified and the course of action necessary to accomplish these objectives must be specified. In the latter process, a whole host of actions which are detrimental to worthy objectives may be recognized. Auditing, then, aims to encourage actions consistent with objectives and discourage actions which hinder their accomplishment or further conflicting goals.

An appraisal of the activity tends to get messy at the operational level, where it unavoidably becomes entangled in behavioral hypotheses and ethical judgments. Moreover, in spite of the work of the American Institute of Certified Public Accountants, a general approach to auditing has not been forthcoming. Early commissions to auditors often called for specific investigations and narrow objectives, and the objectives often varied. A bank lending officer might ask for an investigation to establish the existence of certain assets. Owners might wish to be assured that management's stewardship reports were accurate in these and other details. Managers and owners might be interested in a breakdown of ethics with fraud, embezzlement, and misrepresentation. Insurance adjusters might wish evidence that safety or fire regulations were being followed. The auditing profession has attempted to weld such aspects of its work into a general framework, but progress has been slow, subject to some backlash, and confused by alternative techniques. For example, the auditing professor now emphasizes the objectives of establishing accurate management representations to the extent that disclosing fraud (once a primary activity) is currently a minor objective. Yet many of the techniques of auditing are still aimed at uncovering fraud! In fact, the very earliest techniques devoted to certifying the *existence* of assets and liabilities at a balance sheet date tend to accomplish the "representation" objective about as well as some of the more modern techniques, with the obvious exception of the modern business approach.

Turn now to some of the more obvious objectives. Auditing is generally assumed to be carried on by individuals who are not involved in making the entries (classifying and recording the data). Clearly one can check, recompute, and correct his own work, but, by definition, auditing implies at least one additional individual. This feature is probably built into the definition, because accountants, when feasible, separate individuals who handle assets from those who record information about them. The induced psychological barrier is thought to be considerable. It is doubtful if the barrier is twice as imposing if a third individual enters the cycle, but it must be more formidable to some degree. At this point the inadequacy of the profession's knowledge of behavior becomes critical. Little or no knowledge and often only the most tenuous hypotheses are available. For example, if two parties are involved, does it make a difference in the strength of the barrier if the parties are in the same or different age groups? Same sex? Same levels? Work in different parts of the organization? Are or are not church members? College graduates? Our knowledge is almost entirely limited to a general understanding that the barrier is weak when an inferior passes on the work of a superior and does not perceive the situation as an opportunity for getting rid of the superior. Even this knowledge is little more than a hypothesis. In a similar way accountants are confident that the introduction of an auditor as a third party in the cycle increases the strength of barrier. Moreover, they feel that the barrier is increased if the auditor is a traveling auditor with less opportunity to fraternize with other members. Surviving professional wisdom of this sort should not be dismissed too quickly. The purpose here is to point out that the importance of outside intervention is so deeply ingrained that it is included in the very definition of auditing. A subsidiary purpose is to emphasize the need for systematic, high-level research in the behavioral aspects of this problem.

The probable influence of expected audits on employees and their attitudes toward work has not been investigated sufficiently. A number of graduate students have designed some experiments in this area, but such simulation studies are highly artificial. It is almost impossible to simulate the tremendous personal stresses that are involved in actual conditions. The stakes are often high (especially in embezzlement cases), and classroom simulation reminds one of playing poker with matches. It is in fact extremely difficult to evaluate any control system without considering the reward-penalty system as a whole. With regard to clerical accuracy, the personal advantage to the worker within broad limits is usually small. The consequences resulting from discovery of continued poor work may exceed a tolerance limit and result in loss of the job. Even here the worker can weigh the probability of getting caught and the possibility that the error, if caught, may be considered to be a human error, i.e., superiors may have a high tolerance for errors of this type. The employee's calculation of the probability of being caught is obviously affected by his past experiences with detected and undetected errors and by the reports of others on such matters.

In some cases employees have positive self-interest working in the direction of misrepresentation. These for-interest incentives are in addition to the general penalties of reprimand, loss of status and discharge. These cases may involve bonuses, overtime premium, citations for efficient work, promotion, etc. The auditing process normally is designed to be more searching in those areas (in the direction of self-interest). Yet these areas have not been covered in a systematic manner. We do not know, for example, how important the failure of past audits to discover similar errors tends to be. If this factor is important, a poor audit may be far worse than no audit at all. We are also vague about the influence of slight changes in the firm's tolerance for dishonesty. There may be some reasonably smooth functional relations, or there may be sharp discontinuities and critical areas. What are the consequences, for example, of the profession's general disclaimer of responsibility for discovering fraud?

One of the few bright spots in accounting research in this area is an investigation of embezzlement by Cressey.[1] His findings indicate that knowledge of existing undetected

---

[1] Donald R. Cressey, *Other People's Money* (Glencoe: The Free Press, 1953). This research is concerned with 133 cases of embezzlement at various state prisons. An excellent summary of certain auditing aspects may be found in the book review by Arthur M. Cannon, *The Accounting Review*, January, 1956, pp. 156-157. Cressey summarized some of the conclusions in "Why Do Trusted Persons Commit Fraud?" *The Journal of Accountancy*, November, 1951. (Cannon wryly points out that the study deals only with those who were caught!)

errors is an important factor, because such knowledge points to the possibility of a solution to the employee's problem. "Borrowings" may be undetected until the funds can be replaced so that no one will be the wiser. Perhaps such unauthorized borrowings will never be discovered even if the funds are not replaced. At any rate, knowledge of undetected (or belatedly discovered) errors or shortages undoubtedly suggests a possible solution to an intolerable stress. The need for generous research at this level is certainly clear enough.

Cressey has concluded that one ingredient of embezzlement is a "nonshareable" problem, and Cannon points out the relationship of nonshareability to the auditor's traditional concern with collusion.[2] If the stress centers on the individual and cannot be shared with the other members of the group or with outside individuals, there appears to be less tendency to collusion. According to Cannon: " . . . our general approach to internal control, i.e., of not worrying about collusion, would seem to be on the right track."[3] Cannon's statement seems to need modification. To the extent that prospective embezzlers know that typical internal control systems require collusion, the necessity for collusion becomes an essential part of the solution. The potential embezzler then conducts his search in terms of the operations he must undertake to effect the solution. Collusion is among the operations usually required by an accounting system. It seems therefore that auditors and system specialists should reexamine any tendencies to stop "worrying about collusion." Actually, the thesis of nonshareability has not been established beyond question. Furthermore, it may be possible that the individual problem is entirely personal, but others in the necessary collusion cycle may have their own personal problems, and collusion (with attendant embezzlement) may be a solution for all. Again, acceptable professional procedure seems to call for more empirical studies on the fringes of behavioral science.

Some attention has been given to the field of accounting as a communication system with the usual shortcomings of any language system. Some events are expressed well in the system while others are almost impossible to communicate without supplementary devices. Changing the location and arrangement of items in the statements provides a partial substitute for intonation. The very fact that the consequences of an event are measured and reported has the effect of communicating the firm's *concern* with the matter. Unfortunately, only major embezzlements and frauds are given separate billing in reports to owners and the importance of day-to-day accuracy and honesty must be communicated in other ways. The fact that auditors are employed at all should communicate a message of importance to all who handle records or are responsible for assets. The message is essentially an implicit statement that the direction of organization assets to nonorganization objectives will not be tolerated and that the accuracy of compiling and reporting information is a matter of importance to the concern. The possible deterrent effect of such a simple communication of objectives may be important even without supplementary rewards and penalties. Research with regard to communication systems should prove to be useful.

The use of auditing to assure absentee groups of the reliability of management's reports is now seen to be an extension of the broader functions of establishing the reliability of all reports on organizational activity at all levels. The reports themselves — form and content — are designed to communicate the objectives to members and also to communicate accomplishment of objectives to all groups. The existence of scrap reports argues for

---

[2] Cressey, *op. cit.*, pp. 30 ff. Cannon, *op. cit.*, p. 157.
[3] Cannon, *op. cit.*, p. 157.

the importance of scrap control, and a detailed record of sales returns should convince employees that returns are a matter of organizational concern. There has been some tendency toward a division of labor between so-called internal and external auditors, but the point of interest here is that the entire accounting process may be approached as a tremendously complicated communication network. It contains a web of internal tests for consistency and accuracy, and should be considered with attention to the sanctions that support it. The study of the structure as a system isolated from the attendant rewards and penalties has chiefly academic interest. The strength of the barriers and the importance of positive rewards are influences that (along with relevant behavior patterns) establish the adequacy or inadequacy of the communication system.

The broad systems nature of accounting has complicated the problem of loyalty and responsibility. To some extent the communication system attaches to the entire organization, and one must ask who speaks for (represents) the organization. Clearly, reports are made at all levels of authority, and auditors try to vouch for the general accuracy of all reports. In most cases the highest management level seems to speak for the organization, and many auditors have associated their responsibility with this group. However, the recent emphasis on rendering opinions about management's representations indicates that interested parties other than employees and managers are usually given consideration.

This ambivalence deserves attention because of the current concern with advocacy versus independence in the public accounting profession. The public accountant is certainly an advocate in the sense that he functions by giving service to a client. The difficulty arises in determining who is the client. Past identification with management and management needs has led to a shift in the direction of independence; but independence from whom? In some instances a public auditor is a definite advocate of owners, managers, etc., and opposed to various governmental agencies. In other instances he restricts the freedom of action of management and others in the firm. At first sight, this ambivalence seems to place an impossible stress on the ethics of the profession.

Undoubtedly, uncertainty over the advocacy-independence position does place stress on the ethical standards of the profession. The stress is increased by the fact that it is difficult to oppose the group that engages and compensates the auditing firm.[4] Clearly, some ordering of importance to be attached to various groups (including government agencies, competitors, etc.) is necessary. It is necessary to decide approximately who are insiders entitled to accountability and who are the outsiders with relatively less important claims for information. Perhaps a more useful approach starts with identifying the needs of all sorts of individuals doing the organization's work and forming professional standards around the general objective of furnishing dependable, unbiased, helpful information at *all* levels.

It may be argued that certain types of work call for special qualities and responsibilities. A policeman, for example, is expected to exhibit more bravery than the typical citizen, and teachers should be expected to display above-average intellectual integrity and honesty. Auditors, as a professional group, according to this reasoning, should have a special duty to be accurate, dependable, and honest. Those who succumb easily to requests for special-interest variances should be ruthlessly weeded from the professional garden. The profession's code of ethics and rules for professional conduct should serve to identify the responsibilities involved and to communicate the urgency and importance of professional objectives.

---

[4] Professor Robert Dinman has pointed out that public accountants take an advocacy position when a government agency or tribunal assumes responsibility for protecting the public interest. If there is no intermediary to represent outsiders, the auditing profession functions as an independent intermediary.

As a minor digression, the ethical position and responsibilities of managerial accountants are worthy of comment. One asks whether managerial accounting is *only* a tool of management. Do managerial accountants have responsibilities for reporting to outsiders, measuring income, disclosing plans and estimates? In other words, are they merely "errand boys" (an SEC phrase) for managers? The view expressed here is that members of any service profession or activity *must* be "errand boys" for some groups or some individuals and that such a relationship is unavoidable and desirable. Nevertheless, the layers of management are not homogeneous and a broad view of management incudes all individuals or groups whose decisions affect the affairs of the chosen entity. For example, owners, creditors, suppliers, etc. have been called 'managers.' In order to avoid complete segmentation of an information-control system with different accountants representing each knot of decision makers, we try to establish a whole series of constraints that begin with broad social needs. We can construct consistent rules and actions for each set of restraints, and provide for the necessary coordination of the segments. Certainly, some standards of accuracy, honesty and efficiency can be applied to all levels of bookkeepers, accountants, and managerial accountants.

Limperg's Behavioral Approach to Auditing

One of the most advanced and articulate approaches to the function of auditing in a social order was advanced by Theo Limperg, and it is still modern a quarter of a century later.[5] Limperg's contention is that the reports of a good information system, e.g., auditing, should incite "proper" expectations in the minds of their readers. These expectations should lead to informed and desirable action. More specifically, a social need (function) exists for dependable, reliable information. The self-interest of those who report on their own activities is an argument for unreliability in their reports, and it is unlikely that such reports merit a high level of confidence. The need for reliable information is obvious, and there should be a net social gain resulting from the "raised confidence" in the accuracy of these reports. Presumably, better decisions should more than compensate for the cost of professional accounting service.

For Limperg the social need exists and is independent of the actual profession. Once auditors arise to fulfill this need and are approved by society to do the work, the freedom of the auditing profession is constricted. Society expects the function to be performed properly and expects audits to be professionally made. It is argued, for example, that a partial audit or qualified report is not satisfactory. The explicit qualification may indeed show honesty and integrity on the part of the individual auditor, but the result does not fulfill the social need — the basic function — and it is the responsibility of the auditing profession to do its work correctly and justify the expectations it creates. It is *not* the responsibility of the public users of the audited statements to decide in each case how much confidence is lost as a result of the specific exception, i.e., how much to discount the usefulness of the representations. (Unfortunately, this line of thought led Limperg to support the hundred-percent audit precisely when such audits were already doomed.)

Limperg thus developed a general approach to independent auditing with an ideal standard for judging the quality of its output. Two problems remain. First, how does one go about appraising the behavioral reactions of report users so that proper expectations

---

[5] Theo Limperg, Jr., "The Function of the Accountant and the Doctrine of Raised Confidence," *Maandblad van Accountancy en Bedrijfshuishoudkunde*, February and October, 1932 and October and November, 1933. (Title translated.) Jules W. Muis translates "leer van gewekte vertrouwen" as "The Thesis of Inspired Confidence," *"Wie Was Limperg,"Accountancy*, October 1980, p. 69.

may be aroused? Second, does the responsibility for inciting proper expectations and creating confidence extend to private accountants?

Limperg did not devote much time to the possibility of different psychological re-actions of report users. He seemed to assume that the educational process would provide enough uniformity in individual interpretations to justify his idealistic rule. Limperg, like so many other accountants, hoped that internal accountants would become professiona-lized sufficiently to accept responsibility for creating acceptable public expectations.[6] He expressed serious doubts about the possibility, but obviously rejected the view that in-ternal accountants are lackeys for internal managers and completely subservient to their immediate superiors.

Independence was discussed by Limperg with sophistication. The "function" insists on auditors who are concerned with the expectations of outside groups and therefore requires professional independence from all groups who would profit from creating false expecta-tions at any level. Any auditor who does not accept this objection is not independent, re-gardless of overt relationships which may lead to presumptions one way or another.

Opinion and Other Specific Difficulties

There is a growing feeling that the public accounting profession may be heading for serious difficulties by giving an opinion whose scope is considerably broader than either the extent of the investigation or the area of competence. For a basis for further com-ments, consider the typical short-form opinion.

> We have examined the balance sheet of X Company as of December 31, 19___ and the related statement(s) of income and surplus for the year then ended. Our examination was made in accordance with generally accepted auditing standards, and accordingly included such tests of the accounting records and such other auditing procedures as we considered necessary in the circumstances.
>
> In our opinion, the accompanying balance sheet and statement(s) of income and surplus present fairly the financial position of X Company at December 31, 19___, and the results of its operations for the year then ended, in conformity with generally accepted accounting principles applied on a basis consistent with that of the preceding year.[7]

It should be observed that the term 'consistency' is used to indicate some acceptable sta-bility through time. 'Consistency' in this sense must be related to things that are consid-ered to be important. To be consistent, for example, in using the identical audit team peri-od after period is hardly an important objective. The term 'conformity' is used to indicate the usual meaning of 'consistent'! 'In conformity with' presumably assures the reader that the recognition and measurement rules actually used were consistent with the guiding rules accepted by the profession. It is difficult to improve on this part of the statement and its objective. The difficulties are at the practical level in that the guiding principles are so vague that it may seem to be difficult *not* to be in conformity with some of them.

It seems desirable to discuss in some detail the looseness of the guiding principles to which the reports must conform. Consider the auditor's opinion that $121,171.67 fairly

---

[6] Theo Limperg, Jr., "The Accountant as a Representative of Particular Interests," *Maandblad van Accoun-tancy en Bedrijfshuishoudkunde*, September, 1927. (Title translated.)

[7] American Institute of Certified Public Accountants (Committee on Auditing Procedure), *Codification of Statements on Auditing Procedure* (New York: American Institute of Certified Public Accountants, 1951), p. 16. This statement is known as the standard short form; exceptions to the scope (first) paragraph should be noted, and the resulting modification of the opinion (if any) is noted in the opinion (second) paragraph.

represents the results of X Company's operations. For comparative purposes, the following additional information is available.

1. Depreciation was based on the straightline formula applied to cost with the controller's estimates of useful life. The amount was $180,000.
    a. If depreciation had been calculated as above except for substitution of a declining charge method, the depreciation would have been $160,000. The use of $R = 1 - \sqrt[n]{s/c}$ would have resulted in a charge of $140,000.
    b. If the calculations actually used had been applied to current replacement costs, the charge would have been $310,000.
    c. If the calculations that were actually used had been unchanged except for the substitutions of the plant manager's estimates of useful asset lives, the charge would have been $210,000.
    d. If the only change from actual computations had been the substitution of compound-interest methods for the straight-line formula, the depreciation would have been $220,000.

2. Inventories were costed on a moving-average basis.
    a. If the average had been applied at the end of the period (i.e., moved at the end of each year), the reported profit for the year would have been higher by $5,000.
    b. If LIFO had been applied at the end of the year, the reflected profit would have been lower by $30,000.
    c. If FIFO had been applied, the income would have been greater by $25,000.
    d. Inventories with identified cost of $100,000 were thought to be bordering on obsolescence. Selling prices were estimated to be at least as high as costs, and no write-down was taken. If these items were written down sufficiently to provide for expected normal markup, the write-down would have been $15,000.
    e. Had direct costing techniques been applied, reported income would have been increased $20,000.
    f. Cost or market combinations were not explored but they could induce substantial changes in reported income.

3. Goodwill was written off on the 40-year option. If systematic amortization of purchased abnormal earnings over the life implied had been taken, the further reduction would have amounted to $50,000. Organization costs were treated in a similar fashion, and amortization based on varying estimates provided by different officers would have resulted in a profit reduction ranging from zero to $10,000.

4. Executive estimates regarding the proper percentage to be applied to past-due accounts varied widely. A reduction of $7,000 was approved, but the estimates varied from $3,000 to $20,000.

Clearly the supervising accountant has adequate material for serious reflection. A few of the above alternatives may not meet the nebulous test of accepted accounting principles, but a large number do meet currently acceptable procedures and serve to emphasize the wide discretionary range over which the auditor may roam. The amazing feature of this entire situation is that the profession's integrity and judgment have been respected to the extent that any dependence whatever has been placed on its reports! Except for some recently stated major complaints that arise primarily from price-level changes, there seems to be little lessening of confidence in the public accountants' results. Serious financial analysts are seemingly astute enough to sift the useful data from reports and make allowances for other material. They are no doubt often mistaken in the magnitude of the allowances and certainly could be expected to operate more effectively with information that is more nearly comparable.

Perhaps the saving grace is the phrase, "applied on a basis consistent with that of the preceding year." At least, an attempt is made to preserve comparability from period to period with regard to individual firms. The looseness and variety of accepted conventions still makes inter-firm comparisons risky ventures, but the straight-jacket of "consistently applied" attempts to restore some degree of comparability for intra-firm comparisons and individual trends.

Consistency of behavior through time has interesting implications. Clearly such consistency is not an unmixed blessing. Consistency in unacceptable social behavior is not to be commended. Professor Sidney Davidson has emphasized that if this standard is applied to moral behavior, a higher ranking is automatically given to the steady sinner and lower virtue is assigned to those who are sometimes good and sometimes fall from the wagon. For accounting reports the case is not much stronger. In both cases prediction of future behavior is important, and both investors and probation officers should find stability in past behavior patterns useful in prediction. Perhaps the profession needs to adopt a modified approach that establishes a temporal order for reviewing consistency. Behavior must be examined first to find whether or not it conforms to the broader accepted principles. If it does not, correction is demanded before the consistency-through-time rule is applied. If the particular action does conform satisfactorily or has been corrected so that it does conform, the time-stability test is applied to encourage desirable actions.

An increasing number of accountants are concerned with the scope paragraph compared with the actual operations performed. One may begin by inquiring why such a paragraph is included in an opinion. It seems that this statement would be entirely superfluous in a mature profession or if all parties had confidence in the competence and integrity of the profession. Medical men, for example, seldom enlarge their opinion by including a statement to the effect that they followed accepted medical standards. Giving approval to qualified opinions has the effect of forcing disclosure of the nature of and reasons for the qualifications. But such approval sanctions various grades of opinions and leads to confusion and to sneering remarks about "twenty-five-cent audits."

The scope requirement may amount to a communication device to keep members of the profession constantly informed of the importance of minimum standards. It also has some coercive effect on marginal members of the profession by requiring them to include the scope of their investigation as an explicit part of their signed representations. Otherwise a simple signature should be sufficient.

The more urgent concern is that the opinion paragraph contains a representation of work done (scope and depth) that is not justified by the "standards" and "procedures" applied. Accountants give opinions covering financial position and periodic earnings, but they do not feel it necessary to have "competence" as an "appraiser, valuer, or expert in materials."[8] A balance sheet, as a statement of financial condition, must imply valuation

---

[8] The following statement, while carefully hedged, tends to deny too much, and, many feel, partially undermines the value of the opinion. "In no sense is the independent certified public accountant an insurer or guarantor, nor do his training and experience qualify him to act as a general appraiser, valuer, or expert in materials." *Codification of Statements on Auditing Procedure, op. cit.*, p. 13.

rules of some sort. Widespread use of cost allocation rules as substitutions for value, and their adoption, does not bypass the problem of financial (economic) significance in some mysterious manner. The usual procedure for amortizing costs, such as the usual treatment of damaged, obsolete, and shopworn goods, must consider the decreased sales possibilities — value — of the goods. The fund-raising possibilities are a function of quantities on hand and also of the prices the quantities will command. These prices are in turn related to the quality of the stocks. It is important to know whether the gems are diamonds or zircons, and if the accountant is not expert enough to discriminate the two, he must himself rely on the independent opinion of an appraiser to ensure that his own opinion is not worthless.

There are clues which point to the financial significance of receivables, fixed assets, inventories, and research costs, and anyone who gives an opinion on management's representations in these areas should be prepared to take whatever steps are essential to form a competent opinion. The responsibility may be sublet to specialists or the contents of the accountants' training may be changed, but to disclaim responsibility is not an acceptable answer.

Digression on Sampling

Early auditors were accustomed to detailed audits (100-percent audits) that checked every entry and summary prepared by the bookkeeping staff. The payment of professional fees to have thousands of small transactions "vouched" is obviously a misdirection of society's scarce resources. Sooner or later those who pay auditing fees could be expected to exert pressure to reduce the cost of such duplication. Yet the retreat from the 100-percent audit was comparatively slow. In the case of highly vulnerable cash the retreat was especially slow, but in the area of inventories, for example, the sampling techniques and evidentiary support were reduced below an acceptable level and subsequently had to be strengthened.

The general retreat from the detailed audit was carried on with inadequate statistical knowledge and proceeded on an *ad hoc*, seat-of-the-pants basis. In the early period it is highly doubtful whether the techniques of statistics were developed far enough to be very helpful. An interesting research project could be built around the adaptation of accounting sampling to the needs of nondetailed audits and the concurrent state of statistical techniques. Certainly, quality-control techniques and such helps as the Dodge-Romig tables were in use some time before they were adapted to auditing work. The developments in sequential sampling beyond the older double-sampling technique were picked up by the profession quickly through the writings of Vance, Neter, and others. The available literature in this area is now voluminous.

The difficulties of defining errors are serious enough, but accountants must find a method of weighting the seriousness of various kinds of errors. For example, failure to countersign a check may be extremely important as an indication that internal control has broken down. But is this error as important as a mistake of $100 in the amount of the check? The newer subjective approach to statistics with its provision for assessing utilities and incorporating new knowledge in a systematic fashion offers help to the auditing profession. Some integration of these techniques is now being done in the cost accounting field and may be expected soon in auditing.[9]

There is a related and unsatisfactory area of accounting where the statistician has so

---

[9] See, for example, Charles T. Horngren, *Managerial Cost Accounting* (New York: Prentice-Hall, Inc., 1961).

far offered little help. When fixed assets and inventories and research costs are relatively unimportant, the accountant's income reports are comparable enough from period-to-period and from firm-to-firm to be acceptable. At the other extreme, the X Company illustrates the futility of reporting a net of $121,171.67 when different sets of judgments or conventions yield fantastically different amounts. Conventional reporting is therefore deceiving because in some lines of business the reporting error is low while in others the possible error is tremendous, and no indication (other than knowledge of the business) is given of the differences in reliability.

In some cases the problem may be solved in part by putting an *addendum* to the operating statement or by using a columnar form with the effects of varying assumptions indicated. In most cases it would not be feasible to show statements for all possible combinations of assumptions. In these cases the effects of many minor variations may be disregarded, and a number of firms have indicated by means of appropriate notes to the statements differences in net if alternate assumptions had been used.

Similar procedures may be applied to the financial statements. In fact, traditional methods for handling appraisals tend to accomplish this end, and the inventory difference between LIFO and current market is sometimes indicated.

Some accountants have recommended that the range of executive estimates be indicated on such matters as depreciation and inventories. In this case a reported profit of $100,000 followed by $80,000 - $150,000 would indicate that the consensus (or strongest personality) indicates $100,000 but that estimates range between $80,000 and $150,000. This suggestion has merit and, when combined with supplementary information regarding the use of alternative methods of inventory costing, depreciation bases, etc., could be useful. For new concerns, progress reports in discussion form may prove to be more useful than formal income reports.

A few half-hearted attempts have been made to apply probable error techniques to these matters, but the accounting process for generating data hardly fits the usual assumptions. Applications of normal variate techniques to test for bias run into similar difficulties. Many accounting measurement rules and definitions have built-in bias while others do not. Changes in the "mix" of such rules is only one of the difficulties involved, for the weighting of errors for relative seriousness has not been solved.

Methodological Suggestion

The balance-sheet audit has had a definite association with single-entry bookkeeping. The common practice in the early years of auditing was to establish the existence and measure of the assets, liabilities and ownership contracts at the cut-off date, and to base the opinion on earnings primarily on changes in proprietary amounts at different dates modified for dividends and additional investments. Secondary support was sometimes gathered by "scanning" the operating accounts. If this approach to auditing is combined with refusal to accept responsibility for discovering fraud, there seems to be no reason to get excited about internal control, efficiency, and internal misdirection of organization resources. A strange position! Major frauds and inefficiencies obviously affect the attainment of goals, but if a "certified" statement of financial status is the *only* concern, fraud discovery is of no consequence and internal control is important only to the degree that the figures may require less outside checking.

The following recommendation shifts the emphasis from the audit-oriented toward presenting a balance sheet to an audit based on performance toward budgeted plans. While the emphasis is on operating accounts, financial matters are not neglected. In effect the recommendation is that the firm's budget be "adjusted to level" and its adjusted figures used as standards from which deviations are noted and investigated. If no budget is presented, the auditor may prepare a skeleton budget based on past performance and fixed-variable breakdown techniques. This constructed budget may be adjusted to actual sales or actual physical volume and used as a standard from which exceptions are reported and investigated.

For an illustration, consider a firm that has no formal budget or standard cost system. The focus of attention for the early part of the audit would be in the area of sales. It would be necessary to audit the sales in some detail so that an opinion as to the actual sales volume can be rendered. In addition it may be necessary to work out overall percentage price changes for each major group of items sold. Even before the formal audit begins the staff can prepare provisional breakdowns of costs into fixed and variable portions so that their behavior in response to changes in sales or physical volume can be estimated. The results of past periods may be used as starting positions, and some attention can be given to accounts themselves so that the balances are analyzed and classified into relatively-fixed, relatively-variable divisions. Before the structure is related to the current period, some attention must be given to changes in cost efficiencies and in the unit cost of services acquired by cost transactions. This work requires an overall appraisal of technological change, as well as wage and material-price changes.

After the cost behavior has been estimated and the sales have been audited, the auditor may break the sales into volume and price variations along the lines of the old "gross profit variation analysis," and an estimated earnings report for the period may be prepared according to the budgetary formulas. It should be observed that the budget is prepared by applying the formulas to the period that is to be audited and not to the future, as is the case in orthodox budgetary procedures. The resulting "formula earnings report" may be used for a standard from which exceptions may be measured, appraised, and investigated. Variations in labor, materials, power, various selling or administrative expenses may be significant and call for special investigation or they may be essentially in line with expectations. Unusual charges for revenue expenditures would show up immediately.

It should not be inferred that the audit is over when such exceptions have been resolved to the auditor's satisfaction. The opinion also applies to the statement of financial position, and obviously the auditor must assure himself that the items of the position statement are substantially correct. From the budget of sales and related items it is possible to construct the estimated charges to receivables, and an extension of budgeting techniques to include collection experience helps establish the estimate of credits to the accounts receivable control. Thus it is not difficult to set up a tentative figure for receivables to serve as a basis for checking exceptions and for disclosing large discrepancies. Notice that a careful audit of the sales figures is essential, and notice also that in connection with the sales audit the debit to receivables would ordinarily be checked as it is in ordinary auditing procedures. A study of the collection experience of the firms should help to build up a part of the budgeted cash position.

It is possible to approximate material and other requirements by applying budgetary procedures that start with operating ratios. With beginning inventories determined with satisfactory evidence, it is then possible to judge whether the purchases as represented by management are consistent with the final inventories as stated. Consistent amounts in these areas in conjunction with inventory observation reports should cut the detail work considerably. In these respects the recommendations are essentially those used in current auditing practice. The difference is primarily one of emphasis, but changes in operating effectiveness are disclosed and audited as a part of the usual auditing process.

Essay Five

Some Behavioral Aspects
of Accounting

"Every society keeps the records most relevant for its major values."[1]

One of the most interesting and vigorous developments of the postwar decades has been reflected in the behavioral sciences. This development is a combination of sociology, individual psychology, anthropology and group psychology. An offshoot of considerable interest to administrators and accountants is known as organization theory — a secondary synthesis of aspects that seem appropriate to associations and groups.

Psychology in various forms had long been an important element of the business scene. Traditional personnel psychologists have been with us for decades and have been working with testing, selecting, classifying, and predicting performance, but as Haire states they seem " . . . to have stalled on the problem of selection and classification . . ."[2] Industry has had its quota of engineering psychologists, who have been concerned with finding the abilities of the workers, finding the requirements of the job, and then designing machines and establishing work conditions that tend to optimize the correlation of the two. This type of psychology tends to concentrate on the conditions of work (the environment) and has developed the macabre name of 'human engineering.' Haire states: "The 'human relations' movement is largely a program of development of attitudes among leaders to manipulate the 'climate' . . . . stemming from the early Lewinian suggestion that it is easier to reorganize the structure of the whole group than to change the individual . . ."[3]

Haire is not alone in asserting that business is behavioral science: "a sample of behavior in a particular context." Accounting is the leading form of the communication-and-control language of business, and it would seem to follow that accountants should be at home among the concepts of psychology, sociology, and the behavioral sciences in general. The truth is that accountants have almost no such knowledge, have developed little rapport with these related fields, and have made some fantastically naive behavioral assumptions (along with some reasonably astute ones). It is the purpose of this essay to point out some areas in which accountants must make behavioral assumptions and to emphasize the numerous instances where accountants have solved the problem by default. The essay is concluded with a brief and elementary survey of selected problems in the field of psychology.

Currently the accounting profession is hard pressed to keep control of the information gathering and reporting aspects of enterprises, and accountants need to ask more and

---

[1] Paul F. Lazarsfeld, "Sociological Reflections on Business: Consumers and Managers," *Social Science Research on Business: Product and Potential*, by Robert A. Dahl, Mason Haire and Paul F. Lazarsfeld (New York: Columbia University Press, 1959), p. 108.

[2] Mason Haire, "Psychology and the Study of Business: Joint Behavioral Sciences," in *Social Science Research on Business: Product and Potential, op. cit.*, p. 88.

[3] *Ibid.*, p. 81.

more what can be learned and absorbed from competing information-control systems. To whom do businessmen listen? How do they evaluate information for accuracy and appropriateness? How do they reach decisions? Do they, for example, use unfilled orders more frequently than past delivered sales? How are current production figures used? What sort of rumor and gossip network is at work and how is it used to supplement other information? What officers or executives are in charge of competing information systems and what do they emphasize? Where do the information services overlap? How do competing groups gather, present and control their data? What have statisticians to offer? How can their developments be integrated into accounting? Perhaps one should look at it the other way and ask how accounting can be absorbed most readily into the field of statistics. Whichever way this particular decision goes is relatively unimportant. What is important is that accountants and statisticians deal with information that is relevant to the needs of individuals and society. Only then can one meet competition in the area of gathering, sifting, classifying, and finally reporting information in meaningful ways.

A vast number of questions in the acknowledged field of accounting are based on psychological foundations and require some knowledge or assumptions before they can be discussed intelligently. David Green, Jr., has emphasized this relationship by referring to accounting as the mathematics of behavioral science. Only a few of the possible points are mentioned here. The reader may wish to prepare his own list; it may well be a long one.

We may start with the field of internal control and system design and review our previous discussion by asking again how important and deterring is the need for collusion.[4] In fact, this essay might be composed entirely of a series of questions. How important is it to make opportunities for personal friendship with other key personnel difficult? We often try to separate, for example, the store's bookkeeper as far as feasible from the broad-shouldered men who handle the physical goods. Perhaps there are status barriers which are in themselves sufficient, and white-collar/blue-collar is enough. Does the deterrent stem in part from a feeling of rejection by a friend; an acquaintance from a lower status-level; from a stranger; from loss of face in the neighborhood? Perhaps it stems from the fear of losing the job? From the fear of being disgraced in the firm or community? From fear of blackball by all firms in the region? From fear of prison? Do accountants have any answers to these questions? Accountants assume that documents from other concerns (e.g., invoices) are better evidence than documents generated internally. Apparently the assumption here is that an interfirm barrier has additional deterrent properties. Most accountants feel that it does, but why? How much? Is it geographical? What about the internal control of the other firm? Certainly the barrier is not homogeneous among all organizations.

We have only begun to ask questions about which accountants have expressed only the vaguest feelings. For example, how much extra protection — if any — does adding a third collusive party, or a fourth, or a fifth, add to a system of internal control? Does it make a difference whether the person who would share guilt is a male or a female? Young or old?

---

[4] To my knowledge the only published work worthy of note in this field is Donald R. Cressey's *Other People's Money* (Glencoe: The Free Press, 1953). Cressey digested some of the contents in "Why do Trusted Persons Commit Fraud?" *The Journal of Accountancy*, November, 1951. A perceptive review of the book by Arthur M. Cannon may be found in *The Accounting Review*, January, 1956. According to Cressey one of the preconditions for embezzlement is the "nonshareable" situation that cannot be discussed with others. This feeling of nonshareability in turn is probably related to the image that the embezzler has of himself. Being in a trusted position with dignity and prestige helps establish the image that in turn will not let him share the trouble. With smaller items and at lower prestige levels, the problems may sometimes be shared more readily and rationalized more effectively over beers at the local pub. See the preceding essay for further comments on Cressey in connection with auditing.

Bumpkin or urban slicker? Is the fact that the firm is profitable or unprofitable a consideration? Does the wage rate make a difference? If so, is the rate relative to other wage rates in the firm or in the community a factor? Or is it the rate relative to the level of living desired? Is union loyalty involved? What about prestige factors? Positions of status and role? Can loyalty to the organization be isolated? If so, how does it function as a deterring force? Does anyone care to defend the existing procedure for appraising internal control?

The point to be emphasized is that accountants, as scientists, should have hypotheses covering these points, and should have attempted to scale the relevant variables, measure the effects, isolate critical and discontinuous points. Our current training and educational requirements for the profession are woefully inadequate in these areas. Most of us are simply not competent to appraise the adequacy of internal control and therefore to plan an acceptable audit program.

The systems problem has wide applications to the general society in which the employee lives. For example, does the difficulty or ease of installing an accounting system depend on the degree of organization or regimentation in other sectors of the workers' lives? Does the regimentation of an accounting control system lead to respect for authority? To disrespect? No effect? Can one generalize at all? The rapid growth of industry in hitherto backward countries may make such questions practical and relevant. Does a system tend to lead to bureaucracy or to authoritarianism? Is there a feedback chain from system to organization to system? How do we instill a sense of values to get those who fill in reports to be accurate? Does it make a difference if they are production workers who are not in the accounting chain of command and have no tradition for accuracy in reporting? How does one go about setting up devices to check the accuracy and consistency of these sub-reports within the usual cost constraints? How important is the ease of evading responsibility? Can we construct some sort of coefficient of buck-passing possibilities? Can the tendency be reduced or controlled? These questions are directly related to accounting, and there are many similar questions that are now being investigated by those in management, personnel, and organization theory. For example, what difference does identification with blue-shirt or white-collar make? In what ways and to what extent does identification with the management group change attitudes toward accuracy of reports and conformance with organizational goals?

Some mention of embezzlers is made elsewhere, but how important is their perception of the probability that they will be discovered? How important is the fear of punishment and the expected value of the resulting misery? Perhaps the expected value of the pleasure from stolen funds can be approximated. Is there a middle ground between being caught and being above suspicion, e.g., a stage of fear not of punishment but of being suspected? Is the approval of the auditor as an individual or as a professional a factor in honesty or accuracy? Is approval of the auditor a bigger or smaller factor as we go up or down the line to the controller? Our answers are meager indeed!

Let us now turn to some behavioral aspects of income reporting and their effects on investors and members of the firm. Again there has been less work in this field than is desirable, although there have been some serious studies of investor motives and reactions.[5]

---

[5] The following sample is only suggestive. Myron J. Gordon, "Dividends, Earnings, and Stock Prices," *The Review of Economics and Statistics,* May, 1959, pp. 99-105. J. Hirshleifer, "On the Theory of Optimal Investment Decision," *Journal of Political Economy*, August, 1958, pp. 329-352. Franco Modigliani and M. H. Miller, "The Cost of Capital, Corporation Finance and the Theory of Investment," *The American Economic Review*, June, 1958, pp. 261-297. James Tobin, "Liquidity Preference as Behavior Towards Risk," *The Review of Economic Studies*, February, 1958, pp. 65-86. James E. Walter, "A Discriminant Function for Earnings-Price Ratios of Large Industrial Corporations," *The Review of Economics and Statistics*, February, 1959, pp. 44-52.

Consider, for example, the following types of questions. What differences in investment action result if value increases are reported by means of footnotes instead of treating them as income and showing them on the income report? Notice that normal tests for income realization require an increase in working capital at least equal to the recognized increase in value before the change is shown as income. What are the resulting changes in demand for dividend distribution? What are the effects of showing current appraisals in the accounting reports? Do investors and owners tend to treat such increases as income? Capital gains? Adjustments for changes in the measuring stick? Are reactions different for each interpretation? If so, how much and in what direction? Are devices for smoothing income a blessing or an "artificial tinkering with profits"? How do businessmen respond to higher reported earnings? Does tolerance for inefficiencies increase? Does bargaining resistance to nonprofit sharing groups decrease? If so, how much? Do owners invest more rapidly and managers expand facilities more quickly? Or do they have some sort of internal stabilizer to smooth or to discount the accountant's reports? A good part of the LIFO controversy and the current discussion of price-level adjustments requires knowledge — or in the absence of knowledge, assumptions — on these points.

Expected reactions to stability enter into the arguments about clean surplus and all-inclusive income reports. Many businessmen in the past must have assumed that reported profits are important. At least many have used the back-door (the surplus route) to obscure unfavorable events. Yet perhaps accountants are sanguine, as one old-time professor has always maintained, in believing that investors and businessmen look at the profit figure at all except to estimate the amount of probable income tax. Accountants should not only know such things; they should be able to specify the conditions in which reported income does matter to each group, and they should be able to indicate the relative importance of the fund backlash from inverse tax payments. That such things can be known exactly is too much to expect, but accountants may be able to isolate critical points and reach conclusions with accuracy rated in probabilistic terms. It should be possible to go further and point out attitudes and errors in judgment that affect only transfers of wealth, e.g., more for one individual and less for another, as well as those that bring about a misdirection of society's resources.

A simple question to start an investigation could be: What are income figures used for and by whom? In the early days of accounting, for example, income was assumed to be an index of the amount that could be withdrawn from the organization without impairing capital in some sense. A modern variation is similar in that income is regarded as a guide for consumption. Certainly reported past income influences expectations and is related in some fashion to the price of securities or to the worth of ownership interests. Unfortunately, here as elsewhere there are intuitive feelings but few careful studies and little confidence in the results of such studies. For example, how interested are the holders of fixed-interest obligation in times-interest ratios and retained earnings as support for their position? Do these creditors have critical points that stir action when the times-requirement ratio is above or below some subjective standard? Such a ratio may become extremely important to a firm's survival.

How do *employees* at different levels react to reported profits? Do they look at high income figures as signals for more rigid bargaining for more wages, bigger bonuses, and better conditions? Do they think of high earnings as a factor in job security through membership in a successful organization? Is pride in successful operation as evidenced by profit a factor? Do they identify their own efforts and contribution with the amount of reported income? How do reactions of governmental agencies differ? Do assessors consider earnings in assessing property taxes? Is there a more or less continuous relationship between reported income and assessments? If so, is the relationship direct or is it due to common causes such as larger inventories, etc.? What about suppliers and customers? To what extent do they tie their interests to one supplier or firm? What penalties does a customer suffer if a supplier folds? What are the penalties attached to making changes? At what point do customers tend to leave a supplier who is in distress?

The income figures are, of course, not the only items of interest in income reports. How do readers use sales returns data, for example? In spite of some abstruse and lengthy arguments, the important issue is not where sales returns belong on the income report. Who follows returns, allowances, rebates, kickbacks, etc.? At what level of authority does he operate? What are his action points and how are they determined? Does someone in the organization investigate such relevant factors as poor packing, impossible delivery dates, misleading specifications and qualifications, careless writing of orders with wrong addresses, etc., poor quality, over-selling in the sense of shipping with only faint hope of permanent acceptance? Do businessmen interpret gross profit as the contribution over variable costs and tend to think of expenses as relatively fixed costs? Which officials follow inventories? How do they set action points and what actions do they initiate? Does the usual expense classification of administrative, selling, etc., have meaning to anyone? How is the overall maintained gross-margin figure used and how is it tied in with individual margin figures?

There is a feeling among many accountants that item location on the reports has genuine importance in getting desirable or undesirable action. If, for example, position is an important motivation factor, it would seem to follow that the form of the report should change from period to period in response to the things that most need to be done. Thus, in one period it may be desirable to start with purchase returns. Accounting reports are specialized statistical tables and are subject to the same criteria of usefulness. Moreover, our measurement and decision rules would seem to be variable in a similar way. To be set against this variable approach is the fact that usefulness and prediction are often aided by some degree of uniformity in measuring and reporting. Clearly there is a balancing problem involved, and it may be less expensive to educate users to interpret imperfect general-purpose reports than to tailor the reports to the probable reactions of each reader.

Now and then accountants argue the merits of treating sales discounts as direct sales deductions as opposed to treating them as selling or administrative or even financial expense. Advocates of each classification usually have no personal (self-interest) motives and are sincere about their beliefs. What objectives are involved in arguments of this kind? Do the 'principles' of accounting call for this type of classification in order to be consistent with broader objectives? Perhaps an accountant feels that sales discounts do not meet the definitional requirement for expenses. If the definition of 'expense' is acceptable, it is clear that preservation of consistency with such useful definitions has positive merit in an information-reporting system. Accountants must appraise the possibilities of various alternatives, assign appropriate utilities and devise appropriate definitions.

There has been systematic effort to appraise the impact of some alternate measuring and reporting schemes on investors, creditors, owners, bankers, and others. Within the last decade or two there has been some feeling (in the tradition of Schmalenbach) that the balance sheet is of little use and is merely a list of unallocated costs and another list of possible claims that in aggregate probably never will be paid. Some other discussions have characterized the balance sheet as a glorified statement of fund sources and dispositions from the inception of the firm. This is an interesting approach, but one should ask how, precisely, is this report used and for exactly what purpose? The balance sheet viewed as the 'big picture' of the current liquidity situation is more familiar, but again we are woefully weak on details. There is a well-developed folklore about the two-to-one current ratio with the result that this fraction probably has more psychological impact than it merits. Is a ratio of four considered to be twice as good as a ratio of two, and does a ratio as large as two put curiosity at rest so that no further attention is directed to the liquidity problem? Little is known about measuring the impact of such devices on behavior. Some may have acceptable/non-acceptable or go/no-go application while others may be represented by relatively smooth functions.

For a further example, does anyone use the imperfectly preserved distinction between total contributed capital and noncontributed capital, or capital contributed by preferred holders and capital contributed by residual holders? Are current preferred holders interested in what a previous generation of preferred holders probably contributed? The classification of stockholders' equity in terms of legal restriction may have more merit, for, traditionally, voluntary retained earning restrictions were a device for disclosing general intentions, vague fears and sundry anxieties. Accountants are not positive about general reactions to such items as reserve for contingencies or reserve for reconversion, and there is little information about attitudes toward more specific reserves. What is the meaning to the financial public of a large retained earnings balance? Does it lead to the expectation of continued parsimony in dividends? Larger future dividends? Careless or optimistic bookkeeping? A substitute for specific disclosure of expected unfavorable events? It is difficult to realize also that nearly nothing is known about investor attitudes regarding capital surplus, revaluation and price-level credits, donated surpluses, surplus restricted for treasury stock acquired, etc. The misconceptions of the average investor about ordinary retained earnings should provide interesting and enlightening research.

The views held by various segments of the financial public with regard to book value and its meaning might also prove to be interesting and useful. Many accountants themselves have apparently given up on book value and are still undecided whether the figure is one that is appropriate for liquidation or for a continuing concern. One solution is to abandon attempts to give meaning to such a ratio as book value per share. There is no necessity for finding guidance and meaning in every possible ratio, remainder or total that might be constructed from accounting data. Yet there must be an important difference between a firm that uses many valuable assets to earn a given return and another firm that uses only a few assets and a lot of personality to earn an equivalent return. Do investors believe that an allowance for depreciation equal to one-half the cost indicates that the assets have yielded one-half their expected benefit? One might ask many accountants the same question with interesting results. The point to be emphasized is the almost complete lack of knowledge about the reactions and desires of those who use the output of an accounting system.

Comments on Stedry's Budgeting Model

We have some examples of how research on the psychological aspects of accounting control may be carried on. One such study by Andrew C. Stedry deserves extensive comment.[6] This study does not measure the magnitude of the variables and constants involved, but it does set up a model that may be used as a framework for thinking in this area. Such a model is clearly a preliminary step that must be made if accountants are ever to get beyond such attitudes as: "tight but not too tight," or such inane statements as:

---

[6] Andrew C. Stedry, *Budget Control and Cost Behavior* (Englewood Cliffs, N. J.: Prentice-Hall, Inc., 1960).

"Don't put this carrot too far in front of the rabbit." The Stedry volume deserves careful study for its methodological structure. The mathematical ability necessary for understanding is moderate; in fact the mathematics does little more than provide a convenient notation.

Stedry borrows the concept of aspiration level from Lewin and his associates and uses this concept effectively as a core construct for his model.[7] The aspiration level is an intervening variable operating in conjunction with budgeted levels (set by higher management) and expected actual levels. With the aid of this set of relationships, Stedry then proceeds to set up some hypotheses that are subject to empirical tests, review some of the literature, and speculate about the determinants of aspiration levels.

The following assumptions and hypotheses are paraphrased or quoted from Stedry as an example of his behavioral approach.

> The discrepancy between the expected actual level of expenditure and the aspired level of expenditure is appropriately termed a measure of *stress*, since clearly the department head's "emotional tension produced by frustration," varies with the size of the discrepancy. A compromising of goals is a well-known reaction to stress . . . (p. 25).

It is hypothesized that the existence of a discrepancy between expected actual and aspired levels will often lead the department head to try to reduce the discrepancy by moving the aspiration level toward expected actual at a rate dependent on the size of the discrepancy. Stedry assumes further that in addition to the effect above, the level of aspiration will be lowered as a consequence of lowering the budget level (imposed by outside authority). Further, department managers will be encouraged if the discrepancy between expected and aspired expenditures does not exceed some positive number or band designated as the discouragement point or area. In addition to the discouragement point there is a larger positive value which may be called the failure point. When the discrepancy equals or exceeds this point the department head resigns. "The neurotic response of extreme discouragement will eventually lead to ultimate withdrawal . . ." (p. 26). If the department head is encouraged, on the other hand, he tries to make the discrepancy smaller by lowering his expected actual level, and Stedry feels also that the manager's reaction to a negative discrepancy is to let the expected actual level rise. In each case he suggests that the rate of adjustments depends on the size of the discrepancy, but of course this assumption requires empirical testing. "If the department head is *slightly discouraged*, he will reduce the discrepancy by reducing expected cost at a lower rate relative to a given discrepancy than he would if encouraged. If he is *moderately discouraged*, he will allow expected cost to increase but at a sufficiently small rate that the discrepancy will not be increased. If he is *extremely discouraged*, he will allow expected cost to increase at a rate which increases the discrepancy" (p. 25).

---

[7] Lewin states: "Experimental psychology has shown that the formation of goals depends directly upon the laws which govern the level of aspiration, particularly upon the effect which success or failure has in raising and lowering the level of aspiration . . . . These experiments make it evident that the level of aspiration is greatly influenced by such social facts as the presence or absence of other persons or by the competitive or noncompetitive character of the situation. It has been shown, too, that the goal-setting depends upon certain ideal goals, upon what the sociologists call the 'ideology' of the person . . . emotional reaction to failure can be changed to a great extent by appropriate praise or change in social atmosphere . . . management of tension by the individual depends upon his particular social and cultural setting." "Field Theory and Experiment in Social Psychology: Concepts and Methods," *American Journal of Sociology*, 44 (1939), pp. 868-896. Reprinted in *Readings in Philosophy of Science*, ed. Philip P. Wiener (New York: Charles Scribner's Sons, 1953), p. 221.

From the framework or model set up by Stedry it is possible to organize inquiry in a systematic fashion. One may ask, for example, what means and channels are available for the department head to improve his expected actual level and thereby cut down the discrepancy from this angle. Perhaps diverting effort from nonorganizational needs or nonobjectives to organizational goals can be accomplished and thus help to cut the amount of discrepancy without giving rise to too many other forms of managerial stress. Improvement can arise in a number of ways including the general desire to work harder; the increased feeling that costs are objects of concern and that they matter.

While these kinds of things have wide application in the field of getting the world's work done, it should be clear that they have particular importance for what is now known as the field of budgeting. It appears that a mechanistic approach to the budget in which performance is related primarily to technology does not account adequately for differences in aspiration levels and reactions to stress. However, it is usually not feasible to tailor all budgets, requirements, standards and goals to every member in the organization. Contrary cost functions are at work here, and there is an optimizing problem in which the advantages of tailored budgets are matched against the sacrifices in making them. Usually this problem can be solved on a marginal or incremental basis, with due caution for possible conflicts in "optima in the small" and "optima in the large," i.e., sub-optimization.

The question of budget strategy involves individuals, and the possible effects of budget paraphernalia on aspiration levels, stress, on expected actual costs and finally on actual costs are a part of the process. Stedry concludes that technological constraints must be considered but a stationary budget that is never attained tends to lose effectiveness and be replaced by some other *de facto* element of control. If such a budget is attained, the possibility of lower cost or better performance is never answered. " . . . blanket budget reductions . . . are of dubious merit. Furthermore, the treatment of all subordinates 'impartially' when it comes to budget demands . . . regardless of their motivation structure, appears not only irrational from the cost standpoint but from the standpoint of welfare of the subordinates as well . . . " (p. 41). With regard to implicit (*de facto*) budgets Stedry argues that: " . . . merely because a systematized and formalized procedure is absent supervisors . . . do not then believe that others . . . hold no expectations concerning their behavior . . . the essence of the budgetary control procedures is formulated around such 'external' expectations which become crystallized as a stated goal when formalized in either a budget, a physical or cost standard . . . " (p. 70).

There is little doubt that the externally imposed budget is an immediate factor in setting aspiration levels, and it is reasonable to assume that as a long-run proposition the aspiration levels indirectly and over a long period tend to influence budgets even when imposed from without. It is usually assumed that the aspired level is influenced by positive or negative awards associated with attainment or nonattainment of the budget. These relationships need considerable work, for their interaction is by no means simple. In some cases the awards are in terms of normal satisfactions that are cared for outside the area of work experience. Certainly the reaction cannot be assumed to be straightline or represented by the usual curves for marginal diminishing satisfaction. Short-run and long-run may conflict in that a good performance today may bring an immediate reward (and improvement) but in the long run will lead to tighter imposed budgets that will make future bonuses difficult to earn.

There has been a substantial amount of laboratory work devoted to aspiration levels and their determinants, but much work remains. Stedry points out that: " . . . work in the laboratory has concentrated on descriptions of the formation of goals, taking performance as the independent variable, rather than manipulating performance through the effect of aspirations and external goals . . . . The experiments . . . have generally dealt with the precise interpretation of 'level of aspiration' in various contexts and casual factors in shifts of the aspiration level. The casual factors investigated include social and personality factors as well as temporary situational factors" (pp. 43-44, 50).

Lewin and his group have defined the difference between an aspiration level and the *actual* score as the "achievement discrepancy," and the difference between the aspiration level and score on previous tests as "goal discrepancy." When change in performance is small the goal and achievement discrepancies may be assumed to be identical. Chapman and Volkmann concluded that their experimental subjects did not change their levels of aspiration in response to announcements as to how other groups were doing, and Stedry (p. 46) concludes that: " . . . the experiment casts serious doubt on the possibility of affecting the aspirations of one department head by pointing out the achievements of another."[8] Some work by Wolfe and others has shown that for some animals (notably chimpanzees) the timing of the reward and the manner in which it is given along with the amount of the reward are factors in goal setting. There is some evidence that aspiration levels fall after failures in previous efforts and rise in response to previous success.

Stedry concerns himself with another problem of consequence for budgeting, i.e., the possibility of strong reactions to showing red variances of any kind and the desire to show black (favorable) variances even at great cost. Thus it is possible that the division between meeting and not meeting a standard is akin to passing or failing a course of study. It is possible that organization interests may be sacrificed sharply in order for the individual department head to look good by avoiding the stigma of red variances — failing no courses. An analogous student prefers all D's to all A's and one F. All standard-cost systems are vulnerable to those who are willing to sacrifice more remote goals to make their own variances look better. Such sacrifices may be disclosed in the course of analyzing variances, but intervention by superiors is sometimes necessary. From the view of the individual department head the intervention rules are essentially servo rules, and it is extremely difficult to discuss the setting of aspiration levels without discussing what the subject perceives the intervention rules of his superiors to be and how he judges the expected consequences of failure. In some actual studies, knowledge of goals seemed to stimulate output. Worst performances were generally turned in by groups that did not formulate their aspirations. Considerable evidence has been turned up that feedback in the sense of knowing how they did on previous tries was extremely helpful. Success or failure previously on related tasks obviously has an influence on current aspiration levels, but the effect is hard to generalize and measure. Clearly, competent scholars should be operating in these areas, and accountants, like Uriah, should be among them.

Comments on More General Psychological Matters

Within the last few decades psychologists have taken an approach that is more in tune with operationalism and other tenets of scientific method and have placed less emphasis on such constructs as self, introspection, mind, and other terms that call for nonoperational constructs and lead to " . . . entanglement with dualistic metaphysics."[9] With re-

---

8 Dwight W. Chapman and John Volkmann, "A Social Determinant of the Level of Aspiration," *The Journal of Abnormal and Social Psychology*, January, 1939, pp. 225-238.

9 Egon Brunswik, "The Conceptual Framework of Psychology," *International Encyclopedia of Unified Science* (Chicago: University of Chicago Press, 1955), p. 659. This section leans heavily on Brunswik, who states: "Since sensory experiences are usually supported by the presence of an external stimulus, they are sturdy and persistent in comparison with emotions, imagery, and thought. They withstand observation better, and there is greater conformity of report from subject to subject." *Ibid.*, p. 663.

gard to mind, for example, the modern trend is away from the "bucket" theory (the term is Popper's) of Hume to a modified Kantian approach. "Kant argued that knowledge is not a collection of gifts received by our senses and stored in the mind as if it were a museum, but . . . is very largely the result of our own mental activity; . . . we must most actively engage ourselves in searching, comparing, unifying, generalizing . . ."[10]

The current trend obviously is in the direction of adaptive behavior, but here again some changes have been made. The older approach with a unique response to a stimulus will no longer do in an age of causation defined in terms of repeatable initial conditions.[11]

The simple stimulus-response (S - R) approach has led to variations of 'dynamic' psychology by Woodworth, who stressed such replacements as W-S-Ow-R-W, where O represents the individual and his drives, W for the world and w for the individual's "situation and goals set." Behavior is carried on as an adaptive operation with far from perfect cues in a heavy fog of gestalt-ambiguity. The reduction of search for strict laws and increased attention to probabilistic tendencies seem inevitable.

> Since behavior as an adaptive function is inherently bound to have its imperfections and occasional failures, the traditional nomothetic search for strict laws becomes an insoluble task . . . . The degree of univocality of results cannot exceed the degree of univocality of behavioral achievements themselves . . . .[12]

This nondeterministic, goal-striving approach is apparently the product of a number of able psychologists, but one of the acknowledged leaders has been Kurt Lewin. The following statement is again from Brunswik.

> In his "topological" psychology he [Lewin] attempts graphic representation of the cognitive and motivational central time-slice which he calls the "life space" or "psychological environment." This is in preparation for a "dynamic" analysis in terms of hypothetical directional forces or "vectors" which leads to the development of laws allowing prediction of the future states of the system . . . . The theory contains reference neither to the objective stimulus conditions nor to the motor execution and the further results of a response. The system and its laws thus remain confined to a postperceptual, yet prebehavioral, "contemporaneous field" . . . . The goals have different "valences," and the path to them is more or less "segmented" by "barriers" into gestalt-like unitary "regions" . . . which are anticipated to lie between per-

---

[10] Karl R. Popper, *The Open Society and Its Enemies* (Princeton: Princeton University Press, 1962). Reprinted in *Readings in Philosophy of Science, op. cit.*, p. 358. Note the emphasis on mind as a "patterning of information" in the following. "The Darwinian continuity between man and the rest of nature has now been carried to completion: man's rationality marks only a difference of degree from other animals, and fundamentally, no difference at all from the machine . . . . With communication and control as the key, a similarity of structure can also be traced between an individual (whether human or mechanical) and a society (again, whether human or machines in a well-designed factory) . . . . The analysis of mind and individual personality as a structure of certain information processes renders obsolete not only the 'mind substance' of the idealist, but mechanistic materialism as well. Mind is a patterning of information and not spirit, matter, or energy." Abraham Kaplan, "Sociology Learns the Language of Mathematics," *Commentary* (September, 1952), pp. 274-284. Reprinted *ibid.*, p. 407.

[11] Brunswik emphasizes that one of the attitudes fought by Gestaltists is the " . . . unrecognized 'constancy hypothesis' . . . taking for granted a one-to-one correspondence of sensory stimulus elements and conscious sensations . . . ." He points out that in " . . . the inkblot test by Rorschach . . . gestalt ambiguity is purposely provoked to throw light on the organization tendencies and personality of the responding observers." *Op. cit.*, pp. 662, 666.

[12] Egon Brunswik, *op. cit.*, p. 686. Brunswik appears to be less sanguine about the future of thinking machines than some and also not so enthusiastic about the use of decision rules. " . . . 'thinking machines' . . . can usually be built with a concentration on a few cues of maximal trustworthiness and thus dispense with the services of cues of limited validity," p. 682.

son and goal. . . . It is one of the assets of the system of Lewin that quantification of the life-space is rejected, and Euclidean, metric space replaced by the nonquantitative yet mathematical device of topological space based on relations of order rather than on measurement proper . . . topological representation may be the long-sought answer to the introspectionist dream of finding a mathematical, and thus univocal, "objective" means of communication for data of consciousness in spite of their intrinsic — absolute or relative — nonquantifiability.[13]

Followers of the organismic (holistic) approach to psychology and of cybernetics attempt to explain behavior in terms of needs and objectives, and take a teleological turn. Tolman has been a leader in the use of "goal striving" in psychological work, and has emphasized "persistence through trial-and-error" and "docility relative to some end."[14] Brunswik comments that " . . . a good part of psychoanalysis is devoted to the discovery of environmental conditions of quiescence which play the role of substitute goals or new terminal foci."[15]

The explanation of behavior in terms of terminal ends is sometimes known as 'whither' explanations. These explanations are usually in terms of purposes, needs, desires, wishes, and have a tendency to push inquiry back a step to an examination of these purposes, desires, needs, etc., in order to find how they are fashioned and how they react to efforts to change them. It seems obvious that service professions such as accounting, law or engineering must be approached and analyzed in terms of whither explanations.[16] As opposed to the whither explanations, there is the so-called 'whence' explanation that has historical elements and tends to find initial conditions and associated variables (causes) so that explanations are forthcoming. In many cases, for example, the two cannot be separated. Clearly an explanation of accounting conservatism in terms of objectives may be related to 'whence' explanations as well as to forces that have fostered the tradition.[17]

The assumption of a more active psychological unit (organism) than was formerly suspected now seems to be justified. 'Operant behavior' is currently used along with 'respondent behavior.' The resulting return to motivation may be, as Brunswik thinks, a considerable change from the older view in that a place is now made for the spontaneity of the individual. Brunswik laments the past tendency to treat organisms as closed systems and the assumption that the second law of thermodynamics (increasing chaos or entropy) and the principle of parsimony always apply to such systems. Instead, he argues that organisms need not exhibit the tendencies toward equilibrium inherent in closed systems, for he insists that they function in open systems in a "quasi-stationary steady state."[18]

---

[13] *Ibid.*, pp. 735-737.

[14] E. C. Tolman, *Purposive Behavior in Animals and Men* (New York: The Century Co., 1932). See also *Collected Papers in Psychology* (Berkeley: University of California Press, 1951).

[15] Egon Brunswik, *op. cit.*, p. 717.

[16] The seemingly strange relationship that makes a goal — an effect — serve as a cause has been pointed out by Max Weber. "From our viewpoint, 'purpose' is the conception of an *effect* which becomes a *cause* of an action. Since we take into account every cause which produces or can produce a significant effect, we also consider this one." Wiener, *op. cit.*, p. 334.

[17] Sometimes the initial conditions are assumed and are not actually observed. According to Spence the result is "response inferred constructs." K. W. Spence, "The Nature of Theory Construction in Contemporary Psychology," *Psychological Review*, January, 1944, pp. 47-68.

[18] Egon Brunswik, op. cit., p. 700. Auditors should notice the change of viewpoint toward objectivity. "We may relate the concept of objectivity to what is known to the psychological statisticians as test reliability . . . . 'Objective,' then, is a class of responses yielding maximum reliability coefficients within or between individuals facing a common geographic situation or situational element." *Ibid.*, p. 669.

Many methods now popular with psychologists seem to belong to the current successors of logical positivism. Much of the former talk about self and mind has gone the way of the "I" with the help of Carnap and the Vienna Circle, but the methodological positivism of some psychologists may indeed approach the "methodolatry" suggested by Popper. The use of postulational techniques by Spence and others, the emphasis on functionalism by Dewey, the concern with measurement by Stevens and Torgerson, the concept of mind as a patterning of information, and other operational definitions, all are evidences that psychologists, like their brothers the economists, are returning to a reconsideration of theoretical foundations.[19]

Biologists and others are now approaching psychological problems through biology with a series of postulates and attempts to find and specify the processes that lead to subjective states such as 'pleasant,' 'desirable,' 'unpleasant.' A group of logicians and mathematicians has been impressed with similarities of binary mathematics and computer design to the firing of a nerve. "Since firing nerve elements follows an all-or-none principle and may thus be idealized as dichotomous . . . 'neural events and relations among them can be treated by means of (two-valued) propositional logic' in a strictly nomothetic manner . . ."[20] McCulloch and Pitts have pointed out the presence of feedback loops and have emphasized that the disjunctive features of choice at many points make it extremely difficult to reconstruct initial conditions or preceding states of any organism.

Rapoport, Shimbel and others have developed an approach that is based on the behavior of neurones in synaptic delays, threshold tendencies and probabilistic methods. Clearly most feedback is negative, but Brunswik points out a useful subclassification: " . . . McCulloch distinguishes 'appetitive' negative feedback devices, in which the 'circuit passes through regions external to the system,' from such simpler cases of feedback as the 'merely homeostatic' which keep some internal parameters of the system constant, or the 'servo,' in which the value of the parameter or end sought by the system can be altered from without the circuit . . ."[21]

The application of such concepts as feedback within closed systems and investigations of the accounting information necessary for intervention rules by human 'servos' have received no attention. The movement toward automation should turn accountants toward the possibilities of collecting, classifying, and feeding back information without leaving the closed human (but mechanistic) system. So far accountants seem to have abdicated this area, and development has gone by default to engineers, psychologists and communication theorists.

---

[19] Those interested in the history of psychology may wish to refer to: *Psychological Theory: Contemporary Readings,* ed. M. H. Marx (New York: The Macmillan Company, 1951) or *Readings in the History of Psychology*, ed. W. Dennis (New York: Appleton Century-Crofts, 1948). A highly specialized review of the quantitative and measurement aspects of psychology may be found in Warren S. Torgerson, *Theory and Methods of Scaling* (New York: John Wiley & Sons, Inc., 1958).

[20] Egon Brunswik, *op. cit.*, p. 742.

[21] *Ibid.*, p. 744.

Essay Six

Normative Considerations —
Sociology and Ethics

It may be said that in commercial or investment banking or any business extending credit success depends on knowing what not to believe in accounting. (F. P. C. vs. Hope Natural Gas, 51 PUR (NS), 193-235.)

This essay contains some comments on the sociology of accounting, in the sense of the interplay of accounting conventions with the social forces at work on shaping objectives and the means for reaching these objectives. The essay on simulating a profession is devoted primarily to the mechanics and procedures for introducing change into a profession and the possible reaction of professional conventions to the introduction of change. This essay deals more with the purpose of accounting in social organization and the influence of social institutions on individual and professional behavior. When conventions grow up in response to needs, those who apply the conventions are subject to responsibilities to see that objectives are met. The coordination of these responsibilities, arrangement according to worthiness and the search for inconsistencies and discrepancies may be included under the heading of professional ethics.

In a narrow sense, ethics is sometimes said to deal with the relation of an individual to a given code of some kind. Thus, if one is given the value judgments and codes of rewardable and punishable behavior of, say, the Kwakiutl, he may be able to judge whether or not specified behavior is in accord with the codes. There is always the possibility of conflicting objectives in a given case and therefore the necessity to interpret the established hierarchy of values in order to settle a particular case. This approach tends to bring ethical problems into the domain of scientific method by establishing the laws governing the formation of value judgments and specifying operational rules for comparing actual behavior with the standards. Thus, in the field of accounting one may accept for immediate purposes the code of ethics set forth by the AICPA, and within the usual limits of judgment decide in a particular case whether a given act or series of behavioral events is or is not in accordance with the code. This type of activity is difficult enough and is an extension of the usual scientific and legal problem of gathering the facts, establishing the evidence, interpreting the standard (code or custom) pinpointing the similarities and differences between the established action and the code, evaluating the variances, and finally rendering the decision. While it may be argued that the procedure depends too much on two-value logic and does not provide for enough stopping places in the grey area, the procedure has worked reasonably well through the years, and in fact has no rational alternative. One comment and warning seems in order here. It appears at first sight that this type of procedure is largely mechanical and does not involve 'social welfare' and other related and vague generalities to get a decision. Such is not the case. We have only to ask: How are the similarities and differences between established behavior in a particular case and the standard measuring stick (the code) to be valued? [1]

The advantage of the above procedure is similar to that coming from the application of sequential sampling. If the cases are obviously alike or diverse, the decision is easy and the established hierarchy covers the case simply and adequately. The borderline cases remain, but one may be able to give a more and more complete code and thereby partition the fuzzy area again and again. Certainly this area of fuzziness cannot be completely eradicated, and the problems remain as to who shall do the partitioning (the code makers or its interpreters), whether the partitioning rules are consistent with one another, and ultimately, of course, whether the rules render decisions that can be ordered better or worse in terms of the aims and objectives of the social group.

It is clear that these ethical problems are interrelated, but the primary emphasis of this essay is not one of establishing satisfactory rules for deciding individual cases. Instead, attention is directed to the forces that may be at work to establish the code of values and provide for change. In the essay on psychological reactions, the goals and objectives were more or less taken as given so that the intermediate threads of behavior could be the center of the focus. Here the concern is with the considerations that help to set goals and objectives. Concern at this point therefore is more with the sociological forces that shape and form the objectives and determine the socially acceptable means for attaining them, and less with finding whether a particular action or a particular person fits into the currently accepted pattern. It is the thesis of this discussion that these ends and processes are socially determined, that they are now in a period of a rapid change, and that the perceptors for the accounting profession are not so sensitive as they could be.

The earliest type of accounting apparently arose with the rise of accountability in connection with storage and what are now known as bailor-bailee arrangements. The objectives of accounting were then fairly direct, and the process consisted of the preservation of a record of inventory of the goods to be accounted for, a storage device for preserving the record and a process for comparing the goods returned to the bailor with the record, which at this point serves as a standard to which the returned goods should conform. A type of advance — or perhaps a sidestep — came about when the accounting process was expanded to include, as historical data to be preserved, the location of the goods left by the bailor. Thus the records also became *guides to internal action*.

Up to this point there has been little responsibility that requires valuation, or a substitute for valuation in the form of costs, or for that matter there has been no need for a common denominator. The need for a primitive kind of common denominator (discrimination) arises when the arrangement takes the form of returning the goods in kind and does not imply that exactly the identical goods are to be returned. The historical records then must contain a different kind of description. It is true that the description of the original goods could be used in order to obtain the proper 'kind' but there can be little doubt that a type of abstraction from specific items to 'identical kinds' of items was a tre-

---

[1] It goes without saying that the goals and objectives change and flexibility must be built into the organization. One can try a Kwakiutl case by referring to a Samoan code, but the effects are not likely to be satisfactory. Rudolph Carnap emphasizes two common uses of the term 'ethics.' "Sometimes a certain empirical investigation is called 'ethics,' *viz.* psychological and sociological investigations about the actions of human beings . . . . Ethics in this sense is an empirical scientific investigation; it belongs to empirical science rather than philosophy. Fundamentally different from this is ethics . . . as the philosophy of moral values or moral norms, which one can designate normative ethics. This is not an investigation of facts, but a pretended investigation of what is good and what is evil, what is right to do and what is wrong to do." Quoted from Morton White, *The Age of Analysis* (New York: Mentor Books, 1955), pp. 216-217.

mendous step in abstraction and in descriptive record-keeping. The accountants of the day must have been faced with a problem of some magnitude — they could abandon for lack of need the exact description of items and substitute a general class description. In order to preserve useful class descriptions in the records, it was necessary that elementary measurement be brought to the aid of the accountant. Up to this point discrimination and description were necessary along with the ability to specify number, but no measurement even in the ordinal sense was required.[2]

Additional responsibilities were placed on the profession when the concept of return in physical kind was replaced by the concept of a common denominator of value. To meet such needs new rules had to be devised and incorporated into the conventions of the profession, and these rules are being debated at a lively rate even today. Some present-day accountants seem to assume automatically that 'accountability' means accountability in terms of original costs, or at least in terms of the number of monetary units committed. Thus, by invoking the word 'accountability' they somehow invoke a defense for original cost and a weapon to be used against current costs and specific adjustments for price-level changes. The attitude which uses cost or value at the time of commitment for the recording base rests on a number of assumptions. Who is to benefit by any increase or stand to lose through any decrease? Should the measuring rod be assumed to be constant or permitted to have some deviation so long as the immediate parties have no appreciable control over the changes?

Notice that the stages are all related to objectives or things that are considered to have value to worthy parties — all are *value*-oriented. Suppose for an illustration that a society is interested primarily in the quality that is subjectively interpreted as 'blueness.' The obvious scale for measuring the progress toward the social objectives is then in terms of this quality. In extreme cases one may abstract from all other characteristics and attributes. The advantage of generalized value to weight diverse objectives now becomes obvious. The accountant can use a common denominator of value, abstract from all kinds of physical properties, and concentrate on matters of concern of the individuals involved.

With the growth of large-scale activity the interests of different groups and different individuals become widely varied. The interests are sometimes identical, sometimes adverse and sometimes mixed, and they often vary widely through time and from one social environment to another. In the social organization provision must somehow be made for evaluating these interests and deciding a hierarchy of worthiness. Mechanisms for making evaluations must be set up, and among the mechanisms or processes must be one for recording progress and status in terms of the factors that are considered to be sufficiently valuable to merit attention and to justify record keeping. Such an information system includes among its processes the devices that have for centuries been known as accounting. One of the problems that arises is whether such an information service is to react passively to change or whether it is to take an active part in shaping the ethical structure itself. This problem too is settled in the general milieu of changing social patterns and shifting ethical systems, and an information system can certainly play both passive and positive roles.

The importance of values in a social organization is so great that such organizations are sometimes identified by their value systems. The methods of scientific investigation,

---

[2] It is true that some authors have treated counting as measurement and have defined what are sometimes known as "enumeration variables." Counting clearly requires an ordering of classes (cardinal numbers), requires identifying of units, and matching the units that have been discriminated with the names of classes, but it does not require an ordering of the data. The concept of distance is implied in measurement and is added to the discriminatory effort for identifying units.

the objects studied by scientific methods, the people who carry on the activity and even the procedures of so-called 'causal analysis' may be said to be greatly modified if not determined by the value system and orientation of the social group. Weber, a leading advocate of the "sociology of knowledge," is most emphatic.

> The *significance* of a configuration of cultural phenomena and the basis of this significance cannot however be derived and rendered intelligible by a system of analytical laws . . . however perfect it may be, since the significance of cultural events presupposes a *value-orientation* toward these events. The concept of culture is a *value-concept* . . . . Only a small portion of existing concrete reality is colored by our value-conditioned interest and it alone is significant to us.[3]

The view that is usually identified as the sociology of knowledge may have been overstated and the possibilities of escaping the constraints may have been presented far too simply, but it is impossible to escape the general thesis. The cultural institutions determine what knowledge is to be recorded, preserved and passed on to following generations, and which area of knowledge is to be expanded. By conferring prestige and financial rewards, or by ridiculing eggheads, brain-trusters, and intellectuals as childish incompetents, some societies regulate the effort devoted to transmission and expansion of knowledge. Weber adds:

> . . . the choice of the object of investigation and the extent or depth to which this investigation attempts to penetrate into the infinite causal web, are determined by the evaluative ideas which dominate the investigator and his age . . . . For scientific truth is precisely what is *valid* for all who *seek* the truth.[4]

While we accountants need not pass on the priority or relative importance of sociology and individual psychology, we must be aware of the interaction of the two and be on the lookout for useful approaches that can utilize both aspects of the work.[5]

---

[3] Max Weber, *On the Methodology of the Social Sciences*, trans. and ed. Edward A. Shils and Henry A. Finch (Glencoe: The Free Press, 1949), reprinted in *Readings in Philosophy of Science*, ed. Philip P. Wiener (New York: Charles Scribner's Sons, 1953), p. 329. Notice also: " . . . an *exhaustive* causal investigation of any concrete phenomena in its full reality is not only practically impossible — it is simply nonsense" (p. 330).

[4] *Ibid.*, p. 334.

[5] Weber, of course, assigns methodological priority to sociology. " . . . the procedure does not begin with the analysis of psychological qualities, moving then to the analysis of social institutions, but . . . on the contrary, insight into the psychological preconditions and consequences of institutions presupposes a precise knowledge of the latter and the scientific analysis of their structure . . . . We will not . . . deduce the institutions from psychological laws or explain them by elementary psychological phenomena." *Ibid.*, p. 338. Edward Chace Tolman emphasized a similar view. " . . . the psychologist's independent variables are not in any final sense independent and absolute. They are always immersed in a 'field' constituted by the 'cultural pattern' of the whole group. They cannot be manipulated independently of this field." "It was the Gestalt psychologists who first brought it home . . . that . . . the whole can often be said to govern its parts quite as truly as the parts may be said to govern the whole." "Physiology, Psychology and Sociology," *Psychological Review*, May, 1938. Reprinted in Wiener, *op. cit.*, pp. 227, 228. Kurt Lewin, as might be expected, holds a similar view. " . . . the so-called 'subjective' psychological world of the individual, his life-space, is influenced in a much earlier stage by social facts and social relations than anyone would have expected a few decades ago . . . . Beginning with this early age, the child's behavior is molded in every respect by his social situation. Of course, his morale, his religion, and his political values are determined by his being a part of, and reacting to, the society in which he lives . . . social influences enter every action of the individual, even actions which seem to have little to do with society." "Field Theory and Experiment in Social Psychology: Concepts and Methods," Wiener, *op. cit.*, p. 220.

That serious consideration must be given to the problem should also be self-evident. The general importance of the view is admitted even by critics. For example, Popper states:

> The sociology of knowledge argues that scientific thought, and especially thought on social and political matters, does not proceed in a vacuum, but in a socially conditioned atmosphere . . . . The social habitat of the thinker determines a whole system of opinions and theories which appear to him as unquestionably true or self-evident . . . for there is no doubt that we are all suffering under our own system of prejudices (or "total ideologies," if this term is preferred); that we all take many things as self-evident, that we accept them uncritically and even with the naive and cocksure belief that criticism is quite unnecessary; and scientists are no exception to this rule . . . .[6]

That the training of accountants has been influenced by the tremendous conditioning power of the social institutions, including the rigidity of the methods themselves, is beyond question. The British stewardship principle with its emphasis on charge and discharge of responsibility may be associated naturally with the semi-feudal social arrangements of the time with their emphasis on rights and correlative responsibilities. The venture accounting of the Italian city-states and much later in connection with mining ventures in the western world is appropriate for the purposes and institutions involved. Of more recent date, one finds emphasis on the viewpoint of short-term creditors reflected in the study and accentuation of the financial report. The change of organization type with the rise of important investors and managers brought about a slow and ponderous swing of emphasis in accounting to the income report and to managerial accounting. Perhaps the most striking, and least justified, example of the influence of the environmental framework on accounting is reflected by the still prevalent feeling that double-entry bookkeeping is somehow connected in some fundamental way with the institution of private property. The identification of the recording process with the dominant social institution during the period of development and growth may have limited some otherwise astute accountants in their application of double-entry record keeping to all kinds of alternative institutions, e.g., sectors of socialist economies, cooperative organizations.

An interesting sidelight for accountants may be gained by trying to place the important doctrine of objectivity with respect to the more general aspects of the sociology of knowledge. This problem is also mixed up with the problem of how an individual or group can break through the social environment and free himself from the value system. We must agree with Popper that " . . . the main trouble about prejudices is that there is no such direct way to get rid of them . . . . Is it not a common experience that those who are most convinced of having got rid of their prejudices are most prejudiced?"[7] Popper continues to emphasize the social character of science and scientific method with attention to the fact that theories are set up so that they can be tested and confirmed by others. Thus so-

---

[6] Karl R. Popper, *The Open Society and Its Enemies* (New York: Harper & Row Publishers, 1962), p. 213 ff. Reprinted in *Readings in Philosophy of Science*, ed. Philip P. Wiener, *op. cit.*, pp. 358, 361. Karl Mannheim, a leader in the movement, states mildly: "The principal thesis of the sociology of knowledge is that these are modes of thought which cannot be adequately understood as long as their social origins are obscured." In a more extreme tone he adds: "Strictly speaking it is incorrect to say that the single individual thinks. Rather it is more correct to insist that he participates in thinking further what other men have thought before him. He finds himself in an inherited situation with patterns of thought which are appropriate to this situation . . . ." *Ideology and Utopia: An Introduction to the Sociology of Knowledge.* Reprinted as "The Sociology of Knowledge," *Readings in Philosophy of Science*, ed. Philip Wiener, *op. cit.*, pp. 349, 350.

[7] *Ibid.*, pp. 365-366.

cial institutions govern the methods of science and scientific investigation, and it should be abundantly clear that the methods of today are entirely different from those employed by the Greeks and the Schoolmen. In some cases investigations are carried on and reported by cranks and by those subject to hallucinations or extreme bias, but the social institutions that surround science (and are in turn strongly influenced by scientific method and its success) provide for verification techniques that tend to screen the trustworthiness and applicability of all reports. Not the least of the advantages of such institutions and attitudes is the fact that results are not given credence and investigations themselves are discouraged unless their verification by others with equivalent training and apparatus is possible. Such attitudes are socially determined, for in certain more primitive cultures a variety of reports that have no possible means of verification are encouraged. Many religious groups in the western world interpret certain experiences in a mystical manner that is vastly different from usual scientific interpretations. In a similar manner, mystical interpretations used by Eastern religions, and indeed by the Judeo-Christian tradition, call for considerable ideological grounding before they become apparent.

Thus, Popper concludes: " . . . what we call 'scientific objectivity' is not a product of the individual scientist's impartiality, but a product of the social or public character of scientific method . . . ."[8] Popper apparently accepts Russell's scientific men who are the equivalent of economic men and who are rational in the sense of conforming to the social institutions of science and standards for rationality.[9] The alternative to looking at science and objectivity as "the correlation of experiences common to all normal people" leads to a semi-solipsistic position in which verification is conceived as a repetitive pattern in the results as they appear to the individual.

It is not enough to realize that man is a product of his times in all facets of intellectual and professional behavior, even as to the form of logic he uses, and to muse with Marcus Aurelius that we are a part of all that we have met.[10] How can one recognize the work and the dynamics of the institutions with the hope of anticipating them and of having positive influence (control) over them? To escape seems to be impossible. In various communist countries the party elite is supposed to be able to free itself of the capitalistic environment (ideology) and to recognize the institutions that tend to make "pigs of men." Psychiatry

---

    [8] *Ibid.*, p. 363. Popper emphasizes this point often. " . . . ironically enough, objectivity is closely bound up with the *social aspect of scientific method*, with the fact that science and scientific objectivity do not (and cannot) result from the attempts of an individual scientist to be 'objective,' but from the cooperation of many scientists. Scientific objectivity can be described as the intersubjectivity of scientific method." Popper, *op. cit.*, p. 217.

    [9] The difficulties in even defining rationality are tremendous. Harold Garfinkel has devoted considerable attention to this problem and has isolated at least eight commonly-used variations of the concept. 1. Categorizing and comparing, 2. Tolerable error, 3. Search for 'means,' 4. Analysis of alternatives and consequences, 5. Strategy, 6. Concern for timing, 7. Predictability, and 8. Rules of procedure. This discussion is well worth the effort if for no other reason than to illustrate the difficulties in forming constructs. "The Rational Properties of Scientific and Common Sense Activities," *Behavioral Science*, January, 1960, pp. 72-83. Bertrand Russell's reference to trained scientific observers who are somewhat like the 'economic man' of political economy is found in *Human Knowledge, Its Scope and Limits* (New York: Simon & Schuster, 1948), p. 208.

    [10] The development of historicism under such mystics as Benedetto Croce and Jose Ortega y Gasset is directly related to this view. Ortega is more quotable, and the results are heady stuff for accountants who are concerned with the past. "Man is what has happened to him, what he has done . . . he carries on his back as the vagabond his bundle of all he possesses. Man is a subtantial emigrant on a pilgrimage of being . . . . *Man, in a word, has no nature: what he has is . . . history* . . . . The past is not yonder . . . . The past is I . . . ," *Toward a Philosophy of History* (New York: W. W. Norton & Co., Inc., 1941). Quoted from *The Philosophy of History in Our Time*, ed. Hans Meyerhoff (New York: Doubleday Anchor, 1959), pp. 61, 64.

may offer some techniques and methods, and Popper points out that the sociologists of knowledge (among whom he cannot be counted) hope to develop a sociotherapy.

> Similarly, the sociologists of knowledge hold that the 'freely poised intelligence' of an intelligentsia which is only loosely anchored in social traditions may be able to avoid the pitfalls of the total ideologies; that it may even be able to see through, and to unveil, the various total ideologies and the hidden motives and other determinants which inspire them. Thus the sociology of knowledge believes that the highest degree of objectivity can be reached by the freely poised intelligence analyzing the various hidden ideologies and their anchorage in the unconscious. The way to true knowledge appears to be the unveiling of unconscious assumptions, a kind of psychotherapy, as it were, or if I may say so, a *sociotherapy*.[11]

It seems appropriate to reflect on the needs of society in connection with an information-control system and on the perceptors that a profession employs to receive impressions. The mechanics of this sort of thing are discussed elsewhere, so that the present discussion is devoted to the relationship of the accounting profession to individuals in the society who seem to have a claim for information and merit consideration. This appraisal is a problem in arraying objectives and worthiness and forming hierarchies of merit. Clearly the accountant's rating scale is formed by his own environment, and the individual values he assigns are a part of and must be consistent with the overall value system in which he operates.[12]

At one state in our social development (even at present in some isolated areas) the ethical structure appeared to be comparatively simple. Some supernatural being was explained on the basis of written or other evidence, and the evidence usually included a ranking of the major social values. Such codes share the difficulties of all classificatory schemes, and produce a priesthood whose duty it is to 'judge' in the sense of providing procedures and rules for items not covered in the code. The primary task in this connection is to construct rules that are not manifestly in disagreement with the superior code. The priesthood then attempts to gain status and sanction for its actions by claiming kinship in some spiritual — or even physical — sense with the supreme being. While this arrangement looks foolproof and tends to stability, its performance has been marred in practice by the development of new evidence and the growth of competing supreme beings. Some cultures have divided the responsibility for the ethical codes among several

---

[11] Karl R. Popper, *op. cit.*, p. 215. Wiener, *op. cit.*, p. 359. Notice the difference in viewpoint expressed below in the liberal tradition. " . . . *liberalism takes the individual as given*, and views the social problem as one of right relations between given individuals." Frank H. Knight, *Freedom and Reform* (New York: Harper and Bros., 1947), p. 69.

[12] In some developing countries the chief purpose of accounting seems to be to conceal rather than to reveal information. A contributing factor is a set of laws, sometimes combined with stupid non-price-system directives, that makes honesty in the traditional sense incompatible with economic, and perhaps even physical, survival. The public accounting profession — to the extent that it exists as an independent information service — adopts rules for concealing or reporting that permit its clients to survive. At the same time, many accountants hope for a return of traditional ethical values and look at the current unsatisfactory position as temporary. American accountants differ only in degree. Padded expense accounts, reimbursed personal expenditures, minor thievery of office and other supplies, payoffs buried in selling expense, and a host of similar items are essentially antagonistic to America's professed ethical standards. Yet these items and many more usually filter through the accounting system undisclosed or unreported. Universities are among the worst offenders and often make transfers from fund to fund with less disclosure than is required of the corner grocery. Juggling expenditures against appropriations is a refined art that must be mastered by aspiring young administrators. A now famous question: Professor (practitioner), let me hear again your definition of 'honesty'?

induced beings and then established a hierarchy among them or divided the field of ethics among them.[13]

The transition to natural rights offers interesting points for speculation. The period of feudalism was a period of considerable stability in social institutions and followed a long era of wars, barbarian invasions and the inability of the civilized portions of western Europe to preserve order. A vast hierarchy with a network of responsibilities and authorities was formed. In many cases a supernatural being was placed at the top of the hierarchy to lend sanction to the general ethical code, with the next highest level (e.g., kings) often claiming to be supernatural in some kind of inferior way. As the feudal system broke up, the era of commercial enterprise, the city-state, and nationalism developed. In spite of the established church's attempt to preserve the ethical principles of self-restraint, the 'just price,' and the nonusurious lender, the social institutions changed so that a sharply modified system of social values emerged. The pursuit of self-interest was sanctified and the accumulation of material wealth was considered to be evidence of divine favor. The social order then became success-oriented toward material things. Self-interest became acceptable and even admirable, for by striving for selfish ends the ends of others — indeed of all society and its supernatural leader — were automatically furthered. The justification for this doctrine was apparently based on a number of relationships including the need for a free market of sellers and buyers, an enlightened electorate and judicious court officials. The advocacy principle assumed that the harshness of extreme self-interest in the marketplace would be alleviated by knowledge and competition.

With the assumption of active competition, an informed electorate, and an enlightened judicial system, the need for individual responsibility for the interests of others seemed to decrease. The emphasis in the minor field of accounting changed from the charge-discharge form of responsibility statement with its obvious fiducial overtones to the accounting for gain or loss to the residual group, whose pool of interests could be represented as proprietary equity. Even the fundamental equation, which emphasized responsibilities accepted and responsibilities discharged, changed to assets equals claims to assets or some variation that emphasized ownership. The 20th-century variation of assets equals equities has essentially the same implications, with acknowledgement that creditors have some interest that deserves attention. The relative shift of emphasis from the balance sheet, which could be interpreted as a sort of responsibility statement, to the income sheet is essentially in keeping with the success-oriented times that emphasized self-interest and evidence of supernatural approval. It is only within the last decade or two that the emphasis on fund accounting, assets equals responsibilities, etc., has reflected a return to the cooperative ideal of society with more emphasis on responsibilities to others and less on properties and worth.

The resulting problem for the accounting profession, according to some accountants, is to interpret the new value orientation and to find rules that will help replace faith in the marketplace, the infallibility of judges, and the brilliance of the electorate. This problem was discussed thoroughly by DR Scott a third of a century ago, but his impact was only

---

[13] The development of the movement toward one God is usually counted to be an improvement by those with Judeo-Christian orientation, but not all ethical theorists support this contention. The subsuming of all the rules (pleasant and unpleasant) with all the sanctions under one being makes for a multi-schizophrenic personality. The trinity appears to have incorporated some vestiges of polytheistic religions without the advantage of separation of power and duty. Breasted has emphasized the historical correlation of monotheistic religions and authoritarian political institutions. Hegel's world view (absolute idea) has goals and intentions of its own and needs only a body.

minor.[14] Scott, an economist and a disciple of Veblen, was concerned with the obvious failure of market economics, with its fantastically simplified behavioral assumptions, to mediate the rights and needs of groups and individuals in society. This position in Benninger's words is stated:

> In the coming society, the controlling force over economic affairs would be a subtle but coercive one. Such a force, Scott felt, would be the institution of accounting itself, adjusted to an underlying philosophy based on science . . . . The long-term trend spelled an increase in control over economic life by government. Such control would be effected by the increasing use of commissions of experts . . . . Eventually, Scott seemed to imply, conflicts among different types of commission control would arise and would need to be resolved by some central economic commission charged with planning the major objectives of the social and economic system . . . . The scientific viewpoint would be applied to economic problems . . . partly through dependence upon an institution which had successfully adapted itself to change over the centuries — accounting . . . . Scott felt those in controllership would be the first to achieve professionalization . . . . Accounting would become a dynamic, controlling force wholly in tune with men's larger concept of a philosophy of science . . . . As social principles evolve, it becomes essential that the entire hierarchy of accounting rules and principles also change.[15]

Scott's concern with substitutes for the marketplace because of the growth of large-scale enterprises is echoed by those who are trying to devise intrafirm-transfer-pricing techniques to supplement or to replace the traditional pricing mechanism as a guide to resource allocation and control of efficiency within the firm. His prediction for the growth of professional accounting principles as a substitute for the price system is based primarily on a system-wide breakdown of the pricing structure.

It should be pointed out that the price system as a device for "establishing and preserving equity" among groups has never satisfied all social philosophers. There is no reason to assume that there is special virtue in the *distribution* of shares as the result of paying each factor the value of its marginal product. Nor is there any automatic reason why the payment of economic rents to suppliers or the enjoyment of consumers' surpluses give the best distribution, unless 'best' is defined precisely in this fashion. Nevertheless the feasibility and elegance of such a system, when compared with such nonoperational formulas as Blanc's rule to produce according to ability and consume according to need, is so obvious as to require no comment. As a disciple of Veblen, Scott was not sanguine enough to assume that the price system is without fault. He did maintain that in one stage of economic development, with its concurrent value system, the price system could be relied on to render an acceptable settlement to many obvious conflicts of interest.

It is interesting to observe that the modern organization man of big business — the manager — has outstripped the professional accountant in moving into the vacuum left by the decline of the price system. Many professional managers now take the view that their

---

[14] DR Scott, *The Cultural Significance of Accounts* (New York: H. Holt and Company, 1931). A more condensed treatment of accounting principles may be found in "The Basis for Accounting Principles," *The Accounting Review*, December, 1941, pp. 341-349. Applications to cost accounting may be found in "Accounting Principles and Cost Accounting," *The Journal of Accountancy*, February, 1939, pp. 70-76. Some philosophical backgrounds including Scott's emphasis on science and relativism are available in "Freedom in an Age of Science and Machines," *Journal of Social Philosophy*, July, 1937, pp. 317-326. An outstanding explanation of Scott's system by a former student is contained in L. J. Benninger's "Accounting Related to Social Institutions — The Theoretical Formulations of Scott," *Accounting Research*, January, 1958, pp. 17-30.

[15] L. J. Benninger, *op. cit.*, pp. 20-23.

primary obligation is to the 'organization,' and that one of their first duties is to mediate between the conflicting interests of consumers, laborers, owners, creditors and others. In fact, many are equally sure that the division of spoils between present owners (in the form of current dividends) and all groups present and future who stand to gain by a policy of retaining earnings and — the magic word — 'growth' is a responsibility of management. Apparently management uses perceptors to sense and to appraise the need and strength of desire of each contending group, and after providing for its own needs and, if possible, for survival of the organization, makes the distribution that seems to be 'equitable' and 'proper.' The growth of this feeling and the growth of the importance of the modern managerial class has led — belatedly — to some thoughts about the necessity for training and the kind of training that may be needed. Until recently there has been far too little in the university training of management graduates that would seem to help reach these important decisions. In fact, major courses have so far been devoid of any real substance in this direction, and almost devoid of workable rules to replace the automatic working of the price system — good or bad. Perhaps the ethical training is left for courses in electives or humanities. In any event, some studies have revealed that the student of business is especially motivated by the desire for material things. This tendency might be expected as a result of the selection process, but some current researchers have been surprised by the tremendous number of students in business schools who are not the least concerned with the means by which wealth is acquired.

There has been an unfortunate feeling among many accountants that the accounting profession has no mandate to formulate rules that may interfere with managerial freedom or the interests of stockholders.[16] It should be obvious that accountants must accept such obligations and insist on an area of decision making or they must abdicate the judgmental aspects of their work almost entirely. It is necessary to use "almost entirely" because it is *possible* to hold an intermediate position and maintain that the accountant's recommendations should always be advisory to law-enacting bodies and that accountants should require only that their clients conform to established regulatory rules.

The controversy then is between the view that accountants should make a series of rules and conventions and insist on compliance and the view that they should operate through organized legal and regulatory channels. Whichever procedure seems to be more feasible, it seems that the accounting profession has the responsibility for placing controls on those who render stewardship reports. Even when it is contended that accountants should perform only what the laws and commissions require, it is also generally admitted that the profession should act as eyes and ears — perceptors — for those who make the laws. It seems that this would be the least that society could expect from an independent profession that devotes itself to gathering and reporting information. There is a large and important segment of the profession that holds otherwise.

Scott thought that controllers would be the first to professionalize, and this attitude is understandable in one who is a cost accountant. The second quarter of the century showed a tremendous increase in the attention given to controllership in business gatherings and universities and to the related procedures of internal auditing. Considerable at-

---

[16] Perry Mason states: "Is there any *accounting* reason why adjustments . . . cannot be made in any way desired by the stockholders as long as legal requirements are met and full disclosure is made of the facts? . . . . Why is this an *accounting* matter?" "The 1948 Statement of Concepts and Standards," *The Accounting Review*, April, 1950, pp. 137-138. V. E. Odmark speaks convincingly for the opposing view. "Every decision made by the accountant is a valuation decision fraught with possibilities of justice or injustice to some economic interest." "Some Aspects of the Evolution of Accounting Functions," *The Accounting Review*, October, 1954, p. 638.

tention was devoted to the functions of controllers as coordinators in spite of the fact that managers have long been regarded as coordinators *par excellence*. The controller, it was argued, has an overall organization view and thus has the advantage of both the broad view and the detailed information necessary to appraise and coordinate the diverse interests.

As conceived in the early years, controllership was to be professionalized and be concerned with all present and future interests involved in the organization. Management was assumed to be interested primarily in the welfare of the owners, narrowly interpreted. However, some managers began to insist that their functions covered the interests of all those related to the organization, including suppliers, customers, workers, political subdivisions, and residents of the communities affected. Some teachers of business and related topics felt that the market mechanism had certain shortcomings and that a coordinating group with some degree of integrity and professionalization must be trained. This professional group influences the size of the revenue stream and its distribution among contending parties. This type of manager considers his position to be similar to that of managers of governmental units — a coordinating judiciary that decides how much the taxes shall be, who shall pay them, and which of the hungry contenders shall receive them. The combination of ↙ business and public-administration school thus becomes understandable and desirable, except to those who hold that the function of management is to maximize the present value of the residual stockholder interest.

We may ask what controllers and accounting departments were doing to establish the responsibilities of the profession. It is the opinion of many that the accounting profession was not doing enough; in fact, it may have been going in the wrong direction. Public accountants were so concerned with 'objectivity' and 'consistency' and the desire for uniformity that they seemed to prefer a reduction in responsibility and an increase in professionalization.[17] On the other hand, the tremendous popularity of the phrase 'managerial accounting,' and the defection to this view of many able professors, tended to slow down professionalism.

Emphasis on managerial accounting may be party justified as an antidote for the obvious overemphasis on public accounting in many departments of accounting. The growth coincides roughly with the increase in knowledge about the place of incremental analysis in decision making and with the tendency for management itself to become a profession. Unfortunately the practical effect of the change in emphasis has not been toward the professionalization of managerial accountants or their adoption of a desirable code of responsibilities. It is the belief of many that the emphasis on management needs has tended to make 'errand boys' of internal accountants. The very title "managerial accounting" somehow indicates limited scope of responsibility.[18] It is probably fair to say that mana-

---

[17] It is not meant to imply that they have abdicated responsibility, although to an impartial observer it seems that the profession has decreased its area of judgments and responsibility in order to hold to methods that can be applied with some degree of uniformity. For example, we are not valuers. We are not experts in materials. (But we give opinions on management's representations on materials.) We treat depreciation as a cost assignment, with spreading "in a systematic" manner being more important than value, benefit, or restatement for changes in the measuring stick. We take no special responsibility for finding misallocation of organizational assets for non-organizational ends — fraud and embezzlement. We permit the most fantastic treatments of development and research costs, and the reports rendered by some development firms are as close as a profession can come to sheer nonsense.

[18] It is possible to argue with Billy Goetz that managerial action should be equated to all decision-making, so that anyone who makes decisions is by definition a manager. This view has the advantage of not requiring a line

---

Footnote continued on next page

gerial accounting as it is now taught in universities is concerned primarily with how the accountant should gather information, sift it and present it to further efficient internal managerial decisions. This concentration has reached such a stage of specialization that accounting courses in some modern schools of industrial management fail completely to consider the ethical responsibilities of the profession. Unfortunately, they also tend to duplicate the material taught in related courses in industrial engineering, operations research, industrial economics, business economics, and management.

It is entirely possible that the mastery of procedures and techniques in accounting requires much more student time than is necessary for understanding the rights of contending groups in society, but it is the contention of this writer that it is *precisely the latter* that merit university study and subsidy by political subdivisions and foundations. The mastery of methods and techniques is training that can be learned on the job under direct supervision and should not be allowed to compete for scarce resources that are the only support for study of such abstract fields as ethics.

The ordering of the worthiness of groups for attention and information requires perceptors. The most common type of perceptor in our economic system is connected with the cash register and with expected income. It is important to emphasize this aspect of the problem, for in a profit-seeking social environment such perceptors are highly developed, and the social pressures are not directed against success-oriented self-interest. In fact, social pressure tends to emphasize the desirability of such sensors and to gauge success in terms of the income take. If accounting were to be governed entirely by the price system, its progress, its scope, and its content would be determined primarily by whether someone is willing to pay for the service. Leaders in the profession would be essentially good businessmen who can ferret out new needs and decide what information should sell best and to whom. Accounting leaders, like their entrepreneurial counterparts, would be on the outlook for new possibilities for a profit and would try to divert some of society's resources (in the form of capable associates) to these needs. A process of selection of new leaders would tend to reward those who have highly developed perception by making them wealthy and punish those who appraise the situation wrongly by less wealth and losses.

Many folks have felt that the price system does not operate effectively in certain segments of society. Such a system may develop a canny, efficient, competent businessman, but self-seeking businessmen hardly constitute a profession. In fact the very idea of professionalism is a counterbalance to the what's-in-it-for-me attitude and emphasizes responsibilities to wider groups.

It is important to point out that ethical statements are not subject to the direct true-false machinery of formal logic. Most ethical statements are what is known as pseudo-statements, for they do not contain the usual subject-predicate construction. "The statement 'sin is bad' is not a proposition in the usual sense, for it is quite possible for A to believe the statement to be true and for B to believe equally strongly that it is false. A would be asserting the equivalent to 'I believe that sin is bad.' B, on the other hand, would be asserting the equivalent to 'I believe sin to be not bad.' Both of these statements in this form may be true or both may be false. Similar difficulties arise in the field of esthetics. 'Mary is

---

between internal and external decision makers, but we should remember that learning is a process of carving out manageable portions of experience. DR Scott concludes: " . . . we might well moralize by pointing out that whenever management prostitutes accounts by making them serve its particular ends, it loses the objective, disinterested service which is the greatest contribution of accounting to management." "The Basis for Accounting Principles," *The Accounting Review*, December, 1941, p. 347.

beautiful' is equivalent to the statement: 'I believe Mary to be beautiful.' "[19] Unfortunately, differences between these preference statements and logical propositions have been overemphasized. Propositions in formal logic are true or false by stipulation, but in practice there is often disagreement as to whether a proposition is in fact true or false. This is precisely the difficulty that has led Dewey to replace the true-false dichotomy with the more probabilistic 'warranted assertion.' Presumably the 'warrant' comes from group consensus.

An interesting feature of statements of this type is that disputation can go on at great length without reaching a conclusion. Such controversies are not nonsense, for it is legitimate for A to try to convince B of the rightness of A's view and the wrongness of the other. If, by some outside chance, B is in fact convinced and changes his previous view, it does not follow that his previous statement is false and that A's previous statement is correct. One asks then how one can argue or even talk intelligently on ethical matters. How do we go about convincing someone else that our ethical or esthetical judgments should prevail? If done correctly this type of argument reduces to empirical operations. We must give operational meaning to 'bad' in the sense of getting agreement on what actions *probably* follow from 'sin' and further agreement that these results meet the definition of 'bad'. This type of argument requires induction as to probable results and agreement as to definitions involved.

In a period of technological change, when it is popular to talk about the probable effects and benefits of automation, it is interesting to consider Scott's thesis that:

> The burden of this course runs to the effect that it is the fundamental function of accounts and statistics to so analyze and present the facts that the decisions of the management will be automatic. Instead of presenting accounts and statistics as tools through which management controls operations under its authority, this course presents them as means through which the management is itself controlled by the facts.[20]

At first glance this statement seems to be that of an institutional economist beyond the ken, but it must be observed that some computer addicts of recent years are pursuing the same ideal. The Scott formulation is highly objectionable, for it appears that the facts are the important consideration. It is now recognized that the benefits of this sort of automatic decision-making reside chiefly in the *organization* of the facts. Automatic management — if such a thing is not a contradiction of terms — will come when the decision system is so refined that comparisons are simple enough to be handled by mechanical means, the rules are simple enough to be followed by mechanical means, and the steps for comparison are specified so carefully that mechanical devices can follow them. The required facts are then automatically specified and gathering them is a relatively minor detail. In Scott's formulation, management is 'premanagement' in that the rules for decision are specified and the required facts are preordered and gathered according to the required scheme. There is no doubt that with properly specified rules and appropriate facts, machines, subordinates, or other devices could accomplish the automatic part of the problem. Managers inevitably reappear to specify the decision rules, fit them to feasible gathering devices, and set the rules for weighing sacrifice and determining allowable costs.

---

[19] See Alfred J. Ayer, *Language, Truth and Logic* (New York: Dover Publications, Inc., 1946), Chapter VI, for further examples.

[20] DR Scott, "Unity in Accounting Theory," *The Accounting Review*, June, 1931, p. 107.

Essay Seven

The Accounting Teacher
and the Semantic Problem

Accounting is concerned with communication and is usually considered to be a specialized extension of the symbols that make up language. Accountants, and especially teachers of accounting, are acutely aware of the difficulties that arise in the process of communicating (instructing) and have given reams of attention to reporting difficulties. Yet in spite of this awareness, accounting reports, textbooks, lectures and directives are often guilty of the most obvious kinds of errors. It is the purpose of this essay to discuss on an extremely elementary level some aspects of the trouble. The present discussion, in short, is concerned with some simple concepts of the comparatively new field of semantics. In particular it is concerned with some of the more obvious cliches, stereotypes, meaningless phrases, wrong-meaning labels, unspecified antecedents, vague referents, confusion of abstraction levels, and general tyranny of words. The accounting profession is overrun with examples of these blocks to effective communication, and teachers of accounting have sometimes compounded the difficulties. It is cold comfort that other professions and teachers may be just as bad or worse.

In general terms, semantics may be defined as the relationship of signs to their correspondents in the world of sensory data. It is difficult to overestimate the importance of this branch of learning. "Indeed, it does not seem fantastic to believe that the concept of sign may prove as fundamental to the sciences of man as the concept of atom has been for the physical sciences or the concept of cell for the biological sciences."[1] Morris has been a leader in the movement for the unity of science and is associated with the classification system under which he includes the entire study of science as the study of the language of science. The general study (science) of signs is known as semiotic. In turn semiotic is divided into:

1. Syntactics — the investigation of the relation of signs to signs.

2. Semantics — the investigation of the relation of signs to objects.

3. Pragmatics — the investigation of the relation of signs to people who use signs.

---

[1] C. W. Morris, "Foundations of the Theory of Signs," *International Encyclopedia of Unified Science* (Chicago: University of Chicago Press, 1955), p. 120. " . . . it is possible to include without remainder the study of science under the study of the language of science, since the study of that language involves not merely the study of its normal structure but its relation to objects designated and to the persons who use it." *Ibid.*, p. 80. An acknowledged leader in the syntactical *and* semantical area of semiotic is Rudolf Carnap. See for example: *Introduction to Symbolic Logic and Its Applications* (New York: Dover Publications, Inc., 1958); *Introduction to Semantics* (Cambridge: Harvard University Press, 1942); *Formalization of Logic* (Cambridge: Harvard University Press, 1943); *Meaning and Necessity* (Chicago: University of Chicago Press, 1947, 1956); *The Logical Syntax of Language* (New York: Harcourt, Brace and Company, 1937).

According to this classification syntactics includes the fields of logic, syntax and mathematics, for it is concerned with conventional rules for manipulating signs and abstracts completely from the relation of signs to objects or to users of signs. It is this branch of semiotics that deals with general axiomatic method, abstract geometry, set theory, and pure mathematics generally. Thus syntactics is made up of sentences (propositions) without material or empirical content, and a study of syntactics deals with rules for forming, combining, and transforming signs.

Pragmatics is concerned with how behaving organisms react to signs. Stevens (following Morris) points out that "the interpreter of a sign-vehicle is an organism whose 'taking-account' of the sign consists in a *habit to respond* to the vehicle as it would to the thing designated by the sign. Thus we find the problem of pragmatics cast in such a form that it can be handled by behavioristics — we deliberately avoid talking about the subjective effects of signs unless these effects are disclosed by public operations."[2] There are several facets to pragmatics. A subdivision known as descriptive pragmatics is concerned with the study of pragmatics as a device for the study of the person. Psychiatrists, for example, study in detail the signs that influence patients, for in many cases the patient's signs no longer stand for the objects and relationships that they once did or no longer agree with the signs used by others. " . . . the troublesome world of reality is pushed aside and the frustrated fellow gets his satisfaction in the domain of signs, oblivious to the restrictions of syntactical and semantical rules."[3] His world becomes literally "a theater of the absurd."

We are not concerned in this essay with neurotic behavior, but we are concerned with the response habits of students, businessmen and all other users of accounting information. We want to use signs and symbols that meet reasonable and predictable standards and are subject to systematic and continuing semantical and syntactical rules. We know that human beings sometimes form habits of response to symbols and that these habits carry over to seemingly related situations where the symbols are senseless and not related by stable and predictable conventions. Gibberish is widely used and is apparently attractive to many whose response patterns continue to operate and provide 'meaning' to the terms. Propaganda may or may not violate the rules of syntax, but it normally has confusing semantics and the confusing aspects of the semantic rules are designed purposely to create intended pragmatic effects.

The field of accounting is designed to accumulate and dispense information, and to study the field without recognizing possible semantical overtones is to neglect an impor-

---

[2] S. S. Stevens, "Psychology and Science of Science," *Psychological Bulletin*, 36 (1939), pp. 221-263. Reprinted in *Readings in Philosophy of Science*, ed. Philip R. Wiener (New York: Charles Scribner's Sons, 1953), p. 179. Morris states: "Historically, rhetoric may be regarded as an early and restricted form of pragmatics . . . . Considered from the point of view of pragmatics, a linguistic structure is a system of behavior . . . ," *op. cit.*, pp. 108, 110. Also by Morris: " . . . the snarl [of a dog] is the sign, the attack is the designatum, the animal being attacked is the interpreter, and the preparatory response of the interpreter is the interpretant." *Ibid.*, p. 114.

[3] Stevens, *Readings, op. cit.*, p. 179. Alfred Korzybski has based his *Science and Sanity* (Lancaster: Science Press, 1933) on the theory that the effect of signs on users is so important that inapplicable signs not related to reality may drive them insane. "Korzybski would cure the resulting insanity by renovating the patient's semantics." Stevens, *Readings, op. cit.*, p. 622. The concern with semantics in the Judeo-Christian religious tradition is an interesting study in itself. At least two of the decalogue (three if icons are included!) are semantic in nature and an important gospel begins and has the universe begin on a semantic note. C. K. Ogden and I. A. Richards discuss these matters and the early association of words with magic. "To classify things is to name them, and for magic the name of a thing or group of things is its soul; to know their names is to have power over their souls." *The Meaning of Meaning* (New York: Harcourt, Brace and Company, 1938, 1923), p. 31. Consider: "In Jesus' *name* we ask it."

tant part of the area. The framework of accounting with its reaction patterns constitutes a social institution and is itself a communication system. Reports of various kinds inform members of the organization about objectives and accomplishment. Messages go up or down or crosswise in the organizational hierarchy through traditional channels and in traditional symbols. In some cases the channels are noisy (contain random, distracting symbols) and the symbols are fuzzy. Messages going up the hierarchical ladder may tend to lose overtones and to pick up bias toward favorable reports, while messages going down may be surrounded by all sorts of added and perhaps irrelevant 'meanings.' These pragmatic effects result from the for-interest bias found in most reporting situations. A selective process tends to screen reports and bias them in favor of the sender. The systems accountant should be prepared to establish alternate channels with different patterns of self-interest to counteract bias and outright suppression of information. Without alternative channels, suppression of information may become serious unless the system is safeguarded to assure that those who initiate and convey information have no stake in the contents of the reports. A limited amount of this kind of control results from having an independent accounting department in charge of communications. Internal auditors and independent auditors supplement the controller's staff for this purpose. This structure is usually combined with a limited number of alternative channels in most modern accounting systems, and there is reason to believe that the resulting reports are more reliable than some information and communication theorists have claimed.

Accountants are accustomed to outright bias in the direction of self-interest, but are sometimes deceived by a subtle blend of judgment and fact known as *slanting*. Hayakawa states: "Slanting gives no explicit judgments, but it differs from reporting in that it deliberately makes certain judgments inescapable."[4] It should be noted that slanting may be the result of bias and be done without conscious effort on the part of the writer. Occasionally a writer without attempting to do so will use emotionally charged words that influence the reader's decision making, so that the resulting statements are slanted. On occasion an author attempts to be fair by slanting both for and against to present both sides of the problem. One well-known accounting writer, for example, customarily gives first the arguments for the opposing view, and then presents his own view as a rebuttal. This procedure tends to slant by the order of the arguments. The author's judgments are established by positive arguments and by demolishing those of the opposition, who of course cannot have a direct rebuttal. This type of slanting may become vicious when indefensible arguments are set for the opposition. The demolition of these arguments makes the writer's views appear to be more conclusive, especially if opposing arguments are 'straw men' or pseudo arguments.

Now the field of semantics is concerned with the relationship of symbols to empirical data — the so-called 'rules of correspondence' or instructions for defining a symbol in terms of operations on empirical data. Popular writers in the field are fond of using an analogy based on the relationship of a map to the territory it is supposed to represent. Often the symbols take on a rigidity with regard to the reaction they evoke that outlasts the uniformities in the empirical world. In this case they lose the original relationship that they once held, and the resulting reports may be as useless as road maps equally out of touch with physical conditions. The word 'capitalist,' for example, is associated by many citizens over the world with pictures of ruthless greed that often appeared years ago in the leftist press. These pictures may or may not have been an accurate map a half-century

---

[4] S. I. Hayakawa, *Language in Thought and Action* (New York: Harcourt, Brace and Company, 1949), p. 48.

ago, but it seems safe to say that the *stereotype* no longer represents the territory that it is now supposed to depict. Such accounting terms as 'surplus,' 'profit before taxes,' 'gross profit,' 'reserves,' 'net worth,' etc., may never have been adequate descriptions of actual territories. At present they may be downright misleading to all but the technically trained in accounting.

The task of definition is to communicate by using words that will bring before the listener a situation or object in the empirical world with which he is familiar; in fact, " . . . the goal of semantics might be stated as 'Find the referent.' "[5] Dictionary definitions are necessarily at a high level of abstraction, and seldom specify necessary operations, or point out an object.[6] "We normally beg the hard question of finding referents and proceed learnedly to define the term by giving another dictionary abstraction, for example, defining 'liberty' by 'freedom' . . . [or defining] a 'sofa' . . . as a 'lounge.' "[7] Unfortunately, one cannot point to concepts like 'income' and finding referents for such constructions sometimes requires complicated reductions.

It is difficult to talk of definitions without discussing the process of abstraction and levels of abstraction. For practical purposes in nonscientific work a particular object at which we can point is the lowest level of abstraction.[8] (Some writers feel that such objects

---

[5] Stuart Chase, *The Tyranny of Words* (New York: Harcourt, Brace and Company, 1938), p. 9. It should be noted that 'finding the referent' is equivalent to 'finding interpretations for the calculus' or assigning 'values' to the symbols. The term 'meaning' leaves something to be desired in the way of precision. Morris states: "Meanings were inaccessible to observation from without, but individuals somehow managed to communicate these private (Can he be sure?) mental states by the use of sounds, writing, and other signs." *Op. cit.*, p. 123. Carnap states: "It seems . . . preferable to avoid the word 'meaning' whenever possible because of its ambiguity, i.e., the multiplicity of its designata. Above all, it is important to distinguish between the semantical and the psychological use of the word . . . . We know the meaning (designatum) of a term if we know under what conditions we are permitted to apply it in a concrete case and under what conditions not." Rudolf Carnap, "Logical Foundations of the Unity of Science," *International Encyclopedia of Unified Science* (Chicago: University of Chicago Press, 1955), pp. 44, 49.

[6] "Pointing, despite Emily Post, nails down referents as nothing else can." Stuart Chase, *op. cit.*, p. 173.

[7] *Ibid.*, pp. 10, 104. For an exercise the reader may wish to hunt the complex referents in the following quotations, "In the final analysis, therefore, the great possibility of achieving understanding in the next 50 years is through improved ways of dissemination of the 'economic facts of life.' " Maurice H. Stans, *Handbook of Modern Accounting Theory*, ed. Morton Backer (New York: Prentice-Hall, Inc., 1955), p. 601. "The Eternal Law is a Supreme Being's eternal plan for the universe . . . . The Natural Law is the Eternal Law as known to man by reason. Man knows naturally, by reason, that he must do good and avoid evil." Brother LaSalle, "An Approach to Ethics," *The Accounting Review*, October, 1954, p. 688. " . . . the Committee believes a statement of accounting concepts should give recognition only to its [a fresh start's] conceptual possibility. That recognition is essential if the application of accounting concepts is to be rational rather than arbitrary." Paul J. Graber, "Report of Committee on Revision of the Statement of Principles, Assets," *The Accounting Review*, January, 1948, pp. 15-16. Perhaps the most discouraging aspect of the following quotation is that the writer is a leader in the crusade for more understandable reports. "It would, furthermore, seem to be in conformity with the direction of accounting evolution to move away from a greater degree of personal judgment based on subjective factors (such as costs artfully constructed by the addition of monetary amounts having different values at different times according to the peculiarly internal design or accident of their incidence) towards a lesser degree of personal judgment based on more objective factors (such as market replacement costs constructed by the addition of monetary amounts having the same value as of the same time and a 'free' relationship to each other according to the more external circumstances of that one time)." William Blackie, "What is Accounting Accounting for — Now?" *N.A.C.A. Bulletin*, July 1, 1948, p. 1373.

[8] This is the so-called 'thing-language' to which all definitions, relations and constructs must be reducible according to early logical positivists. For a discussion of "physical language" and "thing-predicates," see Rudolf Carnap, "Logical Foundations of the Unity of Science," *op. cit.*, pp. 52 ff. Brunswik, and most of us, would like to modify the thing-concept into something like a "constancy hypothesis." "Copernicus himself dethroned man's planet as the center of a faraway universe; Darwin dethroned the human species as the absolute master of the animal kingdom; Freud went still further and dethroned the conscious ego as the true representative of our own motivational dynamics. Kant and Gestalt-psychologists complete the picture by showing the subjectivity of the thing - language," *op. cit.*, p. 667.

are not abstractions at all.) Perhaps the next level of abstraction comes when we paste a label on the object, e.g., 'typewriter number 11,189, in the office at 779 Rooney Hall.' We may then rise to a slightly higher level by using the unmodified term 'typewriter' which includes the set of important properties and relations that are common to typewriter$_1$, typewriter$_2$, typewriter$_3$, ... In this process such characteristics as location, color, height of the operator, the thickness of the dust on the covers, etc., are not important and may be dropped by the abstractive process.

Slightly higher in the abstractive order is the term 'office equipment.' This term includes most typewriters along with many other items. The fact that an object can perform the typing function is not a necessary condition for admittance at this level of abstraction. The term 'asset' is at a still higher level that includes office equipment along with many other objects not ordinarily found in offices. It is not necessary that the object be an item of equipment or that it be used in an office for it to qualify as an asset. In a similar fashion one may proceed to social wealth and perhaps to other more general and abstract classifications. The process of abstraction — omitting characteristics that are irrelevant for the occasion — is the basis of classification and is necessary for reasoning. In fact it may be argued that all knowledge is made up of abstractions that result from the *selective* qualities and processes of our senses. Abstraction from all empirical content (if possible) results in a formal syntactical system devoid of all referents (interpretations).

One of the reasons that political platforms and politicians' campaign speeches are so often unsatisfactory is that they are purposely pitched at a very high level of abstraction so that the hearer may substitute his own referents and understand what he wants to understand. Demagogues unfortunately have sometimes been able to predict, and manipulate for their own ends, the interpretations that normally will be made. Some individuals tend to use dead-level abstraction and talk at a uniformly high level or low level of abstraction. One may define liberty in terms of freedom, or God in terms of omnipotent power, while another remains at levels so low that the discussion is in terms of particulars with little generality. Desirable requirements for clearcut communication may be that the terms can be reduced into less and less abstract terms until the listener arrives at empirical referents that give meaning to the statements. "A preacher, a professor, a journalist, or politician whose high level abstractions can systematically and surely be referred to lower level abstractions is not only talking, he is saying something."[9] We must not underestimate the social force of high-level abstractions. Most principles of conduct are at such levels and are difficult or impossible to reduce to simple referents. "A boy in his efforts to live up to the abstraction 'masculine' would try to be virile, dominating, dissipated, chivalrous, overtouchy about his honor, convinced of his intellectual superiority . . . ."[10]

One of the most common confusions of the levels of abstraction is illustrated in the simple statements: This *is* an asset: A car *is* an asset. It should be clear that the first statement makes peculiar use of the word 'is,' for obviously the *word* 'asset' is not the physical object, nor is the *word* 'car.' In the second case the use of 'is' cannot mean identity in the sense that all characteristics are the same in the two classifications. Instead 'is' means in

---

[9] S. I. Hayakawa, *op. cit.*, p. 177. (Original all italics.)

[10] Stuart Chase, *op. cit.*, p. 203. This more sophisticated view is taken by Urban: "The crucial positions of this chapter are: (a) the denial that there is any such thing as empty words — the principle that we cannot talk about anything that is not . . . . The condition of the meaningfulness of an assertion is not that certain entities about which the assertions are made 'exist' — in the sense of being empirically observable — but that the universe of discourse in which these entities have their existence is mutually acknowledged." Wilbur Marshall Urban, *Language & Reality* (New York: The Macmillan Company, 1939), pp. 226, 227.

the second case that any car is a member of the set of assets and is silent on whether there are other members of the set or other admission properties.[11]

Teachers who are fond of the term 'is' are likely to be fond also of a single- or two-valued approach to thought — the single-valued orientation. "This item is either an asset or it is not." "Is it a cost of production or isn't it?" "Smith is a genius or an imbecile." The "either-or" orientation is a useful one for thinking and turns up in formal logic as one of the fundamental rules of formation — the excluded middle. Nevertheless, in a good part of living we are constantly valuing, appraising, and grading evidence. Notice that what could be an extremely unfortunate aspect of any jury system that requires a guilty or not-guilty decision has been modified by giving the sentencing judge considerable leeway to soften the harsh either-or verdict.[12]

Accountants, as a group, have considerable experience in appraising evidence and drawing probable inferences and are traditionally and understandably reluctant to accept reports without some type of verification. However, accountants and everyone else often accept unverified reports from others, including complete strangers. For example, one readily accepts statements that a particular dog is not dangerous, that the rental horse is safe, or that water is available at the next desert stop. To survive in the present complicated world one must accept many reports without verification other than a general faith in the ethical reliability of the general social group. To survive requires considerable discrimination, and such discrimination is in fact exercise of judgment.[13]

Clear comprehension of simple reports may offer difficulties. In addition one of the most common and serious semantic traps results from confusing someone's inference or judgment for a report. We *infer* from a current ratio of seven to one that the firm will have no immediate short-run debt-paying difficulties. We *infer* from the client's attitude toward deficit financing that he is a Republican. From a report that the controller and the sales manager are not speaking we *infer* that there is ill will between them. We *infer* from a sample of 300 inventory items that the inventory value is substantially correct.

It should be clear that an inference may be based on much or little experience, may or may not be aided with the latest statistical pronouncements on sampling, and may or may not have a high probability of being an inference that is useful for living. Simple existence at the animal level requires untold numbers of inferences. (A cat infers danger from the presence of a strange dog.) The fantastic number of required inferences means that not all are made with high degrees of probability. In many cases the care with which the inference is made bears some relationship to the seriousness of making a wrong inference, but this

---

[11] Lee points out four common uses of the word *is*: "At least two uses of the verb [is] are fundamental and necessary in English. 1. As an auxiliary in the formation of tenses in English . . . . 2. As a synonym for existence . . . . 'The Capital of the U.S. is at Washington, D.C.' . . . . At least two other uses the verb we find false-to-fact and instrumental in making for confusions and misevaluation. 3. When the 'is' leads to the *identification* of different levels of abstraction . . . . 'Man *is* an animal' . . . 4. When the 'is' leads to the predication of 'qualities.' Here we make the assumption that characteristics exist in 'things,' whereas they are to be found only in the relation of an observer to what is observed . . . . 'He *is* most charitable.' . . . . This 'is' serves as a synonym for 'appears' . . . . " Irving J. Lee, *Language Habits in Human Affairs* (New York: Harper & Brothers Publishers, 1941), pp. 228-229.

[12] A gentle criticism of the two-valued orientation and logic is implied by this statement attributed to Lin Yutang: "A is right, but B is not wrong."

[13] Different social groups vary widely in the reliability of their reports. Morris Cohen remarks: "Empirically . . . it is true that lying is subversive of that mutual confidence that is necessary to all social cooperation. And this justifies a general condemnation of lying — but not an absolute prohibition." *Reason and Nature* (Glencoe: The Free Press, 1953), p. 433. Most major religions *encourage* accurate reporting.

generalization may be subject to many exceptions. (See the essay devoted to evidence and proof for a more detailed discussion.)

Judgment is used by some semanticists to mean what are commonly understood to be value judgments, e.g., *"expressions of the writer's approval or disapproval of the occurrences, persons, or objects he is describing."*[14] A little reflection shows that difficulties may arise from confusion of a report and a judgment. For example, the statement: "Our client lied about his payables" may easily be mistaken for a factual report, but it is both an inference and a value judgment. "Lied" itself implies that our client was aware that his statement was false and the listener normally draws this inference. Moreover, it is probable that the speaker disapproves of lies and liars, so that for many people the statement is also a condemnation. A 'report' might state simply that the client stated payables to be $8,000, and payables amounting to $11,000 were in existence at that time, yet even the most neutral report is presumably made to facilitate judgment (decision) and complete neutrality may be an impossible goal.

The accountant and the accounting teacher should be especially competent at weighing evidence and rendering reports designed to initiate desirable action. In fact public accounting is a profession devoted almost entirely to weighing reports from individuals, combining them in meaningful ways, and vouching for their reliability. The form and arrangement of reports are designed to evoke desirable action from those who use them. The choice of events to be recorded is the result of value judgments. The degree of abstraction and the amount of detail (particulars) are adjusted to the pragmatics of reader reaction in light of accepted goals. The tentative nature of induction from specific instances is invariably close to the surface. The subjective aspects of evidence, judgment, reporting, and even facts are encountered daily by the active accountant. The weaknesses of human beings under stress and their tendency to color their reports by ego-saving slanting are on display daily for accountants to observe. In spite of these pressing influences, some accountants and teachers of accounting continue to stress archaic techniques for record keeping, and their students often remain ignorant of even the term 'semantics.'

---

[14] S. I. Hayakawa, *op. cit.*, p. 42. Notice the following statement. ". . . even the simplest sensations involve some judgment . . . . When . . . this judgment is of so simple a kind as to become wholly unconscious, and the interpretation of the appearances is a matter of general agreement, the object of sensation may . . . be considered a *fact*." George Cornewall Lewis, "Matters of Fact and Opinion," reprinted in *The Language of Wisdom and Folly*, ed. Irving J. Lee (New York: Harper & Brothers Publishers, 1949), p. 65. Bertrand Russell states: "Everything that there is in the world I call a 'fact' . . . but it is not called 'cognitive' until it reaches a certain level of development." *Human Knowledge, Its Scope and Limits* (New York: Simon & Schuster, 1948), p. 143.

Essay Eight

Accounting: Semantic Difficulties

The previous essay is devoted to some elementary and general comments about the difficulties of semantics, pragmatics and communication.[1] We are concerned here primarily with specific barriers to understanding that are sometimes encountered in discussions of accounting subjects. Some specific quotations and usages are used to illustrate specific shortcomings. These quotations were selected from writers with superior communicative ability.

Perhaps the worst offender in the field of accounting is the term 'true.' The true proprietary equity is $326,600. The true cash balance on December 31, 1962, is $45,000. The annuity method of amortizing costs does not show the true depreciation expense. The use of LIFO does not permit reporting the true periodic profit of the concern. The examples may be multiplied almost indefinitely.

What is the 'true' cash balance? Are the bank balances cash or a specialized type of receivable? Do outstanding checks reduce the cash balance or should they be added to the book cash for presentation of cash in a financial statement? Is the change fund in the registers cash? Are advances in the hands of salesmen cash? Something else?

Which income is the 'true' income? Are all value increases income? Must value increases be supported by realization? Does true income accrue as work progresses? Do LIFO and FIFO both give true income? Do variations in the methods of taking depreciation yield 'false' incomes? Is it necessary to anticipate future sales discounts to procure a

---

[1] It is not the intention to give a general approach to the use of signs, languages, and communication systems. The following references may prove helpful to those who wish to consider the subject more intensively. The outstanding early work is C. K. Ogden and I. A. Richards, *The Meaning of Meaning* (New York: Harcourt, Brace and Company, Inc., 1938). Their well-known illustration of the usefulness of syntax (grammar) (p. 46) may deserve repeating. "Suppose someone to assert: *The gostak distims the doshes.* You do not know what this means; nor do I. But if we assume that it is English, we know that *the doshes are distimmed by the gostak.* If, moreover, the *doshes* are *galloons,* we know that *some galloons are distimmed by the gostak.*" Charles W. Morris in "Foundations of the Theory of Signs," *International Encyclopedia of Unified Science* (Chicago: University of Chicago Press, 1955), argues: " . . . a language is a social system of signs mediating the responses of members of a community to one another and to their environment [p. 114] . . . . Thus the formalist is inclined to consider any axiomatic system as a language, regardless of whether there are any things which it denotes, or whether the system is actually used by any group of interpreters; the empiricist is inclined to stress the necessity of the relation of signs to objects which they denote and whose properties they truly state; the pragmatist is inclined to regard a language as a type of communicative activity, social in origin and nature, by which members of a social group are able to meet more satisfactorily their individual and common needs" (p. 88). An extreme position as to the usefulness of language in society is taken by Leonard Bloomfield, "Linguistic Aspects of Science," *International Encyclopedia of Unified Science, op. cit.*, p. 239. "Much as single cells are combined in a many-celled animal, separate persons are combined in a speech community — a higher and more effective type of organization [p. 233] . . . . The ordering and formalizing effect of language appears, first of all, in the fact that its meaningful forms are all composed of a small number of meaningless elements." Electrical engineers and others have made a major point of the tendency to degeneration (entropy) and have made provision for the introduction of "noise" and probability into the communication system. See, for example, Norbert Wiener, *Cybernetics; or Control and Communication in the Animal and the Machine* (New York: John Wiley & Sons, 1948), or *The Human Use of Human Beings: Cybernetics and Society* (Boston: Houghton Mifflin Co., 1950), esp. Chapter 1.

true profit? Does consideration of imputed interest on proprietary investment make the reported income false? Is the true loss on spoiled units the difference between their sales value as firsts and their value as seconds or scrap? The absurdity of putting fear into the hearts of sincere opponents by implying in this manner that their proposals lead to false results is obvious. Yet some folks are convinced by such statements; otherwise some authors of considerable prestige would be run out of town. Let us now give attention to the terms 'true' and its kin 'truth.'[2] There is certainly an area of discussion in which it is useful to point out the truth or falsity of an assertion, but the important lesson for accountants, and many others, is that this two-valued orientation *is useful when a substantial part of the controversy (argument) is finished* and the parties in opposition are agreed as to what shall constitute meeting the test (true) and falling short of meeting the test (false). There may still be controversy as to whether a particular statement or proposition meets the tests, but this argument is on a different level of abstraction and is apart from setting standards that must be met before qualifying as true. The point to be emphasized is that it is next to foolishness to claim that one *definition* of income is true, so that alternative definitions by implication are false. Moreover, such argument when done consciously is one of the *more unethical* forms of argument.

The difficulty, of course, is that philosophers have had trouble deriving an acceptable concept of true and even more difficulty with truth. One approach tries to tie the concept to the syntactical or logical domain and to limit it pretty much to procedures that are consistent with the rules of logic that happen to be adopted. Truth and falsity, according to this view, are properties of propositions and are therefore linguistic. Even this procedure does not result in a clearcut construct. The true-false of a truth-table, for instance, may be entirely conventional and need not represent true or false at all in any usual sense. Interpretations of T and F need have nothing to do with what most students conceive to be true or false so long as they are by definition contradictories that can not be asserted together, i.e., they meet the tests for manipulating the symbols that have been adopted in the logic. Thus a mathematician may establish a requirement that set membership rules be unambiguous. Notice, however, that pure mathematicians are not able to determine in a particular case whether or not the membership requirements are sufficiently well-defined to permit the necessary discrimination. The latter requirement is empirical and depends on the discriminatory power of the individual. The concept of logical-truth (validity) clearly has no use except to show whether the manipulation has been done according to the rules that have been adopted. It is sufficient to assume that the user of logic has enough discriminatory power to be able to recognize the symbols T and F and to understand the rules for manipulating them. The translation of these symbols into true and false in the empirical sense is an interpretation and not a part of mathematics.

Thus logic and mathematics tend to yield 'truth' by definition or convention. " 'Two plus two are four,' because all that this statement says is that 'four' *is the name* of 'the sum of two and two.' "[3] It is generally understood that both mathematics and logic are verbal

---

    [2] As an exercise, try to find the referents for the motto of at least two great universities: "Seek ye the truth and the truth shall make ye free."

    [3] S. I. Hayakawa, *Language in Thought and Action* (New York: Harcourt, Brace and Co., 1949), p. 240. Notice also: " . . . the only way to guarantee the 'truth' of logically deduced statements and to arrive at agreements through logic alone is not to talk about actual cats at all, and to talk only about cats-by-definition. The nice things about cats-by-definition is that, come hell or high water, they *always* meow (although, to be sure, they only meow-by-definition)." *Ibid.*, p. 241. See also Vilhjalmur Stefansson, "Knowledge by Definition," reprinted in *The Language of Wisdom and Folly*, ed. Irving J. Lee (New York: Harper & Brothers Publishers, 1949), pp. 85-92.

in nature and that the names of numbers, the operations, and the symbols can be defined without any reference to the 'numbers' that we normally assume. The assignment of the number 'two' to the class of all classes that are similar to a given couple is definitional (conventional), but to be useful the definition needs *interpretation* and requires the empirical or psychological ability to determine similarity, i.e., put things in a one-one correlation.[4]

The meaning of 'true' to most readers is probably related to the semantic aspects of language and 'true' or 'false' are used to indicate whether the report agrees or does not agree with empirical data. Morris states:

> . . . discussions of the term 'truth' have always involved the question of the relation of signs to things . . . . In general, from the point of view of behavior, signs are 'true' in so far as they correctly determine the expectations of their users, and so release more fully the behavior which is implicitly aroused in the expectation or interpretation.[5]

While we may not agree with Chase that: "In given context a statement may be true or false, but there is no such entity as 'truth,' "[6] we must be prepared for difficulty when we try to define the generalized term 'truth.' Russell is in essential agreement with Morris: "When we say that a sentence is 'true,' we mean to say something about the state of mind of a person uttering or hearing it with belief. It is in fact primarily beliefs that are true or false . . . ."[7]

If accountants agree with mathematicians and scientists to accept certain terms as having definite meanings and agree on the rules of formation and transformation (logic), the truth or falsity of a conclusion can be established within the framework of the definitions and agreed procedures. Note however that when the empirical or experiential world is considered agreement is relative, and the truthfulness of a report can therefore be only tentative or probable. If all agree that there is only one god, Allah, and that his only major prophet is Mohammad it is not ridiculous to assert the truth of the proposition that Ormuzd (or any other non-Allah) is a false god and that his prophets are imposters. Likewise if all agree that straightline depreciation on a ten-year basis without consideration of residual value is necessary for a true income figure, then it is proper to thunder that the application of activity methods of depreciation will lead to false income figures. True income, in this case, is the results derived from applying the agreed rules of observation,

---

[4] See for example, Bertrand Russell, *Introduction to Mathematical Philosophy* (London: G. Allen & Unwin, 1919), Chapter II, esp. pp. 14-15. The similar concept of mapping is explained by Irving Adler, *The New Mathematics* (New York: A Mentor Book, 1960), pp. 14 ff.

[5] Charles W. Morris, *op. cit.*, pp. 99, 111. The danger of such a relativistic approach to truth is lessened by the interpersonal comparisons necessary for objectivity. Morris states: "A peculiarly intellectualistic justification of dishonesty in the use of signs is to deny that truth has any other component than the pragmatical, so that any sign which furthers the interest of the user is said to be true . . . . Dewey has specifically denied the imputed identification of truth and utility." *Ibid.*, pp. 118-119. Notice also: "Semantics presupposes syntactics but abstracts from pragmatics . . ." *Ibid.*, p. 101.

[6] Stuart Chase, *The Tyranny of Words* (New York: Harcourt, Brace and Company, 1938), p. 88.

[7] Bertrand Russell, *Human Knowledge, Its Scope and Limits* (New York: Simon & Schuster, 1948), p. 112. Hayakawa distinguishes four different meanings of the term 'true,' but he combines pragmatics with semantics. "We may distinguish at least four senses of the word 'true': Some mushrooms are poisonous. (If we call this 'true,' it means that it is a *report that can be and has been verified* . . .) Sally is the sweetest girl in the world. (If we call this 'true,' it means that *we feel the same way* towards Sally . . .) All men are created equal. (If we call this 'true,' it means that this is *a directive which we believe should be obeyed* . . .) $(x + y)^2 = x^2 + 2xy + y^2$. (If we call this 'true,' it means that this statement is *consistent with system of statements possible to be made in the language called algebra* . . .)" *Op. cit.*, p. 292.

recognition, and measurement. Claiming truth for one set of acceptance rules often by implication treats the results of alternative rules as false. Far too often the result is question begging, for the point at issue is usually the superiority of one set of rules over the others.

The terms 'logic,' 'logically,' and 'logical' are often used in accounting literature. Advocates of a particular method of costing inventories are "throwing logic to the winds." Straightline depreciation may not be "strictly logical, but . . . ." "The logic of the situation dictates" that we treat purchase discounts as cost reductions. Examples may be extended at length. What are the writers saying? The reader has some rights and among them seems to be the freedom not to endure — in Chase's words — "unintelligible noises." Too often the unsophisticated reader accepts the authority that the term 'logic' has gathered through the years and renders his decision against superior evidence. The unsophisticated reader who needs to weigh the evidence on an unemotional and nonauthoritative basis is the person who is most easily deceived by the honorific connotations of such words, and unfortunately textbooks are among the worst offenders.

It is the function of logic generally to give the accepted rules for getting new sentences from old. These rules set the path for determining what transformation may be asserted and what other transformations or combinations cannot be asserted jointly without leading to violations such as contradiction. Logic also may help in the manipulations that are necessary to wrangle new sentences (propositions) from old, and it may help in testing whether a given sentence may or may not be asserted from the previous sentences (giving proofs). This function must not be undervalued for it may well lead to new insights. Carnap states:

> Though logic cannot lead us to anything new in the logical sense, it may well lead to something new in the psychological sense. Because of limitations on man's psychological abilities . . . the psychological content (the totality of associations) of one of these new sentences may be entirely different from that of the other.[8]

The point to be emphasized is that logic, strictly speaking, is not concerned with the truth or falsity of empirical statements about the observed world. Logic cannot possibly tell us that if market values are important when they are below cost, they must also be important when they are above cost, or that the valuations used for determining income must also be used for determining financial status. Chase has stated:

> Logic is a set of rules governing *consistency in the use of language*. When we are being "logical" our statements are consistent *with each other*; they may be accurate "maps" of real "territories" *or they may not*, but the question whether they are or not is *outside the province of logic*. Logic is language about language, not language about things or events.[9]

---

    [8] Rudolf Carnap, *Introduction to Symbolic Logic and Its Applications* (New York: Dover Publications, Inc., 1958), pp. 21-22. Notice also by the same author: "The chief function of a logical calculus in its application to science is not to furnish logical theorems . . . but to guide the deduction of factual conclusions from factual premises." *Foundations of Logic and Mathematics* (Chicago: University of Chicago Press, 1939), p. 35. Also *International Encyclopedia of Unified Science* (Chicago: University of Chicago Press, 1955), p. 177.

    [9] S. I. Hayakawa, *op. cit.*, p. 240. Carnap comments: "Logic . . . is concerned with *relations* between factual sentences (or thoughts). If logic ever discusses the truth of factual sentences it does so only *conditionally*, somewhat as follows: *if* such-and-such a sentence is true, *then* such-and-such another sentence is true. Logic itself does not decide whether the first sentence *is* true, but surrenders that question to one or the other of the empirical sciences." "The Condition of Clarity," reprinted in *The Language of Wisdom and Folly*, ed. Irving J. Lee, (New York: Harper & Brothers Publishers, 1949), p. 44.

It is probably true that accountants and other reasonably educated people make comparatively few mistakes in their use of formal logic. Now and then one forgets that a proof of the inverse does not prove the original statement or that the proof of the contrapositive does not prove the converse, but even these somewhat technical details are violated considerably less than one might suppose. When the rules of logic are violated, the violator should certainly be called to task. What is objected to here is the use of the prestige of the term 'logic' as a psychological (pragmatic) weapon. Words have images and 'logic' sometimes incites an intellectual Jehovah image and is thus well suited for propaganda purposes.[10]

Apparently many nonlogicians use 'logical' in a completely different sense. 'Logical' action is often related to goals and objectives. Thus a person exhibits logical behavior when his actions tend to lead to goal attainment. He is illogical when his actions seem to subvert his objectives. In this usage 'logical' becomes a synonym for *rational behavior*, which itself is poorly defined. Thus (by extension) if one argues that the cost-or-market rule is illogical, he may mean that the results derived from applying the rule tend to thwart the objectives of the overall measurement system. In this extended sense logical becomes a synonym for consistency, where 'consistency' means helping and not hindering the goals of the information system.

Far too often, in practice, the terms science and scientific are used in a tyrannical manner and confuse rather than clarify exposition. Most folks do not like to be thought of as unscientific, for in our present society science enjoys — and with merit — the highest intellectual status. Few can doubt that the rigorous application of scientific method has been one of the crowning intellectual achievements of the past few centuries. Science is concerned with organizing and relating experiences by admitting evidence only if it can be checked at the referent (data) level by replication or by any competent individual.[11]

It is not the object of this discussion to examine the possibilities that accounting may be treated as a bona fide science. Instead it seems sufficient at this time to point out that the use of 'scientific' like the use of 'true' or 'real' often results in conscious or unconscious slanting. No one likes to buck the prestige of the term 'scientific,' and the label by implication tends to make alternative procedures or suggestions appear to be unscientific and therefore less acceptable. Certainly not all of traditional accounting meets the tests of continual checking at various levels of abstraction with referents, but accountants are acutely aware of the prestige resulting from being considered to be scientific, and they may cite with approval the following statement by Pearson: *"The unity of all science consists alone in its method, not in its material.* The man who classifies facts of any kind whatever, who

---

[10] This essay avoids the so-called diction and nondiction fallacies of Aristotle. These pitfalls deserve to be studied carefully by any aspiring accountant. Those concerned with diction are: ambiguity, amphiboly, combination, division, accent, figure of speech. Fallacies out of diction are: accident, confusions of absolute and relative, ignorance of the refutation, begging the question, consequent (converse proof), false cause, and that of many questions.

[11] The problems of scientific method are treated elsewhere, but note: "In science, this interplay [between higher and lower levels of abstraction] goes on constantly, hypotheses being checked against observations, predictions against extensional results." S. I. Hayakawa, *op. cit.*, p. 179. Morris Cohen, "The true [*sic*] method of science is to cure speculative excesses, not by a return to pure experience devoid of all assumptions, but by multiplying through pure logic the number of these assumptions, mathematically deducing their various consequences, and then confronting each one with its rivals and such experimental facts as can be generally established." *Reason and Nature, op. cit.*, pp. 39-40. "In order that a conception may have scientific validity, it must be self-consistent, and deducible from the perceptions of the normal human being." Karl Pearson, *The Grammar of Science* (Everyman ed.; London: J. M. Dent & Sons, Ltd., 1937, 1892), p. 49.

sees their mutual relation and describes their sequences, is applying the scientific method and is a man of science."[12]

To the extent that one's opponent is violating certain rules of scientific and rational behavior, we have a right to call him unscientific, point out his failures and let him suffer the unpalatable consequences. Accountants are on more doubtful ground when they refer to the compound-interest methods of amortizing assets or equities as being scientific. Straightline depreciation *per se* is no more or less scientific than the annuity method, and the approach to the Valhalla of pure science is not necessarily measured by the complexity or modernity of the mathematics employed.

One of the common misuses of words in accounting is found in connection with the term 'distortion.' We may use for an example the following statement from Gilman, but similar statements may be taken from many leading authorities. "It is difficult to escape the conclusion that this [LIFO] and its companion, the base-stock method . . . are intended deliberately to stabilize, or in other words distort, profits . . ."[13]

One has only to inquire: Distort from what? The unsatisfactory use of the term becomes obvious with the asking of the question. Certainly LIFO distorts profit figures when measured from the amounts that would result from the application of FIFO as a norm. It is just as clear that the use of FIFO or an average method distorts the figures that would result if LIFO or any other method were used as the standard. Clearly such arguments cannot be expected to improve understanding.

Perhaps the most serious objection to the use of distortion in this connection is that it tends to obscure the fact that the whole controversy is over the definition of income. The problem at issue in these instances is to determine the most desirable alternative for measuring income and for presenting the results. These alternatives are determinants of income, and each implies a different attitude toward the usefulness of the resulting income. It is manifestly absurd to assume a *proper* definition of income and criticize particular alternatives because they fail to conform to this definition. The result is a plain begging of the question — one of the most obvious violations of informal logic.

Accounting literature is full of sinister admonitions for accountants to avoid recording and reporting in such a way as to distort something or other. Suppose that a client who has been reporting reasonably constant income figures encounters a bad year and asks his accountant for permission to hold the sales register open for a few extra days so that his reported revenues and income will not be distorted from their previous pattern. Our quick curbstone reply is likely to point out that a *natural* change in reported income is not distortion and holding open the register would lead to distortion. (We are left with the nasty chore of defining 'natural' and defending the definition.) The difficulty arises from the uncertainty about the base from which deviation is to be measured. Correction of past periods' profits through current income accounts may lead to distortion only in the sense that someone has agreed on what the usual pattern should be or, at least, what the determinants of the pattern are. On most problems that are worthy of discussion we have not reached the required degree of agreement, and consequently such words as distortion confuse instead of clarify the issues.

---

[12] Karl Pearson, *op. cit.*, p. 16.
[13] Stephen Gilman, *Accounting Concepts of Profit* (New York: The Ronald Press Company, 1939), p. 398. Gilman elsewhere explains distortion: "Distortion as used here refers to distortion from a traditional base founded upon original accounting conventions." *Loc. cit.* "Artificial tinkering with reported profits" is a similar objectionable statement.

The use of 'distortion' and similar words has a slanting effect that is highly undesirable. It puts the accused in the light of being an advocate of distortion — by implication an undesirable position. This tyranny of words with automatic slanting is perhaps not as acute here as it is when the terms 'progressive,' 'liberal,' 'sound,' etc., are used. The appropriation of the term 'progressive education' has had a tremendous psychological effect. Many individuals wish to be considered progressive and consequently dislike the thought of being considered unprogressive (or, perhaps worse, reactionary). While many may not be so sensitive, there must be many educators who follow the progressive line not because they are genuinely sympathetic toward a majority of its aims but because they react favorably to the label and negatively to its opposite.[14]

It is not uncommon to observe the use of the terms 'in theory' or 'theoretically' in the literature of accounting. "In theory it is correct to add some fixed burden to machinery constructed for the firm's own use." "Theoretically expected sales allowances should be anticipated and taken in the period the sales were registered." "Ideally, interest paid or accrued during the period of construction should be charged to the asset." And so on without practical or theoretical limit!

The use of 'in theory,' 'theoretically' and similar terms is not objectionable if attention is being drawn to an accepted set of goals and practices that should lead to these goals. If contrasting practices do not seem to accomplish the objectives, it may be the practitioner has weighed the consequences and rejected the goals. Theory versus practice is not refined procedures versus crude procedures. There is to my knowledge no directive calling for wasting valuable human resources in order to conform to good theory.

Theory is, of course, a very highly abstract term — perhaps among the highest.[15] Individuals are divided as to the honorific value of being theoretical. In some circles to be considered theoretical is to be considered brilliant and learned; in other circles theoreticians may be considered to be incompetents who spend their time in emasculating words and meaning. No doubt all kinds of variations may be found, but on balance it appears that to use 'in theory' or 'theoretically' often makes an argument more palatable and convincing

---

[14] Human faith in the benefits of progress, regardless of the direction, seems to be based on the thinking of the Enlightenment. At that time, the leaders of the new movement felt that human beings were essentialy good and that any change was bound to be an improvement. Even today 'progressive' is an 'honorific' term, and its opposites are mild forms of castigation.

[15] The term 'fact' is itself an abstraction, and of course such words as 'principle' and 'theory' are high-level abstractions. Some writers feel that the term 'theory' is so poorly defined that it should be reconstructed or abandoned. As a rule the term 'theory' in science is used to include the entire assemblage of primitive terms, definitions, relationships, logical calculus, and rules of correspondence. Warren S. Torgerson states: " . . . the set of constructs with their formal connections forms a model. When certain of the constructs are connected to the empirical world by rules of correspondence, the model becomes a *theory*, and, as such, is subject to empirical test." *Theory and Methods of Scaling* (New York: John Wiley & Sons, Inc., 1958), p. 4. William J. Goode and Paul K. Hatt are more explicit. "A fact is regarded as an *empirically verifiable observation . . . theory refers to the relationships between facts*, or to the ordering of them in some meaningful way . . . . Theory is a tool of science in these ways: (1) it defines the major orientation of a science, by defining the kinds of data which are to be abstracted; (2) it offers a conceptual scheme by which the relevant phenomena are systematized, classified, and interrelated; (3) it summarizes facts into (a) empirical generalizations and (b) systems of generalizations; (4) it predicts facts; and (5) it points to gaps in our knowledge." *Methods in Social Research* (McGraw-Hill Book Company, Inc., 1952), p. 8. DR Scott states: "Some hold that practice of the profession cannot be controlled by any formulation or general acceptance of principles. Others hold that accounting practice may be standardized and controlled by generalized rules based upon such practice. The first view in effect denies the existence of accounting theory . . . . The second view looks upon accounting theory as a body of rules or generalizations which summarizes the experience of the profession." "Accounting Principles and Cost Accounting," *The Journal of Accountancy*, February, 1939, p. 75.

to the reader. Presumably those who admire theory and theorists would be impressed and those to whom theory is an anathema would be repelled. In most cases the result is probably one of slanting, but the direction of the slant may not be clear.[16]

Accountants and others have vacillated between the extremes of believing that consistency is the *sine qua non* of effective argument and holding with a famous philosopher that consistency is the hobgoblin of small minds. As a rule accountants seem to favor the former attitude rather than the latter, and recently auditors have pegged one of their most iron-clad rules to the 'principle' of consistency. Let us start with the use of the word in formal logic and mathematics and examine the usual meanings of the term.

Mathematicians and logicians are vitally concerned with the consistency of their premises and fundamental operations. Consistency in these areas means that the sentences may be asserted jointly and that there is no contradiction, e.g., it is not possible to deduce that a is equal to b and a is not equal to b from the same premises and with approved operations.[17] Unfortunately in many types of ordinary discourse the wording is so loose and the levels of abstraction so confused that it is not feasible or even possible to perform the necessary operations to show whether contradiction — inconsistency — exists.

The term consistent can also be used to express uniformity in behavior patterns, and it is in this area that accountants, and many others as well, often go astray. This aspect of the term can take two somewhat different courses. First, it can be akin to conservative in that the actor does the same thing in the same way each time as if the surrounding conditions set the pattern, and for the actor to break the routine is to lead to 'contradictory' behavior and therefore to be inconsistent. While the desire to emulate the logicians may be strong, in general this use of the term must be applied with care. Are auditors, for example, inconsistent if they start an audit on January 17 of one year and January 27 of another? Is an auditor inconsistent if he wears a blue suit one day and a grey the next? Are accounting firms guilty of inconsistent behavior when they change the personnel on particular audits from year to year? By this definition *any change* in behavior involves inconsistency from some point of view!

Clearly there are no convincing reasons why each of the above cases should be considered to be inconsistent. In day-to-day operations individuals use the term to indicate the relation of their activities to their objectives. In other words they *select* those areas of behavior where it is considered *important* that there be few deviations and apply the terms 'consistent' or 'inconsistent' to them. It may be desirable, for example, for audits not to start on the same day year after year, and it may be desirable to change the personnel for the audit crew from time to time. The point is that the goals or conditions must be set and that deviate action must be important enough to isolate.

---

[16] Similar uses of 'realistic,' 'real,' and 'appeals to facts,' etc., are so common in accounting that illustrations do not seem necessary. " . . . LIFO has no logical factual basis whatever . . . ." Arthur C. Kelley, "Can Corporate Incomes be Scientifically Ascertained?" *The Accounting Review*, July, 1951, p. 292. "The primary purpose of this procedure [cost assignment] is to insure a realistic valuation for inventories — and therefore a realistic measurement of profit." John A. Beckett, "A Study of the Principles of Allocating Costs," *The Accounting Review*, July, 1951, p. 328. "The real significance of equities of this character is to be found in the restrictions they impose upon the asset fund . . . ." William J. Vatter, *The Fund Theory of Accounting and Its Implications for Financial Reports* (Chicago: University of Chicago Press, 1947), p. 20.

[17] "The first advantage of logical system is that it helps to eliminate inconsistency between the propositions which it includes . . . . Sensitiveness to contradictions is an essential characteristic of the man of science, and logical method is a way of forcing contradictions into the light. Common sense tries to achieve consistency by alleging reasons for what it wishes to believe. But if we fail to bring all these reasons together into a system we are bound to rely on inconsistent reasons at different times . . . ." Morris R. Cohen, *op. cit.*, p. 109.

Let us now look at the famous "in conformity with generally accepted accounting principles applied on a basis consistent with that of the preceding year." The emphasis on undeviating behavior through time is unmistakable. Apparently there is no implication of consistency in the logical sense of contradiction, and none is presumably intended, although there may be some reluctance to sign such an opinion at the end of the first year.[18]

There is still a third manner in which consistency is used by writers in accounting, and it is a most objectionable use of words for tyrannical effect. This strange usage is a kind of reversibility without counterpart in logic, mathematics or the canons of good language. It is asserted, for an example, that if market is important when it is below cost it must also be important when it is above cost. There is of course no imperative in logic or psychology or in accounting usage that supports such a position. We might just as well *assume* that, if market is important when it is lower than cost, under no circumstances should market be important when it is above cost. Which one, if either, shall we use? It turns out that the orthodox cost or market rule is in harmony with the generally accepted rules for recognizing gains or losses. That is, gains must pass the tests of realization and losses require somewhat less rigorous evidence to support their recognition. In terms of the broader doctrines of loss and gain recognition, the cost or market rule may be said to be consistent, for it does not violate the more general rules for such recognition. Advocates of cost or market are not throwing 'logic to the winds' or being 'grossly inconsistent.'

The reader may ask himself some questions of the following type to convince himself of the futility of this type of argument. Is a swimmer inconsistent because he inhales when his face is above water and does not inhale — except on rare and unfortunate occasions — when his mouth is below water? Is anyone concerned about the inconsistency of most animals because they breathe faster and deeper when they are climbing a hill than when they are descending? If plant writedowns are charged to retained earnings does it follow that plant writeups should be credited to retained earnings? Is it inconsistent to develop one set of rules for recognition of profit and another less rigid set for recognition of loss? Is it inconsistent for increases in assets to be debits while increases in equities are credits?[19]

---

[18] The following statements indicate views from accountants on the application of consistency to the field.

"To be consistently in error is to be consistent, to be sure, but it is in defeat of the ultimate goal of accounting: truth in reporting." M. A. Binkley, "The Limitations of Consistency," *The Accounting Review*, October, 1948, p. 374.

"To be 'consistent' with the preceding year, it should not be enough to say that the accounting principles of both the current and preceding year are *acceptable* and therefore the principles are *consistent* . . . 'consistent' as employed in the accountants' opinion should mean reasonable adherence to *the* accounting *principle* applied by the company to a specific item or class of items in the previous year." Daniel Borth, "What does 'Consistent' Mean in the Short Form Report?", *The Accounting Review*, October, 1948, p. 373. "Consistency, it will be observed, refers especially to uniformity of practice in two succeeding years, so that the results shown are truly comparable." Thomas H. Sanders, "Progress in Development of Basic Concepts," *Contemporary Accounting* (New York: American Institute of Accountants, 1945), p. 20.

[19] "Consistency is not necessarily a hallmark of accuracy but where a technique is conceded to be accurate in periods of rising prices, there should be at least a presumption that it will be accurate if consistently applied in periods of falling prices." Edgar O. Edwards, "Depreciation Policy under Changing Price Levels," *The Accounting Review*, April, 1954, p. 278. "As it is a general rule that unrealized profits are to be excluded from income, it represents an inconsistency to account for unrealized losses such as the writedown of inventory values to lower market prices." K. Engelmann, "The 'LIFO-or-Market' Plan," *The Accounting Review*, January, 1953, p. 57. Paton has long been a user of consistency in the sense of reversibility. "In the first place this basis [cost or market] of valuation is inconsistent, and inconsistency is the very antithesis of sound accounting. The rule recognizes the significance of market quotations when prices decline but denies that they have any bearing on the interpretation of the financial condition and progress of the business when the movement is in the other direction." William A. Paton and William A. Paton, Jr., *Asset Accounting* (New York: The Macmillan Company, 1952), p. 83.

Recently a speaker was condemning British policy because, it was asserted, the policy has been fantastically inconsistent. He attempted to convince his audience that the policy should be condemned because the diplomatic machinery has been directed against France under Napoleon, against Russia in the Crimean trouble, with France and Russia and against Germany in the world wars of the 20th century, and now, at least in part, against Russia once more. What could be more vacillating? More inconsistent? British foreign policy may or may not have been objectionable to an American for many reasons, but from a slightly different point of view the policy appears to be a masterpiece of consistency. In each case the attitude has been hostile to what seemed at the time to be the strongest and most aggressive power on the continent. The point to be emphasized is that the kind of consistency to be cherished is consistency of procedures and assumptions toward a defined goal. A skipper of a sailboat is not to be condemned if he veers from right to left when sailing into the wind if his objective requires that he progress in the direction of the wind. We may conclude that in many of its uses the charge of 'inconsistency' is a prime example of the tyranny of words. The uninitiated may be impressed, but intelligent readers may be alienated, and certainly all deserve better treatment.

Let us now turn to another area of misunderstanding and poor communication. The following quotation — which is in no way unique — will serve to illustrate the field. "In general the actual circumstances rather than hard and fast rules as to percentage of stock ownership should be permitted to settle the matter of consolidation or nonconsolidation."[20]

We may skip over the obvious fact that "actual circumstances" cannot "settle" a question any better than "hard and fast rules" alone can settle a controversy. The question that should concern us is how we are to permit "actual circumstances" to influence our judgments. (Presumably "to settle" means to discriminate, to judge, and to classify.)

It seems fair to say that almost all rules and standards except perhaps those in pure mathematics and formal logic relate to some characteristics and circumstances. We judge whether an object is a house or a wheelbarrow, for example, by comparing actual characteristics (circumstances?) with those used in setting up the definitions of 'house' and 'wheelbarrow.' And we judge — to cite another example — whether a soccer game is played fairly or unfairly by *comparing* actual behavior patterns with the "hard and fast" (written and unwritten) rules for the game of soccer. More precisely, we may say that actual circumstances are a necessary part of *any* judgment discrimination or classification unless we are dealing with entirely hypothetical cases. Thus there is no opposition between circumstances and rules and the two are complementary — not alternatives — for reaching a decision. One who avoids the facts or actual circumstances is dealing in abstractions and hypothetical instances, but one without stable rules may be "lost forever in the labyrinths of space-time."

What would happen if the use of hard and fast rules is avoided? How can any decision whatever be reached if there are no rules, standards, conventions, class boundaries, or general guideposts of some kind? Obviously no decision is possible with the usual "if . . . then" restriction. Perhaps with less hard and fast rules we get decisions that are less hard and fast, until with no guides, we get no decision.

For another example the reader may wish to analyze the meaning of the following. "Each case must be judged on its merits, cold comfort indeed for those who need or re-

---

[20] William A. Paton and William A. Paton, Jr., *Corporation Accounts and Statements* (New York: The Macmillan Company, 1955), p. 577.

quire rules and formulas to guide their footsteps."[21] We may ask questions of the following nature. What "merits" are to be considered in reaching the judgment and what characteristics (merits) are to be rejected? How is the judge to weigh various merits (and demerits)? Are not rules and formulas set up to guide the selection, rejection, and relative weighing of merits and demerits? Has the writer (perhaps in related discussion and context) given general objectives and goals so that there are signposts that point the direction?

With regard to these statements it may be concluded that: (1) the objectives and goals are so fuzzy and ill-defined that there is no direction; or (2) the roads are so confused that there is no order in them whatsoever and therefore no guides for our footsteps; or (3) by reflecting long enough on the facts of the case (somehow all good things come to him who cogitates) the light will be revealed.[22]

The last possibility is apparently the view of those who feel that an array of facts sooner or later suggests relationships and guidance. This view is held, for example, by a number of so-called institutional economists and many in the fields of sociology, government and psychology. Scientists realize that gathering all facts in even a narrow field is obviously impossible and that a group of facts may be selected for testing a given hypothesis or they may be selected at random or in any other manner, but it is clear that it is impossible to gather *all* the facts, and it is clear that a more or less random sample may or may not be an efficient method of finding out some relationship. Many investigators seem to be interested in facts themselves (low-level abstractions) and are not interested in relationships or generalizations of a more abstract kind or in predictability, but on balance these folks probably are relatively few and waste an unimportant part of mankind's mental resources. It simply does not make sense to ignore all prior knowledge above the fact level and not use it as a tool for investigation. Moreover, facts require simple judgments, and the selection of rejection of relevant and irrelevant facts must be done even though the goals are not clearly defined and the bases for acceptance and rejection are only vaguely understood. "Just give me the facts" must be interpreted as sheer ignorance or as a request for facts relevant for the purpose.

Let us now turn to references to related fields of knowledge that use the prestige of these fields to further an argument. References to 'economic facts of life,' 'economic income,' 'socially desirable,' 'politically expedient,' 'fair share,' 'ethically reprehensible,' 'historically unsound,' 'psychology tells us,' 'anthropology indicates,' 'ideally included,' 'morally bound,' 'in terms of the engineering involved,' 'mathematically speaking,' may go on without limit. In rare instances the prestige of the deity may be invoked to support our argument or to confound our opponents. The childish nature of many of these appeals to outside authority is apparent. Accountants may be swayed by the force of a seemingly settled and authoritative construct about which economists, or other specialists, have been arguing for hundreds of years and have not yet reached agreement.

It is of course necessary for any field of study, such as accounting, to limit its scope of intensive effort and accept in a nonrigorous, more or less uncritical manner the pronouncements and disciplines of related fields. In this fashion the field of accounting joins law, economics, psychology, sociology, engineering, language, arithmetic and many other recognized areas. It is simply not feasible for accountants to examine these areas with suf-

---

[21] Maurice Moonitz, "Adaptations to Price-Level Changes," *The Accounting Review*, April, 1948, p. 144.

[22] "Wisdom does not come to those who gape at nature with an empty head. Fruitful observation depends not as Bacon thought upon the absence of bias or anticipatory ideas, but rather on a logical multiplication of them so that having many possibilities in mind we are better prepared to direct our attention . . . " Morris R. Cohen, *op. cit.*, p. 17.

ficient care to become an expert in each. What is unfortunate is that accountants sometimes refer to these fields as if their problems were settled and more fundamental than those in accounting.[23] The general relationship of accounting to economics, for example, must certainly be admitted, but this admission does not commit us to accept or permit us to use uncritically such terms as 'economic value,' 'economically speaking,' etc., unless the economists have agreed among themselves on the points. Economists are in substantial agreement on some issues, but exceptions are numerous and cover practically all important areas.

In conclusion, consider for a moment the use of 'arbitrary' in the field of accounting. Many of the endless allocations made by some cost accountants are considered to be entirely arbitrary by economists and businessmen and are even called 'arbitrary' by accountants themselves. If such allocations are arbitrary in the strict sense of being meaningless and completely without purpose, with no constraints whatever on the allocator, then there is not much left of this part of the profession. Certainly accountants have some purpose for doing the things they in fact do. If not, there is no profession at all! If anything at all is acceptable, then by definition the allocation is irrelevant, serves no useful purpose, and should be abandoned immediately by those with professional pretensions. Those with a warm feeling for the profession prefer to use the alternative term 'conventional' and to limit the use of both terms to those cases where there is lack of knowledge or genuine doubt as to the facts or the objectives. If, for example, an accountant has no judgment whatever about the life or value of a property, he may follow a convention of writing it off sooner rather than later. This convention may be out of step with current pressures and objecties, but its adoption has not been arbitrary and its purpose has been to constrain or channel certain decisions.

---

23 We should not let ourselves be compared " . . . to those romantic souls who cherish the persistent illusion that by some new trick of method the social sciences can readily be put on a par with the physical sciences with regard to definiteness and universal demonstrability." Morris R. Cohen, *op. cit.*, p. 350. While many of us have searched surrounding fields diligently to find help for our struggling profession, I, for one, have never been impressed with models and analogies from the physical sciences.

Essay Nine

Some Problems of Disclosure*

The conclusions expressed in this paper are relatively simple and obvious, although the means of reaching them may seem to be complex and ponderous. First, it should be clear that there cannot be anything that closely resembles *full* disclosure in any precise sense. Accountants, even with the help of expected future developments in computers, simply cannot record and report everything everybody would like to know about a business, including profit or loss from specific past decisions or profits that might have been made if various alternatives had been taken. Severe abstraction and selection are therefore necessary. One then must ask: How is the selection to be made? Whose needs shall be considered most worthy and given priority? What are the criteria for selection? It is the contention of this paper that a relativist position is the only possible one in accounting or any other discipline that is subject to change; that all procedures, methods, and disclosures must be judged by their ability to satisfy objectives; that such objectives may and do change and that they are socially determined in the sense that social forces decide who is worthy of information from accounting or other information systems. It is the contention of this paper finally that the success or failure of a profession depends on its being able to appraise objectives, place them into an order relation (hierarchy) with respect to worthiness, and to devise rules for satisfying them in approximate order.[1]

Recently the terms 'accountability' and 'stewardship' have been showing up in the journals more and more frequently. These terms are excellent ones for they tend to focus attention on assigning responsibilities for accomplishing objectives, recording facts and judgments relative to the achievement of objectives, and preparing progress reports to those who have a worthy stake in the accomplishment of the stewards. It is equally important to understand clearly what magic these words cannot perform. 'Stewardship' implies responsibility, but it implies nothing as to the nature of the responsibilities or what form the reports should take. 'Accountability' too has pleasant connotations — at least to accountants — but the label does not answer the questions: Accountability to whom? Or accountability for what? A discussion of these words is included because they may be useful in setting up a framework for a discussion of reporting and disclosure, and because — on the negative side — they are sometimes utilized by certain current writers to defend the

---

* Additional comments with regard to comparative strength of various types of disclosure are given in Essay Ten: Accounting — A System of Measurement Rules.

[1] The relativist approach is not above criticism. Even a relativist must accept the existence of such entities as objectives, individuals to judge, criteria for ordering, etc. The chief advantage of a pragmatic approach is that arguments usually are not decided on irrelevant grounds. For example, cost or market should not be rejected because it is inconsistent with some vague unimportant goal but should be judged on its ability or inability to accomplish its objectives; depreciation for hospitals cannot be defended by showing that depreciation is useful in a shoe repair shop. The search for generality and universal applications is commendable, but uniformity of this kind is only *one* objective. Uniformity is an *important* objective when comparisons are to be made and where ease of learning or understanding is important.

doctrine of original cost. Consider now the possibilities for using stewardship and accountability as defenses for reporting on the basis of original cost.

The reader may wish to speculate on the possible forms of reports and types of disclosure if the accountabilities are in the nature of progress reports for the following commissions. Convert to cash as soon as possible without regard to loss. Leave a stronger concern than was given to you. Become the dominant concern. Drive competitors out of business. Lap the course at more than 200 miles per hour. (Perhaps the most famous example of unadulterated ambiguity in our culture is given in the parable of talents. Our sympathies may be with those who guessed wrong.) Accountants are asked to disclose progress toward all sorts of objectives, but usually the goals are stipulated.

Even a quick look at these charges indicates that original cost is not implied by any of the above commissions, and we conclude that such an inference is valid only when the responsibilities themselves are expressed in terms of original cost. The charge to preserve the assets (furniture storage, wine stewards, goldsmiths) can be accounted for in terms of physical units of wine, jewels, chairs, etc. The charge to increase the assets may be accounted for in terms of increase in the physical units, and, if a common denominator is needed, current values *may* be more useful than some scale based on original or aboriginal cost.

It should be clear that our problem is related to objectives in such a way that the extent of the disclosure, the content of the disclosure and the recipients of the disclosure cannot be determined until social objectives have been selected. Unfortunately in a mixed economy the objectives are sometimes not clear, and those who have legitimate interests in the results have widely diversified interests. The unmodified profit motive – while still dominant – is supplemented by a myriad of motives, nonprofit considerations, and threads of public control. One of the interesting historical developments of the past 100 years or so is the tremendous increase in the number of people who have a stake in the development of business and government enterprises and who are now important enough to support demands for information. Only remnants of the frontier remain, so that the welfare and activities of countless business enterprises are of direct concern to all. Consumers in addition to owners and creditors are therefore interested in the output of accounting and other business information services. Seniority and union rights have tended to increase the identification of workers with specific firms and industries, and their welfare is directly related to the welfare of their organizations. The public is now conditioned to limitations on the privileges that go along with private ownership of property and insists that public agencies regulate, tax, and otherwise police economic activity. Such activities obviously require information reports, and it does not follow that all require identical information. With the tremendous increase in types of creditor and ownership relationships and widely diversified decision requirements, reporting to owners is not always as simple as nonaccountants might assume.

Not only are the groups interested in economic activity now more numerous, but their relative bargaining strength in the market for information changes quickly and drastically. Within the lifetime of most professors textbook emphasis has shifted from the viewpoint of bankers and credit men, to stewardship reports appropriate for absentee owners and then in turn, to a more direct relation to the needs of internal management. Those who teach and practice accounting have awakened to the obvious fact that managers make decisions and that these decisions are sometimes aided by records of past events and by a systematic combination of such facts with future expectations. Accountants have also discovered that labor leaders also need information, and perhaps our current managerial accounting textbooks will be replaced with even more modern laboristic accounting texts whose authors solemnly assert that the needs of labor are now dominant. In a speci-fied environment and at a particular stage of historical development it must be possible to sense the needs of various groups and develop an information service appropriate for these needs. It may be desirable for courses and textbooks to specialize and stress infor-mation most often used by even more diverse groups. But in addition the profession must have devices for appraising the changes taking place and for integrating the shifting infor-mational demands into a reasonably stable structure. The problem is complicated further by changes in the technology for data processing.

We now turn to the question of who in our society makes decisions about disclosure. Potential embezzlers are certainly interested in any deficiencies that might exist in the de-vices for internal control. Others might appreciate and be willing to pay for information about combinations for the various safes, the whereabouts of the checkwriters, the kinds of locks on the warehouse doors, those employees who are least loyal to the organization and therefore easiest to bribe. Some stock manipulators would no doubt relish and en-courage the presentation of erroneous reports to stockholders, potential stockholders, and others.

A recent study by Alan Cerf, of the University of California, indicated that public ac-countants tend to feel that the responsibility for disclosure rests primarily on manage-ment.[2] Perhaps by implication opinions on managements' representations exclude the need for further opinion as to whether sufficient information is given! To adopt such an irresponsible attitude is to invite trouble for the accounting profession. (Traditionally, of course, some provision for the scope of the opinion is implied by the *custom* of including both an income report and a financial status report.) It is the contention of this paper that society has placed far too much third-party responsibility on the public accounting profes-sion to be discharged in such a slipshod manner by what amounts to implicit definition of the scope of the opinion.[3]

The reasons for not permitting management to decide what information must be dis-closed are precisely those reasons why public accounting itself came into existence. The general feeling that outsiders such as creditors, insurance firms, owners and others have enough stake in the future of a business to request dependable information prepared by those without direct interest in the information itself is, of course, the attitude that led originally to the profession of public accounting. It was recognized that those who man-age businesses are among those most strongly motivated by the acquisitive instinct and may therefore be tempted to color the statements. The development of a professional group whose members are able to appraise the needs of outside groups, to rank these needs according to some scale of worthiness set forth by the customs and laws of the pre-vailing social order, and to report without coloration was probably inevitable. Neverthe-less, there has been considerable evidence that lawmakers and others who represent the general desires of society have been impatient with the rate of growth of a professional at-titude among accountants. Prescribed systems of accounts and reports go back well be-yond 1907. Unlike its British cousins the Internal Revenue Service still finds it desirable to employ its own accountants, and the Securities Act and Securities Exchange Act represent

---

[2] Alan Cerf, unpublished research at the University of California, Berkeley. See also Cerf, "A Study of Compliance with Reporting Standards," *The Journal of Accountancy,* February, 1963, pp. 42-50.

[3] Even the implications of changes in the names of statements may be important. The neutral 'balance sheet' apparently makes few if any implied representations other than the statement is a sheet and sometimes balances. The title 'statement of financial condition' may make some implied representations that our present reports do not begin to fulfill.

perhaps the most dramatic vote of nonconfidence ever given to the accounting profession. New laws usually arise because there is dissatisfaction with the *status quo*. The dissatisfaction with corporate reporting must have been great indeed.[4]

It may be less irritating to interpret such regulatory legislation as an aid for a struggling profession which at the time is too weak to impose its will on businessmen and make its orders stick. At any rate, it seems clear that certified public accountants are employed by society for the specific purpose of ensuring reliable and adequate stewardship reports. What shall be disclosed is *not* a decision that is best left for those who directly stand to gain or lose by suppressing information or giving misinformation. Certified public accountants, as a profession, must insist that disclosures be made. If they react to social desires too slowly, their profession will be aided (coerced) by legislation and other sanctions, or what is far worse, the profession may cease to be considered an independent profession and be abandoned as a group of special-interest pleaders (advocates) for the insiders. In the latter event, a new group — perhaps with government direction and control — will arise and will assume the function of independence that society feels is vital for its operation.

It is comforting to hold that the laws and other coercive devices are put there directly to force management to report correctly. Unfortunately this interpretation leads to difficulties, for it leaves little or no place for a profession of public accounting. This interpretation implies that someone must insist that managers conform to the requirements for reporting. This someone *could* be a public accountant, but he *could* just as well be a clerk in a government agency. We have experienced this kind of operation in some regulated industries, and accountants are not alone in disliking what they experienced. It must be concluded therefore that the public accounting profession has the direct responsibility for insisting on disclosure of material information. It must be concluded also that the profession insists on matters determined to a large extent by the political leaders and social subcultures. Yet as an independent profession, accountants have further responsibilities. Accountants are in a position to know the difficulties in measuring and reporting business data and judgments. It follows that the profession can perform an important service by explaining to the lawmakers and social leaders in a relatively unbiased manner the problems involved in requiring certain types of disclosures. In a similar fashion the profession can be of direct service to managers by explaining the necessity for disclosure and the importance of disclosure to those who are responsible for the overall operation of the economic system. Thus, the profession takes on an important educational program in both directions, and it is desirable that educational programs be undertaken in the environment of an independent, relatively unbiased profession. Certainly an independent institution that influences people to understand is superior to one that resorts to direct force and coercion.

The problems of disclosure are closely related to problems of communication generally. Communication channels themselves tend to become stabilized so that interested parties often get their information from the same sources in terms of the same cues and

---

[4] There is evidence of dissatisfaction with the inflexibility of many other professions — perhaps all professions. Dissatisfaction may of course be reflected without new legislation and regulatory commissions. When a group or institution no longer satisfies its objectives, new institutions tend to arise. Certainly the fact that operations research workers are so numerous and prominent in business may be interpreted as evidence of some dissatisfaction with the products of cost accounting and industrial engineering. There are numerous specific instances such as the steel executive who found it easier to start a new cost-analysis division than to reeducate his hidebound cost-accounting department.

symbols and with the same bias or slant. It is widely known that information going to those above (with some degree of dominion) tends to be slanted toward the interests of those reporting. Unless alternative channels are available so that misinformation will be discovered more or less automatically by those above, there will be a tendency to suppress unfavorable facts and judgments, to lie a little. Thus accountants must be aware of the probability of slanted reports and the for-interest, against-interest direction of the probable slanting. Management reports to their superiors — owners, creditors, regulatory agencies — may have a considerably different "stress" from those addressed to lower levels of management and nonmanagement groups. Moreover, the slanting may vary from time to time to correlate with changes in desired reactions from those above. Occasionally the reactions tend to conflict, e.g., higher desired reported earnings to indicate effective administration combined with the desire for lower earnings to lessen pressure for dividends, wage increases and taxes.

Slanting is made possible by the varying shades of meaning commonly attached to language symbols and by the abstraction process in selecting the facts — the consequences of accounting events. The following remarks apply also to the auditing function.

> . . . the recipient of a communication is severely limited in his ability to judge its correctness. Although there may be various tests of apparent validity, internal consistency, and consistency with other communications, the recipient must, by and large, repose his confidence in the editing process that has taken place, and, if he accepts the communication at all, accept it pretty much as it stands. To the extent that he can interpret it, his interpretation must be based primarily on his confidence in the source and his knowledge of the biases to which the source is subject, rather than on a direct examination of the evidence.[5]

The entire process of communication is a process of abstraction, and selection processes usually have been applied at many points before reports reach their destination. It is this feature that permits broad views that otherwise could not be comprehended, but it is precisely this feature that makes slanting feasible and difficult to detect.[6]

The usual problems of abstraction and slanting are difficult enough, but matters are complicated further by the presence of noisy channels of communication. Noise (random disturbances) is the result of contamination from all sorts of interferences and constraints that lead to uncertainty about what the message intends to convey. The results are equivocal. It has been estimated, for example, that the English language is as much as 50 percent redundant, and Brunswik has pointed out that proper coding might save one-half the effort now required if we were assured of noiseless channels, but he concludes that some redundancy is necessary to help overcome some of the effects of unavoidable noise.[7]

---

[5] James G. March and Herbert A. Simon, *Organizations* (New York: John Wiley & Sons, Inc., 1958), p. 165. These writers also emphasize the limitations of the language so that some concepts can be communicated with great difficulty. Psychologists have long been aware of the tendency for messages to take on added connotations and overtones as they go down the line of authority. They tend to have reduced overtones as they go up the line.

[6] Our knowledge of the world turns out to be a construct formed by selective experiences. Facts are thus reports of experiences that are subject to empirical verification. Simon and March emphasize the probable increase in confidence (relative to clues) as abstraction increases, but use evidence in a strange manner. "Uncertainty absorption takes place when inferences are drawn from a body of evidence and the inferences, instead of the evidence itself [*sic*], are then communicated." *Ibid.*, p. 165.

[7] Egon Brunswik, "The Conceptual Framework of Psychology," *International Encyclopedia of Unified Science* (Chicago: University of Chicago Press, 1955), p. 750. Brunswik relates psychological reactions to noisy

Footnote continued on next page

Accountants are subject to a certain amount of fuzziness in making their interpretations of events, in evaluating the magnitude of resulting changes, in translating the interpretations into symbols (language) and in condensing and transmitting the reports. The
transmission channels introduce further interference. Yet a major source of trouble still
remains: the reactions of those who decode the communication, interpret the results in
terms of objectives, and incorporate them in their decision-making processes. While positivists, and perhaps others, have been cautious about the lack of precision and the psychological implications of the term 'meaning,' it is clear that accountants must meet the
problem squarely. In fact, the purpose of communication is oriented toward the user, and
its effectiveness is measured (at least in part) by its ability to evoke desirable responses.
Accounting argument therefore must begin with the objectives and proceed backward. An
important intermediate step is, of course, to explore the possibilities for educating the receivers — teaching them to decode and interpret the message more effectively. Unfortunately we have only begun to enumerate needs and specify users. The finer points must
wait until more groundwork is completed.

Some preliminary groundwork has been done, sponsored by The Controllership Foundation. Simon, Kozmetsky and Tyndall have attempted to classify the uses to which accounting data are put. They isolate: (a) problem-solving questions which ask which course
of action is appropriate to attain objectives, (b) attention-getting questions which bom-
bard the user with information that suggests which problems should be investigated, and
(c) score-card questions which indicate extent of goal accomplishment.[8] March and Simon
have suggested the possibility of substituting "coordination by plan for coordination by
feedback."[9] Accountants have given some attention to this important aspect of their
work. Some bumbling distinctions have been made between planning and control (A poor
opposition!), but a serious attempt has been made to integrate budget plans with historical records and to report exceptions to the plan. In fact, this is the basis for variance reporting in standard costing. Additional work may be done in the area of automatic responses to variance feedback, and almost no work has been done with the possibilities of
integrating plans with feedback at the level of reporting to investors and owners. Perhaps
management should report its budget expectations and deviations to owners. Scattered
clues, such as unfilled orders and union demands, could be replaced with summary budget
estimates. Economists have long made a sharp distinction between planned income and
windfall profit, and have argued that only plans can be conduct-determining. Clearly reported windfalls (favorable and unfavorable) are integrated into future plans. Thus we
might argue that it is only the feedback of *deviations* from plans that leads to new strate-

---

communication channels. " . . . perceptual cues and behavioral means are like 'signals' in 'coded messages.' The
perceived objects and behavioral results which correspond to the message are mediated through 'noisy channels.'
These latter are contaminated with interferences or constraints of their own . . . the crux of organismic adjustment obviously lies in the fact that distal perceptual and behavioral mediation must by the nature of things . . .
rely on overloaded channels, with the ensuing limited dependability." *Ibid.*, pp. 748-749.

[8] Herbert A. Simon, Harold Guetzkow, George Kozmetsky and Gordon Tyndall, *Centralization vs. Decentralization in Organizing the Controller's Department* (New York: The Controllership Foundation, 1954), p. 3 *et
passem*. Simon and March have prepared a more general list:

"1. Communication for nonprogrammed activity . . . .
2. Communication to initiate and establish programs, including day-to-day adjustment . . . of programs.
3. Communication to provide data . . . required for the execution of programs.
4. Communication to evoke programs (i.e. communication that serve as 'stimuli').
5. Communication to provide information on the results of activities." *Op. cit.*, p. 161.

[9] *Op. cit.*, p. 162.

gies and is conduct-determining. One might compare the original plans (as part of the environment) to sunk costs and argue that it is only the feedback of exceptions that leads to interesting, nonprogrammed, nonroutine actions.

The interesting part of the above discussion is that accountants have been doing precisely what their critics contend should be done. Accountants do measure progress toward objectives, compare progress with plans, and report variations to those with authority to amend plans or to force compliance. Our feedback of variances may be too slow and our scope may be too narrow, but even here a start has been made. A slight extension of governmental accounting techniques would provide for variations in sales volume and sales prices from plans, and incorporate a full retinue of variances in the accounts and in published reports. (Profit-charts may provide an intermediate step without bringing about a serious break with tradition.) Some accountants now present such reports, and a more general expansion to include plans, accomplishment, and major deviations is a relatively minor technical job. The added disclosure can hardly avoid leading to major improvement.

At the practical level accountants have devised some techniques to vary intensity of disclosure. The reporting field is divided into a core of information that has wide application and general usefulness and a periphery of information that is needed only occasionally. Core information is collected and reported as the routine output of the accounting system. Other information is collected and reported on an intermittent basis as the specific needs arise. Not enough study has been devoted to this problem of classification, and many misunderstandings have arisen. Interest on investment (normal return), for example, may be included as a systematic expense, but most accountants prefer to treat the comparison of normal and actual as a special study. Incremental costs from a shifting environmental baseline may be incorporated in the routine accounts and reports, but most accountants have preferred to smooth irregular costs and compute unit costs from a zero base with incremental costs prepared as supplementary reports. (Advocates of direct costing wish to reverse the process by showing product costs on a marginal basis and full costs on an intermittent basis.)

A slightly refined approach makes use of a more detailed classification in the form of "layers of urgency." There is of course no fundamental basis for distinguishing layers, and a substitution involving levels of authority has sometimes been made. A general rule that calls for reporting at each level only those items that are controllable at or below the level is commonly used. In addition accountants must "read the water" of information needs for outside groups. For investors, net income figures are considered to be more urgent than individual expense items. Percentages are rated below amounts. Current assets and obligations are given dominant positions.

The use of supplementary devices for disclosure permits a fairly rigid, uniform system of reporting with the obvious advantages of uniformity. Uniform systems and reports have a social advantage due to the ease and simplicity of operating and interpreting them. Such advantages permit the application of rigid rules that can be learned by personnel with fairly low-level intellects, and if for some reason it is necessary to change personnel, the use of uniform procedures involves less social cost for training and from wrong decisions based on misinformation. Investors and members of the Securities and Exchange Commission are well aware of the difficulties of comparing reports for different organizations. The advantages of uniformity are manifest, but the solution is not necessarily an enforced uniformity or the inflexibility of an accounting court.

The chief advantage of supplementary disclosures is that they preserve uniformity in a large segment of the field yet provide some degree of flexibility. The savings in social cost is in the form of better decisions with less error in the allocating and combining of resources. The question of disclosure is unavoidably mixed up with the cost of getting and measuring information, for disclosure costs are normally important.

A part of the cost of failure to disclose useful information takes the form of loss of confidence in the information-control system and a downgrading of its output. The problem of cost is also complicated by the needs and desires of various groups interested in the organization. It may be of benefit to the insiders to give no reports or to give false or misleading reports to outsiders. It is also clear that not all information needed by each level of internal management is useful enough to merit disclosure to widely scattered creditors and stockholders. Some disclosures may be a disservice to one group and a service to others — a transfer of benefit. Other disclosures can be expected to improve the performance of several or all groups. Disclosure of failures of the internal control system and the flow of resources to nonorganizational ends is a transfer of benefit to owners, taxing authorities, etc., and a disservice to those who are misappropriating resources. Information to the wrong levels of authority or a general excess of information can do more harm than good by adding to the confusion and mixing lines of authority. A similar issue arises when there is a possibility of giving too strong a disclosure (relatively) than the information merits. The cost of showing relatively insignificant data in a dominant position is due in part to the necessity for showing more important information in an inferior position where it can be overlooked or misinterpreted.

Some Current Sore Spots

Investors are interested primarily in future fund flows, and disclosure is or is not important to the degree that it is helpful for judging future prospects for funds. The output of several types of information services is available to investors and among them are those offered by the accounting profession. In a sense the results of accounting operations are concerned largely but not exclusively with past results. In this aspect accounting reports are similar to those found in the *Racing Form*, batting and earned-run averages, football scores and other compilations of past performances. While such reports may have some value as mementoes and for inclusion in a scrapbook, their primary value is for predicting the future, and their usefulness must be judged from this direction. Any standard of good disclosure, therefore, must be related to an index of usefulness for future decision.

For the purposes of the present discussion, current sore spots are divided into the following groups:

1. Those that result from asset definitions.
2. Those that result from poor matching of costs with revenues — or valuation.
3. Those that result from realization problems — liquidity problems.
4. Those that result from definition of liabilities.
5. Those related to stockholders' interests.
6. Those that result from failure to report future policies and intentions — problems of the outlook.

Let us turn now to some of the more obvious problems that stem from asset definitions. First, accountants have failed to assign asset values to some extremely valuable considerations. The difficulty is compounded in many cases by a stubborn attachment for valuation at original cost, in the face of overwhelming evidence that such costs are hopelessly out of touch with any valuations or sacrifices that might have relevance to current decisions. Consider the problem of oil reserves. Are they important? If so, to whom? How can disclosure be given? Is extraction expensive and difficult? Extraction may be expensive or inexpensive and the most obvious and direct disclosure is to present the estimated value of reserves. Can a footnote that gives the amount of reserves in physical units without giving expected cost of extraction be adequate? Should the fact that the concern is reducing its reported profit by purchasing crude for its refineries instead of using its own low-cost reserves be disclosed? Should shifts in the mixture of purchased and owned crude be noted? If accounting statements are to be taken seriously, a strong affirmative answer is required.

What shall we do about a particularly brilliant president who may be expected to stay with us for several years and yield an economic rent far in excess of his salary? What about the good morale of the working force? An outstanding and underpaid sales manager? The senility of officers in rival concerns?

It may be argued that these valuable considerations will be reflected ultimately in the income reports. Indeed they will, and so will the benefits from buildings, machines, inventories and many other things that are called assets. But how long must the reader wait? And how long will these benefits persist? At least he can check building depreciation and replacement from the reports and reach some tentative decisions, but how is he to appraise the expected life of contributions that accountants refuse to admit as assets or even report? What then do figures on interim balance sheets mean? What is their purpose?

An interesting current example of our difficulties in asset definition arises in connection with a net operating loss carryover. Should one treat the carryover as an asset and reduce the reported loss by approximately one-half? Is the right to make the carryover valuable? Is it probable? We cannot be positive that the firm can use the benefit, but one can never be certain of any expected benefit. To delay recognition until accountants are certain is a universal argument for doing nothing.

Further difficulties in reporting stem from failure to match costs with revenues in proportion to benefits received and to be received. In part this difficulty is due to our failure to estimate the future correctly — a failing that is not peculiar to the accounting profession — but in part it is due to a resigned and hopeless attitude combined with pressure for immediate short-term tax savings. Currently this problem is at its worst in the area of research costs. The difficulty is well illustrated by many business games that have been so popular in American universities. Team A spends relatively large sums on research and development, and the game charges such expenditures against revenues so that past reported profits are relatively poor. Team B, on the other hand, authorizes meager research expenditures, especially during the later years of play. Profits were relatively high. At the end of the game a controversy arises: Who has won? The team with the better reported profits had the poorer prospects, and the team with the poorer past record had the better prospects. The analyst who attempted to judge the future from accounting records of the past and the latest balance sheets is sadly misled. A part of the strategy of the game is to anticipate peculiarities in the reporting service! We must do better!

In a competitive environment a certain amount of fruitful research must be carried on more or less continuously in order to keep abreast of competition, maintain a suitable environment, and permit the firm to operate with a chance for profits, and thereby justify the going concern values attributed to other assets. For this reason and because of the recurring nature of such expenditures, accountants have tended to expense these expenditures immediately as ordinary revenue charges necessary to maintain a competitive organization and protect the investment. This approach is clearly related to the replacement method of depreciation, and represents a workable set of expiration rules if such expenditures are relatively small. In many of the growth industries of today, disbursements for research are so large that a more careful appraisal of the expected benefits must be undertaken. Undoubtedly many such firms possess valuable layers of hidden fat that are not indicated on the statements of financial condition. The problem is difficult, without question, but there is no excuse for the widespread uncritical attitude toward such important items as patents, trademarks, copyrights, secret formulas and other fruits of successful research.

The depreciation problem offers similar difficulties. As a standard we usually accept the writeoff of cost in proportion to benefits expired to total benefits expected. Under stresses resulting from high tax rates, fear of the allowed and allowable provisions, desire to show immediate tax saving to clients, a general heritage of conservatism, and perhaps for selfish reasons accountants have sometimes permitted the carrying of substantial service potential without corresponding value on the statements of financial condition. There may be ameliorating factors, however, that result from increases in replacement costs and, until recently, a stubborn adherence to straightline even though many assets yield larger services in early years. A generally conservative attitude is certainly understandable, for it is especially humiliating to the profession to have well-reported clients turn up in bankruptcy courts.

In summary, the reader of financial statements may search earnestly and long for answers to questions such as these: How long will the *low original cost* depreciation continue to effect future profits before higher replacement depreciation catches up? How much of the reported past profits is due to low original-cost depreciation? How much valuable existing property has already been written off against past revenues? How much longer can basic patents be expected to operate? To what extent have original cost figures lost all contact with current values? The future may indeed be so obscure that little improvement in disclosure of such matters may be expected. This paper asks only that the accounting profession reconsider its procedures and attitudes with the care the problems so clearly deserve.

Further disclosure problems have resulted from rigid adherence to the concept of realization and original cost. Realization is often connected with the problem of evidence. In fact, realization is so intimately connected with evidence, and evidence in turn is so intimately connected with sale that many accountants identify realization with the sales event. Traditionally accountants have been concerned with problems of liquidity and working capital management. With the support of banking groups, they have built into their definition of income not only the requirement for value increases but also the requirement that such increases be in liquid form. There is of course considerable disagreement about the merits of these liquidity requirements, but if they are adopted and if we insist on carrying assets at original cost until realized, it is clear that a strong force is at work during a period of rising prices to bring about asset figures that are vastly undervalued. Fortunately there is an effective method of disclosure available in the form of appraisal techniques. Such techniques permit asset figures that are in line with current valuations without violating the liquidity requirements for income recognition. Moreover, the appraisal device has wide applications that have not been fully exploited. (The most obvious extension is to inventories on the LIFO basis.) A manager who treats an asset as a free good because it has been completely depreciated and combines it with other productive agents without regard to its current value squanders society's resources and is a poor manager indeed. There is no social requirement to *give away* excess value after the investment has been recovered.

The accountant's approach to income has deficiencies other than those arising from liquidity considerations. Accountants have identified a number of uses for reported income that include: guide to withdrawals, help in allocating resources, indicator of management's ability to estimate future conditions and combine factors effectively. Nevertheless accountants have not faced up to some elementary problems of periodic reporting. For example, should quarterly income reports be a reflection of what can be expected for the year? If so, should *yearly* income reports be smoothed and measured to provide an indicant of future years' prospects? Is a period's reported income a measure of the value added by shrewd decisions during the interval? How can the profession recognize the value added by able management period by period and still have the statements reflect long-run prospects? In other words, how much smoothing is desirable? With regard to these questions the profession's disclosure is obviously weak.

Important disclosure problems may also arise because of the traditional definition of liability. The usual definition of liability is in terms of legal obligation. Any dark clouds that have not jelled into legal debts are considered to be contingent liabilities, and the methods of disclosing contingent liabilities leave everything to be desired. They are atrocious! Some accountants have suggested that the definition of liability be broadened to include expected demand on funds. This proposal has merit in that it should remind us to examine *expected* black clouds and recognize them, but it has the obvious disadvantage of mixing all kinds of adverse expectations in the same classification with more stable obligations. What if the probability is ten to one that the firm wins a lawsuit and has no obligation? Would disclosure rules be different if the probabilities were reversed? Accountants are faced with the problem of how to disclose possible adverse events with all kinds of probabilities. The problem is further complicated because there is not only difficulty with the probability itself, but the amount of the settlement is usually not known and must be estimated. Perhaps Bayesian statistics and expected values may prove to be helpful, but accountants have shown little disposition to use these concepts to define and measure either assets or liabilities. (Incidentally, at one time accountants considered reserves for depreciation to be expected demands in funds for going concerns and therefore classified them as liabilities.)

Retained earnings restrictions inherited the antagonisms that were formerly directed at surplus reserves in general. All reserves, and especially the reserve for contingencies, have some genuine advantages as a disclosure device. They afford management an opportunity to warn outside parties of the possibility of unfavorable events without implying that the amounts shown are accurate or the events certain.

The Cerf study was designed to find out what additional information *investors* desire. The following were mentioned with some frequency, and it is interesting to note that with one or two exceptions disclosure of these items should not be difficult.

1. Disclosure of capital expenditures and expansion plans.
2. Information for fixed-variable cost breakdown.
3. General information on labor contracts and outlook.
4. Basis of consolidation of affiliated concerns.
5. Economic outlook and industry trends.
6. Tax clearances and general situation.
7. Expenditures and attitude on research and development.
8. Sales breakdowns and production prospects.

9. Information on reserves.
10. Directors and their affiliations.
11. Proven reserves.
12. Depreciation methods.
13. Inventory — not just LIFO, but *when* did the firm adopt LIFO.
14. Extent of tax allocation.
15. Marketable securities at cost, market, or market after tax?

An interesting sidelight of the Cerf study from a previous study by Horngren[10] is that only 25 of 200 investments experts considered price-level adjustments important enough to require even pencil adjustments in the margins. Horngren speculated that this lack of interest is due to their disposition to consider recovered depreciation as current funds more or less independent of replacement decisions. Perhaps analysts make allowances for such changes in other ways. Perhaps they need education. Perhaps university professors have been making a big fuss over a relatively unimportant problem.

---

[10] Charles T. Horngren, "Security Analysts and the Price Level," *The Accounting Review*, October, 1955, pp. 575-581. This is an interesting report on research in information needs.

Essay Ten

Accounting —
A System of Measurement Rules

"Written numeration is probably as old as private property. There is little doubt that it originated in man's desire to keep a record of his flocks and other goods."[1] In recent years it has been fashionable to identify the whole of accounting with measurement and to insist that accounting is a subdivision of the total field of measurement. This chapter contains comments on this view and contains also some general remarks on measurement and its meaning in the broader field of scientific method.

Accounting, as now constituted and practiced, is composed of a group of behavioral hypotheses, techniques for appraising and ranking need, and rules for classifying and measuring that are oriented toward fulfilling the responsibilities and objectives of the profession. The first task is, of course, to determine the needs to be filled. This task requires estimates of objectives, decisions, and information necessary for these needs. Once these preliminary tasks have been taken care of accounting leans heavily on the field of classification and measurement. This chapter then contains an elementary discussion of some classification and measurement aspects of the accounting profession.

Measurement in accounting is directed at achievement of objectives and is therefore a purposive series of operations and conventions. Thus the tests of effective measurement are the tests employed by instrumentalists everywhere — the degree to which it satisfies the objectives compared with the sacrifice (cost) of attaining the satisfaction. The first task in appraising the measurement processes and rules is therefore identifying and weighing objectives and fitting the measurement rules to the resulting needs.[2]

In part the eagerness of accountants to attach themselves to those who measure may be due to the esteem with which measurement is held in our scientifically-oriented society. Accountants, and it seems practically everybody else, have been fond of quoting over and over the alleged statement by Lord Kelvin that knowledge of nonmeasurable facts and relationships is in effect sheer ignorance. The benefits of measurement seem to be self-evident, for they include the advantages to be derived from a large part of mathematics, but

---

[1] Tobias Dantzig, *Number, The Language of Science*, 4th ed. (New York: The Macmillan Company, 1956), pp. 20-21. The importance of measurement can hardly be overestimated. Alfred North Whitehead states: ". . . Aristotle by his Logic throws the emphasis on classification. The popularity of Aristotelian Logic retarded the advance of physical science throughout the Middle Ages. If only the schoolmen had measured instead of classifying . . . ." *Science and the Modern World* (New York: The Macmillan Company, 1925), p. 41. (Mentor ed., p. 33.)

[2] This view is in harmony with that expressed by Russell L. Ackoff in *The Design of Social Research* (Chicago: University of Chicago Press, 1953), pp. 69-70. ". . . scientific quantification is a way of assigning numbers to properties, objects, and events so as to yield useful information . . . . Thus 'efficiency in use' is the key to scientific quantification . . . . Ideally the decision to qualify or quantify, and how to quantify or qualify, should be based on a systematic comparison of costs." The view expressed is opposed to that of William J. Vatter, "Contributions of Accounting to Measurement in Management," *Management Science*, October, 1958. "The central problem in any measurement process is the selection of the measuring unit," p. 28. In most cases the selection of the unit is conventional and of minor importance.

a substantial portion of modern mathematics (e.g., topology, axiomatic systems) need not utilize measurement in the traditonal sense, a development that has led Russell to comment:

> . . . the laws of macroscopic physics are topological laws, and . . . the introduction of number through coordinates is only a practical convenience, the laws being such as can, in theory, be expressed without the use of number. The old view that measurement is of the essence of science would therefore seem to be erroneous.[3]

The rigor necessary to identify and bound problems so that they may be subjected to the rules of measurement may have a vitalizing and healthful effect on a profession. Accounting is composed of numerous measurement rules (both implicit and explicit), but unfortunately the applicability of the rules to varying needs has received far too little study and intellectual effort. Let us turn to the operations necessary to carry on measurement and to a brief discussion of some of the more obvious accounting measurement rules.

A discussion of the nature of measurement begins with the ability to discriminate the rules for determining membership or nonmembership of a class (qualitative classification), and moves to the things that have to be done to establish a one-one correlation of the classes with some subset of the real number system (scaling).

In the simplest terms: "Measurement is the general procedure of assigning numbers to the properties of objects."[4] The most primitive operation necessary for classification or indeed for modern scientific method is the operation necessary for discrimination, i.e., finding whether or not a particular object or property does or does not belong to a specified set. This primitive operation requires the subject to be able to distinguish the required property from all other types of properties and to be able to reach a decision as to whether or not the property is present. In a slightly less primitive form, the subject finds it necessary to pass judgment on similarity in the sense that the properties of two sets can be matched as to their presence or absence and, even less primitively, put in a one-to-one correlation with one another and remainders noted.[5]

So far we have not considered what is necessary for inclusion as a member of the class 'property.' The definition of Lenzen is clear: "The properties of things are modes of reaction to conditions that are subject to experimental control."[6] It is obvious that we can-

---

[3]Bertrand Russell, "On the Importance of Logical Form," *International Encyclopedia of Unified Science* (Chicago: University of Chicago Press, 1955), p. 41. A similar view is expressed by William J. Goode and Paul K. Hatt " . . . the most 'qualitative' of social research attempts rough *measurement* . . . the increasing use of statistics is not the distinguishing feature of modern social research. Rather, it is the increasing precision and reliability of research techniques, and higher standards of proof . . . " *Methods in Social Research* (New York: McGraw-Hill Book Company, Inc., 1952), p. 314.

[4] Victor F. Lenzen, "Procedures of Empirical Science," *International Encyclopedia of Unified Science, op. cit.*, p. 289. Essentially the same definition is given by S. S. Stevens: " . . . measurement . . . is . . . the assignment of numerals to objects or events according to rules." "On the Theory of Scales of Measurement," *Science*, June 7, 1946, p. 677. Bertrand Russell defines it as follows: "Measurement of magnitudes is, in its most general sense, any method by which a unique and reciprocal correspondence is established between all or some of the magnitudes of a kind and all or some of the numbers . . ." *The Principles of Mathematics* (New York: W. W. Norton & Company, Inc., 1938), p. 176.

[5] It is interesting to note that some textbooks on modern mathematics require only that a set be subject to unambiguous methods for determining inclusion or exclusion. Many exercises then are of the type: "Do the redheaded male residents of Chicago form a class?" Presumably the problem is to find whether or not the rule for inclusion is unambiguous. These exercises may be useful but, unfortunately, they are not mathematics. These problems require further rules of correspondence for determining empirically (in fact) who is or is not to be included. Psychology, scientific method, physics of optics, legal definitions of 'resident,' and all kinds of nonmathematical considerations are necessary to answer this question.

[6] Victor F. Lenzen, *op. cit.*, p. 283.

not observe and manipulate the whole of experience, and that science must isolate in some way the area under consideration — isolate the conditions that can be used in hypotheses and controlled for experiment. Torgerson makes use of the term 'systems' to indicate a collection of properties.

> Whenever we define or denote a property, it always seems to be a property *of* something. For this something, we use the term *system*. Thus, properties . . . occur as aspects or characteristics of systems. To make the circle complete, we might define a particular system as roughly that which possesses such and so properties.[7]

With Torgerson's expressed belief that there is a distinction between a system and a property, it is difficult for him to agree with the Stevens approach to measurement as rules for assigning numbers to events or objects. His statement therefore is extremely critical.

> Stevens' definition . . . does not mention property. For him, if numerals are assigned to objects according to rules (presumably any rules), we have measurement. And apparently it is the object that is measured and not . . . a property of the object . . . . According to this view, we have measured or scaled a stick, though only at a primitive, nominal level, when we determine that that particular stick is a "two." Thus, for this approach, classification, and even naming of individual instances, becomes a kind of measurement.[8]

Stevens would insist that the assignment of numbers to football players is a kind of measurement — a nominal measurement. The usual rules that try to identify players and their positions by blocks of numbers clearly constitute nominal measurements, but presumably if letters were used to accomplish the same ends we would not have measurement. Thus numbered accounts would result in measurement while mnemonic or lettered accounts would not qualify.[9]

While it may seem that there is much ado about nothing in this area, there are several reasons why we may wish to adopt the approach to measurement that Stevens recommends. Certainly the distinction between qualitative and quantitative tends to diminish. It has already been pointed out that modern mathematics is becoming less and less concerned with the usual quantitative aspects of numbers and more concerned with ordering and relating. Thus it no longer is true that a branch of empirical learning must be directly related to numbers in order to enlist help from the field of rigorous mathematics. For example, functional relations no longer need be related to number, and even the familiar greater-than, less-than may sometimes be replaced by other relations such as dominance, ancestor of, etc.

Most accountants will probably agree that the assignment of numbers to identify classes is a trivial distinction to be used as the defining characteristic of measurement, but

---

[7] Warren S. Torgerson, *Theory and Methods of Scaling* (New York: John Wiley and Sons, Inc., 1958), p. 9. The admitted circularity is, of course, completely unnecessary, and results in part from Torgerson's approach to the definition of property. "Properties are essentially the observable aspects or characteristics of the empirical world" (p. 9). He is emphatic in pointing out that a book is a system construct while weight and thickness are property constructs. Carnap takes a somewhat different view and feels that the distinction should be made according to the type of predicate involved. "A one-place predicate designates a property. (E.g. 'Book' designates the property of being a book; 'Blue' designates the colour blue, a property of certain things.) We shall call this property the *intension* of the predicate." Rudolf Carnap, *Introduction to Symbolic Logic and Its Applications* (New York: Dover Publications, Inc., 1958), p. 40.

[8] Warren S. Torgerson, *op. cit.*, p. 14.

[9] Torgerson is unrelenting: "His [Stevens'] nominal scale refers to the processes of . . . classification, with the trivial restriction that numbers be used to name the objects or name the classes of objects." *Ibid.*, p. 17.

calling 'classification' 'measurement' may serve to emphasize the importance of classification. Certainly, Stevens himself has been one of the most effective advocates of classification and its presupposition of the ability to discriminate.

> When we attempt to reduce complex operations to simpler and simpler ones, we find in the end that discrimination, or differential response is the fundamental operation. Discrimination is prerequisite even to the operation of denoting or "pointing to," because whenever two people reduce their complex operations for the purpose of reaching agreement or understanding, they find that unless they can each discriminate the same simple objects or read the same scales they still will not agree. Agreement is usually reached in practice before these most elementary operations are appealed to.[10]

Torgerson has admitted that classification, when done finely enough, is subject to the procedures of measurement.

> Given that a property is measurable (this is not necessarily true of all properties), the advantages of defining it in terms of measurement, as contrasted with a purely classificatory definition, accrue both in the descriptive and in the explanatory functions of science. In terms of description, it makes for greater descriptive flexibility, since the number of classes is theoretically unlimited . . . . In terms of explanation, it allows for more precise formulation of general laws relating different constructs, and it enables the paraphernalia of mathematics to be extensively applied to science . . . . Theories and laws can be formulated in terms of mathematical equations.[11]

The characteristic of measurement, aside from the nominal measurement of Stevens, is that some characteristic (property) can be separated from its environment, specified and put in a one-to-one correspondence with the real number system, or some subset of it. If such a relationship can be established generally, i.e., the behavior of the property is isomorphic with a subset of numbers, the operations of mathematics may be applied to the numbers assigned to the property and new configurations can be derived. Unfortunately, it is seldom possible to have a general isomorphic relationship, and the measurement scales are usually limited in that only some of the mathematical weapons may be applied. Let us turn now to some of the scales that may be identified in various measurement systems. Torgerson points out some of the characteristics of the real number system that are relevant to measurement and can be used for a basis of classifying measuring rules.

1. Numbers are ordered.

2. Differences between numbers are ordered. That is, the difference between any pair of numbers is greater than, equal to, or less than the difference between any other pair of numbers.

3. The series has a unique origin indicated by the number 'zero.' An important feature of this

---

[10] S. S. Stevens, "Psychology and the Science of Science," *Psychological Bulletin*, 36 (1939), reprinted in *Readings in Philosophy of Science*, ed. Philip P. Wiener (New York: Charles Scribner's Sons, 1953), p. 164. "We combine operations when they satisfy the criteria of a class; and the concept of that class is defined by the operations which determine inclusion within the class" (p. 168).

[11] Warren S. Torgerson, *op. cit.*, pp. 11-12. Many will not admit that "unmeasurable" properties exist. Torgerson's definition of measurement keeps his use of nonmeasurable properties from being ridiculous.

origin is that the difference between any pair of numbers containing zero as one member is the number of the other member.[12]

Torgerson selected the three characteristics because they correspond with a common distinction made in the types of measurement scales that are often assigned. Corresponding with the ordering characteristic is the so-called ordinal scale of measurement which is, next to Stevens' nominal approach, the weakest type of scaling.[13] These ordering measurements are monotonic in the sense that they are order-preserving when translated from the characteristic to the number, and are common in accounting, e.g., the typical account numbering of current assets.

A refinement of the ordinal scaling process ties the scale to a zero point, without implying that the distance between numbers represents equal intervals. Accounting is full of these measuring scales. The length of time an account is overdue is ordered — in the usual case without special explanations — with the probability of collection; the amount of quick assets may be related in such a fashion to the firm's short-term, debt-paying ability.

Perhaps the most common type of scaling makes use of equal intervals and makes use of the distance attribute of the natural numbers. The most common variation of this scale is the so-called ratio scale that has a specified zero point or a natural origin of some kind. For a finite set the numbers that identify the degree of a property along with the assumption of equal intervals will determine the scale completely. As Torgerson points out, on a ratio scale the linear transformations that are allowable are limited to those that leave the natural origin unchanged, while if there is no natural origin with an equal interval scale, we are at freedom to select the zero point. The result then is that we may use any type of linear-transformation mathematics.[14] Let us now turn to some of the devices used to establish scales, especially the devices employed by psychologists.[15] It should be obvious that one should have the property to be measured clearly in mind. Some writers have been concerned with differences between 'fundamental' and 'fiat' or sometimes 'derived' measurement. For our purposes these distinctions and the postulation of some sort of 'natural' law of assignment are not important. One must realize that some properties such as length have operational rules (rules of correspondence) which relate the concept to its measurement rules directly. On the other hand, 'proprietary interest' is essentially a constitutive

---

[12] *Ibid.*, p. 15. Stevens distinguishes four kinds of scales: nominal, ordinal, interval and ratio. Nominal scales require little more than determination of equality. Ordinal scales require the determination of greater than, but the intervals may be unequal. Interval scales imply equality of intervals (differences), but the zero point is conventional. Ratio scales permit the determination of equality of ratios and imply an absolute zero. Clearly accounting uses all types. See S. S. Stevens, "On the Theory of Scales of Measurement," *op. cit.*, pp. 677-690.

[13] C. H. Coombs places a quasi-ordered or partially-ordered scale between the nominal and ordinal scales. The objects themselves can be nonordered or partially ordered, or fully ordered, and the properties can also be of the three types. See "Mathematical Models in Psychological Scaling," *Journal of the American Statistical Association*, XLVI (1951), pp. 480-489.

[14] Warren S. Torgerson, *op. cit.*, pp. 19-21.

[15] Torgerson takes pains to point out the relationship of measurement to theory formation and model building. ". . . fundamental measurement itself is an example of the construction and verification of theories. Any particular scale type can be considered to be a formal model. If rules of interpretation are laid down which connect the model to observable data, the model becomes a theory, and as such can become subject to empirical test." *Ibid.*, p. 25. Note also: "The meaning of the numbers assigned to the elements of the model is specified by the model. Rules of correspondence are established, relating elements and properties of the model to observable data, thus converting the model into a testable theory." *Ibid.*, p. 38. Incidentally Torgerson, in turn, leans heavily in this area on Carl G. Hempel, *Fundamentals of Concept Formation in Empirical Science* (Chicago: University of Chicago Press, 1952).

definition and its passage to the empirical world for measurement is usually done indirectly by its relationships to assets and liabilities which can be measured more or less directly through acknowledged rules of correspondence. Social income, for example, is certainly not going to be measured 'directly' or by any so-called *fundamental* laws of nature. What is done, of course, is to define a limited concept of social income in terms of some properties which *can be measured* by empirical means and which have some intuitive relationship to our feeling of what social income *ought* to be.[16] This limited concept is then substituted for the more desirable one. Theorists in any field may profitably study and appraise discrepancies between the constructs that are in fact measured with the constructs that are desired. In accounting, for example, it is extremely doubtful whether current working-capital measurements are adequate substitutes for debt-paying ability.

Psychologists have divided their experimental approaches to measurement into three groups: the subject-centered, the stimulus-centered, and the response approach. In the subject-centered approach: *The systematic variation in the reactions of the subjects to the stimuli is attributed to individual differences in the subjects.* The immediate purpose of the experiment is to scale the subjects, who alone are assigned values."[17] This procedure is widely used in intelligence testing and general testing of physical or mental accomplishment in school work. The stimulus-centered approach, as the name suggests, aims at scaling the stimuli and the subjects, and on occasion the immediate purpose may be to appraise the importance of each.

In the field of accounting we are confronted with the fitting of information to the uses to which it may be put. Thus, a practitioner weighs the attitudes of the users of information and tailors the information to fit his weights. Yet the problem is a dynamic one, and it is possible to change the attitudes of users. He might therefore wish to simplify the approach so that he can scale the information (the stimuli) with respect to a standardized set of user reactions for different education levels. The aim is, of course, to improve the usefulness of the information service, and the changing educational level along with constantly shifting conditions mean responsive adjustments must be made in a dynamic fashion. In the short run however practically all problems including variations on the price-level problem can be set up to scale user reaction, and the urgency or desirability of new measurement rules may be resolved in a subject-oriented context.

Yet these distinctions are not as clearcut as one would like. All approaches require judgment. The subjects may be asked to judge which assets seem more liquid, which arrangement stresses A more than B, which form of disclosure seems more forceful. If such requirements are transitive, they may be ordered and subjected to an ordinal scale of measurement.

Let us return to some of the methods or procedures used by psychologists and others to establish scales of measurement. Regardless of the method used, the experiment is usually done over and over with the same subjects or with different subjects or with combinations. This *replication* is, of course, one of the tools often used in scientific work, and such repeated samples or judgments help to eliminate errors that may be present.

---

[16] With regard to fiat measurement, Torgerson states: " . . . one or more observable properties are selected which on a priori grounds are judged to be related to the concept of interest. A measure of the observable property itself . . . is taken as the measure of the concept of interest . . . . The discovery of stable relationships among variables so measured can be as important as among variables measured in other ways . . . . The major difficulty with measurement by fiat is the tremendous number of ways in which such defined scales can be constructed." *Ibid.*, p. 24. Notice Torgerson's nonpositivist approach in his use of "natural laws," "fiat," and "a priori."

[17] *Ibid.*, p. 46.

A common approach makes use of the ability of subjects to discriminate and is known as the differential sensitivity method. The "just noticeable difference" is sometimes known as the *jnd* or the difference limon, or the DL. The first problem encountered is that the just noticeable difference may be "noticed" in some cases and not in others so that some supplementary rules must be established. The subject may sense a difference 50 percent of the time almost by chance, so that a noticeable difference is inferred only if he differentiates, say, 80 percent of the time. The second step is the formation of the scale. In some cases it can be assumed that the noticeable differences (the DL's) themselves make up the units of a scale. Explicit allowances and replication may be necessary as the subject becomes more skilled or more discriminating at one end of the scale. In any event, it is assumed that the discriminations are transitive and that they represent equal distances on the scale.[18]

The above form of discrimination requires comparative judgment of related pairs. One is faced immediately with the possibility that discriminations may have different intensity. For example, suppose that A is judged brighter than B 90 percent of the time and B is judged brighter than C 70 percent of the time. Is the distance from A to B greater than the distance from B to C? Thorndike attempted to meet this problem by postulating that the differences in distance are proportional to the normal deviates of the statements. As Torgerson states:

> The general notion "Equally often noticed differences are equal" is thus transformed to the notion that the psychological distance between stimuli is proportional to the normal deviate transform of the proportion of times the (directed) difference is noticed.[19]

In some cases it may be feasible to ask subjects directly for judgment of quantitative distance. This method is demanding and assumes that they will be able to estimate distances and place them on the scaling continuum. This type of scaling is done in examination marking by all teachers, and its most common expression is probably a marking scale based on 100.

The estimating task may be made easier for the subject by applying what are known as "fractionation" methods. In this process the subject is given a standard of some kind (e.g., zero, and A = 100), and is asked to select others that are one-half as great, or twice as great, etc. This differs from the previous process in that the subject need not directly estimate the size of the unit. He is asked for a fraction of the given standard, and the researcher then determines a convenient unit. A variation of this approach requires a still

---

[18] Torgerson states: "If a stimulus *B* is 'just noticeably greater' than stimulus *A*, and stimulus *C* is 'just noticeably greater' than stimulus *B*, then the *distance* on the psychological continuum that separates *A* and *B* is equal to the distance separating *B* and *C*. This notion may be taken as an assumption subject to further test, or as a definition of what is meant by equality of intervals on the psychological continuum . . . . Given the definition of what is meant by equality of intervals, i.e., equality of *jnd's*, we have only to devise experimental methods for obtaining *jnd's* in order to obtain a scale possessing a unit of measurement." *Ibid.*, p. 133. For a more complete discussion of this and following procedures see: P. Guilford, *Psychometric Methods* (New York: McGraw-Hill Publishing Co., 1936, 1954).

[19] Warren S. Torgerson, *op. cit.*, p. 155.

> "1. Each stimulus when presented to an observer gives rise to a discriminal process which has some value on the psychological continuum of interest.
>
> 2. Because of momentary fluctuations in the organism, a given stimulus does not always excite the same discriminal process, but may excite one with a higher or lower value on the continuum . . . .
>
> 3. The mean and standard deviation of the distribution associated with a stimulus are taken as its scale value and discriminal dispersion, respectively " (pp. 159-160).

more limited ability of the subject and asks for estimates of equidistance. This approach assumes that the subject is capable of stating whether the difference between A and B is greater than, say, the distance between B and C. It goes without saying that if he is able to determine greater than or less than, he can arrive at reasonable approximations of equality.

In some cases a preassumption is made about the distribution of scale value of the stimuli. For example, it may seem reasonable that the distribution is normal or some other familiar pattern. If such a preliminary step is feasible and the stimuli are ordered, the fitting of a scale according to the distribution is not a difficult chore.

Before turning to specific measurement problems in accounting, some philosophical aspects of measurement may be summarized. The similarity between simple classification and more colorful quantitative knowledge should be clear. A quantitative scale with differences that can be related to symbols in the real number system can enlist some of the methods and strength of mathematics. Notice however that some concept of distance is necessary. Ushenko points out that all measurement reduces to "observations of coincidences on scales or dials, the problems of measurement are reduced to the problems of measuring length, of which the major problem is how to determine whether graduations on a scale are congruent . . . ."[20] The so-called scientific laws almost invariably call for measurement, and measurement depends on observation and transitivity. With this view there is always the possibility of more accurate measurement with the effect of modifying or setting new laws, equations and definitions. According to Ushenko: " . . . should this happen . . . the [old] correlation, being a definition . . . would not become false. But the assertion that there are physical processes which can be identified with [the synthetic statement] . . . would then become false."[21] In pre-Bridgman times (and unfortunately today in some areas of accounting) one of the rules of the scientific game was not to question the invariability of the rod. "From this point of view the selection of anything as a standard of measurement is equivalent to a *convention* that this thing remains invariant throughout the process of measurement . . . the operationalist theory [is an alternative that] . . . explains measurement as a set of operations performed in accordance with specific but arbitrary instructions or rules, among which there are rules how to select a measuring rod . . . . Whatever happens to the rod is irrelevant to the results of measurement provided the specifications of the rod are in accordance with the instructions."[22]

The fusing of mathematics and logic has helped restore some status to classification. The logical development of classes and the similar development of mathematical set theory now mean that powerful mathematical tools may be applied to qualitative (nonmetric) knowledge. To know that x belongs to the class 'dog' is to know quite a bit about x without having seen him. From our knowledge of the class we know something about his habits, his reproductive cycle and methods, the number of his legs, his covering, etc. At this point we need to remember that the ability to discriminate is necessary for both quali-

---

[20] A. P. Ushenko, *The Theory of Logic* (New York: Harper & Brothers Publishers, 1936), p. 157.

[21] *Ibid.*, p. 156.

[22] *Ibid.*, pp. 158-159. Apparently too many accountants have accepted the instruction to use an historical monetary unit and have not questioned whether the accounting constructs thus operationally defined have any relevance to needs. Physicists have similar problems. "In view of . . . experimental results, one is led to postulate that stretches are congruent at a distance if they prove themselves to be congruent when adjacent. In effect, we postulate that the distance between two points on a solid body is unchanged in a displacement . . . it is meaningless to ask if this convention is really true [or] if there were a more fundamental definition of length or distance." Victor F. Lenzen, *op. cit.*, p. 290.

tative and quantitative thinking. In fact, discriminating is more primitive than pointing (specifying), and pointing is certainly more primitive than naming.

There are many unsettled questions of measurement in accounting. Perhaps the most interesting and important applications arise in scaling future prospects into some system of values. The actual rules for recognizing value changes require the definition of new concepts and operations to be substituted for the value construct. Revenue is defined operationally by *naming* the things to be done to identify and measure it. Expenses are related to rules for measuring cost (sacrifice) and then to further rules for allocating cost to current revenues and to future expected revenues. Thus we agree on a set of instructions for measuring cost and agree to accept the resulting quantity as a measure of sacrifice. Another set of rules is then devised to measure the cost to be matched with revenues. This second type of measurement is an attempt to reflect prospects sacrificed to procure the new values represented by revenues and requires a scaling of expected benefits and the application of the ratio of benefits expired to expected total benefits to the costs to be allocated. The resulting system of definitions and relations is related to time periods and the results are given in income reports. Income, defined in terms of these operations, may differ considerably from nonaccounting definitions! Thus in order to measure value added (or decreased), accountants exhibit a whole series of substitute constructs with rules of correspondence to the empirical world. In each case these constructs themselves require their own scaling and measurement rules. Accountants then devise and issue instructions for combining the intermediate definitions and agree that the result of these measurements shall represent the change in *value* from operations. The resulting construct of value added, for example, is not quite the same as the one defined as income because of disagreement over capital gains and losses and realization rules. (Of course provision is made in the rules for additional investment, where the value added is offset by sharing the future prospects of the business or of claims to be satisfied.)

A little reflection will show that a concept of income in terms of being better or worse off is literally impossible to scale without making substitutions of this type. In fact, the economist's entire concept of discounted expectations is almost impossible to implement in terms of workable rules and needs some support before being substituted for the concept of being better or worse off. In summary, it should be emphasized that such expressions as: "Intelligence is what intelligence tests test," or "Income is what results when accountants apply their rules for measuring income," are true enough in themselves. What such expressions fail to explain is that constitutively defined constructs should be related to our needs and that substitute constructs are to be judged good or bad to the extent that they accomplish results similar to those derived from measuring the original construct directly. There is no need to be ashamed of being unable to measure many desirable constructs from our theoretical space — e.g., constitutive definitions that have value in a context of given objectives. The trick of substituting something that can be measured for something we would like to measure if we were more competent is well established in scientific work.

Several relatively minor observations may be made at this point, although a detailed discussion may fit better elsewhere. For example, the question of a constant interval scale (straightline) as opposed to a scale that takes account of the time value of money (an exponential) must be faced in dealing not only with depreciation but also with expectations in any form, including those dealing with benefits. When we add compound-interest methods we are changing from a linear scale to a nonlinear scale for measuring expected benefits. Notice also that if we change the discount rate we are changing scales, even though each is a nonlinear scale of the same family.

We might also ask whether an additional scale is needed to show confidence in the accuracy of the measurement or in the adequacy of the theoretical construct. Perhaps we should try to incorporate the degree of confidence or lack of it in the measurement scales that represent value. The long-lamented but tenacious doctrine of conservatism is designed to "allow" for uncertainty by a preliminary screening of the data before being carried to the usual scale and perhaps also by weighting the scale itself in favor of poorer current reports. Wholesale conservatism is objectionable not because it is a crude attempt to allow for differences in reaction patterns. The objections are that a general prescription to "tip the scales" in some direction may be opposed to best professional judgment and that it is often impossible to determine the magnitude of the 'allowance.'

A related problem arises through combining measures whose degrees of accuracy are widely different. To some extent this is unavoidable, for the measures that make up complicated constructs contain no reason to suppose that the accuracy can be or should be the same in each case. The measurement rules for taking value declines in buildings for example are less reliable than those for taking interest on government bonds, and the two measures along with others are combined to measure income. Again, the objection is not that they are done with unequal confidence — the objection is that they are combined and all are treated as meriting equal confidence without disclosure of differences.

An interesting and important case of measurement concerns the evaluation of different types of disclosure. We do not have any standards at all for comparing the relative strength of a footnote with a similar statement adjacent to the item. Is there for example an ordering that corresponds with the placement in the statement of financial condition? Are there enough lazy readers to justify the belief that the first few lines of the statement are most likely to be read? Actually accountants have never examined this hypothesis in a formal way. We may also ask whether the last places in the statements are more important than, say, intermediate locations. Is there a sharp break between the body of the statement and the body of the footnotes? How much is the situation helped by such statements as "the accompanying notes are an integral part of the statement"? If such a statement is made, where should it be placed for greatest effect? We have hardly begun to consider these kinds of things, yet they should be tested by experiment, ordered, and if possible scaled. To many outsiders accountants have hardly begun to learn their craft.

Clearly the internal composition of the disclosure note has some connection with the strength of disclosure — at least for those who read it. Our body of empirical information in related fields is so meager that it is of little service. Additional information might be gathered to indicate the importance of subtotals in the statements; the influence of indentations; or the use of heavier print for items that deserve emphasis. This material is in the field of pragmatics, it is psychological in nature, it is important, and accountants are not studying it!

The following discussion of financial-statement arrangements is meant to illustrate the need for careful ordering and to suggest areas of study that students might investigate. Does the order in the financial statement indicate the order of accuracy of measurement of the individual items? A positive case has some support, for it is probably true that cash is the most accurately measured; receivables may well be second best; certainly intangibles rate last. But if we agree that the order of location represents the order of our confidence in the accuracy of measurement, can the ordering of accuracy be scaled? It is doubtful that an ordinary distance scale could be applied meaningfully, but it may be possible to set up some sort of function that would scale the differences. Measurements differ in accuracy among firms and among themselves from statement to statement, but such a scaling might have general validity and be useful to those who use statements. It might even be feasible to place accountants themselves and accounting firms on some sort of scale of relative accuracy, or relative conservatism, so that users of accounting output could apply these indexes to reported statements and gain some measure of comparability. Revenue agents often have the equivalent of an informal scaling of the honesty of professions and types of workers who assess their own taxes. Undoubtedly their knowledge extends to the relative readiness of certain accounting firms to claim immediate deductions for their clients.

On the other hand, perhaps the order of location on the financial statement may be used to scale the relative importance of the items. It may be possible to set up experiments to measure the psychological distance between places on the balance sheet, and it is not inconceivable that an arrangement of items in the order of dollar importance would result in more meaningful statements and better understanding. Unfortunately the dollar amounts may not themselves measure relative importance. For example, when a firm is having short-term financial difficulties the amount of cash on hand may have an importance far out of proportion to its amount. The fact that almost without exception accountants place current items first may be due to preoccupation with current debt-paying ability and the influence of bankers. Study might indicate that the trend toward this arrangement gathers impetus during or immediately after each financial crisis or depression. Fixed assets are normally far more important in terms of dollar amounts, yet even public utilities and railroads have abandoned placing them first.

In a similar way liabilities on the balance sheet might be ordered as to: (a) liquidity — urgency of asset distributions for their satisfaction, (b) definiteness of payment, (c) definiteness of amount— accuracy of amount to be paid, and (d) importance of dollar amount. At this stage we are not interested in the actual scheme of assignment. We are interested in understanding how accountants may possibly increase the number of information facets by classifying and ordering data.

It is also interesting to speculate about the relative importance of positions on the operations report. For example, does subtracting merchandise cost from sales imply that this cost is recovered first? What about putting corrections of previous periods first so that the reader may judge how accurate past reporting has been? The usual argument is that the most prominent places should be reserved for the most important information. The volume of sales is usually given first. Should it be concluded that this is the most important item? What about placing net income first? Controllable costs first? These questions are empirical and can be tested by empirical means.

There is room for considerable study of accounting measurement in terms of whether the methods are response methods or subject-centered studies. In auditing, for example, accountants are trying to appraise the trustworthiness of the individuals who make the representations and also the trustworthiness of the representations themselves. What is the scale of trustworthiness? The amount of checking to be done is related to estimates of the adequacy of the internal controls and on how well they are working. Is there a scale for judging the adequacy of such controls either on paper or in fact? The amount of checking done by an auditor is obviously related functionally to the auditor's appraisal of the trustworthiness of the *system*, which includes controls and the people involved. What kind of scales should he use? J-shaped? Logarithmic? Discontinuous with discrete points? More study!

Recently there has been considerable interest in the attitudes of investors, and at least one writer has tried to establish standards for good reporting, although so far he has not tried to scale deviations from the standards.[23] We need to set up experiments to find what investors read; what they value highly; how adaptable they are to new procedures — e.g.,

---

Footnote on following page

how educable they are. Thus both subject-centered and stimuli-centered methods are needed. We do not know, for example, the importance of ratios in analysis. Is a current ratio of four to one twice as good as a ratio of two to one? Is the measure continuous? Does it match a linear scale? Are there relevant ranges for decisions of various kinds? Are there serious dangers in trying to estimate future plans by scaling static levels at the beginning of an interval?

Finally, accountants may ask whether the debit-credit rules themselves are types of measurement. The purpose of these rules is to indicate changes resulting from certain events in a firm's history. In this sense they correspond to some aspects of plus and minus rules. The assignment of position to indicate direction of change is combined with a natural zero element and qualifies for nominal measurement.[24] Unfortunately there is no ordering in the basic debit-credit rules and we must add further measurement rules to provide higher-type measurement scales. "Assets = Sources of Assets" is true if and only if the scales selected to measure assets and sources of assets make the equation true. Thus it is a tautology only after the measurement rules have been selected. We might, for example, measure sources of assets in terms of the number of individuals contributing or the number of physical items, or by other rules without much purpose. The equation does not specify the exact scales, but it offers a very important constraint on the scales that are selected.

[23] Alan Robert Cerf, *Corporate Reporting and Investment Decisions* (Berkeley: University of California, 1961). George Staubus has shown interest in the subject. *A Theory of Accounting to Investors* (Berkeley: University of California Press, 1961). See also a related study by Cerf, "A Survey of Compliance with Reporting Standards," *The Journal of Accountancy*, February, 1963, pp. 42-50.

[24] Some Chinese-Indonesian bookkeepers place the credits on top and debits on the bottom. Dr. Sohadji Hadibroto has summarized parts of: *De Boekhoudingen van Chineezen, Japanners, Brits Indiers en Arabieren* (Djakarta: Dienst der Belastingen, 1937). See *A Comparative Study of American and Dutch Accountancy and their Impact on the Profession in Indonesia* (unpublished doctoral dissertation, Universitas Indonesia, 1962), Appendix 14, pp. 260-262.

Essay Eleven

Belief, Evidence and the Nature
of Proof I

All professional and intellectual fields have their own problems of evidence and proof. The importance of evidence in legal matters is known to all. Historians have especially difficult problems of sifting evidence from sources that are almost always incomplete and biased. Internal bookkeepers and accountants need certain elementary notions of proof and evidence, but auditing as a profession cannot survive without adequate and comprehensive standards for reaching opinions and judgments. The typical legal curriculum contains a formal course devoted to these matters, and graduate students in the field of history may be required to devote some time (even a course or two) to the area of historicity and historical method. Unfortunately, accounting students are often told that they must develop the feel for adequacy of tests and other evidence from practice. This situation is unfortunate because practitioners are often not interested in philosophical and related matters. It seems clear that mathematicians, logicians, statisticians and philosophers are interested in the more abstract aspects of evidence and proof, and any serious discussion of these relations must include a survey of their efforts. It is the purpose of this and the following essay to present an elementary account of the nature of proof in these fields and to review briefly the kinds of evidence that are available to the auditor. Emphasis is placed on the psychological basis for proof and on the psychological attitudes necessary for the support of belief.

The discussion begins with a general treatment of the problems of establishing belief and weighing evidence. These general remarks are followed by a somewhat detailed examination of the meaning of 'objectivity' and the distinction in science between private and public information. The first essay closes with a brief look at problems of evidence in the field of law. The second and concluding essay on the topic deals first with problems of induction, statistical inference, and explanation. These topics are followed by a brief discussion and illustration of proof in logic and mathematics. Some accountants may wish to omit the second essay entirely or to cover selected sections of it. In order to encourage this time-saving approach there is some duplication of material. Very general comments and conclusions about subjective probability, decision theory and the logical rules of inference are included in this chapter.

Apparently the human mind often hopes to discover absolutes, and the quest for invariant relationships has been an important part of intellectual activity. One manifestation of such an attitude is found in those who hope to find proofs so devastating in their impact that all who understand their structure will be convinced and all doubt will be banished. In general the student is better advised to abandon such an inflexible conception and accept a relative approach that leads to a reduction in, or temporary banishment of, doubt.

In mathematics the truth of some statements appears to be obvious, but the truth of a statement that is obvious to a layman may be highly uncertain to a trained mathematician or vice versa. It is the purpose of *formal* proofs to make the truth of some statements seem to be obvious by relating them to other statements which have already been accepted as true. Kershner and Wilcox express this viewpoint clearly.

> It has already been mentioned that the theorems of a mathematical theory consist of asser-
> tions whose truth is usually not obvious. For this reason it is necessary to give a proof, that is,
> a series of statements which makes the truth of the theorems obvious . . . . When properly
> used, the word [obvious] refers to a statement of implication whose validity will be immedi-
> ately accepted as apparent by the audience . . . . All that is required of a proof is that it con-
> vince the audience of the truth of the implication at hand . . . there is no simple test that can
> be applied to determine the validity of a proof, that is, to determine that an alleged proof
> really is a proof.[1]

The fundamental requirement of a proof is clearly that it be "psychologically satisfying" — convincing — for the persons to be convinced. In this essay we are interested
first in how one goes about the business of convincing, and second we are interested in
speculating about the sociological forces that shape professional attitudes toward proof
and establish the necessary evidentiary requirements. The discussion of the first objective
takes the form of an elementary discussion of proof in logic and mathematics with references to statistical inference. The discussion of the second objective is concerned primarily
with the problem of determining attitudes in the field of auditing.

Accountants and other nonspecialists in the field of formal logic or mathematics are
often surprised to learn that the laws of logic and the rules of inference are 'conventional'
where this term is meant to imply that the procedures are generally accepted in the same
sense as "generally accepted accounting principles." In some cases the realization that such
laws are not outer-directed may lead to a skepticism that is far from satisfying, but it must
be remembered that these laws have been indispensible to the practical business of living,
and the conventions are in no way arbitrary, haphazard or academic. (The reader may
wish to refer again to Essay One, which contains a discussion of the rules of logic as the
product of experience and observation as opposed to the view that considers them to be
beyond experience, i.e. metaphysical.) For our purposes it is essential to recall that there
are alternate rules of logic and that the current acceptable ones are the result of judgment
and belief in their usefulness and adequacy.

Before turning to the more familiar kinds of evidence in accounting, let us emphasize
the psychological elements of proof as applied in logic and mathematics. The somewhat
complicated and impressive apparatus of logic is likely to obscure the psychological implications. It has been suggested by some that even the use of truth tables in the logical calculus is an interpretation in the same sense that algebra, geometry and mechanics are interpretations. To this group the 'T's' and 'F's' of the truth tables could be used in abstract
logic without any implications of true or false. Such interpretations have offered yeoman
utilitarian service, and on the basis of effective results some interpretations that are not at
all obvious have been accepted. To many geographers the following *valid* implication

---

[1] R. B. Kershner and L. R. Wilcox, *The Anatomy of Mathematics* (New York: The Ronald Press Company, 1950), pp. 76-77. Rudolf Carnap is more rigorous. "A derivation without premises is called a *proof*. A
proof is thus a series of sentences of which each is either a primitive sentence or a definition sentence, or is directly derivable from sentences, which precede it in the series," *The Logical Syntax of Language* (Paterson:
Littlefield, Adams & Co., 1959, 1937), p. 29.

intuitively seems to be an unconvincing segment of logic. "If New York is in California, then Los Angeles is in California."[2]

In the field of induction and statistics the nature of evidence and proof becomes more obvious and their relationship to accounting and auditing becomes more clearcut. Modern investigators make use of all the intellectual accomplishments that are available for help in resolving their problems. The most widely used and generally satisfactory development in this line has been the growth of knowledge in the field of statistical inference. This bundle of tools is the legacy of one of the major intellectual achievements of the present century. Although accountants have been slow in utilizing these techniques, the last decade or two has seen a gratifying acceptance and at least nominal utilization of these advances in the auditing field.

An investigator has reached an important threshold when he is reasonably sure that there is only one chance in 20 that the observed data are not accounted for by his recognized factors. But are such odds — even though they be accepted as unquestionably accurate — sufficient to support a belief or to prove a position? At what point do auditors concede that the figure for receivables is substantially correct? It is perhaps fair to say that the typical person has an endlessly complex hierarchy of beliefs. About some of these beliefs he is certain; about others he is less sure, until we may find a rare human who has no opinion on the subject at all. Does confidence develop proportionately with the evidence? Perhaps there are thresholds of confidence — none over a considerable range, then a little, followed by a surge that overwhelms and cannot be resisted. A little reflection will show that the problem and its answers are behavioral and that statistics helps us only in an auxiliary way. This conclusion does not deny that all methods of arraying probabilities and evaluating evidence should be explored and that to neglect them is to neglect valuable intellectual equipment. What is meant is that confidence is a psychological reaction and that proof is a definition — a name given to the level or *degree of confidence* that is convincing and satisfying to the individual or group involved.

Tremendous strides have been made recently in the direction of combining subjective elements with traditional statistics and developing the combination into a theory of rational decision. This approach practically defines statistics as " . . . a body of methods for making wise decisions in the face of uncertainty."[3]

Roberts continues: "The Bayesian approach argues that whether we like it or not, we should first implicitly or explicitly assign a weight to each event. If these weights are assigned according to certain rules of consistency, they deserve to be called *subjectivistic* or *personal probabilities* . . . . It is useful to think of a probability in terms of the odds at which you would be indifferent . . . ."[4]

Among the advances most useful for accountants is the Bayesian technique for modifying early (prior) valuations in the light of further information (likelihoods) and obtain-

---

    [2] The following distinction between judgment and belief is from A. P. Ushenko: "Acceptance or rejection of a proposition is called a *judgment*; it is always an individual act . . . . The psychological disposition to make judgments which assert a proposition may be called *belief* in that proposition . . . ." *The Theory of Logic* (New York: Harper & Brothers Publishers, 1936), p. 27.

    [3] Harry V. Roberts, *Statistical Inference and Decision* (Chicago: Lithoprinted by the author, 1960), pp. 1-2. Roberts points out that the present upsurge in subjective statistics apparently springs from the Neyman-Pearson deviation from traditional statistics. Abraham Wald added utility assessment, and modern Bayesians added "the principle of maximizing expected utility." A rigorous (axiomatic) approach is given by Leonard J. Savage, *The Foundations of Statistics* (New York: John Wiley & Sons, Inc., 1954). For a more understandable exposition see Robert Schlaifer, *Probability and Statistics for Business Decisions* (New York: McGraw-Hill Book Company, 1959).

    [4] Roberts, *op. cit.*, pp. 1-7.

ing revised (posterior) probabilities. It should be clear that a formalized scheme for re-
vising opinions in the light of further information should be extremely valuable. With or
without a formalized approach such revisions must be made. Experience with odd-shaped
coins or dice permits us to revise our predictions. Our accumulated knowledge of certain
regular physical characteristics sometimes permits us to predict with limited revision.

In appraising odd-shaped articles the initial probabilities may need to be modified
drastically as experience accumulates and regularities appear. Auditors review the system
of internal control with the hope of determining the configuration of probabilities for certain errors. On the basis of this review (similar to sizing up the shape of the coins or dice)
we draw elementary (prior) judgments — probabilities. The audit can be started with these
probabilities in mind. Further information is gathered about the actual operation and effectiveness of the control system as the audit proceeds. Probabilities (judgments) may be
changed on the basis of the added information, and the course and extent of the audit itself are changed to meet the changed judgments.

Without dealing with substantive material we may observe the criteria for changing the
course of the audit to meet changed judgments. The Bayesian approach makes use of
utility assessments. A word of warning is necessary to those who are accustomed to dealing with utility in classical economics. The modern definition is general. Roberts states:
"A utility is a conditional value that you attach to a consequence of an act such that you
will always prefer a consequence of higher utility to one of lower utility."[5] This definition
itself does not seem to be very helpful, but the Bayesians have done much to make the
definition operational.

It should be clear that the concept of utility is entirely subjective and that a money gain
or loss may be a poor approximation of the individual utility function. Yet as a starting
point it may often be assumed that the utility schedule is linearly related to income or loss.
Modifications may then be introduced for deviations, critical areas, nonmonetary objectives, etc. The usefulness of utility assessments is increased by providing a framework for
judging widely varying probabilities and consequences. Bayesians tend to use a betting-
odds interpretation of probability and to reduce complex problems of utility assessment to
simple betting situations. Roberts states the case clearly.

> The fundamental idea is to calibrate the utility of any consequence of action by comparison
> with an uncertain situation in which either a worse or better consequence might obtain . . .
> we do not need utility theory to tell us that we prefer more income to less or that we prefer a
> higher to a lower probability of winning a desirable prize. [We assume (postulate) this type of
> behavior.] Utility theory is useful because the concept of expected utility serves as a guide for
> evaluating complex risky situations on the basis of our evaluation of simple ones.[6]

For auditors this advance in statistics offers a procedure for meeting an old nemesis —
the fact that not all errors are equally grave. The betting-odds approach to utility assessment may provide a framework for weighing the complex hierarchy of errors, and, when
combined with the apparatus of prior probabilities (likelihoods) and posteriors, may permit the profession to examine its own structure for opinion formation and change. The
actual weights used, i.e., the seriousness of different deflections, is a subjective matter,
and statisticians as statisticians are not directly interested in the size of particular weights.

---

[5] *Ibid.*, p. 3-1.
[6] *Ibid.*, p. 3-3.

The latter problem is a problem that must be met — explicitly or implicitly — by the auditing profession. It should be clear that all future auditors should have some knowledge of subjective probability, but being good Bayesians is not enough. They must add some study of sociology and social psychology for clues as to why the profession's relative weights are what they are.

It is the contention of this paper that proof — the establishing of belief — is *socially* determined except in the simplest cases, e.g., direct contact with fire leads to burns. Moreover, in the more abstract cases the rigor of the required proof is adjusted to the consequences of wrong conclusions and to the burden — cost — of added rigor. At all times there must be an incremental balancing of the additional cost of an added increment of rigor with the expected benefits from the added peace of mind that comes from higher confidence levels. Once the concept of proof as an absolute has been dispelled, the way is opened for a detached weighing of evidence without the feeling of inferiority that sometimes results from a standard of unattainable perfection. In the simplified model one strives for a higher rather than a lower degree of success in prediction so long as the expected benefit is in excess of the added sacrifice.

No one suggests that such a model is applicable to all kinds of cases. Certainly the probabilistic approach is essential, for we are never sure of the benefits or the probabilities. At first sight it would seem to be ridiculous to spend a hundred auditing man-hours to be a little more sure that a petty cash fund of a few hundred dollars was handled properly. Yet to an internal auditor a comparatively small error in amount may be an indication that the internal control structure upon which so much accounting judgment rests has broken down. If such controls have in fact broken down, then the amount of work done in other features of the audit may be far from sufficient to constitute proof in other directions. If, however, the internal controls are tight in this area, the amount of work already done in related areas may be sufficient to support the necessary judgments. In a general way the seriousness of accepting as satisfactory a set of circumstances which are in fact unsatisfactory or *vice versa* would always be related to the level of confidence that is desired. It should be emphasized that the seriousness of the wrong decision may not be represented accurately by the number of dollars that seem to be directly involved, i.e., the seriousness cannot be scaled on a linear-dollar scale.

Perhaps one can find an example of this type of confusion in the work of some auditing teachers. It is sometimes — fortunately not often — pointed out that students must get the feel of auditing in practice, and now and then it is asserted that such a feel cannot possibly be procured in the classroom. Assuming that the feel of auditing is concerned with judgmental problems and not with the more obvious aspects of observing the documents in a context of filing cabinets, this position is equivalent to holding that the standards for proof are set by those in practice and not by those in universities. In the past this condition undoubtedly has been the case, but it is a deplorable condition. It is imperative that educational institutions encourage those who have the capacity, experience and vision to analyze and to generalize such problems for all professions. Those concerned with the psychology of learning will probably agree that there is some inefficiency in learning professional objectives and value systems under the pressure and bustle of a deadline in a busy client's office and under the coercion of self-interest. No doubt techniques are learned best in concrete situations, but value systems and judgments are appraised better in the detached atmosphere of scholarship uninfluenced by the urgency of preparing to learn a trade or make a living.

The teacher, regardless of whether he is employed by a university or an auditing firm, can explain the nature of proof and the relationship of evidence to proof. An analytical dissection of evidence may proceed by source, by functions or persons involved, by ordering in time, by permanency, by psychological barriers, and by countless other attributes. Most auditing discussions hardly go beyond a simple classification by the individuals who prepared the documents. A classification of this nature may throw some light on the psychological threads involved and may be important, but it is only a beginning of constructive work.

In another essay the conditions determining survival or rejection of ideas are discussed. Those who lead a profession are subjected to new influences, and the positions of contending groups change. Different weights become appropriate and subjective values held by the professional group change. Professional organizations, therefore, must provide channels for introducing change and weighing the advantages of stability against the advantages of change. Failure to react quickly enough to demands from other groups leads to legislative action, to invasion by related professions (e.g., income tax consultants), to split-off of new professions by members more sensitive to social needs than the constituted professional leaders.

Standards are what they are because those concerned have given consideration to the seriousness of judgmental error in various aspects of the work. Certain types of error may help certain groups and harm others, and errors in certain directions may be more serious than similar errors in the opposite direction. Different situations call for a shifting of weights to recognize varying influences on the judgmental decision. The integrity of the profession tends to assure that the agreed standards are maintained in practice and to influence those who might otherwise become overly sensitive to certain groups (perhaps to those who pay the bill). In any case there is likely to be considerable dispersion of individual judgment and integrity. Such dispersion sometimes leads to unprofessional work, but it provides machinery through which suggestions for change often come. It is the primary task of education at the professional and university level to help and to encourage those who have the capacity and vision to analyze and to generalize the problems of a profession in its social context. Some techniques and procedures must be taught. Some knowledge of such matters is necessary before one can analyze and generalize. Unfortunately some universities have become confused, stressed the manipulatory aspects, and neglected all but the more obvious analytical problems. Intellectual failure has not always been followed by oblivion, and intellectual Darwinism has not always escaped the pressures of economic conditions.

Objectivity

We need hardly remind the reader that 'objectivity' is a word. It is a word of unusual interest to a semanticist, because it has high-status overtones, and for accountants to be nonobjective is to be dead. The meaning is thought to be opposed in some fashion to subjective. Our purpose here is to point out the relationship of 'objectivity' and 'subjectivity' to evidence. The whole universe of evidence has been partitioned into subsets that are supposed to be independent and exhaustive and labeled either objective or subjective. But what are the rules for distinguishing types of evidence and classifying them? How do we know whether the boundaries are sharp and there is no overlap? What is the distinction? Is the distinction related to the shopworn distinction between private and public information? How did the favorable connotations so often become associated with objective and the unfavorable with subjective? Why are accountants so interested in objectivity?

Accountants, especially those in public work, have been concerned with giving opinions on managements' representations and intent. The highly private nature of intent and the desire for uniformity in appraising status and prospects have encouraged accountants to tie their own rules of evidence to experiences that may be shared and appraised by others. Thus, the accountant's interest as an independent auditor is almost always identified with *outside* groups! He is interested in adopting rules which reduce interpersonal variety in both auditors and users. A preference for the social-consensus approach to evidence is therefore to be expected.

Objective and subjective in the traditional sense require a division of the events (clues) into a string that is considered to be internal and another string that is external. Clearly one can have all sorts of clues and degrees of evidence. It is equally clear that some clues arise in such a way that by analogy it may be assumed that external individuals can also experience them. With similar training in appraising clues and interpreting and weighing evidence, they can arrive at similar conclusions. In some cases 'objective' applies only to the *possibility* that someone else could sense the clues, and interpretations and appraisals are considered to be subjective. There should be some reasonably sharp criteria for discriminating events and classifying them as objective or subjective. Such is not the case. The above distinction rests on readiness of physical access to the evidence that could lead to similar hypotheses and conclusions. To a nondualist external data simply cannot be used as the discriminating agent. One who thinks of the world as a series of experiences must look elsewhere for a usable distinction between subjective and objective.

The usual approach to the problem is in terms of social consensus. But as is pointed out later, this consensus is of 'rational' observers or of 'educated' observers. The creation of such entities as scientific man, economic man and rational man needs explanation, since they form an elite whose opinion determines objectivity. The term objective then indicates that there is (or could be) agreement and remains subjective until it is accompanied by the additional belief that others could duplicate the experience. These others have already been judged and their stable reaction patterns predicted. The problem has shifted dramatically, and we now must establish the rules for determining stable reaction patterns of others.

Scientists are certainly influenced by the environment in which they are brought up. Each generation sifts the heritage of previous generations and retains what promises to be useful. Accountants also are educated and influenced by the existing institutions in all things they do. In this sense all their beliefs and judgments are conditioned with respect to the nature of evidence and its adequacy. Even though *I make* the particular judgment on evidence that seems to be entirely private, the bases and the procedures for making it are in part socially determined. One assumes that he is a rational scientific observer because he has been trained like others are trained. He can infer (by analogy) how others will observe, judge and conclude, when they are given identical data and are products of the same educational process. He judges interpersonal relations and reactions by constructing an analogy based on presumed physical and environmental similarities.

Before discussing some particular problems of objectivity in accounting, let us turn to the place of replication in judgment formation. Replication is, of course, only one form of getting evidence, and it does not postulate external observers. For this reason it is a solopsist's darling. The test is in terms of observed uniformity from repeated experiments. The initial conditions along with the inputs are reproduced as nearly as possible and the results observed. Considerable effort could be expended to assess the relative merits of evidence observed by several independent observers and evidence from repeated experiments with the same observer. Replication has its own problems — conditions can never be identical and "no one puts his toe in the same river twice." Clearly some tolerance for ambiguity is essential. On the other hand, there is no reason to presume that the perceptual and inferential abilities of different experimenters will be identical. The most rigorous training and indoctrination cannot assure complete homogeneity. Unfortunately little attention has been given to these matters.

Clearly replication can not be used in many cases, e.g., some astronomical observations and in tests that require the destruction of the object. Many parts of accounting may be replicated. Accountants can retake inventory, recheck documents, etc., but no one makes the identical events occur again. In the latter cases they observe reactions to similar events and draw inferences. Historians are in a worse position. Historical events cannot be duplicated (each is unique) and similar events are not *quite* identical in initial conditions or in the impact of their change. Such historical work often consists of going over reports of the same events time after time. The events are therefore inferred from the evidence, and the evidence often consists entirely of reports. Replication is little more than reexamining the records.

A curious condition peculiar to accounting is that many operations that are considered to be objective are, by all definitions, those most highly subjective. The going-concern concept, for example, implies valuations and estimated benefits for each separate asset in conjunction with all other assets and facilities. The replacement-cost and current-cost concepts usually involve estimates by others outside the organization and more nearly meet the consensus test than the allocation of historical costs. Moreover, market values in most cases turn out to involve more outside judgment and be subject to more social "consensus" than the usual writeoff of cost "in some systematic manner." We can check the outside data; others can check it, and some may be able to replicate it. What about estimates of future benefits? What could be *less* accessible to outsiders than the usual writeoff formula of benefits received over total benefits to be expected with the ratio multiplied times the original cost? If benefits are related to the estimated life of some physical property, there is an additional judgment to be made: the judgment of specific economic life. Original cost itself is relatively objective by most standards, but a supplementary subjective decision is necessary as to whether the opinion of marginal buyers and sellers at acquisition is an appropriate measure of accountability for the firm.

Education for accountants tends to instill a uniformity of outlook and judgment among those in the profession. Objectivity, as a social consensus, is easier to establish when the institutions encourage uniform attitudes toward the weighing of evidence. Similar outlooks and professional indoctrination make it easier to get a consensus and therefore tend to broaden the scope of objectivity. In a totalitarian state objectivity must be extremely broad and dense! Clearly this approach leads to difficulties, but so long as evidence is evaluated, the valuations will certainly be conditioned by training and environment.

The entire field of accounting, especially the region devoted to auditing, is concerned with objectivity, and the profession is irretrievably committed to interpersonal analogy and social agreement. It is possible for an individual to confirm his work by repeating the operations or by designing new operations that can verify it. It is true that he is less likely to find his own errors because of peculiar psychological twists that may have developed during earlier runs. Notice however that other auditors have been brought up in a similar environment and may also have a tendency to repeat the errors and to follow a similar path. The danger may be less when different members are included, and any special-interest incentives or desires to misrepresent are averaged over a larger number of individuals. The very diversity of the drives toward falsification may act as a deterrent to falsification.

Objectivity may be approached through stability of observation reports, whether the reports are made by a single person applying replication or by independent observers. We are overlooking the obvious impossibility of ever furnishing *independent* observers from the same environment, i.e., conditioned by similar institutions, although this impossibility weakens the consensus approach. Objectivity is important to many nonaccounting groups. The following discussion is designed to introduce the reader to the reaction of scientists to objectivity, and to introduce some sources for further study.

Objectivity in Science

> Those who have analyzed inquiry from the point of view of science in general have tended to conceptualize inquiry as a *problem-solving* process. Social scientists . . . have tended to conceptualize inquiry as a *communicative process.*[7]

The area of empirical data offers problems of its own. Those with philosophical leanings have been concerned with the psychological overtones of experience and have drawn distinctions of dubious merit between public and private experiences. Certain philosophers such as the early empirical positivists (Wittgenstein, Carnap, Ayer, etc.) wish to use the term 'fact' instead of the more psychologically colored one of experience. Others have taken care to distinguish between epistemology and psychology and to point out that their positions require only epistemological assumptions. The following statement by Brunswik deserves repeating.

> . . . the ideal of "objectivity" . . . [is] finding a class of observations which, although not necessarily of the highest possible subjective convincingness, display the highest attainable degree of consistency in the sense of agreement among different observers and, for the same observer, from one observation to another . . . . We may relate the concept of objectivity to what is known to the psychological statistician as test reliability . . . . "Objective," then, is a class of responses yielding maximum reliability coefficients . . . .[8]

There seems to be no point in belaboring the psychological ingredient of experience. An attempt to escape the inclusion by referring to the less psychologically charged term 'facts' is certainly no escape, for facts are interpretations, and what appear as facts are so psychologically conditioned and so filtered that little can be gained in this direction. Facts are abstractions and for validity must have all sorts of related conditions specified. The fact that an American metal coin is round requires, for example, an understanding about the position of the viewer relative to the coin and a tolerance for irregularities. As will be suggested later the term 'fact' *sometimes* implies public confirmation while the more direct term 'experience' *may* have a more private implication.

Measurement itself must have psychological overtones, for measurement requires identification, search for similarities, ability to match ends, and a whole group of operations of this nature. All operational definitions set forth instructions, and these instructions require discriminations and are therefore psychological. There is no escape by requiring gadgets for measuring. What is measured may appear to be only shadows of what we hope to measure, but regardless of the complicated machinery employed, someone finally has to make the discrimination necessary to determine similarity, congruence, transitivity and related relationships. Qualitative distinctions require the same type of psychological discrimination so that classification, ordering, etc., require similar treatment. It

---

[7] Russell L. Ackoff, *The Design of Social Research* (Chicago: University of Chicago Press, 1953), p. 8.

[8] Egon Brunswik, "The Conceptual Framework of Psychology," *International Encyclopedia of Unified Science* (Chicago: University of Chicago Press, 1955), pp. 668-669.

should be clear that all aspects of interpreting an abstract system or calculus (finding the so-called rules of correspondence) require psychological operations. While there is some question as to whether the formal laws of logic and mathematics are psychological in the sense that their selection and retention is due to social selection, there seems to be little doubt that the main usefulness of logic and mathematics is considered to be in connection with their ability to permit rearrangements of sentences that lead to new psychological insights.

It is possible, with some preliminary assumptions, to have a scientific structure and still hold to the solipsistic view which forbids making assertions or assumptions about the necessity of a world outside the mind of the observer. It is true of course that mind, when used in this sense, cannot be classed as scientific without some special interpretation such as the ability to pattern experience, but it is equally true that the assumption of an external world lacks many characteristics required by scientific method.

A science with only one observer appears to be a possibility with or without a specific ancillary assumption as to the presence or nonpresence of the external world. Inasmuch as scientific inquiry has been considered to be largely methodology (scornfully "methodolatry") it would seem that a world consisting of only one person *could* pursue scientific inquiry as we know it. The only problem here is in connection with communication and the question of how he learned to do what he does and how he got enough background information to be able to interpret his sensory data. Thus, it would seem to be possible for a scientist to continue to be a scientist but it would be difficult to begin without previous knowledge. Yet some very elementary observations are scientific in their construction, and one must admit the possibility that Adam or Tarzan could have developed into rudimentary scientists.

In view of these possibilities it is somewhat surprising to find that almost invariably scientists and writers on scientific method are concerned deeply with objectivity — social consensus — and the necessity for confirmation by others. In the extreme, the field of science has been identified as the field of the language of science without remainder. Here are some typical comments that are essentially 'truth by definition.'

Vatter states:

> Objectivity is the agreement of intelligent persons as to the significance of independently observed data; it implies not only separate experience or observation on the part of the different individuals but also a communal reporting of those observations . . .[9]

Pearson has expounded this point in detail.

> The universal validity of science depends upon the similarity of the perceptive and reasoning faculties in normal civilized men . . . . even if an individual mind has reached a conception, which at any rate for that mind is perfectly self-consistent, it does not follow that such a conception must have scientific validity . . . a conception to have scientific validity must be *deducible* from the perception of the normal human being . . . an inference which is scientifically valid is that which could be drawn by every logically trained normal mind . . . . Stress must here be laid on the distinction between '*could* be drawn' and 'actually *would* be drawn.[10]

---

[9] William J. Vatter, *The Fund Theory of Accounting and Its Implications for Financial Reports* (Chicago: University of Chicago Press, 1947), Note 40 to Chapter V. Vatter gives credit to Frank H. Knight, "What is Truth in Economics?" *Journal of Political Economy*, February, 1940, p. 7. "Objectivity is a social, not an individual phenomenon . . . ."

[10] Karl Pearson, *The Grammar of Science*, Everyman ed. (London: J. M. Dent & Sons, Ltd., 1937), pp. 45, 49, 50, 51.

Popper reports:

> . . . ironically enough, ojectivity is closely bound up with the *social aspect of scientific method*, with the fact that science and scientific objectivity do not (and cannot) result from the attempts of an individual scientist to be 'objective,' but from the cooperation of many scientists. Scientific objectivity can be described as the intersubjectivity of scientific method.[11]

The views of the scientific empiricists Carnap and Morris follow.

> . . . it is possible to abstract in an analysis of the statements of science from the persons asserting the statements and from the psychological and sociological conditions of such assertions. The analysis of the linguistic expressions of science under such an abstraction is *logic of science*. [Carnap]

> It is an empiricism genuinely oriented around the methods and the results of science and not dependent upon some questionable psychological theory as to the 'mental' nature of experience. [Morris][12]

The requirement for interpersonal agreement and interchange, and therefore the requirement for a set of symbols to function as language, is postulated by all who take the social consensus approach to objectivity and scientific method. Much of the discussion about public and private arises in an attempt to abstract from psychological and phenomenalistic aspects and still preserve intersubjectivity. Hempel for example states:

> . . . properties or relations whose presence or absence in a given case can be intersubjectively ascertained, under suitable circumstances, by direct observation . . . we will refer to such attributes . . . as *observation terms* . . . objectivity of scientific knowledge . . . requires that all statements of empirical science be capable of test by reference to evidence which is public, i.e., which can be secured by different observers and does not depend essentially on the observer.[13]

The interpersonal nature of this kind of objectivity has been discussed by Russell, who seems prepared to accept it but realizes only too well the shakiness of the additional postulate required. Thus to accept the social consensus doctrine we are forced to accept some notion of Vatter's "intelligent" man, Hempel's "public" evidence, or Pearson's "normal

---

[11] Karl R. Popper, *The Open Society and Its Enemies* (New York: Harper & Row, Publishers, 1962), Vol. II, p. 217.

[12] Rudolf Carnap, "Logical Foundations of the Unity of Science," and Charles W. Morris, "Scientific Empiricism," both in the *International Encyclopedia of Unified Science, op. cit.*, pp. 43, 68.

[13] Carl G. Hempel, *Fundamentals of Concept Formation in Empirical Science* (Chicago: University of Chicago Press, 1952), p. 22. Notice, however, that P. W. Bridgman has concluded that the creative part of science must continue to be "private" because the proofs upon which it is based must be private proofs. ". . . science is only my private science, art is my private art, religion my private religion . . . ." *The Nature of Physical Theory* (New York: Dover Publications, 1936), pp. 13-14. See also: *The Way Things Are* (Cambridge: Harvard University Press, 1959), Preface v. In the positivist view nothing can be attributed to private experience and such constructs as self, image and mind are not used. S. S. Stevens states: "Only those propositions based upon operations which are public and repeatable are admitted to the body of science. Not even psychology knows anything about private experience, because an operation for penetrating privacy is self-contradictory . . . . Although a particular experimenter may himself become the object of study by another experimenter, and he in turn by still another, at some stage of such a regress an independent experimenter *must be* . . . assumed." "Psychology and the Science of Science," reprinted in *Readings in Philosophy of Science, op. cit.*, pp. 163-164.

civilized" man. Accountants are left with the assumption of an 'economic man,' with whom economists are for good reason extremely unhappy, and with a 'business man,' with whom much of the world is unhappy.

There is little doubt that the cult of objectivity arose in part, at least, to combat the dragon of authority in the institution of the church and in the person of Aristotle and many lesser lights. Yet it is clearly possible for intelligent people to be biased so that they agree on the "significance of observed data" (say, witchcraft) and, according to a definition of objectivity that depends on social consensus, the results are objective. Furthermore, how does one go about finding an "intelligent" man or "normal civilized" man? What are the specific instructions? All too frequently we tend to attach such honorific labels to those who agree with us, for we are all — in the sense of the sociology of knowledge — a product of our institutions and our ideology. Not only can individuals thinking alone come up with some strange beliefs — to paraphrase Keynes — but whole societies of men can come up with some very strange views, and for an individual to break out of his environment may be difficult·indeed.

We may inquire also whether objectivity as a social consensus helps to break the boundaries of tradition and authority. Does social consensus mean, for example, total agreement? Majority agreement? Clearly it is to some degree an agreement of an elite group. Apparently the consensus is usually put in opposition to authoritative pronouncements, and the "weight of evidence" becomes persuasion and ability to perform an experiment instead of fear or possible favor. Thus it might be said that the effect has elements of democracy, but an intellectual discipline can be subjected for long periods to the tyranny of the majority or the tyranny of an outstanding man, such as Aristotle, or an obstinate man such as Stalin. Cohen's argument for authority and tradition in the following quotation applies with equal force to the need for group dependence on research.

> The essence of the argument for tradition and authority is the actual inability of any single individual thoroughly to apply the process of reasoning and verification to all the propositions that solicit his attention. To doubt *all* things in the Cartesian fashion until they can be demonstrated is impossible . . .[14]

Comments on the Legal Approach to Evidence

It seems to be characteristic of intellectual and professional workers to be optimistic about finding solutions to their own problems by observing other professions with similar problems. In fact these essays are devoted in large part to this kind of observation. Heretofore we have looked primarily at philosophers; let us now turn for a very brief look at the legal profession for possible guidance.

The legal profession has attempted to clarify its problems by maintaining a sharp distinction between fact and conclusion (opinion). It is possible that this distinction is so fundamental for legal procedure that legal judgments without it would be chaotic. This distinction is supplemented by a procedural framework that includes rules for expediting the presentation of relevant facts and machinery for promoting judgment formation. The first of these items is concerned primarily with rules of evidence and procedure, and the

---

[14] Morris R. Cohen, *Reason and Nature* (Glencoe: Free Press Publishers, 1953), p. 29. The following note from Whitehead on common sense could also be turned from tradition to consensus. "Now in creative thought common sense is a bad master. Its sole criterion for judgment is that the new ideas shall look like the old ones. In other words it can only act by suppressing originality." A. N. Whitehead, *An Introduction to Mathematics* (New York: Oxford University Press, 1948), p. 116.

second depends on the ability of judges and institutions for reaching judgments. Let us now scan these legal procedures with the hope of finding material to meet similar problems in the accounting profession.

The distinction between fact and opinion is an indispensible one, but like all distinctions it has fuzzy frontiers. It is a commonplace of semantics that facts themselves are low-order judgments and have meaning — are true or false or even relevant — within an operational framework. Whether or not the statement: "*A* was sitting in a chair," is true or false depends on a number of conditions including such obvious things as: Does the support meet the definitional requirement for 'chair'? Is the time interval definite enough for operational purposes? Is the person we now call *A* the *same* person who is in question at the previous date? Certainly changes have been made, but perhaps we are not talking about the present *A* at all but a previous bundle of molecules and inhibitions that was at the specified time known to himself and to others as *A*. What if *A* was sprawling so that his position may be better described as reclining than as sitting?

The legal profession has developed a reasonably workable set of rules to meet these kinds of objections in actual cases. Notice, however, that if the distinction between sitting and reclining (or between any of the other alternatives) is important to the case, a judgment must be made as to whether *A* was *in fact* sitting or reclining. This judgment is over and above the judgment that the material is or is not relevant, and it is not a matter of law. Instead it is a typical low-order judgment that is *always* necessary to determine whether any report is or is not factual.[15] As will be pointed out later, the judge may have some instructions for determining the difference between sitting and reclining from the body of legal material that he is permitted to use. Such material may be available — say, from previous cases supplemented by acceptance of *stare decisis* — and rules for its usage may have been set forth. The judgment takes the form of establishing "similarity" between present and previous cases. If no such information is available the judgment is raw in the sense that it is made from criteria outside or foreign to the legal profession. The point to be emphasized is that the relevance of facts, the materiality of facts, the competence of facts, all require judgment, but far too often it is forgotten that the very existence or nonexistence of the facts requires judgment.

In view of the impossibility of ever having a perfect structure, the legal profession has done an excellent job of setting forth working rules (some of which are crude indeed) for getting facts and aiding judgment formation. The "best-foot-forward" bias of the advocate system is expected and discounted, and special less stringent rules are applied if a statement is "against interest." Certainly accountants must incorporate an explicit and coherent recognition of the self-interest psychologies in setting up internal controls. The rules of hearsay evidence may need modification before being applied to auditing, but they may help our profession establish a more sophisticated relationship between "all-ears" auditing and the well-established legal doctrine that all written documents "speak for themselves." Auditors are familiar with the doctrine of burden-of-proof and the duty of the complaining party to keep the case going. Apparently the doctrine of "judicial notice" has an undeveloped counterpart in "audicial notice." Auditors may find use for the "presumption rules" of many jurisdictions, but three-way classification of none, prima facie,

---

[15] It is interesting to note that some philosophers have given up on attempting to define fact in terms of physical or similar criteria. Instead some define a fact as a true statement. Suzanne K. Langer states: " 'Fact' . . . is that which we conceive to be the source and context of signs to which we react successfully . . . . Science is an intellectual scheme for handling facts . . ." *Philosophy in a New Key* (New York: A Mentor Book, 1959), pp. 225, 232.

and conclusive may need considerable refinement before being directly useful for appraising auditing evidence.

What institutional machinery is currently available for reaching legal judgments? Put in another way, what criteria are used by judges for getting judgments? How are such criteria weighed? And how does the judge decide when the criteria are sufficient to support a decision? In short, how are judges trained to judge? Answers to these questions may help the reader decide how auditors are taught to audit and how the accounting profession decides which behavior is acceptable and which must be rejected. Unfortunately the answers are at best partial and their transfer value may be overestimated.

Clearly the doctrine of *stare decisis* is a rule that is of some importance and is a device that adds continuity to decisions by assuring that members of the profession follow a similar pattern of observing and weighing the past. The appeal to precedence requires that a careful record of past performance be available in usable form. Accounting does not have the advantage of a more or less complete history of past audits, but typically *some* previous audit papers and miscellaneous information are available. Various organizations have tried to generalize and to distill the more immediate and important experience into rules. In general the continuity of *stare decisis* and documented historical cases is replaced in accounting by the continuity provided by these rules, by the tradition of textbooks, by auditing manuals and word-of-mouth instructions from senior members of accounting firms.

The basis for all judgment must be rooted in the past, but the decision to base judgments on formal precedence involves some unusual features. First, the decision to use precedence is itself based on prior judgments as to the desirability of continuity, uniformity, and predictability. The long discussions in legal literature with regard to *stare decisis* testify to the lack of unanimity about these objectives and the tremendous price that must be paid in the form of ponderous inflexibility. Acceptance of *stare decisis* also involves the judgment as to when, if ever, it may be desirable to depart from the rule. If some departure is sanctioned, how can it be done without wrecking the structure entirely? These problems are in turn related to the problem of balancing inflexibility with the need for a structure that will provide enough stability to permit predictions of the most common outcomes and to let contestants know approximately where they stand. Criteria must also be developed so that decisions may be reached as to whether the case at bar is similar to those that have gone before. Perhaps the case method helps prepare lawyers for this duty. Finally, the changing statutes may help the cause of flexibility. To some extent under *stare decisis* the duty to provide flexibility is shifted to the legislative arm, but statutes, too, call for interpretation by the courts and here again judgment is required to steer through the wording and 'intention' of the statutes.

Accountants are probably prepared to admit that the guideposts to help judges reach decisions are more definite than their counterparts in the accounting profession. The rules of evidence followed by a typical court may appear naive to philosophers, but they are operational in the sense that they can be applied, and they are utilitarian in the sense that they expedite the legal process of fact finding and the process of judging. Judges, like auditors, have the benefit of summaries, distillations, rules, conventions and principles, but judges have a somewhat better transcript of pertinent history than auditors. Judges have also the benefit of more numerous and detailed directives in the form of statutes and regulations set forth by others who have been designated by the electorate. Thus, they have available a reasonably current and *direct* set of partial objectives from the social body through its designated decision makers. In other professions including accounting, such objectives are not so clearly set forth. Accounting finds its clues from legislation, court decisions, administrative rulings, political statements, trade association requests, journal articles, textbooks, informal conferences and a host of other sources. Some have advocated an accounting court to serve as a mechanism for selecting, rejecting, and expanding accounting rules and to weigh the needs of contending groups. Others fear that the added inflexibility may stifle some of the vitality of a new profession.

Essay Twelve

Belief, Evidence and the Nature
of Proof II

This essay is devoted to a general discussion of judgment in relation to evidence in a statistical taste and to the concept of proof as used by logicians and mathematicians. The tone of the discussion is nontechnical and elementary, but an attempt is made to deal with theoretical points and to avoid the common tendency to hide behind techniques and complicated jargon. The field of statistics has been undergoing a period of tremendous change since approximately World War II. The literature is bulky and technical, and the reading is difficult. An attempt has been made to point up the issues that are relevant to accounting and to indicate the leaders in the field and their contributions. Little or nothing is said about the specific problems of applying sampling to auditing. Vance, Neter, Cyert and a small army of practitioners have been developing possibilities in this direction. The view here is that accounting itself is a combination of statistical methods and behavioral observations. Accordingly, interest is concentrated on a survey of statistical literature for help in judgment formation, inductive procedures and guides to inference. The expansions of semi-statistical attitudes in the area of decisions, expected value, utility assessment, etc., seem to have relevance and important applications to accounting. After all, the public accounting profession is based on the value of independent opinion and independent judgment. Members give explicit opinions on many aspects of activity, including management's intent, and implicitly they appraise and weigh the needs of different groups contending for specialized information and balance such needs against estimated costs of providing the information. In the field of control they appraise aspirations, reactions to rewards and penalties, ethical climate, fear of rejection, reluctance to share guilt, and many other similar human reactions. How much control is needed? How much information? The questions are endless. Our knowledge is pitiful.

Certainly the problems are not peculiar to the field of accounting, and they are not new.

> . . . there was a rule in Athenian courts excluding hearsay evidence, on the ground of the general untrustworthiness of reported statements as compared with the evidence of eyewitnesses . . . . Curious and distorted survivals . . . appear in . . . the Middle Ages. For example, two witnesses were required for a "full proof," while a doubtful witness counted for "less than half." The object apparently aimed at was to convert the process of rendering a decision into a calculation of the "resultant force" of the testimony submitted.[1]

The transition from analytic or logical inference to inference from empirical facts is not an easy one, and there is a specious aspect to the drawing of conclusions from a formal set of premises with the rules of transformation given. "Mathematics," states

---

[1] Ernest Nagel, "Principles of the Theory of Probability," *International Encyclopedia of Unified Science* (Chicago: University of Chicago Press, 1955), p. 348.

Polya, "in the making appears as an experimental, inductive science."[2] Carnap also emphasizes that intuition and method are important in deductive logic.

> . . . when a mathematician has found a theorem, he wants to give an exact proof for it so as to compel the assent of others. Finding a theorem is largely a matter of extrarational factors, not guided by rules . . . the rules of deduction are not rules of prescription, but rules of permission and of prohibition.[3]

In fact, much of what passes for mathematical proof is not logically rigorous in the sense that every step is outlined and the citation given to the appropriate logical rule of transformation. Suppes has emphasized that students of mathematics typically feel that they are not given adequate criteria for accepting or rejecting proofs and states.

> In an informal proof enough of the argument is stated to permit anyone conversant with the subject to follow the line of the thought with a relatively high degree of clarity and ease. It is presumably intuitively transparent how to fill in the logical lacunae in the proof . . . in giving an informal proof, we try to cover the essential, unfamiliar, unobvious steps and omit the trivial and routine inferences. However . . . the concepts of being essential, being unfamiliar, or being trivial are not precise . . . .[4]

Now inference may be expanded to cover the process of transferring belief in a collection of premises to belief in the conclusion. Clearly we are in need of some method of identifying which of two beliefs is the stronger and, if possible, some method if measuring and marking how much stronger one is than the other. For it goes without saying that we do hold — and should hold — certain beliefs with more tenacity than others.

G. Polya has performed a service by emphasizing and defending the respectability of heuristic reasoning. The heuristic procedure consists of the study of how invention and discovery are carried on and therefore has strong psychological overtones. Heuristic reasoning "is not regarded as final and strict but as provisional and plausible only, whose purpose is to discover the solution of the present problem . . . . What is bad is to mix up heuristic reasoning with rigorous proof."[5] Heuristic reasoning aims at being plausible and convincing, often makes use of analogies with similar relations, and arrives at tentative

---

[2] G. Polya, *How to Solve It* (New York: Doubleday Anchor Books, 1957, 1945), p. vii. The traditional distinction between analytic and synthetic statements is that predicates of analytic statements repeat the subject, e.g., "A small man is small." Such statements are *a priori* in the sense that they are "true by definition" and not true by experience. In synthetic statements, predicates are not a repetition of the subject. To determine whether such a statement is true or false one must have experience and discrimination. Such propositions are known in classical philosophy as *a posteriori* propositions. Unfortunately the distinction is not always easy to make. Take, for example, the expression: "Material bodies are extended." Perhaps this statement reduces to an equivalent analytic statement: "Extended bodies are extended."

[3] Rudolf Carnap, *Logical Foundations of Probability* (Chicago: University of Chicago Press, 1950), p. 195. He also emphasizes: "Scientists carry out their deductive inferences in most cases, especially where mathematical transformations are not yet involved, in an intuitive, instinctive way, that is, without the use of explicitly formulated rules of logic . . . . In other cases, the premises with which he works are so complex that he is either not able or not willing to take the trouble of formulating them explicitly and exhaustively . . . " *Ibid.*, p. 242. Von Mises is not very charitable to those " . . . naive 'pure theoreticians,' in whose mind all of science dissolves into separate systems of tautological transformations . . . ." Richard von Mises, *Positivism: A Study in Human Understanding* (Cambridge: Harvard University Press, 1951), p. 175.

[4]Patrick Suppes, *Introduction to Logic* (Princeton: D. Van Nostrand Company, Inc., 1957), p. 128. He adds: "As some psychologists would put it, in order to make the transition from formal derivations to informal proofs we must develop a tolerance for ambiguity." *Ibid.*, p. 138.

[5]G. Polya, *op. cit.*, p. 102.

conclusions that may later be subjected to more rigor. The form of heuristic syllogism illustrates the difficulties that have faced so many theorists and takes the form:

$$\frac{\begin{array}{l} \text{If A then B} \\ \text{B True} \end{array}}{\text{A more credible.}}$$

We all would like to know just how much more credible A has become by virtue of B's being true, but this problem is extremely difficult and is reserved for discussion in connection with Bayesian statistics. (Such formulations are, of course, not logically valid.) Polya continues:

> . . . they do not have the certainty of a strict demonstration . . . they are useful in acquiring essentially new knowledge, and even indispensable to any not purely mathematical or logical knowledge . . . . The conclusion of the heuristic syllogism differs from the premises in its logical nature; it is more vague, not so sharp, less fully expressed. This conclusion is comparable to a force, has direction and magnitude. It pushes us in a certain direction: A becomes *more* credible . . . . *The direction* is expressed and is implied by the premises, the magnitude is not.[6]

Let us now turn to the possibility of arranging strength of belief in some sort of order and perhaps applying a measurement index to the results. The discussion begins with the more traditional view. Braithwaite, for example, feels that there is only a slight possibility of finding a useful ordering and is convinced that belief is an all-or-none phenomenon. He states:

> It is not a question of being more or less reasonable in adding H to his rational corpus . . . it is more reasonable to believe a hypothesis if it is supported by a greater amount of evidence of the same kind . . . belief is discarded at one blow; it does not fade out of the corpus by becoming less and less 'probable' until it falls below the 'probability threshold.' Similarly a belief is added at one blow; it does not fade in by becoming more and more 'probable' until it rises above the threshold. The notion of a scale of probabilities of a hypothesis with a corresponding scale of degrees of reasonableness of belief in the hypothesis is, I believe, a philosopher's myth.[7]

Braithwaite recognizes subjective considerations; " . . . although I am unable to recognize differences in the reasonableness of the beliefs which are in my rational corpus, I am able to recognize differences in the *tenacity* with which I hold them."[8] There are several serious objections to Braithwaite's views. First, he assumes without offering anything like either empirical or analytical proof that the corpus of rational belief is a go/no-go kind of thing with beliefs of various kinds not distinguishable on the base of reasonableness. 'Reasonableness' is, of course, a word used without instructions for identifying and scaling. Yet the recognition of the "tenacity with which I hold them" indicates that he feels that beliefs (at least within the corpus) can be discriminated and are probably scalable. We then ask what kinds of changes must be introduced in the evidence to change tenacity habits or to overcome the fixed amounts of tenacity in each case. Braithwaite does not discuss this

---

[6] *Ibid.*, pp. 186, 189.
[7] R. B. Braithwaite, *Scientific Explanation* (Cambridge: University Press, 1953), pp. 356-357.
[8] *Ibid.*, p. 359.

matter fully although he points out: "Of course any particular set of highest level hypotheses may be held very tenaciously, being treated as 'functionally *a priori* ' propositions . . . ."[9]

Braithwaite asserts that there is no threshold for admission, and one is then forced to ask: What are the determinants for admission? What exactly are the habit patterns that determine admission and nonadmission or later rejection? What degree of confirmation is necessary? If every instance of experience tends to confirm a particular belief, we have one of the cruder ideas of causation. Ordinarily scientists do not insist on such a high degree of confirmation. Nagel, for example, points out: "A theory is not in general dismissed as false or worthless because the confirmation of its prediction by observation is only approximate — even though *formally* every deviation from a predicted value of a magnitude is a negative instance for a theory."[10] Carnap has worked extensively with the possibilities for an inductive logic and with the nature of confirmation. For Carnap, inductive logic may be summarized: "Given: a sentence *e* as evidence; wanted: a hypothesis *h* which is highly confirmed by the evidence *e* and suitable for a certain purpose."[11]

The point that is most evident in the Braithwaite use of the concept 'mental corpus' is that the construction is entirely psychological, and the behavioral overlays simply cannot be avoided. One then asks, what are the psychological determinants for admission and rejection of attitudes? Auditing is a profession that derives its revenue and excuse for being from selling its opinions, judgments, and beliefs. How are opinions formed? How are judgments rendered? When does evidence become 'evidence'? These may be the fundamental questions for all auditing, and they are related to Braithwaite's admission and rejection rules. The auditing profession has an additional problem. It must communicate the *feel* for evidence and belief to its practitioners so that an appropriate degree of uniformity is procured.

Now the degree of evidence that will satisfy an individual and justify a conclusion is psychological, yet it does not follow that the auditing profession deals entirely with private opinions. The machinery for teaching, for determining the rules of procedure, and for setting the thresholds for admission to the mental corpus is determined by the leaders of the profession in response to what they believe to be social needs. All of this influence in training and other forms of indoctrination means that the individual is so preconditioned that the communicated attitudes are about as 'public' as one can expect to get.

Probability

It is important for nonspecialists in statistics to realize that mathematicians try to develop a completely abstract set of primitive terms and to define the relationships and properties of all new terms admitted to the set. These relationships and properties are based on notions that are considered to be primitive. It is important that the terms have no interpretations except those given in the axioms that relate them to other terms. The axiomatic system for probability can be developed and can remain completely uninterpreted in the empirical world. Later the term can be interpreted (connected to empirical data by rules of correspondence) in any way that does not violate its relation to the other terms

[9] *Ibid.*, p. 359.
[10] Ernest Nagel, *op. cit.*, p. 397.
[11] Rudolf Carnap, *op. cit.*, p. 194. Carnap distinguishes three levels of confirmation. " . . . (i) a *classificatory* concept of confirmation ('the hypothesis *h* is confirmed by the evidence of *e*'); (ii) a *comparative* concept of confirmation (*h*' is confirmed by *e* at least as highly as *h*' by e' '); (iii) a *quantitative* concept of confirmation, the concept of *degree* of confirmation ('*h*'is confirmed by *e* to the degree *r*')" [p. 163].

after they too have been interpreted. While the construction of an abstract axiomatic system is rarely made without reference to some empirical data, it is important to remember that it could be so constructed. Interpreted systems are often derived originally to account for some empirical data, but alternate interpretations of the system are possible and are sometimes plentiful.

Inasmuch as words ordinarily have undesirable overtones, theorists often set up the system entirely with symbols. Suppes for example states:

> Our axiomatization of probability proceeds by defining the set-theoretical predicate 'as a finitely additive probability space.' The axioms are based on three primitive notions: a nonempty set X of possible outcomes, a family F of subsets of X . . . and a real-valued function P on F; for EϵF, P(E) is *interpreted as the probability of E.*[12]

Mathematicians have made tremendous strides toward generalizing the abstract structure of probability, but at the practical level applied statisticians have had difficulty agreeing on the most useful interpretations. It is with this area that accountants are most directly concerned. It should not come as a surprise that several interpretations are in use. Nagel states:

> There are, in fact, three major interpretations of the term [probable]. According to the first, a degree of probability measures our subjective expectation or strength of belief, and the calculus of probability is a branch of combinatorial analysis . . . . According to the second probability is a unique logical relation between propositions, analogous to the relation of deducibility; its most prominent contemporary supporter is the economist Keynes. According to the third, a degree of probability is the measure of the relative frequency with which a property occurs in a specified class of elements.[13]

Let us start with the early understanding of the term, which was associated with the problems of evidence and confirmation of belief, and is of special concern to the auditing profession. Carnap states: " . . . the term 'probability' was meant in the sense of 'evidential support for an assumption (or event)' or 'rational credibility of an assumption,' and more specifically, as 'numerical degree of this support or credibility.'"[14] De Morgan is reported to have said: "I consider the word *probability* . . . as meaning the state of the mind with respect to an assertion, a coming event, or any other matter on which absolute knowledge does not exist."[15] Nagel devotes some time to discussing whether the degree of probability in the classical sense is based on what folks do believe or on what they ought to believe. Certainly finding a scale of belief that is common to everybody or even to one individual is a difficult task. The classical solution, offered by Laplace and followed to some degree by Poisson, De Morgan, Boole and others, was based on the ability to analyze each possible occurrence into a set of "equipossible alternatives." Once the probability space has been determined, the individual probability is found by dividing the num-

---

[12] Patrick Suppes, *Introduction to Logic, op. cit.*, p. 274. Kolmogorov is usually credited with being the first to construct a rigorous axiomatic structure for probability using finite numbers. "In every situation . . . there is an associated probability space or triple (Ω, ξ, p), where Ω is an abstract space . . . ξ is a σ - algebra of subsets of Ω . . . and p (E) is a measure . . . defined for E$\epsilon\xi$, and satisfying the condition p (Ω) = 1." Statement by A. T. Bharucha - Reid in bibliography for A. N. Kolmogorov, *Foundations of the Theory of Probability* (New York: Chelsea Publishing Company, 1956), p. 77 (published originally in 1933).

[13] Ernest Nagel, *op. cit.*, p. 360.

[14] Rudolf Carnap, *op. cit.*, pp. 182-183.

[15] Quoted from Ernest Nagel, *op. cit.*, p. 386.

ber of favorable alternatives (presumably counted) by the total number of alternatives making up the set. Inasmuch as each alternative is "equipossible" the resulting fraction can be taken to be a measure of probability. One does not have to be a philosopher to feel that basing such a theory on the equipossibility of alternatives leaves something to be desired, although it may be possible to work out a practical guide for action on such a foundation. Does, for example, "equipossible" mean "equiprobable?" If so, the circularity is obvious, and the resulting foundation is not as firm as one would like. The circularity is not complete however, for it is possible to calculate "indifference" or "equal-deal" points in the manner of economists' indifference points and to define new concepts that depend on this relationship. If there is available a set of operational rules for determining indifference and another set for combining them to form a construct, the term probability may be applied to the result.

Unfortunately, it is sometimes difficult to resolve the alternatives into equipossible occurrences, e.g., a loaded die that has a larger possibility of turning an ace. The next step or extension is to follow the lead of Ramsey and set up operational rules for handling nonequipossible alternatives. How may this problem be approached? The Ramsey solution, and the solution that is followed by Bayesian statisticians, is to measure the strength of beliefs by the size of the bets that someone would be willing to take, and to scale nonequipossible events in this fashion. The advantages of this system are clear enough, but unfortunately there are difficulties. Certainly, the amount of the bets that a person would make depends on a lot of things other than his feeling of relative expected frequency, but there is *no* inherent need to identify probability with relative frequency. The assessment is subjective, and there is no implication that the betting odds will scale linearly with individual estimates of frequency or that money should scale linearly with sacrifice.[16]

Nagel also points out that to assume that a probability ratio made up of "equipossible" cases is related to the frequency with which they do in fact fall is unwarranted. He points out that the definition is *a priori* and that the actual frequencies are synthetic and *a posteriori*. In order to set "equipossibilities" and assess utility, one may have a convincing model or only information of the vaguest sort. One may ask whether the operational instructions (methodology) for finding the total possibilities of the set and weighting them will tend to establish some relation between the probabilities and the actual occurrences. Those who do poorly — apply the operational instructions poorly — become losers and may be weeded from the betting fraternity. It may also be asked whether there need be any necessary connection between strength of belief before an occurrence and the frequency of the actual occurrence. A close relationship is not essential, but one's subjective weights are influenced by knowledge of analogous physical models or past frequencies. Again the business fraternity rejects decision makers whose assessments of probabilities stray too far from profitable outcomes.

There is no doubt about the desirability of having measures of the "degree of confirmation" and the "weight of evidence." Whether this kind of thing is called logic or probability is not important so long as the facets of the problem are brought to light. Exactly what operational rules should be followed to test the degree of confirmation of any theory or proposition? To some the truth or falsity of a proposition can never be established with

---

[16] Carnap has again treated this topic in a thorough and competent manner. See *op. cit.*, pp. 252 ff. See also Harry V. Roberts, *Statistical Inference and Decision* (Lithoprinted, Chicago: By the author, 1960), Chaps. 1, 2, 3, and Robert Schlaifer, *Probability and Statistics for Business Decisions* (New York: McGraw-Hill Book Company, Inc., 1959), Chap. 2. Apparently the betting-odds approach was well established in 1926. See F. P. Ramsey, *The Foundations of Mathematics* (Paterson: Littlefield, Adams & Co., 1960), pp. 172 ff.

a finite number of positive instances. One negative instance is supposed to disprove a theory. Fortunately to these extremists the possibility of poor measurement or of unidentified factors means that rarely is a theory abandoned because of a relatively few negative instances. In fact, at times this position is carried to the opposite extreme by defending the anti-rational position that "exceptions prove the rule." Nagel wonders why one feels more secure when several samples show a high degree of stability under repeated sampling. The answer is, of course, psychological and is essentially an appeal to experience.

> A theory is "better established" when we increase the number and kinds of its positive instances, because the *method* we thereby employ is one which our general experience confirms as leading to conclusions which are stable or which provide satisfactory solutions to the specific problems of inquiry . . . . As Peirce succinctly put the matter, "Synthetic inferences are founded upon the classification of facts, not according to their characters, but *according to the manner of obtaining them*. Its rule is that a number of facts obtained in a given way will in general more or less resemble other facts obtained in the same way; or . . . "A degree of confirmation is thus a rough indication of the extent to which our general *method of procedure* has been put into operation.[17]

Perhaps the most widely held empirical interpretation of probability is in terms of relative frequencies. The frequency approach has strong appeal to those with bias for the scientific approach. In the early days of worrying about the nature of probability (and even today), a distinction is made between probabilities *a priori* and probabilities *a posteriori*. In Carnap's words:

> If the evidence . . . said only that the die had the shape of a regular cube, the statement would be said to give a probability *a priori*. If, on the other hand, the evidence described the results of 6,000 throws made with the die and stated that 1,000 of them were aces, the probability was called *a posteriori*.[18]

From the viewpoint of some theories of knowledge there does not seem to be very much difference between the two. The relative frequency method is usually identified with the latter approach. It requires no previous knowledge of the shape of the die (no physical model), for it is concerned only with historical results and with the additional very important requirement that probability be interpreted and defined as the limiting value of the relative frequency of an event in the long run.[19] In one sense the *a priori* approach requires a theory in simple form. Past experience has been gathered about the behavior of aces when a symmetrical die is cast. This experience has provided, or someone's intuition has developed, information that such a cube should fall with a given side up 1/6 of the time. It is possible in simple cases, like a coin, to use intuition, to recall the behavior of similar objects, and conclude that the long-run frequencies should be 1/2. That is to say, there is often a physical model or analogy over and above a record of past frequencies. Researchers feel more confident (feel that the relationship is not "spurious") if they have

---

[17] Ernest Nagel, *op. cit.*, p. 414. (Italics in original.)

[18] Rudolf Carnap, *op. cit.*, p. 188. The former case is based on experience with a physical model; the second case is sometimes called 'empirical.'

[19] *"As a basis of an exact theory of repeated events and mass phenomena one may choose a probability concept defined as the limiting value of the relative frequency of an event in a sequence of trials continued indefinitely."* (All italics in original.) Richard von Mises, *Positivism: A Study in Human Understanding* (Cambridge: Harvard University Press, 1951), p. 169.

independent criteria that support any conclusions from counting frequencies or observing correlations. The relative frequency approach does not rule out devices that help find the limiting values, but it holds that such supplementary support is not necessary. The following summary of the relative-frequency position is from Nagel.

> a) No meaning can be attached to any expression which, taken literally, assigns a probability to a single individual as having a specified property . . . .
>
> b) Every probability statement . . . is a factual statement, into whose determination empirical investigations of some sort must always enter . . . they are not formulations of the degree of our ignorance or uncertainty. To assert . . . the probability of a normal coin . . . is 1/2, is to ascribe a physical property to a coin . . . .
>
> c) Since the explicit definition of probability statements is in terms of relative frequencies, the *direct* evidence for them is of a statistical nature . . . .
>
> d) Since a probability has been defined as the limit of a relative frequency . . . (in the long run), every probability statement is a hypothesis; such a hypothesis cannot be completely confirmed or finally verified by the (necessarily) finite amount of evidence actually at hand at any given time . . . they cannot even be completely disconfirmed by any actual evidence . . . .
>
> e) It is perhaps sufficient to note that the use of probability statements requires no commitment, even by implication, to any wholesale "deterministic" or "indeterministic" world-view . . . ."[20]

It should be quite clear that some problems cannot be measured in the framework of the frequency approach to probability, for there are many questions of judgment and belief for which there is no body of data that remotely approaches a frequency collection. Such an approach is simply inadequate for modern decision theory, for example, because decisions worthy of attention are *not* precisely like *any* previous decision. For that matter, frequency theorists must also exhibit tolerance for ambiguity, for no two 'tosses' or other 'tries' are ever identical. Such statements depend on past factual experience and an assumption about the future. From a methodological viewpoint, the concept of limit assumes a temporal ordering, and, when taken with the impossibility of ever proving or disproving such an assumption with a finite number of tries, the ordering assumption may prove to be distasteful; it is a synthetic assumption. Carnap states:

> Statements . . . which assert success in the long run for the inductive method would be true if the world as a whole had a certain character of uniformity . . . . There is no doubt that the principle is synthetic . . . any attempt to confirm inductively the principle of uniformity would contain a vicious circle . . . . Other philosophers maintain that we must abandon the principle of empiricism which says that a synthetic statement can be accepted only if it is empirically confirmed.[21]

It is generally admitted that the frequency concept of probability cannot answer all questions containing the term 'probable.' How shall we evaluate this statement? It is probably true that Lincoln visited the town of Blacksville? Such a question cannot be answered by holding that it is elliptic and therefore a part of a more complete formulation. The evidence can be weighed in the sense that information that seems relevant may be marshalled and arrayed, but this kind of evidence is not in the form of frequencies and cannot be put

[20] Ernest Nagel, *op. cit.*, pp. 365-366.
[21] Rudolf Carnap, *op. cit.*, pp. 178-179.

into such forms. Nagel emphasizes that the frequency viewpoint with its associated probability calculus cannot answer all types of problems of induction and inverse probabilities.

A common objection to the frequency theory of probability is that, although probability statements concerning single occasions or single propositions are often asserted and debated, it is meaningless to assert such statements in terms of the frequency theory . . . . Frequentists have retorted, quite rightly, that such statements *are* without meaning, if they *literally* attribute a probability in the frequency sense to a single proposition . . .[22]

Perhaps the most interesting criticism of the frequency theory of probability involves the argument that it confuses the evidence (subject matter) with the concept. This view is held by Carnap.

. . . the frequency statement is not a premise of the probability statement but part of its subject matter, and hence the customary phrase "derived from frequencies" is misleading. It would be more correct to say that in these cases the probability is determined with the help of a given frequency and its value is either equal or close to that of the frequency.[23]

Thus it makes about as much sense to assert that our knowledge of the design of a die or a coin makes up the *concept* of probability. Unfortunately elementary business statistic texts sometimes convey this impression.

Some variation of the subjective approach to probability has been introduced by Keynes.[24] Probability according to this view is not interpreted as some scale of subjective expectations, and there can be no such thing as the probability of a single proposition. Probability is defined as a relation between propositions of which one is the conclusion and the other or others are propositions setting forth the evidence. The relationship is held to be beyond the capacity of analysis, and the "logical distance" is held not to be subject to scaling and measurement. In fact, it is highly doubtful if probability in this sense is even capable of being ordered.[25]

Return now for a brief look at the modern subjective interpretation of probability that has influenced recent decision theory and promises fruitful extensions in the field of accounting. A type of belief or confidence index may be established and scaled according to willingness to bet variable sums, and the results may be interpreted as a measure of subjective probability. Braithwaite holds essentially this view.

. . . a scheme of hypothetical generalized betting can be devised which will enable degrees of belief to be measured . . . there is no objective empirical probability with which the degree of his belief ought to correspond . . . . Since betting odds can be attached to the possibility of changes in my rational corpus these will serve to define a subjective sense of "probability" (if we choose to give it that name) . . . .[26]

---

[22] Ernest Nagel, *op. cit.*, pp. 402-403.

[23] Rudolf Carnap, *op. cit.*, p. 188.

[24] J. M. Keynes, *A Treatise on Probability* (London: Macmillan & Co., Ltd., 1921). Chapter IV is concerned with the principle of indifference and Chapter VII gives historical perspective.

[25] Braithwaite, who dedicates his book to Keynes, agrees on this point. "Can any satisfactory general criterion be given for arranging beliefs in scientific hypotheses in an order so that one can be said to be more reasonable than another? . . . I do not believe that any criterion can be given for even a non-numerical comparison which is at all satisfactory." *Op. cit.*, p. 355.

[26] R. B. Braithwaite, *op. cit.*, pp. 358-359. The acknowledged treatise on *subjective* probability and its axiomatic basis is: Leonard J. Savage, *The Foundations of Statistics* (New York: John Wiley & Sons, Inc., 1954).

J. Neyman, R. A. Fisher and others have done some effective work along these lines, but have been careful to distinguish "measures of credibility" from probabilities. Carefully worked out rules have been devised for assigning values which must meet stability standards when subjected to repeated samplings. If the process is to be employed for decisions even this sort of stability is not essential, but some sort of consistency of actions with goals may be implied and some sort of cost structure must be added. The attempt to reunite value theory with positive methods will be considered to be an improvement by most philosophers.

It is clear that the purpose of identifying and measuring strength of belief is to help someone make decisions. These decisions usually take the form of selecting one hypothesis or one course of action over others. For this kind of problem, whether or not the process is known as probability and regardless of the particular decision rule, the assignment of values cannot be avoided. Carnap comes to this conclusion and devotes considerable attention to the considerations necessary to weigh relative values. His position anticipates the 'expected value' of modern statistics, but his decision rule is only one among many possible rules.[27]

Braithwaite comes to a similar position that: ". . . depends essentially upon regarding belief in a hypothesis as having desirable effects if the hypothesis believed is true and undesirable effects if the hypothesis believed is false."[28] This too is the position of quality control statisticians and auditors. The consequences of accepting a document as valid when in fact it is a forgery may have variable consequences, and they may be important or relatively unimportant. The cost of rejecting a procedure or document that is in fact good is ordinarily of less consequence, but the values change in different circumstances. Perhaps the chief merit of modern statistical methods in accounting is that they force auditors to face up to the chances they are willing to take of an unwise acceptance or an unfair rejection. Furthermore, auditors are forced to appraise the relative importance of different errors and weight them in some sort of subjective decision scheme. By so doing, auditors organize their thinking and by making use of intellectual advances in sister professions, they are permitted to concentrate on investigations where their competence is better established.

Digression on Logical and Mathematical Proof

It may be worthwhile for accountants to observe how logical and mathematical proofs are developed. The following discussion is extremely elementary and sketchy, but it may help arouse interest in the topic and encourage an occasional reader to turn to the standard works in the field. Careful study of the mathematical process is ordinarily profitable, and with the extension of computers and mathematical models the process promises to become an increasingly important part of an accountant's training.

---

[27] Rudolf Carnap, *op. cit.*, p. 264. " 'Choose that action for which the estimate of the resulting utility has its maximum.' The use of this rule presupposes that utility can be measured and that there is a quantitative law stating the utility as a function of the gain."

[28] R. B. Braithwaite, *op. cit.*, p. 201. He continues: "The choice is to be determined by a comparison of the desirable effects of believing one hypothesis if it is true and the undesirable effects of believing the other hypothesis if it is true or false. Thus notions of measurable *value* cannot be avoided . . . . The gains and losses considered may be quantities of happiness, or quantities of eudaemonia, or of joy, or of absolute goodness; there is no need for the logician in devising a choice-policy to settle any ethical question as to the nature of the ultimately desirable things." *Loc. cit.*

A brief discussion of the accepted laws of sentential calculus is followed by some comments on the rules of logical inference and the combination of these laws and rules to develop analytical proofs. Some points of controversy among logicians and mathematicians will be mentioned. In spite of similarities in training and knowledge, some mathematicians are convinced relatively easily while others insist on more difficult standards of rigor.

The following laws of logic are relatively simple and are familiar and acceptable to most accountants.

1. (Identity) If p then p.
2. (Simplification for addition) If p then q or p.
3. (Simplification for multiplication) If p implies q and q implies r, then p if, and only if, q.
4. (Hypothetical syllogism) If p implies q, and q implies r, then p implies r.

The laws below may not be so clear.

5. (Contradiction) Both p and not p are not compatible, i.e., $\sim [p \wedge (\sim p)]$. The symbolism is read: It is false that p and not p. The wave $\sim$ means 'not' or it is false that.
6. (Excluded middle) Everything must be p or not p., i.e., $p \vee (\sim p)$. The wedge indicates 'or' and the expression may be read: Either p or not p.
7. (Double negation) If not p is false, then p., i.e., $[\sim(\sim p)] \leftrightarrow p$.
8. (Tautologies) (a) p and p if, and only if, p., i.e., $(p \wedge p) \leftrightarrow p$.
   (b) p or p if, and only if, p., i.e., $(p \vee p) \leftrightarrow p$.
9. (Commutativity) Except in rare logical or algebraic systems it is assumed that p and q is equivalent to q and p, and that p or q is equivalent to q or p. Thus: $p \wedge q \leftrightarrow q \wedge p$, and $p \vee q \leftrightarrow q \vee p$.
10. (Associativity) The associative laws for multiplication (a) and addition (b) are usually assumed.
    (a) $[p \wedge (q \wedge r)] \leftrightarrow [(p \wedge q) \wedge r]$.
    (b) $[p \vee (q \vee r)] \leftrightarrow [(p \vee q) \vee r]$.

Particular care should be taken with the use of "implies" or "follows" in logical proof, and as will be pointed out later, there is some disagreement among logicians themselves. The logical usage has a conventional and somewhat specialized meaning. By agreement an implication is true in all cases except one: It cannot be that the first part (antecedent or hypothesis) is true and the second part (consequence or argument) is false. All other truth possibilities make the implication true. For example, the implication: "If an object is tangible, then it is an asset" is true if the particular object is or is not tangible and whether it is or is not in fact an asset. It is a false implication only if the item is tangible and is not an asset. Strange conclusions — at least to a nonlogician — may be derived. Witness the following adapted from Tarski:

"If p is true then p follows from any q . . . a true sentence follows from every sentence;

if p is false, then p implies any q . . . a false sentence implies every sentence;

for any p and q, either p implies q or q implies p . . . at least one of any two sentences implies the others."

The point to be emphasized is that the very apparatus of logic itself is not at all self-evident. Logicians themselves have felt uneasy about the nature of the above "formal" implication, and alternative formulations have been advanced by Lewis, Keynes, Reichenbach and others.[29]

The definition of some further relations may help one understand the procedure for grinding out logical and mathematical proofs.

Converse. The converse of p→q is q→p. The converse of "all assets are services to be received" is "all services to be received are assets!" We can see immediately that the truth of a statement does not assure the truth of its converse. The truth of the sentence 'factory labor is a production cost' does not establish the truth of the statement 'production cost is factory labor.' 'All girls are females' does not imply that 'all females are girls.'

Inverse. The inverse is formed by negating both the hypothesis and the argument of an implication. In symbolic terms the inverse of p→q is (∼ p) → (∼q). Again the truth of a sentence does not guarantee the truth of its inverse. The admission that 'bookkeeping is accounting' does not establish the truth of the inverse 'that which is not bookkeeping is not accounting.' The inversion in this case is obviously false, but some inversions do happen to be true.

Contrapositive. The contrapositive is formed by replacing the hypothesis by the argument as in the converse and then negating each part. The contrapositive is the inverse of the converse, and for the original statement p→q the contrapositive is (∼q) → (∼p). Now it can be established (shown, proved, made believable) that whenever a sentence is true its contrapositive is also true. For example:

Statement: 'Labor cost is factory cost.' (true)
Contrapositive: 'That which is not factory cost is not labor cost.' (true)

Perhaps the greatest advantage and worth of formal or general rules of logic and mathematics is illustrated here. Once it has been shown that the truth of any implication implies the truth of its contrapositive, this rule may be applied to any particular statement or 'interpretation.' If the contrapositive is formed correctly, we are assured that the implication of the contrapositive is valid without further proof. If the reader has wondered why it is that mathematicians and logicians are so intent on establishing the generality of their procedures and relationships, the relationship of an implication and its contrapositive and the resulting economy of intellectual effort should put his mind at ease.

Before turning to other matters it is interesting and useful to observe that the inverse is in fact the contrapositive of the converse. Now if the converse is established, the inverse can be asserted without further proof. This statement assumes that the reader is satisfied with the evidence logicians advance to support the truth of the relationships between the original implication, its contrapositive, and the converse and the inverse. The laws of logic themselves must be satisfying, although sometimes the relationships are so complicated that the reader is convinced by faith. For most folks, however, the establishment of the truth of a sentence and its converse by independent means will be sufficient to establish the truth of the inverse and the contrapositive.

---

[29] For brief summaries of alternative meanings for implication see: Raymond L. Wilder, *Introduction to the Foundations of Mathematics* (New York: John Wiley & Sons, Inc., 1952), pp. 213-214.

In addition to the so-called laws of logic there are *rules* of inference of which the rule of substitution and the rule of detachment are the most familiar. In logic *equality* is more rigid than in common usage. 'A equals B' means that A is another name for B, i.e., that everything that is asserted about A may be asserted about B. The common usage in the sense of a pile A is equal in weight to pile B is a special meaning that is applied when the universe has been limited to matters of weight. Also the expression 'variable' in logic and mathematics is used in the broad sense of a 'place holder.' The statement 'x is green' contains a variable x and the sentential or propositional function is not true or false until the identity of the variable x is specified.

The Rule of Substitution is a method of getting new statements from old ones by substituting for the existing variables either new variables, equals, or *concrete interpretations* of the variables. The Rule of Detachment (*Modus Ponens*) has been stated by Tarski:

> . . . if two sentences are accepted as true, of which one has the form of an implication while the other is the antecedent [hypothesis] of this implication, then that sentence may also be recognized as true which forms the consequent [argument] of the implication.[30]

We are now in a position to see how a formal deductive or axiomatic system works. *Undefined terms* must be agreed on in order to avoid the circularity of an infinite regress that comes inevitably from attempting to define everything. In the abstract — in the most general expression — these terms may be devoid of meaning, but for an 'interpretation' of the abstract system it is necessary to have some intuitive knowledge of these undefined items — something must be known about the undefined terms. This intuitive flavor of semi-definition of undefined terms before an interpretation can get off the ground seems to be an intuitive oasis in a veritable desert of rigor. If for example 'asset' is an undefined term of an accounting interpretation, we must know enough about 'asset' to use it in the system without being allowed to define it in the language of the system. The second requirement of a deductive system calls for *axioms*. These axioms are unproved propositions that in an abstract system may be picked at random but in an interpreted system are formulated from experience and concern the permissible behavior of the undefined terms. Needless to say, the selection of a set of axioms for a field such as accounting may require a considerable knowledge of the behavior of the field, and it is easy to understand why the generalized system in practice so often follows years or even centuries of practical knowledge. Theorems — propositions that have been proved with the aid of axioms, undefined terms, and the rules of logic — are often called the 'theory' of the abstract system. Inasmuch as the truth or validity of the theorems has already been admitted, they can be used to develop further theorems without the need for going back to the primitive elements each time.

The development of an abstract system has often been compared to playing a game. The cards and their behavior are accepted and the rules of logic make up the rules for playing the game. The interpretation of the formal system in terms of accounting is treated in some detail in another essay, but in passing it should be pointed out that if Mattessich and others are successful in fitting the objectives of accounting into an axiomatic framework and employing the methods of logic and algebra, many implications that are not now suspected may be brought to light. For example, if it can be established that accounting or any portion of it meets, say, the definition of a mathematical *group*, immedi-

---

[30] Alfred Tarski, *Introduction to Logic* (New York: Oxford University Press, 1946), p. 48.

ately all the previously developed or proved theorems that apply to group theory must be true also for the 'interpretation in accounting.' These formal theorems then become a part of the 'theory,' and the resulting statements in terms of accounting, mechanics, geometry, physics or even the number system itself are known as proofs by interpretation.[31]

Let us turn to proof in formal systems. The laws and rules of logic are applied to the axioms so that new propositions are established or proved. These new propositions — theorems — are then added to the undefined terms, axioms, defined terms, and previously established theorems to increase the body of theory. But the reader may be impatient with generalities and ask how propositions are proved. Proof may take on many variations but here it may be sufficient to illustrate briefly the methods employed in direct and indirect approaches.

In order to prove that $x \to y$ we may start in a direct fashion to examine all the body of theory that is available. Perhaps in the pool of admissible theorems we can find that $x = y$, i.e., x is another name for y. In this case, we can substitute y for x and derive $y \to y$, and then apply the law of identity. Perhaps instead we find in the bag of existing information that $\sim(\sim x) \to y$. In this case we can apply the rule of double negation to establish the original statement. On the other hand, we may already know that $(\sim y) \to (\sim x)$. By the rule of contraposition we immediately know that $x \to y$.

For a slightly more complicated case, suppose that we have been convinced by previous proofs that $x \to z$ and also that $z \to y$. Now suppose we know x to be valid, then the rule of detachment tells us that z must be valid. Now acceptance of the validity of z forces us by the rule of detachment to accept the validity of y. Thus if we accept x as valid and accept the laws of logic, we are forced to the conclusion that y is valid. It should be noticed that the rule of the syllogism may be accepted directly. Thus $[(x \to z)$ and $(z \to y)] \to (x \to y)$ can be applied. The validity of the hypothesis (antecedent) by a single use of the law of detachment assures the validity of the conclusion (consequence).

The indirect method of proof has several variations, but it starts with the negation of the conclusion. Again, it may be possible to find previous axioms or theorems that show $x \to \sim y$. In this case the law of the excluded middle indicates that $x \to y$ cannot possibly be valid. Instead it may be possible to ascertain that $(\sim y) \to (\sim x)$. Now the contrapositive rule states $[(\sim y) \to (\sim x)] \to (x \to y)$. We have found that if the antecedent is valid the detachment rule assures the validity of $(x \to y)$. In other cases the denial of the conclusion may lead to the denial of the hypothesis (as above), to the denial of itself, or to denial of theorems previously proved or even of axioms.

Suppose, for a more complicated illustration, that we have accepted the mechanics of logic and wish to prove the following theorem in accounting: If cash is an asset, it cannot be worthless. We shall adopt only these three axioms:

(1) Cash is the asset in this instance.

(2) If the asset (in this instance) is an asset, it has value.

(3) If the asset (in this instance) is worthless, then it does not have value.

It should be noted that symbols are not necessary to demonstrate the proof, but, as usual, symbols tend to simplify the demonstration by emphasizing the formal relationships. Ap-

---

[31] See *Ibid.*, p. 117 ff.

plication of the rule of substitution permits us to substitute the identity of cash for the asset in this instance in axioms (2) and (3). Now denote:

"Cash is an asset" by a,
"Cash has value" by b,
"Cash is worthless" by c.

With these symbols the theorem to be proved becomes $a \rightarrow \sim c$. Axiom (2) becomes $a \rightarrow b$, and Axiom (3) becomes $c \rightarrow \sim b$.

The direct proof proceeds as follows. Assume the validity of the hypothesis (antecedent) a of the theorem to be proved. Then from (2), $a \rightarrow b$ is valid and by detachment b is valid. Now (3) states that $c \rightarrow \sim b$ is valid, and the law of contraposition shows that $[c \rightarrow (\sim b)] \rightarrow \{[\sim (\sim b)] \rightarrow (\sim c)\}$. Therefore by detachment we must accept the consequent, i.e., $[\sim (\sim b) \rightarrow (\sim c)]$. But the rule for double negation lets us substitute b for $\sim (\sim b)$, so we may write $b \rightarrow \sim c$. At this stage we have shown that b is valid and that $b \rightarrow \sim c$ is valid, so that the rule of detachment will assure us that $\sim c$ is valid. The theorem is thus proved, for we have shown that if a is valid, then $\sim c$ must also be valid. In words: if cash is an asset, it cannot be worthless.

The theorem can also be proved by indirect methods. Remember that in symbolic terms the theorem becomes $a \rightarrow \sim c$; axiom (1) becomes $a \rightarrow b$; and axiom (3) becomes $c \rightarrow \sim b$. An indirect proof begins by an assumption that the consequence is false, and therefore we replace $\sim (c)$ by $\sim (\sim c)$. But the rule of negation lets us write c for $\sim (\sim c)$. Axiom (3) then becomes by this substitution $\sim (\sim c) \rightarrow \sim b$. We assume the validity of $\sim (\sim c)$ and by detachment $\sim b$ is valid. We now turn to axiom (2) and apply the rule of contraposition to get $(a \rightarrow b) \rightarrow [(\sim b) \rightarrow (\sim a)]$. Now axiom (2) assures us that the hypothesis is valid, therefore by detachment we are assured that $(\sim b) \rightarrow (\sim a)$ is valid. We have already established the validity of $\sim b$ so by detachment again we know that $(\sim a)$ is valid. At this point we have established that $[\sim (\sim c)] \rightarrow (\sim a)$ is valid. The final step is to apply the rule of contraposition to yield $\{[\sim (\sim c)] \rightarrow (\sim a)\} \rightarrow (a \rightarrow \sim c)$ and the theorem is proved.

It should be emphasized that these proofs could be established without symbolism, but they may be considerably more difficult to follow or to construct. The machinery of symbolic logic is available to all who wish to make use of it, and to fail to utilize it may be a waste of valuable intellectual resources. In a similar fashion mathematics has a tremendous arsenal of specialized resources that is available for use by anyone who can profit by their use. Moreover, if our needs as accountants are so specialized that existing logical and mathematical tools are inadequate, accountants along with professionals in logic and mathematics are free to develop new procedures and methods that may be applied. Within recent years the methods of matrices and groups have been applied to and even expanded for the social sciences. Accountants have been a little backward about applying modern methods to their problems. Our mathematics has been confined to the simplest operations of arithmetic and algebra, and our definitions have not been sharp enough to utilize the more powerful logical weapons. In short we have used mathematics to calculate and have largely neglected its potential to further theoretical inquiry.

There is an even greater lack of agreement among logicians. The intuitionist school, for example, accepts the usual meaning of contradiction in the sense that any statement that implies contradiction has to be false, but the intuitionist does not accept the law of the excluded middle with its consequence that the falsity of a false statement implies its truthfulness. For an example, consider the following statement from Wilder.

"There exists a natural number having property P . . . one may resort to the device of showing that the assumption of nonexistence of such a number leads to contradiction and concluding that one has thereby proved the theorem . . . . The intuitionist would not accept such a "proof" as this . . . proof — by *exhibition* of a number with the desired property P — is of the constructive character demanded by the intuitionist . . . . This does not involve a use of the Law of the Excluded Middle, however, nor its corollary that the falsity of the falsity of a proposition p implies p![32]

While the attitude taken here is that proof (even logical validity) requires empirical monitoring, a modified approach that plays down psychological involvement is sometimes used and has some advantages for abstract argument. This concept of proof is highly mechanical and is stated by Carnap as follows.

By a *proof* in L we understand not a train of thoughts of a particular kind, but a sequence of sentences of L which in a certain sense corresponds to such a train of thoughts. The correctness of a given step from the preceding sentences of such a sequence to some subsequent sentence thereof is not tested on the ground that it is a more or less plausible inference in the train of thought, but rather on the ground that it does or does not conform to the transformation rules for L . . . a *proof* in L is a (finite) sequence of sentences of L, each of which is either a primitive sentence or a definition, or else is directly derivable from sentences preceding it in the sequence . . . . If the negation of a sentence is provable in L, we say the sentence itself is *refutable* in L.[33]

At first glance this approach to proof seems to be entirely different from the essentially psychological approach used in this essay. The difference turns out to be less dramatic. A proof in the above sense is defined in terms of the rules of transformation, but how are the rules of transformation determined and when do they apply? These rules are determined by those who make use of the language and are in fact constructed with an eye to their ability to satisfy the needs of those who make use of the abstract language of logic — to satisfy those who must interpret the language in the semantic sense. The plausibility of the proof, to Carnap, apparently is shifted to the plausibility of the transformation rules, and he is not concerned with the intuitive plausibility of the intermediate statements.[34] The advantage and economies of being convinced that the 'tools' and 'processes'

---

[32] Raymond L. Wilder, *op. cit.*, pp. 243-244. Wilder points out that L. E. J. Brouwer is considered to be the leader of the intuitionist school, although many of the ideas go back to Kronecker. Brouwer's intuitionism rejects such nonintuitive concepts as infinity so that a good part of mathematics does not meet his test for proof. It is also interesting to note that mathematics is divorced from the 'social consensus' assumption and is at least partially divorced from logic. Wilder (p. 232) states: " . . . it [intuitionism] recognizes the ability of the individual person to perform a series of mental acts consisting of a first act, then another and so on endlessly . . . . This operation is not dependent upon the use of a language . . . mathematics is basically *independent of language*. For the *communication* of mathematics the usual symbolic devices, including ordinary language, are necessary, but this is their only function. This seems to make of mathematics virtually an *individual* affair rather than an organized or *cultural* phenomenon."

[33] Rudolf Carnap, *Introduction to Symbolic Logic and Its Applications* (New York: Dover Publications, Inc., 1958), p. 90. Notice the necessity for 'preceding' and the implied ordering. A similar approach to the meaning of 'fact' attempts to play down psychological overtones.

[34] *Ibid.*, pp. 85-86. "They [the rules of transformation] consist of rules specifying primitive sentences and rules of inference . . . . Our choice of primitive sentences and rules of inference will turn out to square with the interpretation we intend to make . . . ." That Carnap is aware of the psychological overtones of logic is well understood. For example: "Though logic cannot lead us to anything new in the logical sense, it may well lead to something new in the psychological sense. Because of limitations on man's psychological abilities, the discovery of a sentence that is L-true or of a relation of L-implication is often an important cognition. But this cognition is not a factual one, and is not an insight into the state of the world; rather, it is a clarification of logical relations subsisting between concepts . . . . *Content can never be increased by a purely logical procedure.*" PP. 21-22.

are satisfactory so that intermediate results need not square with our ideas of plausibility at every step are certainly obvious. In fact, in some complicated relationships in physics and elsewhere it may be impossible to give any meaningful interpretation to correspond with some intermediate steps other than to know that the steps were made according to the rules of inference and are therefore valid according to those rules.[35] One's confidence in the results — the plausibility of the results — depends on his confidence in his calculus (language) and at the practical level on the feeling that his interpretations (his semantics) are proper.

Carnap makes a distinction between proofs and derivations. The degree of difference does not seem to be great, but the difference in import is considerable. Essentially derivations are proofs, but the proofs are derived from sentences which themselves may or may not be provable or even true. These sentences are called 'premises' and may be added to the primitive terms and rules of inference. Clearly the conclusions are true only if the premises are true, and the confidence in the conclusions will normally be no greater than the confidence in the premises.[36]

A number of social scientists (and perhaps a few scattered accountants) have been strongly influenced by Hegel's so-called dialectic method as an alternative logic. To the extent that this approach calls attention to the interconnectivity of all events it has holistic overtones. But as Hook points out, the effects are not very startling unless the method helps determine how events are related and "what *kind* of interrelation is meant."[37]

The Hegelian doctrine of polar opposites appears to be a poorly defined substitute for negation. Instead of using 'tin cans' and 'not tin cans' we find ourselves looking for the 'polar opposite' of tin cans. What is the 'opposite of' automobile? A star? Accounting? A debit? Does, as Hook suggests, 'polar-opposite' mean only that there are diffeences in data or experiences that can be isolated? This conclusion is trivial. Hook concludes: " . . . the term 'dialectic' is so infected with ambiguity, that it is not likely to function as a serviceable designation for any concept or intellectual procedure in any inquiry which aims at the achievement of reliable knowledge . . . ."[38]

---

[35] R. G. D. Allen states: "A mathematical proof may be quite incapable of 'translation' though the premises from which it starts and the consequences reached can be, and should be, put in 'literary' form. The testing of a theory can lead to its rejection as inconsistent with the facts; but it can never lead to the 'proof' of the theory, but only to its provisional acceptance as not inconsistent with facts." *Mathematical Economics* (London: Macmillan Co. Ltd., 1956), p. xv. The first sentence technically does not deal with the relationship of sentences to empirical data. Allen is comparing two languages.

[36] Carnap, *Introduction to Symbolic Logic, op. cit.*, p. 92. (There are opposing views. See *Essays*, Vol. III, *Essay One* for statements by Whitehead and Friedman.)

[37] Sidney Hook, *Reason, Social Myths and Democracy* (New York: The Humanities Press, 1950), Chap. 9. Reprinted as "Dialectic and Nature," *Readings in Philosophy of Science*, ed. Philip P.Wiener (New York: Charles Scribner's Sons, 1958).

[38] Hook, *op. cit.*, p. 266. It is interesting to note that Hegel, himself, did not fall into the trap of considering all knowledge a closed system. He recognized "relatively isolated systems" and Hook makes an attempt to show that the dialectic may be interpreted as a type of scientific method. *Ibid.*, p. 194. To be scientific in a dialectic framework requires instructions for recognizing the thesis and the antithesis, and ability to follow the devious paths of their interaction to syntheses that may be far from obvious. Where are such instructions?

VOLUME I
Author Index

VOLUME I
Subject Index

Footnotes, 124
Formalist, 91n
Fractionation methods, 121
Function, 49
Fundamental measurement, 119n
Future, 26

Generalization, 7

Heuristic reasoning, 144
History, 25
Holism, 10

Ideas, 33
Income, 60, 96, 113, 123
Indirect proofs, 157
Inference, 88
Internal controls, 58
Interpretation, 155
Intuitionist school, 158n
Inverse, 154

Judgments, 89
Just noticeable differences, 121

Language, 91n
Laws of logic, 153
Legal approach to evidence, 138
Level of abstraction, 86, 87
Liabilities, 113
Logic, 94, 95
Logical behavior, 95
Logical empiricism, 8
Logical implication, 153
Logical proof, 152
Logical truth, 92

Management science, 1
Managerial accounting, 79
Managerial responsibilities, 19
Managers, 77
Mathematical proof, 144, 152
Mathematics, 8, 117, 127
Meaning, 2, 86n
Measurement, 115
Measurement defined, 116
Measurement scales, 119
Mental operations, 6
Merits, 100
Metaphysics, 4
Modus ponens, 155
Monism, 7

N-tuple entry, 21
Noisy channels, 85, 107

Nominal measurement, 117
Nonsense statements, 2

Objectivity, 73, 74n, 132, 134, 136
Objectivity in science, 135
Operationism, 5
Opinion, 50, 139

Personal probabilities, 129
Polar opposites, 159
Positive instances, 149
Positivism, 6
Postulates, 10
Power, 21n
Pragmatics, 10, 83
Premanagement, 81
Present, 25
Price system, 39, 75n, 77, 80
Probability, 146
Probable, interpretation of, 147
Professors, 32, 34
Progress, 97n
Progressive, 97
Proof, 127
Pseudo propositions, 8
Psychiatry, 84
Psychology, 57
Public accounting profession, 105

Qualitative, 117
Quantitative, 117

Rationality, 74n
Reality, 5
Realization, 112
Reduction, 7
Referents, 86
Relative frequencies, 149, 150
Replication, 133, 134
Research costs, 111
Retained earnings restrictions, 113
Rule of detachment, 155
Rule of substitution, 155
Rules of correspondence, 85
Rules of inference, 155
Rules of logic, 8

Sampling, 53
Scaling, 125
Science, 95
Scientific method, 2
Semantics, 10, 83
Semiotic, 83
Simulation, 46

ESSAYS IN
ACCOUNTING THEORY

Volume II

AMERICAN ACCOUNTING ASSOCIATION

The By-Laws of the American Accounting Association state that the first purpose of the Association shall be "to initiate, encourage, and sponsor research in accounting and to publish or aid in the publication of the results of research." In harmony with this objective, the publication of the Studies in Accounting Research is aimed at encouraging and publishing research. This series is an outgrowth of the research program initiated by the Association in 1965. Under this program research projects and authors are selected by the Director of Research, who is assisted by a Research Advisory Committee.

This project was based on the author's lifework over nearly a half century, in which accounting issues are analyzed from an interdisciplinary perspective, in particular from the standpoint of such basic disciplines as scientific methodology, philosophy, ethics, logic, mathematics, economics, and behavioral science. In preparing the materials for this publication, the author was assisted by a Project Advisory Committee consisting of Yuji Ijiri (Carnegie-Mellon University, chairperson), Edward V. McIntyre (Florida State University), and Stephen A. Zeff (Rice University), as well as by AAA Publications Director, Janet G. Nuñez.

This publication was approved by Theodore J. Mock (University of Southern California), 1982-84 Director of Research. The Research Advisory Committee (1982-83) at the time of publication approval was composed of Joel S. Demski (Stanford University), Daniel L. Jensen (Ohio State University), James C. McKeown (University of Illinois), James A. Ohlson (University of California, Berkeley), Lawrence Revsine (Northwestern University), and William F. Wright (University of Minnesota), in addition to the Director of Research.

ESSAYS IN
ACCOUNTING THEORY

Volume II

by
Carl Thomas Devine

AMERICAN ACCOUNTING ASSOCIATION
1985

TABLE OF CONTENTS

TABLE OF CONTENTS

Essay One

The Unit Problem

The purpose of this essay is to register a mild protest about the general sterility of the entity — proprietorship — fund discussions and to emphasize the importance of unit selection in accounting measurement. Surely there are more important differences in the selection of a reporting viewpoint than whether the accounting equation is to be written A - L = P or A = L + P. Surely the entity approach has more to offer than a squabble over whether interest charges are expenses or income distributions. Just as surely a switch to the entity view does not guarantee the ascendancy of the income report or herald the end of status reports. Certainly the fund approach implies more than reduced emphasis on legal considerations and a highly questionable reduction of behavioral overtones.

Accountants who insist that an accounting entity is an area of interest and that measuring and reporting are purposive activities are on the right track. The entity-selection problem requires identification of the individuals and groups contending for information, and the problem also requires recognition of the kinds of information wanted. It is usually impossible to provide adequate information for all individuals so that a selection process based on an ordering of the contending parties according to importance is required. A further ordering of the information with respect to each party is also necessary.

Now this ranking of psychological entities may be done in an explicit manner, or it may be done implicitly (by default) by selecting procedures on the basis of nonpersonal criteria. The selection of the proprietary approach, for example, tends to rank the needs of residual owners extremely high but need not neglect completely the interests of creditors, suppliers, taxing units, national income computers, workers, etc. The fund approach, at least in the Vatterian version, places the interests of managers in a prime position and views creditors not as individuals with important informational needs but as restricting influences on managerial freedom of action. Creditors and other nonmanagers are outsiders who do little more than make up the environment. The entity approach apparently started on a desirable path by emphasizing the organization in relation to all kinds of individual and group interests. Unfortunately, some advocates have seemed to lose sight of the obvious advantages of the approach and have emphasized the interests of equity holders. The peculiar needs of managers and other groups have been practically submerged. Perhaps each accountant will appraise need and worthiness differently. The merit of the entity view is that it can be based on the concept of an organization with cooperating and contending individuals with diverse objectives. It is impossible to avoid drawing some line between insiders and those outside the organization, for such lines must be drawn for routine measuring and reporting. However, adoption of the entity approach does not imply a fixed ordering of interests and permanent boundaries between insiders and outsiders. These boundaries may be modified through the selection of classification and measurement rules.

This essay examines some accepted recognition and measurement conventions and some of their alternatives. Attempts are made to relate them to different units and to speculate about the usefulness of each. The discussion begins with a broad look at the entity, moves to individual assets and liabilities as opposed to group totals, considers losses on units of inventory when value of total stocks is unimpaired, and concludes with a note on the cost of shrinkage and unsuccessful exploration. We begin with the old, but important, procedural problem: whether to select small units and aggregate them so long as they prove to be useful or to select a large unit and use imputation devices until interest wanes. Of course, accountants in practice are not restricted to one or the other; forunately they may combine both.

Many of the arguments and controversies in accounting result from undisclosed differences in points of view with regard to the accountability units selected. Economists have often considered a business organization, or even an industry, to be a monolithic structure with its components highly synchronized as to objectives and motivation. The accountant, burdened with problems of measurement and reporting, has been less rigid and has generally directed his measurement conventions to parts of the organization that seem manageable and has assumed that the results may be aggregated for the entire organization. Moreover, his approach to behavioral reactions has tended to be of the simple stimulus-response type without the holistic niceties of psychological fields and Gestalt ambiguities. It is also interesting to observe that economists of the older school often adopted a long-run view (a long-time horizon) while accountants, in spite of claiming the going-concern concept as their very own, have often proceeded as if the organization's history is composed of numerous piecemeal conversions and liquidations, e.g., inventories and equipment. Clearly the selection of units has important methodological and theoretical consequences and is too important to be neglected or tossed off in a cavalier manner.

The simplest unit for measuring income would seem to be the entire organization. Some sort of community of interests is selected for the entity and a set of rules adopted for measuring such constructs as financial status, efficiency, and income. The enterprise-wide definition of income, for example, calls for estimates of future favorable and unfavorable events and conventions for coordinating these estimates in some kind of time pattern. At first glance this approach seems to avoid the usual problems of separable services (joint efforts) and the necessity for determining individual contributions to favorable events.

A second glance is likely to reduce optimism over the expected benefits of an overall enterprise approach. What are the rules for anticipating, estimating and especially measuring future favorable and unfavorable events? It might be possible to make such estimates without regard to the existing pile of *individual* resources and the necessity for replenishing and perhaps expanding the pile, but clearly estimates must be tied to manageable factors that have relevance to the future streams of events. Overall estimates of this sort may be possible for relatively uncomplicated activities, but most businessmen wish to examine the individual agents that contribute to the future events and appeal to their intuitive feeling for cause and effect and for responsibility. Thus some attention to the individual agents contributing to the stream of favorable circumstances seems to be indicated. Certainly estimates of future expenditures for an entire enterprise must be related somehow to the individual services needed to preserve the revenue stream, and these services are usually related to *particular* sources — potentials for specific kinds of service. In other words, our present estimating techniques usually proceed *from* specific services needed *to* expenditures required rather than directly from expenditures back to individual services necessary to support the income stream.

Let us turn now to the problem of selecting an extremely long time interval. A long interval combined with an assumption that calls for keeping capital intact means that 'basic' liabilities need never be paid, capital funds need never be returned, and 'basic' assets never depreciate except in the sense that the stream of replacement expenditures is nearer and often irregular. Thus, pensions accumulated for past services under this view can be neglected as a liability except for the change in the present value of irregular out-lays within the time horizon during which discounting is a material factor. Clearly, dis-counting events in the infinitely distant future results in valuations of zero, i.e., their dis-counted value at any rate other than zero approaches zero. While the basic amount of lia-bility need never be paid, it is true that a more or less continuous stream of unfavorable outpayments is necessary, and the discounted value of this series is by no means zero. Thus, if we were to discount the expected stream of individual payments to liability holders in perpetuity at some going rate we would ordinarily have a large number. But what about the favorable effects of the services furnished by incurring new individual pay-ables — the asset effect?

To the extent that services arise from expenditures and the level of services remains ap-proximately unchanged through the years, it may be argued that the 'value added' to the pool of service potential by such expenditures is at least as great as the expenditures them-selves and that they keep the value of the entire pool from deteriorating. To argue that no value has been added by expenditures to keep the expected value near the old level is to hold that the old level could be maintained without effort — a ridiculous position. Thus the series of expenditures keeps the service expectations flowing. Accountants usually as-sume that the discounted increase in expected service potential is at least equal to the dis-counted value of the payments to liability holders. The asset valuation resulting from such procedures is then comparable to the liabilities 'valued' in a similar fashion.

A digression on the much-discussed capital-revenue clearage seems appropriate at this point. This so-called principle gets around the problem of long discounting periods for as-sets and liability values by first establishing a level of service expectations for existing as-sets. (Considerable range in the size of the unit is found.) Expenditures to maintain the service level (maintain service potential intact) are matched immediately with revenue, i.e., not shown as increasing the service potential of the organization. Expenditures that raise service expectations above this level are capitalized to the amount of the expenditure provided value added is equal to or greater than the expenditure. Capital expenditures then tend to increase the potential of the selected assemblage of assets. Revenue expendi-tures are those necessary to keep the environment (or some part of it) suitable for activity, and capital charges appear when such conditions are improved. The clearage is relatively clear-cut when applied to total fixed assets as in the renewal-depreciation method, but it is less successful when applied to individual assets.

In a similar manner, payments to creditors take the form of continuous replacements. The basic amount may be viewed as contributed capital and may be treated as a part of permanent capital without maturity — a kind of permanent capital equity. Payments may in fact be divided automatically into a kind of revenue-capital division. Any temporary excess over the basic long-run amount may be considered to mature and to require repay-ment, while the permanent long-run base may be treated as contributed capital.

These procedures seem complicated and unrewarding to nonaccountants until the con-sequences of alternatives are considered. What about estimating total receipts and expen-ditures in perpetuity? Clearly, discounted amounts have some meaning in a business con-text, even though 50 years in the land of compound interest are roughly equivalent to in-finity. To this accountant, at least, it seems far more simple to adopt a modified capital-revenue approach, establish a level of service potential, and approach the asset problem by estimating value added to or subtracted from such a base. At least the estimates take a different form. Liabilities seem to have less urgent and important consequences. A certain amount of capital is in effect furnished by creditors whose contracts have individual due dates. A broad conception of the liability 'unit' removes it from liability status for a continuing concern! A narrow view that considers each account as a liability seems to adopt an opposing view. Legal definitions aside, the scope of the unit adopted can create or destroy a "liability."[1]

It is often pointed out that long-term liabilities are refinanced — never paid — and thus are clearly instruments for permanent financing. When individual liabilities are actually paid, the situation is essentially the same as long as the total remains practically unchanged. The only way the total could remain unchanged is, of course, to incur new liabilities as soon as the existing ones are paid.

The accounting difficulties that accompany the overall enterprise view are imposing, but any atomistic view encounters special difficulties of its own. That consideration of each individual asset apart from any surrounding support is inadequate has long been understood by accountants and economists alike.[2] The economic concept of value-in-use as opposed to market value dates at least as far back as Adam Smith, and the accountant's going-concern value is among the more ancient of accounting conventions. Both concepts are clearly based on an organismic view of the enterprise and recognize that valuation problems must be considered in a structured environment in which the importance of relationships is dominant.

It seems that accountants have preferred to approach the income problem first by adopting the organismic view long enough to define an entity — an area of interest — and then employing measurement conventions that apply to individual components. The valuation of individual assets is related to their "membership character" and their membership character changes in response to changes in the structure itself and in cooperating members. Classical accounting rules bring the new members into the structure at a figure representing some measure of sacrifice in terms of other members given up instead of at the greater figure representing the incremental addition to the structure's overall ability. In fact, these conventions usually insist that an individual member's carrying figure be no greater than the valuation of alternative members that might be substituted in the structure by exchanging in some sort of external market. These classical (atomistic) accounting conventions mean, of course, that the going value of the organization may be far in excess of the sum of the numbers assigned to the parts. The economic rents are neglected individually and are imputed to the organization. In this case the whole is obviously greater than the sum of its parts. The explanation requires no esoteric Hegelian logic — the accountant simply distributes (imputes) the value that way. He could, just as well, have imputed

---

[1] Paton has argued for years that creditors furnish a part of the "permanent capital" of the business, but the problem flared anew in connection with pension liabilities and deferred taxes. See Maurice Moonitz, "Income Taxes in Financial Statements," *The Accounting Review*, April, 1957, pp. 175-183. Thomas M. Hill, "Some Arguments Against the Inter-Period Allocation of Income Taxes," *The Accounting Review*, July, 1957, pp. 357-361. Sidney Davidson, "Accelerated Depreciation and the Allocation of Income Taxes," *The Accounting Review*, April, 1958, pp. 173-180.

[2] The following discussion of the holistic-Gestalt approach reads like a defense for the accountants' going-concern value. "We shall never achieve an understanding of structured totals by starting with the ingredient parts which enter into them . . . we shall need to understand the structure . . . . There is then some possibility that the components themselves will be understood . . . the law of membership character . . . permit(s) no use of the conception of elements which when compounded into totals remain what they were before . . . . The Gestaltist insists that the attributes or aspects of the component parts . . . are defined by their relations to the system as a whole in which they are functioning . . . . Surely if membership character in so fundamental a sense dominates not only the locus but the very character of every ingredient, then there are no parts or elements or components, and it means nothing to say that the relations between them must be studied." Gardner Murphy, *Historical Introduction to Modern Psychology*, Revised ed. (New York: Harcourt, Brace & Co., Inc., 1949). Reprinted as "Gestalt and Field Theory," *Readings in Philosophy of Science*, ed. Philip P. Wiener (New York: Charles Scribner's Sons, 1953), pp. 210, 211, 216.

the rents to individual sources, and, presto, the whole now equals the sum of its parts. This 'philosophical' problem is largely definitional and is not likely to improve our understanding of the accounting process.

The accounting procedure devises rules for estimating services received and to be received from each component in conjunction with all other relevant components and aggregates them in some fashion for the structured entity. The interdependence of services from cooperating components means that further rules are necessary to allocate joint effort and such rules must be related to the outlook adopted for the enterprise as a whole and for cooperating facilities. Accountants have long tempered their estimate of service life for depreciable units by reference to expected maintenance and upkeep policies. It should be emphasized again that classical measurement rules were not composed to give assurance that the amounts assigned to components will always equal the number that might be assigned to the whole if a different set of measurement conventions were applied to the whole. Unfortunately, even the direct approach to valuing an organization as a whole makes indirect use of techniques appropriate for valuing components, i.e., capitalizes the aggregate expectations for individual assets, factors and products. Such valuations of the structure are highly subjective and are determined in part by considerations outside the accounting area. It should be emphasized again that the formation of rules for valuation and income for the enterprise as a whole is difficult (if not impossible) without recourse to the estimated replacement of parts and the estimated contribution of improvements. This approach requires a scheduling of replacements, and of receipts, and a discounting of the related streams. Such overall estimates involve appraisals of future management and future pressures from increasing or decreasing competition as well as estimates with respect to individual service potentials. Thus, reported past demonstrated services derived from aggregation of contributions from certain constituent parts is a partial determinant of such overall valuations. Traditionally such constituent parts as managerial ability and morale are not separately valued, and their omission accounts in part for the 'excess' value assigned to the organization.

The details of enterprise valuation by aggregation are worth repeating. Traditionally certain constituent parts, such as managerial skill and worker morale, are not valued separately. In fact, it is rare for an accountant to attempt to separate revenues according to sources. With few exceptions, e.g., contractual rent and interest, the revenue figures are measures of joint endeavor and joint accomplishment. Costs of keeping the environment suitable for procuring the stream of revenues are, however, partially separated. In some systems, e.g., renewal depreciation, separation is done with reluctance, but in other systems the breakdown is in some detail. Enterprise valuation is usually based on some assumption with regard to the future of these streams. Thus valuation of the concern as a whole must depend on estimates of outlays, and a detailed record of necessary past outlays would seem to be helpful if not necessary. Actually there is mutual interdependence between outlays and revenues, so that future revenues depend (in part at least) on future outlays. An attempt to reverse the mechanics is often made in budgeting, where the procedure starts sometimes with specifying a desired stream of revenues and proceeds to estimate outlays necessary to procure it. To the extent that estimated outlays are related to individual service potentials, the resulting valuation for the entity is found by partial aggregation. (The possibility that control may be exercised best when the members are considered separately is neglected here, because control *may be* effective even when the only check point is related to overall considerations such as enterprise profit.)

Perhaps the most clear-cut illustration of the enterprise approach to income and valuation is found in a regulated industry with an adequate and steady demand and a seasoned

6 *Essays in Accounting Theory II*

plant. The problem here is primarily one of programming expenditures so that the allowable deductions and profit can be recovered period by period. So long as this happy condition persists it is reasonable to insist that the firm suffers no depreciation in the sense of capital consumption that is not made good by current expenditures.[3]

The replacement (renewal) approach to the depreciation problem is based on the assumption that there is no decline in value of a well-maintained complex of plant assets. For a continuing firm with an indefinite future and expected demand sufficient to make continuing in business worthwhile, a seasoned plant, viewed as a single business good, is not subject to decline in value and to depreciation.[4] Railroad managers, for example, argue either that there is no decline in value in a well-maintained roadbed or that the life of such a roadbed is so long that any periodic write-off would be negligible.

A little reflection will show that this view rests on the assumption that the *unit* for depreciation is the entire plant or class of assets. If a smaller unit — say the individual rail or the annual batch of ties — is taken, decline in value becomes obvious. Depreciating individual assets on a service (or value) basis results in allowances of approximately one-half the base figure for a seasoned plant. If all plant assets are treated as a single service potential and if the plant is assumed to be a continuing service potential instead of a series of piecemeal liquidations, there is no required write-down to reflect service expiration or value decrease and therefore no depreciation on the basic facilities. The implications of this shift to a larger unit of accountability are not traced in detail at this point. Clearly these implications might have some effect on early utility rates, reported earnings during the formative period of any business, total assets, earnings related to investments, fund mobility within the firm and between the firm and the outside, taxes, and even replacement policies.

It may be worthwhile to illustrate how the income measuring process used by accountants utilizes small units and aggregates them to approximate the income for the organization. It became clear several centuries ago that the venture approach to income measurement was not adequate for indefinitely continuing concerns. By shifting the venture approach to the individual units of inventory and summing those that passed the sales (liquidation) point, the resulting sum may be defined as the income for the enterprise.[5] Thus the individual inventory item becomes the unit, and the acquisition — holding — liquidation calculation is made for each such unit. Supporting rules were devised for inventory units that had not met the liquidation (sales) test, and further conventions were added for other services that obviously could not be cycled and summed in the period selected. The period costs too have a long and honorable history, and early accountants who were astute enough to shift the unit to the inventory item were astute enough to understand that the

---

[3] This approach has been widely held and fiercely defended by many in the utility field. Unfortunately there has been a widespread feeling that this position is one of special interest at the expense of consumers of utility services. For a defense of the position by one who has no special self-interest, see my "Depreciation Accounting in Utilities," *The Accounting Review*, January, 1943, pp. 1-9.

[4] The restriction to "seasoned" plant is necessary because before this condition a plant does decrease in value to the extent that the wall of major replacements gets nearer. A new plant is more valuable than a seasoned one (for a continuing firm) because replacements are not so near and the interest factor cannot be neglected. If the pattern of expenditures does not yield a series of periodic income deductions that appeals to users, a smoothing device in the form of replacement reserves may be applied so that the individual members of the series will yield a closer index of long-run prospects. Notice that the smoothing device should build up when replacements are low and return to a small balance when the plant is seasoned. It does not build up to approximately one-half the cost. *Ibid.*

[5] See Stephen Gilman, *Accounting Concepts of Profit* (New York: The Ronald Press Company, 1939), p. 73, and my *Inventory Valuation and Periodic Income* (New York: The Ronald Press Company, 1942), pp. 9 ff.

units of fixed assets will also turn over if the period is long enough. It probably seemed reasonable to break up some of the longer cycles on a straight time basis, amortize the costs in some fashion, and deduct the amortizations from gross income.

An interesting extension of the unit problem may be made for goodwill and such costs as research and development. If one carries the original purchased goodwill as a permanent asset and takes later promotional expenditures to expense, he is taking a broad view of this asset and is essentially advocating a replacement approach to its write-off. The implied argument is that there is no decline in the overall value of intangible items that is not made good by current expenditures. A finer breakdown of such an account (selection of a smaller unit such as a patent) would probably lead to a systematic write-off of the original item and capitalization of at least some subsequent expenditures.

Research and development may be approached through the use of projects (patents, etc.) as accountability units with systematic cost accumulation and write-off. If expenditures of this sort are more or less uniform and continuous, the reported profit will be approximately equal after the firm has "struck its gait" regardless of the method used. The carrying value for financial reporting may be widely different! The renewal approach to depreciation keeps the original book value intact, while the current write-off method (immediate expensing) shows no value in the financial report. Firms using the latter method tend to accumulate 'hidden fat.' It may be argued — not too convincingly — that all growth firms of this type need to make such expenditures to stay in business and to validate the going-concern value of their other assets. The same argument may be used to defend carrying the plant assets at zero amounts. Some shelter is obviously necessary to validate the amounts for equipment, inventories, etc. The argument is therefore too general and is not convincing.

An interesting illustration of the unit problem applied to fixed assets may be drawn from an unusual cold snap in Florida. The freeze destroyed a considerable portion of the current crop and was, in fact, so severe that a number of trees and a few groves were destroyed. Some Congressmen began putting the machinery into motion to have the region declared a distress area (in spite of the fact that citrus land had appreciated some 400 percent in value in 15 years), and tax consultants immediately began to investigate the possibilities of procuring tax deductions for their citrus-growing clients.

If one emphasizes value-of-the-crop, there may or may not have been a deterioration in overall value. Florida at the time was producing slightly over two-thirds of the oranges produced in the United States and foreign competition was negligible. It is well known that the demand for citrus fruits — and most other food products — is extremely inelastic in the regions of normal output. Thus those groves that were damaged only an average amount might be expected to yield a higher income than would have been yielded without the damage. To the extent that this inelasticity operates, no decline in value (loss) has occurred. Obviously some grove owners were worse off than they would otherwise have been, for some of the crops were entirely destroyed, and prospects for revenues were decreased. But from the viewpoint of the industry as a whole there was probably little or no decrease in value. However, in this case as always, it is the individuals who are psychological entities, and there is certainly support for using such entities as units for calculating gains and losses.

The usual accounting definition of loss is in terms of decline of prospects applied to a cost base. Thus, a decline in the future prospects of one-half is assumed to call for a write-off of one-half of the cost. Let us now examine the damaged crops in terms of cost expiration. The conclusions are similar. From the view of the entire industry as a unit there is no deterioration of value (revenue-getting prospects) if the demand is sufficiently inelastic. If there is no deterioration of benefits or services expected, there is no case for taking a loss by a write-down of cost. For those owners whose damage was so great that the demand elasticity would not compensate fully, there was a decline in prospects, so that the antici- pated benefit level was reduced and a loss recognition for the individual was in order. No- tice, however, that the anticipated benefit level for the long pull (over a long unit of time) may have considered a few cropless years so that the long-run level of expected benefits may not have been lowered by the current damage even in the individual cases. If so, there has been no decrease in value — a subjective phenomenon — no decrease in expected benefits and therefore no signal for a write-down of cost. Again it should be observed that from the point of view of the entire industry as the unit of accountability, there may be no decline of even short-run dollar-getting possibilities, and therefore no reason to recognize a loss. The gains in value of the output for some groves may have more than offset the loss in value for others.[6] At the other extreme it is possible to use each tree as the accounting unit (or each orange) and report — in good faith — tremendous losses for individuals and for the industry.

An extension of the unit problem is also found in the oil industry, where it is common to drill dry holes that in themselves as individual units are of negligible benefit to anyone. Accountants for tax and reporting purposes have long been accustomed to adding the cost of a normal amount of dry holes to the cost of the producing wells. Looked at from the point of view of the individual drilling effort the cost is a clear-cut loss! However, if the unit is enlarged to the entire operations of a firm, the same costs may be construed as an asset! Certainly the line between loss — capital reduction — and asset is thin and shifting. So long as a firm can keep from being submarginal, the selling price of the output of the producing wells should be high enough to cover at least some (marginal) exploration costs. By selecting certain imputation techniques some exploratory costs become recover- able and by definition are not losses at all. It seems evident that a wildcatter with funds for only one effort would be required to write off the cost of the single dry hole as an immedi- ate loss. Suppose, however, that he has numerous risky (nonoil) endeavors, and we accept his total activity as the accountability unit. There is a case for adding the cost of unfortu- nate activities to the cost of more fortunate ones *so long as total prospects have not de- creased*. It is even possible to argue that a longer time unit should be employed so that, with a reasonable long-run probability of ultimate success, we might take a man's lifetime of activity as the unit and hold that his future prospects are little changed by this particu- lar failure and that his report should not reflect a loss. Most accountants would probably agree that the universe and eternity are too large and too long to be used successfully as accounting units, but a man-for-a-lifetime is a psychological unit for whom reports of ac- complishment and status may be useful.

In the field of accounting a familiar area of indecision arises in connection with inven- tories. Suppose, to illustrate, that a few units of merchandise have been damaged so that they must be sold for scrap or given to charity. Meanwhile the sales possibilities of the re-

---

[6] The Internal Revenue Service has taken a curious attitude toward such cases and its meaning is difficult to determine. In 1943 the Bureau took the position that in storm damage the land and improvement should be taken as a unit for loss determination and that no separate basis should be attached to trees and shrubbery (30 BTA 1028). In 1955 it was held that for damage due to a freeze, land and trees could not be taken as a unit for determining the amount of loss. Among other things it was held that the land deteriorated in value due to the presence of the dead trees (Bessie Knapp *et al.*, 23 TC 716). Apparently the authorities became so involved in value imputation to types of assets that they missed some of the related problems.

mainder of the stock have increased so that the value — revenue-getting possibilities — of the entire inventory has not declined. Is there need for loss recognition? If the stock were liquidated, the reported net income would report the algebraic total of the adverse and favorable circumstances. Shall we let this possibility influence our attitude toward loss and the units to be selected for an inventory that is not liquidated? The selection of the inventory unit clearly influences the income reported with cost or market and with the retail method designed to simulate cost or market. Moreover, the unit problem is encountered at the beginning of any discussion of base stock or LIFO. LIFO defenders have emphasized for decades that the identified - unit approach implies piecemeal liquidation of arbitrary or conventional inventory units to which the costs are said to attach.

It should be clear that major changes in income from varying the size of the unit arise because of differences in requirements for recognizing gains and losses. If cost or market is applied to individual units, the increased prospects of those items that increased in value are *not* offset against the decreased prospects of those items that have suffered a decline. Thus the prospects for the entire stock may have increased while accountants who follow item-by-item cost or market stubbornly insist on the recognition of an inventory loss in the form of a write-down to market. They find the evidence adequate to support a loss but not sufficient to support recognition of gain.

Application of cost or market to the entire stock of goods permits the offsetting of individual value increases against decreases, and so long as the value of the entire inventory asset has not decreased no inventory loss is taken. Only the area covered in appraising the prospects has been changed — the unit to be measured has been shifted — yet in the one case a loss is indicated and in the other case status has been maintained. If the rules for both loss and gain recognition were identical, it would be a matter of indifference whether cost or market is applied to individual units, classes of stock or to the entire inventory. If the unit is widened until it coincides with the firm itself, no amount of damaged stock, receivables, buildings, etc., whether from fires or any other reason, would result in a loss so long as the total long-run prospects of the firm have not decreased.[7] Long-run prospects are defined to include a 'normal' amount of setbacks of this nature.

The unit controversy is also a part of any discussion about the desirability of burying inventory losses in merchandise cost of sales. If the inventory process is thought of as a method for the assignment of cost of goods available for sale to revenues and to future periods, the entire pool of costs may be assumed to be one unit, and the declines in value of the unsold units may be combined with the obvious decline in utility of those that were sold. A separation of the two elements may be desirable because of evidentiary differences, but there is certainly no serious objection to the assumption of the broad unit for income accountability. Accountants sometimes insist that value declines on units unsold should not be combined with the cost of units that were in fact sold. If so, they are insisting on the use of the individual item of inventory as the accounting unit. Of course, there are all kinds of differences between units that are on hand and those that have been sold, but we are interested primarily in their value changes. Certainly a unit may lose value long before it is sold. Accountants may wish to give recognition in some manner to decline in

---

[7] The propensity of accountants for using more rigid rules for recognition of gains than for recognition of losses introduces lags in the broad enterprise reporting of income as discounted prospective receipts. The discounted stream of value declines would be larger due to the rules for speedy recognition of losses. The discounted value of receipts would be smaller due to the accountants' reluctance to recognize them. It is therefore necessary for one who discounts to separate these two streams or to change the traditional accounting approach.

value due to sale and due to other considerations. Thus it may be desirable to separate the cost of goods available into two or more portions.[8]

The problem of shrinkage loss (loss from lost units) is seldom discussed adequately in cost accounting textbooks, and the reader may not have realized that the unit problem is a major consideration in this area. If one of the requisites for an asset is that services or benefits must be expected (all accountants seem to be in agreement here), then it would be difficult to explain to a judge or jury why accountants are willing to add the cost of *normal* number of *lost* units to the cost of good units. Clearly there are no benefits in a literal (direct) sense to be expected from the physical units actually lost. If the unit of accountability for benefit and loss is the individual pound, gallon or other measure, a defense for capitalizing such costs by their addition to salable units is difficult to construct. (It is doubly difficult to defend by those who prefer animistic embodiment in physical units.) If the unit of accountability for gain and loss recognition is taken to be the entire production, the defense is straightforward, plausible and even convincing. If the shrinkage is *normal* the expected value or revenue-getting possibilities of the entire output are not decreased by the lossage, and therefore no write-off is indicated. Presumably the forces of competition will mean that (in the long run at least) the selling price of the good units will be high enough to cover normal shrinkage, and accountants have in this case apparently agreed to use the entire output as the costing unit for loss determination and to redistribute the cost to smaller units for inventory purposes. If the losses are abnormal, the assumption is apparently that such losses are not recoverable, i.e., that the value increase on the good units is not sufficient to cover the loss of potential in the units lost. In this case not even the selection of the entire output as the unit will be able to conceal the deterioration in value.

What conclusions may be made in regard to the selection of units for measurement? Are accountants hopelessly inconsistent because they do not select a uniform unit and stick with it? Is there help from related fields and disciplines? Which units *should* be adopted? The answers here, as elsewhere in accounting, are not very satisfying. We select the units that promise the greatest benefit to worthy users and are amenable to classification and measurement. The individual stock of inventory or the individual plant asset is usually the most useful unit for control against theft, and for control of maintenance and upkeep. For income calculations the appropriate unit would seem to be the larger alternative — even the firm itself — if measurement could be applied directly and not require aggregation of smaller units. For liquidity purposes the unit may be fairly large. (Usually the firm may be influenced by legal relationships not appropriate in other connections.) Claims may operate against individual assets, against the entity, or sometimes against more than one organization. We may need to look longer and harder at the parties at interest, their areas of decisions, their reaction patterns, and their needs. This kind of scrutiny combined with knowledge of our measurement limitations may lead to a more useful profession.

---

[8] The pool approach as opposed to the unit approach has had staunch defenders and foes. For a friendly approach that considers the utility of the entire stock of goods see: William Morse Cole, *Accounts: Their Construction and Interpretation* (New York: Houghton Mifflin Co., 1915), pp. 118-120. For the views of a fierce foe see: George R. Husband, "The First-In, Last-Out Method of Inventory Valuation," *The Accounting Review*, June, 1940, pp. 190-196. In general those who feel that costs somehow attach and adhere to physical things tend to be foes of the broad approach, e.g., Paton, Woodbridge. The present writer has long been reasonably sympathetic to the pool and utility-of-the-group approach. See: *Inventory Valuation and Periodic Income, op. cit.*, p. 15 and the citation in note 3 of this essay.

Digression on the Organic View of Organizations

There is a theory of organizations, prevalent in Europe and among some organization theorists elsewhere, that tends to impute a separate *will* to the organization in the form of intentions, drives, and objectives. This view is often connected with the worn-out cliché to the effect that the whole is greater than the sum of its parts, and is probably an offshoot of the Hegelian doctrine of "world view" — the "absolute idea."[9] In some mysterious way an organization such as the Notre Dame football team becomes endowed with a will of its own and with intentions and goals and the other paraphernalia usually attributed to individuals. To the extent that an organiation develops any group solidarity, it is said to have some sort of quality that is over and above the qualities of the individuals. There is little doubt that this view is a reversion to primitive anthropomorphism with the equivalent of minor gods who inhabit each organization and presumably account for the excess 'will' that results from the association of individual wills. Nevertheless, this view is widely held, and its basis may be worth reviewing.

The example most commonly cited to illustrate and explain the excess of group will (spirit) is the case of mob psychology. The scientific view is not quite so mysterious, or romantic, or so irresponsible. Individuals act differently in different situations and under different pressures. This conclusion is based on simple observation. Under the stress of hunger, the sex urge, companionship of friends, antagonism of enemies, individuals may be expected to exhibit different reactions and to move in different ways. Variations in behavior from some sort of norm need not be imputed to the mob and not to the individuals. An extension of this sort of imputation would impute behavior to sex and to hunger instead of to human decision centers acting under stresses of passion and lack of food. Therefore, when a group of individuals are together in a mob and are incited by leaders in specific ways, there should be no reason to expect that each individual should continue to act as if conditions were different and he were alone. To expect such a result is to deny the relevance of environment in predicting behavior! In organized society a number of individuals often carry on limited activities and enjoy emotional outlet through, by means of, and around an organization. With regard to athletic teams, some die a thousand deaths when their team loses, and roughly an equal number expire when it wins. Such artificial crises on Saturday afternoon are attractive to many individuals, and by becoming emotionally attached to a particular group the lives of many individuals are drastically changed. An executive of Chrysler feels identification with and responsibility for an entirely different group of individuals than a corresponding executive of General Motors. (The recent, lamentable rise of nationalistic identification is a more dramatic and unhappy example.) The inference that there is an excess 'will' with different objectives from those of the individuals is related to metaphysical things-in-themselves, is animistic, is gratuitous, and is not necessary. If all individuals were stricken from the earth, the wills of

---

[9] "On his [Hegel's] view the universe is not unlike an animate being that has a soul, desires, aims, intentions, and goals. The universe is spiritual; it has direction; and the explanation of ordinary facts, human actions, historical changes, and institutions may be grasped once we recognize how they are embedded in this cosmic organism . . ." Morton White, *The Age of Analysis* (New York: New American Library, 1955), pp. 13-14. White also points out some similarities of Hegel's views with those of John Dewey. "Under the influence of Darwin and James he [Dewey] transformed the antitheses of the Hegelian dialectic into the tensions of a biologically rooted and socially enveloped 'problematic situation.' " *Ibid.*, p. 175. The specific cliché about the whole and its parts is probably related to the Cantorian *definition* of infinite numbers — long a favorite topic of mystical discussion and wonder.

many organizations would doubtless need considerable revision, and if all except one individual were stricken, his behavior patterns would certainly be due for a rapid change.

We ask: how then can scientists reconcile their teleological, goal-seeking approach in biology and psychology with a nonholistic approach generally? Actually, no reconciliation is necessary. Scientists may study changes in individual behavior in response to all sorts of excitations without finding it necessary to impute goals and objectives to the state, the church, the corporation, the mob, or the aged. Scientists try to determine the reacting entity by observation and by deductive methods. The function of a stomach, for example, is studied in relation to its contribution to the body, and the scientist tries to study the clues and messages that excite it to action. So far as we know, however, the stomach has no independent will over and above its physical and chemical components, and no such assumption is necessary. Nor is it necessary to impute a part of the stomach's observed reaction to the will of a larger unit — the human being. The evidence supports a relational hypothesis — nothing more.

In the field of accounting Limperg and other Dutch and German accountants emphasize the social function that results from society's need for dependable information. This function is filled by public accountants, and it is argued that the accounting profession has as its purpose the objective of performing this function. Scientifically the explanation and verification become more manageable if one takes the opposing view that individuals have information needs (that are observable) and that other individuals try to fulfill these needs. In order to fulfill these needs more effectively they sometimes band together and form professional organizations. Moreover, individuals within the organization often permit other individuals of the organization to exert influence over them in numerous ways.

Perhaps the argument can be supported along other lines. Man seems to place himself at the center of willful activity, and he may therefore tend to picture an organization in his own image. No one doubts the influence of organizations and institutions (and other environmental conditions) on the behavior of individuals. No one doubts that certain individuals can manipulate other individuals by means of all sorts of arrangements. This mutual influence is a fundamental doctrine of the sociology of knowledge. These points are capable of being researched. Moreover, in a given sociological setting science can study the influence of many sorts of organizations on many kinds of individuals.

It is our conclusion that the term 'organizational goals' is a rank example of reification at its worst and should be avoided. (Unfortunately the expression is convenient to use and often simplifies otherwise complicated rhetoric.) To hold that an organization — like an institution — is an arrangement of individuals having certain stability features does not deny that organization theory may be useful or that organizations may be used as instruments for the control of individuals. The wills and desires of individuals in stable social organizations may be modified so that all individuals are partially satisfied. This melting-pot operation is a proper and important object of scientific study and is the basis for the type of accounting entity used throughout these essays.

Essay Two

The Doctrine of Management Intent

The extent to which management intention is a determining factor in setting asset valuations, classification and income measurement has received little systematic discussion and seems to merit more extensive inquiry. The present paper is a start in what is hoped to be this desirable direction. There is little doubt that expressions of managerial intention are pieces of evidence that must be weighed by independent accountants, for they are clearly partial determinants of valuation and income measurement. The following quotation states the position of the typical accountant and indicates the influence of intention in the field of business measurement:

> Costs need only to be accounted for in accordance with the intention governing their incurrence (or subsequently modified intention) . . . From the viewpoint of intent the costs of items on hand are properly to be exhibited as assets since they represent the costs of items which are to be disposed of in the future — either voluntarily or in liquidation — for the purpose of acquiring profit. The costs of items disposed of are properly treated as revenues or liquidation costs since upon disposal intent reaches the end of the road.[1]

As all readers undoubtedly know, public accountants render opinion on management representations. Clearly, management representations include statements of its intentions in numerous directions. The problem for auditors is not whether they should give opinions on management's plans (intentions), for they have long been doing so. The problem that requires attention is to find what evidence is necessary before the auditor feels free to give such an opinion and what weight should be attached to management's own statements of its intention.[2]

The problem reduces to the task of finding suitable rules for determining tenacity of purposes — the stability of plans — and for determining the truthfulness of reports regarding these plans. In some cases it may be feasible to appraise the stability of the objectives themselves and then to appraise separately the possibility of changes in the plans (means). If, further, the client is *adaptive* and adjusts quickly to changes in his environment, we may have less confidence in his current intentions than if his flexibility were more limited. These suggestions are very general. What exactly are the criteria for

---

[1] George R. Husband, "The Entity Concept in Accounting," *The Accounting Review*, October, 1954, p. 562.

[2] The going-concern assumption illustrates our confusion. It is one of the duties of the independent accountant *to determine* whether a going-concern assumption or a liquidation assumption (or some other premise) best fits the probabilities and to modify his measurement methods to suit his conclusions. It is true that the going-concern premise is appropriate in many situations and consequently the measuring procedures for such a premise are called for. However, there is no reason for accountants to assume away and neglect the possibility of liquidation by adherence to some pseudo principle that is erroneously considered to be fundamental. Maurice Moonitz uses the German-Dutch term "continuity" in *The Basic Postulates of Accounting* (New York: American Institute of Certified Public Accountants, 1961). See also *The Journal of Accountancy*, November, 1961, p. 72.

determining tenacity of intentions? Can we construct an index of stability? What sort of training is available to improve our appraising techniques? How can we weigh the shifting strength of the numerous outside influences that may operate to change intentions? How can we appraise the truthfulness of representations about intentions? If there should be deviations from truthful reporting, in which direction would the influence of self-interest tend to drive them?

At first glance it appears strange that an independent group would risk its professional standing by attempting to weigh probabilities and issue formal — expert — opinions on management's plans. A little reflection, however, indicates that in many cases the problem is not difficult. Often the evidences of intention are more than adequate. Legal documents and agreements may attest to management's plans. Examples are numerous: sinking fund agreements, stock option deals, purchase commitments, contracts with selling agents, construction contracts awarded, dividend declarations, articles of incorporation are only a few of the more obvious forms of evidence. In these cases the problem reduces to one of establishing the authenticity of the agreements and correlating the intentions which the documentary evidence seems to imply. Clearly the ease of changing intentions is not entirely related to legal enforceability. For example, the firm may be so far committed by expenditures and other cost or profit considerations that major changes in plans (intentions) are highly improbable.

The accountant may assume that intelligent management will intend to do those things that further its own interest, but he can never know exactly what management considers its own best interest, and he may sometimes question its intelligence. The best interest of management may of course not coincide with the best interests of any other group, but in most cases the traditions and standards of stewardship and fiduciary relationships influence management and help harmonize its own interests with those of the shareholders and other groups to whom management is responsible. In an enterprise economy in which each person is supposed to be motivated by what he believes to be his own self-interest, management finds that its own interest is usually furthered by paying some heed to the objectives of all other interested groups. Nevertheless, with the separation of ownership and control and the currently ill-defined lines of responsibility, management objectives may at specific times seem inconsistent if not beyond understanding. Maximizing retained earnings through a reduction of distributions to owners (dividends) may sometimes be an important consideration. Solvency consideration when creditors are aggressive may be more important than immediate profits, and keeping maximum losses within acceptable bounds may appear to be a stronger objective than higher overall profits.

The problem is further complicated by the possibility that even if the overall intentions of management were known, there still would be intentions on individual items or policies that obviously do not square with the overall objectives. How is the independent accountant to resolve these possible inconsistencies? Clearly he should take notice of the inconsistencies and must render his opinion based on his judgment of probabilities. Management's immediate goals may be inconsistent with one another and with long-run goals, and, worse, they may not be consistent with objectives of creditors, government agencies, owners or other outside interests. Moreover, there is always the possibility that the representations do not agree with the intentions. Clearly the possibility of divergences of this kind cannot be neglected. Accountants must have adequate knowledge of the pressures that bring about such disparities and the directions in which self-interest and ego-building pressures operate.

Apparently, the independent accountant must examine the stated intentions of management in light of its own goals and also in light of the goals of outside groups with significant coercive powers. It is with the needs of both inside and outside groups that so-called accounting principles have developed. Management intent is often modified, if not actually formed and molded, by the desires and needs of outside interests who have a stake in the outcome of the affairs of the concern. To the extent that accounting conventions express the requirements necessary for reporting significant information to these outsiders, it is clear that the accounting conventions themselves become coercive restraints on at least some of management's actions and intentions. Therefore, it seems that a primary duty of independent accountants is to examine actions *and intentions* of management in light of the outside needs (and restrictions) and to insist on reporting only intentions that are consistent with (not contradictory to) the common goals of all groups. This position goes counter to the once-prevalent attitude that the accountant is supposed to report on where the firm has been and not on where it is going. The older attitude has never been defensible because, first, the information about the past is accumulated to aid in making decisions affecting the future and, second, one usually cannot measure the results of past operations without making some assumptions about the future.

We may now review some of the procedures and guideposts that are available for appraising intentions. In most cases the auditor places some reliance on tradition — past management behavior. It is probably safe to say that both individual and collective human behavior, in some respects at least, tends to follow patterns — known trails — and therefore the distribution may be predicted with varying degrees of confidence. Whether the typical training for the public accountant includes enough statistical and behavioral training to make him competent in this direction is extremely doubtful, but in limited cases a study of an individual's past behavior may permit the auditor to express his qualified opinions in areas not supported by formalized agreements that are subject to direct verification.

Let us now turn to some specific aspects of accounting that are currently influenced by intent. The field of strongest influence is that of classification, but intent may also be important in asset valuation (income measurement). First, consider the extreme possibility that intent can *create* an asset or an equity.

Perhaps the most notorious and questionable case of asset creation by intent is that of reacquired shares. In at least some instances accountants have held that treasury stock *(and perhaps bonds), which according to intention soon will be convered into cash or used to reduce liabilities or to acquire services, can be classed as a current asset.*[3] To illustrate the position assume that $10,000 each month is to be deducted from wages for employee stock acquisitions by construction workers. Suppose also that the concern buys for $100,000 sufficient treasury stock so that delivery of stock can be made according to contract. There is no doubt about the validity of the charge to construction cost, and the concern, apparently in good faith, has a *bona fide* cost to the extent of $100,000. It is argued therefore that the cost of the reacquired shares is an asset in the sense that the costs of services in the physical form of building, machinery, inventories, etc., are assets. Intention is therefore said to govern the treatment of treasury stock as an asset or an equity deduction, for, if the intention is to retire the reacquired stock, these accountants ordinarily do not wish to show the expenditure as an asset.

---

[3] For example, see: American Institute of Accountants, *CPA Handbook* (New York: American Institute of Accountants, 1952), Chapter 18, p. 12.

Fortunately there are many accountants who disagree. For example: W. A. Paton and W. A. Paton, Jr., *Corporation Accounts and Statements* (New York: The Macmillan Company, 1955), pp. 422-423. Roy B. Kester, *Advanced Accounting* (New York: The Ronald Press Company, 1946), pp. 234-235.

This kind of argument is extremely common in accounting, and the reader must be aware of the semantic implications of truth by definition and assertion. The class, 'assets,' obviously includes what interested parties wish it to include. The inclusion or exclusion of a particular item is a matter of agreement, and the agreement should normally imply that the results of the classification are considered by the profession to be more useful than alternative possibilities. (It is of course possible — at least for short periods — for the agreement to be based on superstition, ignorance, inertia or tradition.)

The point to be emphasized is that intent is evidenced by both contracts and expenditures, and some accountants feel that the definition of asset should cover the service potential generated by the combination of stock and agreements. A small number wish to broaden the definition of asset to include unissued stock, but the majority is overwhelmingly negative and to include unissued stocks or bonds as assets is no longer acceptable classification. Suppose however that a contract has been completed for the construction of a warehouse (the contract is evidence of intent), and that payment is to be made by issuing previously unissued stock or bonds. In the interim should the accountant include the required amount of unissued stock as an asset? The answer here is again definitional. If one insists on cost as a requirement for entry into the asset classification, he must define cost to include *sacrifice* brought about by sharing future prospects. Accountants may wish to abandon entirely the definitional requirement of cost or to reinterpert the meaning of cost. It should be observed that the original cash raised by the sale of stock may be considered to be a cost in the sense that the rights to future prospects are rearranged and shared.[4]

A related problem of asset creation by intent arises in the treatment of subscriptions receivable from the sale of capital stock. Accountants are in considerable disagreement as to whether these claims are assets or deductions from the amount of the ultimate permanent equity. To a nontheorist the question is simple: Do we have an asset or don't we? A number of accountants prefer to meet the question by reference to intent. If management intends to collect the unpaid balances, it is occasionally asserted that the balances are assets. If, on the other hand, management intends to let the balances ride, it is argued that the equity should be reduced. These accountants, therefore, permit asset creation or destruction by short-run intention even though intention may be quickly changed, and its relevance is doubtful.

It is interesting to note that some important intentions even when evidenced by legal contracts are sometimes *not* recognized in the accounting reports. Mutually unperformed contracts, e.g., a contract for the construction of a warehouse, may involve material sums and the intent may be unquestioned, but traditionally accountants have felt little compulsion to show the building to be constructed as an asset and the liability for future construction as a liability. Only recently have some accountants insisted that such items be disclosed in connection with leases. It seems obvious that shifting of material amounts from the working-capital section to long-term assets should call for disclosure if the usual implications of a "statement of financial condition" are to be taken seriously.

Suppose, for another example, that the manager intends to borrow money for a business on his personal note given to a member of his family. Is an asset created by his unmis-

---

[4] The "sacrifice" in raising cash by sales of stock is not always clear. Who, for example, makes the sacrifice? The new investment is presumed to yield more than its cost, so the old owners are in effect getting a share of the new rents, and the sales price of the stock presumably reflects sharing of old rents with the new owners. Notice that this whole argument takes the viewpoint that the entity for which sacrifice is measured is composed of existing equity holders. An interesting collateral question is: How does a steward operating under "assets equal responsibilities" ever incur a cost in the sense of sacrifice? Is his sacrifice in the form of added responsibilities?

takable intent? A negative answer is rendered by the profession even though evidence of his intent may be adequate to establish a strong probability. A further question is in order. Is disclosure of this material financial opinion necessary if the evidence to support intent is adequate? To change the example, suppose that management intends to declare a dividend as soon as it can meet the formalities of having the board give rubber-stamp approval. Assuming that the evidence of intent is satisfactory, is a liability established? The profession's answer again is generally in the negative, for liabilities shown on the statement of financial position are still tied closely (perhaps too closely) to the concept of legal obligation and partly divorced from the concept of probable demand on funds. A definition in terms of the latter may be more useful for guidance than the more conventional definition.

At the present time it seems fair to say that intention, unless supported by agreements enforceable at law (or perhaps by strong custom and usages), seldom supports the formation of an asset or the creation of a liability. Intention plays a much more important role in asset write-down and liability cancellation.

Intention and Measurement. Without doubt intention has long been an influential factor in the measurement of cost expiration and asset valuation. Seldom are fixed assets used until they have no value other than scrap. For prestige purposes a florist, for example, may follow a policy of trading his delivery vehicles each year. Clearly the depreciation and maintenance rates are affected by such plans (intentions), and it is interesting to note that auditors do not call for special or unusual evidence to support such implied or stated intentions. If the client has been in business for some time, his present intention may be inferred from his past actions, and if he is a newcomer in the business, the actions of others in similar lines of business along with a statement of interest from the client may create an inference strong enough to support the write-off.

Intention is a factor in general write-downs to scrap when a fixed asset is to be taken out of service. In some instances the auditor may wait until the asset is in fact removed from service, but to adopt such a rule is to insist that a mistake resulting in a loss cannot be recognized until removal from service by junking or sale — a ridiculous position.

Intent also plays a role in both the definition and valuation of inventories. In the retail field intent to mark-up or mark-down is considered to be hardly sufficient, but as soon as management gives tangible expression to its intentions by reducing the retail tag the accountant accepts the evidence and changes his valuation accordingly. In cost or market, whichever is lower, it is assumed that a decline in replacement cost leads to an automatic and unavoidable intention to reduce the selling price. When goods are damaged, obsolete or otherwise unsalable at regular prices, a cut is often highly probable and the intention to reduce the price in order to move the goods is usually inferred from the physical evidence.

Intent and Account Classification. There is little doubt that the modern controversy over the place of management intent in accounting is concerned chiefly with classification for statements of condition and earnings. It must not be supposed, however, that intent is the only factor that helps to determine classification, and according to some accountants it should be only a relatively minor one. It may be assumed that the primary (and perhaps the only) purpose of the *current* classification is to provide the reader with a crude guidepost to the short-term, debt-paying ability of the concern. The classification has been widely used for this purpose and the division between current on the one hand and all other assets on the other has received more attention than other items on the financial statements. Many accountants hold that management's intent is close to being irrelevant if the debt-paying ability of the firm is not strong. This group argues that the creditors are in a position to change the plans of management and that the current classification should be in terms of assets that *could* be turned into cash within the appropriate period. If conditions are very bad, the possibility for conversion without interfering with the continued operations of the business may be abandoned and replaced with prospects in liquidation. However, except in extreme cases, creditors are usually interested in what items and amounts can be used to meet obligations without liquidation of the concern.[5] The accountant, in such cases, is well advised to look to the creditors for his clues about management's intention.

This viewpoint may be valid if the firm is in a tight working-capital position, but what if the concern is well situated in this regard? In this case creditors may be interested in the current position of the firm *after* deduction for the financial needs of major improvements or capital expenditures to carry out other managerial plans. Thus, if the debt-paying prospects of a firm are favorable, it may be argued that creditors are better informed if the backload of government securities that are temporarily holding funds for plant expansion were not shown as current. Such placement of the bonds would serve to put the public on notice of management's intention to convert the proceeds to fixed assets. In these cases a shift of relative power means that creditors are less important factors for determining plans.

We must not forget that short-term creditors are not the only parties interested in the short-term, debt-paying ability of a concern and therefore influence management's intent in this area. Long-term creditors become vitally interested if the position of the firm is deteriorating, and owners are usually aware that their future dividends depend in part upon management's ability to manage the firm's working capital. Also, it must not be forgotten that the managers themselves are interested in maintaining control, and their stated intentions with regard to liquidity problems and classification may be tested by referring to the direction of their interest. It seems therefore that an investment in land for speculation would appear to be more current as the liquidity position deteriorates, for the strength of management's intention to employ it as a current asset would correspondingly increase. In this case the inferred evidence to support intention would be in harmony with those who insist that it is creditors' intentions that are dominant.

Many accountants conclude that owners and managers themselves (along with creditors and prospective creditors) should benefit by having the current assets include only those assets that can be used for short-term debt-paying without interfering with management's major plans and intentions. Perhaps a dual current-asset division would be desirable to show the amount available if present plans are carried out and also to show the amount that could be available if creditors seriously curtailed management's current intentions. Consider some statements by practicing accountants on this aspect of the problem.

Blough feels that assets that have been or are to be dedicated to a planned program should be disclosed.[6] Wehr discusses some methods of disclosure: (1) If intentions do not impair normal liquid requirements, a note in the President's letter is sufficient; (2) an ap-

---

[5] Notice that the working-capital concept is based on the assumption of a continuing concern. If it were not, a statement of affairs with all assets marshalled for their debt-paying ability in liquidation would be in order. From the going-concern viewpoint a two-to-one ratio might be considered to be adequate because it is a margin that might be reduced for maturing debts *without interfering* with the operations of the business and not because such a ratio is a sufficient margin to provide for liquidation losses and leave enough to take care of the current liabilities. For more detail see my *Inventory Valuation and Periodic Income* (New York: The Ronald Press Company, 1942), pp. 25-27.

[6] Carman G. Blough, "Earmarking of Funds Dedicated to Fixed Asset Expansion," *The Journal of Accountancy*, April, 1948, pp. 345-346.

propriation of assets to be placed among other assets and a "reserve" below current liabilities; (3) a parenthetical note to work in process or fixed assets; (4) the less desirable showing of a restriction of retained earnings.[7] Bliss is an early advocate of pulling cash arising from the sale of fixed assets from the current section if management follows the policy of segregating such monies for reinvestment.[8] He does not seem to be concerned with monies that may be from other sources and still be "intentionally segregated." Foulke points out that cash earmarked for specific purposes should be separated from unrestricted cash.[9]

Apparently the profession is strong in its inclination to show working capital available after carrying out current plans, but it is interesting to note that arguments in support of this position are, for practical purposes, omitted.[10]

Classification of marketable securities in practice has always been influenced to some extent by management intent. The profession is now in substantial agreement that current assets should include those assets which in the ordinary course of business will be turned into cash within a specified period plus those assets that *could* be turned into cash within the period without interfering with the operations of the business. The tests for current inclusions with regard to securities (and perhaps with some standby assets) are: (1) that the asset can be disposed of without interrupting operations of the business, and (2) that the firm must have a high probability of being able to dispose of it, i.e., a ready market or smoothly functioning marketing mechanism. The latter requirement for the existence of marketing machinery recognizes that the firm's outlets for selling its regular merchandise may not be able to move securities or other unusual items without outside selling help.

Nevertheless, a number of accountants still feel that management intent with regard to the investment classification is a determining factor and that there is little reason for insisting that 'expansion money' invested temporarily in government bonds be shown as a current asset. The latter position enjoys some authoritative support. For example, Kester feels that intent is the most important criterion and that classification as current is proper only if it is intended to reconvert to working capital within the near future.[11] Paton states: "Likewise cash funds on hand but dedicated to construction or other noncurrent purposes should in general be excluded [from the current classification]."[12]

Intention seems to have less influence in the arrangement of the earnings report, although it influences the reported profit to the extent that it aids in establishing asset valua-

---

[7] P. N. Wehr, Jr., "Accountant's Responsibility for Disclosure of Fixed-Asset Commitments," *The Journal of Accountancy*, September, 1951, pp. 322-325.

[8] James H. Bliss, *Management Through Accounts* (New York: The Ronald Press Company, 1924), p. 166.

[9] Roy A. Foulke, *Practical Financial Statement Analysis* (New York: McGraw-Hill Book Company, Inc., 1953), p. 72. A similar position is expressed by B. Bernard Greidinger, *Preparation and Certification of Financial Statements* (New York: The Ronald Press Company, 1950), pp. 21-22.

[10] A related problem is interesting. A minimum amount of cash is usually not available for paying existing debts if the concern is a continuing one. Here, it seems, is clearcut restriction on intent. According to Peloubet, this cash "can no more be distributed than can the land on which a plant is built." Maurice E. Peloubet, Correspondence, *The Journal of Accountancy*, October, 1932, p. 310. Woodbridge feels that change funds are as fixed as the registers in which they are contained and subscribes to the view that: "Such amounts —of cash— should no longer be carried as current assets, for it is no longer the intention of the management to use such funds to meet the current debt as shown in the current liability section of the balance sheet." Frederick Wells Woodbridge, *Accounting Basic Concepts (Accounts — Proprietorship Analysis)* (Dubuque, Iowa: Wm. C. Brown, 1948), p. 38.

[11] Kester, *op. cit.*, p. 208. For a concurring opinion written some time ago see: Anson Herrick, "What Should be Included in Current Assets," *The Journal of Accountancy*, January, 1932, pp. 51-62. See also correspondence from Herrick in the *Journal of Accountancy*, November, 1932, pp. 388-390.

[12] W. A. Paton, *Essentials of Accounting* (New York: The Macmillan Company, 1938), p. 787.

tions. There are, however, a number of areas of income classification that may be influenced and modified by intent. The earmarking of unassigned profits in the form of restrictions or appropriations is, of course, an expression of the intent of appropriate directors or officers. We are faced here again with the need for inferring actual intent and using the inference to support an opinion about the directors' representations. The auditor may have confidence in his opinion about restrictions for bond retirement and similar objectives if the restrictions are contractual or are obviously necessary. He may find it more difficult to appraise restriction for expansion, modernization, etc., but even here some opinion should be possible. Management's objectives are seldom completely obscure and individual representations can usually be judged on the basis of their consistency with his probable objectives or the objectives of persons in similar positions.

The 'reserve for contingencies' is an especially interesting case. This widely criticized account conveys management's uneasiness (and uncertainty) about possible dark clouds. But it does more; it expresses management's intention to institute a cautious (perhaps niggardly) dividend policy. This technique includes only a crude effort to measure the amounts and it requires no commitment to disclose the nature of the dark clouds. The public accountant's duty here is ambiguous. Certainly there is no duty to insist on accurate-sounding, specific numbers when round numbers better express the uncertainty. Whether the accountant should insist on disclosure of the nature of the foreboding is an open question. Disclosure usually helps the reader make his own assessments. This problem is most acute in the federal government, where the executive branch is often permitted to withhold details when its bargaining position might be undermined by disclosure.

The problem is certainly complicated by the possibility that specific individual intentions of managers may not square with the overall objectives of management or other parties in the organization. How is the independent accountant to resolve these possible inconsistencies? This problem of judging the adaptability of specific actions (means) to objectives (ends) is a fundamental problem in business administration and is not peculiar to the field of accounting. The independent accountant must render opinions in this area, and the need for a careful and intensive study of business organization and behavioral science should be obvious. The auditor should be aware of the needs of all groups and the pressures that operate on management. In the midst of getting detailed information he should observe the business environment, peculiarities of its influences and the behavioral reactions of managers. To the extent that accounting conventions express the requirements necessary for reporting to outsiders and to members of the management hierarchy, it is clear that these conventions themselves become coercive restraints on some of management's actions and intentions. A primary duty of the accounting profession therefore is to examine actions and intentions of management in light of these pressures and needs, to devise procedures that will isolate inconsistent actions and statements, and to coerce acceptable action by rendering positive opinions only on representations that are closely consistent with enterprise objectives.

One final word: It is my opinion that our profession should insist on *more* policy statements and expressions of coordinated intentions rather than *less*. Accountants are in an advantageous position not enjoyed by the general public, and they should use this inside position to improve disclosure. Insistence that the statements are "management's representations" is a recent step in the right direction. Added responsibility by management cannot help but be salutary! But what are the collateral responsibilities of the accounting profession? How are they to be discharged?

Essay Three

Income and the Case for
Current Costs

It is the purpose of this essay to examine the concept of income and to appraise its relevance to the current problems of economic organization and management. The following observations may be summarized.

1. There are several economic uses to which income measurements may be put, but resource allocation and combination to minimize sacrifice are among the more important.
2. The fact that sunk costs are not relevant to certain economic decisions does not imply that costs of existing facilities are immaterial for all decisions or that the existing resources should be treated as free goods.
3. Income as a master stewardship report for managerial action may be far from being ideal, but is useful.
4. Current costs appear to satisfy the short-term resource-allocation and stewardship functions better than other forms of cost.

Seldom can a discussion be confined entirely within the limits of a single discipline. In accounting, for example, materials from the related fields of psychology, engineering, law, sociology, and especially economics are usually introduced before the argument is hardly begun. Accountants have used references to 'economic value,' 'economic theory,' 'economic income,' and the like to administer the *coup de grace* to opposing arguments, and for some reason these vague references and the prestige of the economist and his generalizations have carried tremendous weight among practicing accountants. The economic burning bush is found to glow brightest in discussions of value and income.[1]

Economists may be in semi-agreement that income is a form of *personalized*, individual expectation. This view, except by chance, will yield a different income for each individual, but decades of conditioning have tended to yield reaction patterns that exhibit some degree of uniformity — products of a common ideology.[2] There is by no means agreement among economists as to the 'central meaning' of the income concept, and there is even less agreement about the usefulness of the concept.

We must allow for differences in meaning, but certainly the enthusiasm of Fisher: "Income is the alpha and omega of economics," is not shared by Hicks: "At bottom they [income, saving, depreciation] are not logical categories at all . . . . They are bad tools, which break in our hands."[3] Hayek is certainly skeptical: " . . . there must go economists' habitual practice of separating out the part of general investment activity which happens to leave the capital stock in some sense constant as something different from activities which add to that stock. This distinction has no relationship to anything in the world."[4]

Footnotes on following page

Pigou seems to be more temporizing and takes the general position that " . . . perfect definitions cannot be found" for income and related concepts; economists should "try to make them as little imperfect as they can."[5] Boulding has supported the anti-income approach by a devastating attack on his fellow economists for over-stressing the importance of income as an explanation of business behavior.

> My main cause for dissatisfaction with the existing theory of the firm lies in its deficiency in capital theory. The usual marginal analysis treats the firm as if it had nothing but an income account; it has no balance sheet, no capital problems, and no dynamics . . . .[6]

These uncertainties among economists should be a warning to accountants to beware of glib references to economic income, but most accountants have apparently never seriously doubted that their profit computations were necessary and important information. While economists were retreating from the income concept, the income report attained dominance over the condition statement, organization men advocated decentralization and broadening the profit point of view, and accountants stoutly affirmed that the measurement of periodic income is the heart of accounting theory.[7]

---

[1] "They [accountants] seem to think the economists have discovered some mysterious type of value with which most people are unfamiliar." D. H. Mackenzie, "Contemporary Theories of Corporate Profits Reporting," *The Accounting Review*, October, 1949, p. 360. Sidney S. Alexander explains: "Economic science has no single universally accepted body of doctrine that need only be translated into nontechnical language in order to tell the layman what 'the economist' believes . . . . It would accordingly be arrogant for anyone to present 'the economist's view of income.' " "Income Measurement in a Dynamic Economy," *Five Monographs on Business Income*, Prepared by the Study Group on Business Income (New York: American Institute of Accountants, 1950), p. 8.

[2] " ". . . if carried to its ultimate conclusion, income becomes a subjective feeling on the part of each individual . . ." Norton M. Bedford, "Need for Supplementary Data in Interpretation of Income Reports," *The Accounting Review*, April, 1952, p. 196. "It is evident, however, that the accountant's lack of capability in the realm of prophecy will probably leave the profit calculation . . . an unfinished symphony." George R. Husband, "That Thing Which the Accountant Calls Income," *The Accounting Review*, July, 1946, p. 253. "To an orthodox accountant, net income is essentially an historical record of the past. To an economist, net income is essentially a speculation about the future." Joel Dean, "Measurement of Profits for Executive Decisions," *The Accounting Review*, April, 1951, p. 185. ". . . the calculation of income at the conclusion of an enterprise is but financial autopsy!" William J. Vatter, *The Fund Theory of Accounting and Its Implications for Financial Reports* (Chicago: University of Chicago Press, 1947), p. 36.

[3] Irving Fisher, *The Theory of Interest* (New York: The Macmillan Company, 1930), p. 13. John R. Hicks, *Value and Capital* (London: Oxford University Press, 1939), pp. 171, 177.

[4] Friedrich A. Hayek, *The Pure Theory of Capital* (London: Macmillan & Co., Ltd., 1941), p. 13. G. A. D. Preinreich discussed many years ago the possibility of defining income as existing only after provision has been made for some percentage of growth, *The Nature of Dividends* (New York: Privately printed, 1935).

[5] A. C. Pigou, "Maintaining Capital Intact," *Economica,* August, 1941, p. 275.

[6] Kenneth E. Boulding, *A Reconstruction of Economics* (New York: John Wiley & Sons, Inc., 1950), p. 27.

[7] "It is generally agreed that the measurement of the periodic net income of the business enterprise, particularly in the corporate field, is the most significant and crucial task essayed by the accountant." William A. Paton, and William A. Paton, Jr., *Corporation Accounts and Statements* (New York: The Macmillan Company, 1955), p. 274. "Income is an important index of economic progress, and its determination is the principal objective in accounting today." *Handbook of Modern Accounting Theory*, ed. Morton Backer (New York: Prentice-Hall, Inc., 1955), p. 209.

The following are considerably less positive as to the virtues of income.

" . . . our [SEC's] registration forms for mining companies in the developmental and exploratory stage and industrial companies in the promotional stage require the submission of statements of cash receipts and disbursements instead of profit and loss statements . . . ." Earle C. King, "Presentation of Pertinent Data in Financial Statements," *The Accounting Review*, October, 1948, p. 353. "No area of capitalistic thought is likely

---

Footnote continued on next page

In spite of the continued claims that income reports are indispensible, accountants only recently have taken the trouble to enumerate and specify exactly the ways in which such reports are useful. A quick glance at the following tabulations will be sufficient to show that the uses are either extremely vague or they arise because certain present institutions (e.g., income tax) have incorporated income in their structures. The list below is more or less representative.

(1) As a basis for taxation;
(2) As a component of the measure of national income;
(3) As a basis for determining the legality of distribution of corporate property to stockholders;
(4) As a measure of the reasonableness of the prices charged by the corporation for its products and services; and
(5) As a basis for managerial decisions in conducting business operations.[8]

A business economist offers the following meager list of management uses of income figures.

Among the more important practical applications of estimates of a company's real economic earnings to top management policies are: (1) dividend policy; (2) capital budgeting; (3) pricing policies; (4) appropriations for advertising; and (5) government negotiations.[9]

---

to be examined more thoroughly and critically than that pertaining to profits. The laboristic society will wish to review how profits are made, what purposes they serve, how efficiently they perform these purposes, how they affect the operation of the economy, how they are used, and how they should be used." Sumner H. Slichter, "Profits in a Laboristic Society," *Harvard Business Review*, May, 1949, p. 346. "It does appear to be too so phisticated a version of management motivation, however, to claim that the profit factor has no significant influence." D. A. Fergusson, "Accounting and the Price Level," *The Accounting Review*, October, 1954, p. 642. " . . . the measurement of income is not the sole, or even the most important, aim of accounting; in fact, there are grounds for the belief that the accountant has overemphasized and overworked the notion of income . . . ." William J. Vatter, *The Fund Theory of Accounting and Its Implications for Financial Reports* (Chicago: University of Chicago Press, 1942), p. 35.

[8] Charles E. Johnson, "A Case Against the Idea of an All-Purpose Concept of Business Income," *The Accounting Review*, April, 1954, p. 227. Johnson concludes: "Such considerations lend considerable weight to the proposition that managerial requirements are of secondary importance in formulating a concept of business income for use in corporate reports." *Ibid.*, p. 241. Recently there has been a flood of statements pointing out that we need different income concepts for different purposes without identifying the purposes or specifying the necessary changes. " . . . the deeper truth is that income is properly defined differently for different purposes. Different treatments may honestly be accorded a given experience when the purposive goals are different." George R. Husband, "Rationalization in the Accounting Measurement of Income," *The Accounting Review*, January, 1954, p. 5. "The concept of business income is dependent on the ends served by the use of the income measurement. There is no one correct method of computing net profit. The question of which procedure to use can be decided only on the basis of the purpose or purposes for which the figures are to be used, not on an abstract basis." Albert L. Bell, "Fixed Assets and Current Costs," *The Accounting Review*, January, 1953, p. 44. "The fund theory does not embrace a concept of income, for the reason that income is not definable unless it includes a recognition of the situation and the purposes that relate to it." William J. Vatter, *op. cit.*, p. 95. His following statement certainly goes too far. "No matter how the general purpose [income] figure is defined, it will still be a single amount, a single computation *fit for only a single use.*" (Italics mine.) *Ibid.*, p. 77.

[9] Joel Dean, "Measurement of Real Economic Earnings of a Machinery Manufacturer," *The Accounting Review*, April, 1954, pp. 255-256.

A business lawyer offers little improvement with the following list: "Let me repeat these purposes [of income measurement]:
(1) to obtain information on economic progress;
(2) to ascertain what they may presently spend in consumption without impairing their future wellbeing; and
(3) to determine property rights and obligations as between and among the different members of society, including distribution of the burden of taxation."
Arthur H. Dean, "The Relation of Law and Economics to the Measurement of Income," *The Accounting Review*, July, 1953, p. 333.

It should be observed that the lists, in addition to being disappointing, avoid the broad aspects of economic resource allocation and factor combination except for a passing reference to capital budgeting. Furthermore, the possible use of income as one of the sources of information for judging whether entrepreneurs have demonstrated ability to appraise potential markets and make favorable factor combinations, and thus whether they should or should not be entrusted with such decisions, is not mentioned. The latter use may be referred to as the stewardship function, and for complex situations accountants so far have failed to come up with anything better than financial statements and earnings reports. Revenues, in general, tend to indicate demand potentials and elasticities, and expenses are a crude measure of ability to combine factors with productive ingenuity. Failure of accountants to mention such aspects of their work makes further discussion of these points highly desirable.

It seems to be generally agreed that economics is concerned with economizing and allocating scarce resources to satisfy wants. In almost all well-developed societies the price (market) system is used with some modification to guide the allocation process and the distribution of the income among individuals and groups. While alternatives — including slavery — may be used, the price system is generally conceded to be the device that *tends* to allocate with the least loss of satisfaction and with the least interference with individual freedom.[10]

Built into the price system in an enterprise economy is a device which tends to make the process more efficient. Price reflects scarcity relative to demand, and in the pursuit of profits, businessmen will economize those items which have high prices (scarce relative to demand) and substitute those with lower prices. The effect is that the individual who seeks to increase his profits in this manner increases the social dividend — output. This degree of substitution is carried on until the price of the less desirable substitute is bid up and the decrease in demand for the other brings down its price, so that a kind of equilibrium is approached.

The price system with a profit motive tends also to eliminate those businessmen who are prone to wrong guessing, to reward the shrewd, and to encourage the successful to administer society's factors of production. As a part of the overall, semi-automatic scheme it is assumed that there is an alert group of entrepreneurs (businessmen) who have access to financial resources and who stand ready to move in the direction of *expected* profits and away from *expected* losses.

In view of the economizing (allocation and distribution of scarce resources) basis for the field of economics it seems that one of the major functions of reported income is to give information that will help to allocate society's resources for a reasonably high level of satisfaction.[11] Unfortunately reported profit figures are predominantly *ex post* computations with limited access to the crystal ball with regard to depreciation, bad debts, and inventories. The result is certainly not *ex ante* income and some economists and accountants may even prefer to abandon the term income.[12] We return to the relationship of *ex post* to *ex ante* later.

While it may not be essential that income reports be used for reaching economic decisions, one of the contentions of this essay is that the accountant's income report is ordinarily one of the more important existing informational reports for channeling new investment and for combining productive agents. For ready comparison of alternative opportunities in different fields the *ex post* income related to the necessary investment *may be* highly desirable, although the decision is, of course, made on the expected rate of re-

---

Footnotes on following page

turn. The usual approach to this problem is to relate the expected incremental return (income) to the incremental investment, but this approach must be modified drastically when the new investment results in the admission of new equity holders who must share the fruits of existing facilities as well as the expected return from the incremental facilities. The complex of existing properties may be sunk costs for some purposes, but their existence and prospects are relevant to new equity holders.

In most cases the investors will prefer recent rather than ancient data.[13] It seems clear therefore that information based on current costs of specific assets is likely to be useful.[14] In practice, all productive agents except fixed assets are substantially at current figures, and depreciation on current values is clearly implied unless we wish to allocate resources in such a way as to economize resources on the basis of heterogeneous costs. Moreover, when comparisons are made with earnings and assets, it seems that both earnings and as-

---

[10] With assumptions of freedom of entry to improve one's position, it can be shown that the self-interest motive will tend to move those with higher preferences for "things" into more work or more lucrative work. At least there is a presumption that more satisfactions result from a free price system. For a discussion see Abba P. Lerner, *The Economics of Control* (New York: The Macmillan Company, 1944), pp. 50 ff.

[11] Davidson is concerned with the allocation problem. "With regard to the allocation of resources as it affects capital assets, there are two major questions to be answered. What use shall be made of existing capital assets and what portion of the economy's productive effort should be devoted to turning out new capital assets in each area of production? To the extent that profit calculations aid in the answering of these questions, a profit figure reached after deducting current cost depreciation would be the more useful." Sidney Davidson, "Depreciation and Profit Determination," *The Accounting Review*, January, 1950, p. 46. Bowers is also aware of this function. "The justification of accounting for real profits as well as accounting for any economic income lies in the more fundamental problem of allocating real resources to their various possible alternatives. We cannot economize either individually or socially by economizing merely dollars." Russell Bowers, "Business Profit and the Price Level," *The Accounting Review*, April, 1951, p. 177.

Fergusson mentions the problem in passing. "So far as corporate management is concerned, the accountant's primary function must be to provide information which will be useful in the making of decisions or choosing among alternatives in such a way as to maximize owners' profits and incidentally attain the socially desirable objective of making the best use of our economy's scarce resources." D. A. Fergusson, "Accounting and the Price Level," *The Accounting Review*, October, 1954, p. 639. (Many will feel that Fergusson's incidental benefit may be the more important one.)

[12] "To the extent that the accountant can eliminate guesses, he is substituting something else for income." But: "A definition which requires knowledge of all future circumstances is obviously of little practical use." Sidney S. Alexander, "Income Measurement in a Dynamic Economy," *Five Monographs on Business Income, op. cit.*, pp. 7, 29. Notice however: "The fact . . . that it is impossible to convert the reported accounting income for an individual enterprise into something that can be called economic income for that enterprise does not necessarily dispose of price-level adjustments of financial statements as nonsense." Raymond C. Dein, "Price-Level Adjustments: Fetish in Accounting," *The Accounting Review*, January, 1955, p. 10.

[13] Notice that in computations of goodwill (and incidentally of the value of the enterprise as a unit) it is usual to assume that the purchaser buys tangibles and intangibles other than goodwill at current values, and projected income is modified accordingly. This procedure is equivalent to holding that the purchaser will be combining labor, etc., with existing factors at current cost. See, for example, William A. Paton and William A. Paton, Jr., *Asset Accounting* (New York: The Macmillan Company, 1952), p. 497 ff.

[14] Many accountants, however, still hold to dollar cost. "The cost of 'consuming' existing capital should be determined irrespective of the intention to replace in kind, to replace with a different type of capital, or not to replace at all. This conclusion appears to rule out, in the determination of income for periodic reporting to stockholders and other nonmanagement groups, the use of either replacement costs or a price index specific to the particular kinds of assets 'consumed' by a given corporation." American Accounting Association, Committee on Concepts and Standards Underlying Corporate Financial Statements, "Price-Level Changes and Financial Statements" (Supplementary Statement No. 2), *The Accounting Review*, October, 1951, p. 471. "As a rule we think and act in terms of current dollars, and when a mixture of current dollars and past dollars is presented without classification we inevitably tend to regard them as homogeneous." W. A. Paton, "Depreciation and the Price Level, A Symposium," *The Accounting Review*, April, 1948, p. 121. "Isn't it true, in a competitive economy, that the only generally influential, 'conduct conditioning' costs are those currently in effect?" *Ibid.*, p. 122.

sets should be on a current basis. Current decisions are made on the basis of current costs, and the reader need not be reminded that gauging the future is difficult enough even with the latest data and trends. To combine depreciation on assets acquired in 1910 with current costs is not likely to help the problem of resource allocation.[15]

On the practical level resource allocation in a market economy is carried out by businessmen who decide to expand, form new firms, shut down, abandon, etc., in response to *expected* demand and *expected* cost characteristics. Clearly, these expectations are influenced by the latest experiences and trends in factor costs and income. Clearly also, these current expectations cannot be influenced by future experiences. We do *not* learn from the future, and future costs are therefore irrelevant for any possible current decision. We measure *ex post* because these are the only data that we can possibly measure and because our experience has shown that our expectations and *ex ante* planning must be based on our experience in similar or analogous situations. It is estimates of the future that are conduct determining, but our estimates are conditioned by the patterns of the past.

For resource allocation in new investment — expansion — it is true that state planing boards often allocate resources on the basis of payout or more sophisticated economy studies of expected return. Existing facilities could be taken as given and new funds placed in those directions that promise to add the most net return when used in conjunction with the existing environment. Capital budgeting is usually done in this manner, and when supplemented with occasional studies as to the overall yield on all assets, the process works acceptably. The purchase of existing facilities by new investors and the decision to abandon, however, must take into consideration the expected profitability of the entire properties. We encounter the common situation of a firm whose overall earning prospects will not support a high capital value but whose prospects for *additional* funds show a huge return on the increment. One of the difficulties of financing such expansions by means of capital stock is thus suggested. A little reflection shows that the situation may also be reversed with existing stockholders not willing to share ownership unless the price is adjusted for conditions that are in part extraneous to the return on the increment. In each case new investors are asked to share a part of the existing facilities and new creditors must also consider their position with respect to all assets and existing liabilities.

Suppose, to illustrate, that producer A has been extremely successful while B has been suffering losses. Suppose that A has an investment prospect that will promise four percent on the increment, and B has a specialized prospect that promises 12 percent on the increment. Assume also that the plans are not interchangeable, i.e., A cannot adopt B's plan or *vice versa*. A can go into the capital market and, by sharing the entire existing financial structure with the furnishers of new capital, can get the necessary capital for three percent. On the other hand producer B may need to pay 15 percent in order to get incremental investors to share the dismal prospects from existing properties. Thus capital would be distributed at the margin with little regard to its expected profitability at the margin, i.e., A can place marginal capital where it earns four percent, and B is unable to finance plans that promise 12 percent. The effect of permitting average prospects to influence capital at the margin can be lessened somewhat by specialized investment contracts for incremental funds, but some misallocation seems to be unavoidable if the equities are intermingled and reported profits enter the calculation. The rigid conditions outlined above may be rare, but the locked-in effect must be very common in milder forms.

---

[15] An opposing view: "Only under assumed liquidation are current costs of appreciable significance at the date of a balance sheet." Perry Mason, "The 1948 Statement of Concepts and Standards," *The Accounting Review*, April, 1950, p. 134.

Curtailed operations on a long-term basis often take place by not replacing existing plants or by the withdrawal of units from production. Such decisions indicate that there are more attractive opportunities available on a current-cost basis elsewhere. So long as the prospect of incremental profit is not sufficient to attract funds, there will certainly be no expansion, and unless the old facilities can earn more than they can earn if they were redistributed throughout the economy, the activity will fold. To the extent that current costs indicate the value of the items in alternative uses, most businessmen will probably conclude that such costs along with some income reports on a current basis will improve allocation decisions.

For short-run contraction, variable costs are usually compared with changes in expected revenue. If depreciation is in part variable, the sacrifice in operating is related to replacement costs when the assets would be replaced with and without operation. That is to say, the cost of using (over not using) is related to the difference between two replacement costs related perhaps with an interest factor. An individual firm may, in fact, never make the replacements at either date, but for the economy as a whole it may be assumed that there are those who are contemplating investment or disinvestment in the field. For guidance of those who are rewarded if they invest in profitable ways, it is current cost that governs combining and proportioning decisions.

Thus for outsiders who are contemplating getting into a business, current (and expected future) costs are certainly the most useful. When obsolescence or supersession is in sight the current value of the assets should reflect the foreseeable portion of the decline. This point deserves emphasis, for it is widely misunderstood. *The current cost of existing assets will be influenced, to the extent that technological changes can be anticipated.* Therefore, it should be clear that whether or not businessmen replace in kind or with physically similar assets is simply beside the point. The impact of new, efficient assets is reflected in the resulting discount (value decrease) shown in the current price of old (existing) assets. For this reason it is important to distinguish between replacement cost and current cost. The latter is, of course, the current purchase price of existing assets. There is an influence tending to preserve the *status quo*. If a broker's margin is involved the buying price of used assets will be higher than the selling price. The buying price must be competitive with values in new assets, but to the seller the old assets will appear to be better values and therefore tend to lock him in his existing position. Weston has pointed out some of these relationships, although his statement refers primarily to output and seems to be unnecessarily restrictive.

> It is sometimes urged that a practical objection to the use of current costs is that the firm might not wish to produce the same assets or products. However, if the firm wished to use different assets because of the availability of improved equipment . . . . the argument that the firm may wish to produce different products is irrelevant. The only question that is raised and which appropriate accounting data seek to answer is how to measure the costs of producing a given set of services that are actually being produced.[16]

Let us now turn to the type of income, if any, that promises to be most useful in gauging the stewardship ability of management. In most economic systems it is important that better managers be rewarded and matched with society's scarce resources. Even in a

---

[16] J. Fred Weston, "Revaluations of Fixed Assets," *The Accounting Review*, October, 1953, pp. 487-488. Oscar S. Nelson, to my knowledge, was the first to emphasize the relation of partial obsolescence to current market values, although the general notion seems to have been used by industrial engineers for some time. See "Testing Obsolescence in Fixed Assets," *The Accounting Review*, October, 1945, pp. 447-458.

socialist economy, it simply does not make sense to match incompetent managers with expensive facilities. There may be other ways of testing managerial efficiency, but careful income reporting — especially in a profit-motivated economy — seems to provide a reasonable approach.[17] How, then, should income be measured for this purpose?

The concept of stewardship is difficult to define, but one of its characteristics is certainly responsibility for accomplishing objectives. An accounting for the degree of accomplishment is therefore necessary if there is to be interpersonal communication between the steward and his peers. Unlike the Biblical story of the talents, modern stewards are likely to have definite commissions with the objectives clearly set forth and the criteria of accomplishment carefully defined. If the stated objective is to operate within certain constraints and to increase the capital, then an income report is a straightforward example of a stewardship report that sets forth — according to recognition and measurement rules — the degree of accomplishment over a period. It is true that the final figures, and probably the intermediate figures as well, are the net of shrewd and stupid decisions, some of which were made during the interval and some of which were made many periods before. Unless the constraints on the steward are extremely detailed, it does not follow that a stewardship report is useless or not a proper summary of activity because all details and results of each decision are not given.[18]

Managers in our society tend to be selected and rewarded for their ability to produce income and thus there is usually some pressure toward low-cost production. In the pursuit of low-cost production, managers tend to economize the dear agents and be prodigal with the factors that are relatively cheap. If the system is out of equilibrium, there will be a shift from the relatively dear factor to the relatively cheap until the former is supplanted, or until the decreased demand reduces prices, or until the increased demand for the low-cost agent raises its prices and it is no longer relatively cheap.

Labor and materials are usually on a current cost basis. If plant is in terms of, say, 1945 costs, managers may be misled into being more extravagant with plant facilities and over-economizing current repairs, maintenance labor and materials. The insidious part of this arrangement is that accounting on other than a current-cost basis may increase *re-*

---

[17] It is of course possible to substitute other measures of efficiency for the income computation. In fact, with recommendations (from Lerner and others) to push short-run output until cost at the margin equals price, profit figures could conceivably be dispensed with. See J. M. Fleming, "Price and Output Policy of State Enterprise," *The Economic Journal*, December, 1944, p. 336. Beckwith comments: " . . . efficiency might be measured by intraplant unit costs, especially if all plants were required to use uniform cost-accounting methods. In making comparisons between plants, it would be necessary to allow for differences in equipment and other factors, but these differences affect profits also, and unit costs are not affected by many factors unrelated to efficiency which do affect profits." Burnham Putnam Beckwith, *Marginal-Cost Price-Output Control* (New York: Columbia University Press, 1955), p. 152. Socialists and anti-income (marginalist) accountants have detailed recommendations for short-run output decisions but they usually have trouble isolating managers who are good or bad at acquiring the "indivisibilities" — the joint services.

[18] "Many a wise and desirable managerial decision is not reflected in the income statement until years after the decision was made. Often, the effects of various decisions are so mingled in a given income statement that the only result is an average of unknown weighting and of therefore dubious significance . . . . Although there may be validity in the statement that entity income does . . . represent a test of over-all management, this test is far too crude and much too vague and general to serve either as an appraisal of over-all managerial efficiency or as a guide for managerial decision." William J. Vatter, *op. cit.*, pp. 34-35. Notice that the won-and-lost columns, without showing the myriads of good and bad field decisions, are often used as a measure of a baseball manager's performance after "standard budget allowances" for inherited personnel and ability of competition are made. An income report may be viewed as a won and lost report that averages sharp and dull behavior and sometimes confuses responsibility. And like the won-and-lost record, the income record is probably the most adequate single measure of progress toward the usual objectives. Vatter's position is in the right direction but extreme.

ported profit as the factors of production are wrongly proportioned. That is, higher short-run profits are reported if managers over-use existing facilities when depreciation-based costs are lower than current costs. In a similar manner if amortization of recorded cost is higher than the charge based on current cost, managers may be led to believe that labor and material costs are relatively cheap and over-economize the use of existing plant. Short-run profit calculations based on original unmodified cost will tend in the short-run to encourage careful managers to move in the direction of less long-run profits and higher social costs through inefficient proportioning.[19]

A serious confusion of stewardship function sometimes results when managers are shouldered with costs for which they were not responsible or when the measurement rules are not formulated carefully enough to isolate the effects of outside influences such as changes in price levels or in replacement cost structures. Failure to make some kind of analysis in this area may also mean that factor proportioning will be badly done.[20]

To the extent that acquisition gains and losses are not separated from other gains, a shrewd acquisition decision may cover a very poor operating or factor-combining record. Moreover, if an entire industry procured its assets at about the same time, capital may be over- or under-encouraged to flow into the field unless current costs are used.

The measurement of relative performance for managers who are shouldered with plants of different ages and efficiencies offers difficulties. If depreciation is on similar fixed assets or on a comparable base, it is possible to compare managers without regard to their ability at fixed asset procurement. To compare the direct or marginal unit cost of each unit, however, may fail to consider that one set of existing sunk facilities may be much more efficient than another.[21] Depreciation on original cost does not seem to help

---

[19] Apparently some accountants disagree. "One of the underlying postulates is that you continue in business . . . . Therefore, the fluctuations in the value of the assets that you have to have to continue in business are immaterial as long as you continue in business." George O. May, *Five Monographs on Business Income, op. cit.*, p. 206.

[20] The separation of the effects of specific major economic factors is well supported by accountants. " . . . to make a forecast of future expectations . . . from an income statement in which price fluctuation effects are not shown separately is nothing short of foolhardy . . . ." William J. Vatter, *op. cit.*, p. 72. "Each nonmonetary asset carried forward is adjusted to current cost with the index number appropriate to the account. The gains or losses on the assets carried forward are called capital gains, and they are not taken to net worth through the regular income statement." Myron J. Gordon, "The Valuation of Accounts at Current Cost," *The Accounting Review*, July, 1953, p. 373. "First, there is the margin between selling price and current cost of acquisition and selling — the cost at the time of the sale. This I shall call 'management profit.' It has been defined as income after the 'recovery' of physical capital . . . . Second, there is the so-called 'gain' or 'loss' arising from the change in price between the time of acquisition and the time of sale, or between acquisition and consumption. This has been called 'price profit,' or 'price loss,' . . . it is not profit at all . . . ." Willard J. Graham, "The Effect of Changing Price Levels Upon the Determination, Reporting, and Interpretations of Income," *The Accounting Review*, January, 1949, p. 16. Dutch accountants have been emphatic about the use of current costs, especially in their Kostprijs calculation. See, for example, H. J. Van der Schroeff, *De Leer van de Kostprijs* (Amsterdam: N. V. Uitgevers - Maatschappij, Kosmos, 1953, 1947).

[21] In practice 'sunk' is used to mean not relevant for *some* decision. For certain decisions some values and costs may be relevant and some not relevant. It is sometimes argued that there is no sunk cost unless it is practically impossible to sell the service potential, lease it, borrow on it, sell the entire business, or take it for a tax deduction. Some *sacrifice* would seem always to be relevant to some decision. What is probably meant is that historical cost *may* become nonrelevant. Alexander perhaps assumes too much mobility for the assets themselves. " . . . to most people . . . market value is the appropriate measure of well-being associated with each item of wealth in a man's possession. If one man feels that some of his possessions mean more in terms of his well-being than their market value, and others less, he is free to buy more of the first type of goods and sell some of the second type until market values and well-being are matched so far as he is concerned." *Op. cit.*, p. 13. In some cases usage of the asset may or may not reduce the interval of immobility. Only in the extremely rare cases in which usage, repairs, and upkeep have no effect whatever on the service potential is it correct to treat the sunk factor as a free good when proportioning it with other service factors.

much unless price levels increase in line with efficiencies. For example, older plants were in most cases constructed at less dollar cost than newer plants. Consequently, depreciation based on original costs would result in less charges for the older plants. To the extent that the *increase in technology keeps pace with the change in the value of the dollar*, unit costs that include depreciation on original cost may be acceptable bases for comparison of relative managerial efficiency.

It should be clear that current costs provide an automatic adjustment for relative efficiencies, and the automatic adjustment *tends* to be in proper amounts. Current costs, as opposed to replacement costs, should reflect — if the market is functioning as a market — the impact of technological changes and perhaps price-level changes. Thus in the valuation process the advantages of using new or more efficient assets — and consequently the disadvantages of using old, less efficient units — are reflected in current cost and therefore in depreciation based on current cost. (It is, of course, true that there may be economic rents arising in either case due to the peculiarities of the asset and business combinations with which the particular asset is associated.)

It seems clear that the use of current cost should aid in determining relative efficiencies of managers and thus should help society to reward efficient managers and to reject inefficient ones. It is true that the measurement of managerial efficiency *may* be approached in other ways, but the possibility of using current costs for better proportioning of factors seems indisputable.

It should be clear that there are many genuine economic problems whose solution might be encouraged by some sort of income computations. This paper is essentially an argument that economic income — if the term must be used — be measured so as to assist in the allocation and combination of scarce resources. It is also contended that current costs of individual agents should be matched with current revenues in order to build a foundation upon which those operating society's resources can superimpose their own modifying estimates of the dim but, to use a Patonian phrase, "not completely inscrutable" future.

> Economic profit, then, is the difference between current revenues and current costs. It represents the difference between the *economy's* current valuation of the goods and services *rendered* by the firm and its current valuation of the goods and services *used* by the firm.[22]

In conclusion, it seems desirable to mention the function of income as an index of the amount that could be consumed without being any better or worse off.[23] This index-of-withdrawal approach loses some of its appeal in a dynamic growth economy and seems better fitted to the corner-grocery activity. If such a criterion for using income reports is accepted, capital maintenance in terms of physical assets or purchasing power seems to be most appropriate of the feasible solutions. The general index for price-level changes applied to original costs may be adequate for this purpose. However, the chief benefit from general price-level adjustments is probably in the area of holding gains.

---

    [22] Edgar O. Edwards, "Depreciation Policy Under Changing Price Levels," *The Accounting Review*, April, 1954, p. 269. Notice that the 'economy's' or 'society's' valuation is due to those members of society who are at the margin. The usual argument that nonmarginal buyers and sellers are price-determining although they are not at the margin is not convincing. Observe, however, that the buyer and the seller on the same transaction have different subjective values. Market value is something of a reification.

    [23] This viewpoint reached its apex in John R. Hicks, *Value and Capital* (London: Oxford University Press, 1939), p. 171 ff. But all bookkeepers are familiar with "drawings in anticipation of profit" and the balance of the drawings account as a measure of living within (or without) the means furnished by the entity.

Essay Four

Income — Discounting Future
Expected Receipts

*But to inquire whether I [expectation I] on the first Monday is preferred to II [expectation II]
on the second Monday is a nonsense question; the choice between them could never be actual
at all . . .* [1]

It is the writer's purpose in this essay to examine in some detail the recommendations
and models that have been advanced — chiefly by economists — for the definition and
measurement of business income. Specifically, the operational definition of income as the
difference between the capitalized value of the prospects at the beginning and end of the
period is examined in detail. The problem is discussed from several angles. For example,
the charge that the definition is circular because capitalized value implies discounted
future income needs reviewing. Moreover, the assumption that a comparison of expectations at two different points in time leads to nonsense — as stated by Hicks — or is not related in any way to what a businessman thinks income should mean calls for consideration. The leverage factor resulting from capitalizing changes in optimism and pessimism
requires attention.

The charge of circularity is an old one and goes back at least to the writings of Irving
Fisher.[2] The usual constitutive (nonoperational) definition of periodic income is often in
terms of the maximum amount that could be distributed without making the firm's future
prospects any worse than they were at the beginning of the period.[3] The usual rules for implementing this definition (i.e., the rules of correspondence or the operational instructions) insist that future prospects discounted at the end of the period should be equal to
the sum of the discounted prospects at the beginning of the period plus the income for the
year. Thus, income is *defined* to be equal to the amount that could be withdrawn and
leave the discounted remaining prospects equal to the amount of the discounted prospects
at the beginning of the period. Clearly this definition is still not fully operational, for it
fails to give specific instructions for specifying the entity, discounting and measuring
prospects, and applying discount rates.

The charge of circularity may be based on two somewhat different lines of argument.
It may be pointed out that the prospects are in effect income, and that in order to find current income it is necessary as a prerequisite to estimate all future net favorable circumstances until eternity (at least in the compound interest sense) or, if the horizon is finite,

---

[1] John R. Hicks, *Value and Capital* (London: Oxford University Press, 1946), p. 177.

[2] Irving Fisher, *Elementary Principles of Economics* (New York: The Macmillan Company, 1923), pp. 107-
143.

[3] The background statement for this position was given by Hicks in the first edition (1939) of *Value and
Capital*. "The purpose of income calculations in practical affairs is to give people an indication of the amount
which they can consume without impoverishing themselves. Following out this data, it would seem that we ought
to define a man's income as the maximum value which he can consume during a week, and still expect to be as
well off at the end of the week as he was at the beginning" (p. 172).

the windup value. Thus the problem of finding current income becomes the problem of applying measurement rules for spreading the total future receipts to periods with the constraint of always having remaining prospects remain equal. Those who insist that what is being discounted is estimated future receipts (net) and not income are breaking the circular chain by giving operational content to receipts and relating both periodic income and capital value to receipts by constitutive definitions and intervening variables.[4] Unfortunately, net receipts over the life of the concern when modified for additional investment and for disinvestment add up to what a lot of accountants and businessmen think the total reported income should be. It is clear, of course, that there is no *a priori* reason why reported income should be defined to equal the total net receipts over and above maintenance of investment, but a large number of persons do insist on such an identification. There is a related way of attempting to avoid the charge of circularity. Current income is not identical with expected future income, although it is defined in terms of expectations of future income. That is to say, it may be argued that current income is determined by estimates of future income and that the estimates of the future need not be influenced by the amount reported as current income. This approach breaks the circle by introducing the independent concept of future income and assumes that estimating rules are available for this concept. Most accountants will prefer Alexander's "expected receipts" as being less confusing and more operational. Unfortunately, it is probable that future prospects (whether called receipts or future income) may indeed be influenced by current income reports, and, if so, partial interdependence and circularity return.

The other line of argument upon which the charge of circularity is based is related to the selection of a discount rate. It may be asked whether the discount rate that is selected is not in fact the operational definition of the rate of income. In other words, is it not necessary to know or to estimate the income rate in order to get a discount rate that is a necessary part of the operation of measuring income? At the very least the discount rate is a leading factor in assigning expectations to periods. Income is also such a distribution.

The obvious way of attempting to avoid this circularity is to deny that the discount rate is equivalent to the income rate. There is a general feeling that the discount rate, however, is a determinant of economic income so that in order to avoid a charge of partial circularity it must be shown that the instructions for determining an appropriate discount rate are independent of the rules for finding economic income. If the discount rate is the rate at which the investor is moved from indifference into investment action, then it is subjective with the investor and presumably also includes his subjective appraisal of the premium for risk. Thus the discount rate may be the *minimum* long-run rate that the investor will need in order to invest. His actual and expected income may be considerably larger, and of course after the investment has been made his actual return may be smaller than the motivating rate. How do these variances get included in periodic economic income?

An interesting characteristic of the discounting technique for measuring income is that the resulting rate of income will be equal to the rate of discount unless the definition of in-

---

    [4] Sidney S. Alexander escapes the charge of circularity by drawing a sharp distinction between expected net receipts and expected income. "Capital can be measured from the anticipated inflow of receipts and then the measure of capital so obtained can be used in the determination of income. Therefore there is no circularity in our definition of income" (p. 30). "If those receipts were themselves income, we would be engaged in formulating a circular definition. But fortunately, for our purposes the receipts need not be income but can be a mixture of income and return (or reinvestment) of principal. The objection of circularity is based on a confusion of receipts with income" (p. 29). Page references are to *Five Monographs on Business Income*, prepared by the Study Group on Business Income (New York: American Institute of Accountants, 1950).

come is broadened to include the results of unfavorable or favorable changes in expectations. Of course definitions may be set up so that the discounted distribution is the normal return on investment, and only the changes in expectation are defined as income. Thus what are often viewed as capital gains or losses (modified by the discounting process) become income.[5]

It must be clear to the reader that the discounting process and therefore the necessity for selecting a rate is somewhat gratuitous. Economists have used this process of valuation as a model of what investors should do, and it may not bear much resemblance to how such values are in fact derived. In fact, the emphasis on future estimates may mean that the construct can never be used widely and given general operational content. Thus, it may be that a particular business is valued at the beginning and end of the period by an index of sun-spot activity modified by selected astrological readings. To the extent that these criteria set values which result in exchanges, it may be argued that the objectivity of the resulting offers should prevail over an abstract model that is based on discounting some individual's estimates of future forces that may or may not act on the entity. Other models may be constructed. Nevertheless, the economist is probably correct in holding that there is a general tendency to value property in terms of discounted return, that most alternative schemes may be translated into the discounting framework, and that results tend to agree with what is usually meant by being no better or worse off.

It is interesting to note that Irving Fisher, the American pioneer in interest and capital theory, was too astute to be caught without a defense against the familiar charge of circularity. He states:

> When values are considered, the causal relation is not from capital to income, but from income to capital; not from present to future, but from future to present. In other words, the value of capital is the discounted value of the expected income. (p. 142) *Income* is derived from *capital-goods*. But the *value* of the income is not derived from the *value* of those capital-goods.[6]

Attention has been directed to the view that a comparison of capital values at the beginning and end of a period is not acceptable because the choice is never available. But is the possibility of a choice necessary before we can escape the current charge — feared by so many scientists and empiricists — of asking questions whose answers are nonoperational? More specifically, how can the absence of alternative possibilities influence the selection of the base from which to measure income? It is entirely possible that the assets are so specialized and buyers are so few that the only alternative available at any time is to abandon the operation. Whichever alternative was in fact followed will influence expectations and therefore reported profit, and unless plans for the future (as well as expectations) are the same for the beginning and end of the period, the change in hopes and plans will usually influence capital values and therefore reported income. To say that new alternatives or ideas may influence future expectations and reported income is not at all identical with holding that the income concept is meaningless because it is based on a quantity determined by applying rules at point A and another quantity determined in a similar

---

[5] At least as late 1952 George May, whose attitudes have long been those of an enlightened accountant, could see no usefulness in what an economist had to offer along the lines of income determination. His comments on Alexander's monograph were, at best, ill considered. See *Five Monographs on Business Income, op. cit.*, p. 205. "There is an economic concept held by a very respectable body of opinion that is of no practical use to this particular group."

[6] Irving Fisher, *op. cit.*, p. 107. See also pp. 133, 142.

manner at point B. How can he know that he is no better or worse off unless he has a choice? To ask the question is to answer it. It is possible for a man to reflect and estimate that his present feeling of being well-off is less than, equal to or greater than a specified feeling in the past. The new capital value is adjusted (according to the definition) so that he judges his subjective feeling of well being to be unchanged. The question then becomes whether one is able to make such comparisons in a dynamic framework; the problem is not one of interpersonal comparisons of well being, which are acknowledged to be most difficult. A man's memory may be bad, but, unless we believe in temporal solipsism, we cannot deny that he has one and that its product may be ordered and compared. Clearly this type of income is highly subjective and cannot be tested by appeal to the social consensus that is a requirement of objectivity. Income is thus truly the result of value judgments, it is personal, and it is private. The search for 'objective' surrogates goes on!

Let us now turn to the fluctuations that may result in reported profit due to changes in subjective appraisal of prospects, i.e., changes in the individual's optimism and pessimism. One of the most serious objections to the economic model of income results from its tendency to enlarge or magnify changes in the individual's estimates through the discounting device. The problem is due to the effects of taking the entire discounted value of changes in optimism about future prospects as income or loss of the period in which optimism changes. Such discounted amounts may be excluded by definition from the income calculation and reported under separate headings, such as capital gains or capital losses. To make such a separation tends to identify the reported income rate with the discount rate and to encourage the charge of circularity.

The change from certain knowledge to some degree of uncertainty does strange things to the economists' model for income. The disposition of such a model to fluctuate wildly due to changes in the discount rate is well known, although it is possible to treat such differences as "capital" gains or losses and to define the smoothed figures that remain as income. Suppose now that we permit the discount rate to remain unchanged and vary only the time interval between the date at which one revises his estimate of the magnitude of a future event and the actual date of that event. If there is no need to revise the estimates at all (perfect knowledge), the reported income is completely smoothed to a constant rate on investment by the discounting process.

If knowledge is less than perfect and a revision of prospects is made, the amount of smoothing will vary with the lead time between revision and event. If this interval is, say, thirty years the fluctuations induced in the reported income of the revision and subsequent years will be small. If only a year or two separates the two critical dates, the fluctuation reported in the period of discovery (revision) is large. (The exact amount obviously will also be influenced by the absolute magnitude of the revision.)

This effect does not seem to be widely understood, but it should be expected. The smoothest reporting results from certain knowledge. The time interval between revision and event may be used as an index of the knowledge horizon or of the degree of foreseeability. The less the vision ahead, the greater the fluctuations. The limit comes when the discovery and the event belong to the same profit-reporting period. In this case there is no smoothing and the full impact of the revision is reported in the period during which the revision is made. Again it may be feasible to define such irregularities as nonincome and maintain the smoothness of the income stream by definition.

The accountant observes these tendencies with interest, because he rarely smooths future expectations with discount rates. So long as he does not discount and does not adopt other rules for smoothing, his reported income figures will tend to fluctuate sharply. The full impact of changes in expectations that meet his recognition standards is reflected in the period of revision. Now this tendency toward fluctuations will always be greater than the tendency shown by the economists' model, even though there may be hope that the fluctuations will be numerous and be smoothed by averaging.

A new problem is encountered in the averaging process. Variations in the certainty (foresight) of accountants may be considerable over the periods, so that more revisions are made in some periods than in others. Moreover, insight into either favorable or unfavorable revisions may be bunched with erratic results. In any event, considerable manipulation may be possible in either case.

Suppose that the only income prospect is $100 to be received at the end of the second year. For the simplest case suppose also that the businessman does not change his expectations about the amount to be received and that a rate of six percent is appropriate for all valuations that need to be made. In this case there are no receipts other than the expected $100 at the end of the second period. We now ask how much income, if any, should be recognized by economists during the first period. The value of the prospect of the $100 at the beginning of the first year is $89 and the corresponding figure at the beginning of the second period is $94.34. There has been, according to the usual measurement rules, an increase in the value of the business of $5.34. This increment may be given the title of income so long as there are no realization restrictions and value added is assumed to be related entirely to the passage of time. If, however, economic activity and value added are related to buying, processing and selling goods, the relationship of an interest factor of this kind may be pretty farfetched. (The income, so defined, is a period income instead of product income, if we may borrow some adjectives from the cost accountants.) Now when value is added, the favorable prospects increase, and the discounted increase appears as income. The point to be emphasized is that, if the decision and the receipts are recognized in the same period, the full amount of the increase is treated as income (capital gain?). If the receipt is in a later period, less is taken in the current period and future intervening periods are credited with the interest factor. It is possible, of course, to call the value increases due to time 'capital gains,' but the reward for lending funds has long been considered income to the rentier and the title 'income' will no doubt continue to be used even though the major activity of the firm has little to do with waiting. This method tends to take up value added when the shrewd decisions are made (or are discovered) while traditional accounting tends to wait until the value is received.

Let us now turn to the first variation. Suppose that the discount rate of six percent is appropriate for both the beginning and end of year, but that during that interval all parties concerned become more optimistic and instead of seeing $100 at the end of the second period, all parties now expect the receipt to be $200. In this case, the value of the prospect at the beginning of the first year is $89, and the value of the prospect at the beginning of the second year is twice $94.34, or $188.68. What is the income to be reported? Obviously, several possibilities present themselves. One possibility — and perhaps the most common one — is to call the entire difference in the value of the prospects, the entire $99.68, 'income' and thereby inform the owner that he may take out this amount at the end of the first year and still have a prospect valued at the *original* $89. Another possibility is to report the $5.34 as before and to name the excess $89 as some kind of capital gain or "gain arising through increased optimism." Still a further approach may recompute the original value of the prospect on the basis of the $200. Thus, the beginning value of the prospect would be twice $89 or $178. The income to be reported would be the difference between $188.68 and $178, or $10.68, which is of course twice the original reported profit of case one, $5.34.

How do economists select among these alternatives? Meaningful answers must be in terms of income objectives. Keeping original values (discounted original expectations) intact may make little or no sense years later when owners have changed and the passage of time has made the original expectations dim and fuzzy. On the other hand, it is difficult and time-consuming to recompute the base from which income is to be measured and to use latest expectations for the beginning base. If the entire value added is taken to be distributable without impairing the capital of the firm, why not call the entire increase income? If a rational means of separation is available, a separation of that part which is due to changes in optimism may be desirable. It should be noticed that changes in optimism are especially important, because relative to the 'time' concept they are capitalizations and therefore employ a leverage factor. Thus with a six percent discount factor the reported gain that results from a doubling of expectations is almost 17 times as large as income defined in terms of the discount factor.[7]

We may digress for a moment and speculate about the problem of selecting proper expressions of optimism. Due to the leverage factor it seems that considerable care should be taken in appraising changes in optimism. One is confronted with deciding whose opinions should be selected and with problems of interpersonal appraisals. The opinion of the closely-knit owners or managers permits the possibility of manipulation to further their aims. On the other hand, the owners (if closely-knit) and managers are in perhaps the best position to estimate such matters. Reference to outside opinion such as market quotations is sometimes possible. With the widespread use of reported earnings to estimate the market value of the concern, looking to investors for values of the concern in order to measure income does not appear to be very promising! Furthermore, it is sometimes alleged that investors tend to project the level of current earnings into the future (perhaps in perpetuity). It may still be argued that to the extent that *bona fide* offers are forthcoming, the sacrifice in not selling is measured by such valuations, and therefore the capital-stock value at the end of the period is a cost of continuing the business. Notice that this line of argument does not need to consider how the prospective buyer values the concern. Such values may be very volatile in thin markets, but this general approach contains merit. Certainly the accounting profession should hesitate a long time before assuming that accountants or economists are always competent to make such valuations.

To change the illustration, suppose that expectation remains constant at $100 at the end of the second year. Suppose also that the rate of discount at the beginning of the first period is six percent, while at the end of the first period the appropriate discount rate is only five percent. Evidently the value of the prospect as seen at the beginning of the first year and discounted at six percent remains at $89. At the end of the first year the value of the future prospect discounted at the prevailing rate of five percent is $95.24. (An equivalent figure resulting from the use of a six percent rate is $94.34.) Again we are faced with the problem of deciding which difference is to be called income. It should be noted that the $89 for the beginning value of the prospect is changed to $90.70 if the beginning value is recomputed on a five percent basis. First, suppose that the investment was made on a six percent basis and resulted in an actual cost of $89. The income may be defined as the difference between $95.24 and $89. The resulting $6.24 is, of course, 90 cents larger than the amount resulting from the application of six percent. Perhaps economists may prefer to continue to use six percent for measuring income and to show $5.34 as the income. The remaining 90 cents may then be considered to be a capital gain that results from buying the prospect on terms more favorable than those now available.[8]

There is, of course, a case for considering such "capitalization-rate" gains or losses as income and burying them in the income measurement. To the extent that five percent now expresses the current effective basis, the owner might be able to sell his prospect at the end of the first year for the larger figure and thereby realize the 90-cent gain. In other words, to the extent that there is a market for businesses of this type and the rate at which they are bought and sold is now five percent, there is a more or less objective gain, and for those economists, businessmen and accountants who are not concerned with realization, recognition is in order. From one point of view, it may be argued that by not selling the prospect discounted at five percent the owner is in effect buying the prospect from himself at five percent and that the relevant cost for record keeping should be the opportunity (alternative) cost or sacrifice involved. This line of argument abandons the fixed psychological base for income measurement that is based on a fixed percent (in this case six percent) and substitutes for the fixed percentage base a series of imputed market values that are inferred from the change in the discount rate and the fact that the owner does not sell. Where the markets are well established, this alternative satisfies in part those who are concerned with objectivity. Current-market values replace the hold-to-maturity assumption.

There is a definite advantage to the traditional approach as outlined above. As a first step it is assumed that businessmen should discount future prospects in arriving at value. It may even be assumed that some calculation of this sort is, in fact, used by businessmen and by those in the market. A whole series of rates of discount for businesses of varying risks are usually available from completed transactions and bid-and-ask quotations of specialized prospects. Thus, approximate rates may be available while overall appraisal figures themselves are not. By assuming in the model that the rates are applied in a specific manner to all prospects that are to be valued, one may make up his own appraisal (valuation) figures. Of course, he is highly subjective in finding which one of the rates is appropriate for his type of risk and in estimating the future service flows to be evaluated, but at least there is an operational procedure that may be substituted for market appraisals. On the surface it appears that estimates of future net receipts are subjective while the discount rates may be determined from objective markets. A little reflection will show that the discount rates depend in part on risk and on the probability features of the expected receipts themselves, so that the selection of the appropriate rate is also subjective.

---

[7] "The error introduced into accountant's income by basing depreciation on a necessarily fallible estimate of the useful life of the equipment will be infinitesimal compared to the error introduced into economic income by the uncertainty of future receipts." Sidney S. Alexander, *op. cit.*, p. 59.

[8] Alexander has also given attention to these matters. " . . . the pure economic income . . . is the difference between the year-end value of net worth and the year-beginning net worth, both valued according to the knowledge and beliefs current at year's end" (p. 20). " . . . for a business corporation, variable income equals the change in tangible assets plus the change in the going value minus that part of these changes attributable to changes in expectations of future receipts" (p. 71). "The difference between the hindsight value of year-beginning equity and year-beginning equity as valued at the beginning of the year may be termed 'unexpected gain.' We must choose between the alternatives of considering unexpected gain as an actual increase in wealth or as a mere revision of an estimate of wealth. As an actual increase of wealth, it should be included in economic income; as a revision of an estimate, it should be excluded.

"The first viewpoint is based on the assumption that a man is as well off as he thinks he is, and not as well off as someone with superior knowledge either now or later may know him to be" (p. 61). *Op. cit.* Apparently, in some way "actual wealth" is not an expectation.

Essay Five

Income — The Accountant's Approach

It is the purpose of this essay to compare the economist's construct of income as changes in discounted prospects with the typical accountant's measurement rules for revenues and expenses. Specifically it is argued that the application of a discount rate to future prospects can largely be dispensed with by a continuing concern; that the practice of assuming that waiting is the primary activity of a firm and that value is added in a compound-interest relationship with time is only rarely necessary; that the usual accounting rules for recognizing value increases will tend to diminish the smoothing effect of interest and to permit total reported income to vary more freely with decisions and activities other than passive waiting; that the assumption of Moonitz-Staehling that accounting rules are poor substitutes for the discounted-value approach and should be used only when the future is uncertain, is not warranted.

As a basis for discussion let us begin with the excellent discussion given by Maurice Moonitz and Charles Staehling, who have made one of the few serious attempts to compare the discount approach to income determination with the more common cost-revenue approach.[1] These authors begin their work by setting out to show:

(1) The determination of the *value* at a moment of time of a prospective series of cash receipts and disbursements, (2) . . . the calculated effect of time-duration in valuation, and (3) set out clearly the evidence of profit . . . in a situation in which all of the necessary facts are assumed to be definitely known.

Their data are summarized below:

Prospective cash receipts and outlays
to occur at the end of each year

	Values at beginning of five-year period	1	2	3	4	5	Total of receipts and disbursements, entire period
Prospective receipts	$43,951	$10,000	$12,000	$11,000	$9,000	$10,000*	$52,000
Prospective outlays	24,577	6,000	7,000	5,000	6,000	5,000	29,000
Resultant value of the investment	19,374	4,000	5,000	6,000	3,000	5,000	23,000

*Includes cash received from sale of remaining assets, $3,000.

---

[1] Maurice Moonitz and Charles C. Staehling, *Accounting: An Analysis of Its Problems*, I (Brooklyn: The Foundation Press, Inc., 1952), pp. 120 ff.

The present value (at six percent) of the series of receipts, adverse interests (payments) and remainders may be detailed.

Year	Receipts	Outlays	Remainder
1	$ 9,434	$ 5,660	$ 3,774
2	10,680	6,230	4,450
3	9,236	4,198	5,038
4	7,129	4,753	2,376
5	7,472	3,736	3,736
	$43,951	$24,577	$19,374

Moonitz and Staehling then calculate the annual net profit with complete knowledge of all relevant future events. At the end of the first year the receipts of $10,000 have been received and the outlay of $4,000 has been made. In addition all future receipts are more valuable as they are all one year nearer to cash. The value of these receipts, including the one for the first period, has increased by $2,637 from the value at the beginning of the year. In a similar manner the outlays are nearer, and their value has changed by $1,475. The difference of $1,162 represents the net value added and is defined as the profit of the first year. The $4,000 cash receipts in excess of outlays is treated as a withdrawal. In a similar fashion the profit for the second year is $991; for the third, $753; for the fourth, $436; for the fifth, $284. Total reported profit for the five-year period is $3,626, which is, of course, the difference between the total net receipts ($23,000) and the present value of these receipts ($19,374).

It must be observed that Moonitz and Staehling *do not define profit as it is commonly defined in accounting*. The typical accounting definition is based on the assumption that the capital of the firm is kept intact, while they assume substantial withdrawals and the reported income is therefore on a variable capital base. The return of capital is summarized (p. 131):

Year	1	2	3	4	5
Withdrawal	$4,000	$5,000	$6,000	$3,000	$5,000
Profit	1,162	991	753	436	284
Return of Investment	$2,838	$4,009	$5,247	$2,564	$4,716

Suppose, to show the effect of a variable capital base and to illustrate the influence of different receipt and payment patterns, that a single payment of $29,000 is due at the end of the first year and replaces the given series of payments. The present value of the receipts would be unchanged, $43,951, the present value of the adverse payment of $29,000 would be $27,358 and the purchase price would then be changed to $16,593. The first year's profit would be ($2,637 less $1,642) $995. The second year's profit would be $2,194 and the remaining years would report $1,608, $1,043, $567. Now, it is clear that profits defined in this manner will be higher after the lump-sum adverse payment is made, for this payment results in additional investment instead of the return of capital for the first year.

Suppose, to vary the illustration, that the receipts are unchanged and that the $29,000 adverse interest is due at the end of the fifth year. The present value of the outpayment would be $21,669 and the value of the business would be $22,282. The first year's reported profit would be $2,637 less $1,300 or $1,337. The point to be observed is that the timing of the receipts and disbursements influences the pattern of reported profits, because with the Moonitz-Staehling assumptions the invested capital changes as the timing of the receipts and payments changes. If their assumption were modified so that the recovered investment were immediately reinvested, the reported income would have been equal period by period.

Period	1	2	3	4	5
Earnings on Original Investment	$1,162	$ 991	$ 753	$ 436	$ 284
Earnings on Reinvestment	-0-	172	410	726	879
Profit	$1,162	$1,163	$1,163	$1,162	$1,163

Of course, it is a well-known fact that the application of compound interest will tend to report a constant rate of return on capital. Net income defined operationally is the result of applying measurement rules to what are considered to be the determinants of income, and the measurements are then judged to be good or bad in relation to the usefulness of the results. Inasmuch as there are no windfalls or estimating errors, net income (so defined) is due solely to the increasing nearness of the returns of remaining capital and is measured solely through the discounting telescope. Variation in business activity therefore brings about no changes in income but changes the amount of capital that *is assumed to be recovered*.

It is at precisely this point that the assumption of a going concern is so important in accounting. One of the decisions required by an auditor is whether or not an assumption of an indefinitely continuing concern is appropriate. If such an assumption appears to be warranted, a particular set of measurement rules is selected and applied to the events affecting the entity. If the assumption does not seem to be warranted, a different kit of measurement rules is used. (Notice, for example, the different valuation rules for statements of affairs and for depletion in a one-shot mining operation.)

Among the subsidiary assumptions that are implied by adoption of the going-concern approach is that the capital, in some meaningful sense, will be kept intact and that only increases in value in excess of that necessary to preserve the integrity of the investment will be labeled income.

The chief advantage of the continuing-concern assumption should now be clear. With capital held intact for an indefinite period in the future, the influence of discounting diversified assets is reduced to a negligible (primarily smoothing) effect. The continuum of future expectations will be approximately the same at the beginning and the end of each period, so that (except for interest) discounting will yield approximately equal values at the beginning and end of the period. In the absence of unusual irregularities and with capital kept intact, the smoothing effect of compound discounting will tend to yield a *constant periodic* income. The influence of this more or less constant factor is not important for the measurement of accounting income and is accordingly neglected. This position has often led to the charge that accountants do not understand the importance of the "time value of money." We may still be concerned about interest on the current period's receipts and outlays and for irregular receipts and disbursements. But if regular flows are assumed to be matched or centered during the year, the amount of current interest should be relatively constant and therefore relatively unimportant.

Thus accountants can neglect the broad discounting approach only if they can derive some measurement rules that will provide for keeping the future prospects approximately equal in perpetuity. These rules consist of a procedure for recognizing new values that arrive in the specified interval (revenues) and the interest effect of approaching future revenues may be disregarded if the stream is expected to be more or less continuous and reasonably uniform. The going-concern approach also presupposes that capital consumption is provided for and that the horizon is unchanged and extends, like a monotonous prairie, indefinitely into the future. If the horizon of prospects remains unchanged, the accountant feels no need to view it with the discounting glass that makes future benefits decrease as a function of the period of waiting.

The accountant's problem is thus transferred from the problem of discounting future prospects to one of finding suitable rules for keeping capital intact *without* using income or discounted receipts to measure capital. He must deduct from revenues an amount sufficient (when reinvested) to insure within tolerable limits that the wall of future prospects will not be greatly changed. This problem consists of finding acceptable conventions for measuring capital consumption and for deducting enough from revenues to guide (encourage?) businessmen toward the reinvestment necessary to keep prospects unimpaired. Traditionally these measures of capital consumption have been related to costs and to specific service potentials that can be estimated *without* also estimating enterprise income, e.g., shelter for buildings, fund raising possibilities for inventories, period of protection for patents.

A few related remarks about irregular revenue streams may serve to direct the discussion toward costs and their expiration. Suppose that in a particular case the revenues consist of a lump-sum receipt well in the future, e.g., a long-term bond with no explicit interest. The discounting procedure for taking up income recognizes a small amount of income in the early years and larger and larger amounts as the maturity date nears. The implied assumption is that we are receiving more benefits for equal intervals of waiting as the maturity gets nearer. This assumption is related to the feeling that income should be associated with the market-value increase period by period and can be tied to activity or benefit only by changing the *assumed investment* each period. Thus the increase is *not* a larger increase in value for identical services — the capital investment is presumed to be larger period by period. If the interest could be withdrawn each period to keep capital intact, it is clear that the income recognized each year would be the same. Or if the investor has a seasoned holding of numerous bonds that mature regularly and are replaced at maturity, his capital investment (by the market test) would be unchanged and his recognized income under the compound-interest method would be the same as if he used a straight-line computation.[2] It is, of course, a consequence of the going-concern assumption that we do not let the bond equivalent (e.g., the facilities) mature; we replace them on a con-

---

[2] Variations arise when yields change. Defenders of the hold-to-maturity assumption ignore interim market fluctuations even for a single asset. The accumulated value is taken as the 'true' value regardless of the market value of the investment.

tinuous basis. Thus the capital base is kept reasonably constant and the use of a discount factor is only marginally necessary. A generalization seems to be in order: the discounting technique is an appropriate measuring device when a shifting capital investment is assumed. The shifting base tends to agree with the probable sales prices at these calculation dates and thus, by not selling, the owner can be said to be making renewed investments of these amounts at each date. The going-concern assumption and the hold-to-maturity assumption traditionally have implied that such interim sales values are not relevant, and they are therefore excluded from the valuation process.

The accountant's rules for additional investment and for disinvestment are relatively simple and lead us to a consideration of cost. To the extent that the (costs) outlays are regular and the plant is diversified (has struck its gait) we can neglect interest and discount factors in determining periodic income. As in the case of revenues, discounting cost streams that are assumed to be roughly uniform and perpetual serves no useful purpose.

The early years before the firm's investment is seasoned give accountants trouble at the practical level. Until the capital assets have had time to season, some sort of compound interest calculation is necessary. In the context of an indefinitely continuing firm a new plant is worth more than a used one of similar output and efficiency precisely because the wall of major replacements is farther in the future. In order to keep a stream of revenues intact the expenditures are likely to be highly uneven during the early years of seasoning. To preserve the prospects it seems essential that accountants deduct an amount larger than current expenditures for replacements from the revenues of early years.[3]

To the extent that the timing of these outlays is not regular, the time-value of money does become important and the discounting problem returns to haunt the accountant. To maintain the integrity of the prospects requires some sort of deduction in advance of outlay during this temporary period. What is the proper amount of this deduction? If we assume that the excess (earmarked) revenue funds will be invested *in the business* we usually assume the earning rate of the business, and partial circularity returns.[4]

The accountant can always use the rate of return on outside investment opportunities as the assumed discount rate. If the funds are in fact segregated and invested the return will be definite enough, and certainly no one would normally be interested in letting funds lie idle. It remains to estimate the amounts which at the rate of return would keep the net prospects unimpaired. If the funds are put to use, it seems clear that their return will tend to increase the revenue stream, and that the expense — the deduction from revenue — can be increased by amounts equal to the amounts of revenue growth. Clearly one of the compound interest methods of cost spreading seems appropriate for what the accountant is trying to do.

It is of course possible for the accountant to neglect the interest factor in this area, and hope that the induced variation will be immaterial and lost in the errors of hundreds of other estimates. In the unmodified replacement method of depreciation it is usually as-

---

[3] This problem is closely tied with retirement reserves sometimes found in connection with the replacement method of depreciation. See my "Depreciation Accounting in Utilities," *The Accounting Review*, January, 1943, pp. 1-9.

[4] Partial circularities are relatively common and seldom destroy the validity of the work, although they can be annoying. Canning, to the horror of some accountants, held that inventories might be valued at net selling price less a profit element related to the firm's rate. "Some normal industrial rate of return converted to an average rate on the concern's own inventories should be found." John B. Canning, *The Economics of Accountancy* (New York: The Ronald Press Company, 1929), p. 222.

sumed that over the long pull for a going concern the periodic variations induced by ir-regular outlays to keep the long-term earning power intact may be neglected completely — that no smoothing is needed. The retirement reserve technique in conjunction with the re-placement method aims only at smoothing these irregular income effects and may or may not include the refinement of compound-interest calculations.

Neither economists nor accountants have agreed on what the ideal income-reporting pattern should be. Should the reported yearly income be smoothed to serve as an index of expected future prospects? Should the annual figure be related somehow to production activity? Sales activity? Planning activity? Which results and specific changes are high-lighted in the income report for all who are interested? Should a quarterly report, for ex-ample, be smoothed by seasonal adjustment to be an indicant of the yearly income? The long-run rate of income? Some other concept of income?

Economists have apparently approved the annual-indicant view. National income and related quarterly figures are adjusted to annual rates. The discounting recommendation tends to smooth erratic tendencies and to present a still longer-run view. Yet at the time of purchase, the economists' approach tends to take up excess values as income or capital gains and to recognize other income evenly over time as if the only contributing factor were waiting. The timing of these excess-value recognitions may induce wide variations in reported income. The correlation of income recognized and value added is an objective of both economists and accountants. The details vary considerably (see the following essay).

The accountant's measurement rules permit the reported income to vary (without the smoothing effects of discounting) from period to period according to *current* activity in the fields of revenues and costs. Opportunities for management's contribution to profit show up in larger current revenues *and* in provision for keeping future prospects intact with lower current costs. In the latter connection accountants tend to look at capital con-sumption as related to past investment as well as to current expenditures; they then try to decide what portion seems to be a capital expenditure to provide for increasing future prospects and what portion seems to be necessary to keep the prospects intact. The oppor-tunities for shrewd management obviously arise from doing either of these jobs with the least sacrifice. If the level of future prospects is maintained at a very low cost, the current profit report will reflect the fact. Unfortunately, except in the renewal (replacement) method of depreciating capital assets, shrewd decisions for maintaining prospects do not show up as increased profit until later. As will be pointed out in the following essay, shrewd expenditures for increased future prospects (capital expenditures) are not reflected in the period in which the ability was exercised, and the value added to the prospects is as-sumed to be exactly equal to the amount of the expenditure. It should be observed that such rules are not necessarily implied by the accountant's approach to income measure-ment. Other rules with less stringent requirements for recognizing increases in prospects could be substituted, e.g., recognizing subjective value added at acquisition.

There is genuine doubt among accountants as to whether income that is reported as a fixed discounted rate on capital plus the net of capitalized changes in optimism is the most useful construct for those guiding society's economic resources. Accountants seem to pre-fer a distribution of reported income that is more closely related to current activity. Thus, they tend to match costs with revenues (where possible) on a benefit basis that is specific for each service potential and to emphasize the periodic contribution of revenues recog-nized over the costs necessary to maintain specific prospects for service. To the extent that depreciation is recognized on a straight-line basis, accountants are assuming equal costs for service consumption and thus tending to accentuate the effect of the variable periodic contribution of revenues over other costs. Thus in the Moonitz-Staehling illustration, instead of equal reported annual profits of $1,162, application of straight-line would yield successively $725, $1,922, $3,118, $315, and < $488 > [5]

In the following essay we will turn to the problem of matching costs with revenues according to specific benefits received compared with the total expected (specific) benefits. This approach has some factors in common with valuation; for example, it is necessary to estimate total benefits expected from each asset. Notice, however, that a discount rate is not necessary, for we substitute the original cost as the capitalized value and proceed to match it with revenue in proportion to service rendered to total expected services. Interim changes in optimism may influence the write-off, but the leverage factor provided by the capitalization process is removed.

In the Moonitz-Staehling illustration a depreciation rate that approximates the benefit process may be derived by relating capital deterioration to contribution of revenues over other outlay expenses. The required rate works out to be $0.81875 of capital consumption for each dollar of contribution. Total capital consumption would be spread to the successive years: $3,275, $4,094, $4,913, $2,456 and $1,638. If recovered funds are reinvested at six percent the reported profits by year would be $725, $1,103, $1,530, $1,282, and $985 instead of the uniform $1,162.

---

[5] The argument that straight-line reports higher rates of return on old assets is more impressive in the single-asset case. It is true that the book value for seasoned assets is lower with straight-line, but the depreciation charges on these assets should be roughly equal regardless of the method used. Incidentally, a zero interest rate reduces compound-interest methods to straight-line, and for steady-state conditions the difference in book values varies directly with the rate employed.

Essay Six

Cost-Value Identification and Income Measurement

It is the writer's purpose in this essay to review the rationale of cost-value identification and to unravel some of the associated threads that are often found in discussions of income. The limitations of cost as a measurement scale for value are discussed. In the jargon of scientific method, accountants accept a construct of value in a constitutive sense with poorly formed and inadequate rules of correspondence to relate it to the empirical area. They also take another construct — cost — which has slightly better rules of correspondence (operational content) and relate the two in such a way that the recognition and measurement rules for cost may be substituted for the more difficult ones for value. In the course of the discussion the identification of cost and value at purchase is treated and the similarities between cost allocation on a benefit basis and traditional valuation are compared.[1]

Cost at the time of purchase is usually assumed to be equivalent to value at the time of purchase — market value — without serious discussion of the point. To many it seems evident that the transfer (purchase) not only establishes the evidence of the amount of the cost, but it also establishes value to the buyer and to the seller. But market value is not equivalent to value in *use* to the buyer. The following offhand statement is typical.

> The condition which validates the cost figure is the simultaneous action of two independent parties motivated by self-interest. The price-aggregate that emerges at the moment a bargaining exchange is consummated is a mutually acceptable "valuation"; hence the quantitative record of the "service acquired" by one party should be in agreement with the quantitative record of the "service rendered" by the other party.[2]

At the time of purchase the buyer must think that the expected value of the incremental discounted services to be added to the expected services of all his other assets will be *at least as great* as the cost of the addition. Thus we may assume that the amount of his discounted *expectations* for the *marginal* services will be as great as the purchase price. It may be added that there is a tendency for the buyer to keep on acquiring units until the discounted expected benefits from the last (least remunertive) unit are about equal to the purchase price. Furthermore, assuming free access to the fund markets, there is a tendency for him to buy all assets until the discounted expected return is approximately equal to the cost of funds. Expectations for intra-marginal units should be greater than cost.

---

[1] I have treated parts of this problem elsewhere. See: *Inventory Valuation and Periodic Income* (New York: The Ronald Press Company, 1942), pp. 34-35. Also: *Handbook of Modern Accounting Theory*, ed. Morton Backer (New York: Prentice-Hall, Inc., 1955), pp. 333-334.

[2] W. A. Paton and A. C. Littleton, *An Introduction to Corporate Accounting Standards* (Chicago: American Accounting Association, 1940), p. 26.

The accountant, realizing that under the profit motive any particular agent of production should be acquired until its cost is equal to the expected value of its marginal product, treats each agent *as if* it contributes to the revenue area only the amount of its cost. After each asset (productive agent) has been treated in this fashion any excess value (chiefly from intra-marginal units) is attributed to the noncost factors — to the enterprise. Entrepreneurship, it must be emphasized, is not considered to be an asset except perhaps occasionally in an incomplete fashion in the goodwill calculation. Where the period of income computation covers the entire cycle of operations, it is natural to subtract costs of specific factors from total revenues and attribute the remainder (positive or negative) to those who under existing institutions are permitted to appropriate it.[3]

Where the accounting period is shorter than the cycle of operations, there will ordinarily be some agents that have already yielded their entire services at statement date and there will be other agents that have yielded only a portion of their benefits. What seems more plausible, in view of the economic precedent, than to write-off each long-lived agent (marginal or intra-marginal) with the assumption that its services are equal to its cost? The total deferred cost on a statement of financial position at any time then should be the discounted services expected to be received from the *marginal* (least important) unit multiplied by the number of units. More accurately — the detailed discussion comes later — the unamortized unit cost remaining after applying the benefit doctrine should not be far from the value often imputed to the marginal unit.

We may ask why cost adherents — and there are apparently many — bother about value anyway. The essential problem of income determination according to the modern cost view is a matter of matching cost and revenue. When one considers the well-nigh impossible task of finding separable value contributions for each asset, in conjunction with a varying background of supporting assets and a shifting business environment, the retreat to the seemingly safe cost approach is at least understandable. However, certain weaknesses appear in the cost approach, and many accountants remain loyal to concepts of value.[4]

While at the time of purchase discounted expected services must be at least as much as the cost, accountants do not feel constrained to put such assets on the records at figures above cost. The expected services from a particular unit depend on a somewhat arbitrary

---

[3] See: *Inventory Valuation and Periodic Income, op. cit.*, pp. 3-4. "The total services recognized for a given enterprise are made up of those contributed by factors purchased from outside groups and those contributed by the enterprise itself. Revenues may be taken as the *total* amount of recognized services rendered from both sources. By defining closely the limits of the enterprise and devising rules and conventions for determining the amount of costs which expire, it is possible to make a reasonable estimate of the services contributed by 'outsiders.' The difference is equivalent to the contribution of the unrecorded factors of production, where this phrase is meant to include services from all the economic factors and agents which have *not* been acquired by exchange transactions. The modern accounting system, then, reflects periodic net income as a residuum after the contribution of the recorded factors has been subtracted from the total contributions recognized."

[4] Not only is there confusion of cost and value in accounting, but there is even confusion as to who among accountants stands for what. The following statement is considerably more representative of Paton's life-long view than later statements under unfortunate joint authorship. "It is the function of accounting to record values, classify values, and to organize and present value data in such a fashion that the owners and their representatives may utilize wisely the capital at their disposal." William A. Paton, *Accounting Theory* (New York: The Ronald Press Company, 1922), p. 7. Many accountants agree with this more recent statement by Norton M. Bedford. " . . . the activities of a business firm may be considered as the process of acquiring values from outsiders, rearranging such values in different forms and in the process adding value itself both types of which are then disposed of to customers." "Using Supplementary Data to Interpret Reported Income," *The Accounting Review*, October, 1953, p. 517.

ordering of the unit with regard to the margin. That is, the value of a particular asset depends on its supporting assets and also on its ordering in the acquisition series.[5] The value of the services actually received may, of course, be far more or far less than the value of the service *expectations* at any time. Furthermore, the separation of value contributions from individual assets is usually impossible. The accountants' compromise is to find some sort of measure for specific services rendered and to be rendered by each asset or class of assets, and to use these measures to assign the costs. Any excess services (economic rents) are imputed to the organization and appear as income.

Even if the above rationale for carrying assets at cost is accepted, a scheme to apportion cost to the individual income periods must still be devised. Vague references to "some systematic manner" certainly do not qualify for professional standards.[6] Unless we are to use some arbitrary rule, we are forced to argue that cost should be written off as the services expire or that some method of direct valuation, which may or may not keep the earning power of the business intact, should be used. Certainly the earning power concept is a typical valuation problem, and, as will be pointed out later, the benefit theory is at bottom also a problem of valuation.

Unless one of these valuation approaches — benefit-cost-allocation or valuation in the accepted sense — is followed, there is no method of assigning cost that is consistent with the usual meaning of income. Certainly, unbridled caprice is not consistent with the accepted meaning of income. One might write off all of the cost at once, or write off the cost according to determinations resulting from the use of dice, cards, astrological readings or other devices. Many hopelessly irrational methods may still qualify as systematic! The forced conclusion is that if we abandon the service (valuation) approach to asset write-off, the usual income construct is abandoned with it.

It is not difficult to understand the desire of accountants to identify costs and values in some way. They wish to preserve the stability of recorded costs and yet present periodic income figures that retain traditional meaning for businessmen and others who might use them. Identification of the two helps attain both aims. Depreciation may be defined as the spreading of a cost to operating periods, and the principle for making the assignment may be based on value determinants in the form of benefits received and benefits expected. It is

---

[5] Imputation of value based on assets at the margin cannot be added to yield the value of the enterprise. In practice the accountant often approaches the problem by looking at individual assets (Edwards) and also by trying to encompass the whole organization (Dean). "A comparison of subjective asset values at the beginning and end of a period is essentially a comparison of past revenue-cost expectations with current revenue-cost expectations." Edgar O. Edwards, "Depreciation Policy Under Changing Price Levels," *The Accounting Review*, April, 1954, p. 268. "In economic terms, he — the individual — finds the present capital value of his entire future earnings and spends as income this year one installment of a lifetime annuity on that capital value." Joel Dean, "Measurement of Profits for Executive Decisions," *The Accounting Review*, April, 1951, p. 185.

[6] The following quotation is from *Accounting Terminology Bulletin* Number 1 of the American Institute of Certified Public Accountants, prepared by the Committee on Terminology. "Depreciation accounting is a system of accounting which aims to distribute the cost or other basic value of tangible capital assets, less salvage (if any), over the estimated useful life of the unit (which may be a group of assets) in a systematic and rational manner. It is a process of allocation, not of valuation." Paton and Littleton are more helpful. "Under accrual accounting, depreciation is not a valuation process nor a means of capturing replacement prices from customers; it is simply a step in the process of associating past cost, which measures the planned effort to produce goods or services, with the revenue actually derived from the goods or services produced" (p. 17). "With costs properly classified and service lives reasonably determined, how shall plant cost be spread? . . . . Since units of plant are conceived as bundles of services the best procedure would be to apportion their costs wherever possible in terms of the stream of services rendered. In other words, some form of production or output method would be the most appropriate base" (p. 84). Page numbers refer to *An Introduction to Corporate Accounting Standards, op. cit.*

unfortunate that some very good accountants have apparently distrusted "benefit expectations" as a partial determinant of amortization and have advocated such nonoperational, pseudo-guideposts as "equitable bases," "systematic manner," "fairness to periods."

Some accountants have become so confused that they consider cost to be *the* fundamental basis for accountability and tend to neglect value altogether. For old-fashioned stewardship accountability it seems clear that we may sometimes even use physical units. The steward may be held accountable for specified numbers of flagons of each type of wine and may be released from responsibility upon authorized withdrawal. Why should cost be an accountability factor?

The monetary unit acts as a common denominator and permits a vast simplification of the accountability report. Instead of reporting each item of inventory separately (which incidentally is still done in some unit-control systems), the steward may classify, combine, summarize, and report in terms of *some* common unit that can be used to measure responsibility accepted and discharged. In the process of abstracting and scaling some attributes are considered to be relatively unimportant for current purposes and are therefore consigned to the vast pool of data about which the information system is silent and mankind remains ignorant. From accountability in terms of physical units the next obvious step is to specify the dimensions of importance and the measurement rules by which the transformation of physical units is to be made. Shall we use costs or current values? Judgment of relative worth by the manorial lord? Social judgments?

A number of present-day accountants, including a recent American Accounting Association committee, appear to hold that accountability must be in terms of original (or aboriginal) cost. From the accounting viewpoint cost is reasonably objective and the valuation decision that worth (value) is at least as great as cost has already been made by the purchaser. There are some valuable properties that are acquired without cost, and occasionally items come under an area of stewardship that are the results of gifts, thefts, or perhaps acts of God. Is accountability to be denied these values because they do not result from a transaction that resulted in a cost? Such a conclusion seems fantastic. If one admits that value is a proper concept for concern, there can be no question about the desirability of integrating the costless items with others. Cost in its usual definition has lost its isomorphic relation to the variable of concern and no longer justifies its role as a scale of value. The fact that the unit is costless means that it is not subjected to the control imposed by an investment decision, i.e., that expected services when discounted must be greater than cost. The discounted expected services from the donated asset may be higher than market or alternative cost, but they also may be very much lower. Recording such items at current market cost fails to recognize that management's service expectations may be unrelated to such a cost figure in the usual equal or greater-than association.

It should be noted that traditional accounting attitudes toward asset write-ups and write-downs are at least consistent with (small comfort!) the cost-service-expectation requirement for original entry. Under usual cost-revenue accounting, increases above original expectations — new surges of managerial optimism — are ordinarily neglected. Original optimism at the time of acquisition in excess of cost is neglected and subsequent surges above the original level are likewise neglected as being irrelevant or lacking in evidential support.

The case is entirely different if original expectations are subjected to extreme pessimism and become so black that their discounted value no longer is above cost or unamortized cost. Most accountants feel that if expectations break through their original level, i.e., the cost barrier, a write-down is indicated. They are consistent in the sense that they wish the value of discounted expected services to be at least as high as cost, and they are not especially concerned about expectation changes as long as the total remains above cost. The extra expectations, if they materialize, must grind through the slow mill of realization before they are shown as legitimate value increases.

A compromise often arises when discounted expectations are definitely lower than originally anticipated, but are still above cost. This situation is often encountered in the inventory field and is met in a forthright manner by those who advocate the traditional retail method of computing inventory. Mark-ups are clearly expressions of increased optimism and are consequently not permitted to influence the inventory 'cost' figure. Mark-up cancellations are taken above the line and do not result in a write-down of cost, because current expectations after the mark-up cancellation are still above original expectations. Traditionally stratospheric soarings of expectations are not sufficient to support an asset write-up and recognition of gain. The presence of goods marked up but unsold may indicate a surge in optimism but such mark-ups are not considered sufficient to support a gain.

Notice, however, the treatment of a mark-down. The mark-down is an expression of a decrease in sales expectations below the original expectation level. Perhaps nowhere else is the accountant's position more clearcut. A mark-down indicates that sales expectations are below those held originally, and the inventory is decreased in proportion (as a rule) to the decrease in expectations.[7]

Accountants are not in complete agreement regarding damaged goods. If an article that cost $100 and was marked to sell for $300 is damaged and is now marked at $180, accountants who hold to the expectation approach will argue for an inventory write-down to $60. Those who do not use the expectation approach may select from several alternatives, but many of them do not recognize a loss unless the sales expectations (net) are below original cost. The equivalent position in retail inventory accounting would define mark-downs in terms of original cost and treat reductions up to the entire original mark-on as mark-up cancellations. Obviously an inventory composed entirely of items whose net sale values are no greater than cost could mislead short-term creditors with regard to the debt-paying ability of the concern. There is some evidence that creditors expect a certified inventory to turn in the usual turnover period and to provide funds equal to the inventory figure plus a normal mark-up.

It should also be observed that the controversy about applying cost or market to each item or to the entire inventory can be approached in terms of expectations. If we consider expectation levels for the entire inventory, we may offset expectation increases on some goods against expectation decreases in others, and apply the cost-or-market rule to the entire stock in trade as a single asset. If an accountant favors expectation levels in terms of individual items, he may apply the rule to each item and not permit *any* increase in expectation to influence the inventory figure.

The retail method clearly uses the latter approach. If the earlier position is combined with the retail method, mark-downs would be subtracted from mark-ups or vice versa. (It should also be recalled that advocates of cost or market, whichever is lower, feel that a reduction in replacement cost is *equivalent* to a mark-down, i.e., a decrease in selling price below the originally marked price will follow a decrease in acquisition cost.)

---

[7] For a more detailed treatment of loss recognition rules in accounting see my "Loss Recognition," *Accounting Research*, October, 1955, pp. 310-320.

Let us now turn to the allocation process for fixed assets and particularly to the residual known as book value. The unassigned costs that have not been charged to operations are sometimes referred to as going-concern value, or, more romantically, as costs awaiting their destiny.[8]

Accountants, like many other professional workers, seem to derive inner satisfaction from defining constructs that cannot be tested outside the profession. In practice the independence of going-concern values from market values is usually stressed. If the firm should actually sell the assets, then the results are, of course, market values, and practically by definition market values are not permitted to be more than a partial determinant of going-concern value. Going-concern value results from applying the accountants' rules for measuring going-concern value. This is operationism at its best and worst. (An equivalent position: "Intelligence is what intelligence tests test.") It appears as if the definition is conveniently broad enough to include the results of doing what the accountants want to do with no chance whatever of being proved right or wrong by reference to data or constructs from without the system.

While going-concern value may well be an after-the-fact definition to give a label to the results of applying rules the accountant wishes to apply, its name does suggest some limitations, and accounting tradition has set some further limitations. For an upper limit, a widely accepted rule assures that the going-concern value of a standardized asset cannot be more than its current market value plus installation costs plus the contribution (marginal income) that could have been earned while the change is being made. This total is presumed to represent the maximum sacrifice that should be involved to keep the earning facilities intact, and expectations in excess of this total are disallowed in a manner consistent with the similar rule for original cost.

A tempting, but nonallowable, lower limit suggests itself. It seems that going-concern value should not be less than what rational management could get for the individual asset by immediate sale. If going-concern value is below the sales value, management seems to be irrational in not following the path that promises greatest profit by selling the item immediately. The asset in question, however, may be indispensable for operations. If all other assets including the nonrecorded value of entrepreneurship were immediately transferable to their next best alternative uses without loss, the going-concern value of a particular asset might be imputed in this fashion, but, if these conditions are not met, the sum of all imputed values will be a larger total than the market value of the individual assets. This relationship follows because each will include in its "going-concern" value the same benefits from avoidance of interruption and transfer.

In terms of idealized operational instructions, going-concern value has been equivalent to the original cost multiplied by a fraction whose numerator is the benefit still expected (remaining) and whose denominator is total expected benefits. Benefits may of course be estimated and correlated with time, activity or modifications of both, and *must* be estimated in conjunction with the surrounding environment. In a similar way the allowance

---

[8] Going-concern value is not to be confused with a phenomenon with a similar name, 'going value.' The latter is assumed to arise at least in part because the waiting period of building and coordinating is over and the anticipated income stream is nearer. The difference between the going value of a firm and the current value of all specific assets is an approximation of goodwill in the Canning sense of "master valuation account." Eugen Schmalenbach shows a good feel for probabilities and a disregard for realization in this connection. "A successful investment can bring big profits; if it . . . fails, it can cause a heavy loss . . . . The gamble has come off . . . . This means that my business, because it has won through, is worth much more than the amount shown by my capital account." *Dynamic Accounting*, translated by G. W. Murphy and Kenneth S. Most (London: Gee & Company, Ltd., 1959), p. 28.

figure when compared with original cost should indicate the fraction or proportion of total expected services that has already been received or wasted. This approach is idealized, but society has the right to demand meaningful constructs and professional competence in implementing those constructs. Accountants cannot build a profession by refusing to accept professional responsibility for constructing workable measurement rules and presenting information that has meaning to those who make society's decisions.

One group of accountants emphasizes that *total expected* benefits should be used for the denominator to allocate the cost under the benefit doctrine. If the *expected* benefits from a warehouse are in terms of five periods' shelter, the fact that the maximum possible benefits might — with different conditions — extend over 20 periods is considered to be irrelevant. This peculiarity of the benefit or service approach needs special attention because a number of accountants are uneasy about the dependence on original expectations, and wish to use *maximum possible* benefits. To these accountants, a life of 20 periods of equal *possible* services calls for a write-off of one-twentieth of the cost each period. Measured from the maximum possible services there has been a decline and these accountants wish to take a part of the cost to product, to idleness, or to the period.

The relationship of cost allocation to the economic valuation model is much closer than many accountants perceive. Both require an estimate of future services to be expected. The allocation approach requires that some measures of services received and expected be available. The measures, it should be emphasized, are usually of specific services and do not need to be in monetary units. The resulting fraction is applied to the original cost figure, which, as pointed out above, is an imperfect monetary expression of expectations at the time of acquisition. The valuation technique requires the estimate of future service expectations in monetary units at each statement date, and requires further the selection of appropriate discount rates. The methods are similar in that both require the identification and measurement of estimated services. They differ in that the cost allocation procedure dispenses with interim discount rates and the necessity for discounting estimates in monetary units each period.[9]

It is interesting to view the direct-versus-absorption-cost controversy in terms of differences in the ways in which expected services are identified. Whether these costs are in fact period or product costs is completely definitional, and no amount of semantic manipulation can prove that such costs are period or product costs. But definitions are not selected by caprice. We stipulate that costs "attach" to product or to periods because it is convenient and useful to so stipulate, not because a specific quantum of sacrifice from a past decision somehow inherently follows the service forever through the endless corridors of space-time. In connection with, say, establishment costs there are benefits to be received from keeping the establishment going. Even if there is no business in a particular interval, we may still assert that future revenues are closer and therefore value has been added by the costs necessary to preserve the integrity of the concern.

---

[9] It may be interesting to compare further the economic model for valuation with cost allocation on a service or benefit basis. Cost allocation requires estimates of expected services at the time of acquisition and subsequent estimates of services expired periodically. Estimates of appropriate discount rates are not necessary and are replaced by the use of original cost (or similar) figures. But notice that the determination of the original cost figure *may* have had as one of its determinants a discount rate! And the continued use of original cost base may be *roughly* equivalent to continued use of the original discount rate and original expectations. The substitution of current replacement costs, in a similar fashion, is roughly equivalent to changing either the discount rates, the expectations or both in accordance with changes in the market appraisal of these factors. Within limits it may be argued that expectations are related to the individual firm under survey and that the discount rate is largely the result of alternatives available elsewhere.

But if we accept this position, does it follow that we must also accept the treatment of establishment costs during periods of idleness as assets with services to be received as future business materializes? The orthodox accountant's position relates these costs to original expectations, and he may indeed feel that it is useful to defer them and match them with revenues when the revenues are realized. The direct coster tends to identify the services from these costs as inexorably related to the period in some esoteric fashion, or he tends to support a valuation doctrine based on total possible expectations instead of actual expectations. Accountants, regardless of their previous persuasion, would be well advised to identify the end-products of their work (the objectives) and to devise constructs and rules that are consistent with these objectives. Vague feelings and doctrinaire assertions may have limited meaning in such a teleological context. Costs and benefits and revenues attach because accountants say they attach, and accountants say they attach because it has proved *useful* to have a directive that reminds them to treat them as if they do attach.

Let us now review the accountant's traditional approach to the income problem. It has been pointed out that his income-determination process is made up of recording and assigning costs to agents of production and then charging these costs against the new values recognized (revenues). Now revenues are the result of all factors — recorded and unrecorded — working together. The excess of revenues over assigned costs (the *assumed* contribution of outsiders) is presumed to "attach" to the enterprise and to be the contribution of the firm, or of human resources. This contribution includes various economic rents and the contribution of (so-called) entrepreneurship in excess of the cost of hiring managers. This conventional (not quite arbitrary) allotment of services to cost factors up to the amount of the cost involved, and to other factors for the excess, seems strange to businessmen and to some economists.[10] The process has one very distinct and important advantage. The procedure may be followed by nonexpert and economically unsophisticated bookkeepers and accountants.

Perhaps the most astonishing feature of accounting to economists is the unexpected shift from incremental value to historical cost. All accountants, businessmen and economists agree on the need for using an incremental approach for capital budgeting and new investments. The existing facilities form a shifting set of initial conditions from which incremental contributions from new investments are estimated. After acquisition, however, the new facility is absorbed in the environment at its cost and becomes a part of the initial conditions for following decisions. The incremental calculation is, in effect, thrown away after the decision to invest has been made and the exchange-price is used for subsequent accounting. The reasons for this behavior have been set forth earlier in this essay. It is simply not feasible to value each acquisition at its individual expected value at the time of acquisition. Different machines of the same type would be valued at different amounts that could vary widely depending on the ordering rule used. Moreover, due to the fact that the increments are measured from a shifting base, there can be a vast amount of overlap in incremental values so that the results could not be additive. The simplicity of the accounting structure should now be obvious. There may be long discussions among accountants

---

[10] Fritz Machlup seems to be at least in partial agreement with the accountants' approach. "If the fixed resources in question had a greater value to the particular firm than to other potential users, so that the purchase price did not capitalize the full rent, then the specific rent (which would be equal to the difference between rent earned and rent paid) would be no cost element to the firm but would be a part of the surplus above normal returns." *The Economics of Sellers' Competition* (Baltimore: The Johns Hopkins Press, 1952), p. 253 and Chapter 8.

about the merits of different types of costs or values, but there is little controversy over the imputation of economic rents to nonspecific factors of production — the enterprise.

Some writers have observed the accountant's procedures and have remarked that accountants are assigning services to agents in a manner that suggests the cost-theory of value advocated by Marx. In Marxists' animistic scheme the services of goods, land, equipment, etc., do not give rise to value except to the extent that they themselves lose value.

> . . . the values of the means of production used up in the process are preserved, and present themselves afresh as constituent parts of the value of the product . . . the means of production . . . give up to the product that value alone which they themselves lose as means of production.[11]

The accountant — ideologically a long way from a Marxist — takes a somewhat different slant. His income is an increase in value that arises from dealing with parties other than those for whom the income is being computed. Long-lived assets are assumed to yield services equal only to their cost; labor by assumption yields services equal only to its cost. Any other value added and realized by the firm is attributed to the entrepreneurial function — the enterprise. In other words, the economic rents yielded by the sources of services that are procured through cost transactions appear as the net income figure. Physiocrats would have attributed such surpluses to land, and Marx to the workers.

It is possible to present a slightly different approach to the cost-value problem. The asset, it may be argued, gives up its services in such a way as to expedite enterprise contributions and is thus a kind of vehicle for the exercise of managerial virtuosity. It is as if the factors acquired by the firm form the instruments upon which the managers play. This view may be associated with the feeling that net income should be recognized "as the contributions of the firm are rendered."[12] Depreciation, according to this view, consists in writing off the cost according to the relative services rendered to total estimated services, and while there is no necessary identification of cost and value, such an identification may be integrated in the system. Services are related to the ability of assets to serve as instruments or vehicles which are assumed to be more or less passive except for their affording opportunities for managers to perform.

The net effect of the vehicle approach seems to be to assume that the vehicle (factor) contributes its cost, and that, if there is a deficiency or excess in the actual contribution over cost, the excess or deficiency by definition is the contribution of management. Inasmuch as the assumption is nonoperational — the procedure necessary to prove or disprove it cannot be measured — we are back to truth by definition. Nevertheless, the vehicle approach with its correlative assumptions may clear the air in one direction at least. The write-off of the cost factor is not determined by isolated market values or by reference to its own physical contribution. The main test of an asset's expected benefit is its expected ability to let managers exercise their ability and play profitable tunes. Needless to say approximations based on time, physical units, and the like will still be with us.

---

[11] Karl Marx, *Capital* (London: William Glaisher, Limited, 1909), pp. 180, 185. An interesting speculation may arise about the similarity of Marx's "socially necessary labor" to the accountant's penchant for putting "prudent cost" ceilings on the amounts he will capitalize and to the Dutch "Kostprijs" with inefficiencies not considered to be product costs.

[12] The present writer was at one time enthusiastic about this formulation. See, for example, *Inventory Valuation and Periodic Income, op. cit.*, pp. 35-36.

In summary, it should be reemphasized that the heralded shift from value accounting to cost allocation is not the dramatic shift that some accountants have apparently thought. The economic-value model implies discounted expected services. Cost allocation also implies expected services and rules for determining expired services. An assumed discount rate is not necessary for cost allocation, but the service estimates necessary for valuation except for the monetary conversion are necessary for cost distribution under the benefit approach.

It is not essential to the income-measuring process that original cost be identified with minimum value at the time of purchase, or any other value. However, book value is usually the result of assigning cost according to expected benefit, and expected benefit itself is a major factor in determining value. But lest accountants exalt in some supposed emancipation from the bogey of value, they should remember that when a service function, such as accounting, gets so far away from what users need and understand, it is time for appraisal and reexamination of underlying assumptions. Business decisions usually involve values and businessmen are rightly suspicious of esoteric terms, operational substitutions, and unfamiliar constructs.

Essay Seven

Recognition Requirements —
Income Earned and Realized

It is the purpose of this essay to examine the concepts of income earned and income realized and to speculate about the origins of each. It is pointed out that economists and accountants with an orientation toward economics are gravely concerned with the traditional requirements of realization and detachability. Consideration is given to the influence of bankers, who have been the chief proponents of realization requirements and who have had much more influence on the young profession than their more scholarly colleagues in the academic field.

Income is defined and measured according to rules adopted by accountants, lawyers, economists and businessmen. Income is therefore what these groups want it to be, and they want what they want because the resulting construct is thought to be useful — to fulfill certain objectives. The following plaintive statement of Canning shows the usual misunderstanding. "And what is set out as a measure of net income can never be supposed to be a fact in any sense at all except that it is the figure that results when the accountant has finished applying the procedure which he adopts."[1] The profession has been taken to task about its lack of uniformity in this regard and in other respects, but professional problems often look more simple to those on the outside, and the difficulties of single-purpose reports are real indeed.[2] Regardless, however, of the disagreements about the concept to be measured and the relative importance of the uses to which it is to be put, the problem of income earned — broadly interpreted — must be met and the problem of income realized calls for attention.

To define 'earned' and to set forth rules for determining when the earning is to be recognized are difficult problems of temporal imputation. The definition of 'earned' is usually related to value increases, and it may be more acceptable terminology to abandon 'earned' with its usual connotation of deserved and meritorious in favor of the less slanted term 'value added.' Some accountants and law makers still associate earned income with the ethical concept of deserved or merited.

---

[1] John B. Canning, *The Economics of Accountancy* (New York: The Ronald Press Company, 1929), pp. 98-99. Notice, however, that there is no reason why net income should be a "fact in any sense." It is possible to have an operational definition that defines income as the result of applying *any* rules of measurement — even ridiculous ones. The simplification that there is *no* purpose or objective to the construct is certainly unwarranted.

[2] Some of the frustration with single-purpose statements is expressed by Greer. " . . . how much is left to the owners in the way of a money return. This may not be the only thing that people want to know about the business, but it is one important thing . . ." Howard C. Greer, "Depreciation and the Price Level, A Symposium," *The Accounting Review*, April, 1948, p. 130. It should be obvious that one figure cannot be used for all decisions. "Isn't this [orthodox income measurement] somewhat like saying, 'our measure of income is correct, but the business manager who relies on its accuracy in determining dividend policy may be sorry?' " D. A. Fergusson, "Accounting and the Price Level," *The Accounting Review*, October, 1954, p. 641.

For practical purposes the term 'income earned' may be taken to mean that the value has been added, i.e., that the value increase has taken place. It is at this point that accountants and economists have one of their most heated disagreements. Almost invariably, economists insist that value increases should be taken up as profit as soon as the evidence is adequate to support a judgment. Paton at one time certainly held this view. "The liberal view that, ideally, all bona fide value changes in either direction, from whatever cause, should be reflected in the accounts has been adopted without argument."[3]

The application of no other test except that of value increase to support recognition leads to some interesting accounting results. Suppose, to give an example, that a corporation is formed to produce the requirements for a single government order. Suppose further that the place to exercise astute ability is in bidding and getting the order on favorable terms and that the manufacture of the necessary items is a hack production job that could just as well be sublet to any number of concerns. It is not unreasonable to maintain that the value is added at the time the master or prime contract is procured on favorable terms and that the income should be taken up at that time. Before the orthodox are horrified, they should notice that a properly functioning stock market would recognize that value has been added, and the value of the stock could be expected to reflect the favorable change in prospects. In this case we have evidence rendered by outsiders (professional investors) who are willing to back their own judgment by investment, and there is no longer any excuse for accountants to refuse to recognize income because they are uncertain. Uncertainty about the increase or the amount of the increase is an important consideration for determining whether the value change has taken place — whether the income has been earned — but contrary to popular belief uncertainty has a much smaller part to play in determining whether the income has been realized.

To change the illustration, suppose that no gain is taken up at the time the contract is granted and no funds are to change hands until the project is completed and approved. The purchaser employs his own engineers to inspect the work continuously and to approve the work at specified stages of construction so that it is not possible for the builder to stray too far from plans. At the end of the accounting period approximately one-half of the construction work has been completed, as evidenced by costs incurred to date compared with total expected costs to be incurred. Would a substantial number of accountants recognize a part of the total expected income at this time? This is, of course, the percentage-of-completion problem in its simplest form without complications regarding the availability of funds.

In this case the 'sale' has been made, but in a similar fashion the sale (in the sense of agreement with outsiders) was made in the earlier example when the firm contract was let

---

[3] W. A. Paton, *Accounting Theory* (New York: The Ronald Press Company, 1922), p. vii. Apparently the realization test was once relatively less important among accountants. "A review of accounting, legal and economic writing, suggests that the realization postulate was not accepted prior to the first World War. In 1913 leading authorities in all these fields in England and America seemed to agree on the 'increase in net worth' concept of income . . ." George O. May, "Business Income," *The Accountant*, September 30, 1950, p. 316. Notice however: "The accountant is very likely to have in connection with this kind of profits [gains on real estate still held] the same opinion as the average lawyer has about all kinds of gains." Paul-Joseph Esquerré, *The Applied Theory of Accounts* (New York: The Ronald Press Company, 1914), p. 229. Hatfield apparently was not enthusiastic about the realization postulate. " . . . the frequently recurring confusion . . . between assets and the credit side of the balance sheet. The assets cannot be distinguished as being this capital and that profit . . . . Hence as Mr. Ernest Cooper has pointed out, the question as to whether the profits are liquid or not cannot legitimately be raised." Henry Rand Hatfield, *Accounting: Its Principles and Problems* (New York: D. Appleton and Company, 1927), p. 286. However, Charles E. Hughes (252 U.S. 195) states, "It is the essence of income that it be realized . . . . Income necessarily implies separation and realization."

to responsible parties. Some may object that no sale is made when a mutually unper-formed contract is signed. This illustration points up the misunderstanding of the func-tion of sales in the income problem. Although the goods have not been delivered, the bar-gained exchange price has been set by a deal between two parties with adverse interests. That is to say, the amount of the deal has been set at least tentatively by the parties, and one of them is an outsider and therefore presumably less susceptible to manipulation. The contract also resembles a sale in that the sales effort has already been applied and the criti-cal problem of disposal has been met and solved. It is true that more uncertainty may re-main than would be present in the usual sales transaction. When goods are stocked the un-certainty arises in estimating the price at which they may be sold, and the uncertainty does not disappear until sale or, on occasion, until collection is made. In a contract of this sort the amount of the sale is known or approximately determined, and the uncertainty lies in how much cost will be necessary to satisfy the buyer. To most nonaccountants the crucial aspect of the sales event is probably the evidence for value added.[4]

We may now ask what effect the moving of the work to completion has on the income recognizing process. It seems that as work progresses toward completion uncertainty as to the expected total cost and total profit should decrease. While this assumed progress toward less uncertainty need not be universal, the tendency is likely to be present. How-ever, the influence of uncertainty on accounting records may not be so great as is some-times thought. Now and then the course of future events is so uncertain that neither man-agement nor the accountant has any judgment worth recording, but usually uncertainty tends to decrease so that adjustments and corrections can be made with some confidence at later dates. If accountants waited until they were certain before recognizing gains or losses, interim reports before the demise of the firm might well be nonexistent. Uncer-tainty can be a universal excuse for doing nothing unless levels of subjective confidence are established and evidential events are specified.

An important argument for value added as work progresses is that the payments that have been made to the date of the report will not have to be repeated, and should (unless they represent outright loss) decrease the total future payments and therefore increase the value of the project. A purchaser of the firm at this point would see a decreased annuity for future outpayments with the prospect of receipts growing nearer. Of course such a purchaser would be getting less working capital or more liabilities (or a combination of the two) equal to the increase in cost of work in progress. Thus, the contract itself be-comes more valuable as it reaches completion, but whether or not the value of the entire firm (with only the one contract) increases more than the amount of the expenditures and an interest factor is open to question.

---

[4] I have discussed the sales basis of income recognition elsewhere. "The introduction of the sales event for the recognition of value increases holds off the recognition of accounting profit until there is no doubt that the change is present and its amount is ascertainable. Moreover, it conforms somewhat unsatisfactorily to the de-mands of those who wish to connect the amount of profit with available funds, as the sales event ordinarily im-plies the receipt of cash or a claim which can shortly be converted into cash. The position of the defenders of in-come recognition at the point of sale is therefore one of compromise. It is probable that waiting until the time of sale will set up a lag between the points in time when the services of the enterprise are added (income earned) and those at which the increases are recognized — to this extent it falls short of the results secured by the use of cur-rent replacement prices. On the other hand, the receipt of cash does not mean that the management has complete dominion over its disbursement — to this extent it falls short of giving an income figure which is an index of dis-posable funds and fails to satisfy completely the demands of those who have interpreted the two as being equiva-lent amounts." *Inventory Valuation and Periodic Income* (New York: The Ronald Press Company, 1942), pp. 8, 9.

If percentage of completion is recognized on a time basis (i.e., to date one-half of the expected total time has elapsed regardless of costs) the primary consideration would seem to be the nearness of the receipt, and the interest factor would seem to be the primary influence giving rise to value added. If the earning rate is much larger (or smaller) than the interest rate, a lump sum gain or loss could be imputed and appear at some time or another — perhaps when the contract is let.

The usual assumption is that the value is added as the work progresses in terms of costs incurred to date to expected total costs for the project.[5] Is there anything about the act of incurring costs that leads to value added in excess of the cost incurred? In general a negative answer is indicated. If we assume that costs are vehicles for managerial contribution, we may make a shadow of a case for this method of recognizing profit, but it should be clear that one of the weaknesses of the vehicular approach is that there are other ways in which management may make contributions and add value. For example, it has been pointed out, and should be emphasized again, that management may make a more substantial contribution (add more value) by getting the contract than in combining the factors of production at low cost. There are other means for managers to show their shrewdness than in factor combination.

If, however, value is added and managers *do* make their contribution to production by combining factors at low cost, and if such savings account for the expected profit, it makes sense to say that value is added — and income is earned — as the factors are combined efficiently. In this case a measure of the extent of efficient factor combination may be the costs to date compared with total expected costs for the entire contract.[6]

At this time it may be profitable to digress for a brief discussion of the accountant's strong distinction between savings and earnings. Accountants have made a sharp distinction between the two, but it is contended here that the distinction is one of realization and not of earning. The statements of Paton and Littleton are representative.

> Such discounts [for prompt payment] are associated with the process of buying, the process of incurring cost in the initial stage, and to recognize revenue at this point amounts to sheer anticipation, an extreme case of booking unrealized income . . . . The answer is that cost savings are in no sense revenue. If the business buys well, costs are simply on a lower level than would otherwise be the case. The special efficiency or luck associated with buying, it is true, will have a bearing on the amount of net income eventually earned, but demonstration of the level of earning power awaits future events.
>
> It should be pointed out, too, that it is very easy for the buyer to assume that an extraordinary bargain has been made when no such assumption is warranted. The only reasonable assumption is that buyer and seller are equally well-informed, equally desirous of trading, and

---

[5] "In view of the fact that the problem is one of asset valuation and income, rather than extent of time or physical volume, it seems clear that a cost percentage is the appropriate measure and that a computation based upon total cost is more significant than one that considers only certain elements of cost . . . . The crux of the matter is the basis for the estimate, and no satisfactory substitute for a comprehensive cost percentage has as yet been proposed from any quarter." William A. Paton and William A. Paton, Jr., *Asset Accounting* (New York: The Macmillan Company, 1952), p. 99. This statement is based on the implicit assumption that value added and income are in fact proportional to costs incurred and clearly begs the question.

[6] W. A. Paton and A. C. Littleton hold: "Revenue is *earned* by the entire process of operation, by the totality of business effort . . ." but hedge slightly in a later statement. "Revenue as the price-aggregates of output sold does not appear full-fledged until the product is completed and the selling price determined by actual sale. Yet it may be reasoned that, in a certain sense revenue is 'earned' during the entire process of operation reflected in the accumulation of costs assignable to product." *An Introduction to Corporate Accounting Standards* (Chicago: American Accounting Association, 1940), pp. 46, 48.

equally strong in negotiation. This assumption may not square exactly with underlying conditions in many cases, but it is more useful than an approach which would permit both buyer and seller to introduce purely subjective valuations not validated by the actual terms agreed upon.[7]

It goes without saying that any gains to be derived from lucky buys and paying bills without penalty do not meet the usual definition for realized income, but the pertinent question here is whether these gains might qualify for income earned. Can there be any doubt that management often contributes value by acquiring assets as well as in combining them and unloading the finished product? Is there doubt that value can be added at the time assets are acquired and the costs incurred? Suppose, to illustrate, that a new concern with no other interests spends its entire amount of assets for government surplus goods at fabulously low prices. Immediately after the acquisition and presumably due to the purchase there are firm offers for the stock of the concern at twice the amounts paid in. Thus, there is no question about the quality of the evidence to support the fact that value has been added. The conclusion is that accountants hold off recognition because of failure to meet the test of realization and not because the evidence is inadequate. As will be pointed out later, the defense for omission of these gains is not always convincing and, as MacNeal and others have pointed out, the practical consequences may be ghastly.[8] Moreover, it is not necessary to assume that buyers and sellers are equally "informed," "desirous," and "strong" in order to defend the failure to recognize income until the value increase has met the tests of realization.

Suppose, to return to the original illustration with only one contract in process, that instead of a lump-sum payment upon final approval of the work there are advances by the buyer at various approved stages of construction. Immediately the concept of realization (liquidity) is involved and at various points the value may have been added and the increase may be in the form of liquid assets. If there is a holdback on work approved, care must be exercised, because the holdback receivable may not be current, and it is the contention of this essay that the realization construct is concerned entirely and exclusively with liquidity. At a later point we will consider whether realization implies that all of the cost of the work in addition to the profit increment must be converted into a current asset or whether just the increment need be subjected to the current test.

Realization

To many accountants one of the major mysteries about the profession is that auditing, as an important independent service, did not develop earlier than it did. To present-day businessmen it is inconceivable that a rational lender would grant credit to an applicant without asking some responsible party to size up the general financial position of the applicant and render a report. The prospective lender might insist that the financial position of the applicant be at least as good as the investigator reported.[9] The fact that the investi-

---

[7] *Ibid.*, p. 64. The semanticist will wish to find whether the horizons for establishing "anticipation" and realization have been specified.

[8] The reader may wish to refresh his memory by reading MacNeal's famous illustrations including his two flour mills and his two investment trusts. Kenneth MacNeal, *Truth in Accounting* (Philadelphia: University of Pennsylvania Press, 1939), Chapters 1, 2, 3.

[9] "The owner was not deceived because he knew his business intimately. The banker and trade creditors disregarded all balance-sheet values except those for current assets and rested secure in the knowledge that these assets were worth at least as much as represented and perhaps a great deal more." Kenneth MacNeal, "What's Wrong with Accounting II," *The Nation*, October 14, 1939, p. 410.

gator's compensation came from the lending institution may have been an important early factor in instilling the dogma of conservation in the accounting profession. It is obvious that lenders are interested in expected future current funds — working capital — from which the loan can be repaid. The dangers from reporting income unless current assets are available for at least the amount of the value increase is obvious. Owners may or may not wish to withdraw assets equal to the reported income, but the measure of income is traditionally associated with amounts that can be withdrawn, and the construct itself is usually related to amounts that are not needed to preserve the integrity of the capital.

Thus the accounting profession has been subjected to conflicting forces and demands. Economists have tended to assume that income is management's chief concern with only minor financial problems and have long been enemies of the realization concept. In general, economists have simply not admitted that the realization concept is necessary.[10] Lenders, on the other hand, have insisted on realization tests and have had little interest in measures of income not supported by current assets. The latter group has been so convincing that many accountants still are reluctant to show acknowledged increase in value even as footnotes. There is, of course, no reason why both groups cannot be satisfied.[11]

Arguments in this area are similar to others in the field of accounting in that they are about definitions. The important question is whether we do or do not want to build liquidity requirements into our definition of income. There is no limit to the number and variety of definitions that *might be* adopted by the profession. The question should be discussed in terms of the needs and objectives of those who are considered to be worthy of information. Everyone admits that strong rules must be applied to the evidentiary aspects of income recognition. The tendency to consider detachability (liquidity) as a determinant of income measurement (and therefore as a part of the definition of income) is widespread among accountants and finds its most rigid supporters among the advocates of LIFO and base-stock methods of inventory valuation.[12] The accountant's emphasis on realizability — value increase in terms of working capital availability — is recognition that his work should help management administer its dividend and working capital problems. However, it is also recognized that modifying the definition of income is only one method of aiding management in this area. Appropriations of retained earnings may be utilized for a similar purpose, and it is generally recognized that income definition in terms of realization is not a necessary requirement for successful working capital management.[13] Nevertheless, the main body of accounting doctrine holds that the recognition of income should be deferred until the receipt of a current asset or even cash. For some accountants long-term claims that can be discounted are sufficient, and gains on exchanges of fixed assets are recognized as one of the rare violations of the rule. Sinking fund earnings are another minor exception.

A few accountants and auditors have tended to use the term 'realization' loosely and to confuse its function with the problem of establishing evidence to support the value increase.[14] Opinion of management, even when supported by independent expert appraisal, is ordinarily not considered to be adequate evidence to support value increases. Evidence derived from arm's-length dealing with outsiders is ordinarily accepted under our present legal institutions, but in case of obvious stupidity on the buyer's side some doubt may arise. Market prices for investments and inventories are often available and are objective in the sense of being able to meet the social-consensus test. Often responsible offers are available for real and personal property, and these offers are relevant to the judgment process. Recent transfers of similar or related properties may be admitted as evidence. In-

---

Footnotes on following page

dependent appraisers make use of some or all of the above indicators to render professional and reasonably unbiased opinions. Finally, representations of management as to value changes may be based on intimate and specialized knowledge and may therefore be especially useful.

Some accountants do not wish to recognize income unless quick assets have been increased. LIFO accountants, for example, argue that an increase in inventory is not sufficient to support a realized gain. Inventories are, by most definitions, current assets, but they still must 'be sold' — undergo further effort. From the formative years of accounting there has been considerable support for not including inventories among the current assets.[15] If realized means that the owners can withdraw the amount of income without be-

---

[10] While economists may not have had very much influence on accountants and the course of accounting theory, it seems that accounting has not had very much influence on economics. "Scientific accountancy has now been developing for some 50 years, but I cannot trace that it has made a single substantial contribution to economic science over its own field of analysis of the results of industry, although it has practically a monopoly grip of the required data." Statement of Lord Stamp in 1921, quoted from Mary E. Murphy, "Book Review of *Precision and Design in Accountancy*," *The Accounting Review*, July, 1949, p. 334. Allocation of fault is not necessary or perhaps even desirable, but notice the following statement from W. Stanley Jevons: "There is not a clerk nor bookkeeper in the country who is not engaged in recording numerical facts for the economist." *The Theory of Political Economy* (2d. ed.; London: Macmillan and Company, Ltd., 1879), p. 11. Quoted from John Wheeler, *Handbook of Modern Accounting Theory*, ed. Morton Backer (New York: Prentice-Hall, Inc., 1955), p. 48.

[11] Accountants may be on the threshold of wide use of the "have-your-cake-and-eat-it-too" approach that has been applied so widely in accounting for appraisals. Recognition of value increases does not necessarily imply recognition of income nor does it imply the defenseless assertions given in Chapter 9 of *Accounting Research Bulletin* No. 43: Restatement and Revision of Accounting Research Bulletins, Issued by the Committee on Accounting Procedure (New York: American Institute of Accountants, 1953).

[12] ". . . the conclusion seems to be that net income to be reported as the basis for possible distribution should be limited to that share of bookkeeping return which is appropriable and consumable . . . " R. G. Walker, "The Base-Stock-Principle in Income Accounting," *Harvard Business Review*, October, 1936, p. 85. "Profits in accounting is a disposable surplus, that is disposable within a period. If profits could be paid away in the form of stock-in-trade there would be little problem involved . . . . On the other hand the relationship of profit to the cash which will be used for its disposal governs our view, and any profit not arising from an actual sale will be left out of the computation, not because it is not real profit, but because it cannot be detached for distribution." P. Taggart, "Stock-In-Trade 'Valuation,' " *The Accountant*, May 18, 1935, p. 726. "For the accountant profit is largely bound up with questions concerning its distribution, with the consequence that he places the emphasis on its realization in terms of cash or its equivalent . . . . " F. Sewell Bray, "Recent British Accounting Developments," *The Accounting Review*, April, 1946, p. 203. There is naturally considerable authority for the opposing view. "No profit and loss statement, however, should stress a distinction between realized and unrealized profits . . . " Kenneth MacNeal, *Truth in Accounting, op. cit.*, p. 300. "The distributability test for income recognition is obviously an unfeasible one; accounting has enough problems of its own without the attempt to apply standards of financcial administration to the reporting of financial events." William J. Vatter, *The Fund Theory of Accounting and Its Implications for Financial Reports, op. cit.*, p. 38.

[13] "Earned and realized income is not necessarily *distributable* income; a distinction should be drawn between income performance and income administration." W. A. Paton, *Advanced Accounting* (New York: The Macmillan Company, 1941), p. 453. This semantic distinction, which tends to beg the question, is expanded in an article by Rufus Wixon, "The Measurement and Administration of Income," *The Accounting Review*, April, 1949, pp. 184-190.

[14] "Realization, as I understand it, is a set of rules devised as a guide in determining when the *quality* of the evidence with respect to prospective net revenues is such that they may be directly valued as an element of the firm's financial position." Charles E. Johnson, "Inventory Valuation — the Accountant's Achilles Heel," *The Accounting Review*, January, 1954, p. 16.

[15] This has been the position of defenders of base stock and to some extent the advocates of the later-day version (LIFO). Yet others who were not interested particularly in the base-stock argument looked on inventories as noncurrent assets. See, for example, Paul-Joseph Esquerré, who included them with stationery and printing in a working-asset section of the financial position report. *Op. cit.*, p. 408.

coming financially embarrassed, then inventory increases may fail to qualify as adequate support for realization. The evidential angle is probably not so important at this point. Some land, for example, may be traded at arm's length for stock in trade with an unquestioned value increase. Some accountants are willing to accept the evidence and insist that an inventory increase is current enough to support income recognition. Those who reject the immediate recognition of profit may do so on the basis of inadequate evidence (unlikely with the assumption given) or on the grounds that the increase is not sufficiently current.

In manufacturing it is common to transfer some of the building cost to inventories. A part of the building cost is now considered to meet the definitional requirements for a current asset, and revenues expected in the next period are assumed to be adequate to cover the amount severed from the building cost. Interestingly enough, few accountants argue for the recognition of income at this point. Again their failure to do so may be for either or both of the two reasons — evidence unsatisfactory or asset not current enough.[16]

We may now inquire about increases in the value of marketable securities that are not owned for control purposes and are quoted on a major exchange. Do increases here qualify as realized income? If not, is the rejection due to lack of evidence? Lack of working capital increase? Or from fear of showing increases so long as there is any substantial probability that they will be wiped away before owners can withdraw or spend the proceeds? The evidence of *bona fide* quotations and the ready operation of an organized exchange is certainly sufficient to support an increase in the eyes of most nonaccountants and quite a few professional accountants.[17] Here the sales act is not crucial in any sense, for the effort of making the sale is not important, and there is little or no reason to believe that the securities cannot be transferred.

In general, it must be concluded that increases in market value of such securities are realized gains whether the stocks are sold or not. The evidence of increase is adequate for all but the most skeptical, and the increase is in a form that can be detached from the business without interfering with its operations.[18]

---

[16] There is an extreme offshoot of the evidence-inadequate approach that merits attention — the terror theory. The evidence may be admitted as adequate for present conditions, but something *might* happen before the owners can get their hands firmly on the increase. This Milquetoast approach requires evidence in the form of cash and is concerned with the possibility that even the cash may be lost.

[17] If the holding is a large block, it is possible that an attempt to feed the securities into the market at a rapid rate will break the price. If the holdings are large enough for this possibility, there may be some doubt that the investment should be treated as a current asset. The doubt arises with regard to the validity of the evidence.

[18] Most textbooks — especially those that lead in sales and are therefore important in shaping the thought of young accountants — do not agree. The supporting reasons are usually not given, but, when given, they make interesting reading. For example: "Since temporary investments in securities are current assets, they should be valued at the lower of cost or market for balance sheet purposes." (No support given.) H. A. Finney and Herbert E. Miller, *Principles of Accounting — Intermediate* (New York: Prentice-Hall, Inc., 1951), p. 518. Perhaps the Patons are nearest to taking such value increases as income. "Accordingly, when the value of listed bonds held has either fallen or risen materially below or above the recorded amount on the investor's books it is not only allowable but desirable to take notice of this condition in the investor's records and statements. The least that should be done is the showing of market value in parenthesis or by footnote in the statement of financial position, coupled with appropriate notations on the underlying records. . . . As noted in an earlier connection, such a procedure doesn't mean treating an increase in value as realized income, and likewise it does not — necessarily — require the charging of an accrued loss to revenue. In extreme cases it may be desirable to go further, and recognize market values as a new basis of accountability, with the historical cost data placed in the subordinate position." William A. Paton and William A. Paton, Jr., *Asset Accounting* (New York: The Macmillan Company, 1952), pp. 167, 168.

Let us now return to the question as to whether the concept of realization as working capital availability is necessary or even desirable in a modern business economy with production carried on chiefly through large industrial and trading aggregations with widely separated management and ownership.

It may be argued that attempts on the part of the accounting staff to help management manipulate its working capital are unnecessary or, at least, of so little consequence that they are not worth retaining at the sacrifice of other advantages. In small businesses owners and managers are often essentially salesmen or production men and have little knowledge of finance or of elementary financial matters. Many lean on their bankers for advice in this field, and bankers sometimes solicit the aid of the accounting profession by asking for the realization test of income recognition. It may be contended that even small businesses today have the advice of public accounting men who are competent and willing to give advice on financial matters. Certainly large corporations have managers who with the aid of treasurers, independent accountants, investment bankers and commercial bankers are competent to manage financial matters.[19] In view of this tendency the profession would do well to examine the sacrifices necessary to cling to the realization concept.

Perhaps the strongest statement is that of Vatter. "The timing of speculative gains on the criterion of 'realization' is simply wrong so far as the investor is concerned."[20] MacNeal (*infra*) is vitally concerned with failure to disclose important financial information and points out the tremendous possibilities for manipulation by insiders who may decide whether to make a value increase public information or not by skirting around the concept of realization. Management does have considerable freedom in which to manipulate, but the area of freedom in this direction, it is generaly agreed, should be supervised if not constricted. Capital gains may in times of rapidly changing price levels be more important than ordinary operating gains, and with the current possibilities for sale-leaseback agreements, changes in current values of hopelessly committed assets are no longer a matter of indifference to be reported or not reported at the whim of the accountant. Moreover, in line with modern technology, which requires tremendous aggregates of capital, the amount of assets held by a business concern is no longer unimportant when related to operating revenues and income. The possibilities of capital gains and losses are greater, and of course many firms are now organized with such gains in mind.

From the viewpoint of the investor in a large concern, a strong case can be made for abandoning the disadvantages of the realization test and placing more trust in the financial ability of owners and managers. The opposing view is taken by many accountants including defenders of LIFO. These advocates hold to the detachability doctrine and insist that the traditional procedures tend to violate the informational rights of both management and investors. It is contended that to report as income value increases that can be severed from the firm only if major policy changes in financing or partial abandonment

---

[19] How many investors and prospective investors, it is asked, spend any substantial time checking the working capital position and trends of a well situated company? Working capital deficiencies may be symptoms of lack of ability somewhere else in the management area, but it is doubtful if many investors spend much time checking the working capital position of, say, General Motors. Small businesses with unproved managers may on the other hand merit concentrated study in the working capital area. It is obvious however that a satisfactory income does not assure solvency. "Over a relatively short period of time . . . profitability and solvency are almost independent of each other, sometimes almost antagonistic goals." Maurice Moonitz, *op. cit.*, p. 376. Kenneth E. Boulding is extremely critical of the view of most economists that businessmen have few if any problems of solvency. See *A Reconstruction of Economics* (New York: John Wiley & Sons, Inc., 1950), pp. 26 ff.

[20] William J. Vatter, *op. cit.*, p. 34.

are made, serves little or no useful investment purpose. Moreover, managers may understand fully the situation and have the necessary restraint in ordinary circumstances, but
there may be such pressure from more or less uninformed investors that management is
forced to acquiesce in spite of its best judgment.

Perhaps the controversy is not so serious as it seems. Regardless of which position is
held, a primary objective appears to be adequate disclosure of pertinent facts. Income
may be defined in terms of value increases without completely disregarding the realization
concept. Reported figures can be supplemented with copious notes that tell the reader why
he may not expect to receive dividends equal to the amount of the reported income.

At the other extreme, an accountant may hew to a careful line for realization and take
what is essentially the LIFO position for inventories and plant assets. In this case, he reports income only if it has met rigid tests for realization, but he also gives extensive notes
to indicate the existence of value increases that have not yet met the tests for realization. If
disclosure is reasonably adequate, the reader may reach his own conclusion as to whether
he probably will be able to cash in on the increases.

The question cannot be resolved by references to income determination and to something else called income administration. The problem is naked enough — which way
should income be defined and supplemented to meet best the requirements of a modern
economy. The tremendous burden of corporate (and individual) income taxes means that
accountants should approach with care any definition of income that does not consider
the necessity for funds to pay the resulting tax. In fact, it may be argued that an income
tax at the current rate practically forces accountants to cling to the realization postulate.
Borrowing on the increase for dividend payments is a possibility, but this financial device
has definite limitations.

There is a related problem of some interest: if we are to hold to realization, is it necessary for all the cost including the increase to touch first base — cash or equivalent — or is
it sufficient for only the amount of the increase to meet this test?

One view is expressed in the following quotation.

> An expenditure for wages was charged to the revenue account at that time, not because it rep-
> resented a periodic expense to be matched against the income which it produced but because
> it represented a loss of circulating capital which had to be replaced before there were profits
> available for dividends.[21]

If inventory is sold for other current assets with a recognizable value increase, the increase could be detached in the sense of supporting a dividend without changing the working capital position of the firm. Suppose that a fixed asset is exchanged for a fixed asset of
equal value plus cash for the amount of the acknowledged value increase. In this case, it
appears that the amount of the increase could be detached without impairing working
capital.[22] If, however, inventory items are exchanged for fixed assets and there is an obvious value increase, the working capital decrease (according to usual definitions) has

[21] D. A. Litherland, "Fixed Asset Replacement a Half Century Ago," *The Accounting Review*, October,
1951, p. 478. Notice the turn to management freedom in the following quotation from Maurice Moonitz. " . . .
the emergence of revenues restores a business to a liquid position, thereby permitting management to shift, if necessary, the precise form of the investment." "Adaptations to Price-Level Changes," *The Accounting Review*,
April, 1948, p. 141.
[22] Provisions of the income tax law and regulations recognize the working-capital characteristics of fixed asset exchanges and make complicated provisions for relating the taxable income to the amount of the "boot."

been for the entire amount of the value recognized from the inventory. If dividends to the amount of the increase are paid from working capital, the total decrease in working capital is the amount of value recognized for the fixed asset.

The fluidity of the entire proceeds may be used as a criterion of income recognition. Now the "ability to shift investment" does not necessarily imply that the entire amount of revenue must be represented by working capital. It is, of course, possible to argue for such a criterion (such a definition), but even traditional accountants seldom insist on complete fluidity. A straight swap of a fixed asset for another fixed asset plus some boot in the form of working capital presents the opportunity for the decision to shift or not to shift the cost commitment from one bundle of services to another and provides considerable freedom with respect to the increment. It is the increment that has the additional dimensions of withdrawal and tax, and therefore it seems to be more critical in the area of liquidity.

Essay Eight

Realization Difficulties — Dividends

In a preceding essay the controversy about the realization concept is discussed in some detail. The merits of the straight value-increase approach are substantial, but realization in both its evidential and working capital aspects will no doubt be with the accounting profession for some time. This essay deals with the realization problem in connection with withdrawals and with some simple equity reorganizations within a corporate structure. Under what circumstances, for example, are stock dividends earned and realized to the recipient? When are cash dividends earned or realized? In this connection some references are made to the voluminous income-tax literature.

The dividend question is obviously a part of the larger problem of interentity transactions. Attitudes about realization tests will be conditioned in each case by the individual's own concept of the proper accounting entity and its relationship to other entities. There is little doubt in most of our minds that the word entity got off on the wrong foot by long metaphysical discussions as to whether the entity is "real or imaginary," or is a "fiction."[1]

It should be clear that informational reports must be relevant to individuals — to people — and to their needs, their interests and desires. This attitude does not deny the continued existence of such organizational entities as the American Accounting Association, Notre Dame football team, the Northwest Mounted Police, The Chrysler Corporation, or the Commonwealth of Virginia. Such organizational entities not only exist — in the sense of influencing conduct and creating emotional response — but such entities are conducted by individuals whose work is directed to the benefit of themselves and other vaguely determined individuals for whom the organization becomes a symbol and an understandable surrogate.

Recently in accounting there has been some discussion about the functions of modern management in terms of organizational survival instead of stockholder agency.

---

[1] Walter G. Kell has no illusions about this point:

". . . a seemingly endless controversy has ensued over the entirely irrelevant question of whether the corporate accounting entity is based on fact or whether it is based on fiction."

"Should the Accounting Entity be Personified?" *The Accounting Review*, January, 1953, p. 40. Canning uses semantic arguments effectively in the controversy. "Imaginary entities have their proper place in the conceptual world of analysis in pure mathematics, but never in the statistical analysis of realities." John B. Canning, *The Economics of Accountancy* (New York: The Ronald Press Company, 1929), p. 55. Husband points out the "artificial" nature of entity but does not let it interfere with his analysis and conclusions. "It is recognized, of course, that the corporate entity is a fiction, an artificial personality, that it lacks objective reality, and that it possesses no power to act or to direct action." George R. Husband, "The Corporate-Entity Fiction and Accounting Theory," *The Accounting Review*, September, 1938, p. 241. " . . . it becomes necessary for the fictitious business entity to account both for the kinds of goods or things making up the property in its possession and for the kinds of ownership claims attaching to these goods." Warner H. Hord, "A Neglected Area of Accounting Valuation," *The Accounting Review*, October, 1942, p. 337.

Especially significant . . . has been the role of management — instead of merely representing the stockholders it has become the custodian *of the enterprise objectives of survival and growth* . . . the stockholders in an enterprise and their rights are subsidiary to the organization and its survival.[2]

This area is overdue for serious consideration, even though discussions of managements' duties and responsibilities have been going on for some time. If management is primarily an agent for the residual shareholders, its duties are primarily toward the shareholder group, and the proprietorship approach to accounting may be in order. One point of opposition should be noted; the fact that management should be responsible primarily to residual shareholders does not mean that the interests of other groups must be neglected. Nor does this position imply that accounting reports should always be aimed at the management group, although improved administration usually benefits all groups with legitimate interests in the organization. It is conceivable, therefore, that an entity or fund approach would be more useful even to owners than the owner-oriented proprietorship assumption.

Husband, who has given considerable attention to the entity problem, apparently has taken the general view that management is directed primarily to stockholder interests and that accountants should be oriented toward an entity-for-management view.

Considerable tendency exists in current accounting to relate basic theory to the presumption that the corporation as an entity conducts its affairs for its own ends. Basic accounting problems are solved in a manner more or less consistent therewith. From the point of view of economics, however, the core principals in free enterprise activity are the individual entrepreneurs who use the various forms of business organization for personal ends.[3]

---

[2] Waino W. Suojanen, "Accounting Theory and the Large Corporation," *The Accounting Review*, July, 1954, pp. 393-394 (italics mine). Apparently Littleton does not stress individual human relationships. He states with approval: "Not all property . . . is capital. To be capital, property must be devoted exclusively to some business enterprise with a view of realizing profit. Capital thus set apart constitutes a business which from its beginning establishes relations between itself and all parties dealing with it." A. C. Littleton, "The Logic of Accounts," *The Accounting Review*, January, 1955, p. 45. The following recommendation is refreshing and shows more appreciation of the human beings involved. "Or, better than 'enterprise' we may say 'human association' . . ." John W. McMahan, "Basic Education for Accounting in Business," *The Accounting Review*, April, 1946, p. 137.

[3] George R. Husband, "The Entity Concept in Accounting," *The Accounting Review*, October, 1954, p. 553. Notice also: "Since the locus of the entrepreneurial function rests in personal individuals rather than in impersonal business entity it would appear that accounting theory would be more realistically hinged to economic reality if the corporation were assumed to be an agency organization." *Ibid.*, p. 554. For a stimulating view see Nelson B. Seidman. "It can hardly be doubted that in the case of the private closely held corporation, an agency relationship does, in reality, exist . . . . But [in the closely held corporation] it is not that here the corporate veil has been pierced; it is that in reality (though given substance before the law) the corporate veil never existed at all . . . . 'What do we mean when we say that the corporation is an economic and social entity? We mean that the corporation as such (like other social institutions) has a tradition, a reputation, a place in the economic process and in the community . . . . It is said that individuals run the corporation, but it can also be said that the corporation runs individuals.' " "The Determination of Stockholder Income," *The Accounting Review*, January, 1956, pp. 64-65. Even philosophers have recently become interested in the problem. "Above all, the administrator thinks responsibly. His first duty is to maintain the activities of his organization; he will improve them if he can, but he must keep them going at all costs. In this respect his professional code resembles that of the doctor whose first duty is to guard the life of his patient . . . . So it is with the administrator; he thinks in terms of the groups he administers and of the individuals with whom he must act. He will test the value of an idea with such questions as these: 'Will it work in practice?' 'Will it benefit or hurt the organization I serve?' 'Will my colleagues go along with me?' For the administrator, in his professional capacity, a valuable idea is nothing more or less than a workable plan. He thinks practically, in terms of concrete situations. Essentially and necessarily a conservative, he welcomes cautious developments provided these lie well within the conventional, accepted framework of his society." T. North Whitehead, "Permission to Think," *Harvard Business Review*, January-February, 1956, p. 34.

While there is something appealing about the simplicity of a doctrine that considers the major function of management to be its duties and responsibilities to shareholders, there has been a growing feeling that such a model is far too simple to represent the relationship of management to outside groups.

> . . . management is indeed far removed from the application of neat theories of authority delegations following the lines of property rights; management is not the servant of the proprietors but rather the conciliatory agency between two or among several . . . groups . . . . Viewed realistically, the corporation is a conglomeration of personalities, resources, conditions, and relationships; and this conglomeration is but faintly if at all recognized in the legal fiction of the corporate "person."[4]

Let us now look at the "organizational custodian for survival" theory of entity. Perhaps the first question is whether or not the custodians are attempting to aid the survival of the organization regardless of equity holders as individuals or as groups or classes. Is it the survival of the entity *name* that is important? The line of products? The jobs and welfare of individual workers or of the working population of the area? The trademarks and products with public acceptance?

While there may be several interpretations as to the meaning of survival and who is to be allowed to survive, one suspects that management is interested in its own survival and gives action to this end high priority. Thus, it seems reasonable that the bondholders and preferred holders will be paid some return if at all possible, for failure to do so constitutes a threat to management survival. Moreover, to perpetuate itself management must keep the common holders reasonably well satisfied. While the common holders may share some behavior patterns with sheep, when stirred up, they have often failed to conform to the Berle and Means pattern. Clearly, if management wishes to continue in power, it must keep common stockholders from becoming mutinous. Furthermore, a management that finds it impossible to get along with pertinent labor organizations usually finds itself unable to earn satisfactory profits and thereby unable to keep all equity holders satisfied. Customers offer a similar example. Certainly, if management wishes to stay in power, it must have workable relations with this group. Perhaps it is not by chance that the new managerial elite follows a fairly definite and predictable pattern of agreeable and impressive personalities.[5]

It is not meant to imply that the chief concern of the dominating group is always its own survival. The general team spirit that makes management want to pass on to its suc-

---

[4] William J. Vatter, *The Fund Theory of Accounting and Its Implications for Financial Reports* (Chicago: University of Chicago Press, 1947), pp. 9-10. Husband expresses the broader view, perhaps not with approval. "Instead of interest being a cost which is paid for a service, the corporation is viewed as an organizational agency earning income for the creditors, as well as for the stockholders . . . . Further inclusion within the aggregate group of the wage earners . . . makes wages also a distribution of income . . ." George R. Husband, "The Entity Concept in Accounting," *op. cit.*, p. 560. While income reports based on the principle of value added are not new, an able defense for this organizational view is given by Waino W. Suuojanen. " . . . if the enterprise is considered to be an institution, its operations should be assessed in terms of its contribution to the *flow* of output of the commuity . . . . The purpose of the value added concept of enterprise income is the measurement of the flow and its division among the participants in the organization." "Accounting Theory and the Large Corporation," *The Accounting Review*, July, 1954, p. 395. Russell Bowers apparently does not hold the "organizational survivl theory." " . . . a fallacious economic theory that the primary motive of a business firm is to maintain its capital in such manner as to enable the firm to perpetuate itself in business without diminishing its scale of activities." "Objections to Index Number Accounting," *The Accounting Review*, April, 1950, p. 151.

[5] T. North Whitehead, *op. cit.*

cessors a stronger railroad is akin to the spirit that makes the footballer willing to die for Rutgers in order to improve her miserable record over Princeton. Moreover, while survival of the name may be important, there are many examples of willingness to change names without tears.

Apparently there is little or no interest in aiding the survival of an individual stockholder or other equity holder. Individuals buy and sell securities regularly, and except in cases where individual holders are important, it is possible that the individual composition of the equity holders' ledger is a matter of no great importance to the management.

The question now arises as to the relevance of management motivation and goals to the selection of the entity for bookkeeping purposes, and subsequently the question as to the relationship of the bookkeeping entity to the concept of realization in the field of corporate distributions — withdrawals.

If the stockholders and their interests are subordinated to the survival of the enterprise, then it seems to follow that the agency approach to corporate relations with the owners is not an acceptable viewpoint. It should be clear that a form of management-centered entity would be appropriate for such relations. From this point of view the owners' interests, like those of laborers, are adverse (the term is Canning's) to the management group or to the organizational entity, and presumably their reward should be minimized. Just as management may try to procure borrowed funds at the most favorable rates, management may attempt to keep the payments to stock owners as low as possible without choking off the supply of new capital or losing its position.[6]

The entity problem, in one sense, involves drawing a line between insiders and outsiders. Many on the outside are considered to have adverse interests to those in the inside. Managements' duty to bondholders, as outsiders, is to entice them into contracts that are most favorable to inside groups. Although preferred interests are usually included among stockholders' equities and income is usually determined from their viewpoint, management and common shareholders often consider them beyond the pale. To the extent that common holders are considered to be a part of the outside environment, policies may be designed to give them as little as is consistent with optimizing managements' overall position.

A little reflection will show that the insider-outsider analysis is far too simple for accounting theory. Even outsiders are worthy of some output from the information system. Creditors, workers, government agencies, customers and even competitors may be entitled to information. In fact, entity accountants are divided at this point. One group of theorists takes the mystical position that the entity is a separate area of accountability quite apart from the contending and cooperating groups that make its existence possible. The other branch of entity theorists takes the association view and looks at the organization as a mechanism for resolving conflicts and furthering the interests of all relevant groups. The accounting rules may be considerably different under the two assumptions. However, it is usually assumed that the interests of all are well served by capable administration and management. With this assumption the two branches of entity accountants may merge in a kind of managerial accounting whose primary objective is to improve ad-

---

[6] Husband almost comes to this decision with regard to preferred stock, but his concern with the agency approach apparently keeps him from applying the same conclusion to common. "Capital is an effective instrument contributing mightily to any success that management may achieve. For this the manager should be charged, otherwise the managerial accomplishment will not be isolated . . . . Consistent therewith preferred stock dividends are best treated as a cost." "The Entity Concept in Accounting," *op. cit.*, p. 561.

ministrative efficiency. We are still shouldered with the old, old problem: Efficiency in accomplishing whose objectives?[7]

This problem of entity definition is given more attention than it would normally receive because of current attitudes in corporation finance. It is now common practice to specify the chief responsibility of management in terms of maximizing the current value of the residual stockholders' equity under conditions of uncertainty. This assumption is a fantastic oversimplification and is subject to its own special difficulties. The necessity for recognizing peculiarities of market behavior is obvious. Moreover, if stockholders of the future are different from present ones, and if the switch intervals are not known, the problem becomes highly complicated. Actually, problems arise at a much more elementary level. For example, a stockholder wishes to retire and the firm buys his interest as treasury stock. Is it the obligation of management to see that the retiring stockholder receives optimal treatment even at the expense of other current holders or of future stockholders to whom the shares may be sold?

Moreover, it is now fashionable to adapt a set of measurement rules for costs of capital that defines the construct in terms of cost (sacrifice) to residual owners. A number of questions clamor for attention. What is known about feasible alternatives (opportunity costs) available to each stockholder? What is known about individual stockholders' desire for more risk or less risk implied by more or less trading on creditor equity? What about differences in the rates on withdrawals among individuals and modes of withdrawal? Why should one measure sacrifice by means of an implied cost derived from *marginal* buyers and *marginal* sellers in a market?[8]

The current position in corporation finance seems to be reasonably close to the original proprietary approach of early accountants. Yet it should be clear that accountants deal with many organizations without stockholders, residual or otherwise. Hospitals, school districts, cities, counties, states, clubs and many other organizations require accounting information. The construction of a theory of accounting must accordingly be more general and be based on information in relation to the varying needs of diverse groups with shifting social worthiness.

Let us now apply these various entity assumptions to the question of income realization to recipients of corporation dividends. The preliminary discussion begins with another look at cash and other property distributions.

From a strict agency relationship it should be obvious that cash dividends are *not* income to the recipients at the time of declaration or payment. The owners, with this view,

---

[7] William J. Vatter has partially brushed aside this question in his interesting fund theory. Assets are segregated for some purposes and the bookkeeping definitions are clustered about assets and restrictions of various kinds. *The Fund Theory of Accounting, op. cit.*, p. 19. Paradoxically, Vatter's condemnation of the entity approach contains one of the most competent statements of its defense.

[8] Perhaps the market price represents some sort of *average* feeling with some potential buyers willing to pay less and some potential sellers wanting more. Such arbitrary positioning of market price on the curves is highly questionable, and the rules of measurement for cost of capital do not specify cost to some average investor. Notice that an average rate derived from using bond rates, preferred returns and common market rates is an average of different interests. If each were exactly arbitraged by the market, the average still might not represent the feeling of the residual holders. Interesting side issues on cost-of-capital measurement may be raised. What, for example, is the "cost" of additional common capital *to bondholders*? Is there a "cost" to existing bondholders when new bonds are sold? Preferred retired? What is the cost *to management* of retained earnings, if shareholders would rather have "growth" instead of dividends? Managers get the benefit from more earning assets without being charged an explicit cost for the use of the funds when retained earnings are utilized. This peculiar effect is the result of the accounting tradition for recording only explicit costs.

have interests in the assets of the concern before the distribution is made, and after the distribution the owners have undivided interests in a smaller amount of corporation assets (by the amount of the distribution) and have an equivalent amount of assets in their own individual pockets. To illustrate, assume that a cash distribution of $100,000 is made to the five stockholders of the corporation. After the dividend each stockholder has $20,000 and a one-fifth interest in a corporation whose net assets are decreased by $100,000 by the dividend action.[9]

We may inquire next whether the concept of realization is useful if the association (agency) assumption is deemed to be appropriate. A negative answer seems warranted. From the more or less continuous flow of financial and operating events that make up a firm's existence the accountant may select with relative freedom those that are to be considered important (crucial) in the income-realization process. It seems hardly necessary to point out once more that the value increase must be conceded before the question of realization — net quick-asset betterment — arises. The realization problem then may be resolved into an attempt to find events that lead to added value and increased working capital. Is there any precedent for considering as the crucial realization test the transfer of funds from agent to principal or vice versa? Clearly not! The precedent in accounting is in the direction of treating transfer of funds between affiliates in an agency relationship as relatively unimportant and of far too little consequence to trigger the recognition of value increases or realization.

A little reflection on the profession's attitudes toward withdrawals by sole proprietorships and partnerships will show how unimportant withdrawals are considered to be. Accountants are so accustomed to thinking in terms of the association view with regard to partnerships that they tend to assume and take for granted that the earnings of the firm are indeed the earnings of the partners. They are accustomed also to regarding the firm's income as the owners' income and considering withdrawals as totally unimportant in the income recognition process and relatively unimportant in most other connections as well. This strong attachment for the association view, it may be added, has grown up in spite of a well-established and sharply-defined distinction between the firm as an *accounting entity* and the individual as a different entity.

It may appear that domination — the power to make withdrawals — is the important difference between corporations and other forms of business organizations for income reporting purposes. But what about restrictions on withdrawals in partnership agreements? Or restrictions resulting from loan agreements? Furthermore, the important reason why domination cannot be used as an argument at this point is that an association or agency view of a corporation must recognize that the owners do have such powers of withdrawal within the surrounding legal restrictions. The association view does not emphasize the importance of freedom to withdraw or even to manage. Thus, the proportional-interest doctrine does not seem to be appropriate from the association view, and no income would be realized to recipients of dividends if such dividends are made in property. What about the association view and stock dividends?

---

[9] The recent emphasis on growth stocks has made this approach more popular. A number of empirical attempts have been made to relate the price of shares to retained earnings, to cash dividends, and to a host of other variates and combination of variates. M. J. Gordon, for example, states: "He receives the dividend in cash and the retained earnings in a rise in the share's value, and if he wants additional cash he can always sell a fraction of his equity. In short, the corporate entity is a legal fiction that is not material with respect to his rights in the corporation or the value he places on them." "Dividends, Earnings, and Stock Prices," *The Review of Economics and Statistics*, May, 1959, p. 103.

Under the association view the earnings would be income to the owners when the income is earned and realized by their agent — the corporation. A decision not to take out assets in the form of dividends would appear to have no important bearing on income to the recipient just as the decision not to withdraw partnership earnings has no important bearing. The decision to have a stock dividend is analogous to the decision of a partner to have a part of his drawing account transferred to his more permanent capital account. One must not overwork the analogy because of legal differences between retained earnings and capital stock and the possibility of different market reactions. If the association view is appropriate, however, market behavior would not seem to be an important consideration except as a mechanism for reflecting changes in expected future corporate policy.[10]

With stock dividends one must remember that the individual shareholder may have an opportunity cost in the sense that if the funds are to remain in the firm he loses larger income or satisfaction than he might have derived from the funds in other uses. An individual holder may be able to derive more benefit from the dividend than he can from his increased interest in the business. This opportunity cost cannot be too great in a well-developed market, however, since each individual can sell his holdings until the tendency to arbitrage narrows the gap. A stock dividend may be interpreted as a statement of intention, but unfortunately the overtones are not clear. Such action may indicate a commitment to growth by freezing retained earnings, or it may indicate the opposite — intention to continue the regular dividend rate on a larger number of shares. One interpretation or the other may strike the fancy of those in the market and change the value of stock. Otherwise it is difficult to assert that owners are better off than if they had received assets. Alternative opportunities vary and the incidence of income tax is certainly not uniform.

Clearly other equity holders are in better positions than if their cushion had been reduced by asset distributions; thus we reach the strange conclusion that stock dividends as opposed to asset distributions clearly strengthen everyone's position except possibly the position of some recipients. (Competitors, who in an enterprise society are supposed to look out for themselves, are not so well off due to the added strength of the firm.)

Suppose we turn now to the separate entity point of view and examine dividend possibilities in terms of the realization criterion. The quotation below is a deserving statement by Husband:

> From the entity point of view the following would seem to constitute the most reasonable line of argument and the most reasonable conclusion:
>
> 1. Income earned by the corporation is entity income and not the income of the stockholder participants.
>
> 2. Any resulting retained earnings constitute part of the corporate entity's equity in itself.
>
> 3. A distribution of assets which reduces the corporate entity's equity in itself (a cash dividend) or the transferring of part of the corporate entity's equity in itself to the stock-

---

[10] At times the Patons take an association view. "As stated above a dividend is basically a distribution of corporate assets, and it is nothing short of ridiculous (or perhaps one should say ironic) to label a procedure which insures the permanent retention in the business of a specified amount of income funds as a 'distribution.'" William A. Paton and William A. Paton, Jr., *Corporation Accounts and Statements* (New York: The Macmillan Company, 1955), p. 95.

holders (a stock dividend) transfers to the stockholders something which was not theirs previously and therefore constitutes income to the stockholders.[11]

From this point of view it may also be argued that a cash dividend is income to the recipient because the net effect is a reduction of the buffer assets for other members of the organization in favor of the residual equity holders. With the separate entity assumption, it is entirely gratuitous to assume that earnings by the corporation without reservations are a part of the equity of the residual holders. In fact, the very term "residual holders" may be ill-chosen, and the assignment of all retained earnings to this interest may be pointless. Under Husband's scheme stock dividends would apparently increase the book value of the common-stock interest.[12] At least that part of the book value derived from retained earnings would now be imputed to the common holders. Instead of using Husband's "entity's equity in itself" it seems more useful to return to the older treatment of retained earnings as "undivided profits" — undivided among the classes of equity holders as well as undivided among the individuals composing the common stockholders. If management is, in fact, a coordinator of interests that are often conflicting and accepts as one of its chief obligations the survival and enlargement of the enterprise, the undivided profits may be considered to be 'undistributed,' and to include the balance with any group of equities serves no useful purpose. It is true that the usual ownership contracts are drawn so that residual holders *seem* to be getting the primary benefits from retained earnings. However, the position of other equity holders is improved, and inasmuch as they have already indicated a willingness to substitute safety for earnings, their subjective improvement may be even greater.

We now ask in what ways the amounts included under capital stock or under bond obligations are different from the amount kept under undistributed profits. Does, for example, the amount under the capital-stock caption represent a claim by the stockholders? An equity of the shareholders? Some other kind of interest? With the assumption of a going concern, it may be argued that the terms 'equity,' 'interest,' and 'claim' should be abandoned altogether. Husband argues that retained earnings do not represent an equity or a claim of the residual shareholders, but he accepts without question that the capital stock balances *do represent* the equity (or claim) of the holders. In what sense is the balance of the capital stock account an equity or claim of the owners? A bookkeeping transfer does not in itself indicate realization of income for the recipients, but it is possible that the psychological reactions of investors could change the value of stock interests and that these value changes in the individual holdings could qualify as realized income to the

---

[11] George R. Husband, "The Entity Concept in Accounting," *op. cit.*, p. 555. Notice the "hard" concept of the entity. The milder organization concept of an entity would interpret retained earnings as an uncommitted pool for the benefit of all groups.

[12] Book value, as is pointed out elsewhere, is a strange computation. Current assets are near current liquidation values, but unfortunately the carrying figures for other assets may or may not have any relationship to any value concept. Book value has some use for judging the value of an enterprise in its entirety, but its usefulness here is probably less than many accountants believe. If two businesses have demonstrated the same earning power in the past, it *may* be that the one with the larger book value depends more on *properties* and other asset considerations. In the former case, it is sometimes assumed that future earnings should be more stable because even a less high-powered management should be able to drain a normal stream of earnings from the larger complex of assets. Needless to say, the importance of the difference and of book value may easily be overestimated. Nelson B. Seidman points out some liquidating features of the book-value concept, which should be constructed from going-concern values. "Determination of Stockholder Income," *The Accounting Review*, January, 1956, pp. 66-67.

recipients. We shall return later to the question of whether the stock dividend action of management may, through a chain of probable psychological reactions, justify recognition of income by recipients.

An approach to reporting and recording that stresses assets and responsibilities (or sources of assets) is certainly in harmony with the view of management as coordinator. In both cases there is no implication that the amounts recorded under 'bonds,' 'preferred stock,' 'common stock,' are interests, equities, claims in liquidation, or otherwise. Furthermore, it is not necessary for an advocate of this system to take a stand on whether the retained earnings *belong* to anyone. Such questions are considered to be irrelevant for a going concern.[13] Unfortunately there are difficulties in defining sources and keeping track of changes in sources. When a dividend in property is declared, accountants transfer from one pool or source — earnings extracted from customers and suppliers and retained in the business — to another pool or source — assets furnished by whoever represents 'dividends payable.' A little reflection should convince one that the financial equivalent of "waving a wand" by the board of directors cannot make the assets come from a new source. A proprietary theorist may reject this position and (with an alternate wand) arrive at the conclusion that the common stockholders furnished the assets all along. However, an appropriation of retained earnings in favor of preferred holders carries the implication that the preferred holders furnished assets to that amount. Bond interest payable does seem to represent an appropriation and thereby to qualify as a source of assets! Of course there is a sense in which all these folks do contribute to an increase in assets. It may be *assumed*, for example, that each group *contributes* financial services to the asset fund equal to the payments that must be made to them, and that such appropriations are recognition of these services. This view, it may be added, is in keeping with the attitude outlined in an earlier essay — that factors of production (outsiders) contribute only to the extent of their costs and any excess is attributed to those who make up the entity. In view of these difficulties in accounting for asset sources and the lack of relevance of many historical events to current decisions, many accountants prefer the assets-equals-responsibilities approach. The latter equation in turn may be criticized for restricting the amount of recognized responsibilities to the amount of the assets.

The individual shareholder, if he is considered to be a separate entity, has no reason for keeping his books (recognizing value increases and decreases) in harmony with the rules adopted by the corporation.[14] If the stockholder is in fact divorced from the corporate entity, there is no necessity for requiring income to the recipient to harmonize with income for the corporation. The stockholder has a right to certain prospects. The value of

---

[13] Louis O. Foster has been an articulate advocate of the asset-equals-sources-of-assets approach. "The Asset Approach to Elementary Accounting," *The Accounting Review*, March, 1941, pp. 8-15. *Introduction to Accounting* (Chicago: Richard D. Irwin, Inc., 1941).

[14] Husband holds this view in emphatic terms. "It may be argued, with some logic, that once the stockholder becomes an integral part of the corporation his accounting thereafter should coincide with the accounting of the corporation and that the corporate book value of the stock dividend received should constitute the basis of income recognition. This view of the case, however, is not consistent with the view that the corporation and the stockholders are separate entities and that the stock dividend transfers to the stockholder corporate entity equity to which he previously did not have title. From the separate entity point of view the basis of accounting for the corporation's experience is not of material influence in deciding what should be the proper basis of accounting for the stockholder. The stockholder as a separate entity may therefore properly use the market basis of the dividend stock received as the basis of income recognition." George R. Husband, "The Entity Concept in Accounting," *op. cit.*, p. 556.

his prospect will be influenced by the success or nonsuccess of the corporation, but it is also influenced by market valuation by others who have different opportunities and may be subject to periods of optimism and pessimism. It is conceivable that a concern would declare liquidating dividends and still have the value of its stock rise in the market. This somewhat unusual situation might arise because regularity of dividends is a highly weighted factor in setting the value of the stock, or for other reasons including sheer ignorance.

Thus, if the market reacts so that a stock dividend increases the value of a share of stock, if there is no compulsion for the individual holder to keep his records in line with the corresponding records of the concern, and if the resulting value increase meets the test of realization, then stock dividends may be considered to be income to the recipient.

Let us now review the criteria for realization and apply them to the problem of stock dividends with the separate-entity assumption. Suppose that the value increase has taken place and is expressed in higher market prices for the securities. The problem is then no longer a problem of establishing the adequacy of the evidence. The presence of an independent market furnishes objective evidence of the existence of the increase and helps measure its magnitude. But are the usual liquidity tests for accounting realization met?

If the stock itself is held as a marketable security and meets the tests for inclusion among the current assets, it seems that the increase is in the form of a current asset and therefore meets the liquidity aspect of the realization test. The actual sale of the securities is an unimportant event and does not seem to be crucial enough in the string of events to merit serious attention. Obviously, if securities are held for control or for community-of-interest purposes, they do not qualify as current assets, and their increased value does not meet the liquidity tests *unless* effective control can be maintained after disposal of the dividend shares. For securities held for control purposes, the conversion of the incremental value into current asset may mean the undermining of the control position and accordingly the dividend shares should be classified as noncurrent assets. On the other hand, if control or communal interest is maintained without the extra shares, the increment meets all liquidity tests and may be treated as realized income.

We now have sufficient background to examine the relevance of control and proportional interest to income recognition. A cash dividend tends to leave the relative interests of common holders unchanged *unless* some of them decide to reinvest their dividend checks in the same company. The decision to reinvest or not reinvest these receipts is an independent decision and is usually considered to be of little or no consequence for income recognition. Reinvestment decisions to maintain proportional position are influenced by a number of considerations not directly related to income recognition, e.g., preemptive rights, management policy, competitors' actions. Common holders have less equity after a property distribution, and their position with respect to holders of other equity contracts is weakened. Unless these holders are also contenders for control, their position *vis a vis* common holders is irrelevant for the income problem.

The relative-position criterion for income realization on stock dividends deserves restatement. At first glance it seems that such a test for realization is an anomaly found nowhere else in accounting. The arguments in support of this criterion are so weak, scattered and confused that no effective defense exists even in the tax literature. The argument advanced here relates the control factor to the current-noncurrent classification of the investment. Thus control by the investor is related to liquidity, and liquidity is an essential feature of realization. In this fashion certain changes in control are relevant to the problem of income recognition by the recipient of stock dividends. At least they are consistent with the usual rules for income realization in other situations.

The presence of an effective market mechanism and the lack of desire to control are both required before accountants classify investments as current assets. A liquidity constraint that requires a working-capital increase at least equal to the amount of income recognized is built into the accounting definition of realized income. (A discussion of this widely misunderstood aspect of realization may be found in the preceding essay.) If retention of the dividend shares is necessary to maintain control or continue the community of interest, clearly such shares fail to meet the tests for working capital inclusion and therefore are inadequate to support income realization even though the evidence supporting increased value is adequate. Now it is possible that the recipient has more than enough stock to assure control. Accountants would ordinarily agree to classifying the excess stock as current. Such stock could be disposed of without interfering with the operations of the firm, and in the presence of an adequate market would qualify as a quick asset. In a similar way any dividend shares not essential for control are current and may be used to support the treatment of a value increase as realized income. The usual change-in-interest rule is not so refined. In fact, it is hopelessly confused. A stock dividend of common on common is not considered to be income even though the value of the holdings may be increased and control is not a factor. On the other hand, common on preferred may be considered to be a change in interest and therefore realized income regardless of the position of the recipient.

Minority holders are usually not interested in control and a test of income that stresses proportionate change in interest would seem to be without meaning for them. One of the difficulties with respect to stock dividends is that all investors (equity holders) are not homogeneous with regard to control. In the same concern at the same time there may be holders who bear a principal-agent relationship with the concern, and there may be several who have no claim whatsoever to such a relationship. For the latter group the separate entity approach with the investment shown as current seems to be appropriate. Thus, in the typical stock-dividend case the accountant is confronted with divergent relationships. Accountants do pass judgment on the relative importance or unimportance of the association assumption in order to classify investments, and the required change is therefore not as great as it may seem to be.

The difficulty should now be obvious. It is the investor's *relation* to the corporation that determines whether value increases from stock dividends are realized income. The entity or association approach is relevant to the extent that it is related to the presence or absence of control. The accountant's consideration of the entity or association view for bookkeeping at the corporation level has little or no relevance to this problem. At least one point should be clear. The traditional interpretation related to changes in the degree of dominance, control, or proportional interest, is not satisfactory, and its usual rationale is even less so.

Essay Nine

Another Look at LIFO

The LIFO material has been covered and recovered for several decades with many extremely competent (and financially disinterested) accountants on different sides of the argument. Many of the publications have been first-rate expositions that explored relevant theoretical and practical aspects of the problem. Unfortunately a number of writers continue to stumble over identical points decade after decade, and it seems appropriate to discuss these shoals again in some detail. Moreover, the environment has changed considerably since the pressure finally convinced members of the Finance and Ways and Means Committees (75th Congress) that nonferrous metal fabricators and tanners were subject to discriminatory taxation unless they were permitted to use LIFO. Later carry-over tax provisions relieved the discriminatory pressure to some extent, but by that time (1942) it was obvious that the old sine-curve assumption of cyclical activity was in for serious modification before it could be applied to post-war activity. The evidence suggested a plateau with future variations around a much higher general level of prices than had previously existed. Accordingly the probable effects of LIFO needed to be reexamined and fitted into the new economic price structure.

The purpose of this essay is to examine the usual arguments relating to LIFO in light of post-war developments. Several original arguments, both for and against, are no longer relevant. The usual arguments against the use of last-in, first-out may be classified: First, arguments based on physical movements of goods with an accompanying assumption that costs are somehow embodied in the physical units; second, arguments that LIFO is in the right direction but is only a weak step that interferes with getting the job done correctly through the application of specific price-level adjustments; third, arguments that point out decisions that might be made to avoid unfavorable LIFO effects but are otherwise not consistent with enterprise goals; fourth, arguments that emphasize possible erratic income behavior and harmful financial reporting from LIFO. A few accountants apparently have objected to LIFO because its application must reduce the tax bill for the particular business concern. Clearly some individuals or groups of individuals must bear the tax burden. This argument should be related to social values and desirable canons of taxation and is not discussed here. We are not concerned here with tax equity, but we shall discuss the other arguments in some detail.

It should be clear to anyone who has observed inventory control in manufacturing and trading concerns that physical goods seldom move in last-in, first-out fashion. For short periods a few items — e.g., those loaded and removed by clams — may perhaps meet this unusual test, but if there is the least danger of physical deterioration, adequate inventory control will require that the old units be removed before deterioration reduces sales value. The point that is so often not understood and needs emphasis is that to an advocate of LIFO the *physical* movement of goods is completely irrelevant. If physical movement were pertinent, then the application of LIFO would be so rare that the controversy could be abated for lack of materiality.

In most textbooks and articles the reader will usually find the implicit assumption that identified unit cost is *the* ideal basis for inventory costing.[1] As a rule, the impracticability of identifying unit costs is pointed out, and the usual formulas (FIFO, LIFO and Averages) are introduced as convenient but imperfect substitutes. On the surface, this assumption seems harmless enough, but it has a very important consequence. If identified unit cost is *the* proper way to value inventory and determine the current merchandise charge, then it follows that LIFO, FIFO, and the averages may be graded good or bad to the extent that they yield results near to those that would have been rendered by the use of identified invoice cost. A standard is thus created by definition, and an ordering scheme is established for feasible alternatives.

Clearly, the numerical result yielded by the assumed standard (identified unit cost) cannot be available in those cases where specific identification is impossible. This situation is overcome by a neat bit of inference. To the extent that the actual physical flow of units is first-in, first-out, accountants infer that FIFO will yield an allocation nearest to the standard allocation resulting from the use of identified unit costs. Since by assumption the standard gives the *right* allocation, FIFO is rated higher than the averages, and in turn the averages outrank LIFO. If the physical units are mixed together, the moving-average assumption most nearly approximates the flow of identified unit costs, and the moving average is therefore elevated to leadership just beneath the ideal itself. Only in rare instances will physical goods move in a by-pass manner, and only in these rare instances would LIFO be rated above its competitors. Clearly, LIFO advocates must undermine the widespread feeling that identified-unit cost is the ideal standard for cost allocation and therefore for income determination.

To my knowledge, J. Chester Crandell was the first to attack seriously the assumption that identified-unit cost is the proper ideal. Crandell was building a defense for average costing, and he realized that an extension of average methods requires the overthrow of identified-unit costing as the idealized standard. The defenses for LIFO and for the various average methods are not identical, and each has its own positive arguments. It is true, however, that each must do away with the assumption that identified cost is ideal before it can enjoy widespread application.

The following statement by Crandell is a classic.

> . . . consider an oil barrel into which is poured successively a certain number of gallons of oil, each of an identical nature and test, and at different costs per gallon — say 10 gallons at 6¢, 30 at 8¢, 10 at 10¢, and 50 at 12¢, a total of 100 gallons at a total cost of $10, an average of 10¢ per gallon.
>
> If one gallon is now sold, the gallon withdrawn cannot be identified, and as a matter of fact it probably actually consists of 1/100 part of each of the 100 gallons which were originally poured into the barrel. The purchaser does not care which gallon he receives and therefore, each gallon commands the same selling price. The seller, whichever gallon is delivered, parts with 1/100 of the total and has 99/100 left . . . and . . . from an economic point of view the remaining 99 gallons stand him $9.90.

---

[1] For a typical discussion consider the following quotation from William A. Paton and William A. Paton, Jr., *Asset Accounting* (New York: The Macmillan Company, 1952), p. 59. "The most *realistic* procedure, of course would be a system of labeling or tagging each unit or particle of cost as incurred in such a manner that it could be specifically traced and identified at any subsequent point in its journey . . . . Occasionally this is practicable . . . . In many situations, however, such a procedure is impossible or impracticable . . . . This means that often it is necessary to adopt some *assumption as to the flow of materials* and other factors which can reasonably be employed in determining the cost of goods on hand . . ." (Italics mine.)

This is, I believe, equally true in a case, where, instead of pouring the 100 gallons of oil when purchased into a single container, all gallons purchased are segregated and continuously identified by being placed in identical gallon bottles, numbered successively from 1 to 100. It is, of course, technically true that if the shipping clerk delivers gallon bottle numbered 15, the seller will part with an identified gallon of oil which actually cost him 8¢, but to use 8¢ in determining the gross profit from the sale would not, in my opinion, measure the change in the economic status of the seller. Under such a plan, by selecting a particular gallon for delivery, the seller would be able to show whatever profit he wished on his profit and loss statement, and yet the fact is that, since he parted with 1 out of 100 identical units, whichever one he chose to deliver would have reduced his inventory assets by an identical value, 1/100 of the previous whole. This, it seems to me is sufficient reason, from the standpoint of principle, to remove from serious consideration the costing of sales on the basis of selected identified purchases of identical goods.[2]

The Securities and Exchange Commission has been reported to favor average costing in some instances, although the Internal Revenue Service unfortunately requires FIFO if securities cannot be identified. Obviously the IRS ideal is identified unit cost.

Suppose, to illustrate, that an investor makes the following purchases of identical common stock:

100 shares at 180
100 shares at 250
100 shares at 140
100 shares at 25

Stock splits and other capital adjustments are ignored, and it may be assumed that the owner is now selling the equivalent of 100 shares at $180. It is clear that he may show no gain or loss, a gain of $155, a gain of $40 or a loss of $70. This ability to manipulate may lead to reports that seriously mislead the reader, for the investor in fact parted with one-fourth of the income-getting power of the asset.

The intellectual basis for identified unit cost is so weak that it is practically nonexistent. For decision making, costs are clustered about the alternatives involved in the decision and their inclusion or exclusion is determined by their relevance to the decision. In determining the information necessary for control, the goals and criteria should normally be those used in making the decision, and the pattern of cost assignment and accomplishment should also follow these lines. Now decisions require mental activity and call for classification, arrangement and appraisal of benefits and sacrifices of many kinds. In many cases these variables may be simplified by relating them to physical properties, areas of responsibility, periods of time, and other familiar concepts. The decision to manufacture a physical unit with revenue-producing properties will usually require an estimate of sacrifice (cost). Clustering costs to be matched with revenues or with other decision estimates is simplified tremendously if the cluster point is a familiar object or area that persists or recurs and can be related directly to the increment of revenue, or to the sacrifice involved. Major decisions may serve as cluster centers, but most past decisions easily become confused in the changing flow of activity, and their cost assignments may be difficult to relate to the future.

---

[2] American Institute of Accountants Annual Meeting, Discussion of "A Statement of Accounting Principles," September 29, 1938, included in *Papers on Accounting Principles and Procedure*, presented at the 51st Annual Meeting, 1938 (New York: American Institute of Accountants, 1939).

In fact, assigning costs to units of output, sources of services of various kinds, areas of responsibility, periods of time, etc., becomes so ingrained in accounting thinking that some leaders have forgotten the utilitarian nature of cost assignment. A slight step further leads to fantastic animistic overtones. The idea that costs somehow attach to units of production like barnacles to a boat may be a useful elementary teaching device, but to argue, among theorists, that costs 'attach' or 'adhere' in some dualistic body-soul relationships is the rankest kind of gratuitous animism. The contention that costs are somehow 'embodied' in physical units and are 'released' (disembodied) at the point of sale to be reincarnated in periodic revenues is the intellectual equivalent of the sleeping princess turned to stone and is consistent with the cruder pantheistic aspects of primitive religions. LIFO advocates are well advised to ignore the flow-of-goods and to concentrate on objectives and methods of arraying sacrifice (cost) to further organizational goals.

Related objections to LIFO stress the difference between income determination and income administration and sometimes include such semantic embroidery as "artificial tinkering with profits" and "flagrant distortion of profits." Advocates of LIFO wish to match current costs with revenues, i.e., deduct from revenues an amount for capital consumption sufficient to replace the physical stocks. With the typical accountants' insistence on documented cost it is difficult to get the profession to agree to the use of current costs, and accordingly LIFO defenders have been willing to compromise and accept the latest invoice cost or its equivalent calculated with the aid of specialized index numbers. Notice that the issue is concerned with matching current costs and that the last-in, first-out formula is a practical device to approximate the objective. In this sense the LIFO formula in itself is no more important than the childish sum-of-the-years' digits rule for measuring relative benefit received from a fixed depreciable asset. It is important to understand that some objections to LIFO are directed at current costing in general, while others emphasize LIFO's shortcomings as a workable approximation of current costing.

Current costing and its LIFO approximation call for a redefinition of income that is based on maintenance of physical capital. Charges that LIFO is 'artificial tinkering' with the profits or that it 'distorts' income miss the point completely and beg the question. The question at issue is whether or not a redefinition of profit that keeps the physical stock intact is a useful one. The individual pros and cons of the redefinition are well known and available in any acceptable advanced text. The American Institute holds generally that the old definition of profit is preferable at this time and that retained-earnings restrictions and other devices may be used to explain dividend and financial policy. This position is defensible and asserts in effect that the old definition of profit with supplementary notification is adequate. LIFO defenders feel that this recommendation is makeshift and resent the implication that the Institute's definition is 'true' profit and that financial matters are a thing apart. To a defender of LIFO the income problem cannot be divorced from its implications and its uses. Clearly financial implications flowing from income definitions and measurement rules cannot be disregarded.

Advocates of LIFO are directly descended from the sturdy defenders of base stock. The reader will recall that the basic amount of inventory is considered to be a fixed asset. There is a strong probability that emphasis on short-term, debt-paying ability was an important factor supporting this position. It is clear that a minimum inventory (or even a minimum balance of cash) is not available for short-term debt payment by a *going* concern. In fact, fixed assets (in the traditional sense) may be a more promising source of short-run funds than either minimum inventory or minimum cash. There is usually some flexibility in making replacements of typical fixed assets, and it may be possible to fend off creditors by keeping replacements below depreciation charges for some time. Inventories, and even cash, may be plundered for a limited time, but by definition it is difficult for a going concern to plunder its minimum stock for any appreciable length of time. In fact, a satisfactory current ratio of, say, three to one may be interpreted as meaning that the inventories and other current assets could be reduced by a factor of x (perhaps two-thirds) and still permit the firm to continue as an operating unit. This interpretation is not based on the assumption that a shrinkage of two-thirds in liquidation value would still permit payment of current liabilities in full. It is not a liquidating concept!

In spite of the debt-paying similarity between fixed assets and basic inventory, it seems unlikely that this feature was the prime consideration for identifying last-in, first-out with base stock, for base-stock accountants were never greatly interested in the balance-sheet effects of their decision.[3] Until approximately World War II, American accountants were in substantial agreement that fluctuations in the market values of fixed assets were not a determinant of enterprise profit. This conclusion probably follows from acceptance of the traditional concept of income realization for a going concern.[4] Even if the cyclical approach is replaced with an assumption of plateaus, any such realization may be interpreted as a restatement of capital requirements. These considerations are mentioned because recently there has been agitation for acceptance of LIFO cost or market, whichever is lower. This agitation has been opposed by taxing authorities and has been supported primarily by accountants who are advocates for tax-paying clients.

If the by-pass (LIFO) method is adopted when costs are low, the effect is similar to base stock. Future market prices are not likely to return to these low levels, and the cost or market reduction will not ordinarily apply to the basic layers. Under a cyclical assumption cost or market would tend to reduce the carrying figure to its lowest point regardless of whether LIFO is initiated in a period of low or high prices. The effect is essentially that of base-stock methods with one important difference. The write-down of basic stock is usually a direct retained earnings adjustment that does not affect reported income. With LIFO cost or market the write-down will normally be against earnings in a piecemeal and irregular way. Thus defenders of LIFO or market — unlike base stock advocates — are in the position of arguing that changes in costs of the basic layers are determinants of income if they are downward and do not affect income if they are upward. This is a strange doctrine, and the conjunction of LIFO and market in this sense cannot be defended.

We now turn to arguments to the effect that LIFO means well but is simply inferior to specific price-level adjustments. It should be obvious that unmodified LIFO may give strange and useless balance-sheet figures. Certainly these amounts normally give no relevant information as to the current value of the stocks or the debt-paying capacity of the

---

[3] The almost total disregard for balance-sheet values by accountants of that day is matched only by the disregard of some present-day accountants. For example, Perry Mason writes: "Once the assets have been acquired the enterprise is committed to their use and their undepreciated balances are of little significance to anyone." *Principles of Public Utility Depreciation* (Chicago: American Accounting Association, 1937), p. 26. See also the arresting statement by Paton and Littleton: "Inventories and plant are not 'values'; but cost accumulations in suspense, as it were, awaiting their destiny." *An Introduction to Corporate Accounting Standards* (Chicago: American Accounting Association, 1940), p. 14. The "dynamic" balance sheet of Eugen Schmalenbach is probably the prototype of such balance-sheet doctrines. See *Dynamic Accounting*, translated by G. W. Murphy and Kenneth S. Most (London: Gee & Company, Limited, 1959).

[4] A firm could make a major policy decision to move its plant and thereby realize the increment on its land. Apparently the concept of piecemeal realization through the sale of product was not brought forth until later. It is interesting to note that the piecemeal approach assumes a same-direction movement between the selling price of product and the replacement cost of plant. Modern sales-leaseback arrangements have changed thinking considerably on the realization criterion applied to fixed assets.

inventories. Price-level adjustments, it is argued, permit useful income determination and also useful financial figures. Of course, similar adjustments may be applied to LIFO balance-sheet figures. There is no reason for insisting that the valuation technique for one purpose must determine the measurement for another purpose. We have a well-established precedent for using an unrealized appraisal increment for fixed depreciable assets in the stockholders' equity section and there is no valid objection to using similar devices to disclose current inventory values.[5] Moreover, accountants have a long tradition for disclosing such information by parenthetical remarks or footnotes to the statements.

Many of those who object to LIFO wish to apply general price level adjustments to all assets and liabilities, i.e., do the "complete job." Defenders of LIFO, on the other hand, often feel that the chief source of difficulty stems from inventories and fixed assets, and if these two items can be adjusted for changes in price levels, the other errors can be tolerated. The former group feels that an identical procedure can be applied directly to all assets and equities and that such specialized techniques as LIFO and individual depreciation adjustments are not necessary. The difference is complicated further due to the use of specialized indexes with LIFO and specific fixed asset indexes. General price-level indexes are usually advocated by those who adjust all assets and liabilities. In broad terms the latter group wishes to assure maintenance of purchasing power before reporting income, while the former group feels that provision should be made to keep physical properties intact.[6] The LIFO advocate ordinarily argues that it is management's responsibility to hedge other inflationary influences by balancing dollar-assets with current and long-term dollar obligations. If management does so, the general price-level problem is less acute.

LIFO is sometimes condemned because its use in conjunction with current tax law and investment policies may lead to decisions and actions not otherwise favorable to the firm's objectives. It is argued, for example, that the fear of eating into low-cost layers and thereby showing large taxable income may lead to intemperate purchasing policies and needlessly large inventories.[7] Moreover, layer depletion may tend to occur when the trade cycle is on a sharp upswing, so that additional purchases for layer protection may increase inflationary tendencies and misdirect scarce resources.

One of the traditional arguments for LIFO has assumed that over the trade cycle the tendency to smooth reported income will encourage businessmen to invest when business activity and costs are low and discourage investment when activity is near the top of the cycle where the effect is to increase prices greatly and output only slightly.[8] The disposition to protect layers from depletion tends to counteract this argument. In addition, a countervailing force results from the inverse flow of funds for tax payments. Thus LIFO

---

[5] F. W. Woodbridge has been advocating such modifications to base stock inventories for at least a third of a century. *Elements of Accounting* (New York: The Ronald Press Company, 1926).

[6] LIFO advocates are essentially defenders of current costs, and are much closer to those who wish to use specific indexes than to general price-level advocates. The failure of general-index adjustments to provide for changes in relative costs of the factors and agents of production means that factors continue to be combined as if there were no changes in relative costs except general changes related to time of acquisition. Dutch and Indonesian accountants several decades ago at Ralin Coy. worked out an interesting compromise. Specific indexes are applied to real assets and a general index is applied to the monetary assets and equities.

[7] Waino W. Suojanen, for example, works out an equation to relate the penalty for layer depletion to excessive purchase prices that could be profitably incurred to escape such depletion. "LIFO as a Spur to Inflation — The Recent Experience of Copper," *The Accounting Review*, January, 1957, pp. 42-50, esp. p. 48.

[8] The most complete and positive arguments for the influence of accounting on business cycle behavior may be found in Fritz Schmidt, "The Business Cycle — An Accounting Mistake" (Die Industrieinkonjunktur - ein Rechenfehler), (Berlin, 1927).

tends to report less profits on the upswing, and as a result out-payments of funds for income taxes are less. To the extent that investment decisions are influenced more by funds available than by reported profit, LIFO may lead to more investment on the upswing. In a similar fashion, on the downswing LIFO normally reports more profits or less losses than competing costing schemes. This result may indeed encourage new investment but the fund flow is again an opposite force. Tax payments would be greater (or tax refunds less) and the fund effect would be in the direction of decreasing investment. The fact that the funds involved are roughly only one-half the reported profit is offset in part by the greater relative impact of a dollar of funds over a dollar of reported profit. (A behavioral scientist might be interested in developing a transformation function between the two.) A similar line of argument may be applied to the probable effect of LIFO on dividend distributions and other forms of capital withdrawals.[9]

The smoothed income reports under LIFO deserve further comment. Backlash may be introduced by layer depletion and by failure of selling prices and cost prices to move in the same direction.

A related question is concerned with whether the rate of turnover has any influence on the paper profits reported by FIFO when compared with LIFO. FIFO tends to approximate inventories at current market as turnover increases. With a faster turn LIFO moves nearer the current costs in expense but not necessarily nearer to current costs as assets. But with faster turnover FIFO also tends to charge later costs against revenue so that the net lag between the two may or may not be closed. (Empirical study is needed here, but there is some reason to expect the lag to decrease.) If the net lag is not changed and if prices are increasing at constant rates a change in turnover would not change relative profit reported by the two schemes as long as physical inventories remain unchanged. Most published comments on the effects of turnover assume that physical inventories are lower as turnover increases. Smaller physical inventories mean that the inventory problem is less important in the firm's overall financial and operating world. Agitation for LIFO and elimination of paper profits is therefore less urgent.

We turn now to the relationship of LIFO to renewal (replacement) depreciation methods, to period costs of direct costing and to David Green's cost obviation.

Cost of the original inventory (the basic layers) may be treated as a capital cost of providing a suitable environment, and thus is closely related to the renewal method of depreciation. Both assume an indefinitely continuing concern, and charges against revenues are essentially self-adjusting for changes in specific price levels, i.e., at current costs. Both continue to carry basic 'environment' costs at original outlays. Additions to basic assets are handled differently on the technical level, but the effects are essentially consistent. Renewal depreciation makes a distinction between capital and revenue expenditures, and increases the cost of the basic complex of assets only for betterments or additions, e.g., when service potential is increased. LIFO accomplishes similar purposes by simply adding a layer to reflect the added cost of increased service potential.

A slight, and normally unimportant, difference between LIFO and renewal depreciation develops when the environment is contracted. LIFO ordinarily charges the costs in

[9] In 1916, E. D. Page defended base stock as a "deterrent to its improvident distribution in dividends . . . ." "Balance Sheet Valuations," *The Journal of Accountancy,* April, 1916, p. 246. The income effects were also stressed by H. T. Warshow, "Inventory Valuation and the Business Cycle," *Harvard Business Review,* October, 1924, p. 34. Executives of International Harvester Company and American Smelting and Refining have long stressed the benefits from the elimination of "paper" profits. The countervailing tax fund argument is a recent development, for the corporate tax burden was relatively unimportant before World War II.

the latest layer against revenues, unless the decrease is considered to be temporary. A more sophisticated report that is in keeping with the current-cost ideal charges revenues with current cost, credits inventory at layer cost and takes the excess credit to an equity account representing a capital adjustment for changes in the measuring rod used to measure capital invested. Under the renewal method retirement of an asset without replacement usually results in a charge to operations equal to the original cost of the asset. To the extent that time is a factor in the retirement decision, the units retired tend to be the oldest units. Thus the oldest costs tend to be taken to operations, while in LIFO the costs of the last layer added are matched with revenues. To the extent that the assets are necessary for operations and that the industrial economy is expanding, these differences are not likely to be important.

The relationship of LIFO to direct costing is not so clear-cut and compatible. The current costs of keeping the environment suitable for profit-making, e.g., keeping basic plant and stocks available, are charged to operations. These costs are essentially the establishment costs of English direct costers. Moreover, these costs are usually matched with revenue and thus have the same temporal distribution as period costs. If an additional LIFO layer is added (i.e., production outruns disposition for the period), some current fixed costs are diverted to the layer and therefore less fixed costs are matched with revenues. The problem is therefore related to the treatment of fixed overhead on fixed assets constructed for enterprise use. Most LIFO advocates are not greatly concerned with temporary excess stocks and are willing to treat them as current assets subject to the firm's own rules for carrying temporary assets. Whether the firm wishes to carry excess stocks at direct cost or at full cost is not likely to become a major issue.

The relationship of LIFO to cost obviation is also indirect. Defenders of LIFO clearly prefer to match current costs with revenues. Thus they charge a measure for sacrifice involved in procuring the revenue, but the charge is only *indirectly* related to the anticipated cost of regaining the former income-producing position. The charge can be said to be an imperfect measure of the cost obviated, but the definitional problems of 'obviation' still remain. Shall we assume, as initial conditions, no plant? If so, the sacrifice of the first sale or of the first period includes major fixed costs. Shall we smooth the cost of a generation of output (e.g., fixed depreciation costs) to smaller inventory units than the entire output? Or shall we always assume that the costs of keeping a favorable environment are period costs and that the sacrifice relevant to a particular sale is short-run variable cost? LIFO is, in fact, consistent with either direct or full costing and yields an approximation of costs obviated.

We conclude with a short comment on the influence of speculation on the report rendered under LIFO and its interesting variant, next-in, first-out. This variation attempts to correct the lag inherent in LIFO by matching unit costs incurred in the next purchase following the sale. Sales near the end of a period may be costed at either latest invoice prices or prices in effect at the statement date.

It is possible to build an argument to the effect that next-in, first-out is superior to the generally accepted ideal of using current costs at the time of disposal. This formula, like LIFO, has the clear-cut selling point of being an actual accounting cost to the firm. And beyond this practical point, the next purchase is technically *the actual cost of keeping the stocks intact* while the cost at the time of sale is *what it would have cost to keep* the stocks intact if purchase orders were placed when the sales were made. NIFO has the obvious disadvantage of permitting some manipulation of profits by hurrying or delaying purchases for replacement. Management already enjoys some manipulative freedom under LIFO. Ability to manipulate is increased under NIFO due to the additional time allowed for inventory replacement. Goods sold at the top of a cycle may not be replaced under normal conditions until costs are much lower. The natural tendency to defer replacement when lower costs are anticipated and to replace rapidly when future costs are expected to rise may be modified to influence the income reports.

Essay Ten

Goodwill — The Problem of Unrecorded Values

Many economists have been critical of accounting routines that yield asset totals with little or no relationship to the total value of the enterprise. There are some very good reasons why the total values assigned to the assets ordinarily do not equal the value of the firm. First, each asset is valued individually by measurement rules related to its own specific cost and service potential. It should be observed further that even if assets are carried at current replacement costs there is no reason to expect their total to equal the value of the enterprise as a going concern. The second reason is then obvious: There are many valuable considerations, properties, attitudes, and relationships, that the accountant does not attempt to value individually. The difficulties of valuing directly such important considerations as the excellent morale of the working force, an outstanding foreman, a salesman's extraordinary ability to move goods, the purchasing executive's astuteness or the stock manager's tenacity are obvious. Another reason for variation is that the discount rate for the firm may be entirely different from that applied to individual assets. Speaking more generally, the measurement rules applied by investors to a business may be entirely different from those applied by accountants to specific service potentials.[1]

It is clear that the accountants' asset valuations need not represent the value of the enterprise, but at least some economists and businessmen have argued that measuring and reporting should be changed so that the two valuations do coincide. The mechanics of such a change are comparatively simple. Given the agreed value of the firm, an entry may be made to charge an asset account for the difference and to credit an account with unrealized proprietary gains. If the recorded amounts are not appropriate at the end of the succeeding accounting period, a modifying entry may be made to record the increase or decrease and thereby keep the asset total in line with enterprise value.

The selection of an appropriate name for the debit offers interesting alternatives. An acceptable title might be: "Unrecorded and Misvalued Assets." In practice the general and briefer title "Goodwill" is often used instead of more lengthy and indicative titles. The following statement by Paton is one of the earliest.

> The intangibles are the residuum, the balance of the legitimate values attaching to an enterprise as a totality, over the sum of the various tangible properties taken individually. That is, the intangibles measure that part of a company's asset total which might be said to reside in the physical situation viewed as a whole, but which cannot be considered — except upon some highly arbitrary basis — to inhere in, or have a residence in, specific units of plant, equipment, etc.[2]

---

[1] This possibility is discussed in some detail in the essays related to income and measurement. Some enterprise valuations are made with the help of strange rules. The accountant must then decide whether any excess is due to undisclosed values or to bad judgments.

[2] *Accounting Theory* (New York: The Ronald Press Company, 1922), p. 310. Paton's inclusion of *all* intangibles may be a little too broad, and his penchant for animistic explanations is clearly evident. Synergists and holists should feel comfortable with the quotation.

Canning has a similar statement under the general heading: *Goodwill - A Master Valuation Account.*

> Goodwill, when it appears in the balance sheet at all, is but a master valuation account — a catch-all into which is thrown both an unenumerated series of items that have the *economic*, though not necessarily the *legal*, properties of assets, and an undistributed list of undervaluations of those items listed as assets. It is the valuation account *par excellence.*[3]

Accountants, as a group, feel that they are not especially prepared or qualified to judge future managerial capabilities, competitive pressure, shifts in consumer attitudes, technological changes and other factors that influence the value of a going business. It is true that they can — and occasionally do — use clues from the past to appraise the not inscrutable future, but they have wisely limited their field of operations. Their position is that a continuing series of revaluations of this nature is not necessary and may prove to be more misleading than useful. The problem becomes critical when a client, or user of information, is interested in selling or buying an entire business, or some share in it. Accountants argue that the man most interested — usually the one who stands to gain or lose — may use his own judgments and apply his own effective investment or discount rates. Purchase and sale of stocks (by investors) imply specialized valuations of entire businesses, and it seems that reporting the accountants' views on such valuation matters might be an important service of the profession. The accountant may decline, with reasonable grace, on the basis that his competence to appraise future tariff trends, rumors of war, demand conditions, and a multitude of other variables, hardly supports a professional opinion. What then is the accountants' role in the valuation of a firm? Are his reports of any use to those who make these decisions? Is his service advisory? If so, in what directions may his advice prove to be beneficial? It is the purpose of this essay to set forth tentative generalizations that may serve as provisional answers to these questions.

Other than carefully prepared income and balance sheets, the chief contribution that an accountant makes toward the valuation of a firm is mainly advisory. He helps with the arithmetic, to be sure, but he should be in a position to direct attention to pertinent factors that might otherwise be overlooked, to collect rates of earnings for similar firms and alternative investments, and to appraise the sources of past earning power. In a few instances accountants are asked to arrive at an 'equitable' valuation to be used as a basis for settlement among clients. In these cases one may supply his own estimates of future conditions and select an appropriate discount rate. It is highly doubtful whether these estimates are a part of accounting in any sense of the word, and the man who makes them is undoubtedly acting as an individual and not as a professional accountant.

It is obvious that goodwill may be defined in numerous ways. Perhaps the definition that has the simplest operational content explicates goodwill as the difference between the amount paid for a business and the sum of the assets (exclusive of goodwill) at current values. This definition does not need any accompanying assumptions about excess earning power or super profits. The reasons why the purchase price is above the current value of the assets may be numerous; for example, the difference may be due to stupidity on the buyers' side or shrewdness on the part of the seller. (If stupidity is evident, immediate write-off as a loss is required — comments on goodwill are not relevant.) From this point

---

[3] John B. Canning, *The Economics of Accountancy* (New York: The Ronald Press Company, 1929), pp. 42-43. Canning's dependence on legal relationships is suggested in this quotation.

of view it is possible to have goodwill in a firm that makes no profit and is not expected to make any profit, for goodwill is thus partially determined by the amount paid for the business. Adoption of this measurement rule means that goodwill is not independently valued, and its value is only an indirect determinant of the purchasing price.[4]

Unfortunately most accountants do not have an unobstructed view of the future and are accordingly reduced to searching the past for uniformities that may be combined and projected to reveal the probable course of events. This combination and projection is tricky business. Some past uniformities may be expected to continue, but it is possible to expect high future profits in spite of low demonstrated past earnings. This combination highlights the fact that the valuation of a business involves expected future prospects and that the past earnings record is only one (and sometimes a relatively minor) factor useful for estimating the future. In some cases past performance reports need to be modified or even inverted to prevent them from doing more harm than good. Nevertheless, there is a certain danger in using the concept of "latent goodwill." If the expected future profits are due to the ability of the new owners, one may wonder why they find it necessary to share the capitalized value of this ability with the old owners. In other words, why should rational, profit-seeking businessmen pay the present owners for abilities that these current owners do not possess and therefore cannot possibly transfer? In fact, the prospective owners may be willing to pay a premium to prevent the demonstrated lack of ability from being transferred.

It may be contended that the new owners wish to have the existing firm as a vehicle for exercising their own abilities. But why should they be willing to pay more than the current value of the assets for this opportunity? There may be some going value in the sense that the new owners can begin to exercise their abilities at once instead of waiting until new facilities are made ready and put into operation. Thus, an aggressive young lawyer may buy an existing practice in order to begin his expansion from the existing amount of business instead of from a zero base. The maximum payment would seem to be equal to the discounted value of the higher volume of business for as long as it exists. The increased earnings are 'excess' or 'super' only in the sense that they are higher than they would otherwise have been.

It should now be clear that goodwill *need not* be defined in terms of valuation techniques that include expected future earning power. For the immediate discussion let us assume that goodwill is to be defined as a master valuation account and is associated with expected future earnings. Past earnings may be useful as a guide for estimating future performance, and past reported earnings may be even more useful if they are modified in certain directions. Why, for example, do accountants usually deduct an imputed manager's salary from past earnings? Why is depreciation often recomputed? How many past years are to be considered?

If the expected future net is not equal to a reasonable salary for the owner-manager, the business is assumed to have no goodwill even though the total value may be greater than the total current replacement value of the individual assets. The buyer is then pur-

---

[4] "Thus, the goodwill of a bankrupt concern was at one time sold for a million dollars . . . . Kester speaks of this as dormant or latent goodwill which he defines as the 'excess earning power that would exist if it were not for poor management . . . which the new management will remove.' " Henry Rand Hatfield, *Accounting: Its Principles and Problems* (New York: D. Appleton and Company, 1927), p. 122. See Roy B. Kester, *Accounting Theory and Practice*, 2nd edition, Vol. 1 (New York: The Ronald Press Company, 1925), p. 357. J. C. Bonbright also points out that many courts have observed goodwill in bankrupt concerns. See *The Valuation of Property* II (New York: McGraw-Hill Book Company, Inc., 1937), pp. 755-756.

chasing the *job*. If job opportunities are numerous at the imputed salary, the salary is an alternative (opportunity) cost, and expected earnings equal only to this opportunity cost would not support a higher valuation. In times of severe depression, however, there may be few other job opportunities, and the buyer (especially if he is over-age) may be willing to pay handsomely for an opportunity to work. The business may yield a wage and thus have considerable value in excess of the current value of the assets. In the interests of useful classification most accountants insist on separating the value of the job from the value of the business.

It must be emphasized that expectations of the future are usually relevant to valuation and are ordinarily conduct-determining. Thus, past reports, if they are to be used at all, should be modified for expected changes in any direction. Specific assets are usually valued at current market prices relevant to the buyer. Depreciation is therefore recalculated on a current-cost basis. The depreciation in past earnings reports may bear no relationship to the depreciation charge that is appropriate for the future owners who are buying the fixed assets at current valuations. Therefore past earnings are modified for this factor to provide a better springboard for appraising future earnings prospects.

How many past years' earnings should be considered? The answer seems simple indeed. The appropriate number of periods is the number that yields the best basis for predicting the future. The ill-considered criticism that accounting is always looking in the wrong direction should not be allowed to instill feelings of guilt. Information from the future is a contradiction in terms and can never be relevant to anything; our *entire* basis for prediction and expectation is derived from experience — and experience is all in the past. These obvious statements are repeated again, because of the widespread feeling that certain disciplines of the social sciences have more direct access to the secrets of the future. Certainly accountants look to the past for guidance, and so do all other individuals except charlatans and practitioners of the occult sciences.

Inasmuch as valuation requires judgments about the future, men of equally good will may differ widely in valuing an enterprise. The buyer might make a goodwill computation that is entirely different from that derived by the seller. The buyer, drawing on his own pool of experience, sees the *new* business with his own super managerial ability involved. The seller draws on a different set of experiences, looks to a different set of alternatives, applies different measurement rules and a different intelligence, and arrives at different valuations. Whose expectations shall govern? Perhaps the buyer is willing to share his own (expected!) super ability with the seller and base his price on his expectations. Instead the buyer may estimate the future income of a business with only ordinary managerial ability and value the concern on that basis.

The seller may also appraise the value of his business in terms of expected earning power with ordinary management, although it is reasonable to suppose that he will value his own superior ability and include it in the value of the concern if past reported earnings support it. At any rate, he may be expected to try to get as much as he can. Thus there is a range of valuations for bargaining and the actual price may be anywhere within the range or, if some irrationality or nonobvious objectives are assumed, even outside the limits of the range. If goodwill is then defined as the difference between the selling price of the business and the current value of net assets, the amount of goodwill recognized may reflect *neither* the buyer's nor the seller's judgment of the worth of the business. The actual amount may even have been determined irrationally, in which case acceptable criteria for subsequent accountability are difficult to establish. Before the purchase, the accountant has the important duty of calling relevant factors to his client's attention, and he may submit a bargaining range that is consistent with his client's aspirations.

Normally the accountant attempts to assign current valuations to each tangible asset *and to all intangibles except goodwill.* These attempts at imputation are made with the hope that major contributing factors to past earnings may be isolated and the terms of their expected contribution projected to the future. For example, it may be obvious that a major reason for above-average past earnings is a patent whose cost to the present owners is small and whose services may terminate in two years. It seems misleading to treat the patent as practically valueless, bury its value in a catchall account with goodwill, and amortize the hidden value as the goodwill is written off. The accountant prefers to assume that the patent is purchased at its current value and that the future expected profits should be burdened with an appropriate amount (based on expected benefits) for patent amortization. The individual write-off reduces the estimates of future profits by a capital consumption charge based on current valuations. For this reason accountants exercise special care with specific imputations.

Unfortunately it is often contended that one reason for the existence of goodwill (excess value) may be the excellent location of the firm. This contention requires a new and strange definition of goodwill that is unsatisfactory. If the location was purchased on favorable terms, the buyer should include the site at its current value. Normally sites will not be depreciated and should contribute to earnings for an indefinite period. If, on the other hand, the site is carried on a long-term lease, the lease may be extremely valuable because the landlord for some reason did not exact the full economic rent. Clearly, original prepayments of future rents may be poor criteria of value, and businessmen are often justified in paying handsomely for the transfer of a favorable leasing agreement. Accountants now are agreed that such service potentials deserve status as individual assets.

The same line of argument may be applied to buildings, franchises, secret formulas, trademarks, and perhaps dealer outlets. In each case the buyer purchased these items, and current values should be imputed and his future expected income decreased for amortization of these specific assets. It should be remembered that accountants traditionally do not treat all valuable things and relationships as assets, e.g., senility of competitors, and the total value (even if crudely estimated) of these items influences the amount of goodwill that is recorded. In rare instances it may be possible to assign the entire cost to specific assets, while at the other extreme it might be reasonable to assign no cost to inconsequential assets and to treat the entire value of the firm as goodwill.

A number of accountants include promotional and general developmental costs in the computation of goodwill. The inclusion of a number of indirectly related items in any classification tends to decrease the sharpness of the classification, and in this case the subsequent treatment of the total may not be appropriate for the individual items. It is true that developmental costs are sometimes expensed in the period of expenditure and are not carried among the assets of the firm. This custom is unfortunate, for there are usually services to be received from these expenditures, and they are valuable considerations that often add specifically to the value of the firm. It is, therefore, preferable to value developmental items separately and to include them as a separable item among the other specific assets to be carried at current values.[5]

Accountants, for some reason, have looked with suspicion on firms that carry development costs as assets, yet in some lines of business the value of such items is considerable. For example, suppose that a firm furnishes background music to restaurants, markets, etc., and spends two years developing locations. Suppose also that a competing firm would find it necessary to operate at a loss or at a small profit for a year before procuring comparable locations. As pointed out above, prospective operators should be willing to pay something for these established connections, and the developed locations may have substantial value although the existing firm is operating at a loss. Excess earning power need not be presented to establish value to the purchasing organization. It appears that this kind of value is a type that accountants seldom record as an asset, even though the value has been added (established) and must be considered when the worth of the firm is to be calculated.

The subsequent treatment of this type of asset need not be consistent with that used for goodwill. The benefits from development costs should persist as long as services from the locations, dealer outlets, etc., are forthcoming. Such benefits will normally not persist forever, and it therefore seems unreasonable to carry such costs indefinitely without amortization. The usual accounting recommendation is to take the write-off against the future earnings of the new organization as the services are rendered.

A variation of the developmental-cost problem sometimes arises when the market is large enough to support only one business organization of the particular kind. A prospective businessman has the alternatives of purchasing an existing firm, of competing with the hope of forcing the existing firm out of business, or of seeking a location elsewhere. If an attempt is made to force the established firm from the field, losses may be sustained by both for a considerable length of time. Regardless of the past earnings record of the existing firm, it may be profitable for the newcomer to pay more than the current value of tangible assets rather than suffer prolonged losses while forcing a stubborn competitor from the field. From one point of view, payments of this nature are equivalent to sharing expected future profits with the retiring owners. The asset therefore takes the form of relief from competition — a cost of procuring monopoly rights.

The possibility of abnormal profits due to successful trading on-the equity remains to be considered. Accountants have discussed the use of rate of return on total assets employed when only the stockholders' interest is purchased, but most of them have neglected the valuation problem arising from trading with capital furnished by long-term creditors.

At first sight it seems that the capitalized value of a firm should not be affected by the presence of outstanding obligations. The rates to bondholders are usually lower than the rates used for capitalizing total earnings, but the presence of prior claims tends to increase the risk for residual equity holders. As a result, the discount rate (desired yield rate) in the presence of bonded indebtedness should be higher than it would be if no bonds were involved. It seems, therefore, that the difference in discount rates should recognize the difference in risk and the stock valuations should be approximately the same whether the bonds are continued or retired — the difference in risk would be arbitraged.

The above argument in its extreme form denies the possibility of profit or loss from trading on the equity. However, to assume that bondholders are omniscient enough to require a rate of return at all times exactly in line with the risks involved is certainly not war-

---

[5] Some accountants apparently hold that such items should remain in goodwill. For example, Robert H. Nelson, "The Momentum Theory of Goodwill," *The Accounting Review*, October, 1953, pp. 491-499. Schmalenbach, the intellectual father of German accounting, takes an extreme view. " . . . the value of a business does not equal the total of the value of its individual parts. The value of a business depends upon its suitability for the manufacture or sale of useful things. If a collection of buildings, machines and stocks are needed for this, then there is a collective value. As long as they are tied up in the business they do not possess individual values . . . . Assuming that we could find out the exact cost of the asset 'organization' and would add it to the values of the other assets, we still should not know the value of the business." *Dynamic Accounting*, translated by G. W. Murphy and Kenneth S. Most (London: Gee & Company, Limited, 1959), pp. 26-27. Many of Schmalenbach's ideas can be traced to the early decades of the 20th century.

ranted. A series of long-term bonds at rates substantially lower than current rates for similar risks may be a valuable property right to the stockholders of the firm and should be considered in valuing the residual interest. In fact a case can be made for treating such favorable contracts as assets and assigning current values to them. The write-off can then be related to a definite period of benefit and not buried in a composite write-off of goodwill.

Valuation complications resulting from trading on the equity have been given special attention by Paton. He has been concerned with implicit interest on noninterest-bearing payables and has advocated deducting such implicit interest from estimated future earnings. This recommendation has merit if one assumes that the new owners will make future purchases for cash and thereby procure discounts equal to the implicit interest, or if one attempts to remove all capital costs from future earnings. Paton has also been skeptical of the long-term advantage of trading on the equity of residual owners and discussed these matters in his seminars of the mid-'30's.

> There is some evidence, incidentally, that the possibility of increasing the amount of income available to a residual interest through the issue of bonds and preferred stock is more limited than has generally been assumed, and that opportunities of this character are likely to be temporary phenomena.[6]

Amortization Considerations

Past and even current accounting theories regarding the disposition of goodwill are hopelessly inadequate and are a serious indictment of the profession. Once goodwill is established on the books, the client within broad limits may write it off immediately; carry it as an asset indefinitely; write-off any part of it; make the write-off against current earnings; or in some cases make the write-off against retained earnings. If he meets the preliminary requirements of quasi-reorganization, he may make the charge to something called "reduction surplus." The public accountant finds it difficult to insist on a definite procedure, for "substantial authoritative opinion" may be cited for each of the above procedures. He may insist that the account not be written up without additional purchases or formal appraisal, but otherwise his freedom is practically unlimited. Surely a consistent doctrine for disposing of recognized goodwill can be developed.[7]

---

[6] W. A. Paton (ed.), *Accountants' Handbook* (New York: The Ronald Press Company, 1943), p. 872. See also his *Advanced Accounting* (New York: The Macmillan Company, 1941). This topic has also received recent attention from some economists. See David Durand, *Costs of Debt and Equity Funds for Business* (New York: National Bureau of Economic Research, 1952) and "The Cost of Capital in an Imperfect Market: A Reply to Modigliani and Miller," *The American Economic Review*, June, 1959. Franco Modigliani and Merton H. Miller, "The Cost of Capital, Corporation Finance, and the Theory of Investment," *The American Economic Review*, June, 1958.

[7] *Accounting Research Bulletin* Number 43, *op. cit.*, offers a beacon with extremely low candlepower. "Lump-sum write-offs of intangibles should not be made to earned surplus immediately after acquisition, nor should intangibles be charged against capital surplus" (p. 40). The more general prescriptions are: "When it becomes reasonably evident that the term of existence of a type (b) intangible including goodwill has become limited and that it has therefore become a type (a) intangible, its cost should be amortized by systematic charges in the income statement over the estimated remaining period of usefulness. If, however, the period of amortization is relatively short so that misleading inferences might be drawn as a result of inclusion of substantial charges in the income statement, a partial write-down may be made by a charge to earned surplus, and the rest of the cost may be amortized over the remaining period of usefulness.

"When a corporation decides that a type (b) intangible may not continue to have value during the entire life of the enterprise it may amortize the cost of such intangible by systematic charges against income despite the fact that there are no present indications of limited existence or loss of value . . . . Such amortization is within the discretion of the company and is not to be regarded as obligatory. The plan of amortization should be reasonable; it should be based on all the surrounding circumstances . . ." These are operational rules of action for professional men? The guidelines deserve consideration for the world's worst!

The Gold Dust case may be reviewed to illustrate the past inadequacies of accounting procedures in this area. On August 31, 1928, the Gold Dust Corporation presented a balance sheet in which Goodwill was carried at one dollar — an accepted practice at that time — and Land, Buildings, Machinery and Equipment were also carried at one dollar. The analysis of surplus for 1926 showed "Goodwill written off $1,447,205.20" and the analysis for 1927 contained "Provision for adjustment of plant value $2,510,971.89." The annual report of the president for the fiscal year ending August 31, 1928, contained:

> In view of the available surplus and of the fact that the corporation carries its most valuable asset, viz., its goodwill at $1, and also because of the uncertain market value of industrial plants, it was concluded that it would be entirely appropriate for the corporation to carry its plants in a similar manner as its goodwill, viz., at the nominal value of $1.

Accountants, financiers, and officials of the stock exchange were horrified at such unacceptable accounting procedures, but the horrification was due to the unorthodox treatment of fixed assets and not to the slipshod method of handling goodwill.[8]

The president obviously considered the intangible factors to be more valuable than the plant, and it is disappointing that he did not follow his statement with remarks along the following lines. Obviously accountants are not concerned with economic values for balance sheet purposes or for income measurement. They permit asset reductions of millions without regard to value, and they permit these write-downs to be taken either to current revenues or to retained income. Moreover, with regard to value they are hopelessly inconsistent. They insist on ritualistic and slavish adherence to schemes for amortizing value assigned to physical properties and completely disregard these schemes if the values are attributable to intangible considerations. Perhaps they disregard values and adhere to the convention of matching expired costs with revenues recognized? If so, how is it possible to justify their treatment of goodwill on a cost and revenue basis? Certainly benefit is not used as the criterion of amortization!

There was at that time no satisfactory answer to such questions, and at present our rebuttal to such statements is only slightly improved. A few writers have advocated acceptable procedures for goodwill amortization, but the majority of writers and certain governmental agencies have failed to provide practitioners with defensible procedures or even with understanding of the problems involved.

It has been argued that goodwill (rationally determined) results from valuations in excess of values assigned to specific assets. The new owners back their valuations by payments, so that purchased goodwill is usually a legitimate cost representing expected benefits and services otherwise unassigned. It seems then that the cost of these expected services should be written off as the services are received. No other procedure meets the demands of an approach based on matching expired costs with benefits, although several problems arise in this application of the rule.

Suppose, to illustrate, that normal earnings are considered to be $100,000 and that the new owners pay $300,000 for values derived from expected above-normal profits. Suppose also that the profits for the first year before amortization are $180,000. Strict application of the benefit rule seems to indicate a goodwill write-off of $80,000. If in the second year earnings are $140,000, a goodwill write-off of $40,000 is indicated. If the firm

---

[8] Professor Paton, to whom I am indebted for the above information, classified the Gold Dust Case under the heading "Appraisals" with the subheading, "Plant Write-Down." *Michigan Business Cases*, Accounting Series B. (Ann Arbor: Bureau of Business Research, 1934), pp. 66-67.

continues to earn abnormal amounts after the goodwill has been amortized, it is usually assumed that the buyers made a good investment, or extraordinary current managerial ability is now yielding returns, or new valuable nonasset items have been developed.

There are practical objections to writing off goodwill as excess profits are received. It should be observed that the reported profits for the firm will be exactly $100,000 each year as long as net before the goodwill amortization is greater than $100,000. This monotonous reporting is distasteful to some accountants, and various substitutes have been advanced. A straight-line or compound-interest write-off may be defended if a suitable service life can be assigned to the intangible. Usually the goodwill calculation itself gives a clue to the minimum term of service expectations. In some cases the deal is consummated on the basis of a definite number of years' excess earnings. If so, the agreed number of periods may be used for amortization purposes. Other methods of valuing goodwill are often used, but in most of these instances it is possible to discover an implied life. At the worst, estimates of intangible service life should be no more crude than similar estimates for long-lived tangible assets.

To modify the illustration, assume that the firm fails to receive the expected advantages (services) during the first years after purchase. The procedure in this case depends on new judgments regarding the future. The accountant may be convinced that the buyer has made a serious mistake and that future benefits will be less than were originally expected. If so, there are certainly less expected future benefits to support goodwill as an asset, and an immediate partial or complete write-off is in order. On the other hand, the accountant may decide that the deficiency in earnings is temporary and that the expenditure is still probably justified. With this assumption, a strict interpretation of the benefit doctrine would require no charge off until the resumption of abnormal earnings. Application of straight-line or compound-interest methods would normally require systematic amortization regardless of earnings. It is unfortunate that accountants sometimes adhere closely to formulas such as straight-line when the results are clearly at variance with the flow of benefits. Certainly there is little or no reason for an extremely rigid application of such formulas when their application violates conventions that are generally considered to be more fundamental.

One further comment on amortization of goodwill may be offered. Many accountants have argued that purchased goodwill is often replaced by a similar asset arising from subsequent efforts of the new owners, and it is then contended that amortization is unnecessary as long as profits remain satisfactory. This contention is similar to that employed by defenders of the renewal (replacement) method of depreciation. Advocates of the renewal depreciation procedure maintain that there is no depreciation other than replacement costs as long as the plant is operating efficiently. The support for nonamortization of purchased goodwill is clearly based on the assumption that future expenditures for maintaining the intangible relationships will be expensed and that the original cost is not subject to write-off as long as profits are high enough to support the carrying value. Unless one is prepared to support the replacement method of depreciation he should be wary of considering purchased goodwill as a permanent asset. In general, a more acceptable approach calls for the amortization of the original expenditure over the period of expected benefit. If these valuable relationships are replaced by new ones, it may be desirable to defer all or some part of the current expenditures and make the write-off as the services (benefits) are received.[9]

Footnotes on following page

A sharp distinction should be drawn between carrying the original cost of goodwill on the books without change on the one hand and adjusting the master valuation account periodically for changes in enterprise value on the other. It now seems appropriate to ask what possible use can be made of a goodwill figure that was determined, say, 20 years ago and has remained unchanged from that date. It is true that an historical record of what someone acting rationally or irrationally once paid for goodwill is maintained, but in the hands of unsophisticated readers such an historical record may be interpreted as current value and consequently may do more harm than good. Accountants are currently not anxious to accept responsibility for valuations, but carrying original goodwill figures as assets is equivalent to implicit valuation and seems to imply that the current goodwill is at least as valuable as the carrying figure indicates.

In general, accountants have not been enthusiastic about valuing the entire business from period to period and adjusting the goodwill account for the difference between the current value of the assets and the value of the entire business.[10] The latter position may or may not be rejected, but it at least represents a positive program and has clear-cut objectives. The same cannot be said in behalf of the policy of carrying the original goodwill figure without modification.

Of course, the unamortized book value for goodwill also may not be very useful. Cost of acquired services that have not yet been received may be an acceptable explanation and is as enlightening or unenlightening as the explanation of book value elsewhere in the statements. One word of warning may be in order. Some accountants have advocated the complete and immediate write-off of goodwill and some other intangibles, because they are not ordinarily relevant for appraising short-term, debt-paying ability. It should be emphasized that an item may not be appropriate for a particular decision and yet deserve to be preserved because of its possible usefulness in other connections. A systematic write-off of such items is a necessity of good income reporting, although the results may not be useful for appraising short-term credit prospects.

Accountants feel that goodwill should not be recognized as an asset unless purchased, although unusual promotional charges often may be capitalized and amortized as the expected benefits are received. In connection with partnership rearrangements, however, accountants condone a direct violation of the purchase requirement. Suppose, to illustrate, that A and B have capital balances of $120,000 and $80,000 respectively and that profits and losses are shared equally. C, an outsider, wishes to purchase an interest in the firm

---

[9] Moonitz and Staehling hold to this view. " . . . suppose the management of a concern concedes that goodwill originally purchased is expiring; however, by dint of present-day advertising techniques, they are creating new goodwill as fast as the old is disappearing . . . . The goodwill itself should be amortized . . . in addition, current advertising outlays should be carefully scrutinized, and classified in part as an asset . . . . In this manner, the investment in 'old' goodwill is properly accounted for; so is the investment in advertising." *Accounting: An Analysis of Its Problems* (Brooklyn: The Foundation Press, Inc., 1952), p. 462. Paton and Paton admit that: " . . . the goodwill of an enterprise may be in part the result of various types of expenditures which have been absorbed in operating charges [but] . . . . the estimating of intangible value . . . can better be accomplished without reference to the costs which may have had a bearing on the creation of such value." *Asset Accounting* (New York: The Macmillan Company, 1952), pp. 495-496.

[10] W. A. Paton, ed., *Accountants' Handbook, op. cit.*, p. 843, summarizes the viewpoint of Yang (1927) as follows: "Adoption of a policy of estimating and recording intangible values from period to period would not only obscure important relationships and run counter to the essential purposes and functions of accounting, but it would tend to encourage juggling and misrepresentation and would result in balance-sheet totals, little if any more significant and stable than those which might be obtained by the continuous introduction into the statements of capitalized values as shown by the market for outstanding securities." See also J. M. Yang, *Goodwill and Other Intangibles* (New York: The Ronald Press Company, 1927).

and is admitted upon payment of $150,000 to the firm for a one-third interest in the business including one-third of future profits (and losses), if any. Two assumptions may be made. C may be foolish to pay even book value for his interest. On such evidence there is certainly no reason to recognize excess enterprise values (goodwill), although the additional consideration over book value may be regarded as a windfall to A and B.[11]

If it is reasonable to assume that C acted rationally in paying $150,000, there is evidence that the accountant has failed to report important items or that his valuations are out of line with current values. If the evidence is considered to be satisfactory, one-third of the firm is apparently worth $150,000, so that the implied valuation of the entire firm after C's entrance is $450,000. Inasmuch as total recorded assets are $350,000, it appears that values totaling $100,000 are not reported by the accountant. According to present accounting practices the accountant or his client at his option may or may not recognize these additional values.

Whether or not the additional values should be recorded depends on criteria derived from one's conception of the usefulness of balance-sheet figures in various circumstances. In the past accountants have insisted that such value increases be supported by a bona-fide purchase. However, it is obvious that an extension of the definition of 'purchased' must be made before this type of goodwill can qualify. It is possible to posit a new organization that 'purchases' the business from the old at the imputed price of $450,000, but this position is hardly adequate to justify a purchase of goodwill. It is equally difficult to understand how any of the $100,000 goodwill was paid for. The new member paid for a part of the current valuation, and this particular part of the value is in fact converted into cash. The $100,000, however, is precisely the excess valuation that was *not* turned into cash. A substantial-change-of-ownership rule appears to offer sufficient justification for revaluation without recourse to some fictitious purchase. A substantial change of ownership tends to improve the quality of the evidence by introducing important adverse self-interests into the bargaining arena.

---

[11] It is unfortunate that many textbook writers are so anxious to get to the mechanics of partner admission that they neglect the judgment involved in estimating the degree of astuteness of the new member. Valuation of an entire business on the evidence of a single transaction can be risky indeed, and the magnitude of the isolated transaction may not be an acceptable criterion. If the entire business is purchased, accountants usually assume astuteness and recognize the need for revised valuations and perhaps recognition of goodwill. If the transaction is for a few shares of stock, no revision is usually made. It should be obvious that big dealers are not always astute and that the question of revaluation should depend on more satisfactory criteria.

Essay Eleven

Comments on the Direct Costing Controversy I
(Non-Income Aspects)

One normally expects the fierce winds of controversy to reduce an intellectual field to barren wasteland in a decade or two. Such has not been the case in the area of marginal costing, and a number of articles have attracted new interest and attention to the subject.[1] Most writers seem to assume that direct costing has carried the day in the decision area of internal management and some are now attempting to establish the superiority of direct costing in the field of income determination.

Clearly this entire area of accounting is in need of serious and relatively unbiased appraisal and review. The present essay is devoted in part to this task. An attempt is made to set the direct-costing discussion in a broad framework that is as wide as the concept of cost itself. What emerges may be construed as a skeptical look at direct costing and a mildly sympathetic discussion of conventional (full-costing) methods. This paper discusses first the problem of fixed-cost assignment for managerial decisions narrowly defined. The discussion then turns to the income problem and the nature of period costs. Both questions — in fact the whole affair — reduce to finding and appraising relevant costs for objectives that are not well defined, diverse decisions whose effects are not readily matched with objectives, and behavior patterns that are not clearly outlined. Furthermore, the search is carried out against a background of general uncertainty that covers the future, the lack of knowledge about alternatives currently available and recognition of past uniformities.

Two preliminary observations may be emphasized. First, there is no inner logic or other metaphysical force that bids us accept one course of action and reject another. It should be emphasized that a decision to accept or reject a set of cost-expiration rules, such as those associated with direct costing, requires careful judgment of needs, reactions, goals, and probable consequences. Cost "obviation," for example, is a possible rule that has considerable intuitive appeal. However, there is no compulsion to accept it, and there may be serious disagreement over its scope of application. The second preliminary point emphasizes that decisions are always related to future actions but that all the information comes from the past. Clearly, accountants are justified in classifying and preserving se-

---

[1] See, for example, Charles T. Horngren and George H. Sorter, " 'Direct' Costing for External Reporting," *The Accounting Review*, January 1961, pp. 84-93. David Green, Jr., "A Moral to the Direct-Costing Controversy?" *The Journal of Business*, July, 1960, pp. 218-226. Earlier discussions include the following: R. Lee Brummet, "Direct Costing - Should It Be a Controversial Issue?" *The Accounting Review*, July, 1955, pp. 439-443. Also his *Overhead Costing* (Ann Arbor: Bureau of Business Research, University of Michigan Press, 1957). Samuel R. Hepworth, "Direct Costing - The Case Against," *The Accounting Review*, January, 1954, pp. 94-99. Oswald Nielsen, "Direct Costing - The Case 'For'," *The Accounting Review*, January, 1954, pp. 89-93. Raymond P. Marple, "Direct Costing and the Uses of Cost Data," *The Accounting Review*, July, 1955, pp. 430-438. For a somewhat idealized approach to full costing and the nature of idle-time cost see William L. Ferrara, "Idle Capacity as a Loss - Fact or Fiction," *The Accounting Review*, July, 1960, pp. 490-496.

lected events from the past so that future decisions can be improved and progress toward goals encouraged.

The final preliminary comment emphasizes that relevant costing is always relevant to some decision to be made by some person or group. Costs (sacrifices) that are changed by taking course A rather than course B are relevant to the choice between them, and meaningful accounting must relate estimated sacrifices to available choices. Why then are costs ever assigned to units, to sources of services (assets) and to periods? The answer is simple enough: Decisions are often related to units, service potentials and periods. Accountants therefore economize their effort by preparing *general-purpose* calculations clustered around these centers. Additional areas of relevancy may be appropriate for some decisions, and, if so, special cost studies with more appropriate centers may be prepared. All costing rules that use traditional assignment centers should therefore be examined occasionally to find whether the results are still relevant to decisions that need to be made.

Direct costers argue that the accounting appropriate for *many* management decisions computes product cost (sacrifice) on an incremental basis with the producing environment (initial conditions) given, available, and costless for the decision at hand except for possible value in alternate uses. It is assumed therefore that the regular output of the accounting system should reflect unit (and project) costs on an incremental basis with the increments measured from the base line of whatever facilities exist at the time the decision is faced. Incremental costs will vary widely as base conditions are changed and are subject to all sorts of critical points that tend to destroy comparability except for limited ranges and conditions. Comparability over wide ranges and under widely differing conditions may be over-stressed, but many accountants do not wish to reduce the field of costing almost entirely to special cost accumulations for special purposes. With some sort of common base and some assumptions about the uniformities of cost behavior, cost accounting, in the usual full-costing sense, smooths some past irregularities and provides a benchmark for estimating future costs for similar projects. Unless there are rules for holding facilities comparable by controlling period costs to provide a more or less stable 'establishment' from which to operate, such information is limited primarily to curiosity value, for one can never be sure initial conditions for the future will be similar. A further (and perhaps minor) consideration is that direct cost essentially *requires* some managers to give up their old pricing methods and adopt new ones. The new ones may in fact be better than the old ones, but definite superiority of marginal costing in all cases has not been established. Clearly all judgments — except extremely simple, routine ones — must weigh probable sacrifice against probable benefits. Let us now turn to the benefits and possible sacrifices from abandoning full costing.

It should be clear that each incremental cost decision starts with an assumed set of initial conditions. In some cases these initial conditions are equivalent to a fresh start and the incremental cost of the decision is in fact the total cost. More often, however, a *heritage* problem is involved so that the relevant costs for a particular decision begin with an environment that includes a carryover of facilities and abilities that may be employed. These facilities may or may not be indispensable or even useful for carrying out a particular decision. Of course the productive facilities themselves can be said to enter the incremental cost decision either directly or indirectly. If they are useful, their usefulness may tend to reduce (obviate) costs, for without the heritage additional costs would presumably be needed to implement the decision. If the carry-over facilities are not useful, relevant costs may be measured from a zero base or at least a base that neglects these particular facilities. What needs to be emphasized is that the accountant's costs, or past costs in any form, may not be an acceptable measure of the amounts by which diverse incremental decisions are affected. This is so likely to be the case that some businessmen assert that the accountant's manipulation of past costs is *always* irrelevant and should *always* be replaced by more direct and cogent estimates. The problem is *not* whether the existence or nonexistence of the heritage has any effect on subsequent incremental decisions. This may be stated as a hypothesis and may be a proper subject for situational study, but the very existence of the organization means that the initial conditions and therefore most incremental decisions are affected by the heritage problem. In fact, fixed establishment costs are always related to incremental decisions in the sense that they provide an environment which makes the incremental decision feasible and worthy of consideration. The relationship is similar to that of a question and answer — the question itself limits the subset of possible answers and puts "broad limits on conversation that is relevant." Our problem is to search for clues that may help us determine when, if ever, the influence of existing facilities may be properly measured by manipulation of past cost figures.

It should be possible to conceive of a situation in which every decision is different and begins from a different environmental base. Such a situation would have *no relevant uniformities* and would require an individualized determination of relevant costs and factors for each decision. With no uniformities there would be no reason to look for past situations that might be similar and therefore offer clues or shortcuts for future decisions. With this assumption there is little or no reason to accumulate and report costs of past decisions that are not expected to recur. Thus files of past relevant costs for nonsimilar decisions would not be worth the trouble to accumulate and might well be thrown away. A situation in which all past information is useless is, of course, a situation of utter chaos. Analogies are simply too diverse to be useful. Perhaps the relevant past information is noncost information. In this case uniformities are expected to persist, but past-cost data are of little or no help in projecting them.

It is certainly possible for all past cost information to be irrelevant. In some branches of government activity, during times of rapid scientific and technical change, practically each item and every expenditure is incremental and is important only with respect to its operational efficiency and its fund requirements. Every project is essentially different and builds on whatever facilities and knowledge happen to exist at the time. Inasmuch as such projects will probably never be undertaken again and the heritage has unknown alternative uses, there seems to be no reason to assign values to the heritage and to include such values in the cost of the new projects. It is certainly not essential to compute the cost of each project *as if* it were started from scratch with no heritage of available facilities.[2]

The arguments for nonincremental cost assignments at the managerial level must therefore rest on the assumption that there is enough pattern in the behavior of costs to make it desirable to keep historical records of past costs. Cost estimates for entirely new projects come from somewhere. Sometimes our experiences are far from clear and our analogies are far out, but direct or remote, they must be used.

There is, however, room for argument about cost allocation at several other levels. First, one may argue that the knowledge of the past need not be in accounting form before it is usable. It may be possible, for example, to use information in some intuitive and un-

---

[2] Clearly, advancement toward objectives must be considered and the progress related to budget constraints, time restrictions, etc., should be revealed. It is tempting to argue that the relevant costs within the budget framework are the sacrifices of accomplishments foregone in the projects that had to be rejected in order to pursue those we do pursue. Yet if one never expects to follow the same paths again, alternatives foregone and even past mistakes become irrelevant.

systematic manner. Second, it may be admitted that cost assignments could conceivably be of some use in estimating the future, but that certain past records need not be used in the routine output of the accounting system. It may be satisfactory, for example, to make such cost assignments and allocations only on an intermittent basis as new decisions seem to require. This position is held by typical direct costers, who wish to put the routine costing process on an incremental basis and to add full costing studies on an intermittent basis.

Clearly there is no reason for assigning costs or revenues (or anything else) unless it is thought that the nature of the activity is recurring enough to make the past figures in some way useful for making decisions that influence future action. Thus, the articles of faith for accounting are bound up with the belief that there are some decisions for which past results will prove useful. A subsequent problem is whether in particular cases the accountant's rules for assignment accomplish the objectives better or worse than possible alternatives. This evaluation requires, of course, estimates of recurring decisions, the behavioral patterns of those who make the decisions, the possibilities of educating them to alternative plans, the availability of past information and perhaps other considerations. It may be argued that accounting must be an effective servant to the established patterns, for its procedures have been determined and honed by historical selectivity — a kind of social Darwinism. Procedures that were not useful and did not pay their way were eliminated from the core of activities and the survivors were those that proved to be useful. This position has limited merit, and the burden of proof should be on those who argue that the procedure should be changed. Criticism of this position may take several forms. For example, it may be argued that businessmen are not using the *right* rules for making decisions and that a serious overhauling process is in order. A slight variation asserts that times have changed and that the old decision rules and their information bases are inadequate. It may even be argued that accountants have influenced businessmen to use rules whose merit is primarily that accountants are able to get the necessary information and to do the required work. It is true that in the past accountants have been somewhat inflexible, but to believe that they have held generations of businessmen in bondage to their calculating methods seems to be farfetched.

Let us return again to the extreme example of a government agency that renders a research service and depends entirely on government budget appropriations for funds. This situation presents the strongest case against cost allocation in the traditional sense. Each new project may be assumed to be largely independent of all projects that have gone before. In most cases the new jobs will make use of existing knowledge, research and other carry-over facilities. It is assumed here that all past costs are irrelevant (are not changed by the decision) and that each new projected program begins with what is in existence and that all plans consider only necessary incremental expenditures. The incremental cost of project A, for example, might be completely different if management were starting with the residue of knowledge and equipment that might have been available if he had in fact pursued a different past policy. Notice that we may neglect past costs, but we must consider the legacy of knowledge and other resources.

It seems evident that the wisdom for estimating future costs of projects must come from somewhere. A degree of uniformity is necessary even for incremental costing. If there is some element of uniformity, it might be useful to compute past costs from a fixed horizon that is independent of what available resources happen to be lying around. Estimates of future jobs then could consider incremental costs by using the derived figures for similar jobs and allowing for the presence of resources available from past operations. We can estimate the incremental cost, but without alternative costs for the available resources we do not know how much to allow. Normally the allowance should be the saving from having the facilities — the costs obviated — but the obviation is the entire amount of replacement cost, it is incremental to each future decision, and it must be specified for each situation.[3]

It has been argued that in the extreme case above the only relevant considerations are the funds (budget availability) and probability of attaining objectives sufficient to justify the effort. Clearly, budget availability must consider sacrifice elsewhere, and equally clearly someone must be able to assemble these estimates of sacrifice for new projects, and they should be accurate enough to keep from misallocating resources by selecting the wrong projects in terms of objectives and future costs. Resource allocation and combination and project selection from a limited budget require programming, for with a fixed overall budget, the problem is to select those products that will contribute most toward objectives. The concern of administrators is directed primarily to accomplishing objectives, to funds still available, and keeping within cost allowances may be only a minor objective. To summarize the position: It is argued that generalized or standardized "start-from-scratch" approaches may not be necessary and that the costs relevant are the incremental costs of each project in terms of the budget available. Yet even incremental costs require estimating bases, and budget constraints require selection based on such costs.

There is, however, some reason for assigning expenditures to budget appropriations so that the amounts still available may be reported. This tracing of expenditures is also cost accounting in the sense that historical costs are assigned for a definite purpose, but it is peculiar in that the difference or unexpended balance is more important than the traditional relating of sacrifice to benefits. Clearly one objective is that of control, for the accuracy of past estimates (even though they are made from the prevailing resource availability) is assumed to be important for the future and is being checked project by project with allowances for changes in specifications and other changes that require additional estimates. Thus some control may be exercised on estimators, and the entire area of aspiration levels and penalties for failure is appropriate. The control feature is exercised in another way in that the assignment of past costs along with some psychological barriers to appropriation increases may help control expenditures and keep those in charge from treating funds as free goods, e.g., affect their future behavior. (Unfortunately such controls sometimes backfire and lead to waste of funds or extremely high estimates.) It is difficult to conceive of situations so diverse that not even control has continuing interest. It may be concluded that the chief function of assigning past cost is one of trying to get some measure of reliability in future estimating and perhaps encouraging a preferable pattern of future spending.

Thus it is clear that the period involved in one decision is not the length of the decision-making act, nor the length of the physical life of the items procured — its life is measured in terms of all future decisions affected. The value of unliquidated decisions should therefore be estimated in dynamic programming terms. A past decision binds us in the future through limiting and changing later decisions that would have been feasible or different if the past decision had been otherwise. Note, for example, the original decision to go into

---

[3] The notion of measuring (defining) benefits received in terms of costs obviated or saved was advanced by Horngren, Sorter and Green. In some cases this substitution has merit and may help to tighten the loose rules for benefit measurements. Clearly the existence of *any* useful facility obviates employing substitutes. Some smoothing is also necessary for making these rules operational. The cost obviation thesis is thus a type of incremental replacement-cost substitution (often lumpy) for the usual smoothed historical cost allocation.

business and the host of future decisions that follow from it or are influenced by it. With the original going-into-business decision and numerous later decisions not to go out of business, the making of numerous future decisions becomes necessary and their pattern is to some degree set — i.e., certain constraints are imposed. The accountant may be helpful in gathering information that will make the task of assigning carry-over values easier. He attempts to do so by assigning original cost according to estimates of benefits received and expected. He smooths the original cost and tries to match the expired portion with benefits. Other rules for determining expiration and carry-over values are clearly possible.

In the previous discussion we have argued that the cost of existing facilities may be irrelevant even though the facilities themselves are highly useful and have emphasized the futility of accounting for irrelevant costs. It seems appropriate to point out that 'relevancy' is a highly debatable term in a context of changing activities. One may begin by asking when, if ever, it seems desirable to accumulate unit or project costs with the assumption that the project is starting from scratch — beginning with no inheritance. Then one may ask when, if ever, it is desirable to begin from some other *uniform* base such as that afforded by some sort of assumed flow of period or establishment costs.

In one sense the entire cost of a plant is incremental to the decision to begin business and all replacements are incremental and relevant to the decision to remain in business. Thus it is possible to argue that each plant replacement is a part of the incremental cost of all the future products to be produced over the life of the plant. If the unit is considered to be the entire output of the generation of plant, the period costs including depreciation become incremental unit costs. It must be conceded, therefore, that the unit selected often influences the relevancy of costs.

Manipulation of the unit to show that period costs become relevant to some kinds of units is not fatal to the direct-costing thesis. First, and least important, it may be argued that special calculations at appropriate times are all that are necessary and that the basis for regular routine accounting should be some other kind of unit. But what kind of production unit or time unit? What are the criteria for deciding? How do we decide, for example, that the unit basis breaks down and some stage-of-completion basis should be substituted? Clearly, for determining income there is some relation between the units on which profit is recorded and the length of the time period. But what is it? How can it be measured? And how does it affect the nonincome aspects of direct costing?

The relevancy of costs for internal management purposes *must be related to the decision* and not necessarily to the unit or to the period. In this context cost would be related to the period *only* when the decision relates in some fashion to periods. Period costs are related to periods *not* because they are somehow fundamentally or intuitively related to time intervals. They should be related to periods because some decision or set of decisions can be improved by clustering costs about periods. Which managerial decisions are improved by this type of cluster? And does the clustering need to be made in the usual output of the system or can it be done intermittently as the occasion demands?

The point to be emphasized is that it is not the unit or the period that determines relevancy. It is the decision that is the center of activity and it is decision requirements operating in a behavioral context that determine the relevancy or nonrelevancy of information. Periods and irregular segments of the time continuum do enter decisions, especially in income matters, but indiscriminate dumping of nonproduct costs into a period-cost hopper seems to be a crude application.

One may argue that decisions of certain types recur more often and that the utility of having pertinent information available for them is greater. It follows then that the information should be clustered about any center that might aid such decisions. The direct coster may feel, for example, that utility is maximized if costs of keeping long-run facilities intact and standing ready to produce may be dumped on a period basis where they do little harm (and probably little good) in order to isolate the costs that are relevant to the decision to raise or lower the short-run stream of output. This decision may be a good one, but is not the only available one. The assumption that the primary purpose of routine costing is to provide continuing information on incremental costs from an established but shifting baseline and the tendency to relegate information for alternative uses to intermittent special-purpose accumulation, seem to underlie the direct cost position. Traditional cost accountants and businessmen have long been committed to a different set of assumptions. Let us review them briefly.

The full-costing approach is based on the assumption that a cost system should include in its routine output a smoothed approximation of unit costs if management were to start from scratch. The decision problem is assumed to be helped by selecting some kind of production unit. In practice the actual units selected are considerably smaller than the output for one generation of plant, and the heritage costs that would be direct and incremental to the entire output are smoothed by being apportioned in some fashion to the smaller units that are selected. The resulting unit or project cost is then composed of the smoothed incremental costs that would be necessary from all kinds of assumed horizons. Among these horizons is the smoothed incremental cost measured from a zero level of carry-over facilities, e.g., with no heritage of facilities available. The resulting unit cost of running an extra train from Los Angeles to Chicago, for example, would not be the sum of the incremental costs of carrying the passengers if the train were already running, but it will include this total. The total, moreover, will not be equal to the total incremental cost of adding the individual cars that make up the entire train, but it will include this total. Moreover, the total cost will not include *all* the costs of providing the entire assemblage of facilities. The total cost of transporting a passenger, for example, will include (perhaps separated and explicitly stated) the incremental cost of transporting him if there were unused car and train capacity. It will include a smoothed amount of the incremental car cost. The incremental cost of adding the train will be smoothed and applied over the "normal" trainload of passengers. Finally, the incremental cost of building the entire railway system for handling thousands of trains and millions of customers will be *smoothed* and distributed to passenger cost.

We may now speculate on the relative usefulness of each approach. Is there any possible usefulness in knowing that the incremental cost of manufacturing an additional crankshaft with all factory facilities furnished and costless is $8.00 and in addition knowing that the cost of providing the environment for manufacturing it — smoothed — is an additional $7.00? Now if the decision area is clearly defined with no interdependence of decisions among projects or in time, the addition would seem to be unnecessary. A *single* element from the domain of cost would be associated with a *single* decision from the range of possible activities. Such is rarely the case.

The direct costing approach consigns the sum of the $7.00 items to period costs and views the decision involved by using a short-run incremental rule for each decision as if it is more or less independent of others. The relevancy of costs (except in the case of period costs) *is defined* in this fashion.

The full costing convention assumes that the smoothing of heritage costs over product permits significant comparisons (in some directions at least) more quickly than direct costing. Comparison of selling prices with full costs by products or by different plants may yield quicker and more direct comparisons than direct costing. In the latter case such comparisons may be made intermittently or on a period basis. Notice, however, the implied

assumption that the degree of recovery per period will normally be slower and less informative than degree of recovery per unit. The case is not entirely clear-cut.

We may speculate at length as to whether pricing policy would be more desirable for
the enterprise and for society if managers would accumulate contributions for time periods and compare the totals with period costs. A similar comparison on a unit basis may be
faster, but the periodic comparison has the advantage of giving explicit consideration to
the turnover factor. The unit comparison considers the turnover factor indirectly by
smoothing at some sort of desired level of production and by assuming that production
and deliveries are in phase.

It is extremely difficult to render a judgment as to the superiority of either method in
the area of pricing. Some businessmen may have a good intuitive grasp of their demand
elasticities and may be able to neglect the temporal relationships that may exist between
today's prices and tomorrow's demand. Other businessmen may have a preference for
price stability and wish to utilize smoothed long-run costs to aid such a policy by introducing psychological restraints to price cutting. This question has been discussed elsewhere and will not detain us here except to serve as a reminder that adverse effects of today's actions on tomorrow's prospects must be included in the relevant costs of all current
decisions. This neglect has been the undoing of numerous economists who have advocated
the equation of MC and MR for each short period of time and have unquestioningly assumed independence among periods and therefore that such behavior must be appropriate
for the long run. Dynamic programming now supports the older technique from the calculus of variations and helps to emphasize periodic interdependence and shortcomings in
the short-run rule.

A further point deserves mention. The usual common-cost problem in which there is
no freedom to vary units is related to direct costing. (We are neglecting the obvious incremental relationship when freedom to vary the joint products is available.) In the genuine
common-cost case it is difficult to identify the elements of production with individual elements of cost. The problem here as elsewhere arises — at least in part — because the costing unit is finer than the obvious effect of the incremental cost impulse. Again we are
faced with the decision of smoothing or not smoothing. Should we record only obviously
separable costs as unit costs and treat the common costs before split-off as establishment
(period) costs? Clearly we may extend the concept of period costs to cover keeping the establishment ready for service and also to include keeping a supply of product available at
the split-off point, i.e., treat the common costs as period costs. It is true that these costs
are related to the period only in the most indirect fashion, but this situation also exists for
practically all period costs. These costs are generally related more closely to the provision
of certain facilities (maintaining the establishment) than to the period of operation.

It seems appropriate to conclude with a note on the similarity of period costing to the
renewal (replacement) method of depreciation. Both treat those current expenditures necessary to keep specified facilities intact as expenses of the period. Neither is concerned
with units other than time intervals related to the general level of facilities. Piecemeal utilization of specific units of equipment or units of production (related to nontemporal
benefits) is neglected. The replacement-depreciation method is directly related to providing a stream of services, but it does not get the issue confused by trying to establish
some sort of direct attachment with periods in keeping with some vague feeling that costs
automatically attach to time intervals. Given the original facility level, the costs of replacements are necessary to preserve the base (plant establishment) and may be treated as
if they are period costs. However, the last step is not necessary, for one may defend replacement depreciation and still argue for the inclusion of such depreciation in unit cost.

Essay Twelve

The Direct Costing Controversy II
(Income Measurement)

Members of the general accounting profession were extremely slow to assimilate marginal techniques into their thinking about price and output problems. Many cost accountants (and industrial engineers) from the turn of the century had made use of differential cost techniques for special purposes but had not generalized the approach for broad output decisions. The younger-generation accountants were far better trained in the techniques of enterprise economics and have been leaders in the drive to get the incremental approach accepted more widely. The term 'direct costing,' while not a happy choice in some respects, exhibited independence from the economist's better chosen marginal costing and related the new concept to the well-entrenched, familiar and vaguely related concept of direct cost. A powerful force tending to encourage direct costing undoubtedly resulted from the shortcomings of conventional costing for income determination and budgeting. A number of discussions of the income aspects of the problem have been published recently, and this essay is devoted to a somewhat detailed (and seemingly endless) discussion of the income effects of direct costing.

As a basis for discussion it is assumed that the usual economists' definition of income is appropriate. This definition is related to certain kinds of increases in service potentials (prospects). The accountant's addition of realization criteria is omitted, and it is assumed that in the absence of direct valuation, cost should be written off as the benefits are received and the value has been given up and has passed outside the boundaries of the organization. It should be pointed out at this stage that the identification of benefits to be received is sometimes more difficult than the subsequent problem of assigning the cost to periodic revenue in some satisfactory fashion. The cost assignment rules are usually based on some concept of service rendered and expected to be rendered. Before we can apply such a rule we must be able to identify and specify the type of service rendered and to design appropriate measurement scales for its quantification.

The accountant's approach to income is centered around the concept of matching expired costs with revenues recognized. The matching must relate to a specified organization, and it must be related to some meaningful unit for comparison and prediction. Our minds seem to operate best when this unit is in terms of activity units, or time units or perhaps an organization-activity unit, an organization-time unit, or a combination of the two. Accountants follow the lead of most economists and measure income or loss from some sort of fixed base of estimated future prospects. In other words they try to devise a set of instructions for determining whether capital, in some acceptable sense, is held intact and for measuring deviations from this stable base. Naturally the quantity of capital that is actually measured may be a far cry from the idealized mental construct of discounted future prospects, and the measured deviations may be poor measures of income or loss as idealized conceptions.

The appropriate point here is that accountants adopt rules for recognizing revenues and amortizing costs that will tend to yield an income figure that approximates the economist's concept of incremental prospects. In practical affairs accountants have therefore adopted a benefit (service) criterion for amortizing costs. In its simplest form this convention sets forth evidentiary and measurement rules for recognizing new values (revenues) and requires that the values given up to procure these revenues should be measured in terms of the loss in service potential weighted by an appropriate cost factor. In practice the original cost is usually modified by a fraction whose numerator is the services given up and whose denominator is the total expected service potential. This somewhat complicated description is described on the operational level as matching costs with revenues on a benefit criterion. This procedure is intuitively appealing, for most accountants probably accept without question a rule which matches one-fourth of the cost of an item when it is evident that one-fourth of the benefits have been recognized.[1] This rule is widely accepted even in the nonphilosophical sectors of the profession, and it certainly does not conflict with the broader view adopted by the economist.

The problems surrounding the benefit doctrine arise from the difficulty in specifying and measuring benefits as well as from the need for appraising the future. For buildings we may sometimes identify and specify the benefits as shelter, observe that services are rendered (and benefits received) roughly in proportion to units of time, and relate total expected service potential to time units. This procedure looks simple, but possibilities for error arise at each step. Specifically in regard to direct costing a real difficulty arises at step one — identifying and specifying the service potential. In all cases it becomes necessary to decide what form the benefits take, when they are rendered, and when the value is added.

To set the problem in perspective it should be recalled that full costers tend to assume that the incremental benefits from fixed charges (costs) are received when the products whose production is expedited by the fixed costs are sold and contribute their bit to the stream of recognized revenue (new values recognized). Thus the period's building cost, for example, is treated as an asset (without change in carrying value) until the production of the period is sold and then is metered to expense (matched with revenue) as the sales value of the product is recognized.

Notice that the full-costing position does not depend on some mystical feeling that the costs somehow attach inherently to physical units. This dualism is totally unnecessary, and its use leads to doctrinal disputes not unlike those encountered by theologians of almost all persuasions.[2] Full-costing advocates feel that effective fixed costs should be retained as assets until the product whose production was expedited by the cost is sold. Such a stand is not required, however, for one may be a full-coster without committing himself to accept the sales event as the crucial event for recognizing new values to the firm. This position does not commit its holder to any particular stand with regard to when the benefits are actually received. One is committed, instead, to the position that the incremental value to a firm (income) is measured best by treating bundles of sacrifice as if they were made when revenues are *recognized*. Thus, full costers need not hold that costs expire or that service potential is released in some mechanical or mystical manner. Costs expire exactly when accountants say they expire, i.e., when the conditions set up in the rules

---

[1] This rule has general appeal even with a liquidating assumption as sometimes found in mining ventures. It is not necessary to assume that capital is held intact.

[2] The doctrinal disputes over dualism have often been bitter. The related and more general philosophical problem of indentity preservation through change is also involved. The doctrine that costs attach is almost completely gratuitous except in the sense that accountants select a member or a limited subset of the total environment and specify that certain costs attach to that member or subset. Such imputation may be arbitrary (capricious) but in most cases such assignments are made in pursuit of definite objectives.

for cost expiration have been met. These conditions are determined by the profession with considerations for the objectives of accounting. The question at issue between direct and full-costing advocates is to find which expiration rules best fit these objectives. To designate some independent criterion for expiration is to beg the question unless this criterion is related to acknowledged objectives. Even appeals to value are not convincing. Direct costing may result in asset values nearer to economic values, but this conclusion is not certain, and indeed such values may not be those the accountant is seeking.

Appeal to *release* of service potential may have some merit but has been improperly used by some outstanding accountants and some otherwise important committees.[3] Cost, as a mental construct, ordinarily refers to sacrifice. Defined operationally 'cost' includes a set of instructions that yield figures which should be constituently related by definitions, relations, or intervening variables to sacrifice. It is certainly true that service potential of some sort is usually acquired by the sacrifice. It is also true that for the *determination of rules for writing off costs* the decline (release?) in service expectation is often used. The processes for measuring declines in service expectations are fairly well developed, and these processes are sometimes used to determine a convention or rule for *measuring* the expiration of cost. It is also true that we define concepts operationally (relate them to the empirical world) by giving the operations necessary to discriminate and measure them. The term 'cost' usually is associated with many properties around which certain kinds of service potential *may* be clustered. Do the service possibilities need to be exclusive to the organization? Scarce? May we have costs without any service potential? For decision making a cost definition that emphasizes sacrifice seems to be preferable.

The preceding paragraphs are devoted to suggesting some limitations of the definition of cost expiration as release of service potential. This discussion does not oppose the doctrine that costs should be written off — assumed to expire — as service potential declines. The benefit doctrine does in fact imply that cost expiration should be measured in terms of service reduction. Except for extremists both direct and full costers accept this approach. The point of contention is over the selection of appropriate rules for determining service decline or release.

One objection to income measured by full-costing conventions is that fixed costs are matched with revenues — at least in part — as if they are in fact variable with revenues. If idle-capacity losses and excess utilization gains are omitted, the procedure does treat fixed costs as if they are variable with production and sales. When the traditional provisions are made for treating idle capacity as an immediate expense, the effect is to meter to profit and loss (match with revenues) an amount which tends to average out as the amount of period costs but which varies from period to period, not in proportion to output, but in response to the difference in production *and* sales of each period. (As long as sales and production are equal the change is equal to the period cost.)[4]

It has not been established just why the period costs give the proper amount to be matched with revenues, and in fact the definition and relevance of period costs are not completely established. Nevertheless, the disadvantages of the full-costing approach are clear enough. Profits on reported projects can be manipulated by merely changing the production rate and not changing the firm's prospects or values. Budgeting is slightly more difficult and requires an additional accounting for that part of the variance which is due to out-of-phase production and sales. These admitted limitations of full costing are well known and widely discussed. We are more interested here in the shortcomings, if any, of direct costing when applied to income determination.

Footnotes on following page

The literature of direct costing indicates that primary concern has been with incremental costs and that the rationale for period costs has been less well developed. Exactly what services are made available? Some direct costers may wish to abandon the benefit approach entirely and to defend their position by trying to establish some sort of cost attachment or embodiment to or in the period. Yet the concept of costs being embodied in a time period makes about as much sense as its cousin which tries to attach costs to tangible service potentials. The mind may soar on wings of analogy, but the explanatory results are meager. We may treat costs *as if* they attach in some manner to the periods, but even this analogy must be pursued with caution. We need to define or at least explicate the term attach. Clearly costs are not barnacles nor are they glued or clipped in some fashion to products, or periods, or structures, or property rights or to anything else. Thus, "costs attach to periods" is not some sort of compelling anthropomorphic argument. Instead the term is a poor attempt to explain by a picturesque analogy that a decision has been made to measure cost expiration in a specific manner. The fundamental question for direct costers is whether or not they are willing to defend the implied assumption that the services rendered by period costs are invariant to short-run changes in output.[5]

Sophisticated advocates of direct costing for income determination ordinarily do not wish to abandon the benefit (service) approach to expiring (expensing) costs. Instead they cling to the service approach by calling for a new look at the form of services received and to be received. What is the nature of the benefits from fixed costs? Why is the cost of a building capitalized and spread to periods that cannot influence the amount of the cost? Is

---

[3] Vatter seems to be the originator of the "release of service" approach: " . . . expense is simply the draining-off or the release of converted services into those channels during some period of time." *The Fund Theory of Accounting and Its Implications for Financial Reports* (Chicago: University of Chicago Press, 1947), p. 22. Robert Dixon appears to have accepted Vatter's approach. "My personal feeling is that in its ultimate [sic] meaning cost is just that — any release of value." "Cost Concepts: Special Problems and Definitions," *The Accounting Review*, January, 1948, p. 42. Notice the change from "expense" to "cost." Vatter seems also to be the originator of the term "embodied" in this connection. "Assets are economic in nature; they are embodiments of future want satisfaction in the form of service potentials . . ." *Op. cit.*, p. 17. How are services "drained off?" When? What are the recognition rules? Which measurement rules are appropriate?

[4] Economists have sometimes referred sneeringly to the accountants' "ability to convert fixed costs into variable costs at will." They forget that the fixed-variable classification, as they use it, is a poorly structured construct that is, at best, a subdivision of the relevant-nonrelevant division. If the costs are relevant to a decision or action they are influenced by the alternatives, and they in turn have an impact on the decision. Traditionally, relevancy of cost with regard to *production decisions* is often called variable cost, and costs not relevant to a particular output decision are said to be fixed. Clearly a cost may be fixed with regard to output decision A and at the same time variable with respect to decision B. Or a cost may be fixed or variable if the initial (or side) conditions are changed, e.g., all costs are variable before they are committed.

For an accountant depreciation on buildings is a smoothing of a cost that *was* relevant (variable) to a big batch of future production. Now if the decision to invest has already been made, how can the accountant argue that its cost is relevant to future periods or to individual production units? The accounting procedure may be criticized but it is not nonsense. He assumes first that the firm is a continuing one and that future replacements will therefore be necessary to generate the income required to stay in business. He assumes further that a future decision similar to the past one will need to be made — a series of irregular capital budgeting decisions. But, more important, he sees the need for a whole new series of decisions that may be improved if income is reported for shorter intervals than the normal replacement cycle. Revenue is usually recognized on a unit basis, and the accountant feels that taking capital consumption on a unit basis will provide useful income figures. He does *not* argue that this cost is relevant to (and therefore variable with) the short-run production decision.

It should be observed that assignment of capital consumption to periods makes this cost *variable* with respect to time periods. Clearly this cost is relevant to the decisions for which periodic income reports are useful and not to what should be done with *time* or time periods.

[5] It would seem that *some* direct costers might acquiesce in charging depreciation as a function of sales (units sold). Clearly they must oppose depreciation on an activity basis unless the depreciation could be avoided by not producing or unless revenues are recognized on a production basis.

the period depreciation incremental or relevant in any manner to specific periods? Does the fact that some wage contracts are related to periods mean that wage cost is incremental to the periods?

Early direct costers were probably not greatly concerned with period costs and probably looked on them as residuals after the more important task of defining product cost for incremental purposes had been settled to their satisfaction. Thus period costs become associated with (attached to) periods due primarily to their being residuals not relevant to short-run decisions. Accountants have long been addicted to a type of conservatism into which pattern the period-cost concept could clearly be fitted. But perhaps more important, there has been an existing tradition for treating only merchandise cost of sales as a product cost, considering gross profit as contribution, and treating other cost expirations as independent of sales or product sold. Moreover, this tradition of period costs was ingrained in the handling of purchasing, receiving, and stock-room costs. Some concerns treated freight-in and make-ready costs in a similar manner. Therefore, it can be seen that the extension of period costs to manufacturing was no serious break with tradition. Apparently little attempt was made to provide independent support for the period-cost notion.

Suppose we look first at the decline in value criteria and examine the form of the services rendered by period costs. First, assume *no* production or sales in the period. What then is the form of the benefits from the fixed costs of depreciation, taxes, salaries of key personnel, etc.? In this case it seems that the services of the outlays are in the form of keeping the facilities and organization together so that the firm will be in a position to take advantage of the favorable future prospects. These costs tend to increase the value of the firm and certainly are not losses. A valuation approach would not only defer the amount of the costs and match them when the ship of better prospects does come in but would probably report an increase in value due to the increasing closeness of these favorable prospects. The only legitimate argument for cost expiration in this case is to insist that there is a loss of expectations measured from some more ideal situation that in fact never was an alternative, e.g., to begin anew at the end of the sterile period.

It is interesting to note that in the above case the period-cost approach is not appropriate and the usual full costing assumption with idle capacity provisions is also highly objectionable. In this case there is little to choose between direct and so-called full costing. With 100 percent idleness the two systems would report approximately the same loss. A variation of full costing that uses no idle-time variance and takes all costs to product (*à la* Earl Saliers) is no better. If only one unit is made, all the fixed costs are added to it and expensed when the unit is sold, and if no additional units are made the effect is that of period costing. Clearly this approach is not desirable. Although one might defer all fixed costs if *no* units were made, the difference between zero and one unit becomes highly critical.

Suppose, to vary the case, that production goes on more or less at an even rate year-to-year, while for some reason sales are made only every other year on the even years. How do direct costing and full-costing methods report income in this case? Full costing could, of course, defer the fixed costs of the odd years and match them with the revenues of the even years. Clearly the firm does not decrease in value in any sense in the odd years. (In fact, its value would tend to increase.) Nevertheless, the full-costing approach yields periodic profit figures that are manifestly absurd even to those steeped in accounting doctrine. The reflection of no gain or loss on odd years and sizeable profits on even years cannot be counted a desirable reflection of changes in the future prospects of the firm — and therefore a desirable measure of income. But how does direct costing fare in this case? The pattern of income reported by direct-costing devices is even more atrocious. The period costs of the odd years would be matched with zero revenues of these years and reported losses would be the amount of period costs. The profits reported on even years would, of course, be greater than those reported by full costing by the amount of the period costs of the odd year preceding. Neither scheme works well in this case, but the direct cost approach introduces a greater whiplash that is clearly not related to the welfare of the firm and its prospects. It is only in the most extraordinary situation or with the strongest assumptions that such a reporting pattern would approximate the pattern resulting from applying valuation procedures. It is highly unlikely that such a pattern would in some miraculous fashion lead to more desirable decisions by anyone connected with the firm or with the economy.

Suppose, for another illustration, that a concern buys machines and other necessary facilities and manufactures a five-year supply of product the first year. Fixed costs are high during the initial period and negligible for the remaining periods. It is assumed that all fixed assets are exhausted in this period and that product is stored at negligible cost and sold evenly over the five-year span. Direct costing apparently would show a tremendous loss for period one and perhaps sizeable gains for the remaining four. Clearly the initial loss is not related in any sense to the decline-in-prospects (value) criterion, and the result is in fact capricious.

Full costing is clearly superior in this case and squares pretty well with the assumption that gains or losses should bear some identifiable relationship to discounted prospects — value. Presumably the firm (assuming no continuity and withdrawals) declines in value about one-fifth each year, and any measuring system that pretends to be related to prospects (value) should not deviate too far from this norm. The argument is not changed significantly when capital is maintained. Full costing tends to accomplish this objective subject to some traditional peculiarities in revenue recognition. Note, however, that thoroughgoing full costing when combined with the usual accounting conventions tends to make reported profits proportionate to revenues.[6] The value may, in effect, be added before the point of sale when the goods are produced or even when the decision to manufacture was made. Yet unless we wish to recognize dismal prospects early (before sale), the direct costing pattern of income reporting should prove to be undesirable. Even if it is obvious at an early date that a mistake was made, it does not follow that direct-costing techniques will yield the desired measure of pessimism. More direct means of estimating the extent of the misfortune would seem to be more appropriate.

The case in which direct costing looks best is one in which the fixed costs are evenly distributed over the periods, and production and sales are fairly constant. This is also the situation in which full costing looks best. In a situation where the firm manufactures to stock in some periods and reduces stock in others, direct costing will give less profits when inventories are being built up and more profits when inventories are being reduced. One usually expects wider fluctuations when more costs are treated as fixed (e.g., depreciation on a time basis rather than on an activity basis). Full costing, although it appears to match fixed costs with revenues as if the costs were variable, gives consideration to the effects of the idle capacity loss or excess capacity gain. This effect in combination with usual inventory management gives wider fluctuations over the cycle.

---

[6] This statement must be modified when costs are applied to units and sales prices change. An enthusiastic full-coster might take the position that the units lose their ability to measure cost expiration in this case. That is, the discounted prospects (value) of activity are no longer measured properly by a scale based on units of product. This is, in fact, the contention of those who wish to change inventory valuations for damaged or obsolete goods or for changes in market value.

An interesting sidelight arises from consideration of periodic under- or over-applied standard overhead in the financial statements. These items in a smoothly operating standard cost system are entirely fixed costs that have not been taken to inventories (production) due to the period rules for recognizing some costs (e.g., depreciation on a time basis) and due to the proportional basis used to move these costs to product. It seems that a consistent direct coster would insist that these capacity-variance balances always be taken directly to operations. The traditional accountant need feel no such compulsion. To the latter the preliminary assignment to periods does not mean that the benefits have been received and that the assigned cost must be treated as expired.

The decision of superiority for direct or for full costing, at least with regard to income reporting, relates to specified objectives and to some sort of ideal or 'central meaning' for income that tends to further these objectives. To the extent that such an ideal is related to value changes, we may judge the merits of the two on this basis. Accounting substitutes revenue recognition rules and cost expiration rules for value changes so that any judgment must first consider the related accounting rules. Inasmuch as the usual measuring convention for cost expiration relates to benefits (services) expired we must judge the programs in this framework. Which program then corresponds best to the immediate goal of matching the cost according to benefit and therefore with the more distant goal of showing value change and thus broadcasting changes in expected prospects? First, what is the nature of the benefits from fixed costs? Second, how can they be identified?

Fixed costs are sometimes known as establishment costs, and are therefore looked on as costs necessary to keep the concern in readiness to produce. Does it follow that these readiness costs yield their services tranquilly and evenly over time or are the services received by spurts and jerks over the trade cycles as opportunities for profit present themselves, or as the products are sold, or as the cash and receivable values are increased? If no product is made or sold during a year and such a state of inactivity has been expected, it has been suggested earlier that value is added by these costs, and the benefits are clearly identifiable in the form of putting the firm in a position to take advantage of future prospects. It does not follow, therefore, that the so-called establishment costs are necessarily period costs.

Many accountants, including the present writer, are on record as favoring depreciation of buildings and certain kinds of standby equipment only when the expected benefits are received or lost.[7] Thus a warehouse designed and constructed to be used for occasional bumper crops would be depreciated only in the periods when the benefits from the bumper crops are received. To argue that these warehouses depreciate proportionately with the passage of time is to hold that the services rendered periodically are related to some sort of *maximum* benefit expectations that were never contemplated by management and probably were in fact never available to management.

Defenders of the direct-cost approach apparently hold that establishment costs are period costs, and this identification seems in turn to imply that the services are rendered (benefits received) proportionately to the measurement scale for time. (Modification for compound interest is a possibility.) Thus one would expect direct-costers to side with ac-

---

[7] Occasional further modifications may need to be made for outright mistakes and incorrect estimates. See, for example, my "Depreciation and Income Measurement," *The Accounting Review*, January, 1944, pp. 39-47 and *Handbook of Modern Accounting Theory*, ed. Morton Backer (New York: Prentice Hall, Inc., 1955), pp. 343 ff.

countants who insist that depreciation is always measured best as a function of time.[8] Moreover, they would probably not be satisfied with a depreciation scheme based on units of sales unless there is marginal plant cost associated with added sales.

The case for direct costing as an aid to income measurement seems to rest on an assumption of smoothing. The benefits received from the fixed establishment costs are assumed to be proportional to time. Thinking might be sharpened if direct costers regarded such costs as payments for keeping the organization intact. It would then be obvious that another decision is necessary. How are the benefits from having a functioning organization measured and received? In many cases the conclusion may be that such benefits are in fact received in proportion to time. But they *may not* be so distributed. The use of period costs glosses over the implied conclusion. Moreover, the term itself is objectionable, for accountants are so accustomed to identifying the name of the cost with the form or source of the service that many may feel that the fixed costs are for the privilege of using time in some sense. It seems to be better classification to treat them as going-concern, or establishment costs and then as a separate decision decide whether the services rendered are, or are not, proportional to time.

In conclusion, the similarity of direct costing and replacement depreciation should not be carried too far. Both seem to charge the current costs of keeping the environment suitable for profitable activity as current expenses. Adoption of replacement depreciation, however, does not preclude clustering depreciation about units of production and possibly deferring some of the cost to future periods' revenues by way of inventory buildup.

---

[8] An interesting and similar problem of service identification arises in connection with fire insurance contracts. The usual approach tends to assume a "peace-of-mind" concept of service rendered and assume that this freedom from worry is proportional to time. One wonders whether accountants would hold to straightline-time allocations if the insurance policies were written to cover a specified number of fires. Similar problems of benefit identification and measurement are found throughout the amortization field. Original organization costs help create the environment and opportunity for profitable operation. Are these opportunities proportional to time or should changes in the trade cycle be introduced to suggest that profit opportunities are *not* proportional to time?

We may extend the discussion to cover bond interest and the write-off of bond discount or premium. The opportunities for employment of funds in a profitable manner may bear no relation to the valuations that are procured through straightline or compound-interest methods. In fact, it may be argued that money is not borrowed "for time" but instead is borrowed to take advantage of opportunities that would otherwise not be available and that the money cost should be so allocated. It happens that the terms of most contracts are related to time, but what about income bonds with long terms? Shall we spread the money cost proportionately to time in this case? A negative answer is indicated. We have also not faced the issue squarely in the field of dividends. Regular dividend payments do not necessarily imply equal benefits from capital funds.

Essay Thirteen

Some Aspects of Scientific Method I

The unity of all science consists alone in its method, not in its material. The man who classifies facts of any kind whatever, who sees their mutual relation and describes their sequences, is applying the scientific method and is a man of science.[1]

The objective now is to discuss the time-honored topics of scope and method. This treatment is unorthodox in that it deals entirely with problems of scientific method and the language of science with the hope that accountants will understand the intellectual tools that are available for the study of accounting. Currently, members of all civilizations have tremendous faith in the powers of science. Those who conduct scientific inquiry have status, and a yearning to be scientific is a characteristic of the 20th-century intellectual. According to Russell there is considerably stronger belief in the ability of science to move mountains (or to help underdeveloped nations) than there is confidence that faith will do the job.[2] It is the purpose here to discuss at an elementary level the empirical and logical requirements for a science and to examine briefly the place of causation, explanation, and hypothesis in the methods of science.

It is convenient to think of science as composed of a body of empirical data and devices for apprehending these data so that they become a part of experience. "Science is *a method of approach* to the entire empirical world, i.e., to the world which is susceptible of experience by man. It is furthermore an approach which does not aim at persuasion, at the finding of 'ultimate truth,' or at conversion. It is . . . a mode of analysis . . ."[3]

Thus, the scientific approach is likely to be disappointing to those who are philosophically inclined and like to have their philosophical systems comprehensive and impressive. A few scientists like Eddington and Jeans have speculated about such methaphysical systems, but their efforts have not been taken seriously by practicing scientists. The primary goal of science is extremely simple: to study experiences and to search them for relationships and correlations and thus be able to form a basis for predicting future states of the system. Perhaps the clearest and most unequivocal position is stated by Pearson.

---

[1] Karl Pearson, *The Grammar of Science* (Everyman ed.; London: J. M. Dent & Sons, Limited, 1937, 1892), p. 16. (Italics in original.) Notice also " . . . science claims for its heritage the whole domain to which the word knowledge can be legitimately applied; . . . it refuses to admit any co-heirs to its possessions, and asserts that its own slow and laborious processes of research are the sole profitable modes of cultivation . . ." *Ibid.*, p. 312.

[2] Bertrand Russell, *The Impact of Science on Society* (New York: Simon & Schuster, 1953), p. 15.

[3] William J. Goode and Paul K. Hatt, *Methods in Social Research* (New York: McGraw-Hill Book Company, Inc., 1952), p. 7. "Science itself rests upon a series of postulates, or assumptions, which are themselves fundamentally unproved and unprovable . . . . Here are some of these 'nonscientific bases of science.' *The world exists . . . . We can know the world . . . . We know the world through our senses . . . . Phenomena are related causally . . .*" *Ibid.*, p. 20. Contrast the following statement by Pearson. "Of what is beyond them [perceptions], or 'things-in-themselves,' as the metaphysicians term them, we can know but one characteristic, and this we can only describe as a capacity for producing sense-impressions . . . This is the sole scientific statement which can be made with regard to which lies beyond sense-impressions." *Op. cit.*, p. 61.

> Science in no case can demonstrate any inherent necessity in a sequence, nor prove with abso-
> lute certainty that it must be repeated. Science for the past is a description, for the future a
> belief; it is not, and has never been, an explanation, if by this word is meant that science
> shows the *necessity* of any sequence of perceptions.[4]

This lack of concern with first causes and grandiose explanations, along with the decision to remove such speculation from the realm of science, fails to satisfy those who long for absolutes. Of course, an individual remains free to speculate to his heart's content and can fashion his own explanations to set his mind at rest. The point to be emphasized is that such explanations are not a necessary part of science or scientific method. The individual may be satisfied by the knowledge that negative and positive charges tend to attract, or he may feel horribly cheated and search for a more convincing explanation. He may con-clude, for example, that a gremlin is at work to bring about the attraction, and he may stop inquiry at this stage. He may wish to find a further explanation to explain the be-havior of the gremlins. He may be satisfied that God's will is at work and rest his inquiry there, or he may look for an explanation in the field of psychology, anthropology, as-trology, etc.

Cohen argues that " . . . explanation is but a developed description"[5] when used in a scientific sense. A classic statement about the nature of explanation is that of Bridgman. " . . . the essence [*sic*] of an explanation consists in reducing a situation to elements with which we are so familiar that we accept them as a matter of course, so that our curiosity rests."[6]

It is probably not enough to say that an explanation or a proof is carried on until the investigator is satisfied and that his curiosity rests. We may want to ask what forces tend to lead to satisfaction? Are such forces from the scientific field or from the cultural envi-ronment? Apparently the "modes of behavior" accepted by scientists admit only those explanations that meet the tests of scientific methodology, but the individual scientist may stop exploring the gigantic web — the appalling regress of explanations of explanations at any point. The usual process is one of *reduction* in which explanations are carried back and checked with the scientist's delight — the facts. Many scientific constructs cannot be subjected directly to such tests, but most scientists feel that they should be defined so that they can be reduced finally to sensory experiences. Bridgman discusses the problem in some detail.

> . . . we must be prepared to accept as an ultimate for our explanations the mere statement
> of a correlation between phenomena or situations with which we are sufficiently familiar.
> . . . the explanatory sequence may be terminated in several possible ways . . . we may
> never push our experiments beyond a stage into which the elements with which we are already

---

[4] Karl Pearson, *op. cit.*, p. 99. Notice also: "It would undoubtedly be of great intellectual interest to know *why* bodies fall to the earth, but *how* they invariably fall is the practical knowledge, which now enables us to build machines and which enabled our forefathers to throw stones, and thus helped them as it helps us in the struggle for existence." *Ibid.*, p. 119.

[5] Morris R. Cohen, *Reason and Nature* (Glencoe: The Free Press Publishers, 1953), p. 14. He continues: "Actually, the search for physical causes or explanations is, thus, a hunt for appropriate major premises . . ." *Ibid.*, p. 226.

[6] P. W. Bridgman, *The Logic of Modern Physics* (New York: The Macmillan Company, 1960, 1927), p. 37. Note also: " . . . we see that an explanation is not an absolute sort of thing, but what is satisfactory for one man will not be for another" (p. 38).

familiar do not enter . . . . Or, secondly, our experiments may bring us into contact with situations novel to us, in which we can recognize no familiar elements . . . . Such a situation constitutes an explanatory crisis and explanation has to stop by definition. Or thirdly, we may try to force our explanations into a predetermined mold, by formally erecting or inventing beyond the range of present experiment ultimates more or less like elements already familiar to us, and seek to explain all present experience in terms of these chosen ultimates.[7]

Structural Elements of Science

It is sometimes held that science is based on a "theory of observables" but it should be emphasized that there is more to science than contemplating facts and sensing empirical evidence. Scientists accept a pool of observable data or a collection of sense impressions as a part of their structure, but it is by no means all of the structure.[8] There is also a theoretical side of the structure that is composed of the constructs and their constitutive relations with one another. It is convenient to think of the connections between the observable data and some of the theoretical constructs as "rules of correspondence" or as operational definitions, or as constructs with direct empirical content. In the theoretical space (realm) it is convenient to think of a series of theoretical constructs, some of which are related to empirical data through rules of correspondence and others that are related only to other constructs by means of constitutive definitions, interpretative connections, and intervening variables. Torgerson explains:

. . . in physics we may pass from one set of observable data through operational definitions into the theoretical space, travel across the theoretical space from one construct to another via constitutive connections, return to the plane of observation via other operational definitions, and finally predict the results of a different set of observations. The theory can then be *accepted* or *rejected*, depending upon the agreement between the predicted and observed data.[9]

---

[7] *Ibid.*, pp. 47, 39-40.

[8] There is some disagreement among scientists about the treatment of these sense impressions. Some, including most of the logical empiricists, seem to prefer the use of the semi-neutral term 'facts' in order to minimize the psychological overtones of the term 'sense impressions.' Facts are abstractions and interpretations and are by no means neutral with regard to psychological interpretations. Fortunately, all a scientist needs accept is that sense impressions exist. Bertrand Russell comments: " . . . if physics is an empirical science, whose statements can be confirmed or confuted by observation, then physics must be supplemented by laws connecting stimulus and sensation. Now such laws belong to psychology. Therefore what is empirically verifiable is not pure physics in isolation, but physics plus a department of psychology. Psychology, accordingly, is an essential ingredient in every part of empirical science . . . . Our perceptive apparatus . . . can to some extent be ignored by the physicist, because it can be treated as approximately constant." *Human Knowledge, Its Scope and Limits* (New York: Simon & Schuster, 1948), pp. 49, 208. New aids to perception such as improved microscopes would seem to modify his constancy hypothesis.

[9] Warren S. Torgerson, *Theory and Methods of Scaling* (New York: John Wiley & Sons, Inc., 1958), p. 7. The present discussion leans heavily on Torgerson and Carl G. Hempel, *Fundamentals of Concept Formation in Empirical Science* (Chicago: University of Chicago Press, 1952). Hempel is more poetic. "A scientific theory might therefore be likened to a complex spatial network: Its terms are represented by the knots, while the threads connecting the latter correspond, in part, to the definitions and, in part, to the fundamental and derivative hypotheses included in the theory. The whole system floats, as it were, above the plane of observation and is anchored to it by rules of interpretation . . . . These might be viewed as strings which are not part of the network but link certain points of the latter with specific places in the plane of observation. By virtue of those interpretive connections, the network can function as a scientific theory: From certain observational data, we may ascend, *via* an interpretive string, to some point in the theoretical network, thence proceed, *via* definitions and hypotheses, to other points, from which another interpretive string permits a descent to the plane of observation." (p. 36).

It should be clear that some sciences are better developed than others in the sense that all or nearly all of the constructs are either directly grounded in observational data or are indirectly so grounded through other constructs. Thus Torgerson continues:

> Constructs, to be useful in a science, must possess both systematic and empirical import. By systematic import is meant simply that the construct must be such as to lend itself to the formation of multiple connections with other constructs in the structure. By empirical import is meant that the construct must be connected, either directly or through other constructs, to the observable data. One of the important concerns in science is the search for or the invention of constructs with both empirical and systematic import.[10]

The following illustration helps explain the relations in a fully developed and a poorly developed science.

Well Developed Science   **Poorly Developed Science**

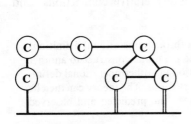   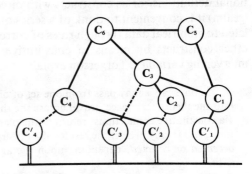

Empirical Data   Empirical Data

Legend and Explanation

Double lines = rules of correspondence between constructs and empirical data.
                   = operational definitions so that the first row constructs have operational content and are empirically meaningful.

Single lines = constitutive definitions and relations among constructs that are logical, mathematical or classificatory.

Dotted lines = relationships among constructs that are not well established and are tentative. ("Intelligence can thus remain the ability to learn, even though most experiments show that intelligence, as operationally defined is virtually un-

---

[10] Warren S. Torgerson, *op. cit.*, p. 11. Henri Poincare emphasized a similar view. "Physicists . . . are not guided in their selection [of facts] solely by utility . . . . The facts that interest them are those that may lead to the discovery of a law . . . . The isolated fact attracts the attention of all, of the layman as well as the scientist. But what the true scientist alone can see is the link that unites several facts . . . the true discoverer will not be the workman who has patiently built up some of these combinations, but the man who has brought out their relation." *Science and Method* (New York: Dover Publications, Inc., n.d.), pp. 27-28. (Translated by Francis Maitland.)

related to learning ability as independently defined . . . '' Torgerson, *op. cit.*, pp. 7-8.)[11]

Example: Suppose that C'_1 represents assets operationally defined and C_1 represents assets as defined in terms of value; C'_2 represents the construct of liabilities operationally defined with rules for identifying and measuring them and C_2 represents some construct defined constitutively in terms of negative assets or adverse interests; C'_3 represents the construct net worth as defined empirically in terms of market values of shares and C_3 represents net worth as defined in terms of the familiar equation involving assets and liabilities. It should be obvious that the constitutive definition of net worth is far removed from the usual definition made constitutively in terms of well being.

We are now in a position to examine the place of logic in the scientific structure. It is clear that observation of isolated facts is not enough to constitute what is considered to be scientific activity. The brief discussion of logic is followed by a brief discussion of the empirical aspects of science including the observation rules and the nature of objectivity. In turn this discussion is followed by a brief treatment of the place of hypothesis and theory in scientific work. The essay is concluded with a broader overview of the possible approaches to science and what makes science a going concern in the Western and recently the Eastern World.

Logic in the Structure of Science

In our present society a knowledge of mathematics confers status, and logic, as a semi-mathematical activity, enjoys prestige in the intellectual community. The inclusion of logic in such company comes primarily from its expansion from the relatively sterile classical logic. The expansion has been so dramatic that Russell and others have argued that mathematics itself is a branch of logic.[12] Clearly logic is a necessary ingredient for scientific thinking and it seems desirable to review briefly what logic can and cannot do.

Logic, in the popular current view, has no relation to empirical data until its terms are interpreted. Logic is thus defined in terms of syntax (language structure) and deals entirely with the rules that are acceptable for transforming one or more sentences into other sentences. A. P. Ushenko states the situation:

> . . . the whole field of logic and mathematics consists of tautologies derived from other tautologies by means of tautologies.[13]

In scientific method the logical apparatus, including its rules for formation and transformation, belong to the classification, definition, explication section that has been labeled as the area of constitutive definitions — the systematic area. It is possible, for example, to agree on a list of symbols, a further list of rules about the formation of such symbols, and further rules about the transformation of such symbols (inference) and to proceed to prove all kinds of theorems in this logical space. These symbols take on empirical content and relate to sensory experiences through 'interpretation' of the symbols. Interpretation is accomplished by the rules of correspondence, i.e., the operational definitions that give us instructions about identifying and perhaps measuring experiences that fit the definitions used in the constructs — the symbols.

Thus if a statement is logically true, it is true by stipulation in the sense that it can be derived according to the accepted rules of derivation (manipulation) from the sentences or

---

Footnotes on following page

propositions that have been accepted. It has been charged then that logic cannot possibly lead to any new knowledge or new truth for all conclusions have already been included in the premises. The practical function of logic then is to set forth some highly mechanical rules for rearranging the sentences and thereby simplify some of the work of reasoning. Tarski explains:

> It should be observed what an extremely elementary form — from the psychological point of view — all mathematical reasonings assume, due to the knowledge and application of the laws of logic and the rules of inference; complicated mental processes are entirely reducible to such simple activities as the attentive observation of statements previously accepted as true, the perception of structural, purely external, connections among these statements, and the execution of mechanical transformations as prescribed by the rules of inference.[14]

The economy that results from applying mechanical means is a clear-cut saving of importance to the intellectual life of a society. Whitehead, for example, states:

> It is a profoundly erroneous truism . . . that we should cultivate the habit of thinking of what we are doing . . . . Civilization advances by extending the number of important operations which we can perform without thinking about them. Operations of thought . . . are strictly limited in number . . . and must only be made at decisive moments.[15]

It should be equally clear that mechanical means of making inferences may lead to less errors. Such formal rules do not confuse the legitimate moves of logic with the emotional connotations of the interpretations, and theorems proved by the logical calculus need not be reproved for each interpretation that may be made.

---

[11] This chart and discussion are adapted from Warren S. Torgerson, *op. cit.*, p. 3. Torgerson, in turn, expanded the illustration by Henry Morgenau, *The Nature of Physical Reality, a Philosophy of Modern Physics* (New York: McGraw-Hill Book Company, Inc., 1950), p. 85.

[12] The standard treatise remains A. N. Whitehead and Bertrand Russell, *Principia Mathematica* (Cambridge: University Press, 1910-1913). A more understandable summary is available in Bertrand Russell, *Introduction to Mathematical Philosophy* (London: Allen & Unwin, 1919). Some mathematicians have resented being treated as specialists in a branch of logic and have pointed out that the constructs of infinite classes and what is quaintly called mathematical induction make the domain of mathematics much broader than that of logic. As a result, they argue, logic may well be considered to be a subdivision of mathematics. For an understandable discussion see Raymond L. Wilder, *Introduction to the Foundations of Mathematics* (New York: John Wiley & Sons, Inc., 1952).

[13] A. P. Ushenko, *The Theory of Logic* (New York: Harper & Brothers Publishers, 1936), p. 131. Rudolf Carnap states: "Such a system [symbolic logic] is not a theory (i.e. a system of assertions about objects), but a *language* (i.e. a system of signs and of rules for their use) . . . . Strictly speaking, what we construct is not a language but a schema or skeleton of a language: out of this schema we can produce at need a proper language (conceived as an instrument of communication) by interpretation of certain signs." *Introduction of Symbolic Logic and Its Applications* (New York: Dover Publications, Inc., 1958), p. 1. Perhaps the best known explanation is by C. I. Lewis: "A mathematical system is any set of strings of recognizable marks in which some of the strings are taken initially and the remainder derived from these by operations performed according to rules which are independent of any meaning assigned to the marks." *Survey of Symbolic Logic* (Berkeley: University of California Press, 1918), p. 355.

[14] Alfred Tarski, *Introduction to Logic* (New York: Oxford University Press, 1954), p. 49. Wilder stresses the same aspect of mathematics. "When we apply algebra to the solution of some concrete problem . . . the steps involved in solving the particular problem have all been provided for; little further thought need be expended . . . ." *Op. cit.*, p. 196.

[15] A. N. Whitehead, *An Introduction to Mathematics* (New York: Oxford University Press, 1948), pp. 41-42.

While it must be admitted that logic is of tremendous benefit in avoiding inferential error, perhaps the greatest benefit of logic is in the realm of psychology. Carnap points out:

> Though logic cannot lead us to anything new in the logical sense, it may well lead to something new in the psychological sense. Because of limitations on man's psychological abilities, the discovery of a sentence that is L-true [logically true] or of a relation of L-implication is often an important cognition . . . the psychological content (the totality of associations) of one of these [new] sentences may be entirely different from that of the other.[16]

However, not all scientists are so enthusiastic about the benefits of formal logic, and those that are known loosely as intuitionists often seem to feel that the slavish following of formal logic can slow down the creative process. While formal mathematics cannot keep from being "exact," it does not solve synthetic problems; instead it pushes them back on the person who is making the interpretations and trying to fit the framework to empirical data. Poincare, for example, states:

> Logistic, according to him [Couturat] lends "stilts and wings" to discovery . . . . On the contrary, I find nothing in logistic for the discoverer but shackles. Logistic forces us to say all that we commonly assume, it forces us to advance step by step; it is perhaps surer, but it is not more expeditious.[17]

Some difficulty arises in regard to the origin of the rules of formation and the rules of inference. How for example do we arrive at such rules that the expression "p implies q" shall be considered to be true in all cases except where p is true and q is false? How do we decide that the expression p v q shall mean p or q or both instead of p or q in the exclusive sense? Here we have a type of analytic truth that is truth by stipulation or convention. If the rules are followed, the results are stipulated to be true even though they may be considered to be tautological and tell us nothing but that the rules have been followed. One approach is that such rules are given from some outside or upper source. One may hold that the selection is arbitrary, and one may select any rules that strike his fancy and operate them in any fashion that is not inconsistent with the rules themselves. (It would be possible to include certain aspects of inconsistency among the rules.) The rules are conven-

---

[16] Rudolf Carnap, *Introduction to Symbolic Logic and Its Applications, op. cit.*, pp. 21-22. Elsewhere, Carnap, in the spirit of a good empiricist, writes: "The chief function of a logical calculus in its application to science is not to furnish logical theorems . . . but to guide the deduction of factual conclusions from factual premises." *Foundations of Logic and Mathematics* (Chicago: University of Chicago Press, 1939), p. 35. Reprinted in *International Encyclopedia of Unified Science* (Chicago: University of Chicago Press, 1955), p. 177. Bertrand Russell states: "By means of such substitutions we really obtain sets of special cases of our original proposition, but from a practical point of view we obtain what are virtually new propositions." *Introduction to Mathematical Philosophy, op. cit.*, p. 151. William Stanley Jevons much earlier held a similar view. "The mind never creates entirely new knowledge independent of experience, and all that the reasoning powers can do is to arrive at the full meaning of the facts which are in our possession." *Elementary Lessons in Logic* (London: Macmillan & Co., 1893), pp. 228-229. Morris Cohen holds: " . . . it is not a matter of definition but a fundamental fact of human experience that we are not actually aware of all the consequences or implications of our statements or assumptions . . ." *Op. cit.*, p. 194.

[17] Henri Poincare, *Science and Method* (New York, Dover Publications, Inc., n.d.), pp. 177-178. He continues: "Must we follow your [logical] rules blindly? Certainly, for otherwise it would be intuition alone that would enable us to distinguish between them." *Ibid.*, p. 178. Notice also the impatience with the syntactical part of scientific method. "The eternal contemplation of its own navel is not the sole object of this science [logic]. It touches nature, and one day or other it will come into contact with it. Then it will be necessary to shake off purely verbal definitions and no longer content ourselves with words." *Ibid.*, p. 183.

tional in the sense that they *could* be widely different from those that are used, and a good many philosophers discontinue the discussion at this point. Social scientists normally are not satisfied and wish to speculate on whether or not there are rules for forming new rules or for discarding old ones. If moreover one has a teleological bent or is an advocate of the sociology of knowledge, he is likely to argue such a rule for selection or rejection of other rules is itself subject to the goal-seeking activities of the society in which the procedures are found. Thus, if one holds that only those procedures and processes useful to the organism survive, he may look for empirical evidence that the surviving rules have met this test and that discarded rules have failed to meet it. Such conventions as those asserting that each set is a subset of itself or the empty set is a subclass of all classes are clearly constructed and have continued in use because they tend to accomplish desirable objectives and to make work easier.

Such empiricists as Mill, Peirce and Dewey (and perhaps such intuitionists as Brouwer) were aware that they were bringing the syntactical structure within the scope of empirical interpretation, but they felt that the determination of rules for analytic truth is essentially synthetic or empirical in content.

> Thus Dewey interprets even logical rules as empirical generalizations embodying methods of inquiry which have proved particularly successful for the purpose of inference and which have therefore been transformed by the users into principles accepted for the time being as stipulations for the carrying-on of future inquiry.[18]

Fortunately, accountants need not decide whether the rules of logic are empirically derived rules that have survived by meeting the needs of goal-seeking individuals. If it is argued that the rules of logic are beyond experience, they are treated as "analytic truths" and as metaphysical entities. In this case one may agree with my former colleague, George Sorter, that the modern separation of logic and empirical data (*à la* Carnap) is a tidy rearrangement that places most of our metaphysical assumptions in the box labeled 'logic' and tries to keep them there. Thus we arrive at such monstrosities as the "metaphysics of logical empiricism" and Sidney Hook's "metaphysics of pragmatism." "Metaphysics" in these cases is essentially another name for "conventions" or "assumptions."

The Place of Hypothesis in Science

We now turn to the question of how research is conducted in the scientific field or in any other intellectual effort. There is an important group of social scientists, including some institutional economists, who feel that *the truth* in the form of useful relationships

---

[18] Charles W. Morris, "Scientific Empiricism," *International Encyclopedia of Unified Science* (Chicago: University of Chicago Press, 1955), p. 67. Charles S. Peirce (1877) stated: "That which determines us, from given premises, to draw one inference rather than another is some habit of mind, whether it be constitutional or acquired . . . . The particular habit of mind which governs this or that inference may be formulated in a proposition whose truth depends on the validity of the inferences which the habit determines . . ." Reprinted in Milton R. Konvitz and Gail Kennedy, eds., *The American Pragmatists* (New York: Meridian Books, Inc., 1960), p. 85. L. E. J. Brouwer states: "The so-called logical principles, therefore, arose as expressions of the structural interrelationships of sentences in the language, and later were found to work when applied to the universe . . . the practical impossibility of finding examples to disagree with the laws, replaced the 'logical impossibility' of the earlier laws of language. The reliability of logical principles, in practice, rests upon the fact that a large part of the universe of experience exhibits far more order and harmony . . . in its finite organization than mankind itself." Quoted from Max Black, *The Nature of Mathematics* (Paterson, N. J.: Littlefield, Adams & Co., 1959), pp. 193-194.

will somehow be revealed to those who gather and contemplate the facts.[19] This faith in revelation is somehow incongruous with the scientific approach, and it is obvious that some rules for selection of facts must be devised. Certainly the facts, being (at least) the totality of recognized sense experiences, are far too numerous to be handled by complete enumeration. What kind of devices are possible? What determines which facts are studied and which are neglected? Who in a society shall do the investigating? Complete answers are not available, but discussion may prove to be useful.

Poincare has discussed this question and has pointed out that: "There is a hierarchy of facts. Some are without any positive bearing, and teach us nothing but themselves." Poincare also is concerned with a requirement for any fruitful research or investigation in the form of intuition, and he speaks of: " . . . this intuition of mathematical order, which enables us to guess hidden harmonies and relations . . . "[20] Again, the entire concept of intuition may not be acceptable to some scientists, and the use of the concept does not help very much with the business of conducting investigations. It is clearly true that the difference between a good scientist and a poor one is the ability to intuit relationships from seemingly unrelated facts and scanty evidence. This intuitive feeling is sometimes treated by laymen as the "imaginative approach," and, while it is undoubtedly good advice for one who wants to succeed, it is approximately in the class of such exhortations as: "Be smart"; "Approach the problem shrewdly"; and "Ever onward for progress." Scientists do get useful generalizations — this much one can see; they use techniques and procedures which can be isolated and catalogued; they may indeed have intuition.

It is generally conceded that scientific inquiry is purposive and not aimless attention to the facts. The usual technique is the hypothesis. An hypothesis states what is being looked for and tries to suggest the operations necessary to find it. Russell, for example, states: " . . . scientific method consists in inventing hypotheses which fit the data, which are as simple as is compatible with this requirement, and which make it possible to draw inferences subsequently confirmed by observation."[21] The point to be emphasized is that useful hypotheses must be limited in their scope to a particular form that can be tested directly or indirectly by empirical evidence. In some cases the scientist can also invent experiments in the sense that empirical data may be manipulated to test the hypothesis, while in other cases, e.g., astronomy, the researcher usually finds it necessary to wait more or less passively until events confirm or do not confirm his conjecture. It is probably desirable to emphasize again that the evidence does not prove or disprove the conjecture (hypothesis) in any fundamental way, but only establishes instances for its acceptance or

---

[19] Joseph J. Schwab, for example, discusses this group in some detail and in fact treats his "anti-principled" approach as one of the "principles" by which scientific inquiry can be furthered. "What Do Scientists Do?" *Behavioral Science*, January, 1960, pp. 9-11. This attitude is apparently an extension of a more general approach to the past known as 'historicism,' " . . . history cannot be cast into a rational system . . . . the special quality of history does not consist in the statements of general laws or principles, but in the grasp, so far as possible, of the infinite variety of particular historical forms immersed in the passage of time." *The Philosophy of History in Our Time*, ed. Hans Meyerhoff (Garden City, N. Y.: Doubleday Anchor Books, 1959), p. 10. This volume of comment and readings devotes an entire section to "The Heritage of Historicism," but the term is also used to imply that there is no rational system or foundation for history — almost the opposite of Popper's usage.

[20] Henri Poincare, *op. cit.*, pp. 284, 50. Notice also: "Method is precisely the selection of facts, and accordingly our first care must be to devise a method." *Ibid.*, p. 19.

[21] Bertrand Russell, *Human Knowledge, Its Scope and Limits* (New York: Simon & Schuster, 1948), p. 311. Alfred Jules Ayer states: " . . . the function of an empirical hypothesis is to provide a rule for the anticipation of experience. And this means that every empirical hypothesis must be relevant to some actual, or possible experience . . ." *Language, Truth and Logic* (New York: Dover Publications, Inc., Revised 1946, 1936), p. 41.

rejection. Acceptance and rejection rules that are in accordance with one's standards of belief must also be established.[22]

One of the uses of constitutive definitions and relationships in the theoretical realm is to suggest further relationships. Thus the existing body of developed relationships (and perhaps the scrap heap of many previously rejected ones) may help the researcher see possible implications and further relations. Logical relationships and manipulations may give new psychological insights and suggest meaningful hypotheses that can be applied to observable data and tested for relative truth or falsity. The tremendous bundle of theorems and other proofs from abstract mathematical systems may be applied in some cases to existing relationships to suggest further connections and possibilities. Definitions, classifications and constructs may be taken apart and reformulated with new properties added and some old properties sheared off by the usual processes of abstraction. (Usually testing is more convenient when only one feature is changed at a time.) The operational rules of correspondence that tie the empirical data to constructs may need reexamination and reformulation.

One must not neglect or belittle the possibility that with relatively poor tools (little more than the desire to find uniformities) a research specialist may look over the observable data (facts) and may find relationships of interest. Thurstone has developed loyal followers and jeering opponents for his intermediate scheme known as factor analysis. Hear him.

> One can invent a hypothesis regarding the processes that underlie the individual differences, and one can then set up a factorial experiment, or a more direct laboratory experiment, to test the hypothesis. If no promising hypothesis is available, one can represent the domain as adequately as possible in terms of a set of measurements or numerical indices and proceed with a factorial experiment. The analysis might reveal an underlying order which would be of great assistance in formulating the scientific concepts covering the particular domain.
>
> In the first case we start with a hypothesis that determines the nature of the measurements that enter into the factorial analysis. In the second case we start with no hypothesis, but we proceed, instead, with a set of measurements or indices that cover the domain, hoping to discover in the factorial analysis the nature of the underlying order. It is this latter application of the factorial methods that is sometimes referred to as an attempt to lift ourselves by our own boot straps, because the underlying order in a domain can be discovered without first postulating it in the form of a hypothesis.[23]

---

[22] Russell L. Ackoff argues that a comparison of two hypotheses requires that they have at least one point in common and one in disagreement. He offers the following advice:

(1) Select a measure of efficiency which is applicable to all the alternative courses of action.

(2) Assign to each alternative course of action a unique set of acceptance conditions based on the selected measure of efficiency.

(3) Reformulate the acceptance conditions as hypotheses; that is, as statements which cover all the possible outcomes of the research and which do not overlap.

(4) Make explicit the assumptions involved in the use of the selected measures of efficiency."

The Design of Social Research (Chicago: University of Chicago Press, 1953), p. 31.

[23] Louis Leon Thurstone, *Multiple-Factor Analysis: A Development and Expansion of the Vectors of Mind* (Chicago: University of Chicago Press, 1947). Quoted from the partial reprint in *Readings in Philosophy of Science*, ed. Philip P. Wiener (New York: Charles Scribner's Sons, 1953), p. 197. Morris Cohen remains skeptical: " . . . it simply is not true that the facts themselves suggest the appropriate hypothesis." *Op. cit.*, p. 80. "Begin with collecting the facts? Ay, but what facts? . . . the relevant facts of nature do not of their own accord separate themselves from all the others . . . " *Ibid.*, p. 76.

Thurstone's extreme sophistication in the general field of scientific method no doubt kept the jeers down to a moderate level. Obviously the field must be narrowed tremendously from the totality of empirical experience before the process of measurement can even be started. Thus a considerable amount of preliminary classifying and delimiting must be done. Clearly also a hypothesis of some sort has in fact been used to give rise to the belief that: "Useful generalities are available from the application of X tools to this Y pile of data." The usefulness of Thurstone's approach is that in poorly developed sciences there may often be such a sorry supply of developed relationships that it is extremely difficult to employ them effectively even as an aid to intuition. His method requires the use of only the most general past developments to delimit the field and to select scanning devices. He then advocates what might be termed a programming technique of examining the results at numerous discrete intervals to find if they can be fitted into previous generalizations. To philosophers with a penchant for a metaphysical world-view such pedestrian attempts to gain knowledge may appear to be base and scrawny. To an empiricist, on the other hand, there may be no other way. The results are impressive.

It is clear that there is no short road or guiding philosophy that will set forth the technique for being shrewd and clever about designing appropriate hypotheses.[24] Yet approaches such as that advocated by Thurstone have heuristic value and should aid investigators in the same sense that explications of prescientific concepts are useful without being definitive. An obvious source of inspiration may be found in related and perhaps neighboring fields. Techniques may be borrowed; definitions may be taken or reworked; classes and methods of subdivision may be used.[25] The pitfalls of analogous reasoning and the dangers of selecting unsuitable analogies are so well known that some investigators have tried to avoid them. Not only are the heuristic advantages of analogies highly useful, but it may be asserted that without the use of analogies there would be no thinking or reasoning, as we know it, at all.[26]

Goode and Hatt have suggested the following possible sources of hypotheses:

1. The general culture in which a science develops furnishes many of its basic hypotheses . . . .

2. Hypotheses originate in the science itself . . . .

3. Analogies are often a source of useful hypotheses . . . .

4. Hypotheses are also the consequence of personal, idiosyncratic experience.[27]

---

[24] S. S. Stevens states: "It [operationism] is not a set of rules telling how to be a bright and original scientist . . . . its method is one which is applied *after* the scientific proposition has been made: it provides criteria for determining whether what *has been* said is empirically meaningful." "Psychology and the Science of Science," *Psychological Bulletin*, 1936, quoted from the reprint in *Readings in Philosophy of Science, op. cit.*, p. 165.

[25] Joseph J. Schwab discusses this possibility. "Thus a psychologist proposes that a society or culture be treated as if it were an organism." *Op. cit.*, p. 13.

[26] We cannot enter into the minds of others to observe the thoughts and emotions which we infer from their behavior. We must therefore accept analogy — in the sense in which it goes beyond experience — as an independent premise of scientific knowledge . . . " Bertrand Russell, *Human Knowledge, op. cit.*, p. 193.

[27] *Op. Cit.*, p. 63-66. (All italic in original.) They continue with criteria for judging hypotheses. *"The hypotheses must be conceptually clear . . . Hypotheses should have empirical referents . . . . No usable hypotheses can embody moral judgments . . . . The hypotheses must be specific . . . all the operations and predictions indicated by it should be spelled out . . . . Hypotheses should be related to available techniques . . . . The hypothesis should be related to a body of theory* (pp. 68-70). (Italics in original.)

There has recently been a flurry of discussion about the heuristic methods. The following quotation from B. E. Goetz illustrates the more informal approaches.

> We investigate any phenomena about which we are curious. We measure all input and output factors which seem at all likely to be significant . . . . By rational derivation, by application of dimensional theory, by intuitive insight, or by fumbling with our tabulated data, we formulate a mathematical model that seems to represent the situation.
>
> . . . we manipulate inputs and observe outputs, and/or we study the network of interconnections until we arrive at a hypothesis — a statement as to how we believe changing inputs will affect output . . . . We can formulate such hypotheses by pure guesswork, and proceed to test our guesses for validity . . . . Since there are at least quintillion of such models . . . . it pays to give much thought to probable relations, to formulate our hypothesis on rational grounds. One help often overlooked is dimensional theory . . . . we finally come out with a hypothesis, usually in the form of an equation . . . we evaluate any parameters . . . . This yields a specific hypothesis . . . . desired objectives are fed into the model, and the model is manipulated to determine the inputs necessary to achieve the desired goals . . . . and a system of controls and feedbacks established which will signal significant deviations . . . deviations are investigated and remedial action is instituted. All this happens over and over again, overlapping, feeding back, branching out, cycling and recycling, in an ever-changing, dynamic pattern.[28]

---

[28] B. E. Goetz, "Mathematical Models of Management Significance," *Advanced Management*, February, 1957, pp. 22-23. In the same informal manner G. Polya has written *How to Solve It* (Garden City: Doubleday Anchor Books, 1957). Unfortunately only those with well-established reputations are usually willing to undertake such informal and popular discussions. Goode and Hatt have expressed it well. "It is necessary to learn the folkways of the field — perhaps to sneer coldly at the scientist who 'popularizes' his work . . . " *Op. cit.*, p. 23.

Essay Fourteen

Some Aspects of Scientific Method II

This essay is devoted to some very general considerations that relate to almost all professions. Here they are collected under the general heading of scientific method and are discussed with little or no reference to the particular field of accounting. The more common difficulties of framing definitions, for example, are treated here; but a discussion of specific accounting definitions is found in the essays devoted to semantics. Also the problem of explanation is discussed at this point in connection with causation and is discussed with different emphasis in the essay devoted to evidence and the nature of proof. Many accountants may pass over the current essay and return to other discussions that relate more directly to their professional interest. Others may find this general discussion worthwhile.

Causation in a Dynamic Science

The concept of causation often appears so obvious to students with accounting training that discussion seems unnecessary. It is precisely this deceptive simplicity that calls for concentrated attention. The uninitiated is likely to associate causation with some sort of compulsion or animism and to spend valuable effort searching for first causes, proximate causes and final causes. Russell wryly points out that scientists do not need to have gods who push the bodies through the heavens.[1] The difficulty appears quickly if one tries to determine the cause of a simple automobile accident. One may follow legal precedent and try to isolate a "proximate" cause or "strategic" action and set up some rules for deciding which individuals had the last "clear chance" to avoid the accident, but for scientific inquiry there must be something more systematic. Why did the driver of the car happen to be there at exactly that time? Why did his wife ask him to make the trip? The point here is to emphasize that the so-called *effect* is a product of its environment, and the assignment of cause to one event as crucial may be useful in some cases, but it may be misleading or dangerous in others.

Hume, a couple of centuries or more ago, observed that what is usually cause and effect is made up of sequences in time, and if the expectation is highly probable the sequential relationship may be considered to be one of causation. Some expressions by Karl Pearson, one of the leaders in the positivist approach to causation, follow.

> Scientifically, cause, as originating or enforcing a particular sequence of perceptions, is meaningless — we have no experience of anything which originates or enforces something

---

[1] Bertrand Russell, *The Impact of Science on Society* (New York: Simon & Schuster, 1953), pp. 9 ff. Notice Morris Cohen's remarks in the same vein. "When we popularly speak of a thing's causing something else, we undoubtedly tend to attribute to the thing something analogous to human compulsion . . . . Such animism is out of place in modern scientific physics." *Nature and Reason* (Glencoe: The Free Press Publishers, 1953), p. 224.

else . . . the idea of causation is extracted by conceptual processes from phenomena; it is neither a logical necessity nor an actual experience (pp. 112, 349).

That a certain sequence has occurred and recurred in the past is a matter of experience to which we give expression in the concept *causation;* that it will continue to recur in the future is a matter of belief to which we give expression in the concept *probability* (p. 99).

No phenomenon or stage in a sequence has only one cause, all antecedent stages are successive causes, and, as science has no reason to infer a first cause, the succession of causes can be carried back to the limit of existing knowledge . . . . Causation, says John Stuart Mill, is uniform antecedence . . . (p. 113).[2]

The awareness of the time sequence is highly developed in popular usage. Suppose, it has been said, that an individual sneezes immediately after hearing a rooster's crow. This correlation and expectation would be treated as a cause and effect relation after experience has verified the sequence a number of times. This kind of temporal correlation is highly spurious to some, but it may help expand existing knowledge of facts and relationships by searching for supporting evidence that makes one feel more comfortable with the correlation, i.e., increases the subjective probability of the relationship's continuing. Many statisticians and philosophers, including Morris Cohen, do not find a record of experienced sequences strong enough to support belief in continuance without independent support and insist on the adjective 'spurious.'[3]

While it is not difficult to understand the different evidence needed for belief in such cases, the term 'spurious' seems to be a little extreme. Some scientists take a somewhat different tack and insist that when the succession relationship becomes familiar, there is no longer a tendency to employ the cause-effect approach. Ernst Mach, for example, writes:

> There is no cause nor effect in nature . . . . Let a fact become familiar, and we no longer require this putting into relief of its connecting marks, our attention is no longer attracted to the new and surprising, and we cease to speak of cause and effect . . . . Acid is said to be the cause of reddening of tincture of litmus; but later we think of reddening as a property of the acid . . . . In nature there is no law of refraction, only different cases of refraction.[4]

This explanation states in effect that among the defining properties (predicates) there may be relationships that can be expressed in the language of cause and effect. Clearly not all temporal relationships appeal to us as cause-effect relationships. Normally we do not assume that the day *causes* the following night. Moreover, we tend to think of table legs *causing* the table top to stand. No succession is involved in this case. In fact, with the involvement of space and time in space-time concepts, physicists were encouraged to reexamine their concepts of sequence and of causation.

Bridgman, as a philosophical physicist, has presented a modern commentary on causation and the complications of modern science, and emphasizes that causation is a type of explanation.

---

[2] Karl Pearson, *The Grammar of Science* (Everyman ed.; London: J. M. Dent & Sons, Limited, 1937), pages as noted.

[3] ". . . we need evidence to support the belief that this correlation is permanent and not temporary . . . . It [science] founds our assurance of a real [sic] connection not merely on the fact that such sequences have been observed, but on an analysis which shows elements of identity between antecedent and consequent." Morris Cohen, *Reason and Nature, op. cit.*, pp. 92, 103.

[4] Ernst Mach, *The Science of Mechanics,* reprinted as "The Economy of Science," *Readings in Philosophy of Science,* ed. Philip P. Wiener (New York: Charles Scribner's Sons, 1953), pp. 447-448.

When a causal analysis is possible, finding the simplest events which act as the origin of independent causal trains is equivalent to finding the ultimate elements in a scheme of explanation, so that here we merge with the concept of explanation . . . . the thesis of essential connectivity . . . is perhaps the broadest we have: it is the thesis that differences between the behavior of systems do not occur isolated but are associated with other differences. It is essentially the same thesis as . . . "explanation," namely that it is possible to correlate any of the phenomena of nature with other phenomena.[5]

The narrow relationship between a single event and its successor is usually too simple for an explanation of causation or even for the simplest stimulus-response patterns that are found so often in psychological writings. One must remember that any result is a joint product in the sense that it is the product of an entire environment. Ackoff states:

The effect that an object, event, or property has on another always *depends* on its environment, and hence the object, event or property is never sufficient for the effect.[6]

A satisfactory definition can be drawn up to characterize causation as a past correlation combined with faith that the correlation will persist. Model makers in the field of economics and business have often been from engineering and other practical fields and have been impatient with fine distinctions of this sort. Whether we call the relation causation or something else, a good hypothesis (or a good model of a complicated system) must arrange the variables so that the effects of a change in the input somewhere in the system can be determined in the measured outputs. It goes without saying that the construction of experiments to test scientific hypotheses and models is usually easier when the inputs [causes] are juggled, for in most cases it is more difficult to manipulate the outputs directly. Goetz remarks:

. . . the physicist observes inputs and constructs models to predict outputs. The more rational branches of engineering reverse this process. The engineer begins with the desired outputs, and uses the physicists' models to predict the inputs necessary to achieve the stipulated outputs.[7]

---

[5] P. W. Bridgman, *The Logic of Modern Physics, op. cit.*, pp. 89, 82-83. Apparently causation here requires a higher degree of probability [one?] than is necessary for explanation. Tobias Dantzig stresses the connectivity feature. " . . . the doctrine of causality, by linking all phenomena into one continuous chain, safeguards our future against all spontaneous disturbances and protects us against the horror of chaos . . . our belief in the continuity of the universe and our faith in the causal connection between its events are but two aspects of this primitive intuition that we call *time*." *Number, The Language of Science* (Garden City: Doubleday & Company, Inc., 1956), pp. 170-171.

[6] Russell L. Ackoff, *The Design of Social Research* (Chicago: University of Chicago Press, 1953), p. 65. Bridgman concurs: "We do not have a simple event A causally connected with a simple event B, but the whole background of the system in which the events occur is included in the concept, and is a vital part of it. If the system, including its past history, were different, the nature of the relation between A and B might change entirely. The causality concept is therefore a relative one . . ." *The Logic of Modern Physics, op. cit.*, p. 83.

[7] B. E. Goetz, "Mathematical Models of Management Significance," *Advanced Management,* February, 1957, p. 21. Model building covers more ground than hypothesis building and includes some looser arrangements, but clearly the objectives are similar and it is not too great a violation of language to use hypothesis to cover models. The following comments by Goetz apply just as well to hypothesis formation. "Often it takes great ingenuity, brilliant technique, and endless patience to identify all of the significant input and output factors, to hold all but two precisely constant, and to measure the varying input and output factors precisely and concurrently . . . . We must vary or allow to vary, every important factor we seek to investigate . . . . We may get rid of others by randomizing . . . . Randomizing this variable . . . cancels it out of our results allowing us to investigate the effects of other variables." *Ibid.*, p. 23.

It should be observed that the desirability of reversing the operation is important in management and in any other behavioral situation where the goals are pretty well established and the problem is to find appropriate inputs. In the field of history reverse operations are a necessity. The problem in history is to explain a set of conditions at time t_n in terms of a series of sets of previous conditions. One set of previous conditions is usually taken as a cutoff and designated the 'initial conditions.' Most changes can be determined with tolerable accuracy, and the problem is to infer causes that account for (explain) the known or assumed changes. Accountants also account for conditions and changes in conditions!

One point should be emphasized. While the current conditions are the results or effects of the entire process of practically everything that went before, in order to get anything done at all, one must narrow the field and define a new system which is small enough to be operational and large enough to isolate and specify antecedents and consequents. In fact, the current situation may not depend on everything that has ever happened, and there is little reason to believe that *all* events are related. It is one of the virtues of science that it does not try to establish a grand scheme of relationships in the manner of the typical metaphysician. Instead, scientists attacked small areas where it was possible to organize sensory experiences into uniform patterns and immediate relationships.

Bridgman discusses the possible inability to use logical precision when initial conditions embrace the entire past history of the system, and he is cautious about the possibility of defining initial conditions apart from the future of the system. In the realm of physics with its mixed-up concepts of space and time, there is also speculation about: " . . . whether we can separate into cause and effect two phenomena which *always* accompany each other, and whether therefore the classification of phenomena into causally connected groups is an exhaustive classification."[8] In this connection, the emphasis on teleological explanation with its system of objectives and available alternatives deserves brief discussion. This type of "means-to-ends" explanation is akin to "whither" definitions and proceeds by specifying the goals to which activity is directed.[9] Explanations are then expressed in terms of the ends of certain accepted goal-directed activity. In biology, the beating of the heart may be accounted for (explained) by reference to the objective of circulating blood. The president of a concern works so hard *because* he wants to leave a stronger corporation than he found. Such explanations are "first stage," are functional in structure, and they may or may not put curiosity to rest. Certainly, they are necessary for one who uses the holistic or organic approaches to scientific enquiry.

Braithwaite states:

> In a causal explanation the explicandum is explained in terms of a cause which either precedes or is simultaneous with it: in a teleological explanation the explicandum is explained as being causally related either to a particular goal in the future or to a biological end which is as much future as present or past.[10]

---

    [8] P. W. Bridgman, *The Logic of Modern Physics, op. cit.*, p. 91. The following comments from pp. 80, 81, illustrate. "We assume in the first place an isolated system on which we can perform unlimited identical experiments, that is, the system may be started over again from a definite initial condition as often as desired. We assume further that when so started, the system always runs through exactly the same sequence of events in all its parts . . . . An alternative way of stating our fundamental hypothesis is that two or more isolated similar systems started from the same initial condition run through the same future course of events . . . . in nature, as we observe it, there is no such thing as an arbitrary change, without connection with past history . . ."
    [9] For an excellent discussion of teleological and other types of explanations, with emphasis in the former case on biological rather than organizational aspects, see R. B. Braithwaite, *Scientific Explanation* (New York: Harper & Brothers, 1960), pp. 322-341.
    [10] *Ibid.*, p. 324.

He stresses further that these ends are related to Aristotle's final causes and that intentions tend to become causes and are also effects. Clearly the ends (goals) return to the reasoning process in the guise of causes if the more traditional causal approach is used. Braithwaite emphasizes also that modern philosophers tend to take either of two paths. They may take the view that: "A teleological explanation is to be regarded as a very poor sort of explanation indeed, to be discarded as soon as the real, physico-chemical causes have been discovered."[11] Some may doubt that physico-chemical explanations can ever be sufficient to explain all teleological behavior and postulate some property for the organism such as purposiveness or drive or operant behavior patterns. This postulated quality may be observed in action so that sufficient confidence is established for it to be used as a so-called cause of behavior in this and other parts of the organism.[12]

It should be noted in passing that accountants use causation most often in the sense of goals and needs. In a similar fashion their use of "logical" is most often related to whether individual *actions* are consistent with objectives. Thus, determining whether a particular action is consistent with goals is an interpretation of the logician's use of 'logical' and is concerned with the consistency of a statement with others and with the allowed rules for manipulating statements. We must supplement the rules for determining the consistency and validity of new statements with rules for determining whether actions are consistent with ends. So far, social scientists and accountants have not developed a vigorous set of such rules.[13]

Some Problems of Definition

> . . . what is set out as a measure of net income can never be supposed to be a fact in any sense at all except that it is the figure that results when the accountant has finished applying the procedure which he adopts.[14]

The problem of definition in accounting and all other fields offers a challenge, and it offers pitfalls that may lead to serious confusion and trouble. To many investigators definitions are the result of applying the process of abstraction — shearing off properties and

---

[11] *Ibid.*, p. 327.

[12] Braithwaite insists on the use of "postulating" in this connection, but it should be noted that observation can establish our belief in the presence of such ends, and that all scientific belief is postulated in this sense. He also stresses that the attribute or property is applied to the organism as a whole, or at least a larger set of its properties than those being explained. " . . . the drive or conatus or nisus or urge — is usually posited not in the separate organ but in the organism as a whole — an urge towards self-preservation, for example . . . . writers . . . agree in postulating something in the organism which is present whenever goal-directed behaviour is taking place and which is to explain it in the ordinary causal way, and agree in supposing that this something cannot be analysed purely in physico-chemical terms." *Ibid.*, p. 326.

[13] Many attempts have recently been made to define rational behavior. These definitions usually stress consistency of actions with objectives in some sense. Garfinkel recently found rational behavior defined in many ways including: (1) empirical adequacy of means; (2) stark fact that experiences are searched for means; (3) degree of attention to the fit between observation and intentions; (4) frequency of review of past rules or procedures that have led to accomplishment; (5) analysis of alternatives and their consequences; (6) concern and rationality for timing and sequence of effects (predictability). Garfinkel distinguishes between "Cartesian" rules of procedure that neglect personal consequences and "tribal" rules that incorporate interpersonal feelings in the decision rules. The question of consistency of means and objectives as an extension of logic is not discussed directly. Harold Garfinkel, "The Rational Properties of Scientific and Common Sense Activities," *Behavioral Science*, January, 1960, pp. 72-83.

[14] John B. Canning, *The Economics of Accountancy* (New York: The Ronald Press Company, 1929), pp. 98-99.

relationships that are not relevant for the immediate purpose. Thus, the expression "truncated descriptions" has been applied.

The accountant must be familiar with the extreme operationalist definition which, for example, can define dexterity as that which is tested by dexterity tests. Bonbright at an early date brought operational definitions to the field of business valuation. "As with other economic terms . . . so with 'value,' the very meaning of the word is conditioned by the methodology of estimating its quantitative amount."[15] Before leaving the subject of definition, we would like to examine some nonoperational definitions for substance and import, and to formulate an appreciation of the usefulness of definitions and the definitional process.

It is convenient to divide knowledge into two interconnected regions, and we will follow the positivists and the operationalists in their division between syntactics and semantics. The sea of observational data which is thought of as the empirical domain is searched for uniformities, generalities, and other bases for abstraction. From this empirical evidence, *constructs* or *concepts* are formed. Constructs that are related directly to observational data are defined in terms of operational definitions. That is, they are defined by giving a package of *instructions* that cover the procedure necessary to identify the concept and to differentiate it from others. These constructs are connected to the empirical data by what are sometimes known as "rules of correspondence" or "rules of assignment." Inasmuch as "facts" are abstractions of an uncomplicated nature, many of these definitions relate to facts, i.e., they specify which data are relevant.[16] There must be no confusion of constructs with phenomena.[17]

Definitions that relate constructs to referents (to empirical data) are known as operational definitions. Clearly, however, there are other types of definitions and unfortunately they often give trouble. These definitions, when properly formulated and stated, give the formal relationships of constructs to one another. Thus, in the framework of single-entry bookkeeping, proprietary interest is defined in terms of two other constructs, i.e., assets and liabilities. These latter are tied to empirical data through rules of correspondence (definitions) that give instructions for identifying and measuring them. The kinds of definitions that tie constructs to one another were named by Margenau "constitutive" definitions, and constructs that are related to other constructs by such definitions and relationships are said to have *theoretical* or *systematic* import. Torgerson points out that a given construct may have several constitutive and several epistemic (operational) definitions. He integrates definitions to a theoretical structure and model.

---

[15] J. C. Bonbright, *The Valuation of Property* (New York: McGraw-Hill Book Company, Inc., 1937), I, p. 12.

[16] George S. Odiorne states: "The predominant philosophy of science held by most O. R. men is one which is sometimes identified as 'positivism.' As positivists, they assume any scientific system is a hierarchy in the form of a pyramid. At the base are the observed facts. The next level above them are simple laws that connect them, a few facts at a time. At the next higher level, are general laws which connect these laws. Finally, above all, are a few grand generalizations which connect these tertiary level laws." "The Basic Limitations of Operations Research in Industry," *The Journal of Industrial Engineering*, September - October, 1957, p. 267.

[17] "Because we deal directly with only the concept . . . it is obvious that we may at times confuse the *concept* with the *phenomenon* it is supposed to symbolize . . . 'reification.' " William J. Goode and Paul K. Hatt, *Methods in Social Research* (New York: McGraw-Hill Book Company, Inc., 1952), p. 41. Susanne K. Langer speaks of " . . . the correlation of symbols with concepts and concepts with things, which gives rise to a 'short-cut' relation between names and things, known as denotation . . . . A name . . . is never *true* or *false*. But if it already has a connotation, then it cannot be given an arbitrary denotation, nor vice versa." *Philosophy in a New Key* (New York: Mentor Books, 1959), pp. 74-75.

As against the constitutive definition of constructs, which must, of and by itself, be circular, a satisfactory theory contains constructs that are also defined, not in terms of other constructs in the set, but rather, directly in terms of observable data . . . . Indeed . . . a model does not become a scientific theory *until* a sufficient number of its terms possess such *operational* or *epistemic* definitions . . . . in order to be useful, *all constructs must possess constitutive meaning* . . . . They must permit themselves to take part in the formation of laws and theories. However, it is *not* necessary that *all* constructs possess a direct operational definition . . . . they must at least be connected with observable data indirectly through other constructs that do. Constructs with neither direct or indirect empirical meaning can serve no explanatory purpose at all.[18]

The chief difficulty of defining concepts in terms of operations, e.g., "Temperature is what thermometers measure," is that the process leaves the idealized concept that is to be defined without status and leaves out of account the obvious motivation of scientists and other intellectuals for trying to refine and improve their measurement rules, e.g., their definitions. From one point of view a thermometer of the ordinary type is a measure of the changes in volume of some material. Apparently we feel that this change may be used as an index or measure of something else that we may be far more interested in than the expansion of the material. It is extremely difficult to appraise operational definitions in terms of the more idealized and purposive constructs they are designed to represent. Feigl states:

Empirical laws enable us to define the same concept by different operational routes . . . . Nevertheless, Bridgman's warning to the effect that different operational routes define *different* concepts is not unjustified: The convergence of operational results is to be taken for granted only until further notice, i.e., until evidence to the contrary emerges.[19]

What is of concern here is the purposive aspect of definitions. How are they formed? In response to what needs? Which ones survive? Why are some rejected or changed or refined? To answer these questions requires some knowledge of the relationship between theory and practice. Constitutive definitions are developed from other definitions, and are suggested by them. To the extent that they can be measured only by their relationships to other constitutive constructs, they may have no specific rules of correspondence (operations). Thus it is possible to derive all sorts of relationships, develop new constructs and definitions without coming down to the empirical level through direct operations at all. These theoretical constructs may, however, be capable of being related directly to the empirical world through an independent series of operations. This possibility offers a challenge to investigators and often plays a major part in hypothesis formation and the direction of new research. Temperature may be defined constitutively in terms of other constructs, but such definitions should encourage the researcher to find direct operations that will also serve as definitions and to compare the definitions and refine them so that the most useful and accessible will survive. As an example, net worth may be defined constitutively in terms of assets and liabilities and then supplemented by additional rules of correspondence that measure assets and liabilities operationally. It is possible alternatively to

---

[18] Warren S. Torgerson, *Theory and Methods of Scaling* (New York: John Wiley & Sons, Inc., 1958), pp. 4-5.

[19] Herbert Feigl, "Operationism and Scientific Method," *Readings in Philosophical Analysis*, ed. Herbert Feigl and Wilfrid Sellars (New York: Appleton-Century-Crofts, Inc., 1949), pp. 504-505.

devise some scheme of accounts that will measure net worth by instructions that relate directly to the measurement of contributions, revenues, and expenses. These alternative operations (measurement and recognition rules) may be consistent so that the measurements turn out the same for either definition. In some cases the rules may not quite be identical so that a balancing factor or estimating error must be introduced. (For a larger *difference* consider a definition of net worth in terms of the market value of the equities.) Notice that the term 'error' implies that one of the definitions is more firmly entrenched than the other.[20]

The insights that come from relationships among constructs help guide research in the quest to find usable hypotheses and to form new definitions. In a well-developed science it is possible to move around with remarkable freedom from construct to construct, none of which can be identified operationally in a direct sense. In fact a number of such concepts may have no empirical meaning in terms of observables, and many of them apparently have no intuitive meaning whatever except as intermediaries between other constructs. This flitting around from construct to construct without being able to identify them empirically is acceptable so long as each is related to others that can be defined operationally and related to empirical data. It is generally agreed that for scientific work all constructs must be related to experience directly or indirectly.[21]

There are certain well-known and circulated aids for construction of definitions. It should be obvious that one does not work up a good supply of them to have handy in case they are needed, for a definition is ordinarily made in response to some sort of need.[22] Feigl has given an excellent summary of the requirements for a good definition for scientific work. It is, in short, a list of instructions for constructing definitions.

> Concepts which are to be of value to the factual sciences must be definable by operations which are (1) logically consistent; (2) sufficiently definite (if possible, quantitatively precise); (3) empirically rooted, i.e., by procedural and, finally, ostensive links with the observable; (4) naturally and preferably technically possible; (5) intersubjective and repeatable; (6) aimed at the creation of concepts which will function in laws or theories of greater predictiveness.[23]

---

[20] Russell L. Ackoff states: "It is not enough to decide that a concept is pertinent. We must make explicit (1) the conditions under which and (2) the operations by which the pertinence can be investigated . . . . The function of a scientific definition of a concept, then, is *to make explicit the conditions under which and the operations by which we can answer questions about that which is conceptualized.* Scientific definitions should be *directive*; they should tell us *how* to investigate . . . " *The Design of Social Research* (Chicago: University of Chicago Press, 1953), pp. 55-56.

[21] Bridgman emphasizes this point. "There are many sorts of constructs: those in which we are interested are made by us to enable us to deal with physical situations which we cannot directly experience through our senses, but with which we have contact indirectly and by inference . . . . We can never experience directly through our senses the inside of . . . a solid body . . . . A stress is . . . forever beyond the reach of direct experience, and it is therefore a construct . . . . The essential point is that our constructs fall into two classes: those to which no physical operations correspond other than those which enter the definition of the construct, and those which admit of other operations, or which could be defined in several alternative ways in terms of physically distinct operations . . . . [the atom] is evidently a construct, because no one ever directly experienced an atom, and its existence is entirely inferential." *Op. cit.*, pp. 53-54, 59-60.

[22] Henri Poincare in *Science and Method* (New York: Dover Publications, Inc., n.d.) has devoted considerable attention to definitions. "A definition is stated as a convention . . . [but not] an *arbitrary* convention . . . . But the choice of a name is not arbitrary either; we must explain what analogies have guided us . . . " p. 132.

[23] Herbert Feigl, *op. cit.*, p. 508. Russell L. Ackoff offers the following guides. "(1) Examine . . . definitions of the concept, past and present . . . . Seek the help of others . . . . Keep the chronology . . . in mind. (2) Try to get at the core of meaning . . . (3) Formulate a tentative definition based on the 'core.' (4) See if the tentative definition covers all the cases you think it should, relative to your research objectives . . . . (5) Submit the definition to as wide a critical appraisal as possible." *Op. cit.*, pp. 56-57.

Many authors have given advice about connotative and denotative definitions, and it is well to examine this advice. In mathematics, for example, the members of a set are identified by giving a list (denoting) of members *or* by giving a rule or set of rules that will permit the identification of a member and the rejection of nonmembers. Some mathematicians, however, have not understood that neither the list nor the set of rules have anything whatever to do with mathematics. Both have bearing and meaning only in the empirical area, and pure mathematicians need insist only that the classification be specifiable and by definition be capable of entering certain types of relationships.

The fundamental operation for classification, to which definition may be compared, is that of *discrimination*; Stevens, a psychologist, points out:

> . . . we find in the end that discrimination, or differential response is the fundamental operation. Discrimination is prerequisite even to the operation of denoting or "pointing to . . ."[24]

Thus, making up a set of rules of correspondence to tie the construct to empirical data very often leads to rules of measurement, but such is not always the case. In some cases the rules call for the recognition of a quality or the absence of it, and the operation is identification instead of measurement.[25]

The accounting profession owes a debt of gratitude to Vatter for bringing a serious discussion of definition to accounting literature, although his own attitude with regard to ideal definitions is not clear.[26] For an illustration to set forth the anatomy of one of the better accounting definitions, let us choose: "An asset may be defined as any consideration, material or otherwise, which is owned by a business enterprise (or in which the enterprise has an equitable interest) and which has a value to the enterprise."[27] This definition — an old one — is selected because Vatter criticized it in the following manner. " . . . it is not operational in content; it does not specify the things that must be done to establish the presence or the absence of an asset, and it does not clearly mark out what tests are to be applied in distinguishing assets from other things. The meaning of this definition depends upon a number of things that are not specified within it. What operations are involved in recognizing a 'consideration,' in establishing the existence of ownership or equitable interest, and in measuring the value to the business enterprise?"[28]

It should be noted first that the definition asserts the necessity of the conjunction of three criteria — the logical product of three sets or collections of which one may be the sum of two alternative classes. First, to be an asset the item must be a consideration. Second, it must be attached to an enterprise in the relationship of ownership or of equitable interest. Third, it must have the relationship of being valuable to the enterprise.

---

[24] S. S. Stevens, "Psychology and the Science of Science," *Psychological Bulletin*, 36 (1939), pp. 221-263. Quoted from the reprint in *Readings in Philosophy of Science*, ed. Philip P. Wiener (New York: Charles Scribner's Sons, 1953), p. 164. Ackoff emphasizes the same point. "Before the individual members of a class can be identified, we must know what properties identify them as class members. Consequently, a connotative definition is a prerequisite for constructing a denotative definition." Russell Ackoff, *op. cit.*, p. 63.

[25] Measurement requires discrimination of differences (jnds. limons) and it has been argued by Stevens and others that classification — discrimination between presence and absence — is also measurement.

[26] William J. Vatter, *The Fund Theory of Accounting and Its Implications for Financial Reports* (Chicago: University of Chicago Press, 1947).

[27] W. A. Paton, *Essentials of Accounting* (New York: The Macmillan Company, 1938), p. 23. A later version and slight revision may be found in the Paton and Paton revised edition of 1949.

[28] W. J. Vatter, *The Fund Theory of Accounting and Its Implications for Financial Reports, op. cit.*, pp. 14-15.

It should be remembered that every definition does not have to contain "within" itself a full set of instructions in order to be considered operational. The first instruction is one of discrimination and delimitation. Does the item under survey meet the tests for inclusion as "consideration" or doesn't it? (The instruction not to be concerned with whether it is material would ordinarily be unnecessary, but in the past accountants sometimes have taken peculiar attitudes toward nonmaterial assets.) This part of the definition is then constitutive in that it relates asset to consideration and assumes that the operational rules for discriminating a consideration are known, are available directly or can be found by continuing the chain of constitutive definitions. Vatter would seem to have a case in that the usual definition of "consideration" is so fuzzy and confused with other similar legal terms that the operational rules for delimiting a consideration are not drawn sharply enough. The rules of correspondence and constitutive relationships of "owned" or "being an equitable interest" are set forth with some definiteness as legal doctrines. While there is always difficulty in making borderline discriminations and as a result there is a *universal* criticism of the discriminatory process, the instruction to find either the relation of equitable interest (or ownership) is a logical requirement with reasonably well-defined instructions for determining the members of the classes involved.

The final constitutive element is also an instruction — an instruction to find the relationship of value to the enterprise — for which there are appropriate identification operations. Unfortunately, economists and accountants often do not agree on the rules that should be followed to measure value, but they are reasonably close to uniform rules for recognizing the presence of the relationship.

We must conclude, then, that Vatter's criticism is considerably more harsh than seems to be justified.[29] A little consideration will show that all accounting definitions are of this type except the comparatively rare nominal definitions which give other *names* for the constructs involved. An example of the latter type of definition with a slight restriction is the definition of debit and credit. When the field is appropriately limited, debit and credit are substitute names for left and right, and are excellent examples of nominal definitions. The terms 'journal,' 'ledger,' and 'accounts' are not nominal for they do not replace another set of appropriate symbols. In each case operations of identification of certain aspects must be performed. 'Ledger' is an excellent example of a constitutive definition in terms of the definition of 'account.' Instructions are indirect and involve the ability to determine the presence of accounts and to group them.

It is the intention to close this essay by considering some of what Schwab calls the "principles" of scientific endeavor.[30] The function of such principles is to analyze the subject matter and delimit its scope so that it can be treated by acceptable methods.

---

[29] Incidentally, Vatter's own structure in the *Fund Theory* contains some first-class definitions even if one does not agree with all the instructions. He defines 'assets' as service potentials, 'funds' as purposive arrangement of assets, 'liabilities' as restrictions on assets, 'revenues' as inflows of restriction-free assets, 'expenses' as releases of service potentials. This is a tidy definitional structure, and the student may wish to separate the constitutive and operational levels as an exercise. Strangely enough Vatter quotes from Paton and Littleton with approval. " . . . those factors acquired for production which have not reached the point in the business process where they may be treated as 'cost of sales' or 'expense' . . . . Under this usage assets or costs incurred would clearly mean charges awaiting future revenue, whereas expenses or costs applied would mean charges against present revenue." See *An Introduction to Corporate Accounting Standards* (Chicago: American Accounting Association, 1940), pp. 25-26. Vatter's approval is expressed in *op. cit.*, p. 15. One of Vatter's own less desirable definitions: "Assets . . . are embodiments of future want satisfaction . . . " (p. 17). One looks expectantly for operational instructions for disembodying satisfaction and for "releasing" service potentials.

[30] Joseph J. Schwab, "What Do Scientists Do?" *Behavioral Science*, January, 1960, pp. 1-27. The present discussion follows closely the ideas set forth by Schwab.

The first specific service of principles to the course of enquiry is to provide it with terms in which to couch its problems . . . the principle then determines what shall constitute the data required by the enquiry and outlines the procedure which will elicit the required data . . . . Finally, the principles of an enquiry restrict the form which knowledge of the subject will take by indicating how the data are to be interpreted . . . . Of principles in this sense we find five kinds: reductive, rational, holistic, anti-principled and primitive.[31]

Thus principles, to Schwab, are the results of decisions as to how the inquiry should be conducted and the area that is to be covered. Principles, in this sense, are closely related to the rules of correspondence that relate to objectives and selection of procedures — they are a part of the theory. The latter term — which appears in the title of this volume — is ill defined and probably ought not to be used in careful discourse. The term *theory*, as has been pointed out earlier, usually refers to the whole logical apparatus including the rules of correspondence and the theorems. Usually when theory is used in the singular it refers to some constitutive relationship between levels of constructs or a relationship that has been demonstrated between the observable data and the constructs, i.e., established rules of correspondence or interpretations.[32]

DR Scott would be more or less in agreement with Schwab in that he relates the term principles with those constitutive relationships that tie a given area to other areas, i.e., bound the field.

General statements relating accounting rules and procedures to underlying social principles might well be called accounting principles.[33]

Schwab explains carefully how the findings of science are ranked and appraised by scientists themselves.

The four criteria [by which judgments are made] are: interconnectivity, adequacy, feasibility, and continuity. Interconnectivity concerns the extensive domain of subject-matters subsumed by the proposed principle. Adequacy concerns its intensive domain, the degree of complexity or "completeness" . . . Feasibility concerns the ease, economy, precision, and consistency with which the data required by the principle can be collected. Continuity concerns the ease

---

[31] *Ibid.*, pp. 2-3.

[32] A good definition of theory in the usual mold is the following from Eric L. Kohler, *A Dictionary for Accountants* (New York: Prentice-Hall, Inc., 1952), p. 467. "A set of propositions, including axioms and theorems, which together with definitions and formal or informal rules of inference is oriented towards the explanation of a body of *facts* or treatment of a class of concrete or abstract operations." W. Stanley Jevons long ago pointed out that the term was an undependable one. "In reality the word [theory] is highly ambiguous, being sometimes used as equivalent to hypothesis, at other times as equivalent to general law or truth . . . . When a word is really used in an equivocal manner . . . it is not desirable to attempt to give it an accurate definition which would be imaginary and artificial." *Elementary Lessons in Logic* (London: Macmillan & Co., 1892), pp. 274-275. A. C. Littleton takes a different angle. " . . . theory, as explanations, reasons, justifications, does not contemplate producing 'a' theory, that is, a didactical arrangement of ideas which persuasively presents a series of compact propositions, beginning with a broad, distant premise . . . and emerging at a predetermined point with a more-or-less predetermined conclusion. "Choice Among Alternatives," *The Accounting Review*, July, 1956, pp. 363-364. R. G. D. Allen relates 'theories' to rules of interpretation (rules of correspondence). "Theories only arise in a particular subject matter . . . . The theories then involve clothing the premises with a certain 'real life' garb and in interpreting the logical or mathematical consequences in the same way." *Mathematical Economics* (London: Macmillan & Co. Ltd., 1956), p. xv.

[33] DR Scott, "The Basis for Accounting Principles," *The Accounting Review*, December, 1941, p. 342.

or difficulty with which the new principle can be made to contain the bodies of knowledge previously formulated . . . [34]

The general distinction and emphasis on the difference between validity and reliability serve a useful purpose, and it is often possible to classify research workers by this distinction. Again, to quote Schwab:

> To many validists, the reliableist is a man without imagination or one of timorous caution, or one who deliberately pursues unexceptionable and frequent exhibition of "research activity" while others take on the difficult tasks. To many reliableists, the validist is unsound or romantic; unappreciative of rigor and precision as the marks of science; too easily moved by the vague claims of common sense; unskilled in the use of Occam's razor. [35]

The methods of science seem extremely simple to philosophers. One of the requirements is that research workers have a tremendous respect for the facts. Whether the rules of logic and mathematics are considered to be empirically derived or metaphysical entities has not greatly influenced scientific development. Those who feel that logic and mathematics are a deeper truth and not empirically determined segregate their "metaphysics" and use it as a possible tool for unearthing new relationships and facts. It is a rule of scientific method that if the metaphysical assumptions are disproved by the data, it is the metaphysics that must be modified or discarded. It was not always thus!

We may conclude by asking what kind of men go into scientific work? What are their individual aims and status symbols? Who supports the activity?

Certain kinds of science will obviously be supported in our present society by those who are following the self-interest or profit path. Even some so-called basic research will be carried on in a society of this kind. Nevertheless, it is extremely difficult for any concern in a really competitive society where semi-monopolies are weeded out ruthlessly to be in a financial position to carry on large activities in the pure fields. Furthermore, there are areas in which the benefits cannot be constrained to one cash register even though the results are beneficial to the community. Dewey argued that science had humble beginnings from trying to expand common-sense knowledge and is still humble in trying to do the same thing in spite of isolated areas of arrogance. Social approval or disapproval is of course necessary to provide the financial support and to confer status on those who carry on the activity. Many have noted the reversal of attitude that moved from calling scientists "gadgeteers" to the high status level since the intellectual war with Russia and the Communist world began.

---

[34] Joseph J. Schwab, *op. cit.*, p. 14. Note also: "Reliability stands for the following cluster: the extent to which the terms of a research program are free of vagueness and ambiguity; the extent to which the referents of the terms are given distinct and unequivocal location and limit; the extent to which the manipulations and measurements indicated by the terms can be undertaken with precision and repeated with uniform consequences . . . . Validity stands for . . . the extent to which the terms of a research program approximate to the presumptive richness and complexity of the subject-matter; the extent to which abstraction, in its sense of simplification by removal from context, is eschewed as a species of cheat." *Ibid.*, p. 18.

[35] *Ibid.*, p. 19. Economists have often taken the position that accountants are the worst kind of reliableists. Perhaps an approximate contrapositive relationship holds.

Definition — A Technical Digression

The leading thinkers for 20 or so centuries followed Aristotle in using the genus and species approach to definition. This method consisted of specifying the genus to which the item belongs and then specifying the additional characteristics which differentiate it from others of the genus. Examples are common: wives = df female spouses; assets = df considerations having value to the entity. This kind of definition seeks to define in terms of logical product. (Overlap in the Venn sense.) Wives are those members who belong to the set of females and also belong to the set of spouses. Assets are members of the set of properties and also members of the collection consisting of things of value to the entity. As will be pointed out later, this type of definition is too narrow and has some other shortcomings for use in the scientific world, although for ordinary discourse it can usually be made to work.

Perhaps the most useful definition in mathematics is the badly named "nominal" definition that is in effect a *stipulation* that the meaning of the terms to be defined — the definiendum — must be synonymous with the meaning of a term — the definiens — whose meaning is already understood. A nominal definition of a liability for accounting purposes could be: Let it be stipulated that the term 'liability' is synonymous with the expression 'legal obligation.' Nominal definitions are "names" (they are often referred to as verbal definitions), and may be substituted for their synonymous expressions at any time. " . . . the nominal definition of a term has to satisfy only one basic requirement: it must enable us to eliminate that term, from any context in which it can grammatically occur, in favor of other expressions, whose meaning is already understood."[36]

Perhaps the instruction to avoid circularity deserves a note. From one point of view, all verbal (nominal) definitions must inevitably be circular. In logic and in rigorous mathematics a theory is set forth by expressions involving primitive (undefined) symbols and other expressions in the nature of axioms. Definitions therefore usually have some order relation. The first defined term must be expressed in terms of primitive symbols. The second definition may be formulated with the aid of the primitive symbols and the first definition, etc. Thus it makes sense to talk about preceding definitions. Clearly, to the extent that the definitions are verbal this ordering is not actually required, for all definitions could be constructed from the primitive (undefined) terms. The charge of circularity is avoided by the introduction of these undefined or primitive terms, but as is pointed out elsewhere, some intuitive knowledge of the meaning of these terms is understood or taken for granted. A further point interests us here: " . . . it is not intended that a definition shall strengthen the theory in any substantive way. The point of introducing a new symbol is to facilitate deductive investigation of the structure of the theory, but not to add to that structure . . . a new definition does not permit the proof of relationships among the old symbols which were previously unprovable; that is, it does not function as a creative axiom."[37]

It would be possible to set up all sorts of verbal definitions that make no sense whatever, but for practical purposes the formation of these definitions is not arbitrary. In addition to the requirement that they be equivalence relations (e.g., the definiendum must be synonymous with the definiens) and that they be reducible to primitive terms, they must

---

[36] Carl G. Hempel, *Fundamentals of Concept Formation in Empirical Science* (Chicago: University of Chicago Press, 1952), p. 6. Our discussion leans heavily on Hempel's work.

[37] Patrick Suppes, *Introduction to Logic* (Princeton: D. Van Nostrand Company, Inc., 1957), p. 153.

be noncontradictory and useful. Hempel emphasizes that scientific concepts are expected to function as "fruitful theories" so that a selective force is at work to reduce the number of arbitrary definitions.[38] This selective process tends to channel concept formation and to limit those who feel that the first task of a discipline is to construct a supply of definitions.

A research scientist or mathematician may therefore make wide use of verbal definitions that are set up in precise ways to meet current needs. The ordinary worker (especially economists and accountants) has more trouble, for he often redefines common terms. Here he is confronted with problems of: (1) *determinacy* of terms in the sense of their uniform usage among different users and (2) *uniformity* of terms in the sense of constancy of meaning from discourse to discourse or through time. There can be no doubt that much useless discussion at the higher levels of abstraction is due to lack of determinacy and uniformity, e.g., ambiguity of terms. There is also a danger of *ad hoc* or impromptu definitions in ordinary discourse, for these definitions may become tricks of argumentation. Many times there is little or no similarity between the meaning of supposedly identical terms, and the unwary may find themselves arguing about entirely different propositions. While such definitions are sometimes used with ulterior purposes, impromptu definitions, if clearly stated *at the beginning*, can reduce fuzziness and point up the contention. The reader should also be warned about the slanted or persuasive definition.

Before proceeding to empirical definitions let us look for possible applications of meaning analysis to highly abstract terms. Carnap has attempted to bring clarity to this generally unsatisfactory area of communication by introducing "explications."[39] In general, explication deals with broad terms like liberty, freedom, etc., and tries to make them more precise by pruning implications that are not relevant for the purpose at hand and perhaps by shifting the meaning slightly so that it will be more precise and, it is hoped, more usable. The method is of course a type of descriptive analysis. Hempel explains the process as follows:

> Explications, having the nature of proposals, cannot be qualified as being either true or false. Yet . . . they have to satisfy two major requirements: First, the explicative reinterpretation of a term . . . must permit us to reformulate, in sentences of a syntactically precise form, at least a large part of what is customarily expressed by means of the terms under consideration. Second, it should be possible to develop, in terms of the reconstructed concepts, a comprehensive, rigorous, and sound theoretical system . . . . Explication is not restricted to logical and mathematical concepts . . . . the notions of purposiveness and of adaptive behavior . . . have become the objects of systematic explicatory efforts.[40]

For purposes of research in accounting as well as in general scientific inquiry, it is ordinarily found that 'real' definitions take the form of empirical requirements, i.e., instructions. These definitions specify the necessary and sufficient conditions for identifying the phenomenon under discussion. They are therefore often stated in the form of a scientific law, e.g., as a kind of explanation. The definition given above: "x is a current asset if and only if x has value and x is converted into cash within the following financial cycle," has empirical content. In effect, the reader is told to take an x (a property in the legal and not

    [38] Carl G. Hempel, *op. cit.*, p. 18.
    [39] Rudolf Carnap, *Logical Foundations of Probability* (Chicago: University of Chicago Press, 1950), especially Chapter 1.
    [40] Carl G. Hempel, *op. cit.*, pp. 11-12.

logical sense), examine it for the presence of value and examine it again for whether it has been converted into cash during the required period (or appraise the likelihood of such a conversion). If x meets both of these empirical tests, it has met the necessary and sufficient conditions for inclusion among current assets. A real definition of this nature gives, in effect, instructions that may be followed to find out whether the item is a member of the class covered by the definition. Mathematicians usually build "constructive" proofs that are analytic in nature. The technique is essentially an instruction to "take an x" which is stipulated to be a member of the specified set and with appropriate application of rules find whether or not a theorem can be satisfied. Instead of empirical content or investigation in the ordinary sense, the testing is done by way of the accepted rules of mathematics and logic — the proof is therefore analytic and not synthetic.

A similar controversy about definitions arises over the requirement for the use of only observation terms. Most accountants and other nonphilosophers probably take a phenomenalist approach to evidence in the sense that immediate sense perceptions are assumed to be the final test of knowledge. What then is more reasonable than to insist that all definitions be expressible in primitive terms that are related directly to our perceptual apparatus — observation terms. Observation terms may in turn be defined broadly enough to include pointer or meter readings of various kinds. It is perhaps generally agreed that such definitions are highly desirable for scientific and other purposes, but some concepts are so complicated that such definitions fail to include all relationships that need to be included for productive investigation. Hempel, Carnap and others have pointed out that there are "at least two kinds of terms which raise difficulties: disposition terms, for which correctness of the thesis is at least problematic, and quantitative terms, to which it surely does not apply." Hempel suggests a conditional *definiens* with the *definiendum* having a "disposition," and appears to follow Carnap who suggested "reduction" sentences that give partial definitions.[41] Regular definitions seem to constitute the limiting case, because reduction sentences give only necessary conditions. Definitions are tightened by adding more and more reduction sentences, i.e., more requirements. A reduction approach to value, for example, is essentially the one used now by economists. The reduction statements concern scarcity relative to desire and ability at a specified time. Nothing is said about many types of value or about whether there would be value with no individuals or at different times with different subjective attitudes. This type of definition is impromptu in the better sense of the word, for most economists are honest enough to explain the narrow meaning by placing the adjective "economic" before the term.

A further objection to the strict phenomenalistic approach is that it cannot cover adequately "numerically measurable" quantities such as length. Clearly it is not possible to apply an observational vocabulary to the mathematical concepts of continuum, limit, instantaneous and other concepts necessary for scientific investigation. While an empiricist from the field of accounting would no doubt assert that the nonobservable aspects are relatively unimportant, most of us would agree with Hempel that it is precisely these constructs which permit science to take such strides as it has taken.[42]

---

[41] *Ibid.*, pp. 24-25. Hempel suggests "magnetic," "elastic," "fissionable" as examples of disposition terms. See Rudolf Carnap, "Testability and Meaning," *Philosophy of Science*, III, No. 4 (1936), pp. 419-471 and IV, No. 1 (1937), pp. 1-40.

[42] Hempel, *op. cit.*, p. 31, " . . . it is precisely these 'fictitious' concepts rather than those fully definable by observables which enable science to interpret and organize the data of direct observation by means of a coherent and comprehensive system which permits explanation and prediction. Hence, rather than exclude those fruitful concepts on the ground that they are not experientially definable, we will have to inquire what nondefinitional methods might be suited for their introduction and experiential interpretation."

Wilder, a theoretical mathematician, expresses the mathematician's attitude toward definitions as follows:

> When a mathematician gives a definition, it is intended that it will be not a mere synonym (such as "aggregation" for "collection") which the reader may happen to know the meaning of, but a criterion for identifying; a *characterization* of the thing defined . . . . Incidentally, this kind of definition is probably one of the most difficult notions to get over to the student of mathematics . . . if he wants to know whether something is a certain type of mathematical entity which has previously been defined, he should *see if it satisfies the criterion given in the definition.*[43]

Before leaving the area of definitions another item requires at least brief mention. Hempel not only holds that observational definitions are too narrow for modern science but he insists that reduction sentences are also inadequate. Some of the measurable entities (metric concepts) are broader and in Hempel's terms *"theoretical constructs."*[44] Terms of this kind — mass, force, volume, proton — are not introduced by definitions or reduction chains based on observables; in fact, they are not introduced by any piecemeal process of assigning meaning to them individually. Rather, the constructs used in a theory are introduced jointly by setting up a theoretical system formulated in their terms and by giving this system an experiential interpretation, which in turn confers empirical meaning on the theoretical constructs.

---

[43] Raymond L. Wilder, *Introduction to the Foundations of Mathematics* (New York: John Wiley & Sons, 1952), p. 52.
[44] Carl G. Hempel, *op. cit.*, p. 32.

VOLUME II
Author Index

VOLUME II
Subject Index

ESSAYS IN
ACCOUNTING THEORY

Volume III

AMERICAN ACCOUNTING ASSOCIATION

The By-Laws of the American Accounting Association state that the first purpose of the Association shall be "to initiate, encourage, and sponsor research in accounting and to publish or aid in the publication of the results of research." In harmony with this objective, the publication of the Studies in Accounting Research is aimed at encouraging and publishing research. This series is an outgrowth of the research program initiated by the Association in 1965. Under this program research projects and authors are selected by the Director of Research, who is assisted by a Research Advisory Committee.

This project was based on the author's lifework over nearly a half century, in which accounting issues are analyzed from an interdisciplinary perspective, in particular from the standpoint of such basic disciplines as scientific methodology, philosophy, ethics, logic, mathematics, economics, and behavioral science. In preparing the materials for this publication, the author was assisted by a Project Advisory Committee consisting of Yuji Ijiri (Carnegie-Mellon University, chairperson), Edward V. McIntyre (Florida State University), and Stephen A. Zeff (Rice University), as well as by AAA Publications Director, Janet G. Nuñez.

This publication was approved by Theodore J. Mock (University of Southern California), 1982-84 Director of Research. The Research Advisory Committee (1982-83) at the time of publication approval was composed of Joel S. Demski (Stanford University), Daniel L. Jensen (Ohio State University), James C. McKeown (University of Illinois), James A. Ohlson (University of California, Berkeley), Lawrence Revsine (Northwestern University), and William F. Wright (University of Minnesota), in addition to the Director of Research.

ESSAYS IN ACCOUNTING THEORY

Volume III

by
Carl Thomas Devine

AMERICAN ACCOUNTING ASSOCIATION
1985

TABLE OF CONTENTS

FOREWORD

In many ways my effort to be an accounting theorist has been a lonely one. Some alienation and sense of frustration with the profession results from my stubborn belief that no activity is more practical than consideration of the functions of a profession in the context of mankind's objectives. What could possibly be more professional or more practical than inquiring about the ends of man and the relationship of our activities to them? At the other extreme, some academic colleagues have postulated a ridiculous relationship between the intellectual worth of a discipline and its subject matter and have assumed that business, and especially bookkeeping, could not possibly appeal to an intellectual. Until the recent appearance of a horde of bright and eager hounds, theoretical foraging had been attractive mainly to the lone wolves of the profession. In my own instance the ability to forage in the interdisciplinary pasture has been greatly increased by a number of fascinating visiting positions. These stations carried few low-level administrative chores, required modest teaching duties, and offered tremendous opportunities for listening, reflecting, and, on occasion, arguing.

My envy of scholars who crisply construct precise and intricate typologies, take x's that exhibit the stipulated attributes, and work out all sorts of astounding relationships is genuine and deep-seated. I too would like to build sharp arguments, but my own abilities, for better or worse, are in other directions, and writing these rambling essays has been an exciting and satisfying experience. A few unfriendly critics have concluded that the style is a conscious effort to make relatively simple ideas appear complicated. Naturally, I feel their conclusion is not warranted. It is true that I try to get away from dead-level statements and to vary the rhetoric slightly in the interests of a supposed literacy. A part of the difficulty undoubtedly comes from lack of understanding. Most of us like to discuss and write about ideas that are new and interesting, and we tend to find the familiar dull and unexciting. Happiness, it seems, is often an unsettled mess of problematic situations.

Approximately ten years have passed since the earlier essays were distributed, and it is discouraging to find so little difference in my thinking and so few changes in my viewpoint. A comparison with my dissertation from a still earlier period is even more discouraging. There is of course some stubborn pride in maintaining a consistent front, but in this fast-moving and psychedelic intellectual environment, consistency of belief may indicate a failure to understand and adapt. Under the influence of Kohl's *The Age of Complexity* and Wittgenstein's torturous soul-searching, I now identify slightly less with Carnap and the logical empiricists. However, during this shift I have steadfastly refused to identify with holists, with organismic organization theorists, or with certain popular inanities related to the total systems approach. In spite of a deep-seated and continuing concern with ethics and mankind's miserable attempts to find workable interpersonal relations, I still am unable to accept the ethical recommendations of philosophers like Singer and Churchman, and I remain restive among exponents of Zen and with advocates of the various branches of existentialism.

The minor shift in belief is reflected in the composition and order of the essays. The first and second deal with principles in the Friedman tradition, with modifications from my long interest in historicism and institutional economics — an interest which has survived in spite of rigorous training in hard-core marginalism. Functionalism and teleology in both narrow and sweeping senses are present, and evidences of Veblen, Mannheim and, yes, Marx show up here. The behavioral aspects of principles (Essay Three) is primarily the result of a rich Indonesian experience, and the essay on phenomenology and mystical considerations is a direct reflection of my search for some organizing scheme for the complexities of human relations. Unfortunately, I simply cannot incorporate these views in my own intellectual outlook. Psychiatrists, as an important intellectual group, have tended to identify with phenomenology, but somehow I cannot believe that their methods are consistent with this methodology. Hopefully others with different orientations and abilities will be able to develop these areas more effectively than I have been able to do.

The essay dealing with continuity began with an uneasiness resulting from Storey's excellent article of a decade or so ago and became an uncomfortable roar with Chambers and his philosophy of generalized and continuous exit relevance. The essay dealing with organizational slack has obvious beginnings in Cyert and March. My effort here combines with two other essays to discuss the problem of smoothing and interim reporting.

I should like to affirm again for the younger generations the belief of Professor Talbot, my first science teacher, that being a bookworm is a respectable activity for mature human beings. Some acknowledgments for help along the way are indicated. Since the earlier volumes I have had many happy hours of wrangling with Harvey Hendrickson, William Andrew Paton, Jr., Gibbes Miller, Richard Arellano, Richard Mattessich, Charles Hubbard and a number of reasonably interested graduate students. Important volumes by Chambers, Churchman, Ijiri, Staubus, Sterling and others have come to my attention. A host of bright and talented young scholars from Chicago, Stanford, Berkeley, Carnegie and elsewhere, with broad interests and sharp tools, now make the road less lonesome. The advisory committee for the ill-fated Green-Devine-AAA project offered some fascinating ideas, and I hope sometime to show my gratitude by means of a fourth volume of essays built around the behavioral theme. Meanwhile, sincere appreciation goes to my typist Marie Payne and to the School of Business of Florida State University for providing clerical assistance.

Beth has joined Drue and Steve as a member of the seething but, so far, nonmutinous crew.

Essay One

Principles, Theories, Systems - Again

For several decades the accountant has had difficulty in specifying even one theory of accounting or one principle of accounting. (Readers may wish to exercise their ingenuity by performing a similar operation for economics or for the physical sciences.) The Institute and the Association have joined the search and have sponsored some interesting documents in this area. The former has appointed a special board to see (among other things) that its pronouncements are properly formulated and enunciated.

The modest recommendations of this paper are that principles be operationally defined and treated as guidelines and that theories be treated as predictions. If these recommendations are accepted, certain appropriate methodological operations and behaviors follow. Principles, for example, should be selected and evaluated in terms of their effectiveness for accomplishing objectives. The adequacy of theories is judged in terms of correspondence between predicted outcomes and actual outcomes.[1] This distinction, like so many others, may easily be overdrawn, for a certain amount of interdependence seems to be unavoidable. A portion of this essay is devoted to an examination of the consequences of this distinction and to the behaviors necessary for organizing and conducting inquiry in each area. The following three sections extend an invitation for the reader to accept the recommended definitions. The remainder of the paper is devoted to the place of assumptions and explanatory systems that include functionalism and teleology.

Principles

In ordinary usage the term principles, along with directives, conventions, and rules, may be treated as divisions of the more general term guidelines. Grammatically, the distinguishing feature of these terms is that they are imperatives; critically, they are to be evaluated by similar procedures. Effective guidelines direct action and therefore function as means, and means are evaluated with reference to their anticipated consequences compared with objectives.[2] Used in this sense, the principles of accounting are the imperatives

---

[1] Students of philosophy will recognize this evaluation of theories as the pragmatic approach to warranted assertions — truth — and the evaluation of principles as Dewey's test for the efficiency of hypotheses for resolving inquiries. In J. N. Keynes' system the former activity would belong to positive science and the latter to normative or regulative science, i.e., " . . . a system of rules for the attainment of a given end." Quoted from Milton Friedman, *Essays in Positive Economics* (Chicago: University of Chicago Press, 1966, 1953), p. 3.

[2] Elsewhere I have discussed attempts to relate principles to honorific terms such as 'basic,' 'fundamental,' 'first,' and even to God himself. These efforts are probably semantic attempts to gain legitimacy and sanction for the directives. *Berkeley Symposium on the Foundations of Financial Accounting* (Berkeley: School of Business Administration, 1967), p. 16. Strangely enough, the feeling that principles ought to be general and pervasive has led to some overly cautious statements. George O. May states: "In these fields [accounting and business law] there are no principles, in the more fundamental sense of that word." *Financial Accounting* (New York: The Macmillan Company, 1961, 1943), p. 3. W. A. Paton and A. C. Littleton have succumbed to the mystique. " 'Principles' would generally suggest a universality and degree of permanence which cannot exist in a human-service institution such as accounting." *An Introduction to Corporate Accounting Standards* (Evanston: American Accounting Association, 1940), p. 4.

(guidelines) for practicing accounting, and the principles of physics and of economics are similarly reduced to rules for carrying on the operation of physics and economics. Acceptance of this simple approach is less glamorous than a romantic quest for basic touchstones with some hypothesized world spirit, but acceptance does give rise to some interesting questions. What, for example, distinguishes principles from related entities such as conventions, rules, etc.? How are such directives accepted and rejected by the profession? By whom? After what delays?

If there is genuine need for distinguishing between various guidelines, the need itself should furnish clues for making the necessary discriminations. A possible need for distinguishing different types of guidelines might be related to their range of applicability. For example, rules might refer to guidelines of limited range. Possibilities are virtually unlimited. A complex series might be introduced so that each term indicates the administrative level with authority to accept, modify or reject the designated imperative. Conceivably, only those directives changeable by Jehovah or his authorized subordinates might be called principles while those adopted by the head of a clan or a household might be called rules. The reader may wish to exercise his ingenuity and devise alternate classification schemes. Some suggestions follow: cultural criteria; relative importance on some agreed scale; level of skill necessary for executing; relative difficulty of teaching and learning; mechanical aids required to comply; length of time already in use.

There is an obvious relation (to be discussed in detail later) between *objectives* and *principles* to guide specific action, and the separation of means and objectives may easily be overdrawn. Some objectives function as intervening means for other objectives, and in turn means may serve as intermediate objectives. In order to simplify the problem, emphasis here is on the necessity to identify objectives, and then to construct principles whose consequences help accomplish the objectives. Justice may be an objective. If so, principles should be constructed to encourage actions that result in accomplishments of justice.[3]

If principles are to be considered guides for action, an appropriate concern is with the evaluation, selection and rejection of principles themselves. What principles do we need for selecting other principles? The suggestion of this paper is to discourage an ordering of principles along a more-basic, less-basic scale. Instead, it is recommended that one identify the objectives that the activities are to perform. Some knowledge of possible means and their relation to objectives accomplished and foregone is necessary, and the ordering of principles according to relative importance is subject to change as these features change. This knowledge requires predictions, and predictions require theories, so that, as is so often the case, conceptual independence is secured only by neglecting various interactions.[4]

The evaluative process must be in terms of norms in the form of accepted objectives. Have either the norms or objectives changed? Are they properly ordered and evaluated? Are the required tradeoffs understood? Are anticipated consequences appropriate for goal achievement? Are improved procedures available? Do the instructions lead unambiguously or probabilistically to appropriate actions? It should be clear that any serious discussion of principles and their formulation must consider the interaction of individual and social values.[5]

Theories

The term theory, in this paper, is used to designate a statement or series of statements which lead to testable predictions.[6] Inasmuch as any proposition (declarative sentence)

Footnotes on following page

claims truth, it should be clear that the adjective "testable" as a defining property for theory is desirable to make the definition operational.[7] It may seem desirable to restrict the definition and to distinguish theory from speculation, hypothesis, law, law-like statements, and related terms. On what basis are such distinctions made? Again, concepts are distinguished for certain purposes, and the purposes should help determine appropriate definitions. Such distinctions could be based on the degree of confidence in the predictions; in terms of the scope involved; on the basis of methods used to suggest them; according to their estimated permanency. In short, if there is genuine need for more detailed classification, the need should help suggest the basis for differentiation.[8]

---

[3] The following statement illustrates: "The purpose of financial statements . . . is the *maximization* of wealth and not the *measurement* of wealth." Myron J. Gordon, "Postulates, Principles, and Research in Accounting," *The Accounting Review*, April, 1964, p. 256. Clearly, if maximization is the objective, measurement is an intermediate necessity (means); and the principles of measurement are recommended operations. W. J. Vatter is in essential agreement with the attitude taken here, " . . . principles are generalizations as to the way in which certain objectives may be reached." "Postulates and Principles," *Journal of Accounting Research*, Autumn, 1963, p. 184. Francesco Barone omits the teleological features: " . . . *principles* . . . assertions which provide standard rules for judgment and for conduct." "Semantic Therapy," Reprinted in *Classics in Semantics*, Donald E. Hayden and E. P. Alworth, eds. (New York: Philosophical Library, 1965), p. 366.

[4] Not only are theories necessary to evaluate principles, but principles help guide the selection of theories, i.e., in Deweyian terms the ends-in-view influence the hypotheses that are relevant. Friedman states the converse: "Normative economics . . . cannot be independent of positive economics. Any policy conclusion necessarily rests on a prediction about the consequences . . . " *Op. cit.*, p. 5. The possibility of self-actualization is expressed by Karl R. Popper. "The idea that a prediction may have influence upon the predicted event is a very old one . . . . I suggest the name '*Oedipus effect*' . . . " *The Poverty of Historicism* (New York: Harper Torchbooks, 1964, 1957), p. 13.

[5] "Charles Morris has recently defined the study of values as the 'science of preferential behavior' . . . [but] . . . A value is not just a preference but a preference which is felt and/or considered to be justified — 'morally' or by reasoning or by aesthetic judgment . . . . A value is a conception . . . of the desirable which influences the selection from available modes, means, and ends of action." Clyde Kluckhohn and others, "Values and Value-Orientations in the Theory of Action," Talcott Parsons and Edward A. Shils, eds., *Toward a General Theory of Action* (Cambridge: Harvard University Press, 1959), pp. 390, 395-396. Incidentally, the most enduring contribution to management science by C. West Churchman may well be in the area of values and their importance for making choices that the culture and environment afford. Many may have overlooked the subtitle to his important book: *Prediction and Optional Decision: Philosophical Issues of a Science of Values* (Englewood Cliffs: Prentice-Hall, Inc., 1961).

[6] Examples of more comprehensive definitions that involve a series of related statements to form theoretical systems follow. " . . . the set of constructs with their formal connections forms a model. When certain of the constructs are connected to the empirical world by rules of correspondence, the model becomes a *theory*, and, as such, is subject to empirical test." Warren S. Torgerson, *Theory and Methods of Scaling* (New York: John Wiley & Sons, Inc., 1958), p. 4. " . . . a clear rounded and systematic view of a subject . . . the coherent set of hypothetical, conceptual and pragmatic principles forming the general frame of reference for a field of inquiry." *Webster's New International Dictionary*. My own attitudes have remained relatively stable through the years. "A theorist in accounting is one who examines the rules and principles and tries to determine the consequences resulting from each and to evaluate these consequences in terms of broad social standards taken from without the field of accounting proper. Theory then, is a type of inquiry, an approach which takes existing principles or advances new principles, points out the probable results, and by comparing with standards from other fields attempts to reach value judgments regarding the relative desirability of various alternative courses." "Current Trends and Persistent Problems in Accounting Theory," *The Controller*, July, 1942, p. 334.

[7] If we throw out metaphysical assertions, the remaining propositions may serve as hypotheses to guide empirical study. C. West Churchman would limit 'proposition' to descriptive propositions. "All description methodologically entails prediction." *Prediction and Optimal Decision, op. cit.*, p. 85. Also: " . . . *facts, measurements and theories* are methodologically the same," p. 71. Kluckhohn is even more inclusive and quotes George Lundberg: " . . . the basic similarity of scientific and ethical statements . . . all 'should' and 'ought' statements as well as scientific statements represent *an* expectation which is, in effect, a prediction." *Op. cit.*, p. 392.

[8] Paul Henle, citing Whorf and Sapir, point out that Eskimo languages contain, "a variety of words for different kinds of snow . . . [while] Aztec is even poorer than we . . . using the same word stem for cold, ice, and snow." *Language, Thought and Culture* (Ann Arbor: University of Michigan Press, 1958), p. 5.

The temporal distinction between explanation and prediction may merit attention. (Other differences are discussed later.) The naive identification of explanation with the past and prediction with the future may lead to serious difficulties.[9] In some cases research attention may be focused on predicting an outcome (past or future) from initial conditions, while in others attention may be concentrated on finding the set of conditions that might "account for" a given outcome. The development of an accounting classification system requires decisions as to which facets of which events are to be recorded and is based on predictions that the selected classes and events will be useful in explaining — accounting for — past accomplishment as well as for planning future accomplishment. The importance of event selection is clearly illustrated in general history where the system is less structured, general outcomes are known, and appropriate contributing events must be inferred. How do historians go about the task of inferring antecedents from known outcomes? Prediction? In the absence of ability to replicate even the verification process is similar. From this point of view "we could have predicted" is not greatly different from "we predict."[10]

Assumptions

We turn now to the place of assumptions in the field of inquiry. From a broad view, assumptions make up all propositions stated and *unstated* that are not included in the explicit theories and principles. They set the conditions for the inquiry.

The unstated propositions make up an open class whose limits are, of course, unknowable. These unstated assumptions have one very important property — they are assumed to be unimportant for the immediate inquiry. That is, they are assumed to indicate that the environment is passive — stable — (or possibly understood as matters of common knowledge) with respect to any unformed propositions. This class of assumptions may be

---

[9] Perhaps "forecast" would be more useful for temporal reference. See: Henry Margenau, *The Nature of Physical Reality* (New York: McGraw-Hill Book Company, Inc., 1950), Ch. 6. Friedman states: " . . . the 'predictions' by which the validity of a hypothesis is tested . . . need not be forecasts of future events; they may be about phenomena that have occurred . . .," *op. cit.*, p. 9. If we look toward the consequences we speak of prediction. Rudner states: " . . . the logical structure of a scientific *explanation* is identical with that of a scientific *prediction*, the only difference between them being the purely pragmatic one of the temporal vantage point of the inquirer." *Philosophy of Social Science* (Englewood Cliffs: Prentice-Hall, Inc., 1966), p. 60. Carl Hempel states: "The explanation fits the phenomenon to be explained into a pattern of uniformities and shows that its occurrence was to be expected . . . " *Philosophy of Natural Science* (Englewood Cliffs: Prentice-Hall, Inc., 1966), p. 50. Hempel also states: " . . . theory . . . explains the empirical uniformities that have been previously discovered, and usually also predicts 'new' regularities of similar kinds." *Ibid.*, p. 70.

    The necessity for at least a part of a language to be so constructed is given by Marvin Harris: "Every natural language contains a set of terms and rules for combining events which are pragmatically appropriate for isolating and predicting important occurrences in the human behavior stream," *The Nature of Cultural Things* (New York: Random House, Inc., 1964), p. 23. Deutsch and Krauss state: "For it to be fruitful, the 'grammar' or logical structure of a theory, and its 'vocabulary' or set of theoretical constructs, must somehow fit with each other in such a way that empirically meaningful predictions can be made." *Theories in Social Psychology* (New York: Basic Books, Inc., 1965), p. 7. With regard to history Morton White states: " . . . a narrative, unlike a chronicle, is a conjunction of singular explanatory statements . . . a singular explanatory statement may be confirmed either by presenting a full-fledged deductive argument of the requisite kind or by presenting good inductive reasons for thinking that such an argument exists." *Foundations of Historical Knowledge* (New York: Harper Torchbooks, 1965), pp. 4-5.

[10] Friedman's approach is similar to the one adopted in this paper. *Op. cit.*, p. 9. Except for induced cognitive dissonance, he, like us, seems to be little concerned with logical consistency and completeness. *Ibid.*, p. 10. The fact that the present writer is not overly concerned with simplicity and parsimony may be inferred from the structure of these essays.

dismissed without extensive discussion except to say that for a different inquiry some of them may need to be formulated and used as hypotheses or as explicit assumptions to limit the domain for prediction.

The class of explicit (stated) assumptions deserves more careful analysis. It is this group of statements that is usually designated as axioms and postulates.[11] These statements cover some of the relevant conditions (preconditions) necessary to limit the range of the theoretical structure. Friedman states:

> . . . the entirely valid use of "assumptions" in *specifying* the circumstance for which a theory holds is frequently and erroneously interpreted to mean that the assumptions can be used to *determine* the circumstances for which a theory holds . . .[12]

Mathematicians are in an especially good position to observe the place of assumptions. A functional relationship between y and a number of independent variates, $x_1, x_2, x_3, \ldots$ x_n is usually simplified by assuming that certain x_i are relatively unimportant for the inquiry at hand, and thus the hypothesis that argument x_i is relevant is laid at rest by assigning a constant impact or, as with unstated assumptions, omitted altogether. Thus the expression $y = f(x)$ assumes that all sorts of independent arguments are stipulated in the functional operator and their variability is not important or that they are dormant for the inquiry at hand. A distinct advantage of the mathematical formulation is that equation formation warns the investigator of possible over-simplification or at least alerts him to the necessity for trading off the simplicity of reduced variables against possible over-restriction of the theoretical system.

In logical terms, the simple implication $p \rightarrow q$ is seen to be a vast simplification of the broader conditional implication that includes several p's. Thus, given the existence of p_1, $p_2, \ldots p_n$ then q may be deduced for convenient predictions, by establishing empirically (or stipulating, in logic) the constancy of all p_i except p_1, then $p_1 \rightarrow q$ is valid, and its contrapositive is valid. We may translate means-ends estimates into p_i's as hypotheses with a specific prediction (or principle) playing the part of p_1. Other means-ends hypotheses (or objectives if one is examining principles) not being investigated at the moment in this sense are "dormant hypotheses," "underlying hypotheses," or "necessary preconditions."

We digress now on the necessity for the assumptions to be "realistic" before they may be used with confidence in a theoretical system. Clearly no assumption or proposition is realistic in the sense of reproducing some part of nature. These statements are verbal

---

[11] *Webster's New International* defines assumption as "something that is taken for granted." A postulate is also defined as a "claim that is taken for granted," but the definition would seem to exclude most unstated assumptions: "an *essential* presupposition, condition or premise." (Emphasis added.) Methods for gaining acceptance for the proposition are given under "axioms"; "a proposition . . . that has found general acceptance or is thought worthy thereof whether by virtue of a claim to intrinsic merit . . . an appeal to self-evidence . . . based on experience . . . synthetic *a priori* . . . self-consistent statement about the primitive terms."

[12] Milton Friedman, *op. cit.*, p. 19. Compare the use of *z* and *t* in the following quotation from C. West Churchman: "One wants . . . to assert that *x* has property *y* under conditions *z* at time *t* in such a manner that the information contained in the assertion can be used in a wide number of other conditions . . . " "Why Measure?" in *Measurement: Definitions and Theories*, ed., Churchman (New York: John Wiley and Sons, Inc., 1962), p. 89. In a broader sense Talcott Parsons states: " . . . science is not simply a reflection of reality, but is a selective system of cognitive orientation to reality," *Toward a General Theory of Action* (Cambridge: Harvard University Press, 1959), p. 167. R. M. MacIver states: "There is an active 'cause' and there is a set of conditions that are conceived of as relatively passive, though necessary for the operation of the cause." *Social Causation* (New York: Harper Torchbooks, 1964, 1942), p. 40.

statements and are highly abstract. To the extent that these assumptions are preconditions that limit the range of predictive machinery or help the predictive process, they relate to some aspect of the environment. If the particular environmental aspects covered by the assumption satisfy our criteria for reality, they are realistic. If they fail to express some relation whose internal operation we fail to understand or have difficulty in intuiting, we tend to call the assumption "unrealistic" even though it is a necessary condition for the operation of the theoretical structure.[13]

A slightly different approach to reality as applied to assumptions of an inquiry explains the term by reference to its provability in the system. It should be clear that if the assumptions are outside the system, it is not feasible to prove their realism by arguments from within the system. If all other aspects of the theoretical system are consistent, and if it is known that p_1 is a necessary condition, we may infer the influence of p_1, but there is no warrant to make the further inference that an "influence" guarantees its own "reality," unless being influential is stipulated to be the defining property of "reality."

Finally, if the assumptions are assumed to be within the system, it does not follow that they should be provable in the system. We are permitted to move from premises, by accepted methods, to conclusions and to compare the conclusions with other statements about the experiential world. Whether the antecedent-consequence relationship is or is not reversible is simply not relevant to that inquiry. Presumably, investigation of assumptions would call for new inquiries with new or different variables in different antecedent-consequence relationships.[14] Meanwhile, the stated assumptions stake out the limits of the system over which predictions are thought to be valid.

Systems: Relation to Scope

In the abstract and in practice . . . the sum of the best solution to parts of a problem is never equivalent to the best solution of the whole . . . The critical thing about large complex systems is that the solutions of the parts do not fit together . . . . a partial solution to the whole problem is a lot better than complete solutions to each of the parts taken separately.[15]

---

[13] " . . . every given content of experience is a reality of some sort or other . . . . The mirage . . . though not real trees and water, is a real state of atmosphere and light . . . . A dream is illusory because the dreamer takes the images for physical things, but to a psychologist . . . these experienced images . . . constitute a reality . . . . The content of every experience is real when it is correctly understood . . . . The 'unreal' is a temporary pigeon-hole for what requires to be sorted or analyzed in some further fashion." *Mind and the World Order* (New York: Dover Publications, 1956), pp. 11, 12, 350. Kenneth E. Boulding states: " . . . for any individual organism or organization, there are no such things as 'facts.' There are only messages filtered through a changeable value system," *The Image* (Ann Arbor: University of Michigan Press, 1964, 1951), p. 14.

[14] The general case for the reversibility of an inquiry and of prediction is weak indeed. Consider the following instances: causation, means-ends arguments, certain types of order relations, and the logical nonvalidity of converse arguments. For comments on transitivity see Mary Hesse, "Theories and the Transitivity of Confirmation," *Philosophy of Science*, March, 1970.

[15] Russell L. Ackoff, Wharton Forum Lecture, "The University Sanctuary or Spearhead?" reported in "Notable and Quotable," *The Wall Street Journal*, August 25, 1969. For a mature, well-reasoned, clearly stated philosophical approach to the obvious merits of systems ("total science") and the limitations of naive positivism and empiricism see: Willard Van Orman Quine, *From a Logical Point of View* (New York: Harper Torchbooks, 1961), 2nd. revised edition, pp. 42-43. For enlargement at a more practical level see Kenneth D. Mackenzie and Francisco M. Nicosia, "Marketing Systems: Toward Descriptions and Structural Properties," *Marketing and the New Science of Planning* (American Marketing Association, 1968), pp. 14-23. R. M. MacIver warns: " . . . the establishment of cause-effect relationships becomes unmanageable if we must attribute every phenomenon, every event, to the whole situation from which it emerges. It amounts to saying that the whole is the cause of the whole, a statement as unhelpful as its correlative that the whole is the effect of the whole." *Op. cit.*, p. 41.

This quotation from the author of *The Design of Social Research* and other well-reasoned monographs leaves a number of questions unanswered. How, for example, does one know when he is dealing with a "whole" problem? How can one be positive that the solutions of the parts do not "fit" together? Specifically what properties of what parts on what measuring scales have a "sum" that is not "equivalent" to the whole? How does a researcher determine if he has the "best" solution? Does a "best" solution for parts always neglect the "indirect" effects on other parts, other combinations of parts, or the "whole?" What decision criteria assign the term "best" to partial solutions without considering important probable indirect effects in different contexts? How much better is a "lot" better? What constitutes a "complete" solution?

It should be clear that a discussion of systems cannot avoid the question of the scope of the inquiry. Most readers will probably agree that there are limits to the scope that can and should be employed in a given investigation. Some investigations are relatively minor. Some inquiries tax our integrating and information-processing abilities and may be pursued most efficiently within a narrow, manageable system. Thus the larger system and the wider scope do not invariably give a more useful framework for investigation, and more variables are not necessarily more useful than fewer variables.

In most cases designing an appropriate system requires serious tradeoffs. Abstraction and simplification are essential even for elementary thinking. Everything of possible importance cannot even be conceived, and everything that we conceive as possibly relevant cannot be included in a useful system of inquiry.

The dangers of shearing off possible relevancies of importance are obvious enough. In referring to the properties of a musical note it is impossible, and undesirable, to specify its possible effects in every composition into which it might become a part. Thus a musical composition is more than the sum of its parts — as the parts have previously been designated. The recent term "synergism" with its 2 + 2 = 5 orientation has interesting overtones and may be of limited help in organizing inquiry. Its chief benefit is probably to serve as a reminder that an additive model may not be appropriate, but it also reminds the researcher of the fantastic amount of abstraction and construction that must be made to define anything; clearly its impact in all possible situations cannot be included![16]

For the objectives of a particular inquiry, many possible influences and features are not important enough to merit consideration. Machlup, for example, points out that Marshall " . . . distinguished between . . . instantaneous . . . shortrun . . . and longrun market equilibrium . . . by extending the list of dependent variables . . . each equilibrium is 'final' on its own terms, though 'temporary' in terms of a model with more variables."[17] The position here is that the size of any system should be treated as a variable until objectives are specified. Specification requires consideration for the cost and efficiency of information and the ability to structure and process information.

---

[16] Personally, I find the term "synergism" a likely candidate for buzz-word of 1965, nominate the term "systems" as a front-running candidate for the decade, and am considering the submission of "decision making" for the century's award. For a man dying of thirst the proper synergistic combination of free oxygen and hydrogen may add potential for satisfying his immediate objectives, but for a shipwrecked individual with an empty balloon disaggregation (dissynergation?) might increase the potential.

[17] Fritz Machlup, *Essays in Economic Semantics* (New York: W. W. Norton & Company, Inc., 1967), pp. 52-53. Note also the variables held constant in both short run and long run by Thomas R. Prince, *Extension of the Boundaries of Accounting Theory* (Cincinnati: South-Western Publishing Co., 1963), pp. 79ff. For a devastating attack on Marshallian price economics for neglecting antecedent factors, see R. M. MacIver, *op. cit.*, pp. 164-168. This statement is one of the best to represent the objections institutionalist economists have to the marginalist position.

Functionalism and Teleology as Systems

We turn now to a brief look at the older, more traditional concepts of functionalism and teleology as frameworks for organizing inquiry. The discussion is concerned with a comparison of these means of structuring research activity with regard to principles and theories. Gauldner states:

> . . . use of organismic models . . . has its major intellectual justification in . . . [the fact] . . . that organisms are *examples* of systems. . . . the two most important aspects of a "system" are the "interdependence" of a number of "parts" and the tendency of these to maintain an "equilibrium" in their relationships . . . . interdependence . . . needs to be taken as problematic rather than as given . . . [18]

From a broad point of view functionalism is a procedure for searching for and isolating manageable subsystems. A gap is suspected, observed, or created between an entity and other activity centers, but the gap is not interpreted as void of interdependent influences. The gap is no vacuum! It is tentatively assumed that pressures from activity centers outside the gap influence or even determine the activities of the enclosed system, and at least some of the goals of the subsystem are treated as if they are dictated and controlled from without the system. An Ackoffian "whole" would seem to be a system defined so that these exogenous influences may be neglected (or treated as stable) *for the purposes at hand*. Thus the entity as a "whole" or a "part" would have meaning only in the context of the particular inquiry and the particular objectives.

As a process for directing inquiry, functionalism is subject to a major objection. It does not provide for investigating and isolating dysfunctional activities. A major contribution of the modern system's approach may result from its format, which does permit objectives of subsystems to be at variance with one another and with the objectives of enclosing systems. The methodology of functionalism usually involves observing the operations and choices of an organ and looking for suspected regularities. Instead of being satisfied with a statement of regularities in the form of observed relationships and predictions, the functionally oriented researcher attempts to go further. He "explains" the regularities and his predictions in terms of responses to forces from without. These responses are sometimes assumed to be drives, yens for equilibrium or survival, urges for release, or specific responses to such general constructions as history, nature, progress, technology. Explanation, or at least the conditions for explanation, is in terms of influences taken as fixed for the system under survey, i.e., it is a method of closing the system.

Clearly the functional approach has possible methodological benefits. Hempel states: " . . . functionalism is best viewed . . . not as the principle of universal functionalism, but rather as a program for research guided by certain heuristic maxims or 'working hypotheses' . . . Tautological use could be based on construing *any* response of a given system

---

[18] Alvin W. Gauldner, "Reciprocity and Autonomy in Functional Theory," in *Symposium On Social Theory*, Llewellyn Gross, ed. (New York: Harper and Row, Publishers, 1959), pp. 241-242, 252. For an attempt to distinguish among eclectic functionalism, empirical functionalism and structural-functional analysis see William Flanigan and Edwin Fogelman, "Functional Analysis," in *Contemporary Political Analysis*. James C. Charlesworth, ed. (New York: The Free Press, 1967), pp. 72-85. Robert T. Holt, following Hempel, states: "Function is not a synonym for effect; it is a subtype of effect. Functions are *system relevant* effects of structures." "A Proposed Structural-Functional Framework," in Charlesworth, *op. cit.*, p. 88. Clearly some effects may be nonfunctional, but some dysfunctional effects may also be relevant!

as an adjustment.''[19] This danger from the use of functionalism is obvious enough, but a possible advantage in the form of helping direct search activity for new inquiries is also obvious. A homeostatic assumption, for example, may encourage one to examine the activities of an observable entity in terms of hypotheses about assumed or known needs of related entities. There should be a tendency to enlarge the scope of the inquiry as long as homeostasis can be applied as a useful structuring assumption, but there may be a tendency to suspend inquiry beyond this point. In the latter case an additional program of inquiry is necessary if the homeostatic system itself is to be expanded or even investigated. That is, the survival hypothesis needs to be applied to a larger system so that the resulting yen will confer functions on its various parts. Incidentally, intuiting a larger unit whose survival needs relate to our object of inquiry may not be easy.

Most readers will feel that there are modest limits to the functional hypothesis of cohesive forces, but Hempel points out that the " . . . hypothesis of self-regulation . . . seems to have a teleological basis.''[20] The typical pragmatist, with his highly developed functional orientation, may be disturbed at being associated with those teleological theorists with emphasis on such constructions as final causes, absolute wills, animistic urges, world spirits, and divine purposes. Yet, he is willing to live with — if not encourage — similar, less inclusive constructions such as drives, needs, functional requirements, operant behaviors and to use them as aids for directing and organizing inquiry.[21]

The tendency to over-expand a functional orientation seems to be widespread, and over-expansion certainly is not a recent development peculiar to systems analysis. Historians investigate a fantastic amount of data, and many feel the need of grand research designs to help organize their investigations.[22] The difficulty with such explanatory devices is that unless we are pretty well acquainted with the specifics of such constructions as the "transcendent intelligence" we cannot use them effectively to predict individual events or classes of events.

A similar sort of grand design is found in the romantic philosophers, especially Hegel. A cyclical (pendulum) approach to history may indeed help the predictive ability if the di-

---

[19] Hempel, *op. cit.*, pp. 295, 298. Friedman too feels that such constructions may be useful. *Op. cit.*, pp. 250-256. Gordon Pask states: " . . . whenever there is a stable system, then, in principle, we can envisage a sub-system acting as a controller that maintains this stability . . . . An organism *is a control system* with its own survival as its objective." *An Approach to Cybernetics* (New York: Harper & Brothers, 1961), pp. 49, 72. Karl R. Popper sounds a warning: " . . . there is nothing in the organism to correspond to one of the most important characteristics of the open society, competition for status among its members, the so-called organic theory of the state is based on a false analogy." *The Open Society and Its Enemies,* Vol. I (New York: Harper Torchbooks, 1963, 1945), p. 174.

[20] Hempel, *op. cit.*, p. 298.

[21] Francisco J. Ayala argues that teleology is inescapable in biology where "the ultimate source of explanation . . . is the principle of natural selection . . . a mechanistic process." "Teleological Explanations in Evolutionary Biology," *Philosophy of Science*, March, 1970, p. 1. It is possible that we are making a sharper than warranted distinction between functionalism and teleological systems. Rudner states: "We are not forced to conclude . . . that the realm of teleological events is inhabited by ghostlike states of affairs — nonexistent, yet somehow causally efficacious." *Philosophy of Social Sciences* (Englewood Cliffs: Prentice-Hall, Inc., 1966), p. 85. J. E. M. Joad attempts to generalize the teleological outlook, " . . . in philosophies of the Bergsonian type, which regard evolution as the key to metaphysical truth, the conception of goal takes the place of reality. A goal is a reality conceived in time . . . " *Philosophical Aspects of Modern Science* (New York: Barnes & Noble, Inc., 1964), p. 252.

[22] Hans Meyerhoff mentions the Judeo-Christian tradition of a universal history as "an intelligible process guided by . . . the transcendent design of a Divine intelligence" and points out some alternatives. *The Philosophy of History in Our Time* (Garden City, N.J.: Doubleday Anchor Books, 1959), p. 3. For a discussion of historicism in contemporary thought see Arnaldo D. Momigliano, *Studies in Historiography* (New York: Harper Torchbooks, 1966), pp. 221-238. See also Karl R. Popper, *The Poverty of Historicism, op. cit., passim.*

mensions of the cycles and counter-cycles can be specified. According to the *Encyclopedia Britannica* the term "dialectic" originally meant discussion. A position was set forth, a counter-position evoked, and the two interacted with the result that the synthesis was "broader" than the original "partial" view. In some cases the syntheses were assumed to be identical with starting points "except that all that was implicit there has now been made explicit."

The more or less static dialectic that returns to the initial conditions in an expanded way is probably not as useful to researchers as a dialectic that adds new information, enlarges the system, and leads to interesting new syntheses. The *Britannica* suggests the latter, scientifically-oriented view. The discussion should make systems theorists feel comfortable and at home, " . . . dialectic considered things in their movements and changes, interrelations and interactions." A thoughtful reader may still ask: *All* the relations and *all* the interactions? Or perhaps: *What* relations and *which* interactions?

Often the complex interrelations of useful dialectics have been submerged in over-simplistic approaches including futile searches for polar opposites. Sidney Hook has emphasized that the dialectic attitude might be related to scientific methods.[23] Any position may be faulted from some conceivable set of evaluative standards. We might hypothesize that any given situation will lead to stresses and to opposition. The scientific process would seek to predict the direction and force of the resulting opposition and hopefully predict the direction and duration of the syntheses.

Not many accountants would agree with Hegel that the actual course of events literally could be deduced from abstract dialectics, but many may agree that new empirical hypotheses may be suggested in this manner. It is perhaps acceptable to interpret the Marx-Engels dialectic in the Veblenian sense of scientific method. Technology influences attitudes in a predictable manner. Changes in these attitudes (also in a predictable manner) put stresses on existing institutions. Once a social scientist has observed and related these influences, he should be able to predict the social consequences of all sorts of changes in technology.[24]

The valuable aspect of agreeing on definite names for *unexplained* relationships is found primarily in their economy for thinking. A little reflection will show that most names are of this nature.[25] Any predictable relationship between inputs and outputs may be given a label even though the process by which the transformation is made may still remain a mystery. For skeptics, such as this writer, no amount of explanation ever removes

---

[23] Sidney Hook, *Reason, Social Myths and Democracy* (New York: Harper Torchbooks, 1966, 1940), "To say that things are 'dialectically' interrelated introduces the conceptions of necessity and systematic connection . . . but [is] . . . ambiguous unless it is indicated *how* they are interrelated . . . in Engel's discussions . . . the critical role of hypotheses is recognized, admission is made of the existence of relatively isolated systems, and the methodological inadequacy of physical and biological 'reductionism' is very forcibly stated," pp. 193-194. R. M. MacIver states: "In all the volumnious writings of Karl Marx there is nowhere any attempt to test the doctrine of the 'materialistic interpretation of history.' " *Op. cit.*, p. 117.

[24] DR Scott's approach might be summarized: Large-scale organization leads to a predictable breakdown of the competitive price system as allocator and distributor of resources. Resources *must* be allocated, and the surviving process will remain a modified price system with administered prices. A desirable, if not necessary, condition for administered prices is cost allocation. Cost allocation, to accomplish desired results in resource allocation, should be based on justice and truthfulness. Accounting is highly institutionalized and may not be able to adapt with the required flexibility.

[25] " . . . we . . . assume the existence of certain entities in order to operationalize others . . . the unavoidable fact [is] that if empirical things are to be the subject of scientific discourse, they must be treated as constructs or abstractions." Marvin Harris, *The Nature of Cultural Things* (New York: Random House, 1964), pp. 5-6.

the labyrinth of misty boxes. Extrication is impossible, but identifying relations between inputs and outputs by labels is necessary and is especially emphasized in the systems' approach.

A System for Predictions — The Theoretical System

Friedman's approach is similar to the one adopted in this paper, although he tends to define "theory" in a broader framework: "Viewed as a body of substantive hypotheses, theory is to be judged by its predictive power for the class of phenomena which it is intended to 'explain.' "[26] However, it should be pointed out that an alternate approach is available. This approach considers predictions as *consequences* of theory. Theory is defined as the persuasive support for the prediction, and the prediction itself is treated as a verbal statement of expectation or belief, which may or may not be considered to be outside the system. Supporters of this view develop a set of operations for testing the prediction and another set of more or less independent operations for judging the quality of the persuasive support, i.e., the quality and strength of the theory. This approach permits its users to evaluate theory by looking at its support as well as by looking at its predictive ability.[27] Clearly the investigatory system itself is greatly broadened, but any net advantage for this dual approach is highly questionable.

The methodological import of the Friedman thesis may be considerable. Specific theory construction is freed from the requirement that each step of the process be amenable to testing against the environment — freed from the necessity to establish independent verifiability for each proposition. While there may be some discomfort over the intuitive element, the release from the requirement of complete verifiability may encourage creativity and incite the imagination. It is, of course, possible that confidence in the predictions may be weakened if the predictions are based on strange and unusual propositions, but one suspects that confidence will be rebuilt very quickly if the predictions of the theoretical system agree consistently with actual outcomes.[28] In the interim the uneasiness

---

[26] Milton Friedman, *op. cit.*, p. 8. Those interested in the controversy over the necessity for premises to be realistic may be interested in the following quotation from Alfred North Whitehead some 40 years before Friedman's publication. " . . . in order to pool our evidence for a body of propositions to the utmost extent, it is desirable that the premises assumed should be as few and simple as possible, and, of course, the more fully they claim our credence the better. But none of these requisites are absolutely necessary on pain of logical fallacy. Our selection of premises is arbitrary, and must be guarded by the purpose which we have in view." Quoted from *A Philosopher Looks at Science* (New York: Philosophical Library, Inc., 1965), p. 37. Original in *Journal of the Association of Teachers of Mathematics for the Southeastern Part of England*, Volume 1, Number 1 (1912).

[27] A related situation may be found in probability and its relationship to relative frequency. Rudolf Carnap accuses relative frequentists of confusing the evidence with the concept. "It would be more correct to say that . . . the probability is determined with the help of a given frequency and its value is either equal or close to that of the frequency." *Logical Foundations of Probability* (Chicago: University of Chicago Press, 1950), p. 188. Nelson Goodman feels an explanatory law should be "acceptable independently of the determination of any given instance." *Fact, Fiction and Forecast* (Cambridge: Harvard University Press, 1955), p. 31. The persuasive aspect of explanation is obvious in Morton White's statement: " . . . the regularists' replacement of the singular explanatory statement by a deductive argument . . . is to show that the explanation rests on evidence other than that which pertains to the particular item before us . . . the explanation may be a shaky one *if* it advocates can present no more evidence in its behalf. But . . . the reformulation . . . will *bring out* the possible shakiness of the explanation." *Op. cit.*, pp. 24, 27.

[28] " . . . great confidence is attached to it [hypothesis] if it has survived many opportunities for contradiction." *Ibid.*, p. 9. William James has written: "Theories thus become instruments, not answers to enigmas . . . . We must find a theory that will *work* . . . . our theory must mediate between all previous truths and certain new experiences. It must derange common sense and previous belief as little as possible, and it must lead to some sensible terminus or other that can be verified exactly." *Essays in Pragmatism* (New York: Hafner Publishing Co., 1948), pp. 145, 167-168.

may encourage research toward finding explanations from broader classes or related systems.

We now turn specifically to the relationship of predictions and explanations in terms of scope of operation. Explanation (either by class expansion or analogs from related fields) is a regress that continues until the investigator is discouraged or satisfied — the system is open and unbounded.[29] Confidence is often increased when the individual antecedent-consequent pattern can be shown to be a singular instance of a similar system that is broader in application. The ultimate in satisfaction would seem to be when all predictions can be subsumed under some great predictor in the sky. The Institute's stubborn pursuit of a *few fundamental* postulates indicates an inclination if not a commitment to this view and toward the goal of a closed system. Unfortunately, as classes get broader, more and more characteristics of their singular members are lost in the abstraction process and the remaining defining commonalities tend to exert less and less influence on the inferences about possible related commonalities, i.e., the loss in homogeneity makes hypotheses from deduction more uncertain.

Before this drive for generality is dismissed as a peculiar mutation, it should be emphasized that the resulting attitude may be a useful instrument for motivating research. The search for wider classes, common properties, and possible analogs may be useful and productive. In a similar way, wondering whether broad and generalized classes do or do not apply to smaller classes and to individual (singular) cases may help generate testable hypotheses. Whether the urge to generalize is in some sense inherent or is culturally evoked need not concern us here, but we mention in passing that deductive explanation of any sort requires notions of classes and that the use of analogs may be an indispensible part of all explanation.[30]

---

[29] " . . . an explanation is not an absolute sort of thing, but what is satisfactory for one man will not be for another." P. W. Bridgman, *The Logic of Modern Physics* (New York: The Macmillan Co., 1960, 1927), p. 38. A similar difficulty relates to proof. " . . . a proof . . . is a series of statements which makes the truth of the theorem obvious . . . . All that is required of a proof is that it convince the audience of the truth of the implication . . . . There is no simple test that can be applied to determine that an alleged proof really is a proof." R. B. Kershner and L. R. Wilcox, *The Anatomy of Mathematics* (New York: The Ronald Press Company, 1950), pp. 76-77. For serious study of this aspect consult R. B. Braithwaite, *Scientific Explanation* (New York: Harper & Brothers, 1960, 1953), especially Chapters I, VI, VIII, and X.

[30] " . . . the method of deductive nomological explanation accounts for a particular event by subsuming it under general laws . . . and . . . to explain the fact that a given law holds by showing that the latter is subsumable . . . under more comprehensive laws . . . " Carl G. Hempel, "Logic of Functional Analysis," *Symposium On Sociological Theory,* Llewellyn Gross, ed. (New York: Harper and Row, Publishers, 1959), p. 274. R. B. Braithwaite states: "In deduction the reasonableness of belief in the premises . . . overflows to provide reasonableness for the belief in the conclusion." *Scientific Explanation* (New York: Harper & Brothers, 1960, 1953), p. 257. Morton White discusses singular historical instances in terms of "contributary cause" and "existential regularism." "A statement of the form 'A is a contributary cause of C' is true if and only if there is an explanatory deductive argument containing 'A' as a premise and 'C' as its conclusion . . . . Existential statements and explanatory deductive arguments without treating the former as elliptical and without forcing us to say that only explanatory deductive arguments are explanations." *Foundations of Historical Knowledge* (New York: Harper Torchbooks, 1965), pp. 60-61.

Essay Two

Principles and Theories: Accounting Orientation

The discussion now turns to specific applications of principles, theories, functionalism, teleology and systems generally to the field of accounting. When feasible, these illustrations include reference to specific leaders in accounting and to their approaches to the field. This essay should be more interesting than the preceding one to professional accountants and students with a bent for practical affairs. Accordingly it is hoped that those interested will wish to expand similar applications to other facets of professional work, particularly to some current inquiries sponsored by the Institute.

Accounting Principles — Systematic Aspects

We inquire now about the necessity to open the traditional accounting system in order to include the objectives that guide the profession. From whence, for example, come the goals to which accounting actions are directed? Recently, some accountants have moved in a behavioral direction, but a number of influential accountants have consistently counseled a relatively limited domain for accounting with the objectives being given exogenously or inferred from actions. Chambers, for example, states:

> Specific ends and the ranking of specific ends are beyond inquiry . . . . It is sufficient, and indeed observers have no other course, to regard specific ends of others as given and beyond inquiry.[1]

In order to generate guidelines, the profession *must* have means for appraising these very ends that Chambers holds are beyond inquiry. It sometimes accepts statements from independent ethical specialists, who study objectives of individuals and groups and rank them as to importance. Accountants may then decide whose needs are important enough to satisfy or unimportant enough to neglect. Professor Carl Nelson has suggested (privately, 1959) that the traditional price system may be used to make these decisions. Apparently, Chambers agrees in part, for he looks to "actions in the market" and exhorts the profession to be guided by these results.[2] The profession's interpretations of market actions are apparently exogenous inputs for the accounting system. The profession then generates the necessary guidelines (principles) to satisfy these inferred objectives. The market actions act as surrogates behind which the profession is not required to look.

For another example, consider (again) the principles of accounting suggested by Scott: justice, truth, fairness and adaptation.[3] The first three of these principles may indeed

---

[1] Raymond J. Chambers, *Accounting Evaluation and Economic Behavior* (Englewood Cliffs: Prentice-Hall, Inc., 1966), pp. 56, 41.
[2] *Ibid.*, Chapter 4 and especially page 101.
[3] DR Scott, "The Basis for Accounting Principles," *The Accounting Review*, December, 1941, pp. 342-343.

come from the environment — the culture — but the profession has the Rabbinical task of assigning weights for relative worthiness to individuals and groups when tradeoffs are necessary. The first and third of Scott's principles may be culturally determined, but the second presumably gives support to those who hold that principles are eternal. For Scott, the accounting task of adaptation apparently includes appraising the importance of contending parties, given the cultural milieu and the three exogenous beacons — justice, truth, and fairness. Adaptation is clearly subordinate, but at least it is endogenous to the profession.

This cultural aspect deserves further comment. For an accounting principle (guideline) to have universal application — as many accountants seem to feel — it seems that objectives would need to be weighted similarly, interpreted uniformly, and the technological alternatives would need to conform to similar standards in each culture. The quest for universal principles that are "basic" to all cultures for eternity is assumed to lead to a smaller list of principles with wide application and a tendency to narrow the areas of difference. This assumption is a hypothesis — conceivably the guideline list may need to be larger in order to encompass a wider range of attitudes and objectives. In a broader context the profession might ponder to what extent it should insist on cultural conformance to rigid professional outputs as opposed to permitting a broad band of accounting differences to accommodate differing cultural influences and interpretations. Some sort of compromise between the limits of narrow rigidity and fluid output tailored to each individual's needs seems to be desirable.[4]

Accounting Theories — Systematic Aspects

We turn now to the problems of prediction in accounting, and this inquiry leads to a discussion of accounting theories. The differences in attitude among accountants as to the limits of their domain are numerous and the variance is surprisingly wide.

To illustrate with a definition of varying scope, consider Ijiri's causative double entry.[5] This approach in the most limited interpretation permits one to predict a family of probable changes — credits — given an identified debit. A debit to inventory, for example, gives rise to an expectation (prediction) that one or more credits are to be found elsewhere in the system of accounts. Most accountants will desire a broader interpretation. The debit to inventory is equivalent to a declarative sentence that creates the expectation that the stock of available goods increased. In the Ijiri sense, it creates the additional expectation that other assets decreased or that obligations increased, and in this respect it resembles a propositional function. In its overall aspect the double-entry structure is similar to the logical rule of detachment (*Modus Ponens*). If one accepts the truth of p and

---

    [4] An optimum "narrowing of differences" would appear to depend on: (1) the diversity of needs, (2) diversity of relevant inputs, and (3) the tradeoffs necessary if general purpose statements are substituted for specialized information, i.e., sensitivity to information. The quest for universal laws that are somehow more fundamental than cultural overlay may be mischievous. With respect to law and political relations Harold Laski states: "A hundred years ago, it was as natural for Austin to stop his discussion of law at the boundaries of the state as it would have been impossible for the medieval thinker to discuss it in other than universal terms." *Introduction to Politics* (London: George Allen & Unwin, Ltd., 1930, 1951, 1962), p. 85. W. Stark emphasizes that the economics of Adam Smith (preindustrial revolution), Ricardo, and Marx were conditioned by the technologies of their times. *The History of Economics* (London: Routledge & Kegan Paul Ltd., 1944), *passim*, especially pp. 32ff.
    [5] Yuji Ijiri, *The Foundations of Accounting Measurement* (Englewood Cliffs: Prentice-Hall, Inc., 1967), Chapter 5, pp. 100ff.

also the implication of $p \rightarrow q$, then he accepts the truth of q.[6] In empirical work he is usually less confident and accordingly forms a hypothesis as to the probable existence of q and designs appropriate activities to investigate. Similarly, an interpretation that permits us to accept the double-entry structure along with the system of accounts as surrogates (language symbols) for principals, also helps us direct our research activity among the principals.[7]

Suppose we enlarge the area of prediction even more. We predict from an increase in earnings per share that the price of the shares will increase. We predict that management will be dissatisfied and take corrective action if sales returns exceed satisfactory levels or that workers will adjust their aspiration levels in response to changes in numbers generated by the accounting process. Are these traditional *accounting* theories? A growing number of accountants feel that no great violence is done by extending the definition of accounting to cover such cases and that positive benefits may result. Traditionally, the tendency has been to use very limited definitions for scope, and some branches of knowledge have practically defined themselves out of existence. The question is not whether behavioral expectations should be considered — of course they must — but rather whether in the partitioning of fields and specializing of work these predictions are best done by accountants. Conceptually, the boundaries may be drawn either to include or exclude such statements, but, if they are excluded, accountants as accountants would never be able to evaluate an existing accounting system or even design one. Predictions of importance — even for chasing errors and recording data — are clearly behavioral in nature.

In spite of some serious confusion, accountants are vitally concerned with still another type of prediction. Some deny that they deal with the future or that their constructions should be governed directly by expected future events. Others ask, to what extent are ac-

---

[6] Until "debit" and "credit" are interpreted the rules of double-entry are tautologies. Milton Friedman states: "Viewed as a language, theory has no substantive content; it is a set of tautologies," *Essays in Positive Economics* (Chicago: University of Chicago Press, 1966, 1953), p. 7. An uninterpreted language (syntax) is often called a "calculus" or a "model."

[7] The question of giving evidential weights to the inferences to be drawn from surrogate clues with regard to principals is also similar to practical deduction. Except for the logical cases of truth by stipulation, the research student goes into a "class" (i.e., finds whether a singular element is a member) by one or more defining properties. He fails to get empirical direction from his "deduction" unless he returns from the class to a singular case by another defining property. That is, he infers that because an element x meets one requirement for class membership, it will share in the other properties common to members of the class. The researcher, of course, must be on guard that the new inferred properties were not among those removed in the abstraction process necessary to establish the class. A more general statement with a different emphasis is given as a summary of Karl Popper's position. "Growth of Knowledge begins with an imaginative hypothesis . . . . It is science rather than myth if it can be tested by observation. *To test we apply ordinary deductive logic to get a singular observation* statement whose falsehood would refute it." (Emphasis added.) Jerome S. Bruner, Jacqueline J. Goodnow and George A. Austin state: "To categorize is to render discernibly different things equivalent, to group the objects and events and people around us into classes, and to respond to them in terms of their class membership rather than their uniqueness." *A Study of Thinking* (New York: Science Editions, Inc., 1962), p. 1.

Fredrick Cecil Mills paraphrases Keynes: " . . . our conclusions should be in the form of deductive correlations rather than of universal generalizations." "On Measurement in Economics," see R. B. Tugwell (ed.), *The Trend of Economics* (New York: Alfred Knopf, Inc., 1924), p. 58. Possible dangers are implicit in Marvin Harris' comment: "Although the process of classification is popularly described as finding the 'same' property in a collection of different entities, this is patently not the case. Sameness is a purely logical relationship which can be demonstrated for logical constructs, but not for empirical entities." *Op. cit.*, p. 8. That all statements of a language may not be of the predictive type has been pointed out by Richard S. Rudner: "Emergentism . . . advances the belief that some events are, in *principle*, unpredictable . . . since they are not connected with other events in any lawlike fashion." *Philosophy of Social Science* (Englewood Cliffs: Prentice-Hall, Inc., 1966), p. 71.

countants' models constructed from past events expected to be predictors of future events? To begin the discussion, it may be useful to point out that *all decisions* are related to a choice of actions to be taken in the future. The clues are *all* from the past and the immediate decision is to decide *what* events from the past promise to be relevant to probable choices to be made in the future.[8]

Accounting clearly is unable to furnish all the information that might be appropriate for all conceivable decisions. Accountants, however, should be concerned when portfolio managers and other decision-makers assert, as they sometimes do, that accounting information is not used at all in their decision processes. To the extent that accountants capture important financial variables, such claims are fantastic. Traditionally, one enters an accounting system with an input vehicle known as a transaction. One's explanation cannot end at this point, for in the long run the definition of transaction is always open. The profession has never been explicit about its rules for selecting certain events to serve as transactions and for rejecting others. Obviously, the events themselves are not "entered" in the system — even in a total system! Moreover, the profession has not always been explicit about its rules for selecting and rejecting the particular aspects of transactions that are recorded. Regardless of the selection rules actually adopted, the system is supposed to account for, or at least register, the effects of inputs on important variables of concern.[9]

More important, we often forget that hypothetical events, e.g., expected return to peacetime activity, may be translated into hypothetical transactions (or aggregates) placed in the system and outcomes predicted. The manager or investor must estimate the effect of an anticipated event on at least one appropriate variable in order to enter the system. The anticipated outcomes may provide an input to a more complete decision system that combines additional expectations with an evaluating mechanism and renders information more immediately useful. The division of information-producing labor along with the diversity of decisions means that accountants supply only a part of the relevant information. With modern office machinery they may sometimes enrich their system by including a wider range of value systems, alternative opportunities and decision rules.

In a broader context, the profession is faced with the problem of deciding to what extent its measures of the past reflect managers' ability to adapt resources to past environmental conditions and to what extent this ability may be extrapolated into the future. To the degree that extrapolation is feasible, the analyst may predict a future impact from an exogenous factor, enter the accountants' model which has been constructed from a selection of past events, and predict the reaction of numerous endogenous variables including the ability of management to adapt to all sorts of possible anticipated conditions. At a

---

[8] I am unable to agree with Chambers' sharp distinction between measurement (of the past) and valuation (of future expectations). They simply are not independent in any respect. Chambers, *op. cit.*, "What is past and present may be able to be measured. But what is future can only be evaluated," p. 42.

[9] Accountants have always been in a preferred position to see the impact of policies and events on many interesting variables including an especially important one — income. In opposition to many engineers and others concerned with physical measures, and at the risk of using strange measurement rules, accountants usually insist that the impact of price, efficiency and volume variances be made explicit and their influence on the overall enterprise accomplishment measure — income — be reported. The desirability of such measures for smoothing the transition to corporate-level management should be clear. That we may miss many important considerations is suggested by Gordon Pask: "To the accountant . . . it means that his model of a company, his precious double-entry stuff, is but a tiny facet of the truth." *An Approach to Cybernetics* (New York: Harper & Brothers, 1961), p. 109. Consider also this statement by Alfred North Whitehead " . . . mere geometry is not the whole tale. Colours are relevant." *A Philosopher Looks at Science* (New York: Philosophical Library, 1965), p. 22.

more practical level, analysts may use quarterly statements to predict yearly results and yearly statements to predict the results of the indefinite future. If they do so, they must face the consequences of assuming the environment as well as managements' adaptive abilities are constant, or be able to predict the degree of managements' adaptability for predicted changes in the environments. The accountants' problem is clear enough: They must account for managements' ability to accomplish objectives in a welter of diverse exogenous influences and to predict reactions to these possible influences in the future.

Inasmuch as accounting theories are evaluated by comparing their efficiency in predicting outcomes, the profession needs specific selection criteria for choosing among theories. In our culture, we sometimes strive to avoid uncertainty. With this norm and neglecting cost factors we might rank highest those theories that predict best. But some theories predict well on unimportant items and may be less dependable on important matters. We choose among competing theories by evaluating their features by reference to normative value grids. We devise principles based on knowledge that consequences from following them can be predicted by our theoretical structure. Principles themselves will be evaluated highly if the predicted consequences of following them lead to desirable results. (Incidentally, one of the most important objectives of control may be in the direction of improved predictions.)

Functionalism Adapted to Accounting

No one seriously considers accounting, or any other information service, to be a closed system entirely divorced from the community it serves. An important question therefore is related to how a professional service perceives the needs of the environment, structures its responsibilities, and develops its processes to meet them. Professional perceptors who sense these needs and understand possibilities for meeting them become especially important, for objectives are from outside the accounting system and must be translated into pressures that are evaluated and treated as professional objectives for the accounting system itself. Thus, the objectives of worthy outsiders must be identified and the importance of each objective and its worthy source must be combined in some way and weighted to form objectives for the profession.

Perhaps the most explicit and interesting application of functionalism to accounting and its related activities has been set forth by the Dutch accountant, Limperg.[10] His methodology is simple enough. First, he wishes to identify existing needs and objectives in a relevant society. Limperg clearly expects the function to be dominant in a service activity: " . . . as soon as the function exists, the engager has no influence over the manner in which the function is fulfilled . . . The accountant is no longer free to choose the means which he may use to fulfill the function."[11]

American accountants would probably not be quite so rigid in structuring their responsibilities. They may express concern that professional leaders often have so many dif-

---

[10] Theo Limperg, Jr., "The Accountant's Function and the Doctrine of Raised Expectations," *Maandblad voor Accountancy en Bedrijhshuishoudkunde*, February, October, 1932 and October, November, 1933. An English translation by Tan Hian Kie (Dasuki Hartano) may be found in my *Readings in Accounting Theory*, Volume I (Djakarta: Lembaga Penjelidikan Ekonomi Dan Masjarakat, 1963), pp. 21-37. The title is Tan's translation of *leer van het gewekte vertrouwen*.

[11] *Ibid.*, p. 34. He admits occasional difficulties of identification: "In periods of transition, new needs of society emerge,and *there is uncertainty regarding the content of the function* . . . . Because of the nonexistence of a general norm . . . the personality of the accountant will play a greater role than usual," p. 33.

ferent perceptions of the objectives and of the most desirable means, but certainly they do not seriously disagree with the functional orientation of the argument. For Limperg, the second methodological step involves the selection of guidelines. "There must be a rule of conduct . . . a guide for action, in order to keep the right track in the unending diversities of particulars."[12] The process is thus seen to be a simple one: Needs exist; needs are recognized; a group moves by means of guidelines to fulfill the needs.

The Sprouse-Moonitz study was weakened by a tendency to derive the "functions" of accounting in a very roundabout and indirect manner from objectives of worthy nonaccountants. The A-Postulates, which were observations about some things that happen in the major host system, are *not* exhibited directly as objectives that the accounting function is to fulfill. Yet, critics may have been over-zealous in attempting to demolish the Sprouse-Moonitz structure. Postulate A-1, for example, relates to quantification, but quantification is stated as being "helpful in making rational economic decisions," and making "rational economic decisions" is assumed to be an objective of the host system. Unfortunately, the remaining A-Postulates (exchange, entities, time period and unit of measure) are more difficult to translate directly into social objectives, and the manner in which they are presented does not tend to emphasize their function as worthy social objectives.

The latter deficiency is partially corrected by later reference to five functions, each of which is said to refer to a specific postulate. Unfortunately, these functions are presented briefly and not systematically, and in fact are turned around. "The first five postulates . . . led to the following statement of the functions of accounting . . . "[13] Quantification (A-1) as an extra-system objective impinges on the accountant's system as a need to measure. Exchange (A-2) translates from a requirement of the social system into the need for the accounting system to keep track of claims and interests. Exogenous needs for entities, time periods, and units of measure translate into the accounting domain as the need for recording changes, assigning changes to periods and using monetary symbols. On the whole this translation is somewhat less successful, and the lack of success is apparently due to failure to emphasize that relevant A-Postulates influence processing rules inside the accounting domain. One concludes that the functional methodology was applied in a casual way, and the bitterness of various functionally oriented critics is at least understandable.

Teleology and Accounting

It may be surprising that several accountants take an attitude that is essentially teleological in the very broad sense. In some cases this attitude is methaphysical only to the extent that certain assumptions of considerable breadth are stipulated. In this sense the specification of assumptions hardly meets the tests for consideration as metaphysical, but on occasion these assumptions may be pretty far from operationally meaningful statements that are stipulated to further a particular inquiry. This semiconfusion carries over to the accepted meaning of 'teleology' as a term. One common meaning is related to ex-

---

[12] *Ibid.*, p. 22.

[13] Robert T. Sprouse and Maurice Moonitz, *A Tentative Set of Broad Accounting Principles for Business Enterprises* (New York: American Institute of Certified Public Accountants, 1962), Research Study No. 3, p. 7. See also Maurice Moonitz, *The Basic Postulates of Accounting*, Research Study No. 1 (New York: AICPA, 1961), p. 23. In this earlier statement the A-Postulates were "related" to one function with five highly specialized guidelines as parts of the function.

planations in terms of purposes ("whither explanations") and is more or less synonymous with functionalism. An alternative meaning, stressed in this paper, treats teleological explanation in terms of broad sweeping causes, i.e., in terms of constructions that go beyond stipulated hypotheses or operational constructions to constructions too broad for empirical testing (history, progress, etc.).

The Mattessich plan of organization is the broad stipulation of a pervasive phenomenon known as a "flow."[14] From this organizing theme, he observes or infers a transaction, and a two-dimensional aspect from which a duality principle that leads to double-entry accounting is developed.

> . . . we may interpret the *duality principle* as the assertion that a transaction or flow has basically two dimensions: an aspect and a counter-aspect . . . a process of giving and taking, input and output, transferring out and transferring in.[15]

From one point of view the uses to which Mattessich puts the concept "flow" constitute an implicit definition of the concept. Must flows be continuous? Discrete quanta? Can transactions possibly be continuous? Which flows serve as bases or carriers for transactions? Apparently, a further organizing schema for selecting useful flows needs to be introduced. If one appraises Mattessich's contribution in terms of teleology — as purpose — he is clearly not teleological or even functional, but if one conceives the term as referring to "bases" below which one does not descend, his work may be ranked as the foremost of teleological systems.

The Spacek approach to accounting principles ranges from a strongly functional orientation in his criticism of the Moonitz document (ARB #1) to the use of an undefined and undifferentiated construction in his own formulations known as "conscience." We are told that " . . . a principle unsupported by sound reasoning is nothing more than any arbitrary rule . . .," but with conscience and the use of "initiative" we are assured of the ability to overcome some of our difficulties with principles. "To do so will require initiative . . . . To develop *initiative*, we need only listen to our conscience. This will inevitably lead us to assume our proper responsibility."[16]

The use of conscience in this connection is highly suspect. Presumably for Spacek, the answers to the principles dilemma are already available, and the problem is one of implementation. The implementation process requires initiative, which the profession by implication lacks. Moreover, the exercise of professional conscience will lead to initiative. Here the attributes of professional conscience are not spelled out. From whence do they come? Why has not professional conscience already led to initiative? Or has it? Is professional

---

[14] Richard Mattessich, *Accounting and Analytical Methods* (Homewood: Richard D. Irwin, Inc., 1964). He quotes Anton (p. 27n) apparently with approval: "The flow concept has universality of meaning . . ." Morton A. Kaplan warns: "A completely general theory would lack explanatory power. It would enunciate only the most elementary truisms about social and political structures . . . . [Yet] highly particularized models lack both generality and relevance to any specific problem." *Contemporary Political Analysis, op. cit.*, pp. 155-156.

[15] *Ibid.*, pp. 26, 27. Specialists in the history of ideas may wish to trace the antecedents of this structure to classical physics? To early Greek philosophers? To Hegel?

[16] Leonard Spacek, "A Suggested Solution to the Principles Dilemma," *The Accounting Review*, April, 1964, pp. 279-283. Again historians may wish to explore the antecedents of this view. The emphasis on conscience is related to natural law doctrines and church dogmas. The motivating role of conscience that leads to initiative is a little more difficult to place. Aquinas?

conscience socially determined? Natural? God given? How is it changed? In summary, the use of conscience would seem to be more useful if it were suggested as a hypothesis along with some supporting hypotheses regarding its probable formation.

For a final illustration, consider the position of Littleton and some of his disciples.[17] The Littleton structure is somewhat ambiguous on the nature of theories and principles. One statement, " . . . theory reasons from purposes outward toward actions . . ." is consistent with our suggestion for the definition of principles. A second statement: " . . . theory consists of explanations and reasons," is consistent with our suggestion that theory be related to predictions and reinforced by reference to broader class inclusion.[18]

A simple functional conception of teleology is evident enough in some references to purpose and objective, but there is evidence that Littleton used a more esoteric integrating assumption for his theory. Theory is constructed, in the Littleton framework, by observing and generalizing practice. In one sense this is an obvious way to start an investigation in this area, but he seems to have expected more. Deinzer speaks of " . . . Littleton's early thesis of a predetermined destiny for accounting, toward which all developments were tending."[19] This "invisible hand" approach as a method of structuring a field amounts to "Darwinizing a profession" and suffers from the same objections.

The difficulty with social Darwinism (or, better, Lamarckism) as an investigating device is that it cannot distinguish functional from dysfunctional activities without further inquiry. Its danger is in assuming that what exists is in fact serving a function. Existence itself may set up the presumption of function and when combined with a further assumption of rational behavior may be a useful research device.

The Littleton habit of identifying theory (principles?) and practices, therefore, provides no way to determine whether either the practices or the principles are good or bad, unless he assumes that both practices and instructions are unfolding with guidance from "good hands" (Deinzer's expression). Given an *independent* appraisal of the ends-in-view one may, of course, evaluate both practices and principles. Practices may not be in agreement with the instructions (principles) and in these cases a comparison may reveal that the practices or the instructions or perhaps both are in need of change. On occasion, deviant practices may suggest reappraisal of the relevancy of ineffective principles. This back and forth comparison may indicate that principles and practices do indeed tend to be consistent, and thus the assumed coincidence may receive a measure of support from the resulting tendency toward adjustment.

Postscript

To conclude we may ask: Where in this endless morass can a free spirit stand? Personally, I am unable to find firm footing in the Mattessich assumption of fundamental flaws.

---

[17] In "Metaphysics of Pragmatism and Accountancy," Nicholas Dopuch, a product of the Littleton environment, derives some interesting presuppositions of accounting including a number of stipulated hypotheses that could be made operational. *The Accounting Review*, April, 1962, pp. 251-262.

[18] A. C. Littleton, *Structure of Accounting Theory* (Evanston: American Accounting Association, 1953), pp. 136, 132.

[19] Harvey T. Deinzer, *Development of Accounting Thought* (New York: Holt, Rinehart and Winston, Inc., 1965), p. 145. Apparently Littleton's essential philosophical tradition stems from Dewey. Certainly the concern with practice and the assumed relationship of theory and practice is Dewey-based. The faith in "progress" is consistent with Dewey, and the use of nonscientific jargon is more Dewey than positivist. Deinzer's philosophical orientation is also strongly Deweyian with overtones from Ryle and Holmes.

Nor can I find comfort scanning the environment with Moonitz and Sprouse without a more definite handbook of functions and objectives to guide my observations. Clearly I do not share Chambers' remarkable ability to choose among alternatives without being able to specify and appraise objectives or to account for performance in the past without making inferences about the future. Nor am I entirely comfortable with Littleton's identification of good practice and good theory and the assurance that progress is in good — if invisible — hands. It is no longer possible for me to accept the traditional Patonian structure with its strength in the area of directives and persuasion and its weakness in predictive theory. My only hope — and perhaps yours — rests with the behavioral scientists. They *worry about objectives* and they advance all sorts of predictive possibilities that qualify as theories. Their output to date may seem to be pretty primitive but, I submit, it is about all we have.

Essay Three

Principles — Some Behavioral Aspects

From certain traditional points of view a behavioral approach to principles may seem to be something of a contradiction. As a rule a behavioralist is not ordinarily concerned with judging "fundamental" things, or "first" causes, or "ultimate origins." Unfortunately, Webster's Unabridged lists ten shades of meaning for the word 'principle' and seven are related to such adjectives as basic, ultimate, fundamental.[1] Equally unfortunately, many practical people have chosen *principium* (ultimate origin) instead of *principate*, which is related to the power and authority of the directive. But most unfortunate are those who have selected "source" definitions but have failed to emphasize the imperative aspect. One would expect that those who associate principles with an authoritative source would also stress the function of principles as guidelines. Instead many have lost sight of the guideline function in a morass of arguments over logical priority, historical precedent, theoretical import and even Platonic essences.

The viewpoint that might have been stressed in order to keep more closely to the attitudes of behavioral sciences generally is given in Webster's *New International* as:

> A settled rule of action, a governing law of conduct: an opinion, attitude, or belief that exercises a directing influence on . . . life and behavior; a rule . . . of good conduct . . .

It is the rule-of-action usage that has been adopted in this essay, as well as in Essay One.[2]

From a viewpoint of behavioral research, the conception of principles as "policy directives" applies best in inquiring about the work of professional leaders who seem to be constructing principles. Certainly behavioral studies devoted to finding how professional leaders relate their work to fundamentals, to essences, to omnipotent beings or to natural laws have so far not been rewarding. Yet this area of behavioral research has tremendous promise, and except for wrong-headed emphasis, might prove very useful to aspiring researchers. These possibilities may be explored further.

Professional leaders scan the social order for clues that might help them select appropriate accounting guidelines to further social goals. Presumably these goals are sensed, delineated or somehow constructed from observed environmental clues. Thus, behaviora-

---

[1] W. Stanley Jevons, writing in the last century, emphasized this view. *"Principle (principium*, beginning), the first source of anything; sometimes especially used to mean the major premise of a syllogism."* His definition of 'postulate' is more useful: *"(postulatum*, a thing demanded), a proposition which is necessarily demanded as a basis of argument; in geometry, the postulates define the practical conditions required." Elementary Lessons in Logic: Deductive and Inductive* (New York: Macmillan and Co., 1893), p. 339. The American Accounting Association's *A Statement of Basic Accounting Theory* is behavioral in orientation but makes use of fundamentalist jargon, e.g., "basic," "in the last analysis," "fundamental."

[2] Talcott Parsons and Edward A. Shils emphasize a similar position with respect to the function of generalizations. "Generalizations are modes of defining the actor's orientations to particular objects of which he has not yet had experience." *Toward a General Theory of Action* (Cambridge: Harvard University Press, 1959), p. 12.

lists should be vitally interested in the observations, the methods, and operations of such leaders. Whom do they talk with? Whom do they regard as worthy influences? When are tradeoffs necessary? How are the consequences of required tradeoffs evaluated? In other words, requirements for professional leaders include antennae for observing the seething, dynamic social order, ability to estimate reactions to alternative accounting rules, and further ability to recognize and adjust alternative rules and new technology to these needs. In terms of the discussion in Essay One, these professional perceptors read the water of social needs and, like the blacksmith, shape the available material to serve their needs. Constant reshaping, or at least review of the process, is necessary to adapt the changing accounting materials (technology) to changing demands.[3]

The work of this essay is concerned first with a brief general discussion of the relation of the source of information to its credibility — an item of extreme importance to accountants and their professional image. The discussion continues with a look at possible outer-directed sources such as religious doctrines and natural laws. A return is then made to the sociological views expressed above, and the work is extended with a brief inquiry into the possible use of existentialism by the accounting profession. The essay concludes with attention to the place of principles in developing the psychological sets that are assumed in existentialism and as a device for bringing discipline to the profession.

Everyone seems to agree that the accounting profession as a social institution can be partially justified because it adds credibility to accountability representations by those who have been held accountable.[4] It should be clear that the image of the profession is especially important. Presumably enough "confidence" should be added to justify the social cost. In turn the confidence added would seem to be a function of society's perception of the ability, judgment and integrity of those who vouch for the representations. Interestingly, professional leaders seem to have done none of the empirical work necessary to support their intuitions.

Members of the profession should know that some work on source credibility has been done, and with this need in mind the discussion turns to an unpublished dissertation by Murray Hilibrand, cited and enlarged by Raymond A. Bauer.[5] Bauer states:

> Since Aristotle's *Rhetoric* there has been for practical purposes no challenge to the notion that the more credible (powerful, honest, knowledgeable, likeable, what have you) a communicator is, the more effective his message will be. Yet there has been evidence in the research

---

[3] Apparently, this process was the imperfectly formed basis for Moonitz' selection of postulates and principles. The environment was observed, and with the aid of an unspecified sifting device a number of requirements became the B-Postulates. The profession's adaptive responses were suggested as B-Postulates and as developed principles. Maurice Moonitz, *The Basic Postulates of Accounting* (New York: AICPA, 1961), *passim*. I have previously discussed the necessity for professional leaders to observe and appraise social needs and adjust resources — and rules — to them. See "Research Methodology and Accounting Theory Formation," *The Accounting Review*, July, 1960, pp. 397ff.

[4] An early but extremely persuasive exposition for this approach is that of Theodore Limperg, Jr. See translation by Tan Hian Kie (Dasuki Hartano) from *Maandblad voor Accountancy en Bedrijhshuiskoudkunde*, February - October, 1932 and October - November, 1933, translated as "The Accountants' Function and the Doctrine of Raised Expectations," *Reading in Accounting Theory* (Djakarta: Lembaga Penjelidikan Ekomomi Dan Masjarakat, 1962), Vol. 1, pp. 21-37.

[5] Murray Hilibrand, *Source Credibility and the Persuasive Process*, unpublished doctoral dissertation, Harvard Business School, 1964, and Raymond A. Bauer, "Application of Behavioral Science," Harvard University, Graduate School of Business Administration Reprint Series. Reprinted from *Applied Science and Technological Progress*, June, 1967.

literature that *perhaps* a communicator could be *too* credible, in . . . that persons listening to or reading his message might accept his conclusions too readily and not examine the evidence. There was also evidence that after a few weeks people forgot where they heard or read messages, i.e., the "source" lost its effect.[6]

The Hilibrand study was designed to test the hypothesis that receivers of messages from those perceived as highly competent and trustworthy would be highly vulnerable to counter-messages delivered a few weeks later. Apparently this singular hypothesis was deduced from a broader belief that receivers generally would substitute authority for substance and accept propositions more or less unthinkingly.

Hilibrand classified message sources as:

1. highly competent and trustworthy,
2. highly competent but not trustworthy,
3. not competent but trustworthy, and
4. not competent and also not trustworthy.

His findings were in line with predictions. Type one sources (both highly competent and highly trustworthy) had highest initial persuasive impact, and Type four the lowest. Moreover, Type one messages were less vulnerable to counter-messages given a short time later, i.e., before the sources had a chance to be forgotten. Interestingly enough, after a couple of weeks Type one messages were most vulnerable. Apparently the most lasting impact is from Type two — those perceived to be highly competent but not highly trustworthy. Tentatively it was felt that such sources encourage careful scrutiny of the evidence, and that those who scrutinize tend to retain.

So far as I know the output of accounting messages has not been tested for persuasive impact and ability to withstand counter-messages. Perhaps it is time some of our more alert graduate students perform such tests. Just how vulnerable are accounting statements (assuming they are even read) to counter-statements by managers, or brokers, or public relations men? One might hypothesize that the investor group would not consider public relations representatives either highly competent or highly trustworthy — perhaps far more competent than trustworthy. Brokers may be suspected of self-interest and a "biased trustworthiness," and in some cases their competence may also be questioned.[7]

Our concern at this point is not directly with the accountant's own resistance to messages from other sources. We feel without extensive research that professional leaders have followed the Aristotelian lead and have toiled manfully to increase their image of being highly competent and highly trustworthy. In many cases the preservation of the desired image must have been difficult. The attributes of neutrality, conservatism, honesty, and objectivity may indeed be useful for internal reasons, but their contribution to image projection may also be important.

Throughout these essays it has been argued that the profession's concern about "generally accepted principles" is an appeal to the public for legitimacy. A democratic order

---

[6] Bauer, p. 102. For an interesting discussion of ethical aspects of persuasion see: Richard L. Johannesen, "Ethics of Persuasion: Some Perspectives," *Marketing and the New Science of Planning* (Blacksburg, VA: American Marketing Association, 1968), pp. 541-547.

[7] Related studies could be directed to internal reports by managerial accountants, consultants' representations, rumors from the invisible (informal) organizations, reports from functional areas, legal opinions, etc.

does not generate great respect for authoritative pronouncements. In fact there is much similarity between the attitudes necessary for successful democratic institutions and the scientific attitude of accepting all statements — except those relating to the process itself — as tentative and subject to change in response to new and conflicting evidence. If this observation is correct, the profession in democratic countries has been ill-advised to emphasize the authoritative aspect of its pronouncements.

The use of "generally accepted" to modify and strengthen the impact of the guidelines is likely to be more successful. Those of us accustomed to the democractic ethic are likely to be impressed with the process of evaluating proposals by majority acceptance. The term "generally accepted" may not entail or imply majority acceptance, but the correlation may have some effectiveness. Finally, in a democratic society we might predict a general shift from inner (or outer) directed legitimacy to the acceptance of peer group approval as sufficient warrant for behavior. To the extent that this shift has been accepted by the age group now concerned with the accounting process, the semantic impact of 'generally accepted' has positive persuasive force. The representation 'generally accepted' does not *necessarily* imply approval from relevant peer groups. However, peer groups themselves are not sharply defined, and a particular member is usually not positive about the feelings of other members of such diffuse groups. To the extent that the member is uncertain about these attitudes, he may be influenced by the assurance that acceptance is widely held. He tends to infer that the breadth of the assenting base is a clue that indicates relevant peer group acceptance.

We return now to professional attempts to gain legitimacy for guidelines by the semantic device of calling them principles and relating principles to the deity and to natural and supernatural laws. Clearly these attempts are aimed at increasing the image of trustworthiness, and perhaps also at improving the image of competence by indirect reference to the competence of the deity or to the efficient and inexorable processes of nature. These characteristics may rub off on — become associated with — the profession and thereby increase the acceptance of its edicts.

Turn now to the possibilities of investigating the importance of the quest for identity with godlike images, natural laws, historical necessity, and other solid and accepted foundations. At first glance such investigations look unpromising, but in an indirect way they may prove to be very useful. To the extent that religious rules reflect relevant ethical standards and life-pattern objectives they may be employed as shortcuts to or surrogates for independent investigations. That is, if the profession accepts the weighting and evaluating explicitly stated in prevailing religious doctrines, its own work in this area may be greatly reduced. Inasmuch as all possible situations cannot be covered by personal word from the deity, or by natural laws, further interpretations, expansions and social surrogates are required. An authoritarian hierarchy of sources ordered according to nearness to the image is sometimes found. The scriptures may be rated higher than the pronouncements of bishops or of the congregations where conflict arises over identical points.[8] Or the specific points may not be treated in the scriptures, so that a body of supplementary doctrine covering commonly encountered tradeoffs arises. (Note the legal analogy with the law, the

---

[8] Such conflict is not likely to occur in a settled authoritarian structure unless there is conflict over the meaning of words involved or perhaps unless "times" have changed and the neophyte is asked to choose between a formal wording and a modern interpretation of the symbols. Sometimes, an additional group — the translators — intervene.

regulations, and opinions in tax matters.) If the authoritarian structure is not settled (stable) or if there has been a division of authority, conflicts are of course expected near the borders, where the elbowing is most obvious.

The point here is that one important set of clues as to the needs, objectives, and acceptable social behaviors may come from seemingly unpromising sources. A hierarchy of closeness is established, and the conflicts that are not resolved by outside cultural sanctions or quasi-religious authority become subject matter to be solved within the sub-culture by the profession. But the profession is not homogeneous, so a hierarchy of judgment centers is also established within the profession. Witness, for example, the Accounting Principles Board as the highest judgment center within the profession, and the organ which mediates with outside authority groups. (Practitioners and professors with less ponderous responsibilities may disapprove of the established order!)

In the case of religious authority, appeal to broader and broader rules of conduct would seem to be more vague rather than more 'basic,' unless the sources of the commandments are employed for scaling such impossible concepts as 'basic.' To the extent that the source of the rules appears to be higher, the resulting edicts may be considered to be more persuasive.[9]

The interpretation of clues from natural laws and from historical necessity is a little more indirect, as there are less well-established hierarchies for appeals. Natural-law advocates ask rule-makers to consider the biological aspects of survival of individuals and species and the psychological aspects of life fulfillment.[10] The clues to proper rule making come apparently from observing the behaviors that lead to survival and propagation, and the goal would seem to be adaptation of the species to survive and prosper in a hostile environment. "Progress" may be taken as an intervening goal even though its direction is not always clearly specified. Presumably, a progressive social group hangs loose and is better able to adapt to changing conditions, although the warrant for this belief is by no means clear. Nevertheless, the current stress in education for business postulates a high degree of uncertainty and recommends the cultivation of skills and abilities required to

---

[9] Incidentally, all religions include some excellent operational rules of conduct. In the Christian area, the golden rule is a masterpiece in rule construction. First, the rule does not need to add legitimacy by using the term 'principle,' for legitimacy is established by the authority of the speaker. Second, the boundaries of its application are unambiguous and clearcut. It does not apply to dogs or trees — only to relations with human beings. Third, its application requires only operational judgments. It requires no looking into other people's minds for clues to interpersonal judgments. The performer looks at his own value structure in every case, reaches judgments on this information and applies it to his actions. The social scientist may wonder whether the effects of such actions will always be consistent with social goals, especially if some of the performers (lookers) are sadists and others are masochists. However, the coordination of the individual actions with social goals is vouched for by an invisible hand — a natural law — the deity himself.

Notice that the rule "love thy neighbor" is a much more ambiguous directive. "Neighbor" is open for definition of a relevant group, and the term "love" has so many shades of meaning that, if the edict is taken in some senses, social condemnation, divine disapproval, and prison sentences may result.

The eye-for-an-eye directive makes use of a *particular* instance to convey a general rule, a prime example of an operational rule that needs an open system for application. Clearly its reconciliation with the golden rule assumes a particular type of personality. It might, however, make the consequences of an action more predictable, although the remedy may not always be the best society could contrive.

[10] But Roscoe Pound warns: " . . . 'nature' did not mean in antiquity what it means to us who are under the influence of the idea of evolution . . . . The 'natural' object was that which expressed most completely the idea of the thing. It was the perfect object . . . . For legal purposes, reality was to be found in this ideal, perfect, natural law, and its organ was juristic reason." *An Introduction to the Philosophy of Law* (New Haven: Yale University Press, 1954, 1922), p. 10.

survive in and profit by such an environment. This uncertainty affords opportunities to prosper and is not always dangerous. Unfortunately, the command to be adaptable is not specific enough to support an entire curriculum.

There have been and are some quasi-priests of the natural-law movement. Aristotle, Leibnitz, Rousseau, Thoreau, Muir, some spokesmen for the medical profession, many environmental planners, and others have been willing to help man interpret his natural requirements. They presumably select rules that encourage consequences consistent with such laws. Behavioralists will find all sorts of interesting research possibilities in natural behavior. Drives, instincts, perceptions, conditioning theories and a host of other devices may be expanded or resurrected to organize investigations.

There are many advantages from having an accepted set of principles. The advantages that arise from less difficulty in training neophytes are clear enough, but the advantages from making the environment more predictable have not been properly stressed. To the extent that uniform rules are applied by all who perform the attest function, the comparisons and predictions necessary for resource allocation are improved. The evaluative task with regard to managers, assets, products becomes less uncertain. Moreover, the knowledge that others (e.g., competitors) are using information and judgments similarly derived, makes their actions and reactions more predictable.

Clearly a system of guidelines (principles) helps a profession instill essential discipline in its own members by broadcasting what is expected from them and making these expectations definite enough so that conformance or lack of it may be measured and appropriate rewards or punishments rendered. Once a pattern of obeying guidelines from above has been established, loyalty is more firmly attached to the ruling authority (accepted principles) and less and less to guidelines that are individual and discretionary. Practitioners should have less loyalty to their own personal habits and should become less attached to personalized rules. Most practical observers of human behavior are aware of the attachment that people feel for their habitual activities and the entrenching effect of the ruts that are so developed. A shifting of loyalty to the professional rule makers should then help get stability and uniformity in activities, and paradoxically make it easier to introduce changes.[11]

Of course, whether the transfer of allegiance to professional headquarters does in fact lead to more rapid changes and quicker adaptation is an open question that depends in part on the attitude of the rule makers themselves. It is conceivable that this group tends to become conscious of its role and takes steps to establish machinery for sensing new needs and adapting to them. A side advantage is that others will find central groups with established procedures more convenient to approach with proposals for change. At least they will know where to present their cases and to exert their pressures.[12]

Theories, following our discussion in Essay One, are sentences that relate phenomena so that predictions may be made and expectations generated. We now digress and speculate about the lack of comparable agitation for uniform theories. Why has the profession stressed uniform *principles* and not also stressed common interpretations and expecta-

---

[11] As we shall see in later essays, 'neutrality' at the operational level is primarily acceptance of rules from the ruling body as superior to the practitioner's inclination to create his own *ad hoc* guidelines in response to whim or pressure. In this sense neutrality is a device for an organization to promote discipline in its membership.

[12] This topic is discussed more generally in Volume I, "Accounting Profession — Simulation and Description." It is conceivable that more adaptive reaction would result if practitioners were given greater freedom to develop and use their own rules, and leaders were to maintain a sharp outlook for the resulting mutations.

tions from specified clues, i.e., uniform theories? If accounting is devoted to accounting for (explaining) accomplishments in terms of antecedent causative decisions and actions, then it seems that the profession should be interested in uniform theories of accounting, i.e., uniform guidelines for evaluation and prediction. Given an antecedent condition (e.g., the presence of assets) we might expect the profession to be interested in predicting probable consequences. Clearly, the profession does a considerable amount of this sort of thing. A given classification of assets speaks for someone's prediction that these resource classes will be useful in explaining and predicting other possibilities, and the fact that expenses are classified at all is a judgment that the classes can be used effectively for disclosing adaptive requirements.

Thus, principles for system installations may be viewed as guidelines for constructing symbols for a model from the past that will yield "accounting for" past accomplishment and also help predict the adaptability of resources to anticipated or possible future conditions. That is to say, evaluation of guidelines must always be in terms of their predicted consequences along variables of concern to those the profession is trying to serve. Without some sort of predictive and explanatory apparatus, guideline selection and the quest for principles would be an aimless and idle search.[13] We return now to the problem of establishing legitimacy for principles.

An approach to accounting principles through the integrating device of historical necessity has been used on occasion. This approach requires professional leaders to observe historical trends, determine the "necessities" involved, and devise consistent accounting rules. In the general field of social science, Hegel would seem to be the most general with Marx, Engels, St. Augustine, Veblen, Ortega y Gasset, and Ayers only slightly less so. The tenets of the sociology of knowledge are similar and hold generally that an individual is shaped and bound by the culture in which he is enveloped. In the words of Ortega y Gasset, *"Man, in a word, has no nature; what he has . . . is history."*[14]

---

[13] The correlation of means to ends by way of consequences is not an easy task. The following quotation is from Abraham Edel, *Science and the Structure of Ethics* (Chicago: University of Chicago Press, 1961), p. 73.

Will the means if acted on produce the end (its *effectuality*)? What is the quality of its performance (*efficiency*)? How does the use of the means affect collateral ends (*constructiveness* or *destructiveness*)? If there is a considerable investment of energy and resources in providing the means, for what other ends can they be used (their *multivalence*)? What is the *liberating-power* of alternative means to the same end? To what human needs or drives may the means-activity itself give expression (its *expressiveness*)? How satisfying or enjoyable is the means-activity itself (its *luster*)? How far will a particular means if utilized tend to become an end in its own right (its *telicity*)? What is the resultant *cost* of employing a particular means, in terms of the disvalue of the means-activity, the end-concomitants and the consequences? For ends: How *attractive* is the end envisaged by itself? How far capable of occurring without means-components (its *purity*)? How long-lasting (its *permanence*)? In relation to other goals, what support does the occurrence of one end give to others *(constructiveness or destructiveness)? What is its area* in the field of endeavor of the given person or group? In relation to means, what is its *attainability* and its *cost*? In relation to the personal and social economy, what is the strength of the underlying drives and problems to which it is addressed (its *depth*)? With respect to these, what is its *role*? In the light of its role, does it prove to be spurious (e.g., rationalization) or authentic (insightful and realistic in grounding), that is, how *genuine* is it? What is the degree of *satisfaction* that it brings?

[14] See Hans Meyerdoff, *The Philosophy of History in Our Time* (New York: Doubleday Anchor, 1959), p. 57. For those who wish to study the subject in some depth, see Karl Mannheim, *Essays on the Sociology of Knowledge*, edited by Paul Kecskemeti (London: Routledge & Kegan Paul, Ltd., 1952). Those interested in historicism as a sociological integrating device may be interested in Volume I, Essay Three. Those with still more interest and a negative orientation may consult Karl Popper, *The Poverty of Historicism* (New York: Harper Torchbooks, 1961). Some American Institutionalist economists followed a similar path. "What ultimately provides direction for the economy is not the price system but the value system of the culture in which the economy is embedded." Allan G. Gruchy, "Economic Thought," *International Encyclopedia of the Social Sciences*, p. 466.

For an accounting illustration of looking at historical precedent consider the apparent thesis of DR Scott.[15] An observation of development coupled with an understanding of history apparently convinced Scott that the free market economy was deteriorating badly. The price system as an allocator, rationer, and distributor was therefore becoming less and less tenable. The resulting pressures were (predictably) leading to a substitute: administered prices. A requirement for administered prices was some sense of justice, and "justice" called for prices based on sacrifice to the social group. Translated into accounting, sacrifices become costs — more specifically, full costs that hopefully include all social costs.[16]

The results seemed clear enough to Scott: A stronger, more flexible, more professional group of full-costing, cost accountants was needed and should be developed. Scott did, however, have certain misgivings about the institutionalized inflexibility of the then existing cost-accounting profession. He ventured the tentative prediction that the profession would be unable to adapt rapidly enough so that an independent group would take over the function.[17]

Existentialism and Accounting

Recently, attempts have been made to relate some aspects of existentialism to the field of accounting, and we turn now to some possibilities of relating this philosophical approach to the selection of accounting principles.[18]

The chief application of existentialism to the profession appears to be in helping to instill a sense of *individual responsibility* in members of the profession. Those who hold a naturalistic view may excuse all sorts of weaknesses with the obvious observation: "Well, after all, I am only a human being." Those of us who are impressed with ideology and the sociology of knowledge, may shift responsibility and reduce feelings of guilt by observing that we are products of our times and generally culture-bound. ("The institutions tend to make pigs of men and of course I too am a pig!")[19]

While existentialism may make it more difficult for individual practitioners to escape responsibility for their own decisions and actions, it may not be quite so useful for leaders of a profession, and it is not exactly consistent with the whole theory of professional discipline as outlined in this essay. Professional leaders should certainly recognize their crucial responsibility to guide the profession, yet the committee form of professional leadership permits some shifting of responsibility for mediocre performance even at the leadership level.

An interesting aspect of existentialism is connected with the development of group identity and the internalization of professional goals. While the development of deep personal concern, commitment and responsibility by members is a requirement of a functioning profession, we need to inquire what forces are at work to shape individual value systems so that the necessary personal responsibility is kindled. Researchers in the field will be interested in how individual value systems are formed and the arrangement by which individuals influence other individuals. We return to some aspects of this group of problems later, and turn now to a short-run dysfunctional aspect of existentialism.

One of the strong reasons for building a profession and a set of binding "generally accepted principles" has been to permit individuals with relatively weak spines to shift responsibility from themselves to a more impersonal group — the profession. A part of any profession is the occasional necessity to serve as gatekeeper and veto certain client requests. For client-oriented professions, the necessity for saying *no* to those who seem to be paying the bills is thought to be fraught with the danger of irritating and losing the client.[20]

Some of us have advocated the development of a strong public accounting profession and the adoption of a set of principles in Southeast Asia primarily as a spine-stiffening device. With a weak public profession, aggressive businessmen, a government anxious to socialize faltering private activity, a long tradition of concealing rather than disclosing information, and a still longer tradition of avoiding direct confrontation, the need for strengthening professional discipline should be clear to all. The responsibility for saying *no* can be widely diffused into the impersonal profession so that personal confrontation and direct conflict are avoided.

Moreover, the profession itself can be strengthened, for accountants no longer risk the discomfort of confrontation. Members can be personally sympathetic and helpful to clients, and clients can be more receptive — their conflicts are directed against impersonal professional leaders back at central headquarters. (The enemy-in-Washington syndrome!) At the same time members can resist personal pressure more strongly and effectively. If the client becomes too aggressive, he must assume the role of placing his helpful friend, the auditor, in conflict with his own superiors and the sources of his professional accreditation. Thus, the insistent client becomes the confronter in a different battle: the battle for the practitioner's integrity and survival.

---

[15] For an understandable summary of Scott's contribution, see L. J. Benninger, "Accounting Related to Social Institutions — The Theoretical Formulations of DR Scott," *Accounting Research*, January, 1958, pp. 17-30. See also DR Scott, *The Cultural Significance of Accounts* (New York: H. Holt and Company, 1931).

[16] Compare the similarity to H. J. van der Schroeff's *Kostprijs*, where the relevant cost is the socially necessary cost at current price levels without cost of inefficiencies. *De Leer van de Kostprijs* (Amsterdam: N. V. Uitgevers Mij., Kosmos, 1947). This text contains approximately ten pages of summary in English — a most helpful and thoughtful addition.

[17] This topic is also discussed in Essay Two. Comments on the development of operations research may be found there. In addition, however, consider the strong current movement to develop managers who feel "responsible" to all sorts of diverse organizations and social groups. So far, operations research has been a little slow in adopting a wide social approach to its responsibilities, but a socially oriented management science may be taking over Scott's accounting principles and their function. Instead of limiting themselves to disclosure for regulatory purposes, the current management leaders seek to change the emphasis, attitudes, and the short-run objectives of managers themselves.

[18] An interesting attempt to bring the overall attitudes of existentialism to business has been made by John H. Rice, "Existentialism for the Businessman," *Harvard Business Review*, March-April, 1960, pp. 135-143. Reprinted in *Accounting and Its Behavioral Implications*, eds. William J. Bruns, Jr. and Don T. DeCoster (New York: McGraw-Hill Book Company, 1969), pp. 71-82. Except for some semi-Freudian attachment to death-wishes, this article should be interesting to most accountants. Disagreement with the selection has been registered by David Green, Jr., in private conversation, and by John J. Willingham in *The Accounting Review*, April, 1970, p. 388.

[19] We may ask what becomes of free will and decision theory in either a natural or ideological framework " . . . if decisions simply registered trends that have already stabilized themselves . . . . Schlick went so far as to assert that the issue of free will versus determinism was a pseudo-issue and that voluntary decision versus complusion from others was the only issue that made sense . . . . in Marxian materialism . . . freedom is identified as the growth of effective consciousness in human life [and] with the evaluation of the material-social world . . . . decision itself . . . becomes seen as pure act. It becomes the absolutely cut off (free) evaluative process, which we may call *the Sartrean leap.*" Abraham Edel, *Science and the Structure of Ethics* (Chicago: University of Chicago Press, 1961), pp. 61, 81, 90.

[20] In my opinion, public accountants have been far too conscious of losing customers who foot the auditing bills and generate income for the profession. In a broad sense, the *public* receives the benefits from required auditing through more reliable and relevant information, and the *public* also foots the bills for the audits. This latter point is seldom emphasized. True enough, the client-firms write the compensation checks, but some of the cost is undoubtedly passed on to the public, through higher prices for products. In any event, the bills are deductible and other taxpayers pay more taxes or some public needs go unserved. Also, some of the cost is normally passed on to custmers, suppliers, laborers, or others who are recipients of organizational slack, emoluments, and quasi-rents.

The side-effect of using professional principles to reduce graft and related payment is also likely to be beneficial.[21] Loyalty to the profession tends to take some of the "personality cult" out of such activity. Graft and similar payments are normally for personal favors, so that graft reduction calls for stronger loyalty to the rules and greater feeling of guilt from variance from the rules. Thus the political problems of forming an acceptable and effective public accounting profession in many parts of the world are considerable. New loyalties need to be forged to overcome the person-to-person attachment. Moreover, businessmen need to be convinced that disclosure works to the public good and to their own good better than concealment. Present government officials are also an obstruction. Their rules and regulations, especially in socialist economies, often made concealment a necessity for business survival, and the officials themselves are usually indoctrinated with the older mores that see nothing ethically reprehensible in the procedures.

Thus, existentialism may be thought to be inconsistent with one of the chief purposes of professional organizations, and in an important sense, this is true. The existence of a strong profession may develop a non-existential attitude in the membership. Dependence on the profession for responsibility may reduce the development of strong personal responsibility. Yet, here again there is danger of oversimplistic answers. The profession wishes to create strong "moral fiber" for resistance to persuasion from clients and equally strong adherence to the profession. In this sense the problem becomes one of channeling the individual's stern responsibility, as advocated by existentialists, into responsibility for following professional recommendations.

Again we are back to the outlook expressed in the sociology of knowledge. The individual makes his own decisions and accepts responsibility for the consequences. But what determines the value system by which he evaluates the consequences? The acceptance of a profession as his reference group and identification with its objectives means that his independence is sharply curtailed.[22] In a very important sense one may ask: *How can an independent accountant possibly be independent*? At best, any individual has a highly limited and highly constrained independence.

The influence of social values on actions of individuals is not a new insight. It has been said that individuals tend to celebrate and enjoy the accomplishments that their culture values most highly. At the accounting level the profession sets up a process for organizing financial data — a system of analytics that relates means to ends. The point that ideologists in the form of historical economists and historicists are trying to make is that the accountant's analytics have a history. This history involves all kinds of pressures and needs from all sorts of interest groups. Clues are identified; tradeoffs are made; commonalities are grouped. The profession has been and is carrying on these activities. It may be argued that they have misread the clues or listened to the wrong sirens, but it is not reasonable to assert that they do not have a process (system) for identifying, measuring, and reporting information.

---

[21] This argument is not to deny that the world's work can be carried on effectively when "favors" from public servants are included in the price system. These favors (graft payments) become institutionalized and more or less predictable, and therefore can be included in planning and controlling operations. For those who are attached to the price system as a rationer and allocator there is something intriguing about extending the concept to governmental favors. Those who need the services most will pay more, so that service prices are set by an improved market system that exploits consumer surpluses with less reliance on one-price policies. Southeast Asians are quick to point out the similarity of these views to the American custom of making substantial contributions to campaign funds and ingratiating themselves with subsequent favors and gifts.

[22] We are all familiar with sociologists who insist that we select our value systems by selecting our reference groups. Of course the operation can be partially reversed. We tend to select reference groups whose values are consistent with our previous holdings.

Essay Four

Methodology — Again and Again

[Russell] . . . criticizes Behaviorism because . . . it is a psychology which bases itself . . . upon the behavior of living organisms other than the observer [and] it overlooks the fact that no such behavior can be observed. It can only be inferred from events taking place in the observer.[1]

This essay started as a mild inquiry into possible reasons why such professional and intellectual leaders as Paton and Vatter have shown so little direct interest in the objectives and behavioral aspects of their profession. Both were clearly opposed to a personalistic approach and for both, inquiry rested with an explanation that resembled organizational Darwinism. Recently, however, we have been subjected to a number of related investigations whose conclusions can scarcely be supported even by complicated and modernized Darwinian assumptions.

The field of methodology is usually assumed to be dull and uninteresting — and so it is.[2] Unfortunately, the benefits are sometimes more important than obvious. The present essay is a belated return to this tortured field with emphasis on the place of objectives and behavioral surrogates in theory formation. Specific comments refer to the work of Littleton, Chambers, Moonitz, Dopuch and Bedford, Mattessich, the ASOBAT Committee, and Sorter. A service that methodology can perform in this area is to emphasize that the adoption of surrogates is unavoidable and that such adoption does not and indeed cannot make the problem disappear. Investigation is redirected to evaluating the adequacy of surrogates for the purposes in mind. Finally it is emphasized that when a surrogate resolution is represented as (or mistaken for) a final solution, genuine harm to the process of inquiry is the predictable result.

The somewhat trite basis of this paper is that a service activity such as accounting *must* be related to user objectives. The question of methodology arises in deciding what sorts of

---

[1] G. E. M. Joad, *Philosophical Aspects of Modern Science* (New York: Barnes & Noble, Inc., 1964), p. 79.

[2] Most of us hope, like Lewin, to derive some benefit from such tortuous studies. " . . . field theory is . . . a method of analyzing causal relations and of building scientific constructs." " . . . it is a set of beliefs about the proper way to build empirical theories; it is, in current terminology, a metatheory." Dorwin Cartwright, "Lewinian Theory as a Contemporary Systematic Framework," Sigmond Koch, ed., *Psychology: A Study of a Science*, Volume 2 (New York: McGraw-Hill Book Company, 1959), p. 9. The first sentence is a quotation by Cartwright directly from Kurt Lewin, *Field Theory in Social Science* (New York: Harper & Brothers, 1951), p. 45. Morris R. Cohen is concerned with those who are satisfied with confining methodology to sensory testing of hypotheses. "According to the traditional account, we verify a hypothesis when its consequences are found to be confirmed by sensory experience . . . . This mode of reasoning, however, is the well-known fallacy of arguing from the affirmation of the consequence. And it seems rather scandalous for logic as a science of consistency to maintain such a double standard, condemning an inference as a fallacy in the part called deductive and glorifying it as verification in the part called inductive." *A Preface to Logic* (New York: Meridian Books, Inc., 1956, 1944), pp. 122-123. However, the fact that a consequence is affirmed gives some reason to believe that the singular case is a member of the class from which the deduction was made.

relations to what sorts of objectives. In some fashion, it is necessary to specify and evaluate the consequences of the relations in terms of the objectives. Furthermore, a device must be found for performing the same sort of specifying and evaluating for the objectives themselves.

Several choices of procedures for performing this chore are available. These choices may range widely and even include random selection, but in some fashion by some mechanism — overt or concealed — they must give consideration to the following:

1. Finding out what kinds of users are available;
2. Deciding which users are important enough to merit consideration;
3. Estimating the objectives of users who count;
4. Deciding the choices and decisions required;
5. Deciding the information requirements for these decisions;
6. Developing procedures for furnishing the desired information.

These requirements have been discussed again and again in the literature, and all will probably agree that solutions in any optimal sense are beyond our abilities — that the optimizing task is an impossible one. Our concern here is in finding out the practical methods by which these tasks do get performed, the assumptions (explicit and implicit) that are made, and the surrogates that are adopted.

The most direct approach would be for the profession to devise some method for identifying and ordering important users and then to ask these users to give their goals, decision requirements, and informational needs. Professional accountants would then select the appropriate procedures for satisfying the needs. Optimal selection may indeed be an impossible task, but workable results must be obtained. While there are wide differences in individuals and the manner in which they make choices and control their environmental conditions, there is clearly *some* uniformity in these processes. We may expect some uniformity from similarity in training and background, the common ideology, and from observed *role* requirements that are imposed on actors at all levels of decision-making. (At least one writer has assured us that management deals with well-coordinated groups and not with a vast horde of individuals, and this view is, of course, widely held by organization theorists.)

Regardless of the possibilities suggested above, the chief task of this essay is to explore the more common *indirect* methods that call for observation of actions, the assumption that actors are rational, are pursuing their goals, have knowledge of the consequences of observed actions and have some ability to make inferences. This approach is clearly followed to some degree by all theorists today. Yet, the approach is far from being uniform. Different actions are observed and used in different ways, and our task is to discuss and perhaps evaluate some variations of these general methodologies.

The Vatterian Fund and the Patonian Entity

Many have wondered why such strong, persuasive leaders as Paton and Vatter have avoided explicit involvement with behavioral hypotheses and objectives. Vatter's position is clearcut enough.

> A fund . . . is a unit of operations or a center of interest . . . in a completely nonpersonal sense . . . . The notion of a fund has not been encumbered by personalistic thinking; it is free from those extensions of meaning which frequently creep into a theory based on personalizations.[3]

Footnote on following page

Obviously assets and collections of assets, regardless of labeling, do not have objectives in the usual sense. A little reflection will show that the transfer of objectives from the *persons* who make such aggregations of assets to the assets themselves removes no personalistic overtones! We need ask only for *instructions for discovering* the purposes of a particular fund to realize that we must look to individuals.

Apparently, Vatter feels that the needs and desires of individuals are clearcut enough so that the very existence of a group of assets operating in an observable fashion is sufficient warrant for *inferring* a stable set of objectives. Thus, a group of assets operating in a particular fashion "speaks" for some dominant personal objectives that were tentatively settled in prior horse trading among the individuals involved. The normal *function* of a building is to generate protection from the elements, and the very existence of the building is an argument for the desirability of this function to dominant personalities in the organization. Thus it is possible to assume that the objectives of individuals can be represented by the more manageable surrogate of fund operations. Changes in individual objectives along with adjusted weighing and reconciling may be expected to find their way into the composition and operation of the fund's assets. To the extent that this hypothesis is accepted, it becomes unnecessary to order and weigh the objectives of the individuals involved — it becomes unnecessary to identify or even specify the personalities involved.

In the Vatterian structure, the manager is obviously the key personality, although for some reason it is not the manager's objectives that are considered to be dominant. The manager appears to be the sensor through which the personal needs of all other parties are filtered and given expression. In this sense the manager is the coordinator of personal desires of other humans in the organizational orbit with certain well-defined constraints or restrictions. Presumably, how the manager transforms this amalgamation into a dominant purpose for the fund is not a part of accounting. (Perhaps this task is to be explained in organization theory.) Vatter's position and his informal enumeration of worthy parties are given in the following quotation.

> . . . management becomes a clearinghouse or administrative agency through which are bent together in a common effort the different interests of owners, long-term and short-term creditors, current suppliers of services or goods, governmental or other social control forces, employees and even competitors and affiliates . . . management is not the servant of the proprietors but rather the conciliatory agency between two or among several of these groups.[4]

We shall return to a possible reconciliation of Vatter's ability to avoid specific personal interests after a brief survey of Paton's entity position.

The fund theory — in spite of efforts to emphasize its novelty — is closely related to the traditional hard entity advocated so effectively by the elder Paton. Listen.

> . . . it is convenient . . . to assume that this enterprise or business situation has a distinct existence . . . through which flows a stream of values . . . . It is "the business" whose financial history the bookkeeper and the accountant are trying to record and analyze; the books and

---

[3] William J. Vatter, *The Fund Theory of Accounting and Its Implication for Financial Reports* (Chicago: University of Chicago Press, 1947), pp. 12-13. Also: "Some . . . unit must serve as the basis for accounting; but it must be a unit devoid of personal implications . . ." *Ibid.*, p. 10.

[4] *Ibid.*, p. 9. Also note the following recognition of personalities lurking in the stage doors. "Viewed realistically, the corporation is a conglomeration of personalities, resources, conditions and relationships . . ." *Ibid.*, p. 10. In previous essays I have referred to this position as the "soft entity" theory. See also my "A Behavioral Theory of the Firm: A Review Article," *Journal of Accounting Research*, Autumn, 1964, p. 204. This approach is clearly consistent with managers as coordinators and as commanders.

accounts are the records of "the business"; the periodic statements of operation and financial conditions are the reports of "the business"; the assets are the properties of "the business," and the equities are its ownership and obligations.[5]

The degree of closeness of the Paton and Vatter formulations can be found in their emphasis on the manager and his needs. It is clear in both instances that the manager's needs are important primarily because he is the instrument through which various personalistic objectives are unified and conflicts resolved. The manager is a conflict resolver and his professional goals become surrogates for the objectives of the others. Paton states:

> The conception of the manager must be exactly that of the business entity as an economic unit; and if . . . the most important purpose which modern accounting can serve lies in the rationalizing of business administration, the accountant must of necessity adopt the viewpoint of the manager . . .[6]

We now are in a position to ask why these theorists were not concerned with examining the adequacy of the manager's will as an acceptable surrogate for the personalities involved. Paton was clearly aware of the surrogate position but preferred not to investigate the adequacy of the substitute. Vatter seems to hold that the substitution of the manager's goal simply does away with the necessity for studying personal objectives.

Paton - Vatter Views: Justification

In both the fund approach and the entity approach there are forces at work that tend to increase the effectiveness of substituting actions for the objectives of the individuals involved.

The very existence of a fund or an entity is evidence that various personal objectives of members were at one time more or less reconciled and some sort of consensus was reached with regard to goals. The continued existence of the organization argues for a continuing agreement on goals and the ability to resolve conflicting interests. If certain individuals do feel that their own objectives are not being served adequately, they may exchange interests with more congenial participants or they may withdraw altogether from the organization. Individuals who are induced to replace the dissident members presumably share the goals of those dominant in the organization. Or in major turnarounds, dissident members may persuade others in the organization to conform to the newly introduced objectives. The influence of this flexibility in entry and exit is in the direction of goal congruence, and it tends to assure (in the manner of an invisible hand) that individual objectives are in fact being melded satisfactorily. The simple survival of the institution combined with freedom of entry and exit is an argument that the institution's activities are approximately consistent with those desired by the diverse interests.

---

    [5] William A. Paton, *Accounting Theory* (New York: The Ronald Press Company, 1922), p. 473. A similar statement is found in paton and A. C. Littleton, *An Introduction to Corporate Accounting Standards* (Evanston: American Accounting Association, 1940). "The business undertaking is generally conceived of as an entity or institution in its own right, separate and distinct from the parties who furnish the funds, and it has become almost axiomatic that the business accounts and statements are those of the entity rather than those of the proprietor, partners, investors, or other parties or groups concerned," p. 8.

    [6] *Ibid.*, p. 478. Notice also the following comparable quotation from Paton and Littleton, *op. cit.*, p. 2-3. "The responsibilities of corporate administration extend widely in several directions . . . . Through bias in favor of one interest or prejudice against another, inequitable results may follow . . . . It is the imperative duty of management, therefore, to strive for decisions based on a balanced consideration of all the rights involved."

Nor is this the end of the defense. In most funds the assets themselves have some flexibility and are not locked in forever as specialized goods wedded to specialized tasks. Many have alternate uses. In other words, if the assets of the fund are *not* fulfilling dominant objectives effectively, they may be exchanged, abandoned, or devoted to alternative uses. In a similar fashion, if the resources of Paton's entity (including skills, abilities, and assets) are not being employed effectively to satisfy members, they may be employed differently. Thus, flexibility in resource utilization helps operations adjust to dominant desires.

We may conclude — as Paton and Vatter have apparently already silently concluded — that the assets of a fund or the resources of an entity are being operated purposively to satisfy objectives that have some degree of unity. If one accepts the equilibrating influence of these factors, he need not inquire specifically and directly about objectives. He observes the operation of the resources and infers objectives from the consequences of the operations. In fact, he can neglect the specific objectives entirely! He does not have to decide which groups are more or less important! He does not even have to identify them! Clearly, this approach is an important methodological innovation. But traditionally this is generally what accountants do; it is what they do best; and in many cases it is the best they can do.

The danger from the above process is possible complacency, and a failure to check from time to time on the efficiency of the equilibrating factors. But there is still another attractive apple in Eden: How does the accountant know which operations — which events — to record and which to avoid? Apparently, the informed manager performs this function for Paton and Vatter. If he, in fact, is the clearing house for diverse goals, and if he unifies them some way, then presumably he knows what sorts of activities he wants from the resources and he calls for relevant reports of progress and of relative interests. The manager is responsible for weeding out dysfunctional activities and for telling the accountant which events to record and which to avoid. The problem has been solved — by surrogate if not by default.

People *do* segregate assets, and people *do* form organizations. Furthermore, it does not strain our credulity to assume that existing combinations are not random, but instead reflect choices of persons with authority and with preferences. Obviously there are cases of irrationality — activities with consequences in conflict with goal systems — but it seems ridiculous to take irrationality as the prevailing case. Instead, we usually start with the opposite assumption — organizational Darwinism — assume consistency in behaviors, and seek evidence for deviations that may serve as clues for inadequacy of the surrogates. Adequate surrogates permit a solution without outright default! Yet, deep inside, some of us remain unhappy with such abject dependence on managerial omniscience.

While the organizational-equilibrium thesis serves Paton and Vatter reasonably well, it is considerably less effective when used by some other theorists. We turn now to a brief review of the applicability of this device in related arguments.

Chambers - Actions in Markets and Neutrality

The Chambers' methodology is not unusual and is obviously similar to the approaches used by practically all theorists who are expected to relate their work to empirical events. The criticisms advanced here are of two types: (1) the common feeling that surrogates are answers in themselves and are somehow independent of their principals, and (2) the goal of neutrality, which demands independence of actions from goals. These attitudes are clearly misleading. Chambers states:

> The corporate system, however complex, does work as a whole through the processes of the
> market; and the measurements emerging from the interactions of the marketplace are alone

relevant to the choices of any participant in corporate business . . . . Statements which embody those measurements are independent of the ends of particular participants.[7]

The observation of markets and a determined effort to use supply and demand schedules as focal points and as surrogates for the attitudes behind them, have a long and honorable history in economics. Economists, however, do not feel that these simplifications have solved problems of personal and interpersonal attitudes and behavior. In fact, many economists with interests in behavioral sciences have been vitally concerned with market operations as surrogates and have directed research activity to focus behind market actions. The quarrel here with Chambers is not that market surrogates are or are not worth observing and may give a framework for all sorts of useful generalizations. The first objection is to Chambers' argument that "interactions of the marketplace are alone relevant to choices." This statement is by itself preposterous. The greater objection, however is to: "Statements which embody these measurements are independent of the ends of particular participants." Clearly, such statements serve as surrogates for *someone's* opportunities foregone or to their accomplishment, otherwise they would be useless for choice making. Does he really mean that statements about market operations are independent of participant objectives? If so, how? Does "embodiment" in a statement remove them? Markets are surrogates — not objectives!

It should be observed that the rule to observe actions in existing markets is usually operational, and it does reduce the need for observing a myriad of actions to a requirement for observing a relatively small subclass of actions. We inquire further: Which markets shall we observe? The answer, presumably, is those markets in which the members of the selected entity are actors or are offered alternatives. Perhaps we should include all markets! A further question arises: What aspects of the various markets shall we observe? We have already asked these questions time and time again about *events*. Now we must redirect these questions to markets.

We ask now whether or not Chambers can depend on equilibrating influences to assure us that his selected market actions do indeed replace a search for personal objectives. Actions in markets combined with the usual assumption of rationality should help express the goals of dominant personalities in the entity — perhaps management working within various loose constraints. Market actions indicate attempts of entity leaders to adapt to the economic environment. In addition, the influence of strong members of the coalition would normally be used to set constraints, guide major actions, and resolve conflicts among less powerful members so that the inference develops some support. Yet is simple action in the market a major goal? What about any kind of action? No action?

We inquire further: What about decisions that do *not* result or have not yet resulted in market transactions? And what about internal divisions and decisions to avoid the market? Internal decisions, it may be argued, find expression sooner or later in market actions. The result is that we may neglect internal decisions *if* we can assume that actions in the market are consistent with them and the entire series is consistent with goals. This consistency needs to be established or at least supported in some manner.

What about *nonactions* in the market? In one sense unsuccessful forays in the market may be interpreted as unliquidated accomplishment, somewhat akin to unsold inventory with reservation prices in the Davenport sense. Here, then, is a sort of realized-unrealized

---

[7] Raymond J. Chambers, *Accounting Evaluation and Economic Behavior* (Englewood Cliffs: Prentice-Hall, Inc., 1966), p. 291.

argument with accomplished transactions in the market being used as surrogates for objectives. Notice, however, that market transactions also are acting in this schema as surrogates for nonmarket actions. The researcher observes market actions and is not asked to decide whether such actions are good or bad — goal-fulfilling or dysfunctional. Furthermore, he is asked to consider only past market actions for unliquidated acts and plans. The relationship of expectations (and the future generally) to past actions in the market is, of course, not accounting according to the Chamberian definitions. (How does one construct a useful accounting model?) For unliquidated deals, subjective values are presumably not recorded until they are referred to the market, yet somehow prices in markets in which we are *not* active may also be relevant, and they sometimes enter the accounting model.

In summary then, a nonaction in the market is equivalent to a decision that the opportunities in some other perceived alternatives will be greater than the opportunities from going immediately to the market and back out on another set of perceived opportunities. To Chambers, at least, this sort of judgment is not accounting. In fairness, he seems to have approached the problem in a different way. The impacts of certain environmental changes are recorded in markets whether or not we are immediate actors in these markets. He seems to believe that these impacts, so measured, should be an acceptable part of the firm's own history. Many of his critics are inclined to accept this position.

The general discussion of Chambers' methodological pitfalls is now approached through the impossible and irrelevant goal of neutrality.

> *Neutrality is the property by virtue of which a statement, singular or aggregative, is relevant whatever ends are selected by the actor for consideration* . . . . Our inquiry, like that of economics, 'is entirely neutral between ends' . . . . Only if he [the scientist or accountant] maintains his independence of the specific users of his discoveries is it possible to formulate them in such a way that they are generally useful . . . . The financial information processor cannot know . . . what may be relevant in the particular sense, for the actor himself cannot know during the interval of processing.[8]

A little consideration will indicate that neutrality in this sense is a Herculean task — impossible for mere mortals. We must search for and select those sentences, and only those sentences, that have universal relevance to all existing decisions and decision makers and also to *all possible* decisions and decision makers. This task seems difficult enough, but there is more. Presumably, to be neutral, the statements should be *equally* relevant to all decision makers in whatever contexts they may find themselves.

---

[8] Raymond J. Chambers, *Accounting Evaluation and Economic Behavior* (Englewood Cliffs: Prentice-Hall, 1966), pp. 21n, 147, 156, 164. The history and development of the concept of neutrality would be an interesting research project in itself. Perry Mason was apparently content to let the courts settle ethical questions. "Is there any *accounting* reason why adjustments . . . can not be made . . . as long as legal requirements are met and full disclosure is made of the [sic] facts?" "Statements of Concepts and Standards," *The Accounting Review*, April, 1950, p. 137. Moonitz apparently hoped to find neutrality in his "problem-oriented" approach. "One immediate advantage of our problem-oriented approach over an ethical one is that it enables us to separate the problems and their solutions from the people who have to recognize and to solve them." *The Basic Postulates of Accounting* (New York: AICPA, 1961), p. 4. Robert A. Dahl discusses difficulties in using a doctrine of neutrality in political analysis. *Modern Political Analysis* (Englewood Cliffs: Prentice-Hall, Inc., 1963), pp. 101-107. The following statement by Karl R. Popper applies to some accountants: "Aiming at objectivity, they feel bound to avoid any selective view; but since this is impossible, they usually adopt points of view without being aware of them." *The Poverty of Historicism* (New York: Harper Torchbooks, 1964), p. 152.

Advocacy of neutrality is still more insidious. It is an offspring of the discredited doctrine of observing *the* (!) facts. Obviously, all facts are not equally important to everybody, and they cannot all be recorded and preserved. Facts are interpretations relevant to a viewpoint. We might, in the interests of neutrality, turn our ears from the clamors of *all* who wish information and select our accounting rules by, say, a random method, where tests of randomness are applied to the results generated by the rules with respect to users and their objectives. A general ukase could then be sent out that all users of accounting information would adjust to the output resulting from these rules. Due to the randomness of the selection process and the definition of the population, all users would count in some manner and be affected in some way. But we randomize to get away from certain possible influences — the very influences we are trying to emphasize in a service profession.

In the random selection case, how could we get changes in rules? Certainly not by looking to the needs or changing needs of users, for this procedure would be preferring one group over another. Clearly, rules that are selected randomly and changed randomly lead to a strange service profession. In fact, the entire concept of neutrality is impossible even in a random sense, for once the rules have been selected, it should be clear that some groups will find them more congenial than others. Perhaps the only way the concept of neutrality can be applied operationally is when the users are entirely homogeneous in their objectives and needs. At a more practical level it seems reasonable to suppose that once a set of rules is adopted and sanctions to conform have been brought into play, users will try to adjust their activity and decision patterns to make use of them. Are we to assume that all parties can make equally satisfactory adjustments to any fund of information? Do we continue to call such rules neutral if parties in some situations find it impossible to adjust? What seems likely to happen is that those parties who are not satisfied with the performance of the accounting information system will set up their own supplementary systems. If they do so, are the pressures on the profession for non-neutrality lessened? We might hypothesize that remaining users would become more homogeneous and that pressures would be reduced, but we must expand the hypothesis to cover the expectation that traditional parts of accounting would become inconsequential to many users. We might, in fact, construct a measure of non-neutrality in terms of the variations in the amounts of the supplementary information that various groups feel it profitable or necessary to provide. Or in Hegelian terms, the antithesis formed by those who cannot adjust might be strong enough to force a more congenial synthesis. This synthesis in turn might provoke an antithesis, and if the unfolding is in "good hands," the resulting rules might be more useful to all. But again when the profession moves to synthesize, it is reacting to needs and pressures — it is not neutral.

Finally, it may be argued that those who need supplementary information should be willing to pay for it and that nonrelevant accounting is therefore no great imposition on them. To continue this argument means complete removal of neutral accounting. If we turn this argument around and define accounting to include these special purpose investigations, then accounting again cannot remain neutral. Apparently Chambers is arguing that actions in the market are equally relevant to all decision makers. If so, then it makes sense to support neutrality as a goal, and actions in the market as a surrogate. Again, which actions in the market?

What is probably meant by the term neutrality is an imperative for practicing accountants at the operational level to adhere to the *accepted rules* of accounting and not to depart from them to help a particular person or group. In this sense, the concept is an implicit ordering of importance. In times of stress and under powerful persuasion, *practi-*

tioners of accounting are exhorted not to yield but instead to stay loyal to the processing rules agreed upon by professional leaders.[9] One interpretation might consider neutrality to be an instruction to practitioners for departing from other instructions — a rule telling when to depart from the main body of rules. The Chambers advice would be relatively simple: Do not depart!

The effect of neutrality in the latter interpretation is to strengthen the ability of practitioners to follow rules, to resist temptation, and thus to shore up the entire body of professional discipline. This interpretation may be good or bad, and its merit depends on a number of considerations including optimum flexibility for the given conditions. One item should be abundantly clear, however: neutrality is not an acceptable guideline for those who are engaged in making the rules themselves! At this level the total bankruptcy of the neutrality concept should be obvious. Numbers simply cannot be relevant and at the same time independent of objectives.[10]

Sorter's Events

We turn now to Sorter, who has publicly advocated an "events" approach to accounting. Sorter speaks:

> Proponents of the "Events" theory suggest that the purpose of accounting is to provide information about *relevant* economic events that might be useful in a *variety* of possible decision models.[11]

A further reading of Sorter indicates confusion about events and their selection. His first interpretation calls for " . . . summing the effects of all [sic] events on the names used in describing these events . . ."[12] Taken literally, this methodological guideline is a nonguideline. Clearly one cannot get the effects of *all* events on named classes. We must specify what is meant by "effect" and indicate rules to tell when the names are affected. The troubles are still not over; even if we can decide on the types of effects that are to be recorded and summed, we must inquire further into who decides which names (classes?) are to be used. This task is, of course, the old task of deciding which variables are of con-

---

[9] This is clearly *not* what Chambers meant, for he wants to establish the rules under independence. *Op cit.*, p. 156.

[10] It is sometimes said that scientists must be neutral. The practicing scientist may be neutral as to the outcome of a particular experiment. He is never neutral with regard to the rules of verification, to the weighing of evidence, to honesty in reporting the outcomes.

[11] George H. Sorter, "An 'Events' Approach to Basic Accounting Theory," *The Accounting Review*, January, 1969, p. 13. Emphasis added. Note the veiled neutrality implied by "useful in a variety of . . . models." Sorter (p. 12, n. 2) attributes the "events" idea to Vatter. Certainly it is consistent with Vatter's stubborn resistance to "personalistic" guidelines. A decade earlier John H. Meyers advocated the selection of "critical" events, although his instructions for determining "critical" were not exactly clear to this reader. "The Critical Event and Recognition of Net Profit," *The Accounting Review*, October, 1959, pp. 528-32.

[12] *Ibid.*, p. 15. Following Chambers, Sorter does limit the range of events, but he departs from Chambers with regard to the future and nonactions in the market. "Under an events notion this means simply that acquisition and consumption events, but not environmental changes are recorded . . . . *each event should be described in a manner facilitating the forecasting of that same event in a future time period given exogenous changes,*" p. 16. How does one specify the entity and separate it from the environment? The present writer has been sympathetic (See Volume I, Essay Two) with the forecasting guideline for a decade or more. But we are concerned in accounting primarily with forecasting the entity's reaction to exogenous events of various kinds and less with forecasting the events themselves.

cern and which changes in them need to be explicitly accounted for in terms of the causative creatures known as events. We may not need to specify decision models if we accept all conceivable events, but we do need to know something about objectives before we can decide on decision requirements, and we must know something about the information needs for the decision requirements. Knowledge of information needs will then help us select classes (and names for classes), and, given the classes, we can select event identification rules, decide on aspects (effects) of the events to be recognized and devise measurement rules to recognize them. The guideline as given is therefore too general. "All events" and "the effects of all events" can become useful subsets only after the classes are named, and the classes cannot be named until decision models are known, and these decision models cannot be known until worthy decision makers and their objectives are known.

In the earlier quotation, Sorter indicates the need to get "relevant" economic events that might be useful in a variety of decisions. Relevance, whatever definitions are used, must be related to objectives. A cost, for example, cannot be relevant or nonrelevant in a world without objectives. The decision process and the goals of interest must be specified before a decision can possibly be made as to the sacrifices — the goals given up or compromised.[13] If the events are in fact relevant to a variety of these models, so much the better. But variety is not an imperative. From whence comes this commitment to variety?

The Sorter approach is related to the attitudes of some institutional economists, some events-oriented historians, and perhaps to L. L. Thurstone and other psychologists.[14] At least some institutional economists seemed to be committed to gathering facts with the hope that the facts themselves would suggest various inferences and generalizations. In this sense, Sorter would apparently observe the events, and the events by interacting with objectives in some fashion would make "valuation" (evaluation?) unnecessary.

In rare cases the data may be so incoherent that the researcher does not know enough about them to construct a substantive hypothesis. It may be beneficial to consider fumbling with the data (Billy Goetz's term) by using different kinds of methodological hypotheses until enough knowledge is accumulated to support substantive theories. For example, the decision to consider the data in the first place requires a prediction of possible benefits. Moreover, there is a more obvious hypothesis that fumbling will prove to be fruitful. But what is "fumbling"? The investigator may now know enough to make meaningful substantive hypotheses, but he may know some generalized procedures that might prove to be useful when applied to the data. Taking means, variances, ranges, samples, etc., has proved useful so often in analogous investigations that a vague methodological hypothesis may be warranted. The results of applying these techniques may or may not lead to substantive hypotheses.

The possibility of applying this approach to Sorter's work is clear enough. He suggests no selective hypothesis to apply to the myriad of events that impinge on those connected with an organization. But he might take a big sample of existing "names" or he might

---

[13] The nonaccountant may wonder why cost accountants persist in calling some nonrelevant items costs at all. Clearly, a nonrelevant cost is not functioning as a cost in the given decision context, but it may function as a cost in other decisions. The accountant therefore continues to label the item a cost. Fixed cost, for example, is not relevant to the short-run production problem and is independent of the decision to make a small change in output, given appropriate initial conditions. It is not necessarily independent of a host of other possible decisions, e.g., its own control, measuring income, tax considerations, cash flows.

[14] The poverty of this position has been emphasized by A. B. Wolfe, "Functional Economics," *The Trend of Economics*, ed. R. B. Tugwell (New York: Alfred Knopf, Inc., 1924), " . . . a mind of a superhuman power [a modern computer?] . . . [would proceed] as follows: First, all facts would be observed and recorded *without selection* or *a priori* guess as to their relative importance. Secondly, the observed and recorded facts would be analyzed, compared, and classified without hypothesis or postulates," p. 450.

take a long list of decision models and fumble with them until a selection criterion emerges. Certainly he will not be able to fumble with all events until their relevance somehow becomes clear, but "decision models," "names" and information needs are not completely diverse and standardized procedures may be tried.

Most accountants probably use a type of Darwinism to help set up this type of hypothesis. This approach starts with the assumption that what exists does so for some past or present purpose. Thus, inquiry can be directed to looking for ends for which the events might be appropriate. In organizations he may assume rationality and knowledge of antecedent-consequence relations, but he must be prepared to face frustration from lack of rationality and knowledge. In human organisms, the organs are discarded or developed so slowly that difficulties from obsolescence and undiscovered needs may be expected. Perhaps there are reasons to expect faster reactions in organizations.

With this possibility in mind, we ask whether there are automatic factors tending to equilibrate Sorter's events with objectives. Mobile members of organizations can withdraw if they are in disagreement with objectives, but events do not have this power. However, those who select and reject events have some leeway, so that we might in a roundabout Darwinistic fashion assume that the actual event patterns are controlled and retained because they are serving a need. A similar assumption can be made for "names" and for their relevance to goals that count. Those who perceive needs (professional leaders) are analogous to the assets of a fund or the resources of Paton's entity: Those who perceive badly are directed to other uses — to other jobs. Whether these leaders are more mobile and have more alternative opportunities than fund or entity assets is still a question. There must be some ability to make events happen so that the inquirer is justified in believing that the events that do happen are contrived to accomplish objectives. Tentatively he may assume that the consequences in fact are consistent with goals. But what about dysfunctional events? Or what about (non) events that were avoided to accomplish goals? Why are only "acquisition and consumption but not environmental changes" defined as events?

The question of determining the goals that are in fact accepted — by whom and how strongly — remains a primary problem in accounting. The fact is that consequences of considered actions and contrived events *do* speak for goal acceptance. But how strongly? What other evidence is there for goal acceptance? I am on record as being sympathetic to the simple task of asking those in command of the decision-making machinery about their goals. But how do we identify those in command? By their ability to influence acquisition and consumption events? The Sorter surrogate is simple enough: Events not only speak for themselves, they speak for the goals of the organization members as well. There is always the possibility that the events speak more reliably than those who respond to the symbols that make up questionnaires. Finally, how do we decide who is to receive the questionnaires?

As usual, the procedure most theorists employ is a compromise. Actions may be observed with the idea of trying to predict their consequences. A study of the consequences of actions will probably permit some inferences about goal systems that would be consistent with the actions. These inferred consequences help identify the power centers — those whose objectives determine the policies of the organization. These decision makers can then be questioned about the relative strength of their goals, and a tentative hierarchy of importance of the organization's members may be established. These two grids can be compared with the idea of finding if the actions are rational, if the statements about objectives are consistent, if the ranking of power centers is appropriate, or if some combination needs attention.

Potential for Choice — Churchman's Surrogate

We have already discussed the possibility of a bookkeeping Darwinism. This orientation can range from an outright impediment to a useful heuristic device for getting an inquiry underway. The impediment arises from the possibility of using the existence of a concept or procedure as a defense for its existence. Thus, there tends to be a *universal* presumption of usefulness for what exists and an influence tending to retard change. The possible advantage comes from aid in directing inquiry toward a functional base. The existence of a procedure speaks weakly for the existence of some function that the procedure might fulfill. Search can then be directed to find possible functions that might have existed or might continue to exist. If the functions are no longer present, the procedure may be a useless vestige or it may be existing as a relatively inefficient substitute for other objectives. If the primary function remains, the investigation may turn to possibilities for better means to accomplish the objectives. In either case the inquiry begins by observing a procedure or concept, treats it as a possible means, tries to infer functions that it might perform, and finally considers alternative means. Obviously, this sequence is not the only one that may be employed. In fact, for many types of inquiry it may be an inefficient one. But, the sequence *may be* efficient and it may sometimes be applied to historical and social problems.

We turn now to a Churchman formulation that resembles the Chambers-Sorter-Sterling orientation in that it assumes a rational attitude that directs activity along functional lines toward specific objectives.

> . . . by maximizing potential one does not have to concentrate on specific goals, because any goal can be pursued if the potential is great enough . . . . The wealth he might accumulate beyond these objectives may be irrelevant. His life's goals, then, are not equivalent to maximizing his assets.[15]

The content of this statement is obvious enough, but its implications are strange indeed, and especially strange for a philosopher of science. In the tradition of mathematics, it may be possible to select a finite upper limit such that if the potential exceeds this limit, the probability of fulfilling anyone's goals approaches one. The mystic, the collector of material things, and those between should be able to satisfy their goals with something less than an infinity of options. "Power" is the common denominator for all values. But how much power?

Reaction to such a shotgun approach leaves some of us with a feeling of outraged concern. What sort of potential is being "maximized?" (Incidentally, the term "maximize" seems a little inconsistent with the tenets of many management scientists.) How great is "great enough?" What are the motivational consequences of "potential beyond objectives?" Perhaps the entrepreneur desires one primary goal and is not as interested in the number of options as in increasing the probability of accomplishing one major objective.

Perhaps if one accumulates generalized potential and is not guided by objectives, he would accumulate cash — obviously the most general and the largest asset (by Churchman's definition of "size"). Yet most organization theorists would rather be caught dead

---

[15] C. West Churchman, *Prediction and Optimal Decision: Philosophical Issues of a Science of Values* (Englewood Cliffs: Prentice-Hall, Inc., 1961), p. 329. Apparently all objectives reduce to "power." " . . . whoever values must value power . . . . any value-seeker values power." *Ibid.*

than found espousing such a simple goal surrogate as cash — or income. Some assumptions about time patterns must be hidden, otherwise an entrepreneur would hesitate to reduce his options by moving from a liquid position. His immediate options would seem to be at a maximum when he holds cash. Perhaps he takes a longer view and assumes that by immediate investment he can increase his options at a later date. The discounting process would seem to need clarification, and the problem of optimizing options over time reminds one of Fisher's problem of finding future consumption patterns.

Assets make feasible certain options that otherwise would not be available, and this point is nowhere more obvious than in capital budgeting. All accountants are familiar with costs as measures of the opportunities that are foregone due to commitments already made. Suppose then that we accept Churchman's definition of asset in terms of *power* to command meaningful options. (Compare economic "welfare" as used in development theories.) How are we to measure the options and by indirection the assets? How are we to write off assets? Account for them?

The methodological consequences of the Churchman recommendation — apart from the nonoperational aspects mentioned above — are similar to those of Sorter. In the Sorter sense the accountant records something about events and apparently the events (or certain aspects of them) enter into all sorts of interesting and useful decision configurations that are somehow obvious. The events — like facts — speak for themselves, and specific objectives are not necessary. In the Churchman methodology, as I understand it, the accountant records aspects of events that bear on their potential to exert power to make choices. These potentials are general enough so that the specific views or objectives of the organization need not be given attention. So long as there is potential of some recognizable kind, it is asserted that an asset exists and should be accounted for. A little reflection will show that the potential must be relevant to someone's goal satisfaction or it is not an asset.

The maximization problem should follow the accepted accounting doctrine of trying to maximize subjective values. The entrepreneur obviously must have goals and objectives in order to make these decisions. To maximize generalized potential is simply not adequate. However, it is possible to argue that the entrepreneur needs specific objectives, but that the accountant should record assets at some figure for *generalized* nonspecific potential. This is often what accountants do by using such surrogate measures as exit values and historical costs. If the exit numbers are used, there is the usual argument that the values represent at least one opportunity — at least one potential. Exit values represent the "power" to command resources in liquidation.

To conclude the immediate discussion, the instruction to maximize potential apparently is equivalent at the operational level of increasing options for *power* regardless of whether or not specified options are needed or even wanted. Apparently all options are weighted equally and are equally valuable. Yet the potential above "objectives may be irrelevant." Do we account for irrelevancies? Or is *power* always relevant? If we assume that the entrepreneur quits accumulating when options become irrelevant, what does he maximize? Are we to assume that he is to maximize only relevant potential? If we do not know his personal goals, how do we know whether the potential we are dealing with is or is not relevant? The profession is not asked to account for accomplishment in terms of individual goals but for the number of generalized external potentials. Clearly, generalized potentials form an open set of possibilities. What criterion should we use to select a surrogate measure for this open set of potentialities if we do not accept guidance from the entity's own objectives? Do market values express the "number of options" and therefore the "size" of the potential?

The Churchman methodology at this point is not clearly set forth, but it appears to be similar to that of Paton, Vatter, Sorter, Chambers and Littleton, who hope to solve the monumental task of objectives by reference to equilibrating forces or by more or less avoiding them. The least that a reader should expect is a rationale of the forces that act as surrogates for the desirable knowledge. Deinzer has pointed out that the Littleton approach depends on the belief that the evolutionary process in accounting is "in good hands,"[16] and earlier in this essay we have discussed the possibilities for equilibration in the other cases. The Churchman beliefs and surrogates, as I understand them, need considerable expansion — perhaps in the following direction.

Presumably, the rationality of businessmen will mean that they stop accumulating generalized potential when an amount sufficient for personal goals has been accumulated. This assumption is then taken as warrant that any generalized potential already accumulated is needed and wanted and is therefore relevant to personal goals. Thus the acquisitive actions of clients can be taken as speaking for their own relevancy. Potential, like actions in the market, activities of a fund, and operations of an entity, speaks for its own worthiness and relevance. The Churchman approach, unlike the orientation of Paton and Vatter, does not have the same flexibility of movement to support its integrating assumption. In the Churchman case *each* entrepreneur seeks power and is operating rationally, while in the other two cases flexibility is attained by the possibility of substituting members with different goals or by shifting resources and their operations. Finally, the measures to be used for generalized potential are assumed to be adequate for each individual case. The reader, like this writer, may still wonder why the "size" of an asset — the number of generalized options — speaks for the "size" of the asset for the individual's choices.[17]

We turn as a digression to an expansion of the Churchman approach to assets along the lines of entity delineation and the unit problem.

> . . . the proposed definition of an asset makes the denotation of the concept very broad. The assets of an urban dweller include streets, lights, stores . . . . an individual wishes only to maximize absolutely possessed assets . . . . In contrast, some individuals and societies want to maximize shared assets.[18]

Generations of accountants have wondered under what conditions such favorable circumstances as good climate, stable government, well-educated leaders, efficient workers, etc. might be treated as assets. (Professor Paton was concerned with this problem at least as far back as the middle '30's.)

A manager may be evaluated against a higher return on investment if these favorable side conditions of a social nature are not included in his costs. If such conditions are valued and included in the investment base, he will automatically be evaluated against this higher norm. Inasmuch as the business may find it necessary to bear some costs of stable government, schools, pollution control, etc., the exclusion of these valuable considerations from the base may not be ridiculous even for comparisons that involve activities in

---

[16] Harvey T. Deinzer, *Development of Accounting Thought* (New York: Holt, Rinehart and Winston, Inc., 1965), p. 141.

[17] "The *size* (or amount) of an asset is determined by the number of choices in a set of alternatives which the asset potentially produces at one time. Churchman, *op cit.*, pp. 324-325. Do all choices count equally or is there an equivalence factor for converting options into power?

[18] *Ibid.*, pp. 325-326.

different environmental situations. To the extent that the manager does not bear such costs and the advantages are not passed on to customers and others, his image will of course be improved by way of higher income.

If society wishes to maximize shared assets instead of individual assets, it may arrange subsidies and taxes to make it profitable for a self-maximizer to adopt the shared view. When the benefits are dispersed throughout the social order, bounties can be arranged to compensate for benefits that otherwise would escape the businessman's cash register, e.g., investment credits. Traditionally, the alternative has been public ownership of such undertakings.

If *cost* is a requirement for asset definition, a natural, pollution-free climate may not qualify as an asset at any entity level. (Unless somehow the costs of taking and settling the region are included.) The costs of pollution and pollution protection are of course borne by someone. The ill effects of contamination usually fall directly on the citizens. If a governmental unit makes the expenditures for protection, the cost falls on taxpayers generally, and a part no doubt ends up in the expenses of the offending firms. Educational costs, as a rule, are borne by governmental units, and in some developing economies are treated as capital expenditures for the funding units. Private concerns operating in the region receive benefits from such social assets and presumably pay for them through taxes and related levies.

Of course, not many accountants nowadays argue that cost is an important requirement for defining an asset. Value is ordinarily taken to be a crucial defining element, but clearly value alone is not a sufficient condition. A good climate is common to all enterprises and is valuable to all. Why doesn't this value establish an asset? More generally, what warrant does the accounting profession have for excluding such valuable attributes from the asset corral? If a manager has an edge — an advantage — over his peers with whom he may be compared, accounting leaders feel that he should be held *accountable* for maintaining the differential advantage and for using it effectively. Notice that the cost to the manager is not relevant unless it has been decided that the measure to be maintained and used for evaluation is to be cost. For comparative analysis, the necessity for holding managers responsible for these differential advantages is more obvious. If competitors have similar advantages and if the advantages are maintained by nature or by the state, accountants seemingly are not concerned with including them at the enterprise level.

Protocol Statements

Recently a methodological alternative of sorts has been advocated under the general title of the "protocol method."

A so-called "protocol method" has been developed for studying people's thought processes by having them think out loud while they are working on problems. The "decision rules" inferred from such protocols are then validated by building a model for computer simulation to test whether the model produces the same results as the human.[19]

From a methodological viewpoint this method consists in getting subjects to say aloud what they think they are thinking. From this line of patter plus observed actions some sort of inferences as to decision rules and relative goal importance are reached. Observe that this method tends to combine the procedures discussed previously. By observing and knowing the consequences of actions, and by using the integrating *assumption* of rational behavior, the observer may order and hopefully scale a subject's preferences. Alternatively, by sifting and evaluating a subject's statements about his preferences, either the subject or the inquirer or both may order and perhaps scale the subject's value system. The protocol method apparently combines the observation of actions and the collection of reports more or less simultaneously.

Both the advantages and disadvantages of the protocol method result from the simultaneity of actions and reports. The advantage, presumably, is that the subject is busy acting, has no time to fabricate reports that he feels the inquirer would like to hear, and accordingly the conversation tends to reflect accurately the subject's decision processes. The inquirer can be alerted if the statements do not agree with the actions, although he may not be certain whether the subject's knowledge is defective or his veracity suspect.

The possible disadvantages over a more leisurely statement of objectives may be serious. First, the protocol sentences are made while actions are being performed. Now some actions are more or less automatic and require little specific thinking, but many of the more cognitive processes require concentration on the actions and on the calculations for fitting the process together. As a result, many of the statements may be related to the mechanics of the process, and the researcher may need to work through much irrelevant data. Careless and fragmented statements may result from processes that require concentration on the details of the action.

An advantage of the protocol method — perhaps the most important one — results from avoiding the formal structuring of questions to be asked. Researchers have long been aware of the dangers of "leading" subjects by the types of questions asked. At first sight the ramblings of the protocol reports seem to avoid this undesirable structuring. To some extent they undoubtedly do, but one is certainly not justified in assuming that subjects do not sense what they are expected to say and react accordingly. Whether they do more anticipating when the questioning is more relaxed is doubtful, but whether they will volunteer more useful information when they are relaxed than when they are busy is questionable. The researcher may evoke more relevant information by careful questioning than by sifting protocol statements, but this too has not been established. Psychiatrists apparently think otherwise, although they clearly use both approaches.[20]

Some Personal Methodological Commitments

Perhaps some comments on my own attitudes may be of interest. Bedford and Dopuch seem to feel that my approach is piecemeal, that interrelations are neglected, and that the

---

[19] Raymond A. Bauer, "Application of Behavioral Science" (Harvard University Reprint Series, 1967), p. 122. The term 'protocol' and the general usage have apparently been suggested by members of the Vienna Circle. Protocol sentences, to the Vienna Group, were observation reports. Deductions were L-Statements which gave rise to meaningful hypotheses, and these hypotheses were in turn tested by reference to reported outcomes in the form of observation reports, i.e., protocol statements. Rudolf Carnap states: "Syntactical rules will have to be stated concerning the forms which the *protocol-sentences*, by means of which the results of observation are expressed, may take . . . . A sentence of physics . . . will be *tested* by deducing consequences on the basis of the transformation rules of the language, until finally sentences of the form of protocol-sentences are reached. These will then be compared with the protocol-sentences which have actually been stated and either confirmed or refuted by them." *The Logical Syntax of Language* (Paterson: Littlefield, Adams & Co., 1959), p. 317. (Translated by Amethe Smeaton and first published in English in 1937 by Routledge & Kegan Paul, London.)

[20] James M. Carman has suggested a comparison of attitude changes with "diary panels" (for purchases) and a concept of "freezing," in which subjects tend to preserve consistency of statements about attitudes that have obviously changed. "An Experiment in Bias from Repeated Questioning in Longitudinal Survey Research," *Marketing and the New Science of Planning* (Blacksburg: American Marketing Association, 1968), pp. 303-308.

process of abstracting from normative considerations in some operations and adding them back for other inquiries is unacceptable.[21] Deinzer has stated: "Initially the requirement for realism was to be subordinated to that of rigor. Subsequently, however, the mathematical systems were to be 'interpreted' by introducing those meanings for variables which seemed to correspond to real-world patterns of affairs."[22]

In some ways my stated approach appears to have a stronger deductive flavor than intended. I have never been greatly concerned with the uses of deduction as a means of getting formal truth by definition or stipulation. The deductive process, in my opinion, is a fantastic engine for generating hypotheses. The cognition that a singular instance belongs to an identified class has important heuristic and behavioral consequences. Membership in a class confers all of the *necessary* defining properties on the members. Thus, deduction in these directions gives a high degree of probability to the inferences. (The possibility of only one defining property with the result that no new knowledge is provided by knowing that a case is a member of the class is discussed in Essay One.) In most investigations there are usually a number of necessary, sufficient, and probable attributes that go along with membership. Going into a class by a sufficient condition then permits one to form all sorts of expectations about necessary and probable attributes. I maintain then that practical deduction is more than a device for *auditing* intuition — it is a helpful device for *facilitating* intuition by sorting out commonalities and analogous features and providing hypotheses.

Some purists may feel that inferring possible analogies from class membership is not deduction. For these individuals it should be emphasized that formal deduction is a useful endeavor for science only so long as the logical or mathematical structure is adequately isomorphic to the sensible data, i.e., is adequately interpreted. Rich and ingenious manipulations are often available at the formal level, and the results of these manipulations, when interpreted, may provide fertile areas for grubbing — suggest new analogies and insights. Observe that formally the implications may have been entailed and therefore valid by stipulation. In most cases, one does not expect a complete isomorphic interpretation, so that the interpreted inferences are only probable — not true by entailment. The confidence one has in the digging operation thus turns on some perception of the goodness-of-fit of the formal model — the effectiveness of the rules of correspondence, the degree of isomorphism.

My commitment to a means-ends (antecedent-consequence) approach may also deserve comment. Except perhaps for a period in which I was trying to replace the concept of primitive causation with associative correlation, at no time could one question my means-ends orientation. The assumption of some kind of connection among events is simply not arguable in the confines of a service profession. For genuine Dewey devotees, I may not emphasize sufficiently the possibility that means and ends may change roles for different inquiries or even within the same inquiry. (Incidentally, the boundaries of a particular inquiry are especially difficult to define in a Deweyian or a systems framework.)

Personally, I have always been a warm supporter of the Dewey approach, yet I prefer a *functional* positivist framework for my own work. The sharp distinction between the

---

[21] Norton M. Bedford and Nicholas Dopuch, "Research Methodology and Accounting Theory — Another Perspective," *The Accounting Review*, July, 1961, pp. 351-361. The other perspective, as I understand it, recommends stable accounting concepts, e.g., income, that accountants are able to implement and requires businessmen to adjust their decision models to these concepts.

[22] Harvey T. Deinzer, *Development of Accounting Thought* (New York: Holt, Rinehart and Winston, Inc., 1965), p. 143.

famous two roads — ideational and existential — has never been as appealing as the syntax-semantic cleavage. The asserted "constant interaction" between the roads is interesting imagery, but the process of a Deweyian inquiry has always reminded me of a shark in a school of tuna — a mighty churning of the intellectual water. My own preference — and I do not wish to imply superiority to others or even for me — is for a more orderly structure of activities, symbols, operations and models.

This latter point may need emphasis in view of the Bedford-Dopuch comments. By most modern standards I am not a systems devotee or follower of holistic methods, but my orientation has been functional from the beginning of accounting study. How can an accountant's approach be otherwise? The optimal area for inquiry depends on a number of variables, including such items as communicational and organizational abilities. Constructs are cobbled together by abstracting from certain experiences and grouping various common remainders. Certain normative overtones may not be dominant in many inquiries, e.g., the consistency of certain treatments, and may be removed from consideration for the immediate ends-in-view. Clearly the model may later be enriched to include them — if relevant — or the outcomes of the more simple model may be subjected to a separate inquiry to determine the desirability of normative or behavioral results. Extreme positivism without ends-in-view (values) is simply not appropriate for research in the social sciences. Most scientists agree that *complete* abstraction from normative influences is impossible, but some separation is usually possible and *necessary* to simplify inquiry and make it manageable.

Bedford-Dopuch may disagree, but I still believe that creating subsystems for logical, inductive, behavioral and normative aspects for my purposes in 1960 was a useful expository device. Moreover, I still believe that the necessity for ordering user needs according to perceptions of relative importance should be emphasized throughout the profession. These interpersonal comparisons I have chosen to call ethics. As a heuristic device I am willing to depend heavily on the Paton-Vatter emphasis on managers as screening agents for weighing and coordinating interpersonal needs and conflicts.[23] Yet reliance on management as the exogenous voice from the burning bush tends to obscure the responsibility of the accounting profession. *It is our responsibility and our decision!*

My earlier concern for the use of broader if-then propositions that may later be filled in with specific objectives probably resulted from numerous discussions with Richard Mattessich, an arguing companion of many years. His published position may have shifted slightly but is relatively clear. Following Popper and Papandreou, he was concerned with the possibility of *falsifying* a hypothesis by a negative refutation instance, and he accordingly drew a distinction between scientific hypotheses and pragmatic hypotheses.

> A scientific hypothesis is invalidated by instances (acceptable to the experts) which testify reliably to the *falsity* of this hypothesis. A pragmatic hypothesis is invalidated (rejected) by demonstrating (or believing) that, *in the long run* or *on the average,* the actions based on it yield results that are *less satisfactory* than the results of actions based on another variable or procurable hypothesis.[24]

---

[23] Mr. Maloo, of Florida A & M, has suggested that both Paton and Vatter listen carefully to managers for clues about objectives, but their reporting differs widely. Vatter reports to managers, while Paton, in spite of a hard-entity orientation, stresses income and the importance of investors. Apparently, to Paton management speaks for one segment of user-needs and investors for another.

[24] Richard Mattessich, *Accounting and Analytical Methods* (Homewood: Richard D. Irwin, Inc., 1964), p. 235.

A slightly broader position is expressed in *Modern Accounting Theory*, where he views assumptions as sentential functions and advocates a relatively value-free set of if-then propositions.

> If . . . it is possible to formulate some of these basic assumptions as sentential functions (i.e., sentences containing variables as placeholders for further propositions) into which purpose-oriented empirical hypotheses can later be inserted . . . the very nature and great diversity of accounting objectives prevents the creation of an "ideal accounting system" serving all purposes equally well . . .[25]

Observe that Mattessich retains a residual skepticism about the possibility of a general set of sentential principles that apply to all cultures and to all situations. There is an important difficulty here: How can we preserve common features that *might* apply in many instances? The propositional function (i.e., Carnap's and Tarski's sentential function) may serve as a useful framework. If the functions are too general, they may of course become trivial, e.g., justice, while, if they are too specific, they may not fit the situations adequately. The point to be emphasized is that some sort of solution to the problem of specificity must be derived.

Systems engineers and others concerned with such concepts as data banks are rediscovering the old accounting problem of what to preserve about what events. The data bank approach requires a set of criteria for judging what is to be included in the bank and what is to be excluded. Clearly not all aspects of all events that could possibly be useful are to be stored. The user requirement is apparently to determine the data requirements for a specific inquiry or judgment. A messenger is then sent to the bank to retrieve appropriate data. But what if the desired data are not available? Presumably, specific needs and the resulting calls for information will be combined with some data rejection rules for stale information and the resulting interaction will assure us of a useful and dynamic banking facility.

The process required for a useful storage bank of data is not difficult to understand and, in homogeneous situations, not difficult to implement. What is disappointing is that many accountants apparently are unaware that this is precisely the process we have been employing in traditional accounting for centuries. Systems specialists may be excused from this oversight because they may not understand the accounting process or may wish to divorce themselves from older disciplines, but for accountants there is no acceptable excuse. They have had far too much experience with accounts, ledgers, journals, daybooks, summaries, recapitulations, and filing arrangements to be carried away with the novelty of new devices and esoteric jargon.

We return to the scientific-empirical division of hypotheses. This classification bears some relation to my own distinction between theories and principles (Essay One). The scientific hypothesis is confirmed (partially) or refuted by comparing expectations generated by the hypothetical proposition with the observed consequences or outcomes. This

---

[25] Richard Mattessich, "The Impact of Electronic Data Processing and Management Science Upon Accounting Theory," *Modern Accounting Theory*, ed. Morton Backer (Englewood Cliffs: Prentice-Hall, Inc., 1966), pp. 513, 515. But listen: "Yet, I believe *this curse of model-building* [atomism] *can be overcome by embedding a group of similar models into a common super-model and by recombining similar super-models into a pattern of still higher order and so on, until a general theory, embracing all the ultimate and specific models, is formulated.*" Mattessich, *Some Thoughts on the Epistemology of Accounting* (Vancouver: University of British Columbia, Reprint No. XXIV, p. 50.

approach appears to satisfy Mattessich's factual verifiability as well as Dewey's process for deciding warranted assertions — truth. Moreover, the scientific hypothesis conforms pretty much to Friedman's use of the term theory. Apparently Mattessich, along with Friedman and most scientists, is not willing to reject a theory on the basis of one refutation instance.

Empirical hypotheses bear a remarkable similarity to my own definition of principles. The selection of principles requires an evaluation of alternative guidelines. This evaluation is in terms of ability to accomplish objectives. Clearly appraisal of adequacy requires some knowledge of consequences, i.e., of theories. We have already speculated on the operational nature of these judgments. Mattessich appears to feel that the evaluation of scientific hypotheses is somehow different from the evaluation of empirical hypotheses. " . . . 'invalidation' for a pragmatic hypothesis, means: 'not acceptable because not good enough,' while, for a scientific hypothesis it means: 'not acceptable because not true.' "[26] Unless Mattessich means analytical truth by definition, he should agree that scientific hypotheses are also judged by whether they are "good enough."

---

[26] *Accounting and Analytical Methods, op. cit.*, p. 235.

Essay Five

Comments on Empiricism, Phenomenology
and Nonscientific Inquiry

"To say that metaphysics is nonsense is *nonsense."*
Waismann*

This essay is more or less a continuation of the previous essays with emphasis on the singular case and the individual fact. The accounting rule of "neutrality" has its counterpart in the broader philosophical doctrines of phenomenology with its ambivalent relation to metaphysics on the one hand and to the empirical sciences (e.g., psychiatry) on the other. The task of reconciling phenomenology with empiricism and pointing out the affinity and opposition of both to a broad systems approach is a chore for professional philosophers, but some specialized extensions in the direction of accounting are certainly materials for our profession.

We begin with familiar material and accordingly discuss the modern empiricist and his outlook. The relationship of this outlook to that of modern systems builders is given some attention, and finally the empiricists' debt to the phenomenologist position — as I understand it — is evaluated. In the process of assessing this debt a somewhat lengthy discussion of certain esoteric aspects of phenomenology is included. Many accountants can rapidly scan this portion without great loss to their problem-solving ability or perhaps to their understanding of the accounting process.

A Look at the Empiricist Position

A brief review of the accepted idea of theoretic systems may be of interest. In general, researchers who feel that a theory is more than (or somehow different from) a "mere" prediction, tend to downgrade empirical uniformities, and to stress theoretical systems in which the individual prediction is more or less a special (singular) case of a broad class of uniform members. In this sense the development of a special prediction should be deducible with some confidence from its membership in a broader class. In some cases, the particular hypothesis might have been derived or intuited from other sources. If so, its verification and its similarity to others that are known to be members of the broader class may lead to a search for other class properties associated with the broader theoretic system. In short, a particular membership relation may or may not be the source of a particular prediction.

Certainly, no methodologist is going to go on record as being opposed to theoretical systems with broad applications through a network of commonalities and related categories. The obvious dangers of "diffuseness" from wide-open systems may be accepted as

---

* Quoted from G. J. Warnock, *English Philosophy Since 1900* (New York: Oxford University Press, 1966), p. 88.

a small price to pay to counteract the restrictions of empiricism and the scientific process generally. We turn for a moment to the older definitions of empirical, and sooner or later everyone seems to turn to Webster's *New International Dictionary* for specific help. Here, for example, is a selected definition: " . . . physicians who disregarded all theoretical study and based their knowledge and practice on experience alone . . . *empirical* depending on experience or observation alone, without due regard to science and theory . . . *empiricism* . . . pursuit of knowledge by observation and experiment." There is some current evidence of overstressing the opposition of empirical to theoretical. For example, Dewey, long an enemy of any distinction between theory and practice ("Theory separated from concrete doing . . . is empty and futile.") states: " . . . *empirical* means that the subject-matter of a given proposition which has existential inference, represents merely a set of uniform conjunctions of traits repeatedly observed to exist, without an understanding of *why* the conjunction occurs; without a theory which states its *rationale*."[1]

Merton also stresses the need for arranging uniformities into some sort of systematic pattern.

> . . . theoretic pertinence is not inherently present or absent in empirical generalizations but appears when the generalization is conceptualized in abstractions of higher order . . . that are embodied in more general statements or relationships . . . . By providing a rationale, the theory introduces a ground for prediction . . .[2]

This statement is typical of writers who emphasize theoretical systems. Obviously, any researcher would like some sort of persuasive independent support for his prediction. This support is hardly "embodied" — a dangerous term — in a relationship. The desired support comes from analogies of various kinds or from the belief that the particular empirical investigation is a member (in some relevant aspect) of a set that has been generalized to include other actual or possible elements, and finally that the other empirical elements would have permitted the particular prediction.

We summarize this discussion by doubting seriously that any effective researchers make the speculative and vacuous predictions that have sometimes been attributed to empiricism. Modern empirical researchers have *some reasons* for speculating and predicting, and: "Wisdom does not come to those who gape at nature with an empty head."[3] It may be fruitful to inquire about these reasons, and the reasons themselves may exhibit patterns

---

[1] John Dewey, *Logic: The Theory of Inquiry* (New York: Henry Holt & Co., 1938), p. 305. F. W. Westaway states: " . . . the very notion of an empirical law implies that it is not an *ultimate* law; that, if true at all, there must be an explanation which should be sought and found. An empirical law, then, is an observed uniformity, presumed to be resolvable into simpler laws . . . " *Scientific Method* (New York: Hillman-Curl, Inc., 1937), pp. 234, 235. Dorwin Cartwright mentions "dust-bowl empiricism" and comments on the "low status . . . given by American psychologists . . . to a 'merely phenomenological analysis' . . . " "Lewinian Theory as a Contemporary Systematic Framework," in *Psychology: A Study of a Science*, ed. Sigmond Koch (New York: McGraw-Hill Book Co., Inc., 1959), Volume 2, p. 12. Robert A. Dahl in political science contrasts empirical theories with "trans-empirical" theories. *Modern Political Analysis* (Englewood Cliffs: Prentice-Hall, Inc., 1963), pp. 101-103.

[2] Robert Merton, "Empirical Generalizations in Sociology," in *Handbook of Research Design and Social Measurement*, ed. Delbert C. Miller (New York: David McKay Co., Inc., 1964), pp. 9-10. Originally published as "The Bearing of Sociological Theory on Empirical Research," *Social Theory and Social Structure* (Glencoe: The Free Press Publishers, 1957). Morris R. Cohen states: "But the reflective mind cannot stop with so-called empirical knowledge, for the more we reflect, the more uncertain become the assumptions on which our empirical judgments rest." *A Preface to Logic* (New York: Meridian Books, Inc., 1956, 1944), p. 138.

Footnote continued on next page

that will permit expansion. Thus, in some fashion inquiry is initiated, speculation becomes prediction, data are brought to bear, prediction becomes belief. At some point the inquiry is "concluded," but it must be extremely difficult for the empirical researcher to walk away from the outcomes of concluded inquiries without at least trying to develop correlations and point out possible extensions.

We turn for the moment to the recent development of empirical research in accounting. One might ask if there *is* any other type of research, or if 'empirical' has *any* meaning apart from research, or whether the devotees of this trend in accounting follow the spirit of the older definition of empirical. Does 'empirical' mean a particular here-and-now observation at the event level? Is searching the library for intellectual antecedents empirical? Must there be numerous instances so that statistical sampling methods may be used to support belief? Is legal research (the search for legal and social precedents) empirical research? Astronomical inquiry? Is comparison with standards or norms empirical research? Analysis of financial statements? Analysis of historical documents? If empirical research requires hypotheses with operational content, are special kinds of operations implied? Or special *objects* to which the operations are to be applied? Is controlled experiment necessary? Will "pseudo-experimental" designs qualify?[4]

With respect to accounting research the emphasis on empirical seems clear enough. Yet, how can a service function possibly avoid being empirical? We may or may not agree with Sterling[5] that auditing is primarily concerned with verifying inputs and that the process is quite different for verifying scientific theories. Yet accounting systems are designed to fulfill functions, and the analysis of a system to appraise the extent to which it is fulfilling its function requires verification of outcomes against predictions in the scientific sense. How could such evaluation possibly not be empirical? It certainly is operational!

The attitude expressed in this essay is that the comparison of outcomes with norms is operational, and further that even the procedures necessary to find whether the rules of syntax are being followed are operational and require observation. It follows that the writer believes the rigid distinction between syntax and semantics and the related distinction between analytic and synthetic statements to be overdrawn — useful, perhaps, but overdrawn. According to some definitions, evaluation processes do not qualify as empirical activities, but I hope to support the contention that in the broader sense of bringing observational apparatus to bear on hypotheses, all evaluation is empirical.[6]

---

[3] Morris Cohen, *Reason and Nature*, 2d ed. (Glencoe: The Free Press Publishers, 1953), p. 17. Nevertheless, a return to the vacuous concept of empiricism may be underway. For example, Manfred Bleuler states: "The existential analyst refrains from evaluations of any kind." Quoted in Herbert Kohl, *The Age of Complexity* (New York: New American Library, 1965), p. 170. It is clear that neither operationalism or empiricism need to be goal oriented — at least in a faraway teleological sense. Accordingly I cannot understand the distinction between these two concepts or the use of "constitutive definitions" by Floyd A. Beams. "Indications of Pragmatism and Empiricism in Accounting Thought," *The Accounting Review*, April, 1969, pp. 382-388.

[4] Morton White takes a general view which probably reflects the thinking of most empirical accountants. ". . . empiricism in history . . . the notion that one can establish laws of history by the direct examination of instances falling under the law." *Foundations of Historical Knowledge* (New York: Harper Torchbooks, 1965), p. 38.

[5] "The individual propositions [of accounting reports] are verified every time the statements are audited . . . . With minor exceptions none of the outputs of an accounting system are *separately* verifiable . . . . The auditing process is not a verification of the outputs; instead it is . . . a *recalculation* of the outputs and [a] . . . check on the accuracy or verity of the inputs." Robert R. Sterling, "On Theory Construction and Verification," *The Accounting Review*, July, 1970, pp. 450-451.

Footnote continued on next page

Suppose, for an illustration, that an accountant is asked to "verify" an income report. At one level of abstraction, he carries on the process of verification by determining whether the operations specified for defining income were or were not properly followed. This process is certainly operational at the low practitioner level. The profession — through its leaders — has a more important job, i.e., to determine whether the income concept as defined by the operational instructions is an adequate tool for accomplishing the purposes at hand. How does a profession decide this matter? Clearly by specifying another set of operations! It is possible to speak of methodologies instead of operations, and it is true that the accounting profession has not been clear in stating the required behavioral observations, but to hold that investigations of the adequacy of concepts are not operational is fantastic.

It should be clear that empiricists in the recognized sense are not systems oriented, but it is not altogether clear how they wish to admit and qualify evidence. It is just possible that the distinguishing characteristic of empirical work is not related to the methods of verification — to the methods for establishing proofs and admitting evidence. Instead, the crucial difference may be the empiricist's desire to *limit the generalization* of his results. In this respect he may be considered to be a disciple of Pearson, who was more concerned with predicting results than with accounting for them in some broader system of explanation, i.e., in finding why the predictors predict.[7] The modern empiricist may then be one who generalizes with caution and takes a cautious if not defensive attitude toward extensions of his results. He seems to be in the Friedman tradition, but he is also in a larger and longer tradition of those economists who segregate and manipulate limited facts from the infinite variety of activity, and tend to let the results of the inquiries, if not the facts themselves, speak for an open-ended and undefined class of data.

Yet this difference, like so many others, can easily be over-emphasized. Empiricists may not be primarily interested in broad theoretical systems, but they must somehow construct hypotheses — *little systems* with possible antecedents and consequences. It is probably unfair to emphasize that they search for uniformities and not for explanations. Their decision to search for possible uniformities is based on some sort of expectation. What expectation? How is the expectation framed? On empirically based evidence? Is not the selection of a topic for empirical inquiry related to previous inquiries and to "fitting" with possible future inquiries? It is also unfair to overstress their reluctance to generalize, for obviously they or anyone else can and do arrange the predictive assertions any way they

---

[6] Thomas H. Williams and Charles H. Griffin place empirical research in accounting in five classes, but explicit evaluation of value sytems is not among them. Their classes are:
  "I. Effects of Accounting Measurements on Users [What effects?]
  II. Relationship between Accounting Measurements and Selected Dependent Variables
  III. Behavior Patterns of Accounting Measurements
  IV. Effects of Users on Accounting Measurements
  V. Miscellaneous Research Papers"

"On the Nature of Empirical Verification in Accounting," *Abacus*, December, 1969, p. 143. Incidentally, they too have shown interest in Webster's comments on empiricism as quoted at the beginning of this essay. Perhaps they, like many others, feel that empirical studies can never lead to the prediction of *specific* events.

[7] Karl Pearson, *The Grammar of Science* (London: J. M. Dent & Sons, Ltd., 1937, 1892), *passim*. William Flanigan and Edwin Fogelman state: "Empirical functionalists remain limited in their use of a functional perspective . . . . they show no concern with fundamental requisites at the level of the system as a whole . . . . They isolate particular elements within the total system and treat them as discrete units . . . . it is upon the validity of their empirical findings rather than the analytic power of a possible functional theory that they rest the case for functional analysis." *Contemporary Political Analysis, op. cit.*, p. 75.

wish. A grouping according to the property of similarity in predictive ability would seem to be useful in helping intuit (or deduce) further hypotheses. But is the process of grouping activities empirical? Apparently *deduction* of singular possibilities from group properties is not traditionally considered to be a major part of empirical activity. What bases for grouping (classifying) are important for them? Satisfaction of immediate goals? Furthering practical inquiry?

This difficulty gives rise to a more general question: How does an empiricist evaluate anything whatsoever other than the simple predictive ability of a statement? How are guidelines (principles) evaluated? It may be possible to infer from actions or from preference statements a set of objectives for an individual or for a professional group. Only a narrow definition of empiricism would exclude this type of inquiry.[8] Certainly it is necessary for someone by some process to predict the probable consequences of various alternatives. The estimation of value systems seems to be operational, although a number of accountants feel that personal objectives are beyond scientific inquiry.[9] A few accountants may go further and insist that such evaluations are not only beyond scientific and empirical inquiry but beyond all other types of inquiry as well.[10]

One suspects that accounting empiricists are on the side of economic positivists in the positivist-welfare controversy. Certainly their outlook has been largely behavioral. (In fact, some of us have lamented the substitution of 'empirical' for 'behavioral' in this activity.) They are willing to render judgments on the predictive force of theories, but are less willing to judge the relative adequacy of various predicted consequences for satisfying objectives. If this appraisal of their position is warranted, they would have difficulty in evaluating a guideline of any sort, e.g., legislative action, judicial decision, administrative efficiency. This position is obviously extreme. Interpersonal comparisons must be made; empiricists may abandon such decisions entirely, but, if so, they put politics, legal processes, family decisions, and cost-benefit studies outside the pale, even though such situations are not completely chaotic. There seems even less excuse to abandon evaluation of goals when no interpersonal comparisons are necessary.

Digression on Replication

We turn now to the empirical processes and conditions necessary for replication, the use of control groups, and some special problems of putting an experiment together. The

---

[8] A related question as to the operational character of such evaluations has been raised earlier. There seems to be wide variation in the meanings attached to 'operational.' Kermit Larsen discusses the adequacy of surrogates and related means for their purposes in terms of the traditional statistical term, 'validity.' "Descriptive Validity of Accounting Calculations," *The Accounting Review*, July, 1967, pp. 480-489.

[9] This position is especially difficult to understand in view of the popularity of expected values and standard-gamble procedures. It is, of course, the duty of those with philosophical inclinations to question the suitability of probability tradeoffs as a major part of the measuring process of evaluation, but the usual objections seem not to consider these possible shortcomings.

[10] For example, Chambers, who also uses valuation with regard to the future. I am not clear as to whether he would wish to apply "measurement" or "valuation" to the problem of estimating relative importance of objectives. (Certainly this chore requires no more inferences about the future than estimating current cost equivalents.) Perhaps he wishes to distinguish between evaluation and valuation. Morris Cohen warns: "The positivist theory of science conceives of facts as all on the same level, namely that of existence. But . . . human facts have the additional character, not shared by most physical facts, of being emotionally polarized . . . . That is what makes them causes of various levels of activity . . . . the determination of what the facts are is the end rather than the beginning of enquiry." *A Preface to Logic* (New York: Meridian Books, Inc., 1960, 1944), pp. 168, 170. Dewey would probably put them near the middle!

replicated outcomes are important precisely to the extent that the relevant conditions are similar in each case. Thus a judgment is necessary regarding the similarities of the two cases and the unimportance of the nonsimilarities.[11] If, as is so often asserted, everything is unique and different, then the simplest classification must allow for the presence of some nonsimilarities among the elements. Similarities become the basis for grouping, and conclusions about elements from class membership are justified only in the areas of these similarities.[12] (The dangers of inferring similarities of items that are not defining properties for class membership are discussed in some detail in a preceding essay.) The case of replication is certainly not unique in this regard. The validity of deducing singularities from a model depends on the ability to capture the similarities of the elements in the model. In model testing it is common to infer from similar outcomes that the important variables have indeed been captured. In practice all sorts of variations in fit are common, and the modern expansion of replication into sensitivity analysis provides an organized process for the comparisons. In some cases the use of isomorphism as an ideal may do more harm than good.

We may ask *how* a researcher decides to do a replication, but this question is a part of the broader one of *why* he undertakes any kind of study. One might guess that he begins with a recognition of the commonalities of the situations. (Dewey disciples may wish to begin with a "felt need" or "tension.") An interesting speculation is why researchers decide to test whether the deductions of a general theory do or do not apply in a specific case. In some instances they may wish to test the range of the theory and find the details of the specific area relatively uninteresting. Others may be primarily interested in the specifics of their area, and enlist possible aid from general relationships either to buttress their belief in their particular predictions or to make the predictions themselves.

The replication problem is related to judicial opinion in a manner analogous to prediction-explanation. The judge compares situations with the help of guidelines. This process involves determination of resemblances (and differences) and evaluation of the relative importance of these similarities and differences. In a similar manner a historian uses *ex post* data and attempts to evaluate the relative importance of common antecedents. In the design of a replication the inquirer evaluates by making predictions of the probable influence of factors included and factors omitted. A further evaluation is made after a nonconfirming replication has been run to decide whether the determining conditions were analo-

---

[11] In a broader context George O. May remarked: "But events and transitions are many-sided, and it is not always easy to decide whether resemblances or points of difference should control the accounting treatment of them." *Financial Accounting* (New York: The Macmillan Company, 1961, 1943), p. 16. For a discussion of the place of analogies see Norman R. Campbell, "The Structure of Theories," reprinted in Herbert Feigl and May Brodbeck, *Readings in the Philosophy of Science* (New York: Appleton-Century-Crofts, Inc., 1953), pp. 297-299. Also see Peter Caws, *The Philosophy of Science* (New York: D. Van Nostrand Company, 1965), Chapter 19. F. W. Westaway warns: "analogy supposes that two things, from resembling each other in a number of points, may resemble each other in some other point . . . . analogy rarely gives more than a slight presumption of proof . . . " *Scientific Method* (New York: Hillman-Curl, Inc., 1937), pp. 250, 253. He might have extended the warning to all forms of deduction and pointed out that all reasoning, except formal logic, involves analogies. "No two leaves are identical — no two blades of grass make the same sounds." Some tolerance for ambiguity is essential!

[12] For a related discussion see James M. Buchanan, *"Ceteris Paribus:* Some Notes on Methodology," *The Southern Economic Journal*, 1958, pp. 259-270. An unfair method of argument is often found in these discussions. If a proof, to be convincing, must exhibit exact conditions, no one would ever be convinced. An example: Not even identical twins have exactly the same environment, therefore no one can assert that differences are not due to environment.

gous and the theory is wrong or whether the theory is not disconfirmed because the situation did not capture the determining variables.

Historians, jurists, and accountants — ordinarily — do not have the ability to replicate, i.e., set up what they feel to be similar situations. However, they do have access to all sorts of happenings from which they may find similarities to the situation under inquiry. Their judging process identifies similarities and differences, and attaches relative importance to them. Jurists and professional accounting leaders have a factor not found so directly in historical work — the selecting and weighting process has normative overtones. The historian's commitment is sometimes to a goal of accuracy, although many historians feel that knowledge of the past is restructured by each generation to fit its changing goals.

Some Objections to Traditional Scientific Investigation

The elements of scientific inquiry should be familiar to all accounting readers. The process is simple enough: On some basis or other, speculations (hypotheses) are made; the observational senses are brought to bear on the hypotheses in order to provide supporting or refuting instances; the conclusions are held conditionally and subject to further supporting or nonsupporting evidence. When the predictions from accepted hypotheses disagree with outcomes, the usual procedure is to modify the hypotheses by restriction of range or improvement in design to account better for the observed outcomes. The latter approach — beginning close to what has been successful in the past — is certainly not essential, for it may be more fruitful to strike out boldly in new directions with daring new hypotheses. The process may indeed be "dinky," to use Hector Hawton's descriptive term, but the results have been remarkable.

The chief objections to the scientific process are usually in the area of reductionism, i.e., the specification of shareable sensory evidence as the primary test of truth, or in the area of the implicit assumptions that are necessary for the conduct of scientific inquiry.[13] Science undoubtedly assumes entities that themselves are not subject to investigation by the methods that make up the scientific process. All thinking scientists admit the necessity for stipulations in this area although some may call such questions pseudo-questions — simply define them away as not legitimate questions at all. It is asserted that they are arrangements of the syntactical language system, have no sense content, are not related to identifiable referents in experience, and therefore cannot be answered within the language system of science.[14]

A major difference between scientists and other investigators is likely to be in the attitudes taken with regard to these preconditions. But the differences may be wider. The following statement illustrates the ambitious program of Husserl, Heidegger, Jaspers, and their followers in the area of phenomenology.

---

[13] Some scientists have apparently overlooked the implicit stipulations about the existence of a world, the uniformities of experiences, etc. that are a necessary part of the scientific apparatus. Sidney Hook has performed a service in pointing out some presuppositions of the scientific process in *Metaphysics of Pragmatism* (Chicago: The Open Court Publishing Co., 1927).

[14] The tendency to treat many expressions of language as emotive will be discussed later. The single classification of all nonpropositional expressions as emotive is entirely too simple, as many philosophers (especially Wittgenstein and his followers) have pointed out. It may well be that analysis of nonpropositional (emotive) expressions may prove to be more useful in social science than traditional logical analysis. See Herbert Kohl, *The Age of Complexity* (New Haven: Yale University Press, 1967) for a general discussion.

Phenomenological philosophy intends to provide a methodological basis for all fields of inquiry, a basis which satisfies the criteria of precision and verifiability and which is fundamental to all methods — regarding the scientific method, narrowly conceived, as a special case.[15]

This position does not admit that all *facts* are related to experience in a shareable sense and holds that such physical anchoring severely limits the framework of inquiry. Moreover, it argues that rigorous scientists tend to dismiss as meaningless many questions of great importance simply because they have not developed criteria of acceptance that they themselves are willing to accept. For example, according to Husserl, emphasis on some sort of "bodily presence" tends to give certain objects priority over objects that involve memory or, say, imagination. At the cognition level he "opposes the affirmation that there is more than one *certain, evident*, immediately given object of cognition."[16]

In this age of complexity scholars are rightly distrustful of simplistic answers and simplistic approaches. The Gestaltists in psychology have performed an enormous service in attacking the simple stimulus-response structuring of human behavior. Systems specialists apparently are concerned with expanding the number of endogenous variables and reducing dependence on exogenous factors. Holism with new and striking labels like 'synergism' is widely accepted by social scientists as an appropriate device for structuring inquiry.[17]

Where does the use of hypothesis and the deducto-hypothetical method fit into these views? Traditional scientists feel that hypotheses are suggested *after* a certain amount of preliminary explanation and are used to burrow farther into a complex mass of data. Thus hypotheses are a device to structure anticipations so that they become simple enough to handle by our relatively limited intellectual and observational apparatus. The dangers of such devices should be clear enough to all. They tend to limit the field of interest, expose themselves to a great deal of possible refutation, and to preset the inquirer's mind so that he tends to overlook relevant possibilities. Some tradeoff of such possible dangers against the benefits of structured direction seem to be essential. What, if any, are the alternatives?

It is in the area of exposing alternatives that phenomenology makes a contribution, and this rival to the deducto-hypothetical approach has application in judicial work, in psychology, and in the thinking of many young activists in the soft sciences. The phenomenological rival is at first sight a simple contrary — entering the investigation with *no* preconceptions, *no* guidelines, and with judgment withheld — a preposterous objective.[18]

[15] Anna-Teresa Tymieniecka, *Phenomenology and Science* (New York: The Noonday Press, 1962), p. xx.

[16] *Ibid.*, p. 9. " . . . the components of perception which prejudice us about its object are: its factual existence, the preconception that the object belongs to the natural world, the preconception that its cognition results from a psycho-physiological stimulus-response relationship . . . " p. 11. But how does one handle more refined preconceptions? Kohl remarks of Husserl: " . . . he affirms that there is an enormous . . . *a priori* in our minds, an inexhaustible infinity of *a priori*." *Op. cit.*, p. 262. Also: "Positivists were still talking of all nonverifiable statements being meaningless while Hitler pounded on table tops . . . " *Ibid.*, p. 15.

[17] Herbert Kohl continues: "Life has become too complex for simple answers; hence philosophy insofar as it is modern does not consider religion as an issue . . . there is no cheap hope for man," pp. 271-272. Karl R. Popper warns however: "It may even be said that wholes . . . can never be the object of any activity, scientific or otherwise . . . . holists plan to study the whole society by an impossible method . . . . it is very hard to learn from very big mistakes." *The Poverty of Historicism* (New York: Harper Torchbooks, 1961), pp. 77, 79, 88.

[18] The relation to the currently fashionable Zen movement should be clear. However, the latter does have a major preconception — there are *no* useful generalizations or explanations. The Zen doctrine may spring from an extreme commitment to the adage that "everything is unique and different" and lead to the belief that there are no commonalities or predictive relationships that can be expressed as symbols. A milder warning: " . . . our liability to be swayed or even 'enslaved' by what Wittgenstein often calls 'pictures' or what could also be called *models* or *standard cases*." G. J. Warnock, *English Philosophy Since 1900* (New York: Oxford University Press, 1966), p. 54.

The courts, operating in a free civil judicial system, are supposed to withhold judgment until a preponderance of evidence — as defined in the legal system — supports a decision. Judgment is withheld! There is no prejudging! But just a moment! A judge in the Anglo-Saxon tradition starts with a guideline — the defendant is innocent until "proved" guilty and the burden of evidence is on the plaintiff. Is this attitude a commitment to unbiased investigation?

What about the psychiatrist who sees a person walk into his office? Presumably he is not supposed to make the "prejudgment" that the newcomer needs psychiatric help. It is indeed possible that he is a bill collector or, more likely, a donation seeker. The psychiatrist presumably listens to the newcomer with an "open" mind. On the basis of his evaluation of the remarks he begins to structure the situation. Or does the situation structure itself? (Popper states: " . . . the *Gestalt* theorists apparently wish to assert the existence of two types of things, 'heaps,' in which we cannot discern any order and 'wholes,' in which an order . . . or a structural plan may be found." *Op. cit.*, p. 83.) It is tempting to say that he lops off nonrelevant possibilities, but this approach more or less assumes a criterion for relevancy. Early in the session the psychiatrist may decide the newcomer is not a bill collector, but what else does he decide and how does he decide it?

Apparently, the psychiatrist has a typology — a series of categories that are relevant to the decisions society expects him to make. These class definitions are relevant to his therapeutic duties and have properties that are operational. His trained discriminatory powers must be able to interpret the client's behavior, and his statements about behavior place the inference in some of these classes, and hopefully suggest clinical recommendations.

The auditor's "neutrality" takes on a similar pattern. The auditor sits down to a bundle of representations and a mass of data in order to give an opinion on the acceptability or nonacceptability of the representations. The representations tend to suggest if not delineate the data that may be useful, and the auditor "withholds judgment" until certain characteristics of the situation "speak" strongly enough to permit a decision.

In one sense the auditor is expected not to prejudge the representations, but what does 'prejudge' mean? Presumably it means to withhold judgment until the evidence is sufficient, but this begs the question: *When is* the evidence sufficient? If prejudge means to reach a judgment without sufficient evidence it is not a useful expression until the level of sufficiency has been determined. If the term is used in the popular sense, then any judgment may be called a prejudgment if the guideline for sufficient evidence is not accepted. In either event, the term is loaded and tends to obscure the important preliminary decision about a proper level of evidence for judgment.

Scientists, it has been argued, do precisely what its critics feel should be done for proper inquiry. They are "neutral" (flexible?) although they have hypotheses to guide them. The hypotheses are undoubtedly "expectations," for resources are limited and the ability to inquire is limited. The scientist is neutral only in the sense that he has no overriding involvement or commitment *except* to follow the rules for evaluating evidence in terms of its support for the truth of the conjecture.

The scientist, the judge, the psychiatrist and the auditor thus are alike in that they sift evidence and reach judgments in order to perform the functions society expects of them. All use an informal Bayesian approach of modifying their attitudes as new evidence is available. All have rules for qualifying and evaluating evidence, and all have norms that the evidence must meet before judgment is rendered. Thus it appears that the so-called alternative to the deducto-hypothetical approach is not a clear-cut alternative. All investigators use categories and their work is often clinical in that they investigate singular cases to find whether or not they belong to predetermined classes. We are back to the philosophical problems of setting norms and deciding the required evidence for determining whether individual cases do or do not fit the accepted classification system.

Digression: Phenomenological Approach to Science

The phenomenologists wish to establish criteria for truth that science itself cannot provide.

> Scientism [of Mach] regarded scientific statements as premises in philosophical arguments . . . [but phenomenology is] expected to provide the foundations for the existing sciences by providing clear explications of the concepts which the sciences use but do not themselves explicate.[19]

The coherence criterion of truth is rejected. "Statements are true *not* because other statements are true but because they describe phenomena correctly." Moreover, "a phenomenologist does not form theories, he describes phenomena . . . free from preconceptions . . . . [his] only duty is to describe . . . . The truth of all premises are tested by examining phenomena." Now this presuppositionless type of inquiry may be what science needs, but exactly how is a scientist expected to carry it on? It is not enough to tell him to: "resist the temptation to make assumptions and define his terms to be consistent with them." Even belief in the existence of objects is suspended until an essence-determining *epoche* is performed, and objects become phenomena only after being "bracketed." Clearly phenomena are not objects and they are not propositions.

The process requires intuition, but intuition is "not psychological in giving causes of certain statements but epistemological in showing what evidence is relevant to them." The investigation arrives at "essences," but strangely enough essences are not empirical and the " . . . truth or falsity of statements about essences is not dependent on the truth about empirical statements" (p. 140). In wonder, we proceed in more detail.

Very few scientists now accept Hume's "blank page" approach to learning and instead more or less follow Kant by assuming that the experiencer exerts a strong positive selective and interpretative influence on the experiences. Thus, most of us assume that the senses construct some important aspects of a perception. That the perceiver abstracts (or filters out) all sorts of overtones and aspects is accepted in general scientific work. The question of an Aristotelian "essence" that may be wrung out of a "bodily presence" is something else. The phenomenologistic essence is not exactly a Platonic "ideal" for it is assumed to be separate from the exhibited phenomena and at the same time a part of them. The realization of an essence is apparently an "immediate perception" of self-evident structures. These permanent and self-evident structures are more than the *formal relational structure* that Mattessich and others have tried to separate from the "facade," but they are obviously similar.

> . . . the *absolute certainty* of the phenomenological method and cognition is held to consist in the immediate grasp of self-evident objects displaying their rational structures, free of all

---

[19] The earlier portion of this section leans heavily on "phenomenology in *The Encyclopedia of Philosophy* (New York: Crowell Collier Macmillan, Inc., 1967), Volume 6. Citations with only page numbers refer to this reference. The Patons and Moonitz occasionally ask to be included with practicing phenomenologists. "In general the actual circumstances rather than hard and fast rules . . . should be permitted to settle the matter . . ." "Each case must be judged on its merits . . . " *Corporation Accounts and Statements* (New York: The Macmillan Company, 1955), p. 577. The second quotation is from Maurice Moonitz, "Adaptations to Price-Level Changes," *The Accounting Review*, April, 1948, p. 144.

preconceptions and the contingent aspects proper to simple natural cognition . . . . the phenomenological reduction eliminates presuppositions . . . it simultaneously opens the field of the permanent structure of objects.[20]

According to Tymieniecka, Jean Piaget makes use of a multilayered design in differentiating emotive, volitional and cognitive aspects. She argues that Claude Levi-Strauss did not try to move from natural to cultural facts but found "culture" to be an irreducible structural essence that cannot be deduced but only described. She too feels that Jean-Paul Sartre's "reflective cognition" results in certain, indubitable knowledge and that an aware image maker cannot possibly deceive himself. Dilthey, she argues, used the approach to replace atomistic psychology by the idea of a descriptive psychology.

Perhaps the most prominent use of this approach is said to be in psychiatry, and it is in this field that the anti-theory bias is most apparent. Generally, however, the newer phenomenologists seem to feel that Freud started with rigid preconceptions and tended to overgeneralize. Consider the following.

> The phenomenological approach . . . consistent with its conception of man and its method, does not consider the psychopathological experience of the patient as a species of a psychopathological *genus*. Nor does it reduce it to extrapsychological causes . . . . Instead of forming theoretical conclusions, on the basis of the connections between symptoms, about their hypothetical, possibly organic origin, a phenomenological psychiatrist searches only for such characteristics as are immanent in the patient's abnormal experience itself . . . . [He] aims at perceiving the vast personal background and the entire mental state of the patient without reducing it to theoretically assumed sources and conditions of disease.[21]

Those of us subject to other persuasions wonder how one can even conceive or define the "abnormal" states without exhibiting their relations in other connections. By fumbling with the data (using simple laboratory or field techniques) some order may indeed arise, but it appears that a conceptual framework of some kind might suggest some appropriate orderings. Perhaps scientists need to inquire about the processes that might influence this ordering. Most of us suspect that this process stems from "outside" knowledge and sets. At the extreme this view is similar to Hume's blank piece of paper on which the phenomenologist has impressed an etching of ability to discern essences. Most scientists have been highly skeptical. Nevertheless, those with the modern systems orientation may be placed on guard, and naive positivists should be duly warned of the shortcomings and excesses of pure reductionism.

We turn now to the application of so-called phenomenological methodology in the social sciences. One might expect that economists who employ the method are few indeed. Schmoller and the German historical group were clearly suspect (by phenomenological

---

[20] Tymieniecka, *op. cit.*, p. 15. "Phenomenology, by concentrating solely on the analysis of the structure of phenomena, has superseded the construction of explanatory hypotheses . . . . [by] differentiating fields of inquiry by their specific nature, followed by analyses limited to aspects appropriate to the particular objectives . . . establishing 'models' of inquiry consisting of multilayered structures . . . determining irreducible elements, qualities, patterns or norms," pp. 19-20. Compare with Richard Mattessich, "Towards a General and Axiomatic Foundation of Accounting," *Accounting Research*, October, 1957, pp. 328-355, esp. 329-330.

[21] *Ibid.*, pp. 54-55. "Entire mental state" reminds one of modern systems analysts and the concept of a "total system." For more discussion of an "anti-principles" approach see Joseph J. Schwab, "What Do Scientists Do," *Behavioral Science*, January, 1960, pp. 9-11.

standards) because they looked to cultural and intellectual history for extra-disciplinary clues for economic explanation in (scornfully) ideological terms. Obviously, phenomenologists could not identify with deductive economists, although strangely enough the tendency of some later marginalists to become strictly positivist may have struck a responsive chord. These economists did not seek to explore extra-disciplinary reasons for demand and similar constructions, but they did subject the discipline itself to a rigid explanatory structure that carried generalization far too far for phenomenologistic tastes.

A closer look at their views suggests the approach of a degenerate and pedestrian wing of American Institutionalists. At times institutionalists have seemed to be "working the data" with few if any guiding hypotheses to aid them. Yet, institutionalists tend to use institutions not as essences but as the integrating theme for their investigations, and they tend to use the stability and movement of institutions as predictors as well as explanators. The phenomenologist approach as set forth in the following quotation is certainly far removed from modern socioeconomics.

> . . . the necessary interrelations among various economic factors establish permanent and universally valid structures of economic reality . . . . Thereby we can obtain access, through ideal, invariant structures, to the analysis of the changes occurring in the economic process, and of the process itself . . . to a morphological system of pure economic types.[22]

The inability of most of us with positivist leanings to use, or even understand the phenomenological approach seems to be widespread. Most agree that a dual-valued logic does not capture all of the complexities that scream for inclusion and that the inclusion of all nonreducible propositions in a single class of "emotive" expressions is far too coarse for effective use. But what are reductions supposed to reduce to? Positivists attempt to reduce constitutive terms to observational terms that can be tested by experience. The phenomenologist also makes reductions, but the process remains obscure to most scientists and perhaps to others as well. Marvin Farber states: "The phenomenological reduction . . . . consists of (1) eidetic reduction, which means that only essences, or essential structures, are of interest, and not particular facts; and (2) transcendental reduction [epoche] with its technique of 'elimination' and 'bracketing,' which leads one back to the 'pure' consciousness of an individual knower . . ."[23]

Accountants — practical souls — may be interested in the precise steps necessary for performing an epoche and finding these kernels of truth known as essences.[24] The following quotation from Alfred Shütz illustrates both the job that abstraction requires and the fuzziness of expression that is so common in this area of inquiry. The quotation is a set of instructions for finding Weberian "ideal types' but the kinship of such types to essences should be clear.

> The scientist observes certain events within the social world as caused by human activity and he begins to establish a type of such events . . . . he coordinates with these typical acts . . . motives and in-order-to motives which he assumes as invariable in the mind of an imaginary actor . . . . he constructs a personal ideal type . . . gifted with a consciousness . . . restricted . . . only to all those elements necessary for the performance of the typical acts under consideration. These elements it contains completely, but nothing beyond them. He imputes to it constant in-order-to motives . . . . finally he bestows on the ideal type such segments of life plans and such stocks of experiences as are necessary for the imaginary horizons and backgrounds of the puppet actor.[25]

Recently, some accountants have been inspired by the term neutral, and this attitude seems to be relatively near to what phenomenologists recommend. "Genuine reflection requires epoche in any field of discourse. In ethics, the first condition for clear and critical thinking is that the student suspend all beliefs and theories that have been accepted, whether on authority, or naively, or even for 'reasons.' Philosophical reflections require a consistent effort to apply this procedure universally."[26]

Mystical Inquiry

We turn now to the task of qualifying evidence and establishing belief in some mystical areas — notably in the religious area. "To convince a Hindu mystic of a 'fact of science' one must do more than perform an experiment before him."[27] We may not be directly concerned with the truth-criteria of the Hindu mystic, but we may be more interested in relation to Judeo-Christian mystics. We approach this area by returning to the pragmatic problem of deciding when statements are warranted or unwarranted.

The mystical approach clashes with science directly on the possibilities of withholding judgment — on the impossibility of being an agnostic. To most religious persons the choices are inevitable and: "There is no question of remaining aloof, taking no position on the character of reality."[28] Certainly scientists do not remain aloof on the metaphysi-

---

[22] *Ibid.*, p. 103. The following quotation of F. W. Meyer by way of Euchen by further way of Tymieniecka seems to express the attitude: "A morphological system is equivalent to an alphabet of individual letters, combinations of which can without great difficulty be made as needed for concrete problems . . . to construct theories for every possible combination of conditions would be a gigantic utopian enterprise like printing a book with a special alphabet for every different word," p. 103. The thoughtful reader may wish to reverse the charge. What about those invariant structures?

It is interesting to note that Marxist doctrine seems to take such matters as the existence of the dialectical process and the relationship of quantitative and qualitative progress as invariant, but: "Not a single principle of dialectics can be converted into an abstract schema from which, by purely logical means, it would be possible to infer the answer to concrete questions." Quoted from John Somerville, "Dialectical Materialism," in *Living Schools of Philosophy*, ed. Dagobert D. Runes (Paterson: Littlefield, Adams & Co., 1962), p. 429. See also Joseph Stalin, *Dialectical and Historical Materialism* (New York: International Publishers, 1940), p. 13.

[23] Marvin Farber, "Phenomenology," in *Learning Schools of Philosophy*, ed. Dagobert D. Runes, *op. cit.*, p. 308. Notice that the "reduction" does not reduce to objects and it does not lead to syntax!

[24] It should be clear that a simple classification such as double entry is unable to capture the richness of many abstracted qualities. A number of current accountants seem to feel that the essence is captured in flows, transactions, financial values, etc. Yet most of us do not claim to have captured a general essence that has universal or even wide application. E. A. Singer, whose influence in the business area has been largely through Churchman and Ackoff, apparently defined *truth* in terms of suitability of means for purposes at hand and an *answer* as a "perfectly" confirmed truth that is suitable for any and all possible objectives that might appear on the horizon. Shades of the Platonian ideal and various holistic wholes! See C. West Churchman and Russell L. Ackoff, *An Introduction to Experimental Method* (Mimeo, 1947), pp. 283ff. See also E. A. Singer, *Experience and Reflection*, ed. C. West Churchman (Philadelphia: University of Pennsylvania Press, 1959).

[25] Alfred Shutz, "The Social World and the Theory of Social Action," *Social Research*, Summer, 1960. Quoted from edited reprint in David Braybrooke, *Philosophical Problems of the Social Sciences* (New York: The Macmillan Company, 1965), pp. 65, 66.

[26] Farber, *op. cit.*, p. 314. In one sense the recommendation is to look for similarities and differences in singular instances. Essences may be interpreted as commonalities that serve as defining properties of classes. But what classes? What determines the classes selected? Essences with regard to what objectives?

[27] Frederick Ferré, *Language, Logic and God* (New York: Harper Torchbooks, 1961), p. 162. The following section leans heavily on this reference. Eastern mystics have long made use of miracles to support their views. One wonders whether miracles are considered to be *evidence* that convinces the mystic himself, or whether they are used to persuade others. Perhaps the belief of others reinforces the belief of the mystic, although the highly subjective criteria for mystical truth would tend to argue otherwise. In any case, miracles are emphasized to undermine reliance on natural-law concepts, determinism, and objective phenomena.

[28] *Ibid.*, p. 165. " . . . even inaction may be a culpable choice . . . [making] agnosticism in life an absurdity." Observe the existentialist overtones.

cal preconditions of their craft, e.g., the assumption of other external observers. Yet, the opposition is not a direct one. Scientists are not necessarily aloof even on matters of investigation. They do use hypotheses for direction, but they take a tentative position regarding their warrantedness, and they take a similar tentative position with respect to their assumed preconditions. Unfortunately they seldom get around to investigating their preconditions, if indeed they can do so with the weapons of science. Their assumptions often appear as metaphysical stipulations.

Ferre, and most metaphysicians, would probably agree that: "Like any conceptual schema, a metaphysical system is required to have relevance to experience, but not necessarily the *kind* of relevance . . . which scientific method demands . . . . When we speak of metaphysical 'facts,' therefore, we need not suppose that these are 'given' independent of the creative powers of intelligence. On the contrary, the 'facts' of metaphysics are supremely dependent on the conceptual activity of mind . . . . 'metaphysical facts' are always facts relative to a specific metaphysical system."[29]

A religious proof for some Christians is furnished by the evidence of the scriptures, even though some of the positions set forth cannot be supported or replicated by the usual scientific means and may, in fact, seem to contradict them. Dewey has argued that a statement of history claims truth and should be investigated by methods appropriate for other propositions. Predicted outcomes compared with actual outcomes may be difficult to arrange in history, but in the subjectivity of religious experiences certain outcomes can be and are predicted, and clearly the outcomes are close enough to warrant belief by many. With respect to historical statements in religion, the authority of the scriptures speaks more convincingly to the faithful than, say, the available evidence to support the existence of our American founding fathers. In both cases, the belief in their existence and importance may help structure our world outlook, loyalties and behavioral patterns. Thus, not unlike science, "Every religion, every particular religious language within the general class of theological discourse, possesses its own ultimate criteria."[30] Those who accept an ideology have their actions guided by it, and antecedent-consequence relations are established and believed by reference to its guidelines. Interestingly enough, the intervening mystical "black box" is similar to related boxes in science — e.g., in science the outcome of a combination of chemicals with specified valences can be predicted without being able to exhibit "essential" reasons for their combinations. It may be argued that all social science is of this type, with mysticism and ideology being influences that must be considered in predicting human behavior and changes in institutions.

A concluding note on the methodological use of analogies, parables and paradoxes may be interesting. It should be clear that rigorous logic needs negation in the sense that T's and F's are not permitted to be asserted in certain ways. Nevertheless, when paradoxes are stressed the process is likely to be Hegelian, in that finding "opposites" may become a major part of the investigations.[31] The proper mode of operation in this case is to find uniformities that would lead us to predict the opposites. If the paradoxes are considered to be outcomes not explained by the theoretical structure, then the appropriate procedures include reexamination of the structure for range and explanatory power.

The usual procedures for testing consistencies and paradoxes is through means of verification or falsification. But in matters of broad belief it is extremely difficult either to falsify or verify statements. If each case is "considered on its own merits" — an obvious absurdity — no amount of contrary instances would falsify a conclusion, for they would be dismissed summarily as nonrelevant. Of course, a world without any uniformities

---

Footnotes on following page

would be a world of chaos. Yet if the problem of "verification is the exclusion of rational doubt," then by rearranging the subsets of believers we can verify anything whatever! The set, it should be emphasized, might be composed of only maniacs.

We turn now to the related question of emotive signals. Ferré, for example, feels that the informative function is only one function of language and that dumping all other aspects of language into an "emotive" hopper is an outright failure to analyze an important part of the situation. Is the appropriate response to "Ouch!" "Prove it"?[32] There is of course a reformulation that can be made. Does the verbal signal indicate the state of conditions that it usually indicates? For example, we may feel that the signal "Ouch" permits the hearer to make a prediction of the utterer's condition, and it is possible to check the accuracy of this prediction. In a similar fashion, a command can be reinterpreted as a statement of the commander's desires, and an esthetic statement can be reinterpreted as a statement that implies a reference scale with which it is consistent. Any ethical position may be evaluated (verified?) with respect to some scale of values.[33]

The use of analogy is common in all sorts of languages. If one assumes that every event is different from all others in some respects, he must be careful to specify the defining properties that establish class membership. It is usually not satisfactory to generalize from one concrete case to another whose elements are analogous without careful attention to related similarities. We must check our warrant for inferring that similarities in one area suggest similarities in another. The usefulness of analogy is that there *may* be some likeness of the two events with regard to the property under investigation. This likeness (whether in terms of similarity or probability) may be an extremely useful guide for further inquiry. An accepted degree of similarity with respect to property P_1 may permit us to wonder about the possibility of similarity with regard to property P_2 and to form a hypothesis. The force of the analogy may or may not be convincing and may or may not incite inquiry about goodness of fit, range of similarity, conditions for transfer, etc. In this sense deduction itself is a type of analogous reasoning.

In religious and related work, wide explanatory use is made of analogies in the form of parables.[34] The possible benefit from parables in conveying knowledge is clear enough — usefulness results from selecting a related situation with which the learner is already familiar. The related situation contains resemblances or common features with the unfamiliar situation. Some caution is necessary to ensure that the learner does not construct similarities where they do not exist or latch on to nonrelevant aspects of the situations.

---

[29] *Ibid.*, pp. 161, 163. If a fact is a "true sentence" then many physical as well as metaphysical constructions are facts in that they are constitutively related to and help predict other facts. For an interesting discussion of Einstein's physical laws as free creations of the human mind and his strange combination of positivism and metaphysics, see Philipp G. Frank, "Einstein, Mach, and Logical Positivism," in *Albert Einstein, Philosopher-Scientist*, ed. Paul Arthur Schilpp (New York: Harper Torchbooks, 1949), Volume I, pp. 269-87.

[30] Ferré, *op. cit.*, p. 142. Science considers sense reactions to be the most convincing evidence available to support belief. In religious matters pointer readings count less than soul stirrings.

[31] Antinomies are, of course, common in science and formal logic, and experimental methods usually indicate such inconsistencies. Thus, antinomies are usually signals that the explanatory hypotheses do not cover the points under consideration. Russell, as a young man, spent some time studying Hegel, and his fondness for paradoxes may be one of the results. The Marxist uses opposites to create unities: " . . . the unity is of opposites; the opposites through their interpenetration form dynamic unities . . . which generate . . . contradictions . . . on a different qualitative level." John Somerville, *op. cit.*, p. 429.

[32] Ferré wonders about the proper response to "I pronounce you man and wife" and points out "speech here is not being used to inform but to *perform*." *Ibid.*, p. 56. (Emphasis added.)

[33] For some ethical considerations along this line, see Charles L. Stevenson, *Ethics and Language* (New Haven: Yale University Press, 1944, 1967), especially Chapter 1.

[34] See Gilbert Highet for examples of parables and analogies in Judeo-Christian teaching. *The Art of Teaching* (New York: Random House, Inc., 1950).

The usefulness of analogy in teaching is readily granted, for all learning proceeds effectively from the familiar to the unfamiliar. Thus, its effectiveness in expanding knowledge through suggesting new hypotheses should require no detailed support. The creative act of generating new hypotheses — sensing new relationships — is undoubtedly aided by guided intuitive insights — often small ones. (Even modern artists start with some analogy that they hope to suggest.) Observe that usefulness arises from the understanding that intuition is guided by similarities and the nearness of analogs. It is entirely possible that intuitive flights start not with new but with far away analogs, but the evidence seems to support the reverse, and it is widely agreed (at least by ideologists) that concepts and ideas are conditioned by if not captives of the cultural past.[35]

In summary, analogs may be used as persuasive support for prediction, and in the non-Friedman tradition they may be used to establish confidence in any resulting theory. Thus they may be called 'explanations,' for they tend to create confidence that is independent of the outcome of individual predictions.[36]

Nonscientific investigators search for continuing similarities — essences — that are somehow constant and unchanging. They appear to be willing to conclude only after taking an individual situation and observing it until its essences are somehow revealed. But if essences are interpreted as classes of observed antecedents, the method is essentially scientific. The scientist's faith in the auditing function implicit in interpersonal observations is clearly played down in favor of more intuitive (subjective) support.

What about the accounting artist?[37] Is he the person who perceives that the profession's integrating structure is functional? Are the "essences" the objectives that are "revealed" as commonalities in the human condition? A person with unusually sensitive response to symbols? One who investigates the permanency and relevancy of essences? Are accounting leaders artists in sensory reactions and in designing hypotheses? Intuiting user reactions and needs? Certainly if the defining property of 'artist' is the ability to abstract from a complex reality, then all those who design accounting systems (and everyone else) are practicing artists. Perhaps one who knows when to depart from accepted rules is an artist. But departures should exhibit pattern and conform to objectives, and if so, they are simply rules for modifying rules — imperatives about the permanency and relevancy of other imperatives.

Are those who determine the limits of the accounting domain artists? Do artists intuit more sharply than scientists? Abstract with more abandon? Does their broader perspective permit them to "see" the structure better? (Marxists generally have argued that some indoctrination is necessary before the elite — party members — can get free of stultifying institutional influences.) What precisely in the metaphysical approach permits us to transcend experiences and better organize the profession? A perception that transactions are a flow is a metaphor — certainly not a direct observation. Does an artist organize more ef-

---

[35] On the practical level Cyert and March have pointed out that search activity in business usually starts with specific exogenous events, begins near the trouble, remains fairly unstructured during much of the investigation, and usually moves according to feasible rather than optimal guidelines. See *A Behavioral Theory of the Firm* (Englewood Cliffs: Prentice-Hall, Inc., 1963), pp. 52, 59.

[36] An interesting possibility arises here. If two situations can never be "alike," then without abstraction no two aspects would ever be "alike," and no two items could ever be placed in a class. Any kind of classification device (typology) clearly requires some tolerance for ambiguous similarities. There are always questions at the extreme edges as to whether the element is or is not a member.

[37] I have touched on this topic elsewhere. See: *Berkeley Symposium on the Foundations of Financial Accounting* (Berkeley: University of California, 1967), p. 18.

fectively than the usual antecedent-symbolization-consequent process? Do metaphysicians tend to go back to hypothesized sources rather than to consequences? Do they stipulate the assumptions more definitely than others? Do they defend them from change more vigorously? Does the metaphysical attitude allow for changes in essences? Perhaps it stimulates change by encouraging a restless searching for ultimates in a world where ultimates are obviously difficult to come by. If the restless search for common features, common explanations, and common sources stimulates inquiry and does not over-compensate by downgrading other scientific methods, there can be little objection to metaphysics and its artistic practitioners.

One observation is crystal clear: Accounting (like science and language generally) is a symbolic system only distantly related to physical things. As a symbolic system it *must* be evaluated in terms of the effectiveness of its metaphors — not with reference to mental constructions masquerading as physical facts. In this respect accounting is similar to poetry and other artistic activities and should be judged by the same sort of criteria, adapted to its specialized objectives.

Poincare and others have argued that logic performs an audit function — attests to the legitimacy of the intuitive leap (inference) which leads to new and exciting knowledge.[38] Many seem to feel that the intuitive leap is an art and the more pedestrian tracing of consequences is science. It should be clear to the reader that the ability to intuit new hypotheses from little evidence and scattered clues is an important skill. In certain areas clues may be clamoring for recognition, and professional leaders may be too insensitive to recognize them. In this sense the leaders may indeed be "artless fellows." Popper has argued that science is not concerned with the techniques of getting new hypotheses. Scatterbrain sources are as good as others, if they provide useful bases for experiment.[39] Do we need to abandon this part of inquiry to the artists? Or should we try to include useful items of this sort in the body of science?

A broad integrating system — a grand design — may be an extremely useful device for helping intuit relationships on more mundane levels. Enthusiasm is cooled, however, when the possibility of limiting and conforming aspects are considered, and broad integrating schemes may help or may hinder the process of inquiry. This writer, for example, is committed to a functional theme that requires comparison of anticipated consequences with objectives. Moreover, the organizing scheme of functionalism helps direct "intuition" in specific directions. Alternative organizing themes are available; but those that survive tend also to direct the artist's use of his intuition.

Notice, however, that relationships of a very limited nature *may* lead to new inquiry. When, for example, a minor outcome does not agree with predictions, the broad integrating theme of consistency is seen to be violated. The required examination may be con-

---

[38] Henri Poincare states: " . . . it is by logic that we prove, but by intuition that we discover . . . . Logistic according to . . . [Coutarat] lends 'stilts and wings' to discovery . . . . On the contrary, I find nothing in logistics for the discoverer but shackles . . . . It is not wings you have given us, but leading strings." *Science and Method* (New York: Dover Publications, Inc., n.d.), Maitland Translation, pp. 129, 177, 178 and Chapter 1. Also see Morris Raphael Cohen, *A Preface to Logic* (New York: Meridian Books, 1956, 1944), especially "Logic and the World Order," pp. 192-200.

[39] Karl R. Popper, *The Poverty of Historicism, op. cit.*, p. 135. " . . . it is irrelevant from the point of view of science whether we have obtained our theories by jumping to unwarranted conclusions or merely by stumbling over them (that is, by 'intuition'), or else by some inductive procedure. The question, 'How did you *find* your theory?' relates . . . to an entirely private matter, as opposed to the question, 'How did you *test* your theory?' which alone is scientifically relevant."

sidered to be scientific, but the original burst of insight that suggested the importance of consistency itself, and the *recognition* of alternatives that might satisfy the condition of consistency, may be considered to be artistic.

We return to the function of logic as an auditing device that checks the legitimacy of operations. This important function of logic is far too restrictive. Logic should help bring to light all sorts of possible implications that might not otherwise be discovered. The misdirected emphasis in logic is also misdirected in accounting. Many accountants emphasize the audit function — justification through adding confidence to stewardship reports. They insist that accounting deals with the past — with facts. Yet, as all budget officers know, the usefulness of messing with the past is to help make decisions about the future. One suspects that the body of accounting principles, like the rules of logic, have been modified and have survived precisely because they have been effective instruments for evaluating and intuiting future courses of action.

Finally, what can we conclude about the restless search for idealized life-patterns and religious living? Certainly these attitudes have fantastic consequences, some of which can be observed. How are these doctrines to be judged if not by their consequences?[40] By consistency of required beliefs? By methods of qualifying and weighing evidence? By introspective requirements which are not permitted in science? The writer's positive pro-science leanings should be obvious, though they are filtered through a curtain of deep respect for the richness and complexities of life — complexities that slip through the loose-meshed filters of the scientific process.

---

[40] Unfortunately, monitoring consequences of earthly action in the spiritual after-life is difficult, and the feedback leaves something to be desired. The scientist limits his scientific inquiry to consequences that can be observed, and, as usual, removes himself professionally from some fascinating speculations.

Essay Six

Entity, Continuity, Discount, and Exit Values

It is the purpose of this paper to review selected attitudes of Sterling, Chambers, Staubus, Storey, Moonitz, Dicksee, Hatfield and others toward the going-concern assumption and its implications for discounted values, exit values, entrance values, and for performance evaluation and resource allocation. It is argued, for example, that the continuity judgment is a special case of the general abandonment decision that must be made periodically by auditors and at more irregular times by managers and investors. Further, it is argued that adoption of the continuity assumption sharply partitions possible opportunities and behaviors into those that have relevance and those that are not immediately pertinent. More specifically, the relevance of current exit costs to measure enterprise performance *after* a positive continuity judgment has been made is seriously questioned.[1]

Early in the audit assignment practicing accountants usually visualize an entity with some commonality of interests and a relevant time horizon. If the interest seems to focus on continuity, the usual auditing, evaluating, amortizing and related accounting methods are tentatively considered to be appropriate. If the decision is against continuity, it is generally thought that alternate methods may be more acceptable, but as Sterling points out, acceptance of a long horizon does not *necessarily* entail acceptance of alternative procedures for accounting. These procedures are means and the evaluation of alternate means with different objectives is an important part of this paper and of accounting itself.[2]

From a broad point of view the continuity decision is a judgment to the effect that opportunities from liquidation are *not* preferred alternatives and merit no further immediate consideration. Interested parties will, it is assumed, prefer to continue the specialized activities. Curiously enough, the operational details that auditors use for reaching the continuity decision have not been spelled out. In fact, they have hardly been mentioned.[3] Early

---

[1] Persuasive opinion in favor of using some form of current entrance or exit cost for measuring enterprise performance has become tremendous. See, for example, Raymond J. Chambers, *Accounting Evaluation and Economic Behavior* (Englewood Cliffs: Prentice-Hall, Inc., 1966), *passim*; American Accounting Association Committee Report on Long-Lived Assets," *The Accounting Review,* July, 1964, pp. 693-699; *A Statement of Basic Accounting Theory* (Evanston: American Accounting Association, 1966), especially pages 28-32; Edgar O. Edwards and Philip W. Bell, *The Theory and Measurement of Business Income* (Berkeley: University of California Press, 1961). For counter views: "It [the going concern assumption] rules out the use of liquidation values in statements . . . " Reed K. Storey, "Revenue Realization, Going Concern and Measurement of Income," *The Accounting Review*, April, 1959, pp. 232-238. George J. Staubus, "Current Cash Equivalent for Assets: A Dissent," *The Accounting Review*, October, 1967, pp. 650-661. George O. May, for example, states: " . . . the value of the enterprise is seldom a material fact; and . . . when it is, it can *only* be measured by looking ahead. *The sole relevance of accounts of the past is as throwing light on the prospects for the future.*" *Financial Accounting* (New York: The Macmillan Company, 1943), p. 8. (Italics added.)

[2] Robert R. Sterling, "The Going Concern: An Examination," *The Accounting Review*, July, 1968, especially p. 485. The present version of this essay has been modified in several ways to incorporate ideas from the Sterling and Staubus articles.

[3] Howard F. Stettler, for example, lists neither "continuity" nor "going concern" in his index to *Auditing Principles*, 2d ed. (Englewood Cliffs: Prentice-Hall, Inc., 1961). Maurice Moonitz states: "In the absence of evidence to the contrary, the entity should be viewed as remaining in operation indefinitely." *The Basic Postulates of Accounting* (New York: AICPA, 1961), p. 53. (We are also warned not to confuse continuity with permanence.) Nothing is said about recognizing and evaluating the quality of the evidence necessary for decision.

textbooks seem to have elevated continuity (in the absence of convincing negative evidence) to the honorific status of principle and have been practically silent about suggestions for evaluating factors that tend to establish belief.[4]

The interrelations of continuity and entity are especially complex. Accountants are not always clear about the entity whose continuity is in question. Clearly the continuity decision cannot be made at all without consideration of *someone's* objectives. Even with given overall objectives, the continuity decision must be shaped, reshaped and supplemented with a series of related decisions concerning lines of product, territories, and individual resources employed. These decisions, to be emphasized later, are usually within the scope of management's responsibility, are usually done on an *ad hoc* basis, and are only indirectly related to the auditor's opinion about the appropriateness of assuming continuity for the overall firm.

There is, however, an especially difficult discrimination required of an auditor. Whether change of *ownership* combined with continued operation of the *facilities* violates the postulate apparently has not been decided. The hassle about "proportional change in interest," and more recently the long discussions over pooling and purchasing, illustrates the lack of agreement. The 'firm' is so ill-defined that those who argue that survival is *the* goal (or even a major goal) have encountered difficulty in convincing others. Some stockholders, workers, creditors, customers, suppliers, and line managers change often or at least from time to time. On occasion accountants seem to be interested in semantic survival. Yet survival of the corporate name — as a hyphenate or a division of a complex — does not seem important enough to support an accounting postulate.[5]

In the Lytton case (Note 5) it must have been obvious to the auditors that the president and most of the board were on their way out, and changes in creditor-stockholder relations were imminent. Loans to householders would no doubt continue and be administered by *some* financial institution, and certain office equipment and other assets would probably survive. Stockholders unquestionably desired the survival or growth of their investment values, and in spite of the reorganization most of them who wished to survive probably survived, although the market values of their holdings certainly did not. Managers and employees normally would be interested in the survival of their positions. Most depositors were protected and probably were not greatly concerned one way or another. Yet the most powerful group — the secured creditors — were clearly unhappy and survival of their relationships was in serious question. We conclude that 'survival' is extremely vague and difficult to interpret. The term must be related somehow to organizational structure, and the roles and needs of dominant groups. We conclude further that the accounting profession has largely evaded the problem and has remained at the simple proprietorship level with little regard for modern organization theory and the so-called managerial revolution.

---

[4] Even Sterling, *op. cit.*, lists going concern as "one of the most important concepts in accounting," p. 481.

[5] The difficulty is illustrated at the practical level by the opinion of Touche, Ross, Bailey and Smart with regard to Lytton Financial Corporation. (Audit Report to the Directors of Lytton Financial Corporation dated March 21, 1968.) The auditing firm prepared the financial statements of the holding concern under the assumption of a continuing operation except for notes to the balance sheet that indicated insolvency and an explanation of the condition in the opinion itself. The SEC in Release No. 5049, Accounting Release No. 115 (February 2, 1970), turned down the following qualified opinion: "In our opinion, subject to the company's ability to attain profitable operations and/or to successfully obtain additional capital, the accompanying financial statements . . ."

Opportunity Costs and Enterprise Continuity

Moonitz, following the AICPA Committee on Accounting Procedure, asks the accountant to look for "evidence to the contrary" and with no contrary evidence, to assume continuity. Evaluating direct evidence to support an assumption of indefinite operation is probably beyond the abilities of most accountants. Evidence does not speak for its own relevance and does not order itself with respect to other possible evidence. Someone must evaluate the situation in terms of objectives and weigh relevance and importance. The evaluator is usually the accountant, although the decisions to continue or abandon are usually made by others. Not only must the accountant reach a judgment about the probable liquidation intentions of others; he is the functionaire most directly concerned with seeing that the information necessary for making this important set of decisions is available to those who do make them.[6]

Except in certain bizzare conditions abandonment is always a possibility, and information regarding abandonment values *may* always be useful and relevant. Unfortunately, information is not costless, and the accounting profession must make some sort of choice between making this information an output of the regular periodic reporting process or of reporting it only when preliminary decisions indicate the net value of the information is likely to make it worthwhile. A going-concern decision ordinarily means that a well-nigh universal alternative — the opportunity to liquidate the entire firm — is not important enough to displace other types of information that are considered to be more appropriate. The decision about abandonment must be made in order to decide the relevance of alternate information flows in the future, and the abandonment decision here is similar to its more general relatives elsewhere. Implicitly or explicitly these decisions *must be made*! In some cases the weight of evidence is so overwhelmingly for continuance that further attention is not profitable or even rational. We try now to isolate the *entities* that are required to make abandonment (continuity) assumptions.

The Investing Entity

Assume for the moment that an investor group has the power necessary to decide whether to continue or abandon the specialized group of assets and abilities that makes up an operating entity. Assume in addition that these investors have the freedom to decide whether to continue or discontinue their own investment. Investors as individuals have all sorts of opportunities, some of which may be shared and some of which are peculiar to each individual. They place their own valuations on their specific alternatives and follow their own selection rules. Most investors will probably adopt a process that compares the expected future return from the specific going concern with various other subjective valuations that could be obtained by disposing of their interests in the entity and using the funds elsewhere. In order to make meaningful comparisons of this nature, each individual investor needs to know the current value of his holdings in each entity so that he can compare alternatives that would become feasible as a result of liquidation. Thus *his* personal abandonment decision is whether to abandon (sell) the securities and to make appropriate switches. It is the liquidation value of his securities and not the current cash equivalent of the firm's assets that is relevant for this switching decision.

However, if an individual investor is important enough to influence the future of the specialized enterprise directly, he may find that the liquidating values of the firm's assets

---

[6] Sterling also emphasizes this point. *Op. cit.*, p. 482.

are relevant to his own switching decision. In our economic society, an investor of this importance makes this decision by comparing three situations. He places a value on his expected benefits from continuing the enterprise. He places a value on the firm's assets and other valuable considerations in liquidation — the estimated CCE, the current cash equivalent reinvested. He considers the market value and expected market value of his securities in the enterprise. A comparison of the first two will show whether to continue or abandon if either is higher than the value of the third. Of course the value of the third does not remain constant and depends on other opportunities for using funds, but if it is higher than either of the others, he should sell his interest.[7]

Assume now that a dominant investor has no effective market for his security holdings in the specialized enterprise. In this case his decision area has been reduced and he will be interested in a comparison of his perception of the best uses for the CCE of the assets with the expected throw-off of benefits from continuing the specialized operation. He should therefore insist on measuring and reporting rules for the specialized operation that will help him make this decision. Unfortunately, these are not the only dimensions of his decision situation. He may want all sorts of accounting help in deciding how to *improve* the operating prospects, the CCE, or both. He must make subjective valuations in all cases, and he needs informational clues that will help him appraise possibilities for improving performance (and therefore expected throw-off) of the going entity as well as to help him select and evaluate alternative prospects. Except in the sense of a constraining measure that helps estimate the alternative possibilities, the CCE seems to be relatively unimportant. Alternatives for the use of such funds are subjective valuations of possible reinvestments and a broad information service should provide materials to permit the comparison of all sorts of existing and imagined entities.

In summary, it should be clear that current liquidation values of assets and other items may be useful for making the decision to continue or to abandon a specialized operation. If an individual holder does not have power to make the abandonment decision, he may still be interested in clues to help him predict whether those with the necessary power will be likely to liquidate the specialized operation, and he may wish to enter a minority protest if his own opportunities seem to be less attractive.[8]

Performance Measurement and Expectation for Locked-In Operations

Before deciding if abandonment of the firm is desirable, we need information to help estimate the firm's future prospects as a continuing assemblage of specialized resources. For this purpose the concepts of income, earnings per share, and return on resources in some form are likely to continue. Inquiry may be directed toward improving and implementing these constructions or perhaps directed to finding preferable substitutes.[9]

---

[7] With respect to individual assets, George Staubus states: "The asset should be held if its net realizable value is less than both value in use and replacement cost; it should be sold if either of the latter is less than net realizable value. If it is sold, it should be replaced if value in use exceeds replacement cost." "Current Cash Equivalent for Assets: A Dissent," *The Accounting Review*, October, 1967, p. 658. This statement may be expanded to include the investor by assuming that "replacement" refers to buying a similar security.

[8] Staubus has discussed some aspects of this material. *Op. cit.*, especially pp. 633ff.

[9] We disregard here the importance of income as a guide to consumption. Traditional bookkeeping technique for drawings against anticipated earnings stressed consumption, and John R. Hicks, *Value and Capital* (London: Oxford University Press, 1939) resurrected or at least reinforced this hoary approach. Emphasis on withdrawal tends to highlight the liquidity aspects of realization, while emphasis on performance measurement tends to move income recognition closer to decisions and implementing actions.

Current cash equivalents (exit values) measure the firm's command over society's resources under a highly specialized set of conditions. The difference between this specialized commanding ability at two points of time *may* be used as a surrogate for, a measure of, or even a definition of, income. We seriously question the usefulness of income so defined! There is certainly a long tradition for considering assets (resources) as vehicles for exercising entrepreneurial ingenuity. With the traditional view all quasi-rents and realized excess present values are attributed to the enterprise and included in income. These quasi-rents in excess of a normal return on comparably employed assets are used to evaluate managerial performance.[10] Even when this traditional view is accepted a serious question remains: Should the accountability base for managerial ingenuity be measured by exit values, entrance values, original costs, price levels applied to costs, or what? The discussion now turns to an exit value (CCE) in this framework.

CCE for Performance Measurement

It is argued, in summary, that acceptance of the continuity assumption requires the use of opportunity costs in an appropriate context and it is argued further that operating performance measures based on exit values (nonrelevant opportunities) are almost invariably wrong for the purposes for which such measures are employed. More generally, changes in command over resources in the limited sense of *command through disposal* is thought to be a poor basis for evaluating operating performance or for predicting future benefits from operating resources — the usual functions of income. But how can one implement a concept of "command through operations"?

The objections to using exit values at two points of time center around the obvious motivation for managers to obtain good performance marks by selecting assets with the highest exit values even though exit is *not* a feasible alternative. Thus playing the periodic CCE game becomes implicitly a goal of management even though the intermediate CCE's are otherwise not relevant. Moreover, this irrelevant game becomes a determinant of resource allocation to the extent that financial markets allocate funds in response to expected income figures.

Consider a specific area. Typically, specialized assets have unique installation and removal costs and few alternative uses. One might expect, therefore, that the commitment of liquid assets decreases exit values and consequently leads to reported losses. Constructing a railroad, for example, should result in fantastic reported losses during the construction period! In such cases the result of measuring income by changes in CCE would be similar to the velvet approach to depreciation that charges all capital expenditures to expense in the period of incurment. Management might well avoid such specialized commitments in order to avoid unfavorable reports, and if businessmen avoid such decisions for this reason, the economy might suffer a substantial and unsought slowdown of ac-

---

[10] The attribution of income to an abstraction known as "human resources" instead of to an equally abstract "enterprise" is an interesting recent development. In each case, assets are assumed to contribute only to the extent of their cost. Students of Marx and of the physiocrats will recognize the possible difficulties in such computations. For the "human resources" imputation see: Roger H. Hermanson, *Accounting for Human Assets* (East Lansing: Michigan State University, 1964). For the older, enterprise view that treats resources as vehicles for entrepreneurial virtuosity, see my *Inventory Valuation and Periodic Income* (New York: The Ronald Press Company, 1942), *passim*, especially pp. 35ff.

tivity. Domestic private investment might be expected to decrease and the introduction of capital-intensive technological development to lag.[11]

It is true that after heavy initial investments have been made, future periodic income would be reduced less. Future depreciation might conform more nearly to the old-fashioned "decline-in-value" model with intermediate holding gains and losses buried in the charge. Observe that as plants get older, they are "converted" to liquid assets — and when reinvested would again tend to reduce reported profits. (Notice that buying specialized assets from others has a similar micro-effect.) While it is possible to have near-perfect markets for specialized goods, such a possibility seems to be more remote than for liquid assets. In any case installation and removal costs of specialized assets would both be deducted from income (expensed) in the period of commitment.[12]

The interesting aspect of this method of recognizing income is that discouraging prospects are reported precisely when subjective value is usually being added, and reported progress is inverse to the change in prospects as perceived by the managers themselves. Investments of liquid funds are made when subjectively valued prospects from the specialized commitment (discounted) are greater than similarly valued prospects from all other commitments, including a precautionary commitment to liquidity. However, to the extent that subjective value is converted into market value of assets,[13] recognition tends to agree with such conversion. With CCE one may expect reported profits to be more nearly in step with liquidity realization rules than with subjective value added. In terms of disclosure it is difficult to assess superiority. Outsiders do not have access to subjective values in either case, and so long as all are aware of the shortcomings of exit values for assets that are not going to be liquidated, perhaps little harm is done. Certainly the use of un-amortized original cost also fails to disclose subjective value effectively.

We turn now to the influence of CCE on one specific measure of performance — return on capital. In the early years with CCE, reported losses are probable, and the balance sheet valuation of the assets should be less than if usual methods were employed. The introduction of CCE gains in later periods will tend to give a higher and more volatile return on investment due to reflecting the entire realizable liquidation gain in *both* income and asset valuations. As a firm reaches maturity, its assets should become more liquid and increase in exit value. If the CCE increase is at a constant rate, the rate of return on investment should decrease unless compensated for by reinvestment earnings. This tendency may be welcome for those who are disgusted with the increasing rate of return inherent in most depreciation methods as assets get older, but on balance the CCE influence on rate of return does not seem to promise much improvement. Intuitively, it seems reasonable to

---

[11] It is, of course, conceivable that a switch to more specialized goods would increase the current cash equivalent rather than decrease it. The fact that the firm actually buys an experimental asset makes the asset more visible and possibly more desirable to others in the used-asset market. This prospect is thought to be rare. It can be argued that the CCE should be applied to combinations of assets including the entire assemblage necessary for an enterprise. In this case the CCE of the entire assemblage of railroad assets might increase due to the nearness of the expected operating receipts. But this view is not consistent with Chambers' position. Apparently his position is that such excess is attributable to the enterprise, is not transferable and therefore is goodwill — an asserted nonasset. Chambers, *op. cit.*, pp. 209ff.

[12] Carl Nelson has also pointed out the above pattern of reported income for expanding and contracting firms. "Use of Professor Chambers' method would result in decreased profits as a result of a physical expansion . . . . Conversely the contracting firm would be . . . having a relatively low . . . charge against revenue." *Berkeley Symposium on the Foundations of Financial Accounting* (Berkeley: University of California, 1967), p. 52.

[13] Edgar O. Edwards and Philip W. Bell, *The Theory and Measurement of Business Income* (Berkeley: University of California Press, 1961), pp. 48ff.

hold management responsible for earning on the opportunity value of the resources it employs. But in view of the nonrelevance of the opportunity involved, assets and managerial talents are more or less locked in, and it is difficult to understand how nonrelevant possibilities can possibly be useful for evaluating performance of either managerial talents or of the assets. Opportunity costs are unquestionably the relevant costs for decision making. But which opportunities? The best one foregone? How do we know our search has uncovered the *best* one? What about opportunities that are considered not worth taking?

Current and Expected Costs for Locked-In Performance Measurement

Consider now the possibility that some form of past, current or expected cost is more pertinent for evaluating performance than exit costs. First, it should be clear that the continuity judgment must presuppose some sort of subjective expected value for the entity of specialized assets and also for alternative candidates for which the cash from liquidation might be used. (The latter includes opportunities for turning up still better alternatives and better means of operating through further search activity.) It should be clear that CCE from immediate liquidation may be only a small item in this overall decision process. However, the concept may be useful in two somewhat different functions. First, knowledge of specific sources of fluid funds may help in a heuristic way. Second, the amount of cash available from liquidation may help determine the size and range of feasible alternatives. All possible alternatives, of course, are not equally desirable, and there is no reason to assume that they are limited and screened by reference to the amount of cash that might be available from existing liquidations. Unused credit lines and all sorts of other possibilities are relevant for switching decisions. In fact, it may be more reasonable to concentrate first on other forms of financing and use the possible liquidation value of existing assets in reserve as relevant only to more dramatic alternatives. The point is that CCE is only one form of possible financing of alternatives. It may not even be the most important form, and it certainly does not often set limits on the range of alternative undertakings.[14]

The relationship of current cash equivalents to financial "power" is not entirely clear. It may be argued that modern financial arrangements make possible convenient sale-lease-back agreements so that liquidation values of owned resources are indeed relevant for financing, and should be monitored more or less continuously. Yet the liquidating value of an asset is not the only support for financing, and it may be considerably less important than the opportunities available on the basis of earning reports. In most capital budgeting decisions the opportunity to reduce capitalization by retiring debt or buying stock is a universal candidate among the proposals, and for evaluating short-run budget constraints the possibilities of selling or encumbering assets certainly need to be explored. As a result the exit value of currently held resources may be a partial measure of the financial power of the firm.[15]

An interesting application of the use of current values without the implication of liquidation has been expressed by the deposed management of Ling-Temco-Vought. The usual consolidated financial statements were supplemented by statements showing all investments at current realizable values in order to: " . . . increase our visibility . . . . While we have no intention of disposing of our subsidiaries, these figures are significant since they are representative of the collateral base we have from which to finance future growth."[16] While this approach has an unusual flavor, it is clearly related to the arguments for show-

---

ing assets at current values in order to inform readers of the fund-raising potential of the concern. Judging from subsequent events it seems that effective earnings and attention to maturities might have been even better indicators of fund-raising power.

Let us now assume that liquidation has been ruled out as an advantageous behavior. If the firm is continuing, it seems that individuals will be interested in expected future throw-off of benefits from the assemblage of resources — the going entity. Current entrance costs begin to take on increased relevance in this context.[17] Yet, as will be pointed out later, current entrance costs are not ideal. First, terminal benefits to many investors are received when they dispose of their securities and not when the firm is wound up. This possibility establishes the relevance of all sorts of short-run nonaccounting variables in the security markets. To repeat, the opportunity cost for an ordinary investor to stay in the firm is not likely to be either the entrance value or exit value of the firm's assets. Second, a continuing firm will need to make expenditures to replace current assets in some sense, but these fund requirements may bear little relation to interim current entrance costs. Current entrance costs for a continuing firm are surrogates for expected future fund outlays. Indeed they may be poor surrogates, and therefore it is strange that the profession has not undertaken the research necessary to estimate the adequacy of such predictors.

If we take the assumption of long-run continuity seriously, we should be interested in estimating both the timing and the magnitude of *future* receipts and expenditures necessary to validate continuance with roughly equal or other baseline potential. These future expenditures might be approximated by historical costs or by current entrance costs, but unless conditions are relatively stable neither is an ideal predictor of future outlays. For several decades this writer has accepted the locked-in condition of continuity, and has suggested that periodic depreciation be based on *expected* economic replacement cost (estimated future expenditures) so that these deductions from revenues might be sufficient to keep capital in some sense intact.[18] The effect of this recommendation is to consider the

---

[14] Calling some activities "measurements" and others "valuations" does not seem to be important or even useful. Chambers states: "What is past and present may be able to be measured. But what is future can only be evaluated . . . . A valuation is an incident in a continuing stream of experiences and actions. It has no permanence; it may never recur." *Accounting Evaluation and Economic Behavior* (Englewood Cliffs: Prentice-Hall, Inc., 1966), p. 42. One wonders just how CCE has "permanence" or if it is sure to occur. Chambers is also concerned with financial status because present conditions determine future abilities. A little reflection will show that past trends, decisions, and actions along with asset potential make future activities feasible.

[15] See Essay Four for a discussion of assets defined in terms of managerial power by C. West Churchman, *Prediction and Optimal Decision* (Englewood Cliffs: Prentice-Hall, Inc., 1961), p. 324. Compare, "Property means anything that can be bought or sold, and since one's liberty can be bought and sold . . . liberty is property . . . . The sale of liberty is a necessary part of every sale. John R. Commons, *Legal Foundations of Capitalism* (Madison: University of Wisconsin Press, 1959, 1924), pp. 22, 26. Specialists in economic development often define economic improvement or betterment in terms of meaningful alternatives rather than quantity of material things.

[16] "Balance Sheet Spells It Out," *Barron's*, March 4, 1968.

[17] Edwards and Bell point out that realizable profit with opportunity costs may be preferable in the short run but business profit with current entrance costs is likely to be more useful in the long run. *Op. cit.*, p. 26. "So long . . . as the liquidation of the firm's assets is not imminent, current cost data would appear to be more useful to the firm than opportunity cost data." *Ibid.*, p. 102. Apparently they feel the support is too obvious to warrant detailed support.

[18] See my "Depreciation and Income Measurement," *The Accounting Review*, January, 1944, pp. 39-47. I have always been uneasy about keeping *capacity* intact. It was also pointed out that an advocate of base stock or LIFO, to be consistent, should take depreciation on expected replacement costs rather than interim current costs. Yuji Ijiri's justification of historical cost by way of "causal networks" approaches the predicting function by searching for some "underlying causal networks." Of course "causal" implies predictor, and the search for causability is a search for antecedent clues. He fails to mention the possibility of direct estimates of *future* replacement costs except for the immediate future. *The Foundations of Accounting Measurement* (Englewood Cliffs: Prentice-Hall, Inc., 1967), p. 64.

expectations of irregular expenditures over the intervening periods and perhaps smooth the resulting income figures more than regular depreciation methods.[19] This method of accounting does not separate holding gains from operating gains. Instead a smoothed portion of expected holding gains or losses is included in the depreciation charge, and therefore in the overall income figure. Changes in the original capital investment, as in double-account accounting and base-stock accounting, are not determinants of periodic income.

With expected-replacement cost as a depreciating base return on investment, ratios would be a mixture of historical cost (capital expenditure) with the allowances in terms of future cost expectations. From one point of view past performance in acquisition markets is poorly measured, for performance in making original capital expenditures is reported only on liquidation. Yet it is possible that *future* prospects may be predicted more successfully from measures that do not include the original investment. Return on original-cost investment without price-level modification leaves most accountants uneasy, for the relation of currently reported income to original investments made years ago is acknowledged to be of little use.

It is possible that depreciation on current replacement costs may be roughly equivalent to depreciation on future expected costs. Current entrance costs — with a "rational" market — should reflect expected changes in technology and future production costs.[20] Thus depreciation on current entrance costs tends to use market evaluations instead of management's evaluations for the depreciating base. These current evaluations may also operate as a more acceptable base for appraising management performance, e.g., return-on-investment computations.

Historical Costs as Predictors

Storey has pointed out: " . . . valuation at cost has traditionally been associated with the going concern, but, as a closer examination of the convention discloses, the going concern convention is quite neutral with regard to such valuation. It merely rules out liquidation and requires asset valuation according to intended use."[21] The historical-cost procedure proceeds in a series of piecemeal liquidations of "units" with changes of base recognized upon expenditure. Thus performance responsibilities are changed only upon the basis of added expenditures, at which time new accountabilities are assumed to arise. Thus the accountability and performance of management are measured with respect to the costs already incurred for its resources.

Bond-valuation technique may have been the original support for adopting historical cost in evaluating progress. In the hold-to-maturity bond situation, interim liquidation

---

[19] While accountants tend to deny — with indignation — that they smooth anything (least of all income), it has been pointed out in previous essays that the concept of income itself may have arisen because of dissatisfaction with irregular cash flows as measures of either past performance or future prospects. If this hypothesis is true, income was specifically designed to divorce accomplishment measures from the irregularity of cash flows, and depreciation is clearly a device for smoothing irregular capital budgeting outlays. Those of us sympathetic to renewal-replacement depreciation are especially aware of the smoothing function of "depreciation accounting." In this framework any distinction between income determination and income administration needs to be modified from the older relationship to administering funds to include such items as growth in earnings per share, tax considerations, etc. Moreover it becomes obvious that current income is not a temporal allocation of future income but a spreading of expected fund flows.

[20] See Oscar Nelson, "Testing Obsolescence in Fixed Assets," *The Accounting Review*, October, 1945, pp. 447-458. Unfortunately this contribution seems to have been generally overlooked for a couple of decades.

[21] Reed Storey, "Revenue Realization, Going Concern and Measurement of Income," *The Accounting Review*, April, 1959, p. 237.

values are completely disregarded and income is computed as if the firm were locked-in and intending to hold until the bond matures. The resulting income by definition is a smoothed portion of the expected increase in value that should be realizable at maturity. The accountant's historical cost is based on a similar locked-in assumption with the liquidation (maturity) value of the firm so far into the future that its liquidation value is deemed to be unknown or inconsequential. With the future value unknown, income is difficult to define in terms of discounted value increases. Accountants have substituted a value-intact assumption by assuming that the value at the beginning can be preserved in some fashion by labeling a portion of the fund flow return of capital before assigning the remainder to income. (See last section of this essay.)

A variation of historical cost makes use of some sort of general price-level adjustment. From the viewpoint of smoothing expected future expenditures, this modification is roughly equivalent to assuming that the expected changes in prices of specific assets and changes in technology of such assets can be expressed well enough by changes in the general price level. (A further assumption is necessary: that the original cost relationships are likely to hold for expected replacements.) If these assumptions are granted, income measured from current historical costs is understandable and rates of return on investment can be given a goal-measuring interpretation. The conditions required are not necessarily those of unmodified historical cost, but the assumption of parallel price and technological movements is on the heroic side. Unmodified historical costs would seem to be good predictors of future fund outflows to preserve continuity only under static conditions or with technological advances offsetting price changes.

Continuity and the Discounting Process

Most of us in accounting have been charged time and again with failure to consider the time-value of money and criticized for not making more extensive use of discounting techniques.[22] Samuelson has pointed out that businessmen of the Middle Ages got around the religious taboo on interest by expressing their deals in terms of so many years purchase of a perpetuity.[23] Historians of accounting may be interested in the application of perpetuity thinking in one of our long-used models for valuing an enterprise and its goodwill. This traditional procedure begins with the past as a clue to the future, modifies past reports for items that are not expected to recur, adjusts further for items expected in the future which have no clues in past reports, and assumes the resulting stream can be generated uniformly. The results may then be turned into "values" by using a further judgment as to a target rate *or* a number of years purchase. The perpetuity concept is well entrenched in accounting thinking, but the religious taboo on interest no longer seems to be a reason for its continuation. With an assumption of continuity, along with some related stipulation such as maintenance of capital, the techniques for perpetuities become relevant, and the need for periodic discounting is greatly diminished, i.e., the continuity assumption in conjunction with an assumption of fund-flow regularity tends to make compound discounting on a regular basis unnecessary. To the extent that these conditions are accepted, the common charge that accountants "neglect the time value of money" is not valid.[24]

---

[22] In capital budgeting the average-rate-of-return method, which projects an average projected income stream, is usually referred to (scornfully) as the "accountants' method."

[23] Paul A. Samuelson, *Economics, an Introductory Analysis*, 4th. ed. (New York: McGraw-Hill Book Co., 1958), p. 592.

[24] This matter is discussed briefly in Volume II of the *Essays*, p. 41.

For a simple illustration, suppose that indefinite operations are likely and that the estimated stream of receipts and disbursements is reasonably regular. We are assuming that the "time" distributions of receipts and expenditures are regular, but we are not necessarily assuming that the progress of the firm, the richness of managerial decisions, and the efficiency of operations are regular. Suppose further that the indefinite future stream of net favorable circumstances is discounted at some nonzero rate at the beginning of a period and again at the end of the period. With regular receipts and disbursements the capital value at each date is independent of the date and in fact depends entirely on two variables: the discount rate itself and the size of the stream of net expected receipts. This situation at the extreme with normalized returns and rates is equivalent to discounting in perpetuity, in which a capitalized value for the firm is found by dividing the estimated equal periodic net throw-off by a discount rate. The denominator requires a judgment of a normalized flow of benefits, and the denominator a judgment of a satisfactory rate of return. If confidence in the regularity of the normalized flow in the denominator is small, the method may be abandoned or modified for major expected irregularities by ordinary discounting procedures. Unusual flows such as major rehabilitation and bond amortizations have traditionally been treated separately in this manner.

An obvious condition for continuity is that something or other should be kept going. Infinite operations are not a necessary condition, and 'going' does not necessarily imply going at the same level. However, accountants tend to use these assumptions in order to support their methodology, and if the assumptions are not stipulated some modification for discounting becomes necessary. Suppose for the moment that accountants do interpret 'intact' to mean maintenance at the prescribed fund-flow level.[25] To the extent that such suppositions are realistic and that appropriate rules can be designed, specific attention to the time value of money can be eliminated *except for material irregularities*. The function of this special discounting is to make these irregularities more consistent with the norm used for income reporting, i.e., value added.

Smoothing through discounting deserves further explanation. With certainty assumed, the income reported would of course be smoothed (per unit of investment base), no further opportunities for unusual contributions by management or the environment would exist, and the income reported thereafter would be a function of accounting for the inevitable. In this case there would be no need for additional information anyway. With uncertainty the situation is different. To the extent that a windfall or shrewd maneuver is not discovered until it happens, it is not smoothed regardless of the appropriate interest rate, although by definition it might be excluded from income and treated as a capital gain. On the other hand, discovery ten or so years in advance with a high rate of discount means that little of the effect is felt in the period of discovery; the main force is spread over the intervening periods.

Consider now the actions accountants take to provide the conditions necessary to validate their process. Due to all sorts of decisions and actions, it is clear that the actual throwoff of funds may be highly irregular. Instead of trying to estimate the indefinite future with regard to fund flows, the accountant assumes that he is able to decide the fund outlays necessary to keep the possibilities for long-run net inflows intact. Current contribution is divided into that portion necessary for keeping the future prospects intact and

---

[25] We are not now considering the long doctrinal disputes as to the nature of the stream to be kept intact. Many accountants are interested in maintaining physical facilities, others are concerned with maintaining cash flows, while still others are interested in stable expectation levels.

that portion available for expansion or withdrawal (income). This process permits reported income to vary with all sorts of influences from management and from the environment without abandoning the assumption that deductions are adequate to maintain future prospects.

In summary, it may be desirable to compare the accountant's traditional matching approach with the usual discounting approach. Fisher,[26] one of the fathers of the discounting process, divided the contribution for a period into the amount consumed (income) and the amount reinvested. Investment appeared as income only when it was consumed. Current capital values depended on expected income, i.e., current capital values were discounted future expected consumption. The Alexander variation,[27] which seems to be widely accepted currently, requires the estimation of future cash (or equivalent) throw-offs. These net future cash flows are not themselves income, but are the chief determinant of the smoothed numbers that are called income. Fisher disciples need to estimate future consumption while ordinary discounters need to estimate future fund flows. Accountants look at the assets, decide how much cash will be required to keep them *intact* for future operation at approximately the same scale, and by definition the remainder of the contribution is income. Readers of accounting reports are then at liberty to make further inferences. Among them is the inference that the deductions are or are not sufficient to maintain future opportunities, i.e., the reader is expected to draw on his knowledge of the environment for an opinion as to whether future income is likely to be maintained with the resources provided. Increased assets (additional capital expenditures) are interpreted as providing a larger facility for prying loose future funds. Past income figures, if available, give the reader some clue as to the effectiveness of the intangible managerial function. The reader is then expected to make his own judgment about the environment and make his investment decisions accordingly. Thus, the accountant by default passes on many estimates about the environment to the investor.

Continuity and Discounting — Some Particulars

In order to emphasize the necessity of objectives in any definition process, consider the following situation. A client at the beginning of period one procured the right to $100,000 at the end of period five. No uncertainty as to time or amount is involved, and the opportunity rate of funds is and remains ten percent. The primary question is: How should we measure income? Possibilities are numerous: take the full amount at the beginning of period one; take the full amount when the cash is received at the end of period five; prorate the gain over the periods from zero value to $100,000 by internal-rate-of-return methods; discount the certain amount at ten percent (the client's opportunity rate); discount the $100,000 at some market rate; distribute the total to the periods randomly; distribute part of the $100,000 as income and the remainder (say, the discounted value at the beginning of period one) as capital gains or windfalls.

Reasonably alert students should worry over the possible reasons for giving information (the objectives), and they should also worry about possibilities of being locked in as

---

[26] Many references to Irving Fisher are available. For example, see *The Theory of Interest* (London: The Macmillan Company, 1930).

[27] Sidney S. Alexander, "Income Measurement in a Dynamic Economy," in *Five Monographs on Business Income* (New York: American Institute of Certified Public Accountants, 1950). Also see an expansion of this article by David Solomons in W. T. Baxter and Sidney Davidson, eds., *Studies in Accounting Theory* (Homewood: Richard D. Irwin, Inc., 1962), pp. 126-200.

opposed to freedom to exit at will. The problem is certainly not clarified by calling the results of calculating as if the asset were held to maturity with the yield rate implicit in the original purchase price "true income."[28] The results of this calculation presumably yield "true" income even when exit market values (opportunities) are available at all times.

Sidney Alexander also points out some difficulties in discounting subjective prospects in order to calculate private income.[29] It is precisely at this point that Chambers' approach generates merit. If the investment were locked in with exit before maturity impossible, the intervening changes in interest rates seem to be nonrelevant. It is in this sense that traditional accountants considered current values of fixed assets to be unrelated to income determination. If exit is not feasible, if fund-getting potential is independent of resources used, and if changes in capital costs are recorded only when made, then accountants assume that interim changes in capital asset values are not a legitimate component of income.

As one might suspect, the relevance of exit values to management's activities and performance becomes acute when exit is a more or less continuous opportunity. In the discounting procedure the ability to exit has equally strong importance. If such ability is present, then the individual is no longer controlled by the initial yield rate. But much more importantly, if exit is possible the market can also appraise the solidarity of the expected $100,000 so that the subjective estimate is supplemented or replaced by market estimates. Now market estimates are subjective also, but their importance is not alone in reducing dependence on the client's own subjective representations. The importance of market values when exit is feasible is that they express the ability to switch to alternative opportunities. Exit values do not, of course, indicate individual opportunities for reinvestment and in this respect Chambers' expression "command over resources" has a more general tone.

In a broader context we may ask whether a manager who cannot exit should be evaluated in terms of exogenous changes which were not available to him. (The question as to whether he should be informed of such changes so that he can be motivated to hold different asset combinations and to combine them differently has been treated elsewhere. See Volume II, Essay Fifteen.) Traditionally, managers *are* given credit and charged for noncontrollable changes in the environment in the usual accounting process. As pointed out in a later essay, the firm's reaction (adaptability) to these exogenous inputs is precisely what the accounting process needs to measure and what investors need to evaluate. To be locked in, therefore, is to have zero adaptability, and lost opportunities due to restriction on freedom to adapt should be associated with the types of actions and decisions that originally led to the restrictions. Finally, these associations of specific lost opportunities and specific past decisions should be made available in case similar decisions come up in the future. Future situations will involve some differences, but the accountant's necessary commitment to continuities and resemblances should be clear. Perhaps the process should record a measure of the cost of opportunities lost by being married to specialized assets.

---

[28] One of the worst offenders in this regard has been Ezra Solomon. See, for example, "Return on Investment: The Relation of Book-Yield to True-Yield," *Research in Accounting Measurement*, eds. Robert K. Jaedicke, Yuji Ijiri and Oswald Nielsen (Evanston: American Accounting Association, 1966), pp. 232-245.

[29] There is evidence that Irving Fisher was concerned with market rates of interest and assumed that most individuals would adjust their personal consumption patterns to be consistent with applicable market rates. Apparently he was concerned more with the determination of interest rates and overall capital accumulation than with individual capital budgeting decisions. I am indebted to my former colleague James King for this clarification.

The cost of inability to adapt could then be evaluated in terms of the outcomes that resulted from actually operating the specialized assets in the locked-in position.

The point to be emphasized is that an evaluation of resource performance requires measures of objectives accomplished in the given context and it also requires measures of what might have been accomplished under different conditions. What different conditions? Presumably the different conditions should have been actual opportunities available or perhaps future opportunities expected to become available. Even the relevance of available past opportunities is related to future decisions in that they give clues as to the ability of the resources to adapt. The older defenders of historical costs argued that the accounting process could not give *all* the information necessary to evaluate resource efficiency. We return then to the problem of scope and domain — what exactly should be included in the accounting process?

Comments on Risk, Exit Values, and Security Values

We digress for a short section on the relationship of asset preference and particularly liquidity preference to business management. As a rule, businesses require specialized assets and the substitution of inflexibility for generalized opportunities. It is usually assumed that some sort of reward is expected by those who sacrifice liquidity. One might speculate that the expected rewards are in some manner proportionate to the distance from liquid funds — to the degree of locked-in-ness.[30]

An interesting empirical question arises at this point: Do managers require a higher subjective value for commitments that are relatively inflexible? One might suspect a positive answer from those who use "bail out" techniques in their capital budgeting process. These techniques, it should be recalled, consider the sum of the expected cash flows plus liquidation value of the asset period by period, and presumably attach special significance to the time required to recover the outlay with possible liquidation of the asset included in the cash flow. Personally, I am not familiar with users of bail-out thinking, but apparently they are especially sensitive to locked-in positions. Bail-out sensitivity should be expected only when exit is feasible, and the procedure seems to be an appropriate capital-budgeting adjunct to the exit-value approach.

It is tempting to argue that the risk is a direct function of distance from liquidity. This statement needs some elaboration. If liquidation is said to be impossible, what is usually meant is that the liquidation value is low or negative. In most cases liquidation at some figure below cost is feasible, and in these cases the risk would seem to be related to the expected loss in exiting. Unfortunately the investor's risk is also related to the possibility of missing opportunities, and a measure of risk without consideration of this feature is seriously deficient.

The risk of technological change and partial obsolescence would seem to be included in the expected loss from either staying locked in or from exiting. At first sight it is difficult to understand how risk of obsolescence is relevant when exiting is anticipated. But

[30] Burlington Industries apparently recognizes this possibility by expecting ROI's ranging from seven percent on receivables to 22 percent on long-lived assets. This evaluative process may have interesting motivational overtones, in particular a reluctance to move into long-lived assets and a desire to lease or subcontract to other organizations. See Donald R. Hughes, "The Behavioral Aspects of Accounting Data for Performance Evaluation at Burlington Industries, Inc.," *The Behavioral Aspects of Accounting Data for Performance Evaluation*, ed. Thomas J. Burns (Columbus: Ohio State University College of Administrative Science, 1970), p. 56.

clearly bail-out is relevant for operations with some possibility of exiting, and just as clearly bail-out values are influenced by technological changes. Both entrance and exit values are influenced by obsolescence and changes in the technology — neither is influenced by a small firm's own subjective prospects. The change in risk factor from being a going concern would then appear to be related to the spread between current entrance costs and exit receipts, and with relatively perfect competition this spread would be a function primarily of removal-installation costs and market fees. The risk from being nonliquid arises from somewhere else — the risk of not being able to exit a part of the organization (an asset) without incurring some important indirect effects such as decreasing the value of a lot of other assets in the operation. This observation opens up the whole problem of the "feasible" exiting unit and the possibility of leasing or subcontracting. The optimum exit value would require consideration of various combinations of assets along with possibilities of leasing certain assets for continuing the firm. Thus liquidating the entire firm is not a necessary condition for use of exit values.

In certain respects having an alternative (exit) market for a firm's assets nearly equal to the value of the concern as an entity tends to reduce the risk of investment in the securities of the entity. A valid high-valued alternative reduces the down-side risk if operating prospects turn sour. To the extent that others in the securities market recognize this factor the value of the entity's securities should be higher. Thus the exit value of a firm's assets may indeed influence the switching possibilities of investors in the sense that switching can take place with little expected loss.[31] If, however, the exit values of the assets are well below expected value in operation it would seem that exit values would become progressively less important to everyone. Perhaps an index of relevance for exit values might be constructed in terms of the spread between value of a going concern and liquidation value of the assets. In one sense the amount of Chambers' goodwill might be a reasonably close measure of this discrepancy. More importantly, the presence of a high liquidation alternative may be similar in some respects to the related problem of marketability. Scholars have speculated that the relative marketability of a security is related to its value, and the presence of a high-valued liquidation alternative may produce a similar effect.[32]

The conclusion that liquidation values do have an impact of varying importance to investors argues *for* the desirability of making these values available. Many have argued that the accountant has no special competence in this area and should defer to others. Nevertheless, the accountant must have *some* skills in this direction or he would never be able to make the required judgment as to whether or not going concern measurement rules are appropriate.

---

[31] I am indebted to William A. Paton, Jr. for this observation and for subsequent concern over the possible manipulations to make the tax expectations comparable. Notice too that a general decline in operating prospects will tend to depress the exit value of the productive assets. In turn the decline in exit values should be slowed by the alternative uses for the assets themselves.

[32] Some consideration of marketability as a determinant of bond values has been given by Lawrence Fisher in "Determination of Risk Premiums on Corporate Bonds," *Journal of Political Economy*, June, 1959, pp. 217-237.

Essay Seven

Organizational Slack, Hidden Reserves and Smoothing

The purpose of this essay is to explore the role of accounting in the creation, manipulation and extinction of organizational slack. In the discussion, it will be useful to give attention to the more general role of information symbols in the economic process, especially with regard to their effect on expectations. If accounting has any function at all it should exert some influence on aspiration levels and thus on the interesting field of organizational theory and incidentally on the special area of organizational slack.

Organizational Slack — Generally

The development of organizational slack is a product of the Carnegie-Mellon group and has been defined too simply as: " . . . the difference between the payments required to maintain the organization and the resources obtained from the environment by the coalition."[1] The present discussion is a brief summary of the Carnegie-Mellon position.

Many economists, including Smith, have observed that firms sheltered from fierce competition tend to entrench and fortify their position against possible future adversities.[2] Practical businessmen and accountants of the older generation observed this tendency at work during World War II with the added incentive of an 82 percent tax rate. Interestingly enough, little serious consideration has been given to trade-off decisions between short-run and long-run objectives. It is possible, for example, that in order to maintain control important future profits are sacrificed by"overexploiting" the current situation. The Carnegie-Mellon position is concerned primarily with the short-run and is based on the assumption that businessmen search and decide in response to short-run "problemistic" situations and avoid, when possible, the necessity for long-run forecasting and planning.[3] That is, slack advocates assume that there is short-run *underexploitation* of possibilities due to satisfaction with the current situation. One may ask if slack may be stored for future use. If so, how may it be exploited at a later date? Finally, can it become negative?

Classical economists for two centuries or so have been familiar with the related concept of economic rent — payments to rentiers in excess of the amounts necessary to induce them to perform their productive duties. Roughly a century ago the rent concept was ex-

[1] Richard M. Cyert and James G. March, *A Behavioral Theory of the Firm* (Englewood Cliffs: Prentice-Hall, Inc., 1963), p. 278. To my knowledge the first published references to organizational slack are in James March and H. A. Simon, *Organizations* (New York: Wiley, 1958), pp. 126, 149, 187. The Carnegie-Mellon group gives credit to M. W. Reder for the notion of slack. See: Cyert and March, *op. cit.*, p. 241, 15n. The Reder reference is "A Reconsideration of the Marginal Productivity Theory," *Journal of Political Economy*, October,1947, pp. 450-458.

[2] For a detailed discussion and a suggested model see Oliver E. Williamson, *The Economics of Discretionary Behavior: Managerial Objectives in a Theory of the Firm* (Englewood Cliffs: Prentice-Hall, Inc., 1964). Williamson's historical perspective is somewhat limited; for example, no mention is made of G. L. S. Shackle's writings in the *Economic Journal* and other journals in the early 1950's.

[3] Cyert and March, *op. cit.*, pp. 102 *passim*.

panded to include quasi-rents and payments to any supplier in excess of the amounts necessary to induce him to supply.[4] A recipient is getting more than enough to induce his cooperation if he receives anything more than his supply price — his "exploited" supply curve. In the short-run, this supply curve must of course include opportunity costs from possible alternative uses of fixed factors, although the specialized nature of such factors means that a number of longer-term alternatives are not included. Thus, the short-run supply price might include some opportunities foregone from not switching specialized assets, while the long-run might include other opportunities foregone, including the limiting case where all the specialized assets are considered to be liquid funds.

It should be clear that classical profit in excess of an economic normal return necessary to attract capital may be interpreted as rent available to owners, and under certain circumstances this rent is transferable and is capitalized as goodwill.[5] Economists generally expand the concept to include availability to all groups connected with the organization, and the Carnegie group wishes to include all sorts of behaviors that are not designed to optimize possible returns. Certainly in most cases the environment is not so hostile as the stipulations of perfect competition imply.

> Many forms of slack exist . . . dividends in excess . . . prices . . . set lower . . . wages in excess . . . executives . . . provided with services . . . subunits . . . permitted to grow . . . public services . . . provided in excess . . . virtually every participant in any organization obtains slack payments.[6]

Cyert and March point out the functions that such slack performs in an economic system. After acceptable goals are met it is asserted that managers seek to create slack — a type of safety cushion. The reader may wonder if the creation and extinction of slack do not require ordinary economic decisions, i.e., various trade-offs in an allocation system.[7] The primary use of organizational slack is asserted to be its function as an uncertainty buffer. In performing this function its economic nature becomes obvious to all. The following expression seems to overstate the case.

> A firm that can absorb the consequences of uncertainty in slack does not need other devices for controlling the environment.[8]

With this clear-cut economic function for slack, the reader may be surprised to read: "This is not to argue that slack is deliberately created for such a stabilizing purpose . . . *it is not*. Slack arises from the bargaining . . . *without conscious intent* . . .''[9]

---

[4] In the latter sense, the combination of a one-price policy and upward-sloping supply curves makes such payments unavoidable. Only under fantastic conditions of equilibrium would an economy be free from such payments.

[5] For a good discussion of the fact that industrial rents are likely to be included in costs while the firm's own excess expectations tend to show up in profits and, in certain cases, in goodwill, see Fritz Machlup, *The Economics of Sellers' Competition* (Baltimore: The Johns Hopkins Press, 1952), p. 253.

[6] Cyert and March, *op. cit.*, p. 37.

[7] Apparently Cyert and March do not wish to handle the slack concept as an economic manipulation. Yet all sorts of considerations affect goal systems and influence the allocation of resources in the economic sense. The argument that "slack" is not manipulated "economically" is not convincing unless one is prepared to accept lack of rationality in this decision area.

[8] *Ibid.*, p. 296. Also: "Organizational slack absorbs a substantial share of the potential variability in the firm's environment," p. 38.

[9] *Ibid.*, p. 38. The support for such unbusinesslike behavior is not given and the evidence for the dogmatic conclusion is not convincing. (Emphasis added.)

The chief function of slack is stated to be its ability to act as an uncertainty buffer, and if true, this function requires the ability to utilize slack when the environment becomes unfavorable.

> Under the pressure of failure . . . the organization discovers some previously unrecognized opportunities . . . . [Managers] . . . can ordinarily find possible cost reductions if forced to do so and . . . the amount of the reductions will be a function of the amount of slack in the organization.[10]

Again support for the reversibility of the process is not entirely convincing. We shall return to the problems of utilizing slack in unfavorable times after a discussion of the factors that are given as determinants of slack. It is at this point that the accountant's role becomes important.

The Carnegie-Mellon approach to slack relates the environmental and internal opportunities to the Lewinian structure of aspiration levels and their adjustments.

> When the environment outruns aspiration-level adjustment, the organization secures, or at least has the potential of securing, resources in excess of its demands. Some of these resources are simply not obtained . . . . Others are used to meet the revised demands of those members . . . whose demands adjust most rapidly . . . . The excess resources would not be subject to general bargaining because they do not involve allocation . . .[11]

We return to the possibilities for utilizing slack in lean years. Williamson has pointed out some methods of burying slack in good times, and has assumed that it is possible to bring about substantial economies by pruning staff, decreasing "emoluments" and other devices without seriously impairing efficiency. No one questions management's overall ability to hide favorable circumstances either by making expense payments that are not essential or by simply not exploiting all possibilities. The reverse procedure is a little less clear.

If conditions are less favorable, some freedom to chop heads and reduce noneconomic or semi-economic costs should be available. But some of these slack-concealing devices may become institutionalized and less susceptible to discretionary reduction. Moreover, some of the nonexploited (external) advantages may simply evaporate (disappear) when conditions get worse. It is certainly unreasonable to assume that worsening conditions apply only to opportunities similar to those that have been exploited and that unexploited opportunities remain unaffected.

The exploitation or nonexploitation of such opportunities is not a major part of this paper, but they must be considered in connection with aspiration levels, and aspiration levels are certainly related directly to the accountant's work and to information generally. Even if the opportunities from the environment were constant, slack could be created and destroyed by manipulating aspiration levels. And the environment, as everyone knows, is far from constant!

Accountants' Role in Slack

The model for aspiration levels is a very simple one: " . . . the demands of participants adjust to achievement. Aspiration-level adjustment, however, tends to be a relatively slow

---

[10] *Ibid.*, pp. 38, 91.
[11] *Ibid.*, p. 37.

process — especially downward adjustment.''[12] The relationship between demands and levels of aspiration requires examination. If demands are in a lagged relation to achievement and achievement itself is under-exploited, then obviously slack can appear. But demands may be greater than achievements! If so, the continued existence of slack depends on the spread between *unexploited* opportunities and amounts necessary to satisfy the demands.

One might suspect that early demands will be above aspiration levels, but, if so, the bargaining demands may be comparatively soft until aspiration levels are threatened. In this case aspiration levels can become relatively stable standards that are related closely to minimum demands. Complete stability is not possible or even desirable, but aspiration levels are apparently assumed to be relatively inflexible. Accountants are especially concerned with the adjustment process, its speed, and its major determinants. A first approach might emphasize concealment as the policy to mask hard-core anchor points. A second approach includes active manipulation of the information.[13]

We assume for the moment that aspiration levels are more or less stable standards above which bargainers bargain less aggressively or fold. We then inquire about the role of information in determining these levels. The accountant, for example, has more rigorous rules for income recognition than for loss recognition. But for an expanding business the accounting tendency to report more and more inventory gains (paper profits) as income may mean higher and higher *projected* earning expectations. The natural increase in physical inventories will add to the tendency. The accountant's failure to adjust for changing price levels may be even more important. Depreciation on historical bases with revenues and costs at current levels will ordinarily feed holding gains into income at an increasing rate. Schmidt points out:

> *If now . . . the entrepreneur regards this amount as profit, he transforms capital into income . . . . if he believes his apparent profit is genuine he must believe that his enterprise is more profitable than it is . . .*[14]

Conservative accounting rules should tend to offset these factors and become more or less neutral overall. The tendency to admit gains with reluctance and only upon strong evidence should tend to offset the inflationary influences. Most accountants are probably uncomfortable with such sloppy measurement rules, for they would agree that reports of past operations tend to influence aspiration levels.[15] Yet the effect of this tendency is not

---

[12] *Ibid.*, p. 38.

[13] "Anchoring points" for positioning the judgment scales is used in a related sense by Dwight W. Chapman and John Volkmann, "A Social Determinant of the Level of Aspirations," *Readings in Social Psychology* (Rev.; New York: Henry Holt and Company, 1952).

[14] Fritz Schmidt, *Die Industrie Konjunktur ein Rechenfehler* (Berlin: 1927). Translated as *The Business Cycle — An Accounting Mistake* and included in my *Readings in Accounting Theory* (Djakarta: Universitas Indonesia, 1963), pp. 150-156. (Translated by Frederick Swartz.) While I consider Schmidt to be an unofficial godfather to behavioral accountants, not everyone is so enthusiastic. Gottfried von Haberler devotes one page to bookkeeping influences on the cycle in *Prosperity and Depression*, Revised and Enlarged Edition (Geneva: League of Nations, 1939), pp. 49-50. However, he cites Eric Schiff, *Kapitalbildung und Kapitalaufzehrung im Konjunkturverlauf* (1933), Chapter IV, pp. 113-134. Delmas D. Ray also concluded that accounting probably had little influence on the business cycle. See his *Accounting and Business Fluctuations* (Gainesville: University of Florida Press, 1960).

[15] Chapman and Volkmann, " . . . the general law that success tends to raise the level, failure to lower it." *Op. cit.*, p. 394. Morton Deutsch and Robert M. Krauss emphasize the influence of past experience, especially its trend and latest impact. They expand; " . . . social revolution tends to occur only after there has been a slight improvement in the situation of the oppressed groups — the improvement raises levels of aspiration, and goals which were viewed as unattainable can now be perceived as real possibilities." *Theories in Social Psychology* (New York: Basic Books, Inc., 1965), p. 53.

entirely clear when compared with the influence of a reporting process that vacillates between favorable and unfavorable reports. Can we predict that a smoothed trend of reporting favorable attainment will be projected and lead to higher and higher levels of aspiration?[16] If the levels are indeed slow to adjust and if they adjust to trends, a smoothed reporting system would not seem to be so important except to make the trend more obvious. But if, as suggested by Deutsch and Krauss, the latest attainment is weighted heavily (i.e., adjustment is rapid) then smoothing should be very important. Accountants therefore need to know the relative importance of later information on aspiration levels before they can appraise the effects of alternate reporting rules. Firm conclusions are not warranted until considerably more is known about the dynamics of aspiration levels.

The affluent accounting profession might consider serious research directed toward finding the sensitivity of aspiration levels to the content and timing of accounting reports. Return again to the failure to adjust for price levels. The typical historical-cost emphasis tends to smooth price-level changes and also to recognize good buys as realized by means of lower depreciation methods. Compromise appraisal methods that do not treat the appraisal increase as realized income but do increase expenses will partially correct for general price-level changes but may bury the effects of good purchasing as well. A general price level adjustment will correct for the capital-income shift and will permit the effects of good acquisition policies to be shown in income piecemeal on both upswings and downswings. Appraisal schemes which take the changes to income will of course tend to make the success reports more variable over cycles.[17] The point to be emphasized here is that accountants are not presently in a position to reach firm conclusions about the effects of these differences.

Schmidt has been seriously disturbed by the probable user effects of reporting gains slowly and reporting losses rapidly. He states:

> Increases in value can only appear as increases in income gradually, while decreases in value work out immediately . . . . In this fact doubtless lies the reason why the development of the prosperity period is gradual while the crisis is sudden . . . . The sudden decline in profitability kills all optimism completely.[18]

The Schmidt interpretation is in terms of induced optimism and pessimism, the demand for money, and the business cycle. Slack theorists may change the emphasis and even argue that an opposite effect is dominant. In any event, Schmidt appears as an early accounting behavioralist and predates this belated movement in the United States by a third of a century or so.

On the upswing, slack theorists may argue, demands of participants may be relatively high, but when their objectives are met the bargaining becomes less fierce, the payments necessary to maintain the organization relatively less. If so, management may be able to develop some organizational slack. Presumably on the upswing possibilities from the environment are greater than organizational demands. A conservative reporting service would tend to help managers conceal the results of favorable opportunities that were exploited. Thus, this combination tends to underplay accomplishment. To fail to exploit op-

---

[16] Here we are not suggesting a scale that is based on the subject's perceived *difficulty* in attaining the levels. See Deutsch and Krauss, *op. cit.*, p. 51.

[17] Edwards and Bell's business income and Chambers' exit values add to the variability, i.e., take the entire capital changes to income instead of utilizing the piecemeal approach.

[18] Fritz Schmidt, *Readings, op. cit.*, pp. 153, 156. (Italics except for last sentence in original.)

portunities to the fullest extent, and to delay favorable performance reports, should combine to provide strong resistance to runaway aspiration levels. Failure to exploit opportunities operates on one facet of the problem, and discretionary spending to conceal how well the firm has done also influences the aspiration level facet of the problem. A conservative reporting service can reinforce each.

Williamson has emphasized both these aspects, but he has failed to emphasize manipulation of the accounting rules themselves. His classification of profits indicates that he understands the reporting problem.

"Maximum" profits . . . are profits that the strictly profit maximizing firms would obtain . . . . "Actual" profits . . . are profits actually earned by the firm that has its objective function augmented to include a "staff" component . . . . "Reported" profits . . . are the profits the firm admits to and are actual profits reduced by the amount of management slack absorbed as cost . . . . "Minimum" . . . profits . . . are profits negotiated by the other members of the coalition that are just sufficient to satisfy their demands.[19]

With respect to revenue and other possibilities that are *not* exploited accountants have understandably done a miserable job. This assignment is undoubtedly an impossible task, but the challenge can lead to interesting speculation. Operational procedures must of necessity be crude and simplistic, for it is clearly not feasible to "account for" all *known* alternatives not taken much less the open-end set of all possible alternatives that might become available. Once the course of recognizable events has been set the accountant attempts to report accomplishment, but in limiting himself to the "actual" course of events he presents no systematic report card on management's ability to make good choices among alternatives.[20]

In a general way accountants have tried to limit their domain by a two-stage operation. First, the capital budgeting operation is designed to screen a limited number of alternatives and to compare various alternative prospects with some generalized acceptable norm. Second, once the alternatives have been selected and the operations more or less frozen the accounting process provides a measure of progress that utilizes those alternatives that were actually selected. It is true that the accounting process does not render an accounting report on whether the firm is selecting the best opportunities afforded by the environment. The process does however provide a framework with some merit for arranging certain expectations and evaluating certain actions. It should be clear that the capital budgeting area is closely related to (if not an integral part of) accounting. Expectations are arranged and weighted so that the results of alternatives actually selected may sometimes be compared with expectations. This evaluation should offer some help for identifying good "proposal evaluators." No direct check is made on the quality of the search activity for alternatives, and no specific report — other than the capital budgeting proposals — is made on the profitability of alternatives not selected. These tasks are performed indirectly and evaluated crudely. If individual A consistently is accurate in his anticipations, it may be assumed — with some caution — that he is predicting more successfully. Yet he may have more predictable opportunities than other forecasters. If his search

---

[19] O. E. Williamson, "A Model of Rational Behavior," in Cyert and March, *op. cit.*, p. 243.
[20] C. West Churchman has been a relentless critic of this aspect of the accounting process. "Accounting does not reveal the profits which would have occurred had alternate decisions been made." *Prediction and Optimal Decision* (Englewood Cliffs: Prentice-Hall, Inc., 1961), p. 322. He might have added: Nor does any other information service except in rare, isolated situations.

turns up more profitable alternatives, he may be a better searcher or he may be bombarded by more attractive opportunities than the others.

The second aspect — the lack of reports on alternatives not taken — is also handled crudely and indirectly. Some sort of profitability norm for resources in similar economic activity is taken as a general target for average attainment over a number of decisions. This target is often a modified average or standard for divisional or enterprise performance. The actual target may relate to average, marginal or some other measure of return for competitive firms, or it may be set and modified by more direct consideration of the perceived opportunities facing the particular firm.

Clearly it is impossible to account individually for the effects of numerous interrelated decisions and actions, and some sort of average or aggregation *must* be used. This compromise seems to be difficult for the profession to make. If businessmen can separate the sources of their expectations to the degree necessary for capital budgeting decisions, it seems that the accounting profession somehow should be able to measure the results and perform a post-audit of the decisions. Attempts are made to arrange a framework for the budgeting estimates that coincides with the framework for reporting. But a little reflection will indicate that the capital budgeting estimates are of an incremental nature from a shifting set of initial conditions. That is, the entire increment is attributed to the decision and none to the cooperating factors that make up the shifting initial conditions.

Management normally enjoys wide discretion in such matters as timing introduction of new products, launching major promotional efforts, modernizing the technology, developing markets generally, and it is a difficult assignment for accountants to include alternate possibilities of this sort into their accounting framework. In the future accountants may be given responsibility for disclosing probable effects of these prospects "waiting in the aisles." In the past professional leaders have felt that the traditional approach plus *ad hoc* analyses are adequate. Nevertheless, on a practical level there is a long governmental accounting tradition for bringing estimated (budgeted) revenues into the records and isolating variances from revenue plans. Accountants for profit-seeking firms have been slow to adopt and expend these techniques, although variances from sales list and sales volume standards were emphasized by Eric Camman a third of a century ago.[21] To my knowledge, however, failure to book the loss of sales volume from not exploiting full market potential has been given no attention. To measure this type of loss the investigator must look beyond the books to capital budgeting proposals not yet implemented or perhaps not even made. In the latter case, the investigator has an open-end group — his search may never develop the best opportunity not taken.

We return to the Williamson classification of profits into maximum, minimum, actual and reported. This interesting classification can be expanded considerably even within the traditional accounting framework. A more complete classification begins with maximum income as defined and then introduces an intermediate concept that indicates the income that would be reported with actual sales and no slack buried in discretionary spending. This intermediate concept is similar to the traditional accountant's reported income before variance writeoffs, i.e., sales less standard cost to make and sell. (This statement requires that no slack be buried in the standards.)

The difference between this intermediate figure and Williamson's "actual profit" would indicate the amount of slack buried in inefficiencies and discretionary spending. In

---

[21] Eric A. Camman, *Basic Standard Costs* (New York: AICPA, 1932), especially Chapters IX and X.

a crude sort of way the amount of the variances will indicate this slack if the standards are relatively slack-free and are comprehensive enough to include selling and administrative effort. Clearly, slack is not buried effectively when it is included in unfavorable variance reports so that one might predict that the most common burial grounds would be in the standards themselves, where investigation is more leisurely and less urgent. Standards are usually short-run in that they are set with regard for existing technology. Nevertheless, to the extent that they include an allowance for long-run discretionary spending for technological improvements they contain long-run — and dynamic — elements. The burial of slack in standards is normally accomplished by including an acceptable amount of inefficiencies in the standards themselves. The amount of normal foolishness seems to be highly flexible and may indeed vary with management's desire to conceal organizational slack of various kinds.

The most serious shortcoming of the Williamson analysis is its failure to consider the influence of the accounting rules themselves on the development and extinction of slack. The *reported* income with absorbed and undisclosed slack is obviously an influential variable on the subjective (aspiration) side of slack creation. Thus reported income depends on accounting rules, and to the extent that members of the coalition understand the operation of these accounting rules, the reported income can be related to some minimum profit that meets their demands. In most cases it is the amount of cash payments and perquisites granted that hold the organizational components together, and it is not clear exactly how minimum-profit levels exert their influence. True enough, reported income may relate to cash and perquisites granted over a long period, but for the interim fluctuation the relationship is less clear. Managers may perhaps build up additional, even excess, job security if income and liquidity are above minimum levels. In the dynamics of the organization all members of the coalition will presumably raise their bargaining sights and anchor their minima more firmly, so that over a long period minimum profits are not independent of past reported income.

Return now to the downswing and the onset of difficult times. Opportunities from the environment would seem to dry up whether or not they have been previously exploited. (Researchers might be interested in the determinants of this shrinking process and their relation to whether or not exploitation has already taken place.) Managers presumably attempt to exploit all sorts of remaining opportunities more effectively and also try to reduce the slack absorbed in discretionary costs. Williamson insists that attitudes toward costs are not homogeneous and "expense preferences" exist; nevertheless, the reduction of some slack-absorbing expenses may prove to be difficult.[22] If the recipients are members of the firm it seems likely that past perquisites and emoluments have been incorporated in the subjective side of their aspiration levels. Thus, the bargaining on these cuts may be extremely hard. Due to the typical lags in accounting reports, knowledge of the adverse situation facing the firm may be delayed, although other influential clues may become available.

But if the accounting rules report the influences of unfavorable circumstances quickly and emphatically as losses, the reduction of slack-absorbing expenses may be accomplished more easily and be accepted with more tolerance. Cost or market, for example, dumps the entire effect of reduced expectations from unsold goods into the current income report. This adverse influence in connection with other clues and propaganda may

---

[22] Oliver E. Williamson, *op. cit.*, pp. 33ff.

lead to more rapid reduction in aspiration levels, to softer bargaining and to acceptance of emolument reduction.

If aspiration levels are *not* reduced rapidly, organizational slack will tend to be destroyed quickly. The existing aspiration levels may well be influenced by sustained improvements on the past upswing and, if so, unless something fairly drastic is done, the possibilities from the environment contract faster than aspiration levels, and slack is rapidly destroyed.

Some propaganda possibilities may be mentioned. Expense preferences may be built up and manipulated consciously, and it has been hypothesized that certain expenses can be reduced with less organizational turmoil than others. For example, some members of the organization are considered to be *in* more solidly than others, and it has been widely suggested there may be an industrial army of heads that can be severed without undue remorse or trouble. There are, however, many more subtle methods of keeping slack-absorbing emoluments from becoming entrenched in longer-run aspiration levels. The use of bonuses is a common example. In a similar way, overtime premium is isolated so that aspirations may not lead to a feeling of permanence. Dividends are often stipulated as extras to keep stockowners from building them into permanent expectations. Management obviously would exhibit preferences for reducing these types of expenditures. Not only are they likely to involve less personal confrontations on reduction — they almost reduce themselves — but they are effective places to absorb slack and may include as a bonus an expectation of getting some economic return in the form of loyalty and more efficient operations from those who remain.

Income Smoothing, Secret Resources, and Slack

We turn now to the influence of income smoothing and secret reserves on slack. It should be emphasized that the income concept is based on the desirability of uncoupling progress reports from the accidental features of cash-flow statements. In this sense income measurement is an attempt to smooth the irregularities and accidents of cash flow to satisfy certain objectives.[23] We are concerned here primarily with attempts to construct this less erratic measure and its probable effects on organizational slack. Nonaccounting attempts to smooth the measure by Williamson's methods of overexploiting or underexploiting opportunities and raising or lowering slack-absorbing expenses are not considered here.

The smoothing controversy in accounting has been more or less unproductive because of lack of agreement as to when income is considered to arise. Shall we say income arises from waiting? Manufacturing? Buying? Selling? Collecting?[24]

---

[23] The income concept was constructed to replace cash flows as a measure of performance, and the surviving *liquidity* aspects of realization may have been compromises to those who abandoned cash flows with reluctance. The necessity for theory builders to specify objectives is especially important. Recently Arthur L. Thomas has deemphasized the objectives aspect of this problem. He feels that income measurement, except some of Chambers' CCE's and fund flows, requires arbitrary allocations. But exit values and fund flows are also arbitrary allocations with respect to objectives and perhaps periods as well. Or does a "happening" allocate without allocating? *The Allocation Problem in Financial Accounting Theory*, "Studies in Accounting Research," No. 3 (Evanston: American Accounting Association, 1969), Chapter 6, especially p. 104.

[24] The very expression "smooth income" betrays an implicit definition of income that has the potential for not being smooth. Observe the title: "Smoothing Periodic Income," by Samuel R. Hepworth, *The Accounting Review*, January, 1953, pp. 32-39.

Suppose to begin that successful counter-cyclical bias is built into the measure. Tremendous slack should then be present in good times due to greater environmental opportunities and reports that tend to retard aspirations. On the downswing, the opportunities may in part evaporate and in part be exploited. The reporting service would then retard the reduction of aspiration levels, but due to conservative reporting in prosperous times the levels would never have been as high as they otherwise would have been.[25]

An interesting question arises as to the probable behavioral effects of a smoothed performance record. First, management *might* be more aggressive with the knowledge that effects of individual mistakes would be obscured by being mixed with the results of good decisions. Perhaps this offsetting would lead to the broader, longer-range attitude of "winning-a-few-losing-a-few." A sequence of good decisions might lead to greater chances and more daring subsequent decisons. The slowness of reporting inherent in averaging might encourage a long-run view, but it might also encourage retention of bad managers for longer periods and a delay in recognizing good ones. Moreover, managers might react by exploiting external slack more effectively on the upswing to procure good current reports along with favorable carryover to future reports, but the influence might be the opposite. Managers might fail to exploit because the effects would be delayed and not show up until later. Empirical study is needed here to compare the alternatives of exploiting now with credit delayed until later, or exploiting later. Again, longer-run effects may prevail, for it may be difficult for management to decide when external opportunities should be effectively exploited, and its decision may be influenced by the accountant's scoring system.

Schmalenbach, as a "dynamist" concerned with income reports, is somewhere between accountants who wish to smooth by hidden reserves (available but unreported resources, i.e., internal slack) and those who wish to use a more fluctuating measure.

> The dynamists are far from supporting the thesis: the more hidden reserves the better. . . . On the other hand, it is incorrect to accuse the dynamists of being fundamentally opposed to all hidden reserves . . . . the dynamist is opposed to all fortuitous variations . . . will be in favor of hidden reserves in provisions for contingencies.[26]

Certainly, the technique of hiding resources makes the manipulation of slack more convenient, and in the Carnegie-Mellon structure the presence of organizational slack helps make the concern more stable, reduces uncertainty, and increases chances of survival. One plaguing question remains without solution, and it applies to exploiting both actual opportunities and playing the reporting game. If we can specify and order the objectives and if we can predict membership reactions, we should be able to devise a scheme for exploiting the environment and reporting the results that will tend to improve (if not optimize) operations and survival. But how?

---

[25] Efficient market theorists probably would argue that this sort of information would already have been discounted by the market and that accordingly whatever accountants do is only of indirect importance. Could this be extended to include everything except insiders' reports?

[26] Eugen Schmalenbach, *Dynamic Accounting*, trans. G. W. Murphy and Kenneth S. Most (London: Gee & Company, Ltd., 1959), pp. 151-152. Note also: "For the sake of the profit and loss account let's fix them [depreciation rates] too high rather than too low . . . . those who tend to overestimate depreciation are better served . . . than . . . those who underestimate; the latter find their profit and loss accounts distorted from year to year," p. 124. Interestingly enough Schmalenbach (Chapter VIII) advocated separating "market profits" from "operating profits" several decades before Graham, Nickerson, Gordon, Edwards and Bell, and various AAA committees joined the fight.

A second look at the structure is likely to reduce optimism about professional accomplishment to date. Accountants have not done the preliminary research necessary to find out and predict user reactions to various performance reports. Do users employ their own built-in stabilizers to smooth fluctuating reports? Do they tend to weigh the latest reports more heavily? Do they consider, through their filtering systems, the fact that accountants report success more cautiously than losses? Perhaps they over-compensate. Do users allow for sluggish managerial exploitation of a favorable environment and for slack buried in staff and elsewhere? Do they have independent clues by which they judge the presence of slack? Without such ability, how do they compare alternative investments? Through variable price-earnings ratios? How does the investor decide whether the management of Firm A is less competent than management of Firm B, or whether the team at A is busily creating more slack? Perhaps comparison over a longer period would disclose the nature of the difference. It is true that some managers *seem* to work best in good times while others do well under adverse conditions. Perhaps their perceptions of user reaction to fluctuations are different.

The study of user reaction is indeed a difficult assignment, but it is not an impossible one. Users, it has been argued, are not undisciplined hordes; they do have some attitudes in common. They are subjected to similar indoctrination from educational and professional pressures, and one might expect a high degree of homogeneity in attitudes. This kind of investigation has empirical content and can be carried out with existing research weapons. Yet even if such research is carried out, long-smoldering and difficult problems of accounting research still remain. The necessity to measure benefit, sacrifice and relative significance when different people are involved should test research ingenuity for some time to come.

Digression — Income and Maximizing Security Values

Assume for discussion that the charge given to managers is to maximize the present value of the common stock equity. Assume also that the bail-out prospects of the owners are highly variable and that the current market of the common equity is taken as the surrogate to be maximized. From a manager's viewpoint the charge complicates his responsibilities, for he must estimate the reactions of investors and prospective investors, exogenous market conditions and related variables. In making decisions that involve trade-off of short-run and long-run prospects he needs to consider probable market reactions. This situation seems strange, but one aspect of it is not unusual. Most managers recognize the value of good relations with gatekeepers and specialists in the security markets. In a marginalist economy dollars devoted to public relations in this direction should yield an expected return at the margin equal to dollars at the margin devoted to other objectives. These costs appear in the expenses of the concern, and the benefits are buried in the advantages of lower capital costs, access to capital, etc.

The problem of maximizing market values is more complicated. It certainly is not inevitable that actions and strategies appropriate to maximize the value of the stock at the end of each short interval will maximize the value of stock at the end of longer intervals or at more distant cutoff points. It seems at first sight that if the value would be maximized more or less continuously that it would also be maximized at the end of any arbitrary cutoff. Clearly such is not the case. The problem of interdependence of intervals is with us again, and the problem is similar to that of trying to maximize income over time by matching MR = MC for each instant of time. In the absence of idealized markets it simply does not follow that the managerial behaviors and strategies that maximize market value at point t_0, t_1, t_2, . . . will be those that maximize market values at point t_n. Note that the problem is not necessarily one of maximizing total market values summed over a longer interval. The usual charge to managers is not a clear directive. Some owners may want strategies that will give the greatest market values at t_4 and others at t_6, and the strategies that peak at these two dates may not be consistent.

Accountants are plagued with further difficulties. If managers do have a responsibility to maximize current security values in some understandable fashion, then it seems that accounting measures of managerial performance should include some appraisal of the effectiveness of management in meeting this responsibility. Finally, market values themselves are partially dependent on the performance of managers, so that the performance measure influences the values and the change in values influences the market values. We may speculate that the ability of management is relatively constant or unimportant so that the changes in market values are relatively independent and reflect the influence of other variables. But this is speculation.

Recently there seems to have been a reaction from the function of income as an index to withdrawals to its function as a measure of executive performance in adapting resources to changing environments. Thus income and its derivatives (EPS, P/E, etc.) are now considered to be primarily measures of managerial performance.

Suppose, as a basis for discussion, that a firm has been reporting (on traditional bases) $100,000 annual income and the price-earnings ratio has been consistently 10. Suppose also that investors reassess existing prospects and bid up the ratio to 12. After an annual lag the accountant would report net income of $100,000 + $200,000. How would the investing public react? Empirical evidence is lacking and, of course, we simply do not know. If investors should value these new-type earnings as equivalent to old, the price of the securities (P/E = 12) would go from $1,200,000 to $3,600,000. To continue an unchanged ratio of 12 for another period would result in reporting earnings of $2,400,000 + $100,000, and a capitalized value of 12 × $2,500,000. Needless to say, this is an explosive situation and some dampening influences are clearly and urgently needed. (There is some evidence that explosive effects may have been present in the conglomerate boom of 1966-1968.)

Consider now an opposing case. Suppose that investors considered the earnings from changes in market value of common to be worthless. In this case, the old 12 to one ratio to operating earnings would be reasonably stable if other conditions in the market were stable. That is, the firm would continue to report $100,000 (after the original jump of $200,000) simply because there would be no internally induced changes in market of common to consider. Investors would of course continue to adjust the P/E of 12 to be consistent with their opinions in other directions, so that it is more accurate to say the firm's P/E would not be influenced by the reporting. There is no point to including market changes as income.

In most cases, investors *probably* would be influenced to some extent by the reported gains and losses in market values, but would evaluate such changes differently from earnings from other operations. If so, how much difference in quality would be imputed? At present we do not know investor reactions to quality differentials of this sort, but the conglomerate debacle provides some interesting material for empirical research.

Some technical accounting aspects of the suggested redefinition may be interesting. Suppose changes in stock values are allowed to influence the income figures. Suppose also that at the end of the first year there is a debit to goodwill, or some equally vague substitute, of $200,000. In what sense is this account an asset, and when, if ever, is it to be treated as a deduction in proprietary interest? If the item is considered to be an asset, presumably management's adaptation of the resources meets the defining requirements for inclusion among the assets. Clearly general stock-market changes in optimism and pessimism become determinants of asset value.

For accountants brought up in the cost tradition the inclusion of increases in market value of common equity as an asset leaves an uneasy feeling. What might be the alternatives? One alternative is to construct an independent measure of management's ability to increase the value of the residual equity. Simply do not include this measure as a part of reported income. A simple series of common stock prices multiplied by common stock equivalents might serve this purpose. A refinement might include only the excess of the increase over some general market effect. Other possibilities should be available.

Perhaps the most interesting alternative considers the goodwill substitute as a deduction from the propreitary equity. The net effect is to increase current and retained earnings and to offset the increase on the financial statement by a proprietary deduction. If the deduction is to retained earnings, the net effect appears only in current earnings. (Presumably some net of taxes measurement is used in all such cases.) In these cases we have the strange (by double-entry standards) situation of reported income without an accompanying increase in assets or decrease in liabilities. Income is thus measured by a different set of values from those used to reflect the resources in the financial reports.

Finally, suppose that investors have been making a relatively efficient market and can be expected to continue to do so — an extrapolation that may be unwarranted. In order to accomplish this considerable task they would be expected to incorporate the effects of their own actions in the market immediately. If the valuation cycle were to explode, would it tend to explode quickly? If various dampening influences were present, how quickly and how effectively would they operate? Rapid oscillation? Smooth transition and adjustment?

In the past there has been an overly simplistic distinction between valuation of the firm on the one hand and valuation of the firm's assets on the other. This digression tends to show that some sort of report on how management utilizes its traditional opportunities separated from how the investing public appraises management's performance (along with a host of other variables) may be an equally important distinction. Given the existing evaluation process it seems simpler to give a measure of management's performance that is reasonably independent of the appraisal itself and of the other market variables.

Essay Eight

Interim Reporting and Smoothing — General Comments

Before starting a discussion of interim reporting it seems desirable to begin with a digression on the objectives of the reporting activity. We ask, for example, the reasons for ever reporting at the windup of any venture. Satisfaction from preparing a chronicle of certain aspects of certain events is hardly adequate support for the work required. What, then, is the objective of giving any final accounting? In short, what are the purposes of financial autopsies (Vatter's term)? The venture, it may be argued, is a node (a part) of a larger area of interest, and a report on venture performance may be considered to be an interim report for a longer continuing entity. If the individual venture is the end of activity for all interested parties, and no decisions about the future will make use of the results of this past activity, it should be evident that no "accounting" should be required. If future investment or consumption were not contemplated, even the ending cash balances for the venture would not be relevant and would not justify an accounting. Accounting for a venture or a time-segment of a venture therefore seems to be related to possible uses of the resulting information in decisions about possible future combinations. Other interim reports are subject to similar considerations.

Often in venture accounting there is a close relationship between the decisions and acts on the one hand and outcomes on the other. That is, the ability of management to adapt and operate in definite ventures (situations) is discriminated and isolated in venture accounting, while such ability is usually hidden in aggregated reports that cover definite time periods. There is, therefore, considerable loss of information when reports are aggregated over intervals, but there obviously must be some expected advantages to support the change from venture-based reporting to time-period reporting.[1] What were these expected advantages? It should be observed that percentage of completion calculations are a modification of venture accounting for more useful aggregation. This "distribution of anticipation" is, of course, the result of dissatisfaction with the pattern of reporting that results from summing activities for completed contracts to provide a measure of periodic income. Why should there be dissatisfaction? With this question awaiting discussion, turn now to an assumption that is more or less dominant throughout this essay.

For many decades the chief objective of income measurement was assumed to be its use as a guide to withdrawals.[2] So long as withdrawals were a primary consideration, the tendency to build realization (a requirement that the value increases be liquid and detach-

---

[1] Stephen Gilman discusses the shift to time periods. *Accounting Concepts of Profit* (New York: The Ronald Press Company, 1939), p. 73.

[2] This attitude may well have been reflected in antediluvian bookkeeping for drawing accounts. Drawings in "anticipation of profits" appeared as debits and "profits" generated by the business appeared as credits with the balance being a reflection of the owner's ability to live within his means. This position received major intellectual support from John R. Hicks, *Value and Capital* (New York: Oxford University Press, 1939), p. 170ff. However, see p. 179 for a broader emphasis.

able) into income definition is understandable.[3] An early alternate emphasis — income as a measure of managerial effectiveness — was given support by Poor and others, but even today this approach is sometimes relegated to a secondary position.[4] The usual attitude of modern accountants is that income reports should help society allocate its resources among enterprises and within enterprises.[5] An eager entrepreneurial group that has access to society's resources is assumed. But reflection should show that past demonstrated profits help decide the flow of resources only to the extent that past profits are harbingers (predictors) of conditions in the future. Investors have developed some more or less mysterious evaluators, which supposedly indicate the quality of past reported earnings as predictors. Decisions of the investment community are reflected in the market and in variations in price-earnings ratios.

This paper is developed from the assumption that income reports are reports that measure the performance of management *and the other resources* entrusted to it with the *primary* purpose of showing how these resources *adapt* to changing environmental conditions. Thus the objective of income measurements is taken to be the evaluation of the adaptive ability of management and other resources of the firm. But our concern does not stop here. It is hoped that the measurement of adaptive ability in the past can be related to recognizable exogenous environmental influences, so that the *probable future* adaptive ability of the firm can be appraised. It is from this viewpoint that the following discussion is developed. Thus, future considerations become a direct and *important* part of income definition and measurement, and the objectives of the users are assumed to be known or to be inferable.

The Framework

The influence of particular events from the environment on success measures of the firm is not, and perhaps cannot be, accounted for completely, but accountants are expected to use their professional judgment to account for influences and responses to help appraise adaptability to possible future impulses. Thus the impact of certain exogenous events on resources and the ability of the resources to react to these impacts are primary objects of accountability. But which impacts? What kinds of responses?

Some impacts from the environment enter the accountability system by way of transactions — the results of an interaction along certain interpersonal dimensions. These results are then classified, reclassified, combined and manipulated by procedures within the system. But how are transactions selected and what about impulses from the environment that do not result directly in transactions? What about broad general impulses such as wars, major shifts in technology and demand? How are these influences accounted for?

---

[3] A liquidity requirement of some sort is to be expected even when income is the major measure of accomplishment. One dimension of managerial accomplishment is undoubtedly to keep the owner-manager in control and not succumb to creditors and bankruptcy. To some extent accomplishment in this dimension is reported by balance sheet classification and to some additional extent by supplementary statements of fund flows. Nevertheless, many feel that a definition of income is highly suspect unless the increment is available for possible disposal without weakening the liquid position of the enterprise. (Note the current concern with reporting income in the real estate sector!)

[4] For an interesting discussion of Charles Poor and the attitudes that led to Standard and Poor's and perhaps to the adoption of the SEC, see: Alfred D. Chandler, Jr., "Henry Varnum Poor, Philosopher of Management, 1812 - 1905," in *Men in Business*, ed. William Miller (New York: Harper & Row, 1952), pp. 254-286.

[5] William A. Paton and A. C. Littleton, *An Introduction to Corporate Accounting Standards* (American Accounting Association, 1940), pp. 2-4 stress the needs of absentee investors and responsibilities to the public.

Accountants have faced up to the event selection problem largely by default, but they have made a positive move by classifying results as recurring and nonrecurring. Exactly what is it that is recurring or nonrecurring? For what possible purposes is this distinction made? What are the implicit assumptions in supposing that members of a class are recurring? The following discussion should indicate that the recurring-nonrecurring division is a minor step that needs expansion for effective use. The discussion begins with comments on recurring items.

A major objective of accounting is to isolate the influence of exogenous impacts of various kinds on the objectives of the entity. Turned the other way, the complementary accounting objective is to measure the ability of resources to react to stable, recognizable influences from the environment.

When an accountant makes a decision that certain conditions are recurring, he may feel that the recurring nature is unavoidable or he may decide that the situation will tend to recur unless controlled and consciously avoided. In the first case, there seems to be less need for accountants to account for the influences, but such a conclusion is not warranted. In the second case, some accounting is definitely necessary to help make the decisions to abandon, modify or accept the firm's present stance.

In each case, a considerable amount of aggregation usually takes place. Unavoidable impacts may not recur in the future in the same combinations and mixes, and the recurring may be irregular and in various combinations. Prediction therefore calls for estimates of the periodicity and critical points of recurring items *and* also calls for information about the entity's reaction to each of these stresses. The environment of the future may not be expected to impinge with constant force, and prediction calls for isolation of the stresses. The forecaster may then anticipate an impulse from the environment, feed it into the accounting model, and predict the resulting responses.

The treatment of nonrecurring items is more interesting. Again the problem is to distinguish between items that recur at irregular intervals and those that are not expected to recur at all. To assume that they will not recur at all seems to remove any need to measure the force of the past impact. There is no reason to account individually for past events that never are expected to occur again. Yet such items need to be separated from the impact of ordinary events in order to assess the firm's behavior on steady-state conditions. If they need to be segregated, should they be shown individually or grouped in some fashion? Randomized? We return to this practical question after a digression on a more general level.

Accounting for Abnormality — General Overview

The case for identifying and reporting the influence of the unusual — the unexpected — the abnormal — is not confined to accounting alone. In fact accountants may be cited as prime resisters of the notion. The treatment of unusual items as "surplus adjustments" that are excluded from the income measure has a long and, until recently, honorable support. The entire commitment to smoothing that is behind the divorcement of income from cash flows has a tendency to aggregate and to reduce sharpness of reporting the results of abnormal conditions.

Perhaps the broadest emphasis on abnormal events is in the field of causation. Mill has pointed out that the selection of a single cause from a number of cooperating influences is a delicate job that is usually guided by the simple rule that the *abnormal* antecedent is to be identified and labeled *the* cause.[6] One is likely to attribute the proximate

---

Footnote on following page

cause of an automobile wreck to the blowout rather than to design of the wheel, the skill of the driver or the need to make the trip.[7] In a similar manner accountants are likely to attribute losses to exogenous factors in the environment rather than to the inability of management and its resources to adapt. The abnormality approach is undoubtedly a useful heuristic search device, but it has certain shortcomings. How, asks White, do we go about deciding what is abnormal?[8] For research purposes it may be useful to begin the search by looking first for unusual outcomes, and these unexpected outcomes may incite search for antecedents (causes) that explain or account for them. The observation of an irregular outcome is taken to be the reaction of a system to some unexpected changes in the inputs or in the systematic apparatus. This approach is widely used in quality control, where variations are given a preliminary test for normality. If a particular variation fails to meet the test, it is taken as a clue that some exogenous (nonsystematic) factor is at work, and search activity is directed to find the abnormal factor — the cause.[9]

The abnormality approach has been used widely in managerial accounting. The typical variance approach is an example of management by exception and usually proceeds from an abnormal result to a search for contributing factors that may account for (explain) it. In income accounting the exception principle has been less widely and less directly applied.[10] In fact economists have been much more aware of the broader possibilities than professional accountants.

Economists have been consistently in favor of including opportunity costs — especially for capital — in the accounting costs and defining profits and losses from the resulting base. Clearly income can be defined from different benchmarks, and the verdict of users has been solidly against the recommendations of most economists in this regard. There are, however, some important aspects of the problem. If *profit*, for example, is defined as unplanned windfalls, a serious question arises as to the ability of planners to maximize it.[11]

In fact it is difficult to understand whether economists would define income in terms of the normal rate of return offered by opportunities of similar risks or in terms of excesses or deficiencies between this base and actual outcomes. Assuming for the moment

---

[6] Morton White, *Foundations of Historical Knowledge* (New York: Harper Torchbooks, 1969, 1965), p. 235.

[7] My early negative attitude toward causation was influenced by Mill, Pearson, Russell, Poincare and Cohen. Nevertheless, as an accountant, I am compelled to use a variation of the concept, and I have tended to follow Dewey's usage as the least objectionable. R. M. MacIver states the position clearly: "In an entirely intelligible sense we cause things to happen, we manipulate certain things, we control certain things . . . . philosophers who . . . reduce causation to uniformity or regularity of sequence seem curiously oblivious to the fact that it is precisely the interruption of uniformity that stimulates our search for causes." *Social Causation* (New York: Harper Torchbooks, 1964, 1942), pp. 56, 63.

[8] White, *op. cit.*, p. 247. " . . . when one does report an unusual event, it is unusual or abnormal only with respect to the way in which the central subject is regarded . . . "

[9] See W. A. Shewhart, *Economic Control of Quality of Manufactured Product* (New York: D. Van Nostrand, Inc., 1931), Chapters 1 and 2. See also Dudley J. Cowden, *Statistical Methods in Quality Control* (Englewood Cliffs: Prentice-Hall, Inc., 1957), p. 2.

[10] Some attempts have been made to incorporate normal rates of return in the accounting system as baselines or norms from which profit is defined as a variance. See, for example, Clinton H. Scovell, *Interest as a Cost* (New York: The Ronald Press Company, 1924).

[11] See, for example, J. Fred Weston, "A Generalized Uncertainty Theory of Profit," *American Economic Review*, March, 1950, pp. 40-59. Also Frank H. Knight, *Risk, Uncertainty, and Profit* (New York: Harper Torchbooks, 1965, 1921), especially Chapter IX. Armen A. Alchian, "Uncertainty, Evolution, and Economic Theory," *Journal of Political Economy*, June, 1950, pp. 211-221.

that he wishes to maximize the combination of the two, how should the businessman go about it? Should he abdicate and make no attempt to predict or respond to (if not control) the windfalls? Should he attempt to find regularities and continuities in the windfalls themselves?

It should also be obvious that many exogenous events may not conform to recognizable patterns but instead may follow a more or less random process. Even in these cases some help can come from the accounting department. If the inputs are not individually predictable the entity's response to all sorts of semi-random inputs may be registered, perhaps combined, and reported. Thus the translation of possible exogenous events into their probable effects on enterprise variables should be facilitated. Moreover, even if these events are unpredictable individually, it may still be useful to incorporate simulation procedures into the planning operation. If past responses are registered and made more or less predictable, the inputs may be treated statistically and incorporated in the budgeting process. (A world of utter chaos is not considered at this point.)

We may be overestimating the usefulness of the accounting function — there just may be too much residual uncertainty to make classification worthwhile. But if there is any basis for the above argument, the case for at least some attention to abnormalities and windfalls seems to be justified.[12]

Now it should be clear that those who "account" are in considerable trouble when they try to specify all the environmental conditions as assumptions, so that a particular consequence can be said to follow given antecedent in a one-one relation or even with high probability. Yet, this is the "accountant's impossible task."[13] Unfortunately, by these standards *anyone* who tries to account for *anything* has an impossible task. Yet, human beings — and others — do evaluate. How do they accomplish the impossible? The answer is not very mysterious. Humans live and work with some degree of uncertainty and loose guidelines. Certainty is not only impossible, it is undesirable!

This question of recurring-nonrecurring is related to the problem of profit maximization, and as we have seen, some economists have suggested a definition of profit in terms of unexpected windfalls. If this definition is accepted, it is difficult to argue that profit maximization is a tenable goal for businessmen. This point needs further attention. It is clear that businessmen should be happy to receive information about sequences and regularities in their environment so that they can plan to adapt or perhaps avoid them. Yet recurring items do not need to be deterministic and inevitable and both those that can and those that cannot be influenced should be centers for accountability. In one sense, an important difference between planning and control may be reduced to the feasibility of avoiding or reacting to impacts from the environment. The definition of control may be limited to cases with choice of responses to impulses regardless of whether the impacts themselves could be anticipated or whether they could be avoided. This distinction turns

---

[12] B. S. Keirstead points out the relation of gambling profits to windfalls: "All these speculative gains resemble my 'windfall profits,' but differ in this respect . . . they are the result of pure speculation and are not, like windfalls, incidental to a process of production. However, I would admit that entrepreneurial behavior, based on expectations of windfall gains or losses, is frequently barely distinguishable from pure speculation." *Theory of Profit and Income Distribution* (Oxford: Basil Blackwell, 1957), p. 15. Does "pure speculation" about exogenous impulses mean that the entity's reaction is also "pure speculation"?

[13] This view is attributed to Kenneth Boulding. Arthur L. Thomas is gloomy about our prospects. *The Allocation Problem in Financial Accounting Theory* (Evanston: American Accounting Association, 1969), *passim,* especially Summary, p. 105.

out to be relatively uninteresting, yet avoiding the impact rather than accepting it and controlling reactions call for different types of strategies.

The reactions to nonrecurring items may also be aggregated, but the case is not quite so simple. The unexpected events that led to the windfalls may have been recurring with the pattern of recurrence misinterpreted. Or they may be expected to recur in the future although they are not yet a part of recorded past experience. In the first case, the planning may have been bad and the control of the reaction either good or bad. The variance from plan needs to be analyzed into a part that was due to bad estimating and a part that was due to failure to control the response. That is, there is the problem of reaction to unanticipated impacts and the problem of unanticipated responses to impacts — both anticipated and unanticipated.

The process for maximizing anticipated subjective income may now be approached more directly. Generally speaking, it is assumed that a profit maximization goal is best pursued by maximizing subjective values, although *whose* subjective estimates may offer some problems. In order to maximize favorable expectations it is usually desirable to anticipate all recurring items whose periodicity has been determined. In addition, any new anticipated events about which there is no direct past history need to be accounted for in the expectations. That is, the importance of the impact on goals needs to be inferred from similarities to other impulses and to related responses generally.

The question, it should be emphasized, is how to anticipate the effects of inputs that are not expected and whose effects may or may not be a matter of past record. Accountants, as writers and keepers of history, should be able to provide a substantial part of what past knowledge is available. Even events that have been thought to be nonrecurring may be objects of accountability, in case they might sometime recur. The latter possibility (a general data bank) probably peaks out rather quickly, for the cost of trade-offs of isolating and preserving peripheral information may be considerable. Clearly if the events are completely unexpected, the problems of maximizing the entity's responses to them is difficult. Moreover, if efforts to maximize such possibilities are costly in the sense of causing the firm to forego advantages of more immediate opportunities, the difficulty is compounded.

Nevertheless, there is an interesting sense in which firms include unforeseen events in their overall maximization plans. The need to hang loose in order to take advantage of unexpected opportunities or to withstand unexpected adversities has a long history in economic thought and is usually related to precautionary liquidity and to under-commitment to specialized goods.[14] The problem in this perspective becomes a problem of selecting that mix of resources whose expected values (some of which are very vague) are most desirable. Economists may be correct in asserting that the unanticipated windfalls cannot be planned, but it is a poor approach that permits the maximization of events specifically anticipated to serve as a surrogate for the maximization of both planned and unplanned. How can the accountant help in this situation?

Some Practical Suggestions

The accountants' role is to help construct a model in which unanticipated events are included either directly or as constraints. Management probably has the more important

---

[14] John Maynard Keynes incorporated these possibilities as important parts of his general theory under the "Precautionary Motive" for holding liquid resources. *The General Theory of Employment, Interest and Money* (New York: Harcourt, Brace and Co., 1936), pp. 1966ff.

role at this point, for it may sometimes arrange its environment so that the impacts are more predictable. Members of the Carnegie Group have emphasized uncertainty absorption and avoidance by pointing out attempts to establish common and predictable attitudes among competitors, customers, etc.[15] The relevance of this tendency for the accounting profession should be clear enough. By reducing the area of uncertainty, the accountant may trace the consequences of various events and reduce more of his work to comparisons of performance with plans.

The discussion now turns to various practical means that have been suggested to make the predictive value of reports more valid. This task not only is concerned with providing historical response patterns, it also is concerned with finding periodicities of similar events. Clearly accounting cannot give all the clues that might be relevant for prediction, but if the profession is able to separate recurring from nonrecurring items, it must have some competence in this direction.

The simplest procedure involves comparing this month's or quarter's results with the corresponding month or quarter of earlier periods. This procedure is a method of eliminating environmental impacts that are thought to be common to such periods and not common to others. That is, comparison of the first quarter of Year B with the first quarter of Year A tends to allow for the impacts that are common to the quarters including accounting peculiarities such as full costing.[16] This type of comparison is related to the statistician's seasonal adjustment inasmuch as the commonalities due to several influences are automatically allowed for and concentration can be focused on noncommon factors.

Comparisons that allow for common impacts are not limited to seasonal comparisons. The continuing effect of an important government restriction, for example, may continue over several seasonal quarters. If so, a direct comparison of such intervals may sometimes be used to remove the influence of the common factor while leaving in the seasonal differences. It should be clear that a simple comparison of the two periods may not be an ideal way of removing such influences. For example, the impact may be much more important in one of the quarters due to its interaction with noncommon features, i.e., one quarter may have been a more responsive vehicle for registering the specialized influence than the other.

A second common form of allowing for (if not specifically accounting for) the impact of certain exogenous influences is to make comparisons with other firms in a similar industrial group. Thus, to recognize that the resources of a railroad may already be specialized and solidly committed to a relatively unprofitable area may suggest a comparison of management's rate of return on resources with the results for comparable firms instead of for industry as a whole. In effect, the evaluator is trying to evaluate managements' utilization of *opportunities* given him without directly modifying the asset valuations to reflect opportunities. At the practical level these problems are closely related to accounting for variances from standards. If industry generally is expected to earn 15 percent and railroads only six percent, the accountant might include a six percent return in the costs so that the performance of the individual firm is measured from the six percent base. Instead he might measure from a zero base and let the analyst evaluate the poorly situated re-

---

[15] See Richard M. Cyert and James G. March, *A Behavioral Theory of the Firm* (Englewood Cliffs: Prentice-Hall, Inc., 1963), especially pp. 118-120, also pp. 295-297.

[16] See David Green, Jr. and Joel Segall, "The Predictive Powers of First-Quarter Earnings Reports," *Journal of Business,* January, 1967, p. 44 and *Idem:* "A Replication," *Empirical Research in Accounting, Selected Studies,* 1966, pp. 21-36.

sources in terms of the six percent rate. The latter case allows for the unfortunate commitment in the evaluation process. Most accountants would perfer to recognize the loss from poor commitments at once and evaluate performance at 15 percent on the lower base.

It should be clear that standard cost accounting is a systematic attempt to account for deviations from plans in various areas. A calendar variance, for example, may be used to isolate (account for) the effect of varying temporal measures. What is not so clear is that in setting the standards the accountant is already accounting for the anticipated effects of technology and at least some environmental factors. Indeed it may be preferable to set the standards on the basis of an ideal technology and then break out (evaluate) that part of the variance due to the firm's inefficient facilities. It may also be useful to recast standards *ex post* on the basis of the best opportunities that presented themselves and to separate a variance due to opportunities offered and missed.[17]

The above discussion needs amplification. If accountants set standards with given technology, the loss due to inefficient fixed resources is not isolated and accordingly becomes a cost of product. The advantage of ideal standards for all cost factors is that the allowance for human frailties in operations, plans, resource acquisition and combination is brought into light and accounted for. The use of *acceptable* standards for the available markets and technologies tends to bury these items.[18] Variations from *any* base may be evaluated *ex post*, and such evaluation has the advantage of being made after knowledge of new opportunities has become available. Setting standards to include anticipated changes in opportunities loses some information but may gain by sharpening the entire planning process. Moreover, allowances for new influences during the period can usually be added during the evaluation process. If ideal standards are used, both anticipated and unanticipated influences turn up in the analysis, but in most cases degrees of confidence in the anticipations themselves are not isolated.

Smoothing — Still Another Orientation

A discussion of standards leads naturally into a discussion of the tendency to normalize, and normalization brings up the charge of editing news. Clearly, we should relate the terms smoothing, normalizing, or editing to some objectives. Accountants measure conse-

---

[17] Joel S. Demski is apparently working in this direction at a more sophisticated level. "An Accounting System Structured on a Linear Programming Model," *The Accounting Review*, October, 1967, pp. 701-712.

[18] Dutch accountants have a long tradition of imaginative variances with emphasis on *Kostprijs* — product cost in terms of socially necessary sacrifices. (They were also leaders in professional responsibilities and price-level adjustments that employed both specific and general indexes.) I am especially indebted to Tan Hian Kie (Dasuki) for translating and explaining the works of Theo Limpeg, Jr. and to Suhadji Hadibroto for introductions to *Maandblad voor Accountancy en Bedrijjshuishoundkunda (Monthly Journal for Accounting and Business Administration)* and to the arguments of van der Schroeff, Polak, and Mey. See Hadibroto, *A Comparative Study of American and Dutch Accountancy and Their Impact on the Profession in Indonesia* (Djakarta: Unpublished doctoral dissertation, Universitas Indonesia, 1962). Some of Hadibroto's suggested readings: H. J. van der Schroeff, *De Leer van de Kostprijs* (Amsterdam-Antwerpen; N. V. Uitgevers, Mij. Kosmos, 1953, 1947). His English summary of approximately ten pages is reprinted in my *Readings in Accounting Theory*, Vol. III (Djakarta: Universitas Indonesia, 1962); J. L. Mey, Jr., *Theoretische Bedrijjfeconomie* (Gravenhage: N. V. Uitgevers, Mij. v/h C Dewel); N. J. Polak, *Verspreide Geschriften* D1 I and II (Purmerend: J. Muusses, 1953). Dual price-level indexes are advocated by L. A. M. Renz, "Winstbepaling en Winstbepaling," *Maandblad*, September 1956 and applied to Philips Gloeilampen Fabriek. Theo Limperg has, in my opinion, the best discussion of professional responsibilities to be found anywhere. For translation by Tan Hian Kie (Dasuki) see my *Readings in Accounting Theory*, Vol. I, *op. cit.*, pp. 21-37. Original in *Maandblad*, February, October 1932 and October, November 1933.

quences of selected past events with the expectation that such measurements will be useful in predicting future responses. All are aware of the impossibility of recording the influence of all events and the necessity for selecting (editing) the inputs.

The uncoupling of income measures from cash flows may be interpreted as an attempt to remove the accidents of expenditures from our performance measures.[19] Methodologically we might take periodic cash flows and then in a subsequent operation account for the effects of items that are not expected to recur over the horizon of interest. Each user would then do his own (evaluating) accounting, and the unmodified cash flow might (or might not) be a good measure of accomplishment and predictor of future accomplishment. To the extent that major replacements are imminent, the immediate past cash flow may be inverse to requirements for the immediate future. The cash measure alone is often a poor predictor of solvency, of future cash flow, or of operating and sales efficiency.

If each user is to do his own accounting, he will select the events that he feels need special treatment and try to isolate their effects on variables of importance. But this task is precisely the task of accounting! The accountant is close to the affairs of the business and is supposed to be competent in these matters. (He often "hogs" access to important information.) Clearly, however, some users are in positions to have relatively private information and will want to make special evaluations of their own. Thus, the responsibility for evaluation tends to be a divided one, although it seems that accountants should make a special effort to arrange their operations to expedite further evaluations by those with additional information. Outsiders (nonaccountants) may anticipate a happening with a higher probability, but they also need information as to the probable consequences of the happening and traditional responses to it.

Smoothing is related to the case for averaging the effects of certain events rather than omitting them altogether. If they are omitted from income but disclosed elsewhere, e.g., retained earnings adjustments, users can read the reported income as an indicator if the event does not happen and read the past retained earnings adjustments if it does happen. Two types of earnings (F. W. Woodbridge [1928] and currently AICPA) may be a better solution. A single smoothed income that includes these items buries the results of specific events, and includes the assumption that these events will recur more or less randomly in the future. A practical application: Shall we include a past labor strike in our estimating equation so that future estimates will include an implicit strike allowance? If so, how many past periods are needed to average the effects properly? What about omitting consequences of the past disorder, deriving a strike-free estimating equation, and adding expected effects when a similar conflict is expected?

We might assume that the consequences of all nontrivial events that are likely to recur (regardless of the cycle of recurrence) should be isolated at least one time in order to improve the planning function. These findings could be stored away so that planners could estimate the impact of all sorts of possible related influences. If a large enough pile of such data exists or the events can be grouped by common elements for a large number of future expectations, a general aggregated income need not be reported. A comparison of the actual individual events might be compared with the forecasts to evaluate forecasting

---

[19] The relations of accidents to objectives is an interesting excursion in itself. " . . . the metaphysical distinction between substance and accident rests on nothing more than the grammatical peculiarities of Indo-European languages." David Braybooke refers to Carnap and Black for support. *Philosophical Problems of the Social Sciences* (New York: The Macmillan Company, 1965), pp. 16-17.

ability and with past findings to evaluate their reliability or effectiveness in controlling responses.

Now it should be clear that the interdependence of events, decisions, and actions makes complete identification of each event and its consequences impossible. This impossibility confronts all evaluators whether or not they are called accountants. Some degree of aggregation and combination is necessary and, with our limited mental resources, desirable. Perhaps the accountant can follow a course between the two extremes. He may be able to group some of the influences into a hypothesized standard or normal input stream. This standard stream may be composed of a stable, more or less constant mix of events with only major exceptional items separated for special evaluation. In addition to the minimum ability to separate such a stream at all, he needs criteria for judging the quality of the process. The constant mix composing the standard must be constant enough so that its response can be predicted. Notice that it is not necessary that the stream itself be constant, but its mix with respect to its influence on objectives must be constant enough so that predictions are worthwhile. To the extent that irregularities become regular, the accountant may wish to include them in the income mix but he still must decide whether to smooth them or not. If they are included without modification in the mix, the evaluator must make the periodicity judgment and allow for it in his analysis, and if these items are averaged, the judgment has been made at the cost of some loss of information. The facts of the business in some pretty important areas may be obscured.

Summary Comments

We have argued that the accounting profession should devote special attention to abnormal items in order to provide clues to the firm's ability to adapt its resources to unusual exogenous events. As an intermediate step managers, owners and others, using their own special clues, construct probability beliefs about the occurrence of exogenous events. The accountant may have little to offer in this area, but he should be able to offer an informational base to help predict how the resources should react to such estimates.

This division of labor between those who make predictions of happenings and those who predict the entity's responses can easily be overdrawn. The accountant classifies and records aspects of past events that should be relevant to future decisions and judgments, but he must make decisions about possible future inputs in order to decide on an appropriate classification and reporting system about the *past*. The all-inclusive, one-step income report represents the ultimate in cross-section averaging, and an interval report covering the entire history of the entity would represent the ultimate in longitudinal averaging. Again it may be difficult to specify an optimum in either case, but it should be clear that average responses are not likely to be useful for predicting the effects of specific impulses. In a similar way the total for the firm's life may not be an efficient predictor of such impulses.

Consider for a moment the present state of the art. Given an input in the form of a predicted change in sales volume of a specified mix, the accountant should be able to predict the firm's probable response in terms of income, liquidity needs, structural changes in other assets, etc. The traditional process requires that an independent estimator estimate the nature of the exogenous event and then translate it into some average effect so that the accounting system can become effective. Thus the high probability of war in a given region might be translated by nonaccountants into, say, effect on national income. The national-income change would then be converted by way of an income-elasticity index to predicted changes in the entity's sales, at which point the accounting process can be brought to bear more directly on the predictive process.

For an illustration consider a copper producer in a South American country. Consider an impulse from the environment — a strong possibility of immediate expropriation at much less than book value. We are interested in reviewing some possibilities. In one case, the effect on production would be estimated by an outside decision center. The accounting system would then indicate — would predict — the effect of lowered production on all sorts of financial and operational variables. With this approach specific additional information needs to be added for responses in the areas of writedowns, tax implications, etc. Of course, the accountant himself may estimate the impact of expropriation on some production variable such as tonnage. Salvage needs to be considered before reinvestment can be estimated and the net reduction in tonnage predicted. Thus in most cases forecasting an entity's response to a specific unusual impulse requires a combination of routine accounting output and other special information. From whence comes this special information? It is the contention here that a part of the regular accounting routine should be devoted to situations that may be expected to recur irregularly but in reasonable configurations. In this regard the problem is a minor part of the more general problem of what to report routinely as a part of the output and what to relegate to *ad hoc* special studies. These two possibilities are not completely independent, and the accountant should strive to select situations that tend to recur in total or in part for clustering his information. (Labor hours and production units are examples that enter all sorts of expected decisions.)

Turn now to the possibility that accountants attain the equivalent of an efficient market in such information. In the copper illustration clairvoyance would traditionally indicate a more rapid depreciation rate for the facilities from their installation date. Lower past earnings and lower book values might have made the shock less disorganizing and the transition easier. The reporting of more depreciation and less income may prepare readers for less favorable expectations and may help the firm prepare for reinvestment elsewhere or for distribution, e.g., dividends.

With less than complete knowledge of the future, one might assume a type of Bayesian incorporation of new estimates. Depending somewhat on the lead time, the new information will change the reports and the profession must decide whether such changes should be treated as ordinary or extraordinary items. The problem here involves a trade-off of breaking out a specific response to an event that is not likely to recur identically against the possibility of having a conglomerated report that might help decisions in a lot of directions. We may wish to evaluate the past in order to establish responsibility, but why do we wish to establish responsibility? The exogenous shock may not be controllable, but the entity's reponse to it may be controllable in whole or in part. If some executive has the responsibility for adapting the resources to exogenous shocks, we will ordinarily wish to judge his performance in this capacity. But even this judgment is made as a basis for a future decision about him. Shall we fire him? Commend him? Commiserate with him? Shall we investigate the possibilities of modifying the response pattern? Or shall we decide that the environment itself can be changed and set about trying to change it?

Digression: Holding Gains and Their Evaluation

The concept of operating gain, in which current costs are matched with current revenues, has a long and respected history.[20] Defenders of base-stock inventory methods and of charging asset replacements to expense in lieu of depreciation obviously favored matching current costs with current revenues to provide a measure of operating performance.

Footnote on following page

Intellectual advocates of LIFO almost universally considered latest invoice cost to be a surrogate for matching current costs at the time of sale. Defenders of traditional appraisal techniques combine the desire to report operating income with a tendency to offset the difference by realized holding gains. The usual advocate of historical costs apparently is not interested in separating operating gains and prefers to feed the results of good acquisitions into reported income as resources are utilized. The holding gain (if any) is recognized over the holding period by way of lower amortization charges based on historical cost.

Evaluation of operating performance may or may not make use of return-on-resources ratios. Appraisal methods probably can be used most effectively with these ratios. Base stock, LIFO, and renewal depreciation, unless supplemented by balance-sheet adjustments, are less susceptible to meaningful ROI ratios. Unless current adjustments for the resource base are incorporated in the measures, some severe modifications are necessary in the analysis. It is not failure to admit the possibility of holding gains that causes trouble!

The present trend among accountants is apparently in the direction of abandoning traditional realization guidelines and reporting holding gains periodically.[21] The holding-gain dimension has been subjected to very little independent study. In most cases, the term "acquiring gain" would seem to be more appropriate, for often any differential edge results from the buying function rather than from the comparatively passive holding function.

Managers clearly are expected to acquire resources effectively as well as to combine them efficiently. If this managerial function is accepted, the activity should be monitored and evaluated. The fantastic and incredible part of this story is that so little attention has been given to the evaluation of holding gains. What standards are to be used? What exogenous conditions call for modification? Is responsibility divided and mixed? Do rate-of-return measures apply? If so, what bases are appropriate?

We may dismiss one comparatively simple case without extended comment. In many situations leasing is a feasible continuing alternative, so that the relevant decision is not between holding or not being in business at all. Even here it is not feasible to switch on a

---

[20] For example, see Fritz Schmidt, *Die organische Tageswertbilanz*, 3d. ed. (Leipzig: Gloeckner, 1929); W. J. Graham, "The Effect of Changing Price Levels Upon the Determination, Reporting and Interpretation of Income," *The Accounting Review*, January, 1949, pp. 15-26; Clarence B. Nickerson, "Inventory Valuation — The Use of Price Adjustment Accounts to Segregate Inventory Losses and Gains," *N.A.C.A. Bulletin*, October 1, 1937. It is interesting to note that William A. Paton and Russell Alger Stevenson recognized the problem, but wished to include holding gains with regular income ("net revenue") on the grounds that the functions of combining, acquiring and transforming were too interwoven. See *Principles of Accounting* (New York: The Macmillan Company, 1918), p. 241. *Zeitgeist* observers may wonder what took Edwards and Bell and various AAA committees so long. Two articles by Fritz Schmidt appeared in *The Accounting Review*, "Importance of Replacement Value," September, 1930, pp. 235-242, and "Is Appreciation Profit?" December, 1931, pp. 289-293.

[21] The evidence of this trend is convincing in spite of some serious second thoughts in the fantastic world of real estate. Here is some well known evidence from the academic world. Edgar O. Edwards and Philip W. Bell, *The Theory and Measurement of Business Income* (Berkeley and Los Angeles: University of California Press, 1961); American Accounting Association Committee Reports: *A Statement of Basic Accounting Theory* (1966); and the subsequent extension by the AAA Committee on External Reporting in *The Accounting Review*, Supplement to Vol. XLIV (1969), pp. 79-123. "Accounting for Land, Buildings, and Equipment," Supplementary Statement No. 1, *The Accounting Review*, July, 1964, pp. 693-699. "The Realization Concept," AAA Committee on Realization, *The Accounting Review*, April, 1965, pp. 312-332. The AICPA attitude on banks, insurance, and (before modification) real estate firms seems to be primarily evidential. See, for a sponsored but unofficial statement: Robert T. Sprouse and Maurice Moonitz, *A Tentative Set of Broad Accounting Principles for Business Enterprises* (New York: AICPA, 1962), pp. 13ff.

day-to-day basis, so that some reporting interval must be devised. The construction of some measure to permit evaluation of holding as opposed to leasing should not tax our abilities, but the old question of whether to make such reports on an *ad hoc* basis or to include them in the routine output of the service is still with us.[22] We return now to the more general case of acquiring and holding gains and losses.

Assume a continuing firm with an indefinitely long horizon. Ordinarily many acquisitions and renewals of long-lived resources will be necessary for continued survival, and in the normal case these acquisitions will be made at irregular times and in irregular amounts. The question then is how to devise a measurement system that can be used to monitor and appraise performance of management in timing expenditures and adjusting resource acquisitions to technological change. Holding, in this context, does not seem to be an important variable.

An evaluation of the above activities should be made with consideration of the opportunities available. In ordinary evaluation the norm is often some sort of generalized rate of return on resources. Ideally, it seems that the base amount should be an expression of the opportunities that the resources afford. If the resources are badly placed, they afford fewer opportunities and their valuation base would be lower. As discussed previously, an alternate possibility is to maintain a stable valuation base and vary the target return to reflect short-run changes in opportunities available. This latter approach is similar to the use of relatively stable standards with detailed variance analysis in cost accounting.

If the facilities are valued to express the opportunities they afford for operating successfully, how and when should acquisition gains and losses be isolated? Should they be isolated at all? Should they be reported as value is added in some fashion? As they afford opportunities for *operating* income? As the funds go out? Come in? As time expires?

What about holding gains? As specific price levels change, operating opportunities available from holding capital assets may or may not change. Operating *contribution* (the excess of fund receipts over immediate fund outlays induced) will probably move in the same direction as capital replacement costs. If so, current values of capital assets may be acceptable measures of cash-flow opportunities furnished by long-lived assets. It may be argued in these cases that both target return and provision for maintenance of capital should be related to fund-flow opportunities. Certainty amortization should be related to some pool of opportunities to be maintained, and *if* opportunities *are* related to current replacement costs, then depreciation may be related to current costs.

If the entire period-to-period change in value of the opportunities afforded by capital assets is taken to income as holding gain, is there an appropriate assumption about the permanency of the changes? The opportunity base may be increased with respect to normal operating income by manipulating replacements even on a temporary basis. Observe, however, that the entire increase in replacement cost (available holding opportunities?) is taken into holding income. Is permanency implied? Changes day by day? For evaluating either measure, what is the appropriate standard to be used?

It is probably true that the larger the investment in long-lived assets, the greater the opportunities to gain or lose through holding and ownership. That is, the normal base for evaluating holding-gain performance should be in terms of the ability of the resources to

---

[22] The exit-value approach is clearly related. In a sense the decision to quit holding and do something else is assumed to be an active and relevant topic. Notice, however, that if consumption is not the alternative, the choice is between holding and switching to alternative holdings including various combinations of leasing and holding.

provide opportunities of some kind. But should opportunities in all directions be included? What about opportunities for making holding gains alone? Operating gains? Both? To become more liquid? Can an adjusted current base provide a satisfactory norm for any of these dimensions? In each of these dimensions the opportunities provided may change widely from period to period. If the current replacement base does not provide the desired degree of flexibility in an area of interest, we can change the surrogate base or make allowances in the acceptable rates of holding return. What warrant then do we have for using a shifting current cost as the opportunity value? We can return to a relatively stable base and return to this environmental allowance method by shifting the standard rate from period to period. But this method can be used with *any* base! Perhaps a better plan is to devise a method of comparing the amounts spent for capital assets with minimum feasible amounts to provide the opportunities and forget the base. Or finally, in the spirit of F. W. Woodbridge and perhaps a host of other base-stock supporters, if we cannot evaluate it, why take the trouble to measure and report it?

A part of the difficulty should now be obvious. Income is the result of shrewd performance in a number of directions and also of exogenous conditions from the environment. To assert that the chief objective of income measurement is to evaluate managerial performance requires one to argue that one facet of management's performance is to appraise the environment and get his resources into position to take advantage of it. Instead of the distinction between operating and holding, perhaps the division should be between combining resources and positioning resources in appropriate economic situations. In some cases we might have placed the resources in identical positions at lower costs. In other cases, we simply misplaced the resources. We need measures to discriminate these situations.

Essay Nine

Full-Costing, Idleness and Pricing Strategies

This essay is concerned with certain behavioral aspects of capacity, idleness and full costing as they relate to pricing strategies, new-product introduction, and search activities generally. The discussion is therefore related to the earlier essay on smoothing and organizational slack. In discussing the area we will give attention to the alleged circularity — "virtuous or vicious" — in using full costs for pricing, to the hoped-for psychological barriers to cutthroat pricing, and to such matters as motivation and serial independence of decisions.

The accounting mechanism is said to be weak in signaling when individual prices or entire pricing structures are or are not optimal, in giving little or no direct consideration to alternatives, and in pointing to the kinds of actions that might lead to improvement. It is clear to all that our accounting process has deep-seated weaknesses. Linear programming specialists have helped make some of these weaknesses visible with spotlight intensity. Yet, the charge that accounting has been useless in these decision areas is unfounded, and it is the purpose of this discussion to review accounting's strengths and weaknesses on these matters.

Before turning to specific problems in this area, it may be well to discuss briefly the usual criticism that accounting does not signal whether the present state and progress of the firm are or are not satisfactory. This charge is always a difficult one to counter although it borders on the ridiculous. It is usually possible to include some status and progress standards in the system and to report deviations from them directly. In general such standards should be based on alternatives and opportunities available. However, a little consideration will show that the opportunities and alternatives available to each reader differ widely. Thus each individual needs to evaluate such professionally adopted standards in terms of his own opportunities in addition to his evaluation of the firm's progress. A serious question arises for the profession. Inasmuch as the generalized norm must be evaluated individually, why not adopt a zero base and omit other norms entirely from the accounting output?

Accountants have traditionally been willing to include certain standards and budget norms in their records and report deviations from them. The norms are included after some sort of consensus on alternatives has been reached by those in authority, and a technological commitment has been made. Once this commitment has been put in force the accountant feels free to neglect all the specialized technical alternatives that were rejected and to report progress in terms of the objectives and combinations selected. On the other hand, when the opportunities are diversified for each user, or not restricted by the specialized resources, accountants are reluctant to establish generalized norms and include them in their record keeping. In the latter case, they tend to measure progress from some sort of zero (or natural base) and leave the task of evaluating the progress to those who have available the diverse choices. Thus accountants often include cost standards for manufacturing in the records and seldom show a normal rate of return on investment as a cost.[1] The cost standards relate to a production process that is stable in the short run, while the opportunity rates of return differ with each investor. No doubt if a particular investor with reasonably stable alternatives were dominant, the profession would be more interested in including "normal" return in the record keeping.

Pricing Considerations

It is the contention of this paper that businessmen traditionally have preferred relatively stable prices and have been distressed by and afraid of cutthroat competition in the form of variable-cost pricing. The research necessary to establish this contention is unfortunately not a part of this paper.[2] Instead the truth of this proposition is assumed, and consequences in the form of pressures on the accounting profession for assistance are stressed. The presence of resource idleness has not invariably led to lower prices for existing products, and businessmen have apparently asked accountants for help in signaling distress and in explaining alternatives.

First, the profession has been asked to provide an explicit measure of plant utilization, and idle-time measures have a long and respected history in accounting literature. Serious questions have arisen about the basis of measurement and all sorts of notions of capacity have been advanced. In addition to disagreements about setting capacity, further problems have arisen about the meaning and measurement of plant activity. Some accountants advocate effective (earned) hours, while others have suggested the use of actual hours whether or not the activity results in effective output. A further question has concerned the desirability of converting hours of idleness into dollars. In the early years of accounting, variations from standards (including activity standards) were translated into monetary units and were often called "profit or loss" from abnormal activity. The effect was to translate idleness into monetary terms so that the influence of the plant load factor on income — the generalized surrogate for organizational goals — could be determined. The impact of the variance is probably increased by this scheme, and, as pointed out elsewhere, this systems orientation toward enterprise activity might encourage operating executives to think in terms of corporate-level goals instead of in terms of operating tasks and allowable hours.[3]

---

[1] Many accountants of the younger generation may not be familiar with Clinton Scovell's semi-classic *Interest as a Cost* (New York: The Ronald Press Company, 1922). This volume is a persuasive plea for including opportunity rates of return in the accounts. Other readers may not be aware that the annuity method of taking depreciation can be viewed as a form of intra-management transfer pricing. The treasurer is given credit for return on funds that his superiors force him to provide for operating facilities, and production managers are charged with a cost for the funds they employ. See Morton Backer, ed., *Modern Accounting Theory* (Englewood Cliffs: Prentice-Hall, Inc., 1966), pp. 151-152.

[2] J. Maurice Clark states: ". . . the same argument which is used to show how competition brings prices down to cost . . . can be used to prove conclusively that competition tends to force prices down to the level of differential cost, if existing productive capacity will supply the demand at that price." *Studies in the Economics of Overhead Costs* (Chicago: University of Chicago Press, 1923), pp. 434-435. Advocates of direct costing and contribution pricing are requested to ponder this quotation carefully and to review again certain aspects of our anti-trust legislation.

[3] See *The Behavioral Aspects of Accounting Data for Performance Evaluation*, Thomas J. Burns, ed. (Columbus: The Ohio State University, 1970), pp. 270-271. Incidentally, there may be serious questions about the advisability of using fixed costs to make the translation. Operation researchers have found direct estimation of opportunity costs more useful in programming. The product-mix problem is, however, only one of the many possibilities involved.

While the accounting process currently monitors and reports resource utilization, unfortunately it does not disclose whether product-mix possibilities are being exploited wisely, or indicate what alternatives are available. The presence of unused capacity is a signal that conditions are less than ideal, but disclosure of capacity variances does not indicate whether the existing mix of products is a good one or whether the pricing of products actually manufactured is optimal. Yet here, too, traditional accounting disclosures may lead to activities designed to improve the situation. Disclosure of full operations at what originally was thought to be a satisfactory product mix may serve as a clue for possible consideration of plant expansion and further capital expenditures. But this disclosure may also serve as a short-run clue that, until capacity can be adjusted, some shifting of prices and mixes may be profitable. Certainly, bustling activity and an accumulation of unfilled orders do not go unnoticed, and it is unreasonable to assume that managers are uninterested in getting greater interim returns while expansion is being considered. What might such managers do?

Product mix has long been a concern of business, and mix variances can be traced to the early stages of standard cost accounting.[4] Yet for some reason accountants have been slow to incorporate suggestions from economic theorists. In the United States the long period of economic development with tremendous demand relative to production facilities tended to make accountants and businessmen naive about demand elasticities. Many early businessmen and their accountants recommended concentration on the goods with the largest mark-ups, and more or less disregarded possibilities of insufficient demand. This policy may have encouraged the unwary to substitute higher mark-up goods regardless of differences in utilization of bottleneck facilities. This shortcoming was discussed and simple rules were recommended before World War II, but a sophisticated approach appeared only when the techniques of linear programming became available.[5]

We conclude that the gross rule to utilize capacity in the direction of goods with highest mark-up was an oversimplification, but we must conclude that the capacity report can be an important factor for instigating search. Its function as a signal to experiment with prices is not so clear. To the extent that managers have been trained to be satisfied with traditional margins on lines of products and to think in terms of "fairness" of selling prices related to costs, they might interpret the full-capacity clue as a signal to shift the mix or to explore new capital expenditures rather than as a clue to raise prices of existing output lines. It is extremely difficult to generalize on these points, but they have empirical content and can be subjected to rigorous research methods. A relatively unsupported hunch suggests that many managers will be satisfied with traditional margins, will feel that products meeting this test are "doing all that has been asked of them," and will be satisfied with a modified contribution approach where "contribution" is assumed to appear only after all overhead has been absorbed. At full capacity the feeling that neither the plant nor the products "owe us anything" may well be widespread and encourage the exhilarating feeling that there is no longer any overhead to be earned. Only at this point do some businessmen perceive the relevance of the marginal-contribution approach.

---

[4] For example, Eric A. Camman, *Basic Standard Costs* (New York: American Institute Publishing Co., Inc., 1932), especially Chapter IX.

[5] See my own preliminary rambling in *Cost Accounting and Analysis* (New York: The Macmillan Company, 1950), pp. 120-121. Naive users of linear programming, like early cost accountants, may also be trapped into accepting the stability of contribution margins.

These feelings of exhilaration can be expected only where full capacity is set below ideal capacity. The mental shift from full costing to contribution costing could motivate attempts to reduce operating interruptions and bunching of sales orders, and to remove related output restrictions from existing facilities. Thus, the perception of a unit contribution of $20 to income may well be a stronger action-producer than the perception of $8 of income plus $12 of earned overhead.[6] To the extent that this supposition is effective, the incentive from under-capacity production would seem to be in the direction of tidying up operations, cutting absenteeism, reexamining costs of materials stock-outs, working on preventive maintenance, considering manufacturing to stock and other regularizing techniques. Unfortunately, for less than capacity operations the motivating influence is less effective. Direct costers wonder why the motivating force of a $20 contribution should not be applied long before capacity has been reached.

A technical digression on the mechanics of calculating overhead variances may be of interest. The more sophisticated (and more modern) process computes efficiency variances in terms of variable-cost rates and capacity variances in terms of fixed costs only. A few systems, however, still insist on using full costs for both of these variances. Look for a moment at the probable consequences. It seems reasonable to approach a manager responsible for inefficiencies with a measure that uses only variable costs *because*, the argument goes, the fixed costs go on anyway and the loss is therefore only the amount of the variable costs. (Incidentally, there is the additional assumption that the hourly variable costs of grinding out product also measure the sacrifice (hourly cost) of operating inefficiently, in spite of an obvious need for less porter service, power, scrap, etc., when no product is coming out.) This depression-based reasoning clearly rests on the assumption that plant capacity is not scarce and is not functioning as a constraint. If inefficiencies appear after capacity is reached, the sacrifice (cost) is clearly seen to be the contributions foregone. Predepression cost accountants lived in a period of high output, and a measure of sacrifice that included only variable costs must have looked ridiculous. Yet, it should be clear that their answer — using both fixed and variable costs — is only a partial answer. The addition of fixed costs does not necessarily and automatically bring the accountant's total cost up to the contribution sacrificed by the sloppy activity. Nevertheless, the result is certainly closer than variable cost alone and should be a stronger motivator for more efficient operations. The motivator — to the extent it works at all — should also operate at less than full capacity, although charging fixed costs to foremen in this situation may lead to important morale problems.

We turn now to further possible effects of measuring capacity variances in terms of full costs. Inasmuch as the measure often includes full costs both below and above capacity, the impact, when compared to fixed cost measures, is likely to be magnified. Managers, above capacity, should be excited with their favorable volume variance and may be motivated to undertake the behaviors necessary to increase it. The momentum to reach capacity should continue beyond it. Each additional unit of progress results in a greatly improved report card and it appears as if the excess capacity hours are adding full cost increments to profits. Again this measure may be less than the contribution added, but it is obviously closer than a measure in terms of fixed costs alone. At less than full capacity the reported penalty is harsh indeed, and the result should be to incite action toward increas-

---

[6] "Look at it this way . . . On the standard volume alone, you net eight percent of selling price; on all cars above the standard volume, you net 25 percent." *Business Week*, April 6, 1957. "How Detroit Figures Auto Prices." (Marketing Section.)

ing activity by whatever means seem appropriate. We return now from the digression to the main argument and the alleged circularity when prices are based on full costs.

Circularity of Full Costing Examined

It has sometimes been asserted that full-cost pricing is circular in that the unit cost depends on the quantity moved and in turn the quantity moved depends on the unit prices charged. This so-called dilemma was well understood by Clark, who stated:

> A price policy has to be based on typical conditions . . . . Goods might seem to cost more in time of depression merely because constant costs are divided among fewer units of output . . . . In partial recognition of these facts, cost accountants commonly charge each unit of goods, not with the actual burden divided by the actual output, but with a "standard rate," covering what the burden ought to be at normal or "standard" output.[7]

Clark's statement needs little elaboration. It may well be that full costing with traditional mark-up is not an optimizing pricing model, but accountants have seldom (in my time at least) advocated full-cost pricing without some sort of smoothing factor. The erratic nature of such prices based on unadjusted seasonal and other variations would be untenable.[8]

The charge of circularity is seen to have little practical import in modern accounting and business administration. Even if the actual fixed burden were distributed to products and prices fixed accordingly, it is not the alleged circularity that hurts; the pain results from not recognizing price elasticities in the output markets. That is, it is always possible to relate cost variables to product value and then relate sales price to cost by *some* expression. If the demand elasticity is a given parameter, the problem is not circular and the expression is subject to maximization. A short-run optimization requirement means that it is impossible to base individual prices on assigned common costs without consideration of the individual demand elasticities.

Legerdemain: Fixed into Variable

We turn now to the related sneers that take the form of wondering how an accountant's legerdemain can turn the straw of fixed costs into the gold of variable costs. Under traditional cost-revenue matching, depreciation and other definitional period costs are considered to expire as the product is sold. Thus, it is common to meter the annual con-

---

[7] J. Maurice Clark, *ibid.*, pp. 39, 65.

[8] Clark was also aware of this aspect of the problem. "A customer has to be charged in proportion to the worth of what he gets, not to the accidental variations in what it costs the producer to turn out things of the same value." *Ibid.*, p. 39.

Stephen Gilman states, "One of the early American pioneers in the use of normal burden rates . . . was William J. Gunnell . . . as early as 1906. By 1908 C. E. Knoeppel, H. S. Gantt and A. Hamilton Church were using and writing about normal burden . . . " *Accounting Concepts of Profit* (New York: The Ronald Press Company, 1939), p. 379.

The same sort of argument is applied against identified-unit inventory pricing by advocates of average and LIFO methods. To an average coster a seller gives up one-tenth of his economic power regardless of cost marking when he sells one of ten identical units of inventory. To a LIFO advocate he gives up the cost of replenishing the inventory if replenishing is relevant. Neither approach finds differences in identified-unit costs relevant.

stant depreciation charge to income as if the charge were largely variable with units sold. (The idle-capacity portion has traditionally been treated as a period cost.) In some accounting systems the charge is originally based on output and is treated as variable from the beginning. Even buildings can be amortized on a use basis. This aspect of accounting clearly needs examination. What is the nature of, or how shall we define, a variable cost? A fixed cost? Are they related to future sacrifices obviated in some manner? Fund requirements? Relevancy to objectives? What objectives? Does potential service *not* utilized qualify as a cost? Services *not* utilized (wasted) would seem to be nearer to 'sacrifice' than service actually used. In what sense is a cost recovered in selling price a sacrifice at all? If a cost is relevant (and therefore variable) to a particular decision, is it necessarily relevant to other decisions?

We turn first to some questions of terminology. In the Paton-Littleton sense cost is related to effort exerted and arises operationally when the firm moves from a more liquid to a less liquid (committed) position. (An exception seems to arise with the issuance of stock, but even here the cost to be imputed to the specialized asset is taken to be the liquidity equivalent of the securities given.) Thus, the test for an accounting cost is a movement from the generalized opportunities of liquidity to the more specialized benefits of a particular service potential.

What then does "expired" mean? From one point of view expired means that services have been received from the acquired potential. At another level expired indicates the assumed reconversion of specialized services into generalized services, i.e., a return to liquidity. The latter view requires that a realization test be applied to revenues, i.e., to the total of revenues and not just to the value increase — the income element.

The Paton terminology has an advantage: The items on the income sheet are not costs — they are expenses. Thus, the accountant may match all sorts of 'expense' items in various time configurations without being accused of misrepresenting fixed *costs* as variable *costs*. If cost is to consider irregularities in the period in which the constraints (commitments to specialized service potentials) are made, then the smoothed 'expenses' shown in the income report are certainly not incremental costs, i.e., sacrifices from decisions made in the particular period. There is, however, a relation of the total expenses taken to the total costs incurred over the entire life of the entity, even though this relationship is often obscured by costs that are treated as losses and never reach the expense hopper.

We ask now in what sense there can be a variable cost for a period. If cost is defined in terms of difference in sacrifice from a decision or action, how can a period possibly be subject to cost? In other words, how is an analyst ever justified in using variable cost per period? Two possibilities may be suggested. The period may be a convenient unit for aggregation, and the variable cost for the period when related to other aggregations for the period (e.g., revenues) becomes a smoothed representative of the mix of decisions and actions of the interval. In some cases totals, averages, marginals, etc. for a period may form better comparisons, controls, and forecasts than alternative planning units. Second, activity for a period may be the object of a decision. That is, the decision may be whether or not to continue operations for a particular period. This use is related to the shutdown decision, and management is not often faced with the decision to suspend or add a period. We conclude that the variable costs for a period are not likely to represent the incremental costs of operating in some fashion over suspending operations for the year. The variable expenses do not represent such costs, for they are smoothed parts of liquidated and non-liquidated cost commitments, rather than estimates of differences in expenditures between operating or shutting down.

We return for a more general look at the meaning of relevancy — a modern buzz word for a functional relation. To be relevant to a decision a cost must operate as a constraint in one or more options. (Even here we might prefer an expression that permits a comparison of more or less relevancy.) This constraint or restriction leads to expected unfavorable consequences or sacrifices that are present in the one case and not present in the others. These unfavorable consequences normally take the form of loss of possible achievement of other objectives or goals. Costs then are goals foregone or compromised. Why then do we speak of nonrelevant costs or sunk costs or fixed costs as costs at all?

Justification should be clear enough. A recordable item of cost has *already* resulted in the compromise of certain objectives. In fact, the exact amount of sacrifice is not known at the time of expenditure *nor at any later date*. That is, the sacrifice has already been made when the movement was made from liquid to specialized goods (or from one specialized set of opportunities to another), and in accounting the measurement surrogate is usually the amount equivalent to an expenditure. An important problem still remains: The acceptance of limited possibilities, i.e., the locking out of some desirable goals is the *cost* of what? Presumably, the voluntary limitation of possible achievements was made in order to open new possibilities that did not exist and otherwise would not have existed. Some prospects are made feasible that otherwise would have been outside the possibility set. In short, the accountant must decide the decision context before he can decide what items will function as costs.

At this point accountants have at least three problems. First, they must set up rules for deciding which costs shall be recorded and which not. A manager who sits on cash is letting all sorts of opportunities slip by, yet most accountants do not feel compelled to record the costs of staying loose and keeping options open. The opportunities that slip by management also slip through the accountant's recognition net.[9] Second, when management decides to change positions, i.e., make a positive move for a different, more restricted possibility set, the accountant must decide what measurement rules to employ. For example, if the subjective value of alternative A is $600,000 and the similar value for B is $500,000, and the firm can take advantage of either by parting with general liquidity (cash) of $300,000, most economists would insist that the relevant cost of A is $500,000. Enlightened accountants might insist that a separate cost *of poor capitalization* be isolated for the $200,000. In this case $200,000 of the $500,000 is specifically related to the sacrifice from general lack of liquidity, and the "cost" assigned to A ($300,000) is what the sacrifice would have been if the firm were in some sort of optimal financial position.

This second point deserves further consideration. To the extent that the firm has ready access to the money markets, situations with $500,000 in opportunities that can be acquired for $300,000 should be rare. In hypothesized perfect markets they should cease to exist. However, in practical cases all purchases provide some expected excess subjective value or money should flow outside the entity in the form of withdrawals or liquidating dividends. Uses of the assets in alternative ways by others would be included in the market price, but special advantages in the particular circumstances would appear as subjective value in excess of cost and would (if actualized) become a part of the income figure.[10]

---

[9] For a more general discussion of some items that slip through the usual scientific net see Arthur Eddington, *The Philosophy of Physical Science* (Ann Arbor: Ann Arbor Paperbacks, 1958), pp. 17ff.

[10] The following well-known quotation from Machlup may bear repeating. "If the fixed resources . . . had a greater value to the particular firm than to other potential users, so that the purchase price did not capitalize the full rent, then the specific rent (which would be equal to the difference between rent earned and rent paid) would be no cost element to the firm but would be a part of the surplus above normal returns . . . . On the other hand, some . . . specific rent items may have been switched into cost, for example, if administrative expenses contain salaries above the 'opportunity values' of the particular human resources." Fritz Machlup, *The Economics of Sellers' Competition* (Baltimore: The Johns Hopkins Press, 1952), p. 253.

The accountant tends to take the cost to the firm — which includes industrial rents — as given, and under stable conditions these explicit costs *tend* to be the earning opportunities for these assets in their next best alternative use. If our firm is a monopoly, these next best opportunities would be outside "the industry," but if our firm is a member of an accepted industrial family of firms, the industrial rents (opportunities) would tend to be capitalized in the individual costs. To the extent that conditions are relatively stable, the cost of assets to a particular firm would include the best alternative value of these assets to other firms, but when, if ever, would they represent the best alternatives available to the firm itself?

Clearly, a particular firm may at one time have a number of prospects that look better than the cost of funds in a generalized sense. Presumably the gatekeepers for funds have sized up the firm's opportunities in terms of other possibilities. Management probably accepts the judgment of the financial gatekeepers and adjusts its purchases accordingly. In order to find costs, individual proposals are seldom compared with one another, but instead they are evaluated in terms of the gatekeepers' rates. If this were not the case, the cost of any proposal would always be the expectation from the next best proposal. Yet, the case is not quite so simple. Gatekeepers' positions are not static. They tend to identify those firms that can find and select good proposals and to make capital available to them. To the extent that gatekeepers do so, the sacrifice to the firm is its market cost of funds, and consequently identification of good alternative prospects does not increase the cost of the proposals accepted but instead tends to reduce the relevant cost for all funds to the firm.

Third, in a specific sense the accountant must decide *which* sacrifice is *the* cost of *which* prospect. The cost of a building, for example, may be viewed as a cost of the decision to build, or as a cost of future shelter, or as a cost of good future worker and customer relations, or perhaps as a cost of other considerations. To whom and for what reason is the sacrifice relevant? In simpler contexts efficiency variances are usually considered to be costs of dysfunctional activities and only rarely as costs of product, and purchase discounts lapsed are usually treated as costs of poor financial arrangements and not as costs of merchandise. Clearly the determination of cost is a problem in definition and classification, but what determines the definitions and classifications?

The notion of relevancy needs more general attention. Any past event can be relevant to present and future decisions only to the extent that past events are conditioners or predictors of future events — to the extent that there is temporal stability in the antecedent-consequent process. From the vantage of the present some past costs may be seen to have some bearing on past consequences and therefore to possess some relevancy to them. Past relevancies are useful in evaluating past actions, past judgments, and past decisions, but with widely different expected future conditions such matching would hardly be worth the trouble.

Accountants accept as an article of faith that there is sufficient stability in the economic order to justify keeping some records of the past. There is some homogeneity in the types of decisions that need to be made, some continuity of personnel and attitudes, some stability in objectives. (Some accountants are understandably not enthusiastic over certain crude interpretations of the random walk process.) This homogeneity helps decide which records of the past should be preserved.

We return for a moment to the possible relevancy of past smoothing to future decisions. First, the smoothing of accidental and irregular happenings may make the evaluation of enterprise progress and management decisions more understandable, and therefore add an increment of helpful information for the forecasting process. But there is a more subtle relationship of smoothing to relevancy. Decisions are far from being independent, and determination of relevancy of each antecedent to each outcome may well be impossible. If so, then a certain amount of averaging, aggregating and disaggregating may be necessary to delineate manageable decision areas that can be used effectively. For example, the period convention is an aggregation for an understandable span of activity. The accountant might use a predetermined volume of sales, the life cycle of major products or any number of other possible substitutes for the annual period convention.

Regardless of the aggregating unit, the smoothing of some joint services to remove accidental timing of the costs and benefits seems desirable and necessary. Thus, a smoothed periodic charge for depreciation might possibly be relevant to one who is appraising management performance or setting prices.

The point to be emphasized here is that relevancy must be related in some causative fashion to objectives. The manner in which this association is accomplished may not seem to be ideal to observers with different views of objectives and available technologies. For economists who argue for the relevancy of marginal costs alone for price determination, the use of smoothed full costing is clearly not relevant. Others, who accept the identical objectives of maximizing long-run income, may disagree on the appropriate means, opt for normal policies, and insist on the relevancy of full costing methods.

Return now to the use of fixed and variable costs. A fixed cost is obviously not called "fixed" because its total remains unchanged indefinitely. The usual meaning is that a fixed cost remains fixed for the decision at hand, i.e., is independent of the decision or activity under consideration. There is no implication that it will remain fixed and cannot function as a cost in many other decisions or actions. Why then call a nonrelevant (nonfunctioning) cost a cost at all? Nonrelevant costs are by definition not functioning as costs! The accountant's justification is simple enough. The fixed cost is a sacrifice held in suspense. So long as the decision or action the cost was expected to expedite is not liquidated (the consequence has not been registered), the accountant keeps the unassigned cost account open. In the meantime, a myriad of decisions and beneficial actions may transpire for which the cost is not relevant. The term 'cost' is attached in a general way to remind the reader that future benefits to which the effort is relevant will sometime be registered.

The fixed-variable classification is clearly a specialized terminology used in a particular decision context. The decision arena has already been specified. For example, the implicit decision in marginal-cost analysis is whether an additional unit is to be produced or removed. The initial conditions are taken as given, and the decision is then scrutinized to estimate what will function as an associated sacrifice and what will not. Obviously all possible sacrifices for whatever reasons cannot be included. Why then are some costs recorded and carried as 'fixed' and some totally neglected? This latter question seems to depend on whether sacrifices have met other tests for admission. Variable cost in this connection is a restricted name for a particular relevant cost, e.g., sacrifice for those decisions involving simple production changes with specified initial conditions.

What then do critics mean when they question the accountant's ability to shift a fixed cost to variable cost? Clearly he cannot make fixed costs into variable costs capriciously and at will. Nor is it within the accountant's authority to change relevancy to nonrelevancy at will. But it is a part of his duty to decide — given the decision context — which costs are and which are not relevant for the objective. Unfortunately, as suggested above, decisions and objectives are not always clear and the antecedents and consequences are not always independent. Yet there is no reason to expect that the costs relevant for measuring income for a period are identical to those relevant for individual decisions made during the period. In one sense this problem is a part of the larger unit problem. Over a long period most decisions are related to (relevant to) both costs and revenues. The accounting problem is to construct a measure for shorter interdependent subintervals that will express this association best for the objectives of evaluating and planning both short-term and long-term progress. Some smoothing and period-chopping is necessary for such an activity.

Suppose, to illustrate, that there exists an explicit recorded cost that was made in response to a decision which made certain prospects possible and rendered other prospects virtually impossible. In what sense precisely was the sacrifice a cost of a particular decision? In what sense was it caused by the chain of all past decisions? What do we mean when we speak of costing income? If we cost decisions individually we require a division of the activities of a business into decisions rather than into the usual departmental and action centers. The life history of a business requires separation of a series of identifiable, relatively independent decisions and the process of recording accomplishment and sacrifice should be clustered around these decisions. Clearly, it would be desirable to aggregate and report the performance of individual decision makers, of groups of such deciders ordered in various organizational sequences, or for various time intervals. Traditionally the cost of income recognized for a period is cobbled from aggregating parts of the costs of all sorts of decisions that were made during the period as well as in previous periods. Obviously, income is a joint outcome with respect to decisions.

Suppose that the accountability structure is changed slightly and that costs are identified with benefits indirectly in, say, physical terms, i.e., the organizing scheme uses a production or machine unit instead of the more intricate decision network. Sacrifices necessary for accomplishment are clustered about the surrogate unit or work unit and matched with benefits. As before, the surrogate units are aggregated in some fashion by organizational structure and by time intervals. For those who want to account for decisions, the use of production or other surrogate units arouses mixed feelings. These units may be used to help plan and forecast *ex ante decision* costs, but inasmuch as decisions vary widely in context, the selected units may not be flexible enough to be used as effective planning and evaluating blocks. Nevertheless, decisions must be implemented by various work arrangements, and the relative stability of work units can be a distinct advantage.

It is clear that a cost may be relevant to a number of decisions and not relevant to a number of others. If we substitute fixed-variable for nonrelevant-relevant, we can understand how costs that are clearly fixed from one view are clearly variable from another. From the viewpoint of making or not making an additional unit, relevant means incremental, and one who matches fixed periodic depreciation with revenues on a unit basis violates one accepted rule of relevancy. Even if variable means that the unit enters as a cause of an incremental future replacement expenditure of a like amount, fixed periodic *depreciation* is not functioning as a cost and therefore is a noncost (fixed cost) for the replacement decision. To make sense as a relevant cost, fixed periodic depreciation must be relevant to some activity or decision pattern that is being aggregated and evaluated by periods. Direct costers admit that periodic depreciation may be relevant to the appraisal of management's income performance but insist that there is no necessity for grinding it through the indirect matching process and making it appear to vary with incremental sales. Observe that both groups agree that some accounting for these efforts is desirable and that such sacrifices are relevant for measuring managerial and overall entity performance over various time intervals and different planning horizons.

Variability to most folks probably means that the action or event or decision in some sense caused the cost to occur — in some way created it or created the necessity for it.[11]

Footnotes on following page

The ability to produce and sell normally requires various sacrifices and the resulting costs are made in order to make these activities feasible. But a further question arises: Once a sacrifice is made, in what sense is it a one-shot affair and in what way is it a continuing sacrifice subject to leisurely amortization? The traditional rationale is that the cost (and its associated expenditure) continues to be a burden on the entity until it generates its own return. Thus the usual defense for periodic amortization is that entity performance is lower than it otherwise would have been due to the expenditure of resources to acquire the capability until the benefits from the acquired capability are received. In short, the original sacrifice *continues* in a reduced way so long as the entity is frozen out of alternative opportunities by the original commitment. This rationale is the traditional one used to support the assertion that fixed costs are somehow *recovered* through sales of product.

Most accountants will probably grant that many costs (sacrifices) persist in whole or in part over considerable stretches of time. These sacrifices are related over these intervals to resources by the assumption that the sacrifices to the entity should be reduced as the potential from the resources is received. If this approach is accepted, what can be said about such measures as return on costs and investments? The returns registered are related to sacrifices liquidated and not to the unliquidated portion of the sacrifice. The ROI measure relates them to the latter. In most cases it probably does not matter greatly, but there appears to be a bias in favor of firms with short-run commitments. Most accountants are aware of this effect, and assume that ROI motivates toward leasing and low capital outlays.

There is, however, a positive side to the use of ROI as a performance measure, and it relates to opportunities foregone — sacrifices. Relating liquidated benefits to the cost of unliquidated benefits may *appear* to be wrong in principle, but the support has considerable merit. When a manager commits liquid resources to long-lived resources he is locking the entity out of immediate benefits that might have been received. Thus the firm foregoes opportunities for immediate gain elsewhere. The ROI measure — not so ridiculous as it seems — holds managers responsible for these opportunities foregone. It expects the net benefits registered (received) to be sufficient to make up for the benefits sacrificed by the long-term commitment. The standard return on investment against which the comparison is made does of course require the entire commitment to yield the standard rate.[12]

For a more traditional summary, the cost of a plant is a sacrifice to be associated with the decision to own the plant and with the decision to be in the resource business. It is a cost to be associated with a large unknown batch of future output, or with numerous feasible future decisions, or with large anticipated fund receipts. The sacrifice is assumed to be made when the funds are committed and to continue in part as long as some restriction persists. In a far-out sense the sacrifice is forever. It is variable with (incremental to) the commitment to specialized activity in the future, and in a special sense it remains a sacrifice indefinitely. In what manner then is such a sacrifice ever liquidated or matched? The

[11] Many accountants may prefer to think in terms of correlation instead of causation. In most cases it is reasonable to assert that the costs or sacrifices 'caused' the conditions to become favorable for goal pursuit. I have vacillated between admiring and abhorring the concept of social causation. Scientists are more comfortable with less demanding 'functional' relations.

[12] I have previously used this type of argument to answer the question raised by Hatfield in the steer case and by Robert L. Dixon, "Decreasing Charge Depreciation — A Search for Logic," *The Accounting Review*, October, 1960, pp. 590-598. Henry Rand Hatfield, "An Accountant's Adventures in Wonderland," *Journal of Accountancy*, December, 1940. My own discussion is in *Modern Accounting Theory*, ed. Morton Backer (Englewood Cliffs: Prentice-Hall, Inc., 1966), p. 154.

usual model (outlined above) assumes that the *benefits* from the commitment will become available to mitigate the sacrifice, i.e., the benefits made feasible by the sacrifice reduce the cost. This return to freedom (liquidity) takes place whether or not a part of the receipts is labeled a return of capital — a mitigation of sacrifice — and a part return *on* capital — a reward for sacrifice.

Our problem here is to find situations to which this big restriction (outlay) is relevant and incremental and can be said to be variable. Advocates of the double-account approach argue that there is no depreciation for a maintained plant, and seem to be happy to charge management with only upkeep broadly defined. The past sacrifices to make production feasible are a part of the evaluation standard and *not* a part of management's current performance. Even these advocates may feel that return on current costs is a better component of the evaluative machinery than historical costs, and the more critical among us may wonder why management is not evaluated in terms of the *opportunities given* him rather than on sacrifices necessary to make the opportunities available to him. Historical costs *may* be relevant predictors of future outlays. Otherwise they seem to be relevant only to those who made the decision to enter the business, and as individual owners change, historical sacrifice to original owners is no longer relevant to anyone except perhaps a hypothesized entity. (Goodwill sometimes remains unliquidated and unmatched, but American accountants have been reluctant to extend the thinking to other assets.) In summary, the relevance of historical cost is primarily in its ability to serve as a surrogate for expected sacrifice, and this statement remains applicable even if the original unit of cost has been subdivided and matched bit by bit.

Fairness

We have discussed and rejected the case of fairness as the universal accounting principle. (See Essays One and Two.) Not only is such a grandiose principle too broad and too diffuse to guide our accounting actions, there is a serious question whether our profession intends to be, or wants to be, fair to all who may have an interest in an entity, e.g., thieves, embezzlers, competitors, disloyal employees, and various confidence artists. This position is similar to that encountered in the discussion of neutrality. *Fairness* is too broad to serve as an objective much less a guideline, but if fairness is taken as the primary objective of our profession and not as a banal slogan, we must make it operational by asking for rules to identify the parties of concern and to weigh their relative importance in case of possible trade-offs. Furthermore, our practitioners need instructions that are operational and are consistent with our concept of fairness to the *right* people. Finally, many object to the term because it is slanted, claims moral sanction, obscures the necessary professional attitude of advocacy and the problem of identifying deserving advocatees, and I have concluded that Scott, Spacek and perhaps others made important contributions to the profession in spite of and not because of their commitment to the attitude that good guys like accountants should be fair. In addition, accuracy is a similar slogan posing as a righteous principle. To question fairness vaguely suggests that one is advocating unfairness or even crookedness, and to question accuracy, except in an absurd absolute sense, is to align oneself with inaccuracy and by indirection with untruthfulness.

Historically, there has been an association of full costing with fairness. When businessmen are indoctrinated to feel that each product should bear its *fair* share of fixed costs, they invoke the usual ethical aversion to unfairness and favor a pricing policy that is roughly proportionate to full costing. Fixed cost thus becomes relevant to fair pricing! In recent investigations of medicines and drugs there was strong public resentment to pricing policies that varied from below cost to hundreds of times above cost. The Robinson-Patman Act and a number of state laws encourage prices that are proportional to costs, and some socialist countries (e.g., Indonesia) use full costing to help measure the amount of state subsidies granted. The Dutch tradition of *Kostprijs* tends to include all socially necessary costs at current prices, and full costing is usually assumed to lead to the poorly defined concept of "good business administration." The United States Supreme Court has considered prudent costs in rate-making cases, and utility regulation has been based in part on full-costing techniques. Finally, trade associations have often encouraged full costing and discouraged selling below full costs. Such expressions as "we refuse to give away our profit" are common in all lines of business.

What is the significance, if any, of the folklore that holds that each product or each department should bear its fair share of fixed overhead? Specifically, why would fixed costs distributed to inanimate objects such as products, activities, and departments be a necessary ingredient of the pricing process? For that matter, why should prices based on variable costs alone be fair? Who should "in fairness" bear the fixed make-ready and establishment costs? The most obvious explanation is that *people* are involved in all such cases. Departments have departmental managers, and to the extent that such managers are being compared and held to an accountability for performance, it is argued that they should in fairness be held responsible for the opportunities afforded them. The accountant and his clients usually assume that assigning costs to organizational subunits according to *responsibility* is fair. It is where responsibility is no longer a direct factor that implementing fairness becomes sticky. For example, why are divisional managers "responsible" for recovering pro-rate fixed assignments? If they are responsible for providing a contribution over incremental costs, should they also be responsible for a contribution adequate to cover the cost of opportunities afforded them? How are they held responsible for designing new products and improvising effective marketing methods that will utilize the opportunities given them?

Businessmen brought up in the full costing tradition tend to follow the long-established rules of traditional allocation: assign to the cost center the costs that are directly and indisputably relevant, i.e., for which the activity is obviously responsible, and also assign costs for which the activity is not directly responsible according to relative service rendered or relative opportunities afforded. Indirectly, it is asserted that anyone using the facilities is responsible for utilizing the opportunities and is therefore assessed a charge based on these opportunities. This is the traditional "fairness" rule in full costing, and during wartime stress billions of govenment dollars are paid on the basis of such allocations, instead of the more easily understood rental arrangements. It is interesting to note that even when rental contracts are negotiated, the rent is often related to full costs or, if not, excess proceeds are subject to recapture through renegotiation until the remainder bears an acceptable relationship to total costs.

It is generally argued that fairness is especially desirable when a number of persons are connected by joint ownership or by joint usage of some facility. The interesting behavioral overtone to many arrangements of this sort is that they in fact transform a part of entity fixed costs into variable costs to the owners. If a mineral spring with high fixed costs is owned by A and B, and if the cost to each is allocated according to service or benefit rendered, then the usage cost to both A and B is variable with a decreasing unit charge. If the basis is "opportunity afforded," it may be argued that a fixed total is appropriate. In public utilities, for example, it is common to assign fixed costs on a fixed ratio of opportunities afforded.

For a socialist state interested in allocating resources for maximum social benefit, it has been argued that fixed allocation tends to inhibit optimum short-run allocation. Can the same be said for all such allocations? It has been so argued. To the extent that the government price includes a part of the fixed costs, the costs are above short-run variable costs and the product will tend to be restricted in its use. The general feeling is that once facilities are in operation their fixed costs are independent of output, and each output decision and asset combination should not have to be referred back to the sunk cost through inclusion of some smoothed fixed-cost portion. In other words, each interim decision should be on its own *immediate* relevant costs, and the capital budgeting decision for the indivisibilities should be made on other criteria (bigger batches?) which are relevant at the time and in the proper decision context. Between major capital budgeting expenditures for renewal and replacement, the optimum utilization is said to be on a mix of prices based on variable costs.[13] We return later to a defense for the opposing position: that for an indefinitely continuing concern past costs may be related to future irregular costs and that inclusion of some past costs of these sorts may be a better "decision prompter" than complete neglect.

In private sectors the use of full costs, combined with a feeling of guilt about being unfair if individual prices do not include full costs and a feeling of frustration over the necessity of "give-away profits," may indeed create an important *psychological barrier* to price cutting. To the extent that these attitudes prevail there is little doubt that businessmen would seek other opportunities (e.g., new products, sales pressure) rather than price cutting in attempting to improve their lots.[14] The ability of firms to disorganize markets and industry by differential cost invasion has led to apprehension, but in addition to the disorganizing influence, it is not always clear that marginal costing will maximize profits in the long run. The incentive to search for new products that will absorb the unused capacity and also provide a normal mark-up over full costs may not only slow down the cutthroat invasions but may increase the individual firm's short-run profits as well.

It is now understood by even the most doctrinaire economists that the simplistic and dogmatic rule to equate short-run marginal costs with marginal revenues needs modification. At best, this rule will optimize long-run profits only if the sequential decisions are independent. In the typical case, the revenues of tomorrow will be influenced by prices charged today, and in a similar manner future attitudes toward costs and cost control may react sharply to current price and control policies. It is generally understood that the traditional marginal approach needs to be interpreted in three-dimensional terms for effective application. The demand curve of alternatives at some short interval of time becomes a demand surface (or family of demand surfaces) through time. Cost curves take on another dimension in a similar fashion, and the maximization problem turns out to be the maximization of a volume (or series of possible volumes) through time rather than a series of two-dimensional areas to be optimized.[15]

---

[13] For applications to planned economies see: Abba P. Lerner, *The Economics of Control* (New York: The Macmillan Company, 1944), especially Chapters 15, 16; or Burnham Putnam Beckwith, *Marginal-Cost Price-Output Control* (New York: Columbia University Press, 1955), Chapter VIII. An interesting feature of the latter volume is a recommendation for charging admission fees for covering fixed costs, e.g., department stores (p. 254). Recently Myron J. Gordon discussed the relationship of intra-firm transfer pricing to planned economies but referred to neither of the above references. "A Method of Pricing for a Socialist Economy," *The Accounting Review*, July, 1970, pp. 427-443.

[14] Inasmuch as industry is full of joint products and common costs, the tendency to invade other areas on a differential cost basis is a universal threat. Almost all products, except major production classes, may be considered to be by-products and, without full costing, the temptation to invade other fields is a genuine threat to stability in the invaded industry. This tendency has long been recognized as a possible aspect of cutthroat competition, but Robert Dixon has dramatized this well understood situation in "Creep," *The Journal of Accountancy*, July, 1953, pp. 48-55.

[15] For more detail see my *Cost Accounting and Analysis, op. cit.*, pp. 712-713. For an earlier discussion see G. C. Evans, *Mathematical Introduction to Economics* (New York: McGraw-Hill Publishing Co., 1930), p. 143.

Unfortunately, some economists have contributed to the widespread feeling that businessmen are completely stupid to adopt any pricing strategy other than the rule to equate marginal revenues with marginal costs in the short run. Some maintained that successful businessmen were those who by chance or otherwise tended to approximate the pricing policies of MR = MC. It is, of course, just possible that the methods used in business are in fact superior to those recommended by economists of the marginal persuasion. That is, instead of proceeding from the assumption that businessmen who follow full costing and related procedures are not following their own interests, it may be more useful to question the assumption of independent time intervals. Darwinism is on the side of the businessmen. If they have been stupid, the way should be open for sharp MC = MR advocates to drive them out of business. All survivors would have to conform in some manner. Traditional business methods have changed very little, bright young MC = MR advocates have not run them out of business, and there is little evidence that the surviving methods conform to the marginal rule either directly or indirectly.

It should be clear enough that a decision to maintain prices is *not* in any way *automatic*, and neither, if the sales price does not cover costs, is cutting prices an automatic reaction. There does seem to be some sort of identification of cost as a floor beneath which prices will not be allowed to go except in dire distress. Trade associations and perhaps other organizations (including many cost accounting texts and teachers) have tended to reinforce the flooring function of cost in the pricing decision. By carrying on an educational program designed to strengthen this feeling, such groups can create an important barrier to price cutting on the downward side. Emotionally charged semantic symbols have been employed. To cut below full costs has been known as "cutthroat" competition, with overtones of dark alleys and gutter methods. Such persuasion tends to encourage search for alternatives other than price cutting and may serve as a motivator for successful search in addition to the obvious alternative of shutting down the factory. In summary, the pressures brought to bear by group leadership in order to enforce pricing discipline should encourage all sorts of new activities, including a number of dissertations on behavioral activities.

To the extent that full costing calls early attention to sick products and areas, the results will normally be beneficial. However, it is conceivable that slower signals and responses might give a chance for the demand to develop and might turn out to be the preferred course. Full costing may incite action sooner but in so doing may incite action in less desirable directions or in wrong directions. For example, full costing might block experiments in cutting prices, in cases where such action is precisely what is needed to explore demand elasticities. Finally, it might be more profitable in the long run to direct attention away from such products. That is, experiments with dealer helps, new packaging, advertising pressures, etc. may conceivably be pursued more profitably on products that are moving well at good margins. Nevertheless, earlier signaling devices in themselves are difficult to fault, especially if they signal both strong and weak areas.

In summary, a good accounting system should contain some built-in devices to indicate whether the combination of prices and goods moved is going according to plan and providing satisfactory contributions. Perhaps the simplest approach is through contribution, in which the contribution over variable cost is computed by products, lines, territories, etc. As a guideline, a norm in the form of an acceptable amount of contribution will normally be compared with the actual results as monitored through the accounting reporting service. In order to get some idea as to the amount of contribution that is acceptable, fixed costs are sometimes assigned. In fact, profit — when interpreted for subunits of an organization and even for the entire organization — may be interpreted as contribution in excess of some assignment of indirect costs. Much of the disgust with traditional full-costing methods may be traced to this assignment of joint costs to products or processes by some accounting clerk who is following rules and conventions that neither he nor many others fully understand.

It is possible to defend certain fixed cost assignments, and Professor Jeremiah Lockwood pointed out a motivational objective of fixed-cost assignment to a generation or two of Wharton students. He, like most accounting professors of his time, believed that a benchmark of contribution over joint cost assignments of various kinds is often a more useful measure of performance than a benchmark set at zero contribution. According to this view, unless a product, a display center, a line or a salesman can contribute enough to cover allocated costs, operations are submarginal and the activity is a candidate for investigation and perhaps extinction. Apparently the average-rate-of-return capital budgeting cutoff is based on similar reasoning. Unless an activity can provide a rate of return equal to the average, it becomes a candidate for review or rejection, even though it would make a short-run contribution well in excess of assignable direct costs.[16] Unfortunately, those who advocate average rates of return may cut off some good opportunities, and the use of past averages as standards for future performance sometimes borders on the ridiculous. While such a norm may lead to unprofitable decisions, it is obviously consistent with the entrepreneur's assumed desire to improve and do better. Of course, this approach does not mean that an activity is automatically discontinued if it fails to cover its fixed costs or to provide for an average rate of return. It does mean that signals are sent out periodically to managment that the activity is not meeting the goal and that further, more detailed, studies that involve long- and short-run objectives may be in order. Most of us probably feel that such important devices deserve more careful attention and expression.

---

[16] Robert Dixon, *op. cit.*, p. 51.

VOLUME III
Author Index

VOLUME III
Subject Index

VOLUME III
Subject Index